ALICE GUY
FIRST LADY OF FILM

In memory of Francis Lacassin

With our sincere thanks to Laure Albernhe, Gabriel Andivero, Leïla Ayachi, Bernard Bastide, Laetitia Bocquet, Emmanuel Bodein, Frédéric Bonnaud, Brigitte Boujassy, Charlotte Boujassy, Thierry Briez, Serge Bromberg, Manuela da Silva, Kathy Degreef, Carlos Fereira, Claude Franck, Charlotte Gallimard, Romain Gallart, Stanislas Gaudry, Emmanuelle Gaume, Philippe Ghielmetti, Emma Hayley, Frédérique Lambert, Mathilde Lepostec, Benoît Mouchart, Cathy Palumbo, Thierry Peeters, Nathalie Rocher, Martine Saada, François Samuelson, Julie Scheibling, Line Scheibling, Elodie Sécheret, Lili Sztajn, Dominique Thiéry, Christophe Vilain, Nathalie Van Campenhoudt, Estelle Verner, Marie-Thérèse Vieira, and all the teams at Casterman and SelfMadeHero.

This book was made possible with artistic support from Elléa Bird, Jeanne Idatte, Julie Larrans, and Margot Sounack.
Marie-Anne Didierjean was the grey wash colourist.
Nicolas Sécheret lettered the original pages in Catelnéo and also oversaw coordinating the sequencing of the chapters.

ALICE GUY
FIRST LADY OF FILM

CATEL
& BOCQUET

Art by Catel Muller
Written by José-Louis Bocquet

Translated by Edward Gauvin

SELF MADE HERO

Alice Guy lived in the first half of the twentieth century, and *Alice Guy* contains offensive and racist language which reflects some of the attitudes and prejudices of the period.

SELF MADE HERO

First published in English in 2022
by SelfMadeHero
139–141 Pancras Road
London NW1 1UN
www.selfmadehero.com

Written and illustrated by Catel & Bocquet
Translated from French by Edward Gauvin

INSTITUT FRANÇAIS
ROYAUME-UNI

This book is supported by the Institut français (Royaume-Uni) as part of the Burgess programme.

English edition
Publishing Director: Emma Hayley
Editorial & Production Director: Guillaume Rater
Publishing Assistant: Stefano Mancin
Publicist: Paul Smith
Designers: Txabi Jones and Kate McLauchlan
Textual Consultant: Nick de Somogyi
With thanks to Dan Lockwood

A CIP record for this book is available from the British Library

ISBN: 978-1-914224-03-4

10 9 8 7 6 5 4 3 2 1

Printed and bound in China

1 July 1873 – Saint-Mandé – France

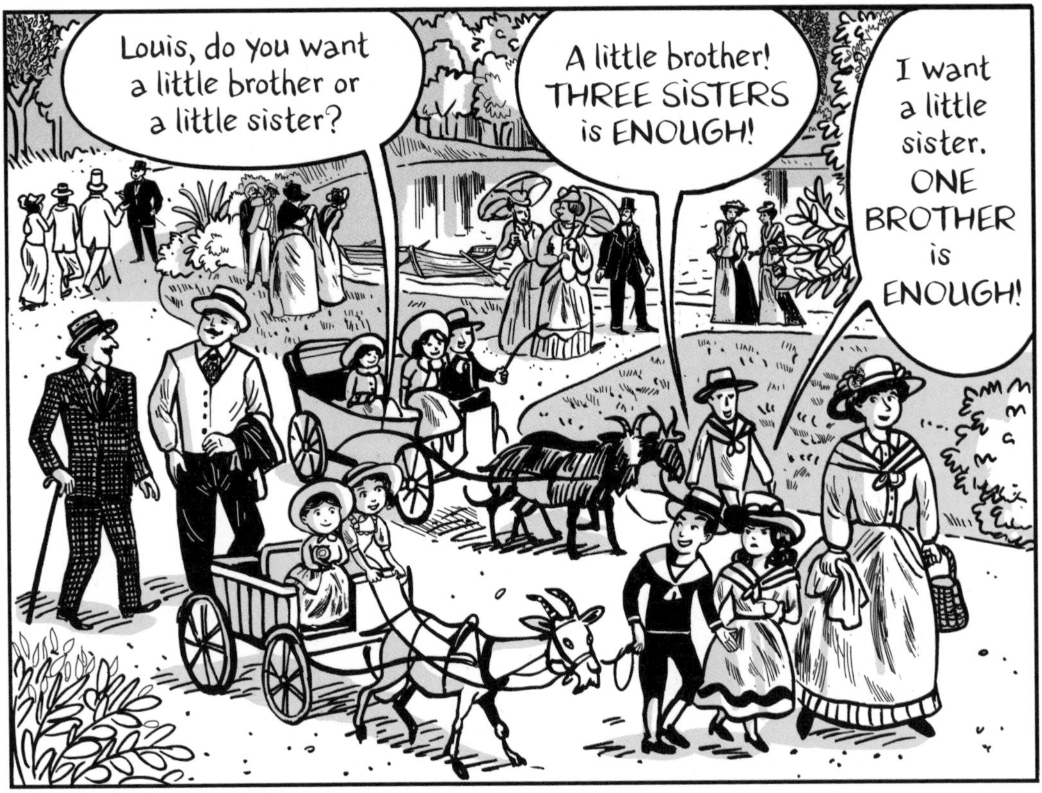
Louis, do you want a little brother or a little sister?
A little brother! THREE SISTERS is ENOUGH!
I want a little sister. ONE BROTHER is ENOUGH!

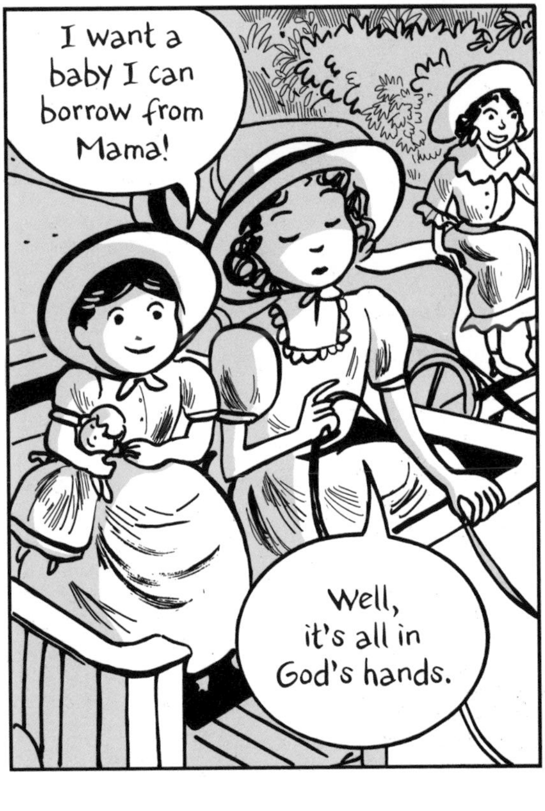
I want a baby I can borrow from Mama!
Well, it's all in God's hands.

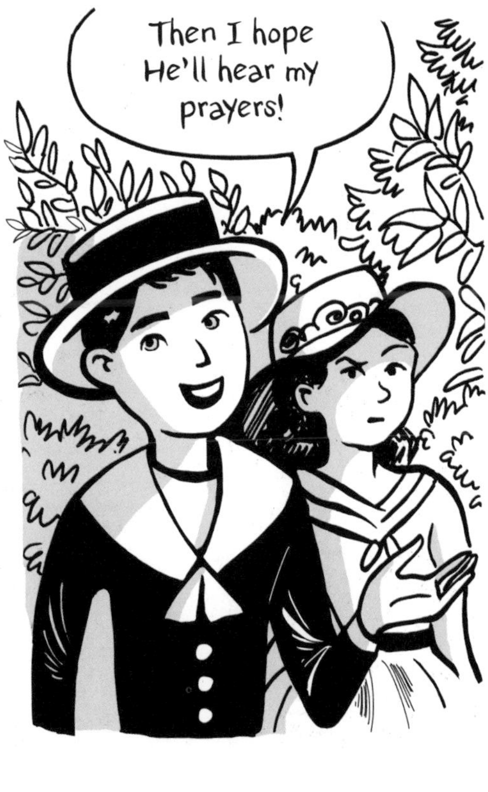
Then I hope He'll hear my prayers!

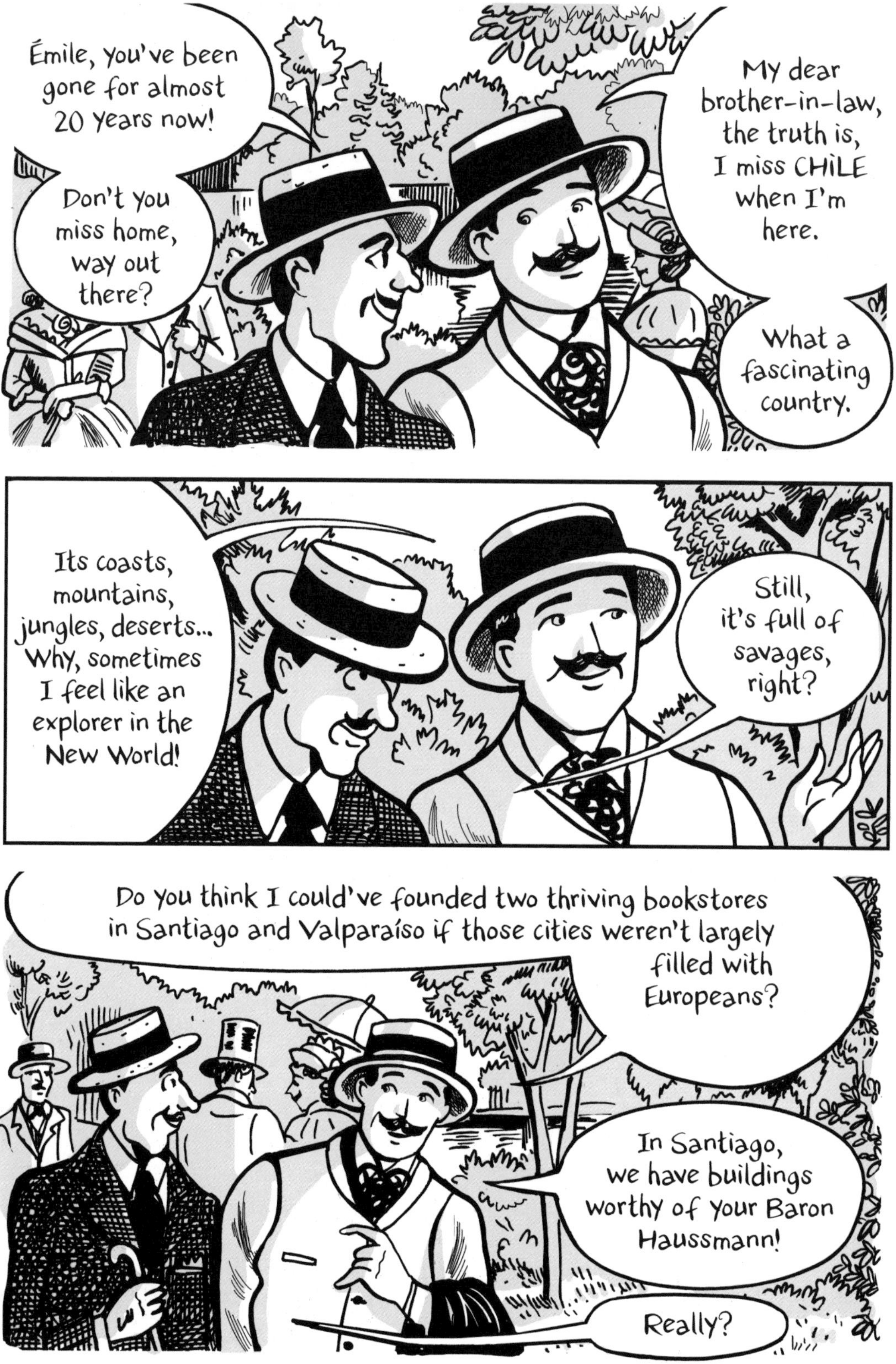
Émile, you've been gone for almost 20 years now!
Don't you miss home, way out there?
My dear brother-in-law, the truth is, I miss CHILE when I'm here.
What a fascinating country.
Its coasts, mountains, jungles, deserts... Why, sometimes I feel like an explorer in the New World!
Still, it's full of savages, right?
Do you think I could've founded two thriving bookstores in Santiago and Valparaíso if those cities weren't largely filled with Europeans?
In Santiago, we have buildings worthy of your Baron Haussmann!
Really?

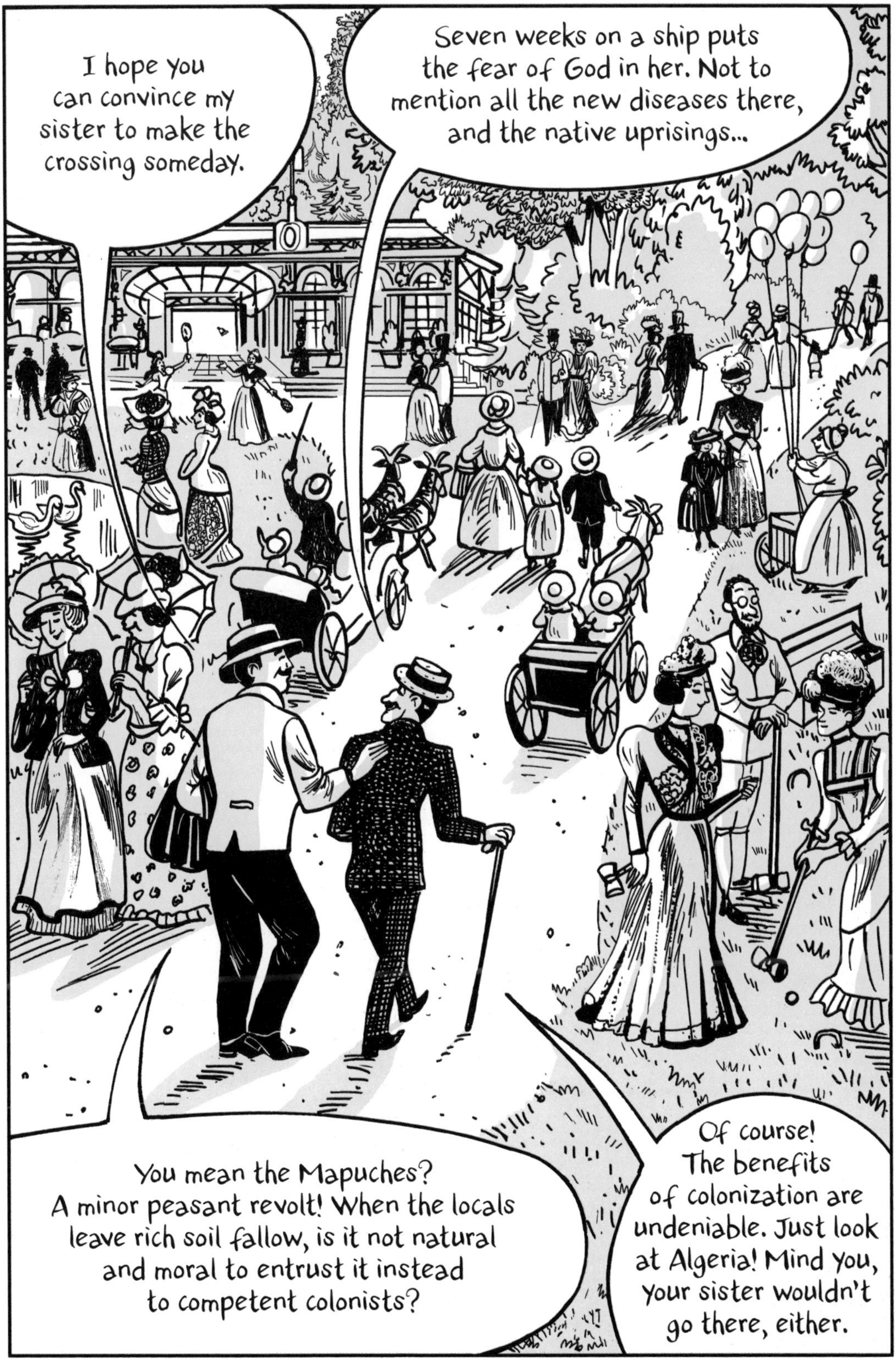
I hope you can convince my sister to make the crossing someday.
Seven weeks on a ship puts the fear of God in her. Not to mention all the new diseases there, and the native uprisings...
You mean the Mapuches? A minor peasant revolt! When the locals leave rich soil fallow, is it not natural and moral to entrust it instead to competent colonists?
Of course! The benefits of colonization are undeniable. Just look at Algeria! Mind you, your sister wouldn't go there, either.

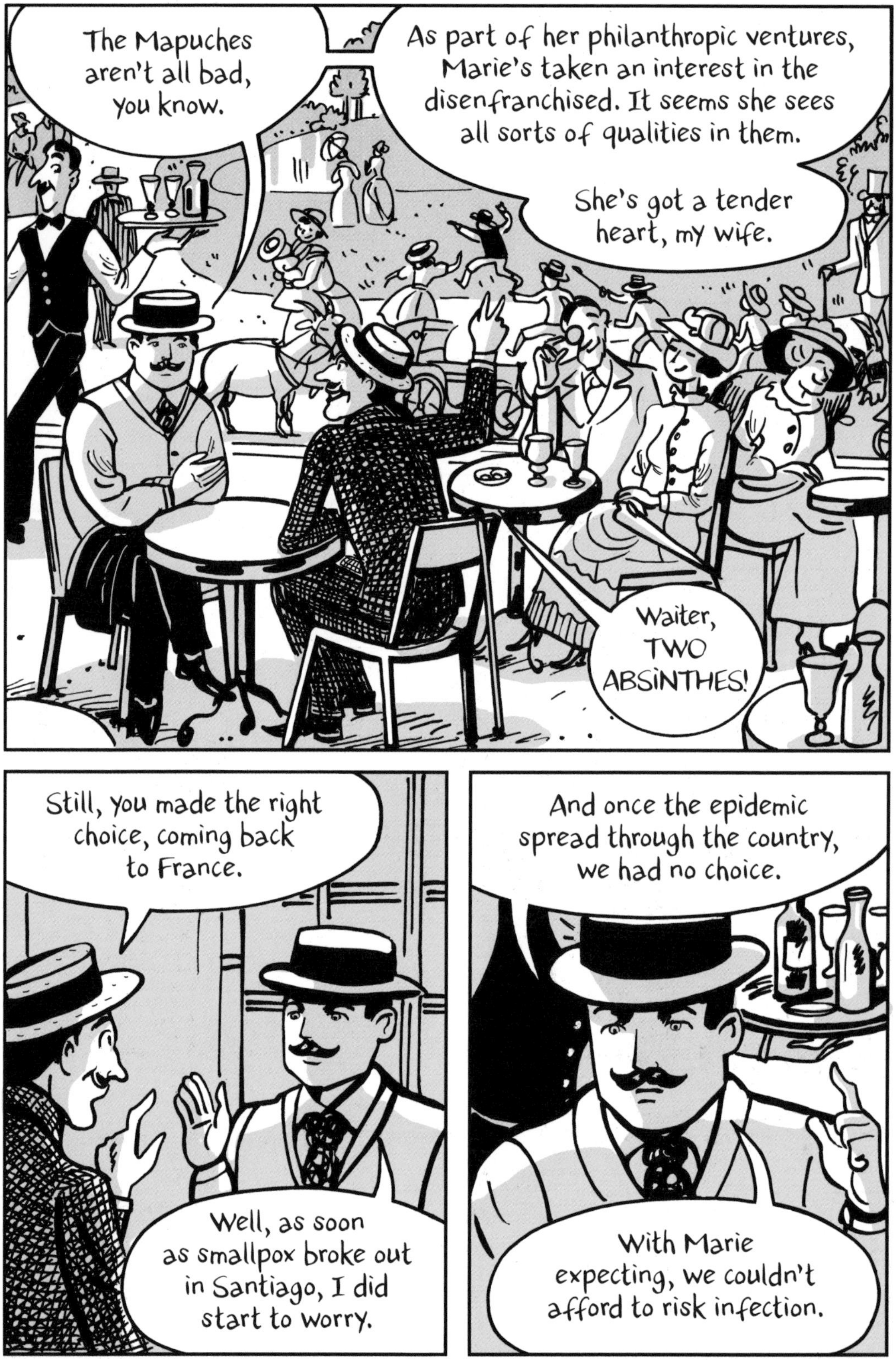
The Mapuches aren't all bad, you know.
As part of her philanthropic ventures, Marie's taken an interest in the disenfranchised. It seems she sees all sorts of qualities in them.
She's got a tender heart, my wife.
Waiter, TWO ABSINTHES!
Still, you made the right choice, coming back to France.
Well, as soon as smallpox broke out in Santiago, I did start to worry.
And once the epidemic spread through the country, we had no choice.
With Marie expecting, we couldn't afford to risk infection.

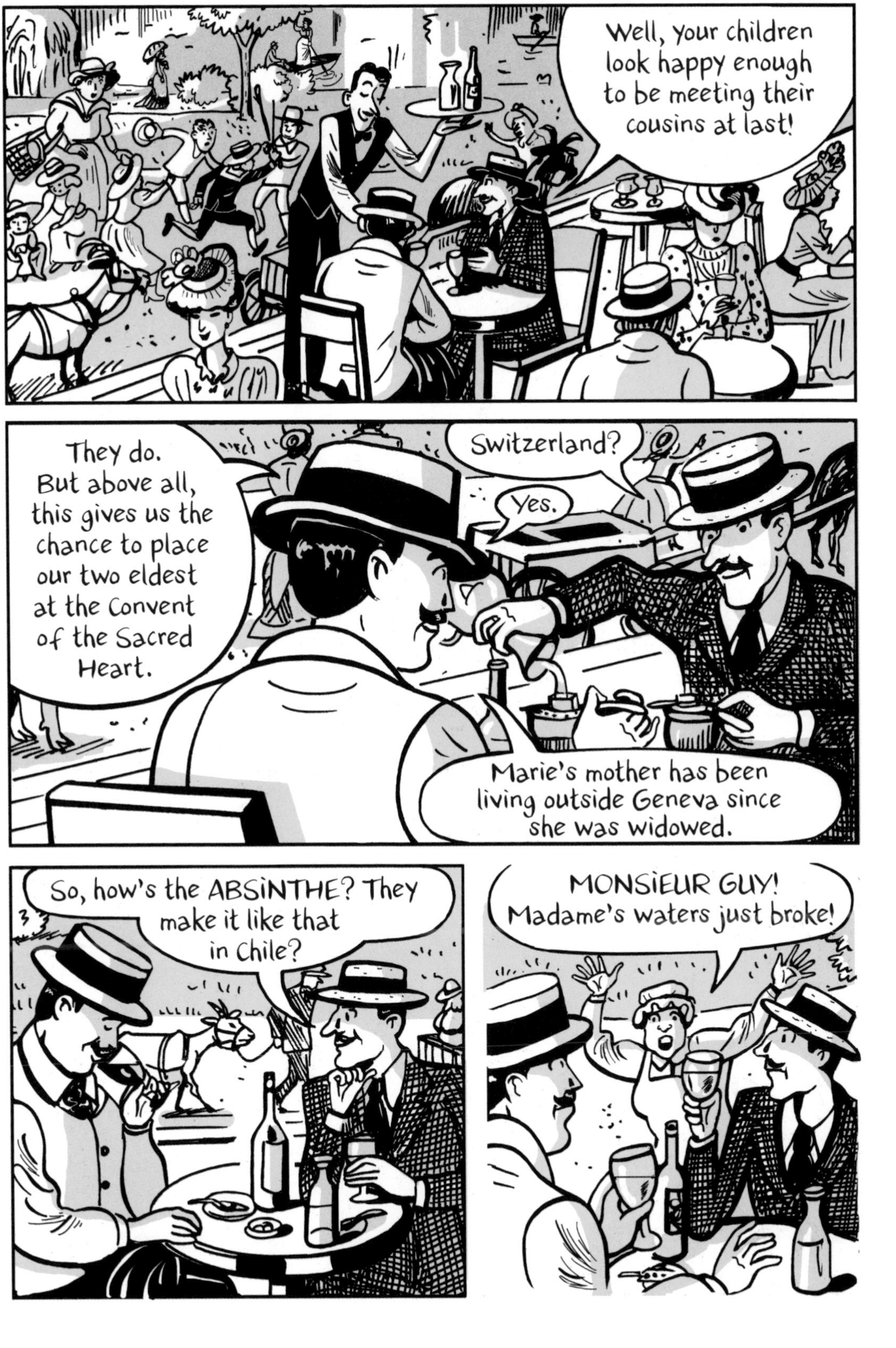
Well, your children look happy enough to be meeting their cousins at last!
They do. But above all, this gives us the chance to place our two eldest at the Convent of the Sacred Heart.
Marie's mother has been living outside Geneva since she was widowed.
Switzerland?
Yes.
So, how's the ABSiNTHE? They make it like that in Chile?
MONSiEUR GUY! Madame's waters just broke!

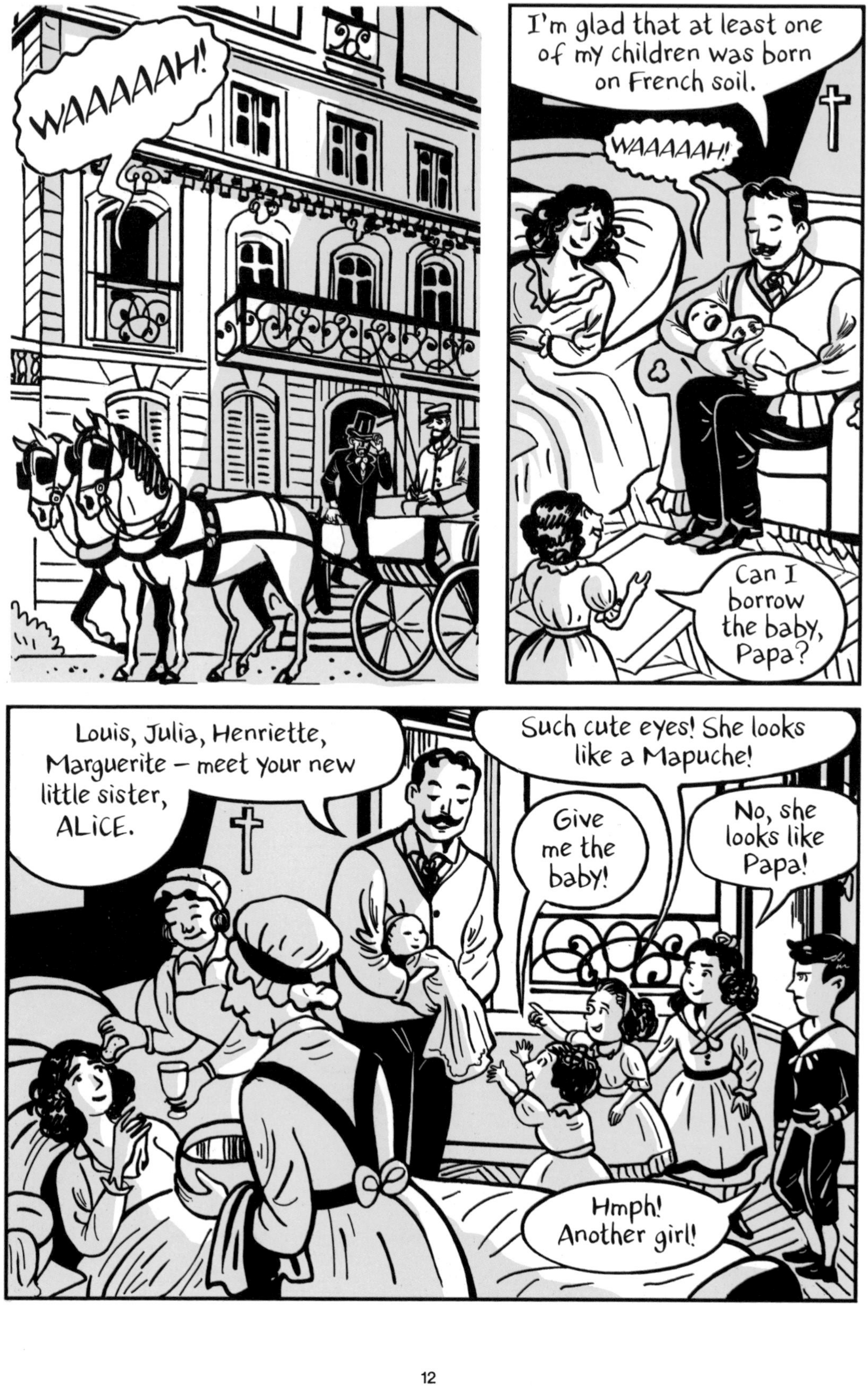
WAAAAAH!
I'm glad that at least one of my children was born on French soil.
WAAAAAH!
Can I borrow the baby, Papa?
Louis, Julia, Henriette, Marguerite – meet your new little sister, ALICE.
Such cute eyes! She looks like a Mapuche!
Give me the baby!
No, she looks like Papa!
Hmph! Another girl!

1876 – Carouge – Switzerland

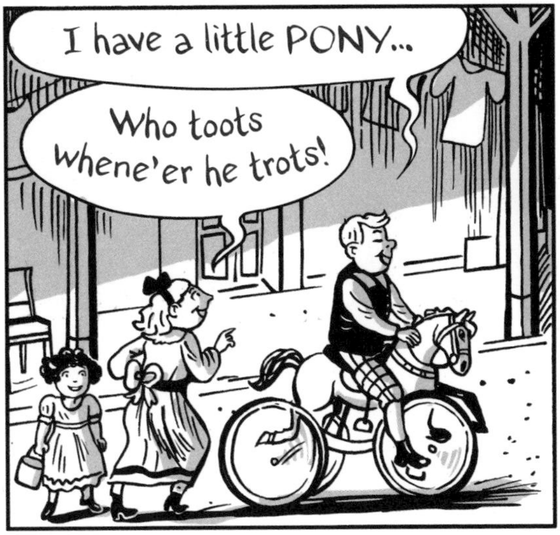
I have a little PONY...
Who toots whene'er he trots!

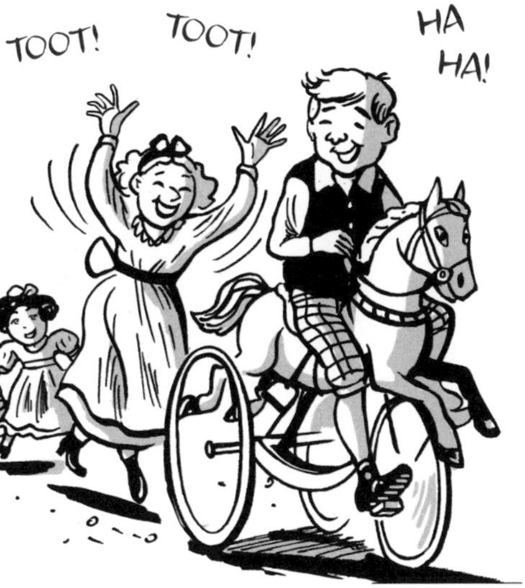
TOOT!
TOOT!
HA HA!

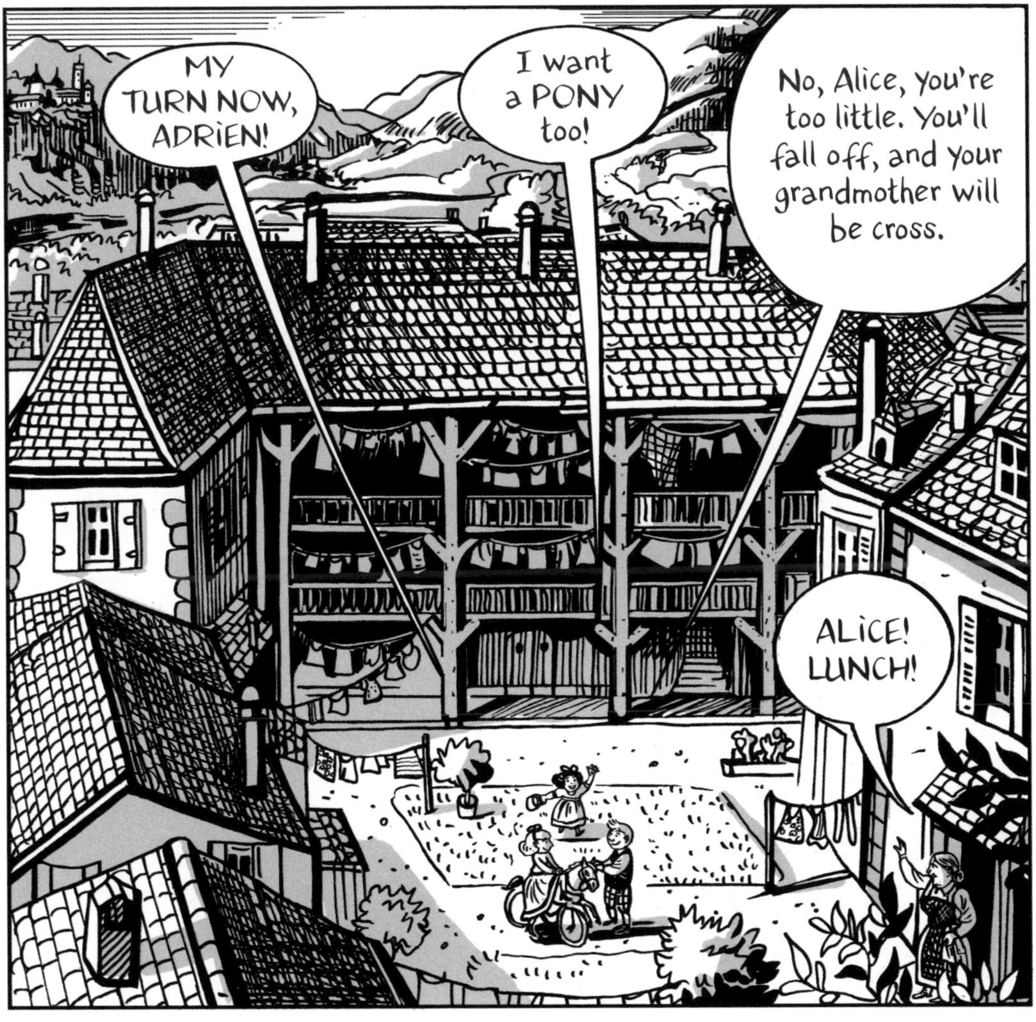
MY TURN NOW, ADRIEN!
I want a PONY too!
No, Alice, you're too little. You'll fall off, and your grandmother will be cross.
ALICE! LUNCH!

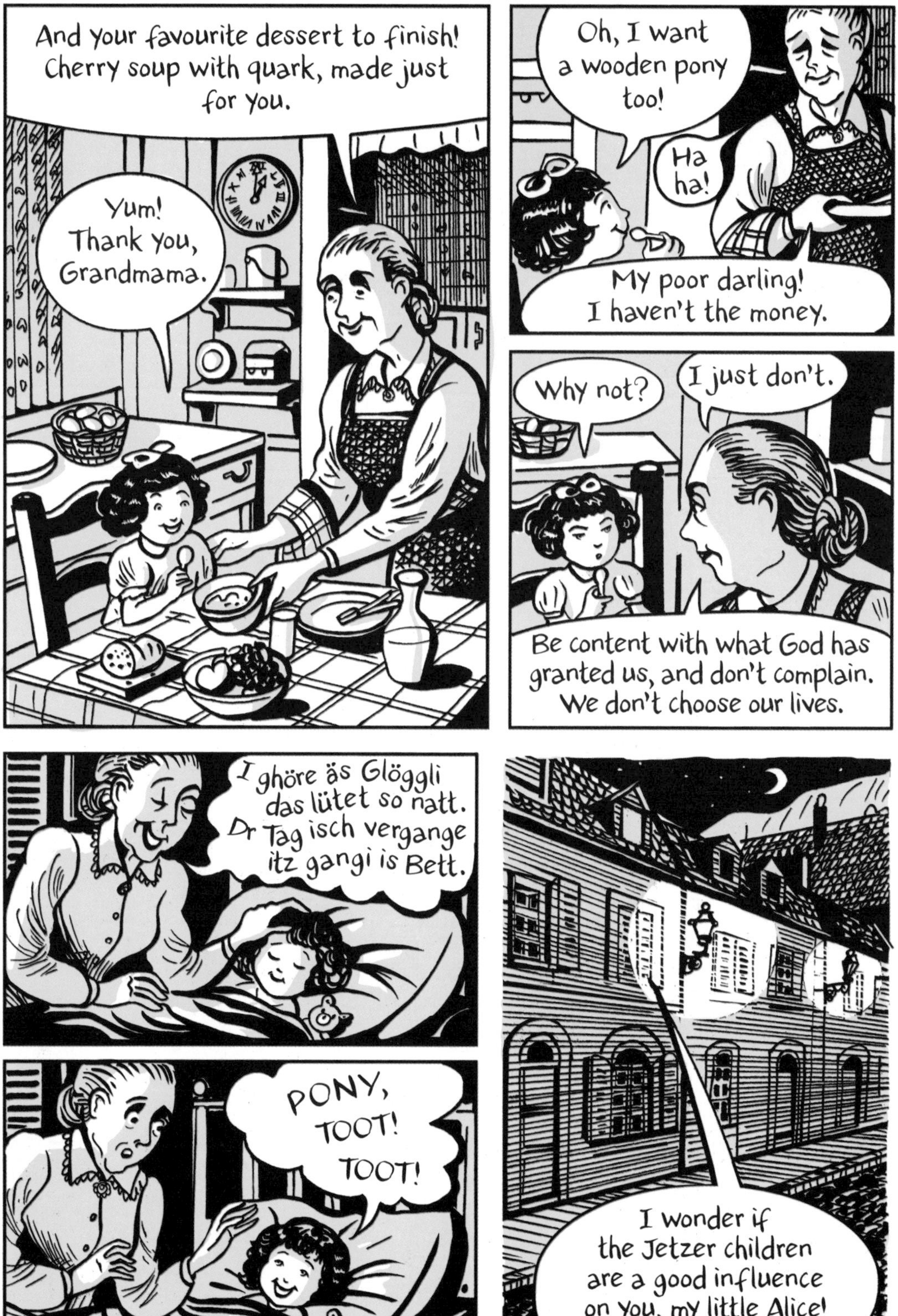
And your favourite dessert to finish! Cherry soup with quark, made just for you.
Yum! Thank you, Grandmama.
Oh, I want a wooden pony too!
Ha ha!
My poor darling! I haven't the money.
Why not?
I just don't.
Be content with what God has granted us, and don't complain. We don't choose our lives.
I ghöre äs Glöggli das lütet so natt. Dr Tag isch vergange itz gangi is Bett.
PONY, TOOT! TOOT!
I wonder if the Jetzer children are a good influence on you, my little Alice!

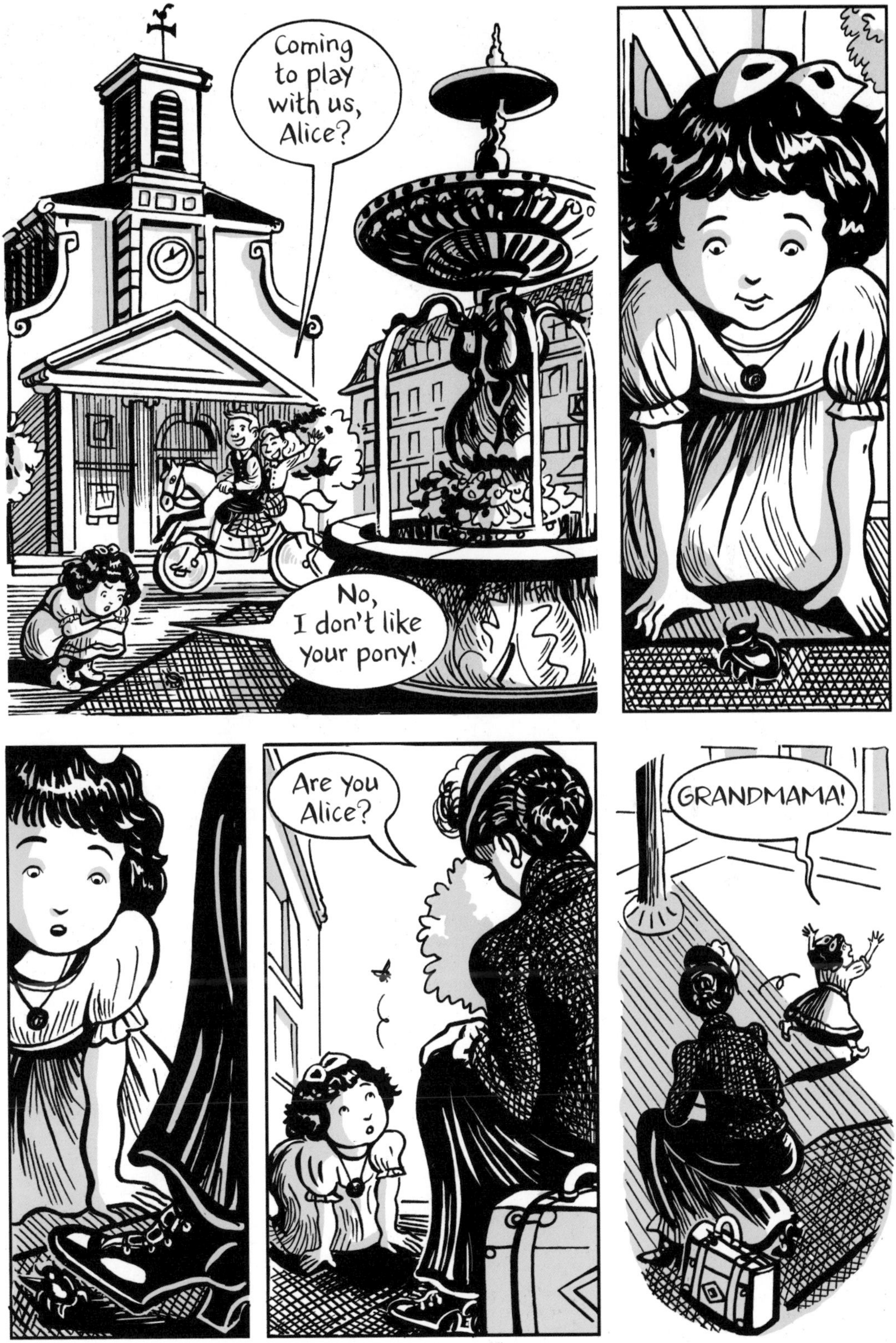
Coming to play with us, Alice?
No, I don't like your pony!
Are you Alice?
GRANDMAMA!

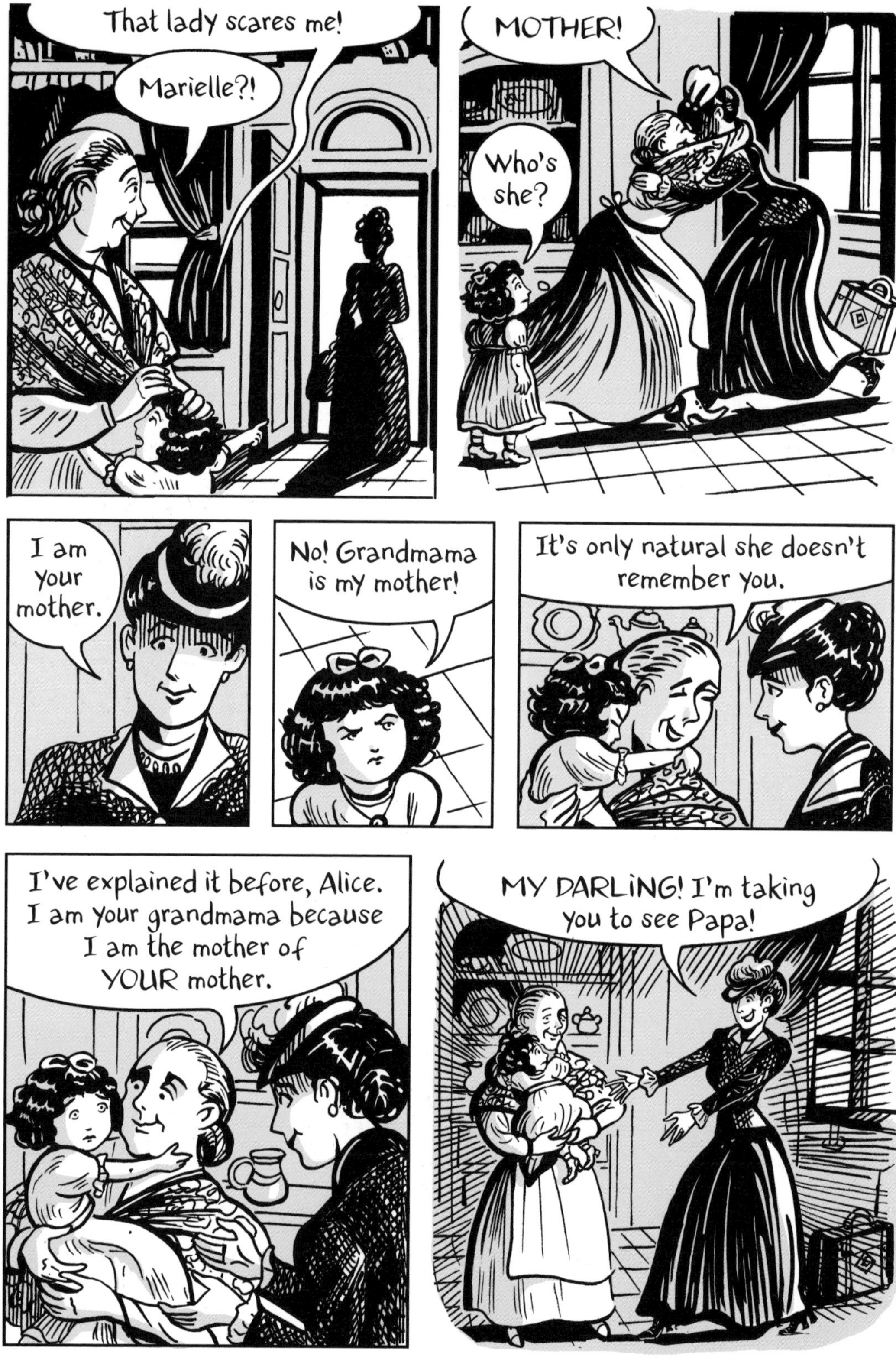

That lady scares me!
Marielle?!
MOTHER!
Who's she?
I am your mother.
No! Grandmama is my mother!
It's only natural she doesn't remember you.
I've explained it before, Alice. I am your grandmama because I am the mother of YOUR mother.
MY DARLING! I'm taking you to see Papa!

1876 – Valparaíso – Chile

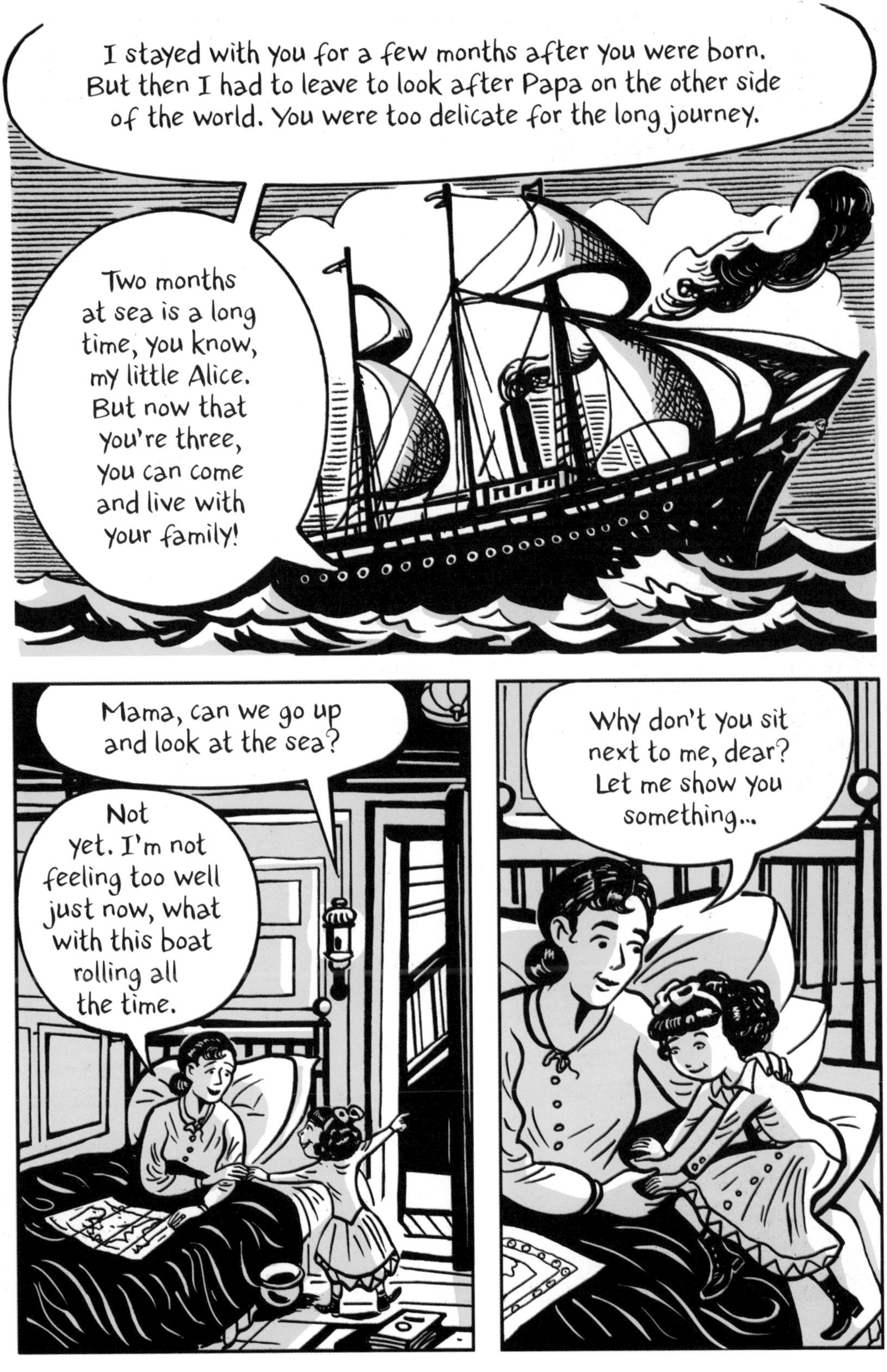
I stayed with you for a few months after you were born. But then I had to leave to look after Papa on the other side of the world. You were too delicate for the long journey.
Two months at sea is a long time, you know, my little Alice. But now that you're three, you can come and live with your family!
Mama, can we go up and look at the sea?
Not yet. I'm not feeling too well just now, what with this boat rolling all the time.
Why don't you sit next to me, dear? Let me show you something...

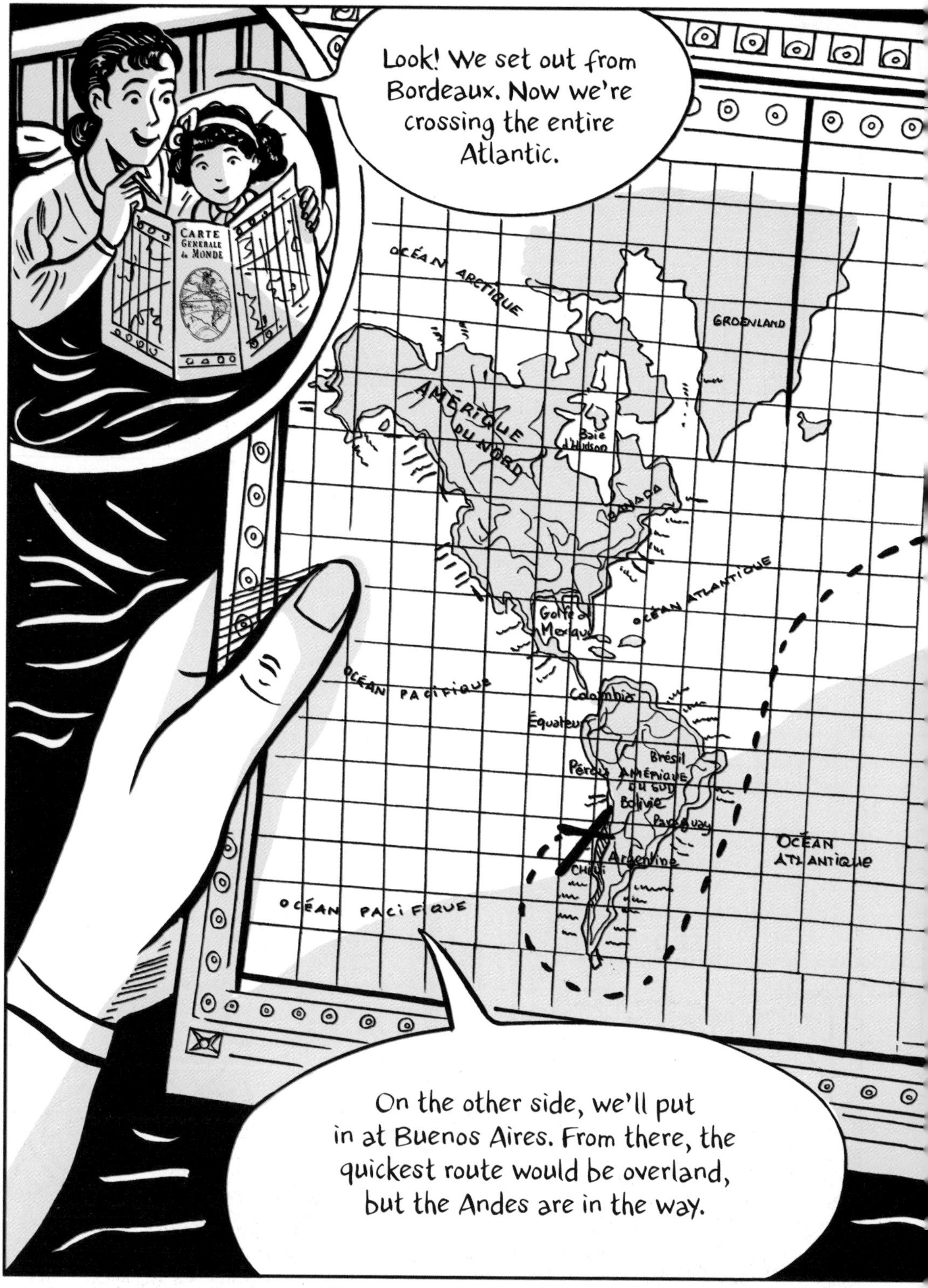
Look! We set out from Bordeaux. Now we're crossing the entire Atlantic.
CARTE GENERALE du MONDE
OCÉAN ARCTIQUE
GROENLAND
AMÉRIQUE DU NORD
Baie d'Hudson
CANADA
OCÉAN ATLANTIQUE
OCÉAN PACIFIQUE
Équateur
Brésil
Pérou
AMÉRIQUE DU SUD
Bolivie
Argentine
OCÉAN ATLANTIQUE
OCÉAN PACIFIQUE
On the other side, we'll put in at Buenos Aires. From there, the quickest route would be overland, but the Andes are in the way.

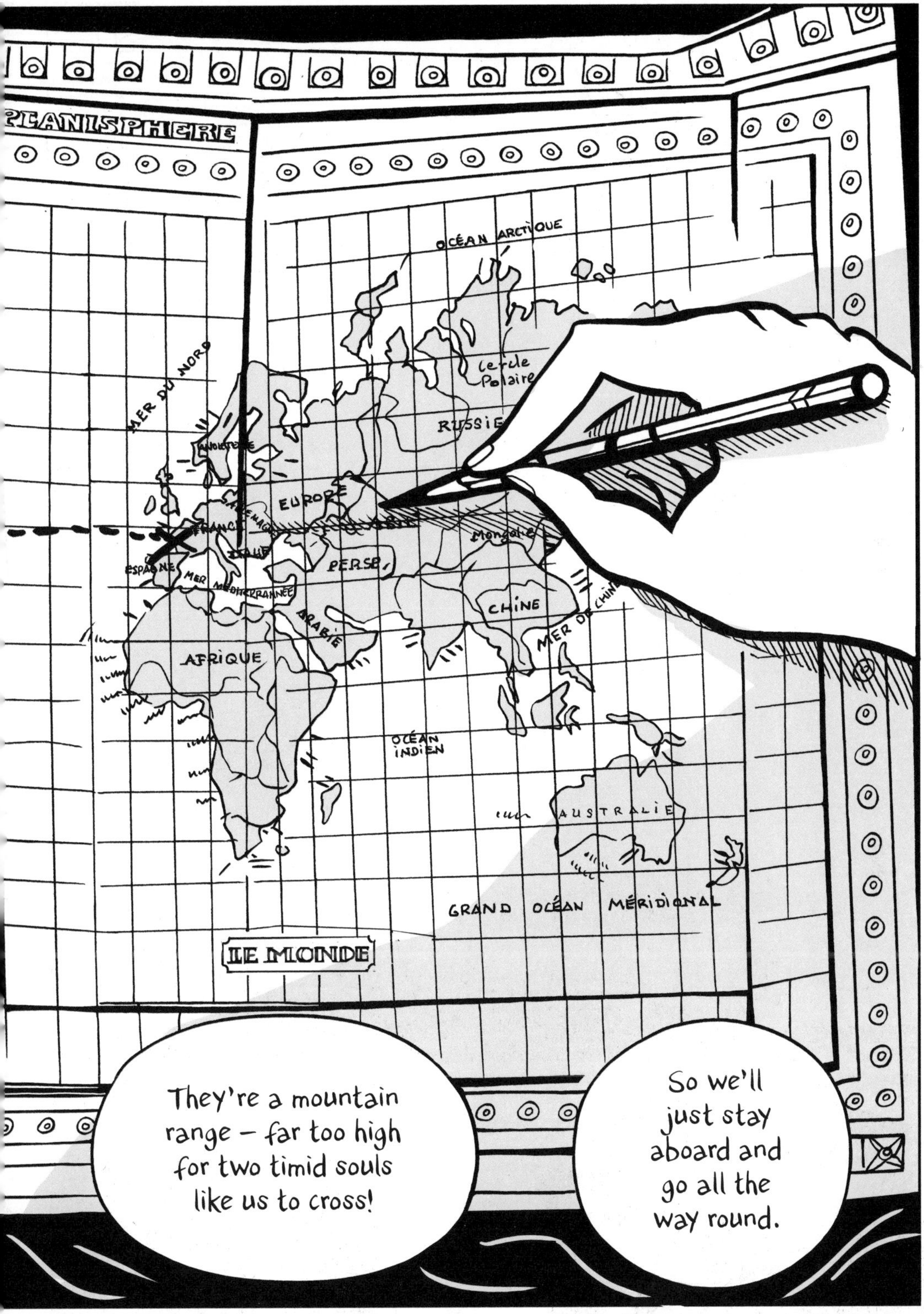
PLANISPHERE
OCÉAN ARCTIQUE
Cercle Polaire
MER DU NORD
RUSSIE
EUROPE
FRANCE
ESPAGNE
MER MÉDITERRANÉE
PERSE
Mongolie
CHINE
MER DE CHINE
ARABIE
AFRIQUE
OCÉAN INDIEN
AUSTRALIE
GRAND OCÉAN MÉRIDIONAL
LE MONDE
They're a mountain range – far too high for two timid souls like us to cross!
So we'll just stay aboard and go all the way round.

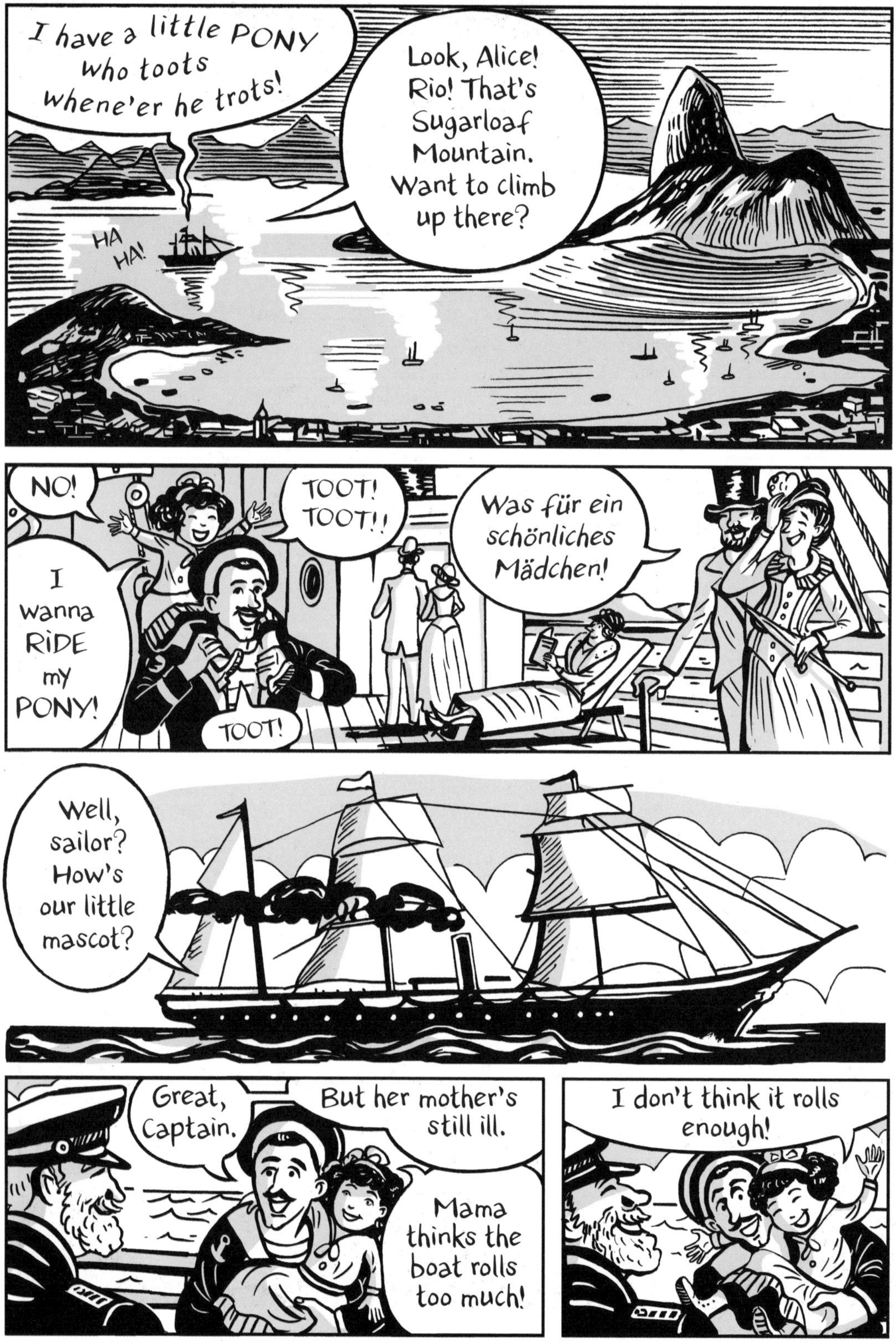
I have a little PONY who toots whene'er he trots!
Look, Alice! Rio! That's Sugarloaf Mountain. Want to climb up there?
HA HA!
NO!
I wanna RIDE my PONY!
TOOT! TOOT!!
TOOT!
Was für ein schönliches Mädchen!
Well, sailor? How's our little mascot?
Great, Captain.
But her mother's still ill.
Mama thinks the boat rolls too much!
I don't think it rolls enough!

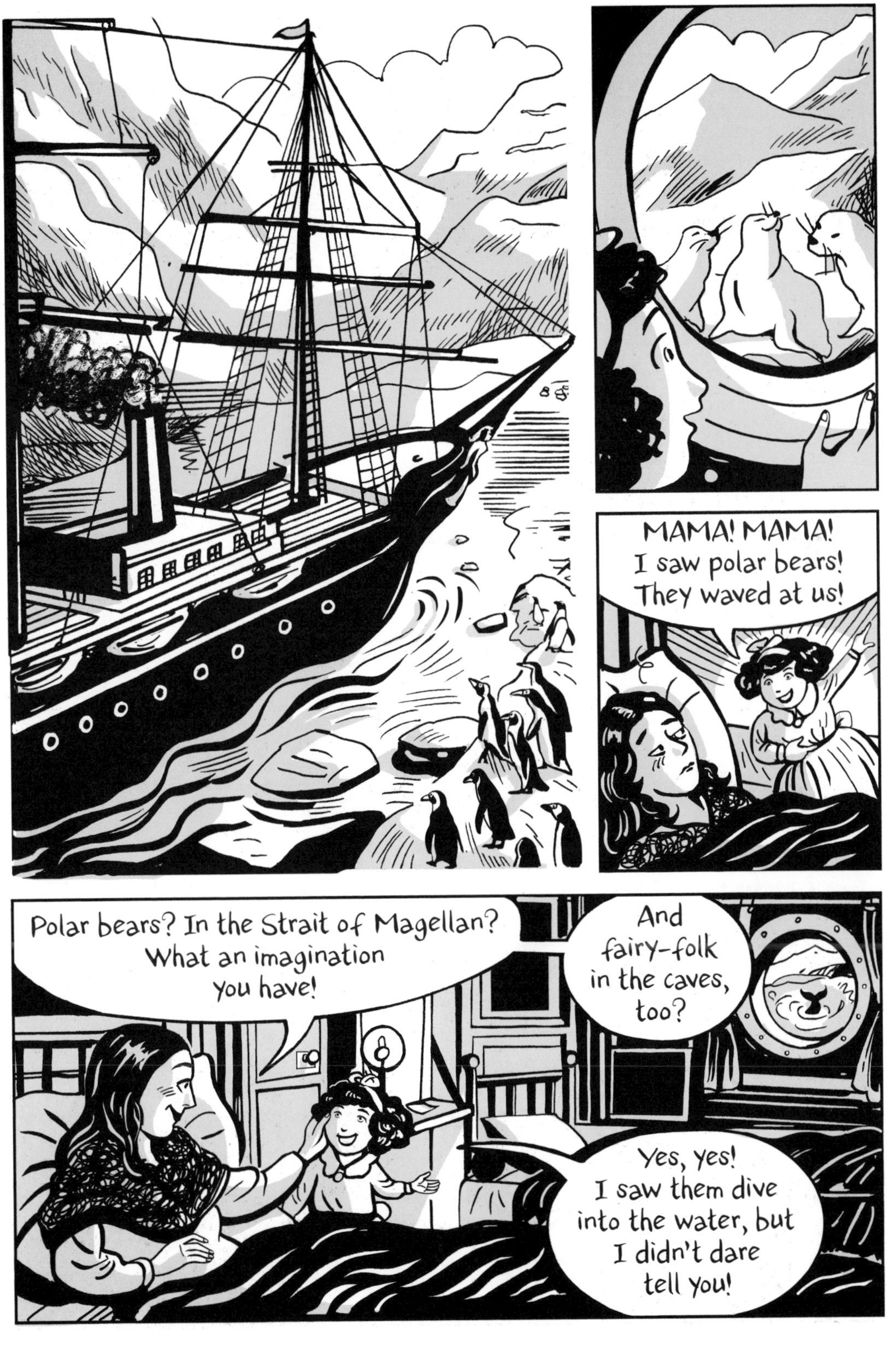
MAMA! MAMA!
I saw polar bears!
They waved at us!
Polar bears? In the Strait of Magellan? What an imagination you have!
And fairy-folk in the caves, too?
Yes, yes! I saw them dive into the water, but I didn't dare tell you!

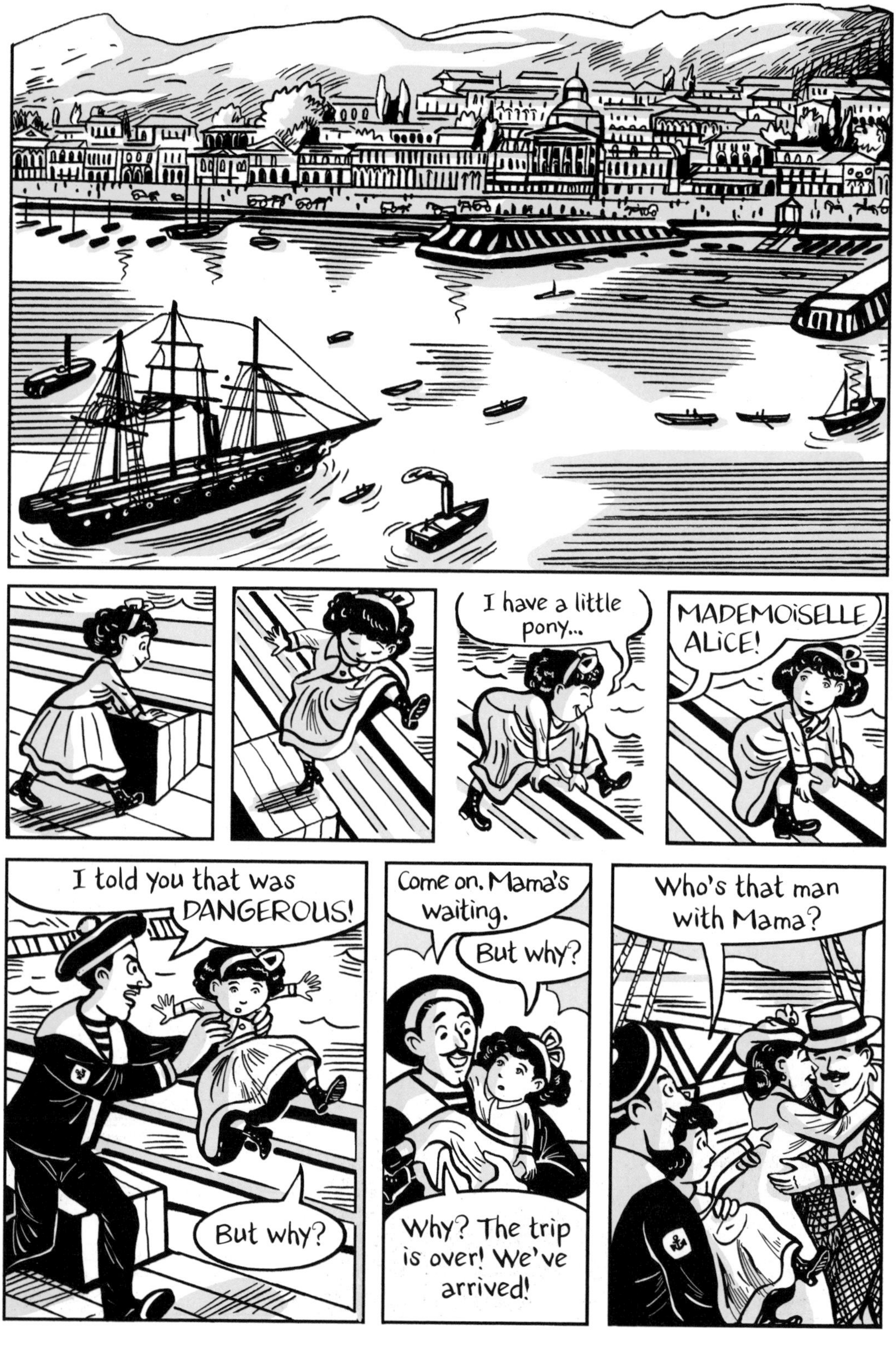
I have a little pony...
MADEMOISELLE ALICE!
I told you that was DANGEROUS!
But why?
Come on. Mama's waiting.
But why?
Why? The trip is over! We've arrived!
Who's that man with Mama?

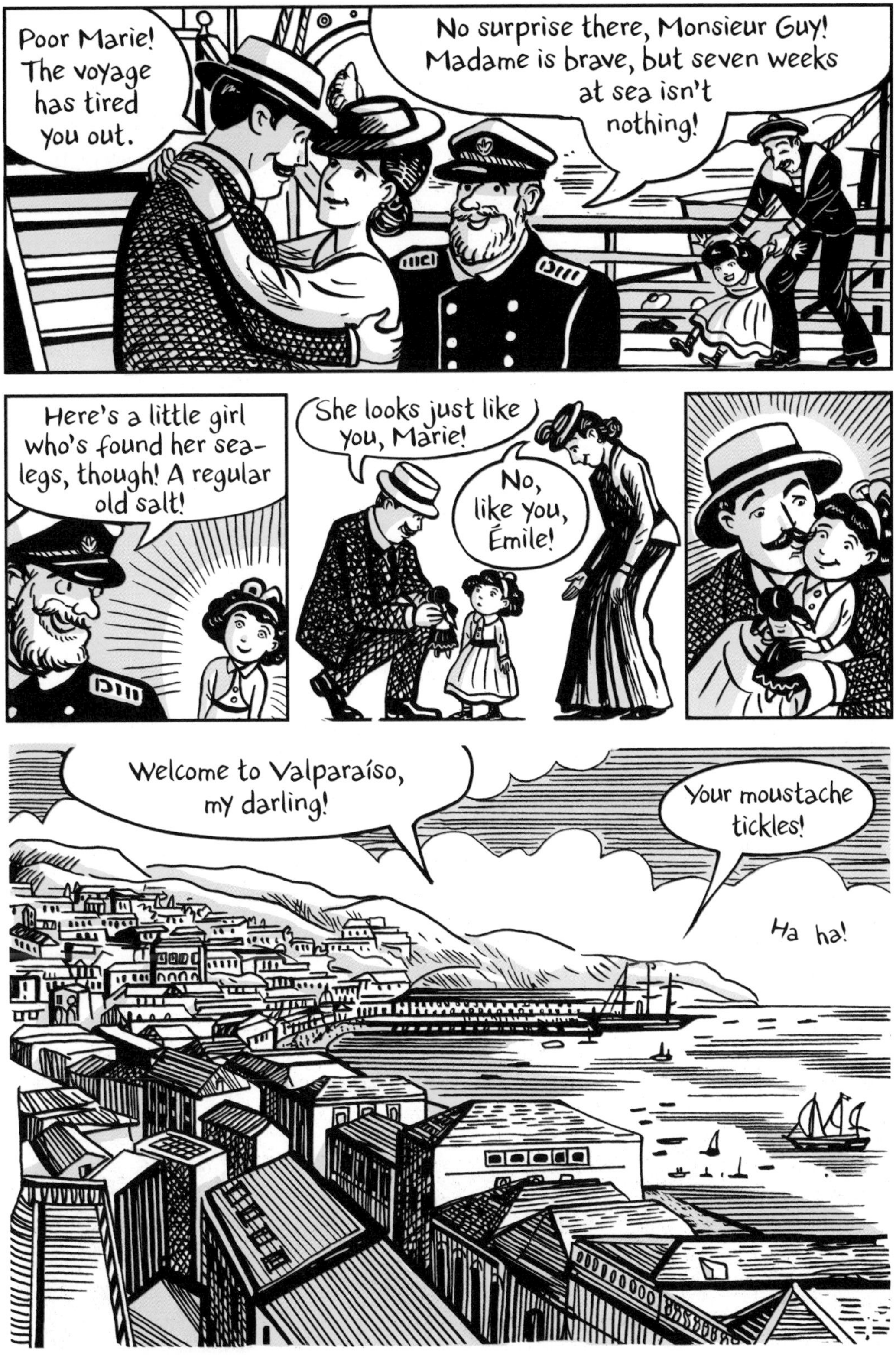
Poor Marie! The voyage has tired you out.
No surprise there, Monsieur Guy! Madame is brave, but seven weeks at sea isn't nothing!
Here's a little girl who's found her sea-legs, though! A regular old salt!
She looks just like you, Marie!
No, like you, Émile!
Welcome to Valparaíso, my darling!
Your moustache tickles!
Ha ha!

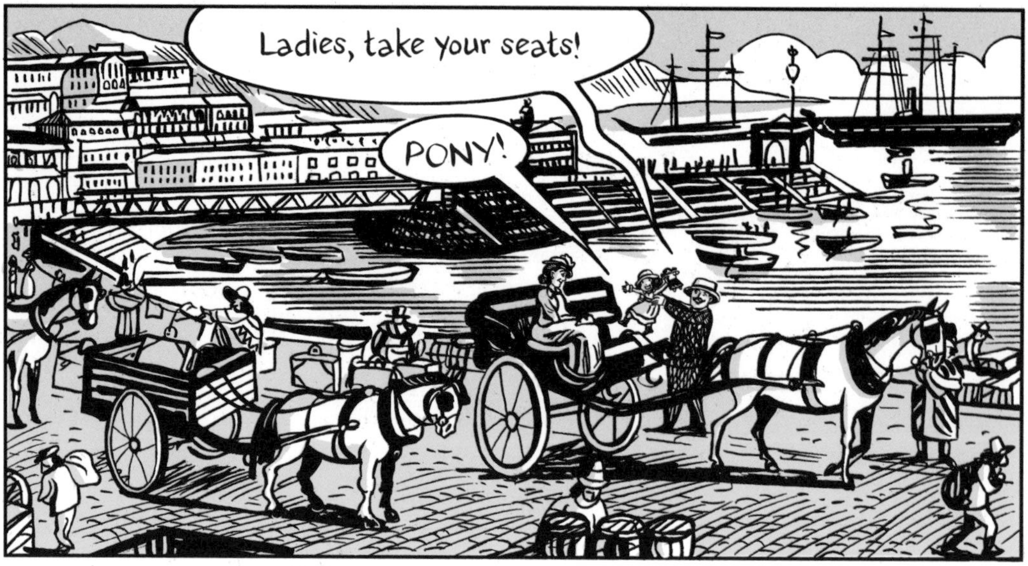
Ladies, take your seats!
PONY!

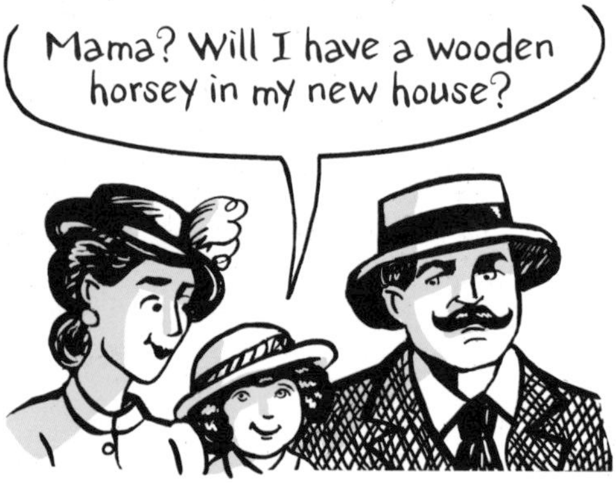
Mama? Will I have a wooden horsey in my new house?

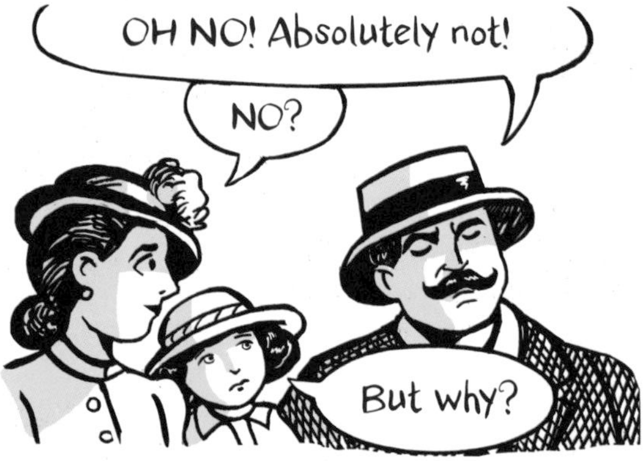
OH NO! Absolutely not!
NO?
But why?

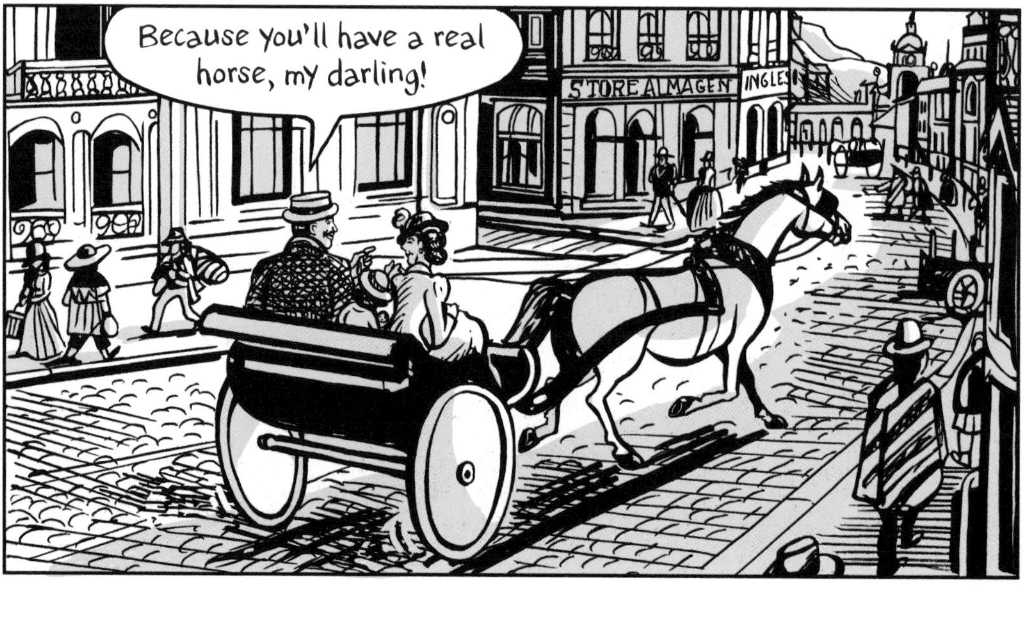
Because you'll have a real horse, my darling!
STORE ALMAGEN
INGLES

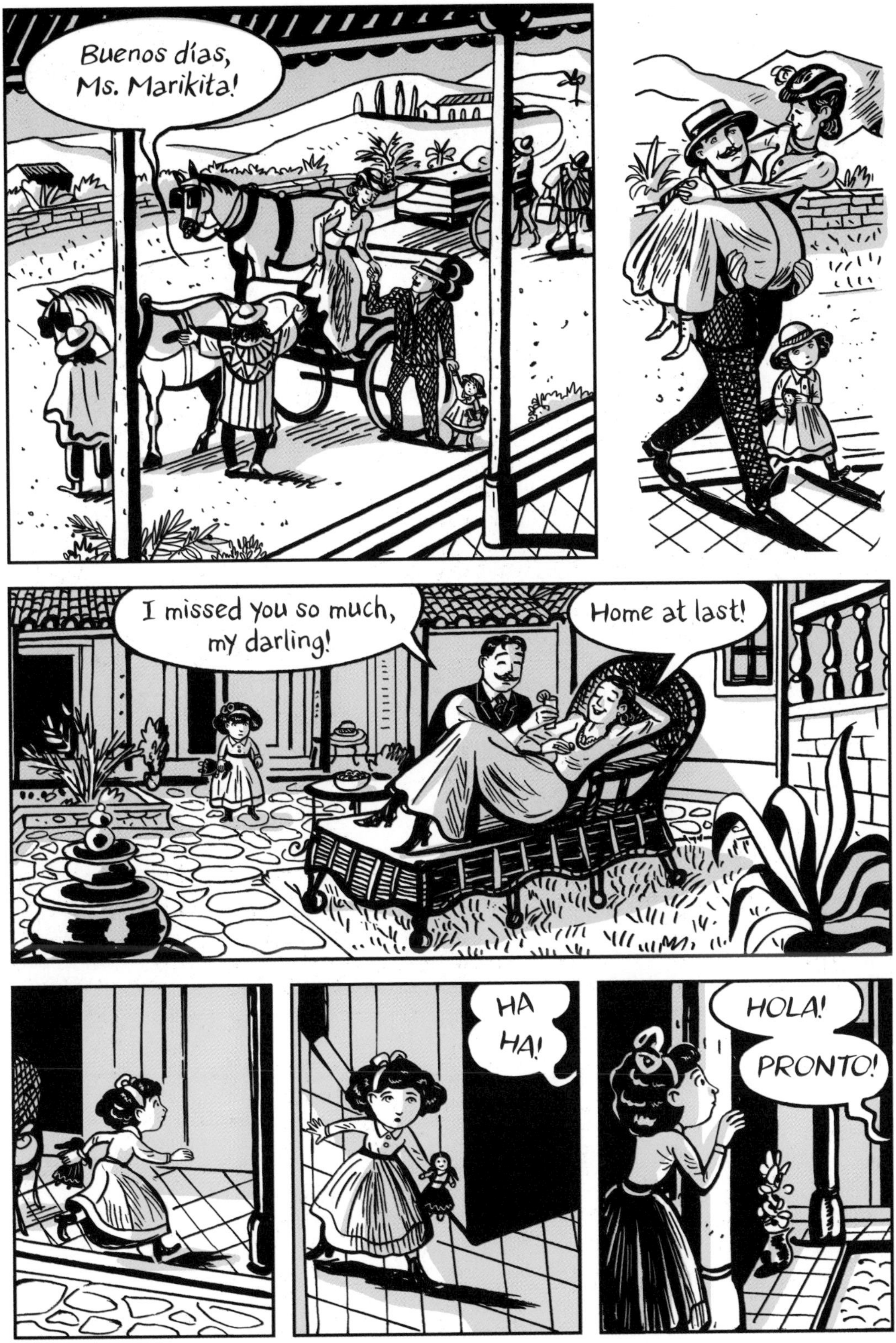
Buenos días,
Ms. Marikita!
I missed you so much,
my darling!
Home at last!
HA
HA!
HOLA!
PRONTO!

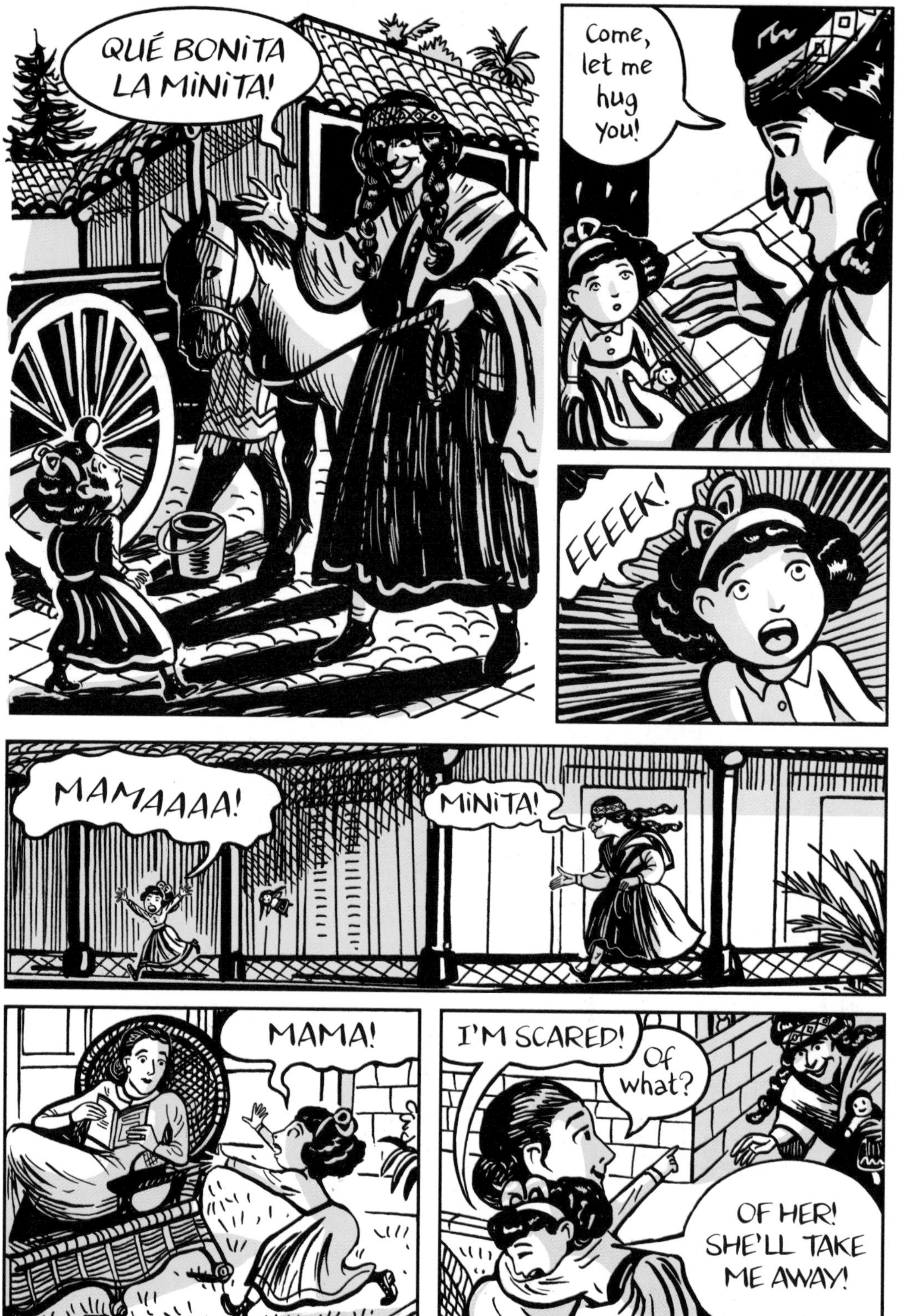
QUÉ BONITA LA MINITA!
Come, let me hug you!
EEEEK!
MAMAAAA!
MINITA!
MAMA!
I'M SCARED!
Of what?
OF HER! SHE'LL TAKE ME AWAY!

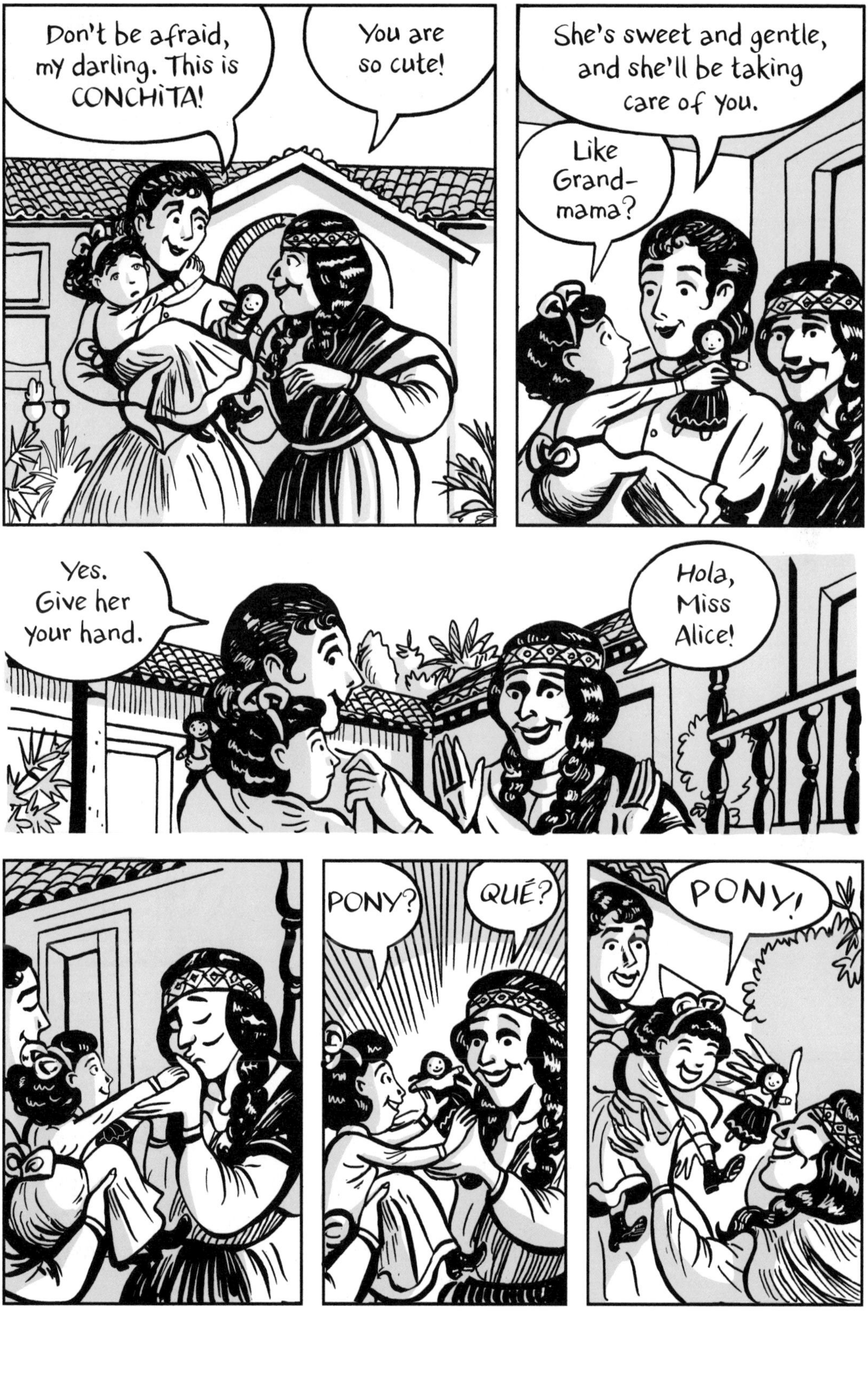
Don't be afraid, my darling. This is CONCHITA!
You are so cute!
She's sweet and gentle, and she'll be taking care of you.
Like Grand-mama?
Yes. Give her your hand.
Hola, Miss Alice!
PONY?
QUÉ?
PONY!

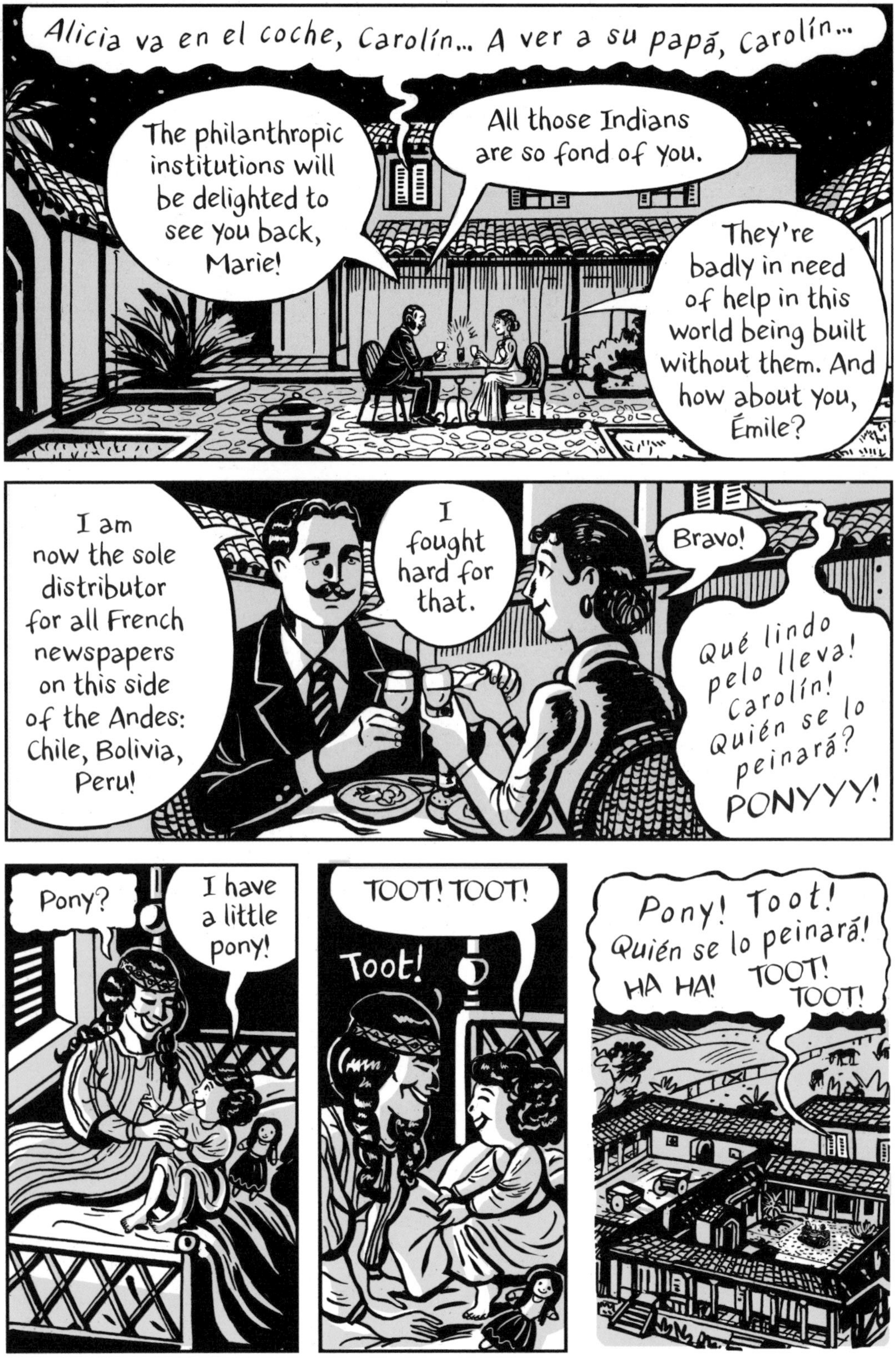
Alicia va en el coche, Carolín... A ver a su papá, Carolín...
The philanthropic institutions will be delighted to see you back, Marie!
All those Indians are so fond of you.
They're badly in need of help in this world being built without them. And how about you, Émile?
I am now the sole distributor for all French newspapers on this side of the Andes: Chile, Bolivia, Peru!
I fought hard for that.
Bravo!
Qué lindo pelo lleva! Carolín! Quién se lo peinará? PONYYY!
Pony?
I have a little pony!
TOOT! TOOT!
Toot!
Pony! Toot! Quién se lo peinará! HA HA! TOOT! TOOT!

1879 – Bois-Salève Boarding School –
Le Pas de l'Échelle – Switzerland

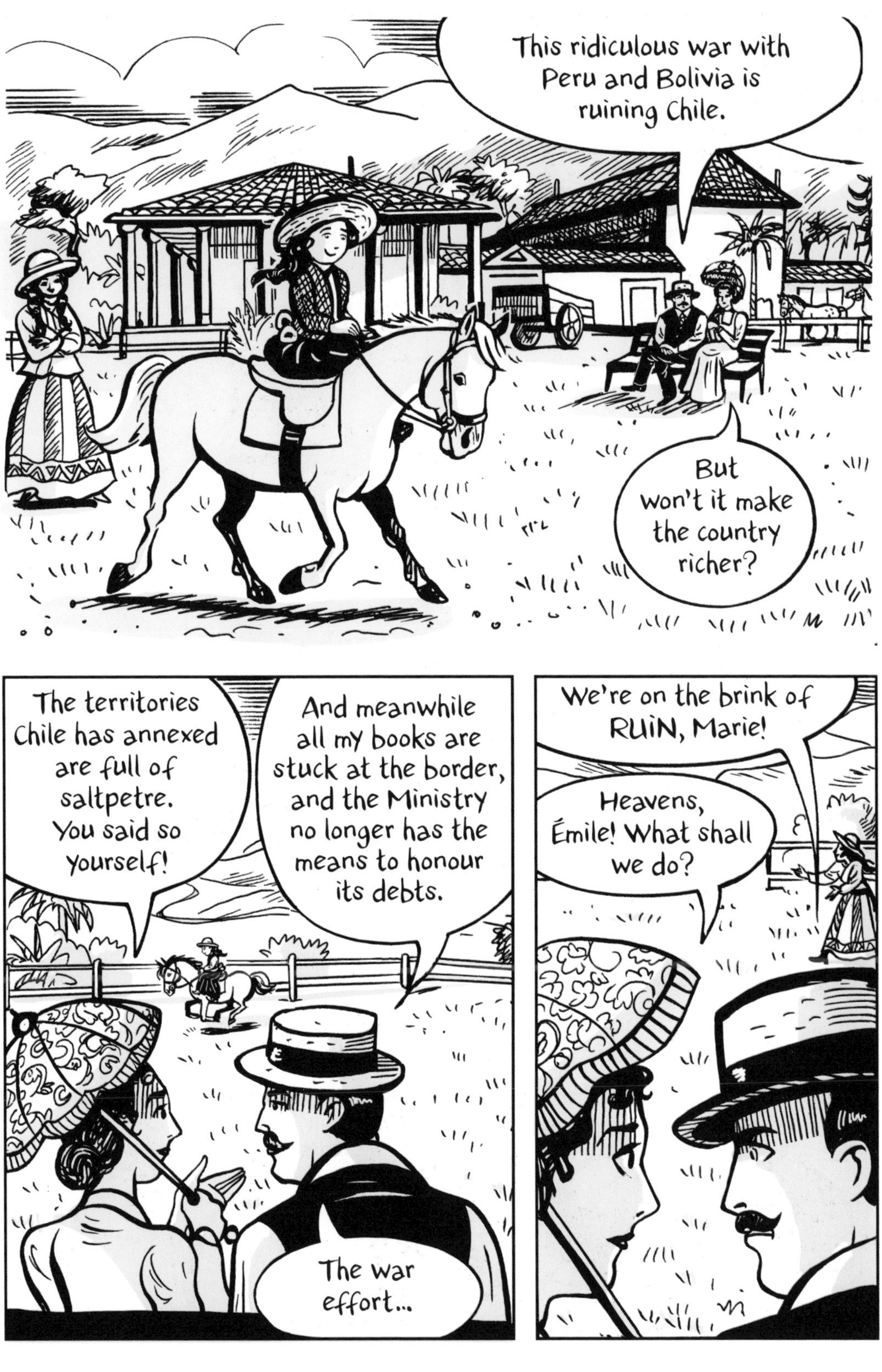
This ridiculous war with Peru and Bolivia is ruining Chile.
But won't it make the country richer?
The territories Chile has annexed are full of saltpetre. You said so yourself!
And meanwhile all my books are stuck at the border, and the Ministry no longer has the means to honour its debts.
The war effort...
We're on the brink of RUIN, Marie!
Heavens, Émile! What shall we do?

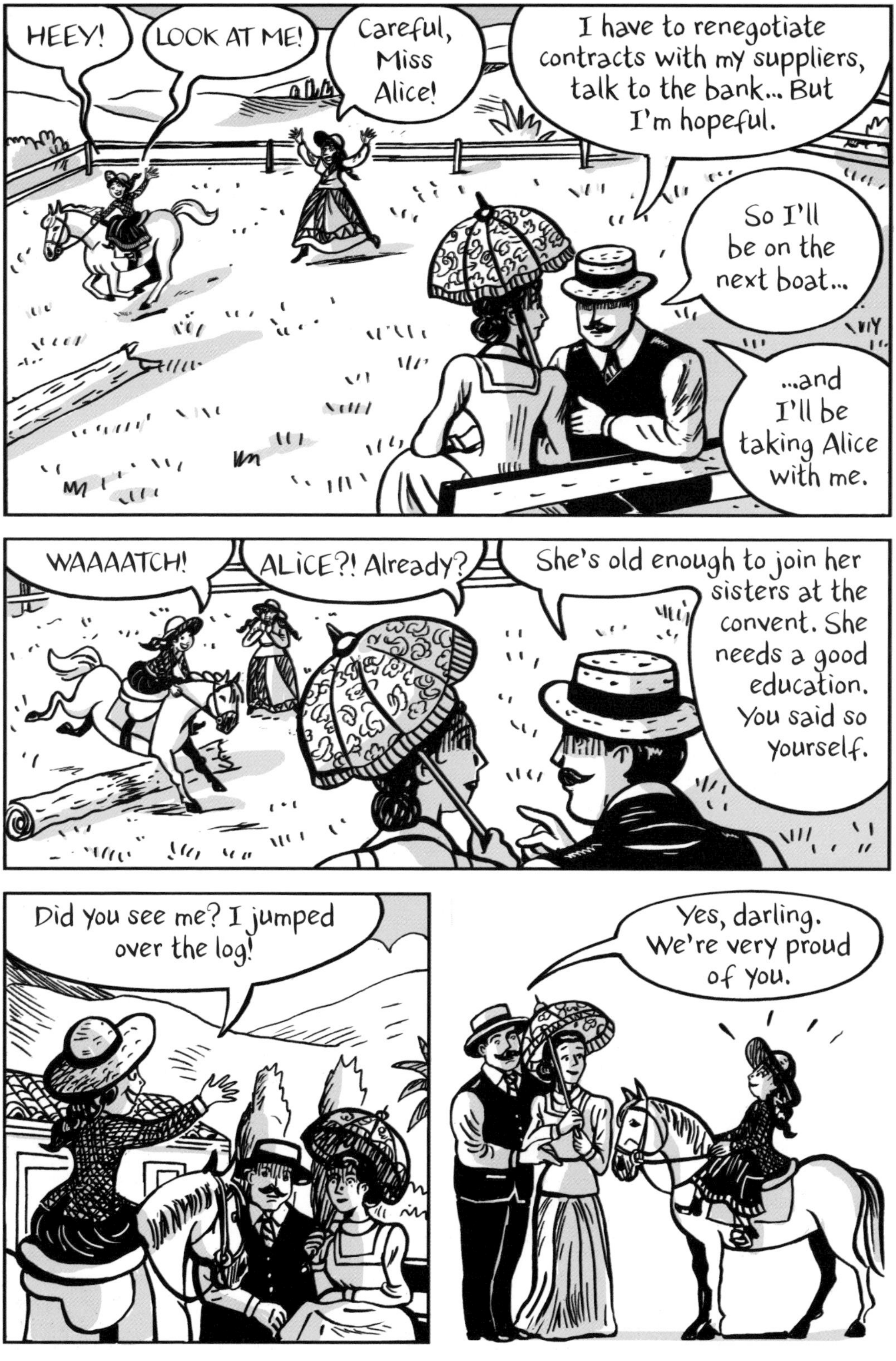
HEEY!
LOOK AT ME!
Careful, Miss Alice!
I have to renegotiate contracts with my suppliers, talk to the bank... But I'm hopeful.
So I'll be on the next boat...
...and I'll be taking Alice with me.
WAAAATCH!
ALICE?! Already?
She's old enough to join her sisters at the convent. She needs a good education. You said so yourself.
Did you see me? I jumped over the log!
Yes, darling. We're very proud of you.

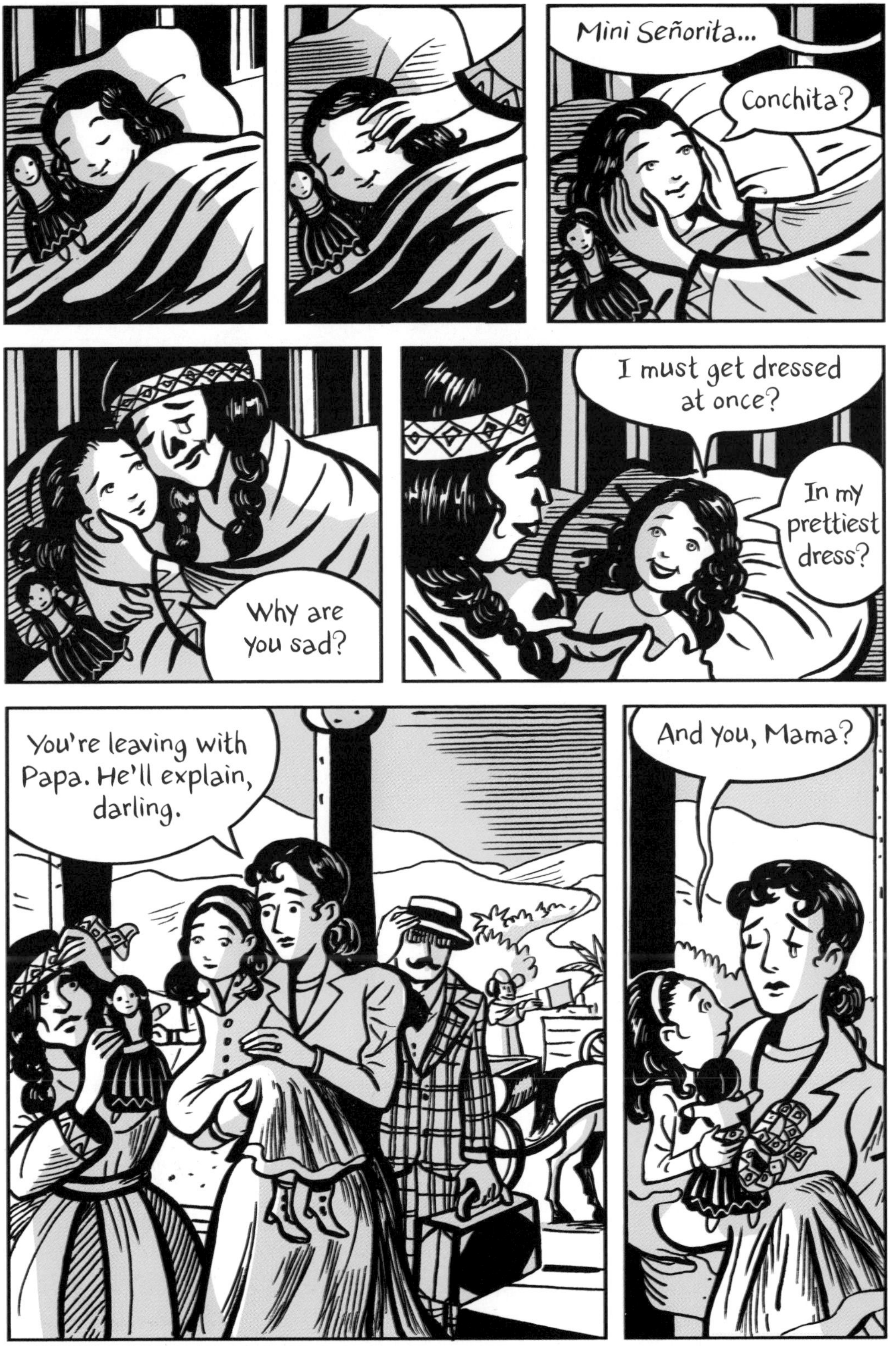

Mini Señorita...
Conchita?
Why are you sad?
I must get dressed at once?
In my prettiest dress?
You're leaving with Papa. He'll explain, darling.
And you, Mama?

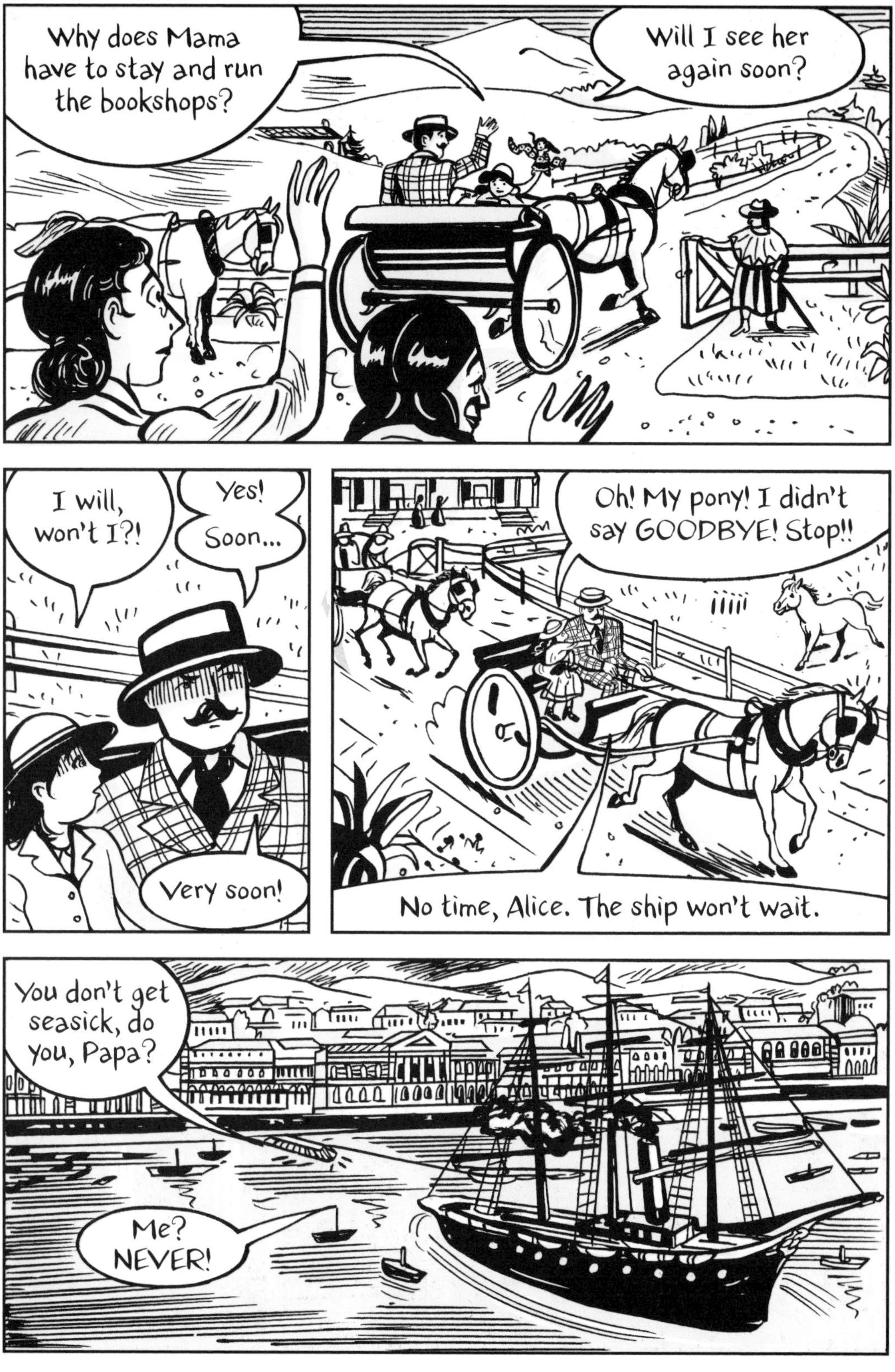
Why does Mama have to stay and run the bookshops?
Will I see her again soon?
I will, won't I?!
Yes! Soon...
Very soon!
Oh! My pony! I didn't say GOODBYE! Stop!!
No time, Alice. The ship won't wait.
You don't get seasick, do you, Papa?
Me? NEVER!

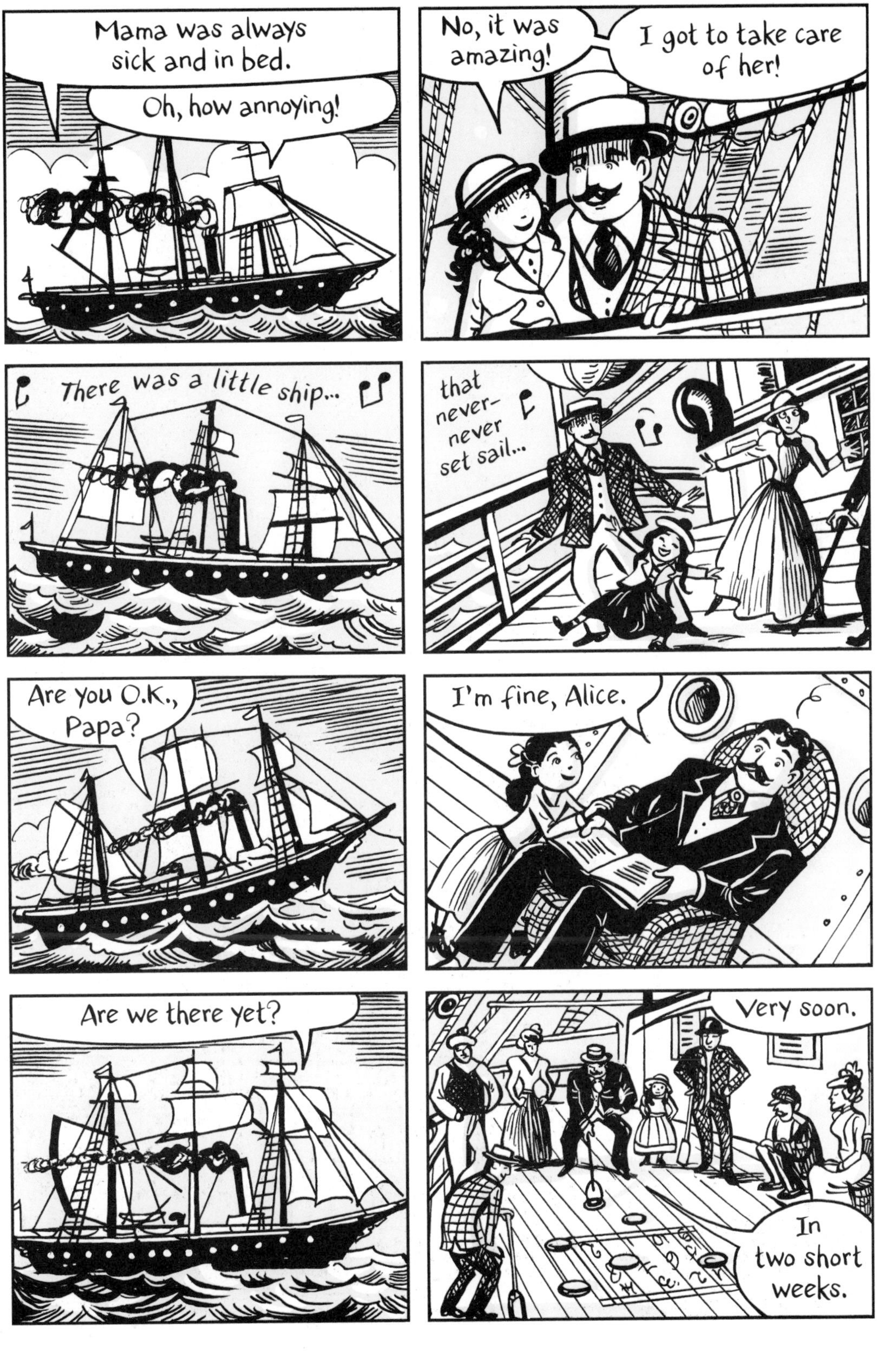
Mama was always sick and in bed.
Oh, how annoying!
No, it was amazing!
I got to take care of her!
There was a little ship...
that never-never set sail...
Are you O.K., Papa?
I'm fine, Alice.
Are we there yet?
Very soon.
In two short weeks.

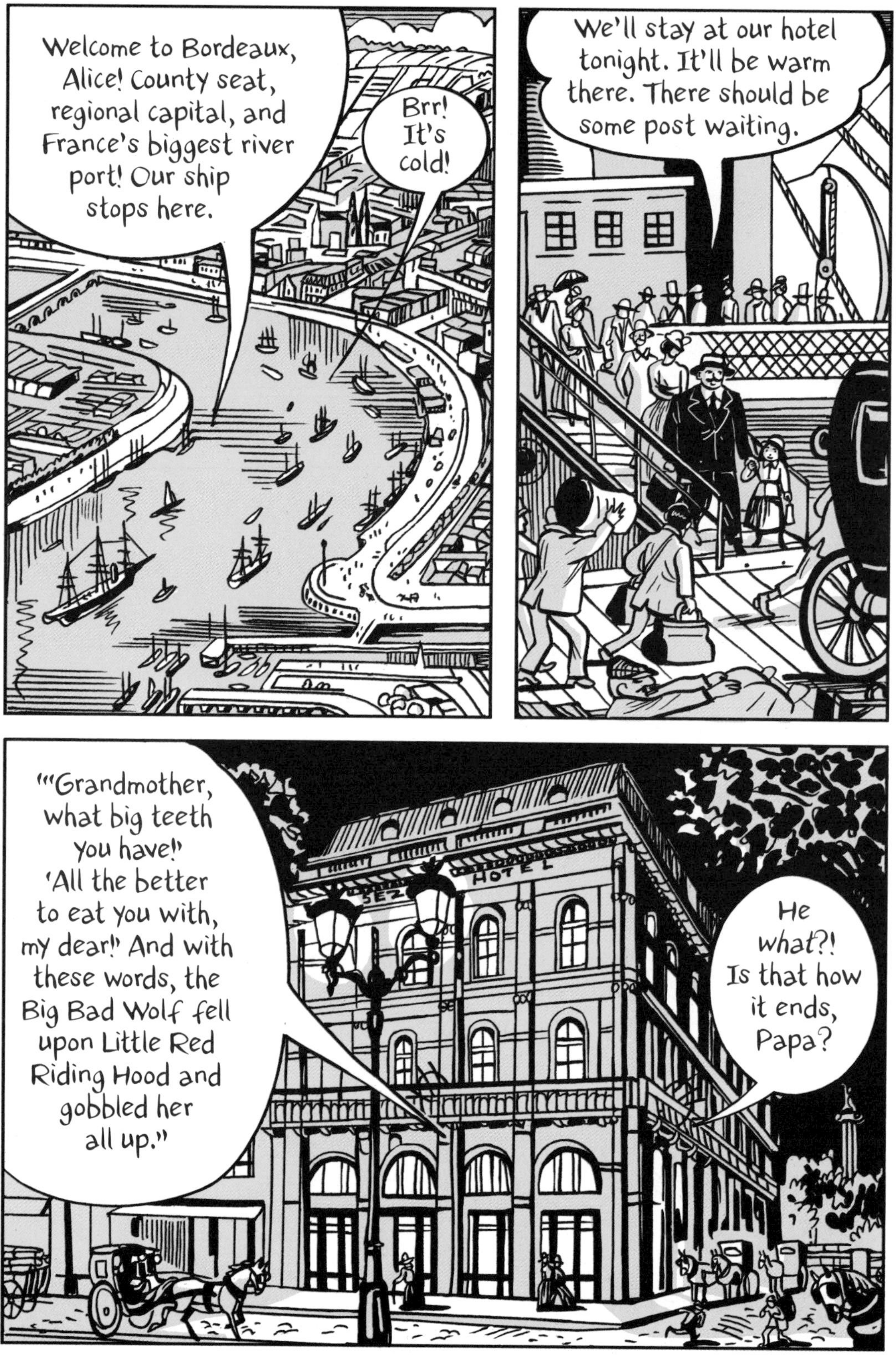
Welcome to Bordeaux, Alice! County seat, regional capital, and France's biggest river port! Our ship stops here.
Brr! It's cold!
We'll stay at our hotel tonight. It'll be warm there. There should be some post waiting.
HOTEL
"'Grandmother, what big teeth you have!' 'All the better to eat you with, my dear!' And with these words, the Big Bad Wolf fell upon Little Red Riding Hood and gobbled her all up."
He what?! Is that how it ends, Papa?

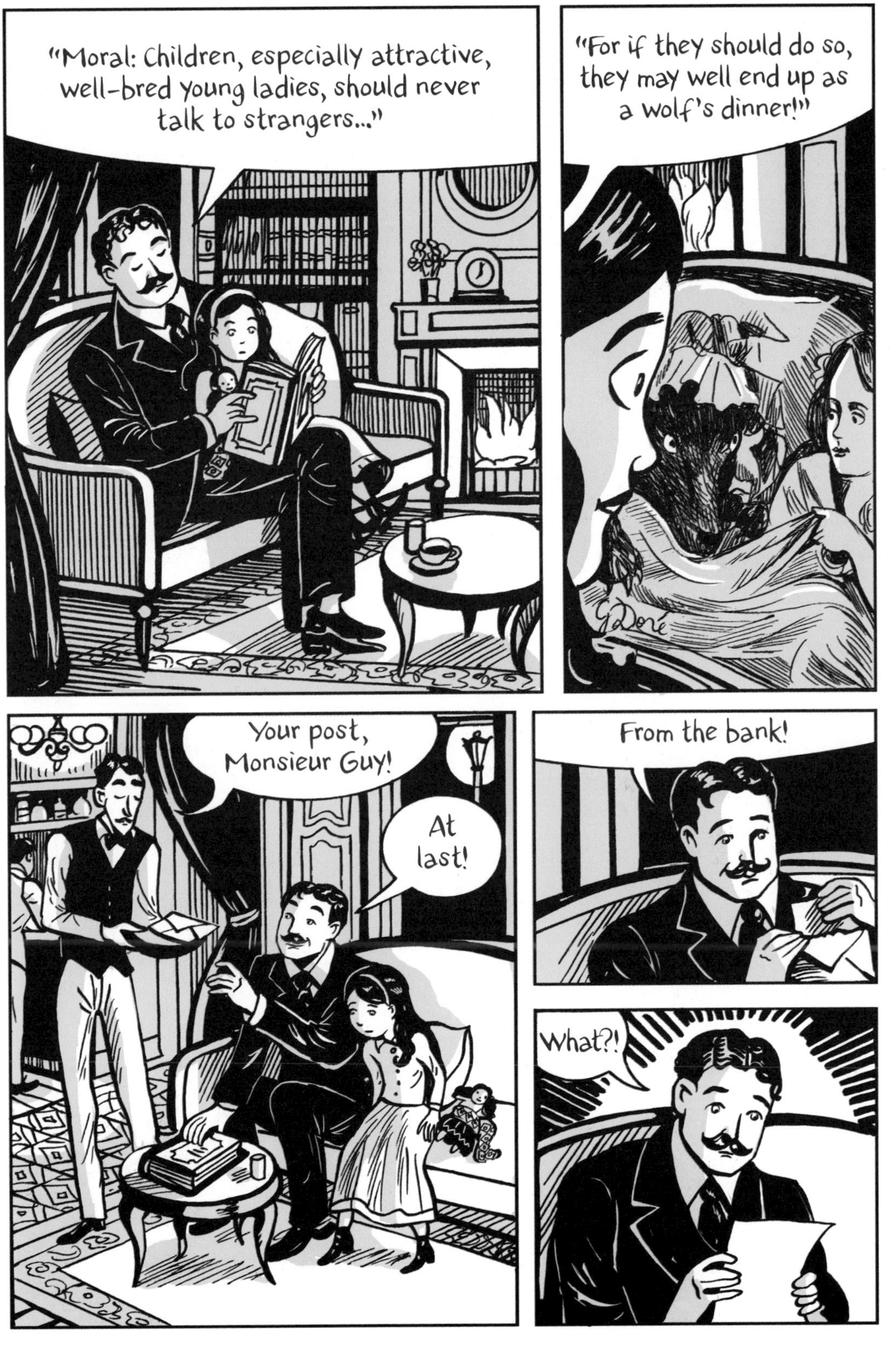
"Moral: Children, especially attractive, well-bred young ladies, should never talk to strangers..."
"For if they should do so, they may well end up as a wolf's dinner!"
G. Doré
Your post, Monsieur Guy!
At last!
From the bank!
What?!

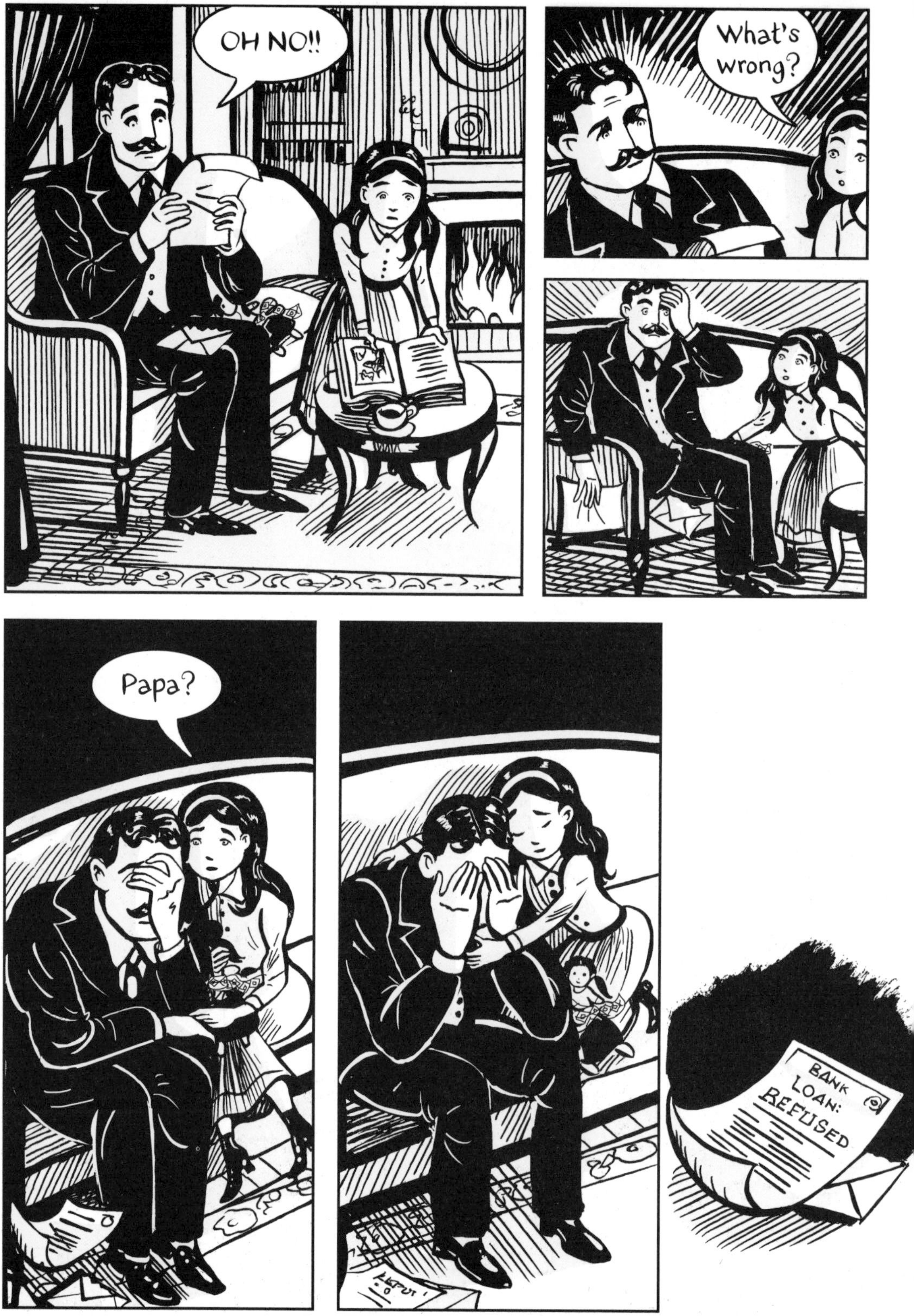
OH NO!!
What's wrong?
Papa?
BANK LOAN: REFUSED

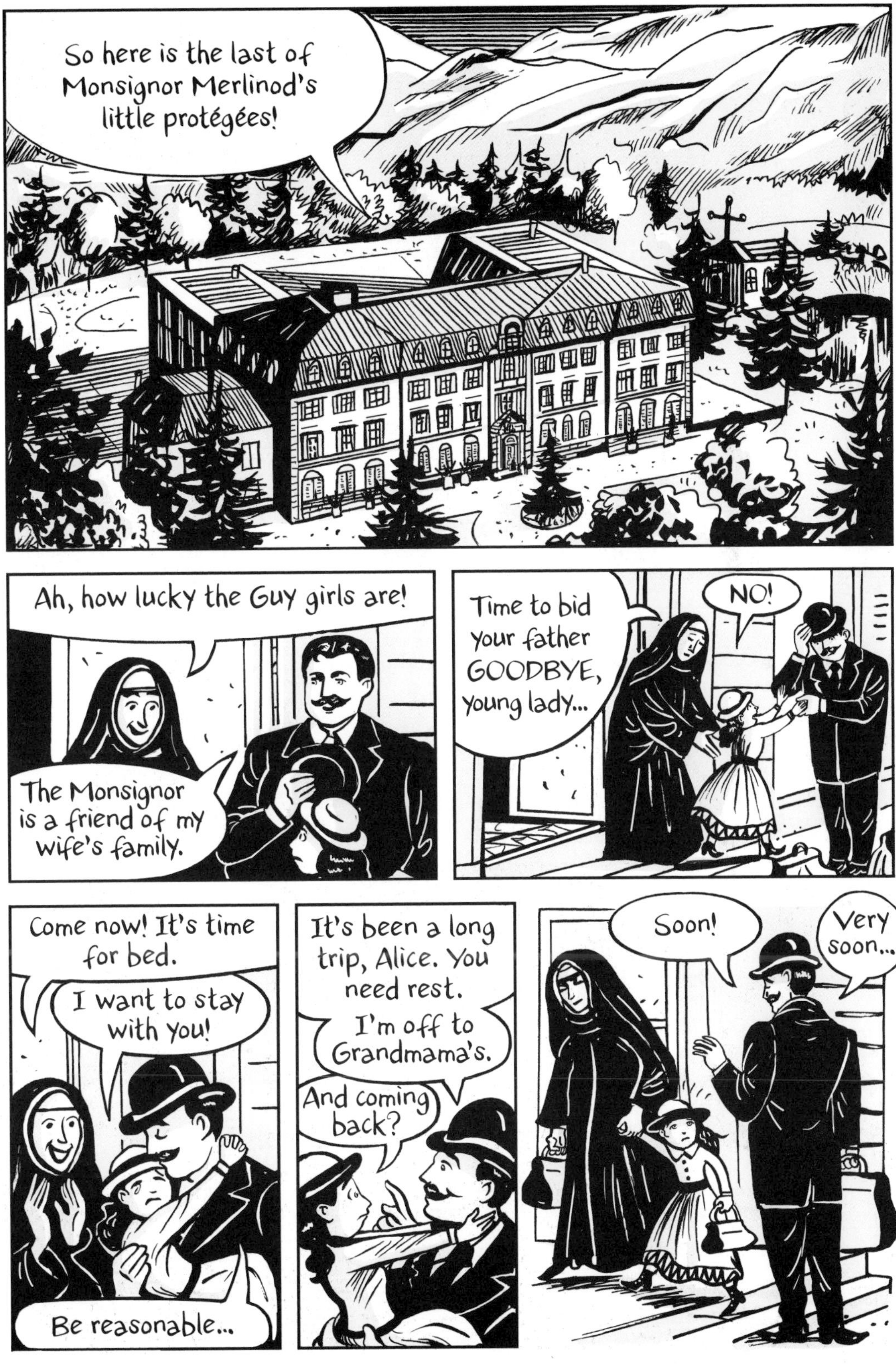
So here is the last of Monsignor Merlinod's little protégées!
Ah, how lucky the Guy girls are!
The Monsignor is a friend of my wife's family.
Time to bid your father GOODBYE, young lady...
NO!
Come now! It's time for bed.
I want to stay with you!
Be reasonable...
It's been a long trip, Alice. You need rest.
I'm off to Grandmama's.
And coming back?
Soon!
Very soon...

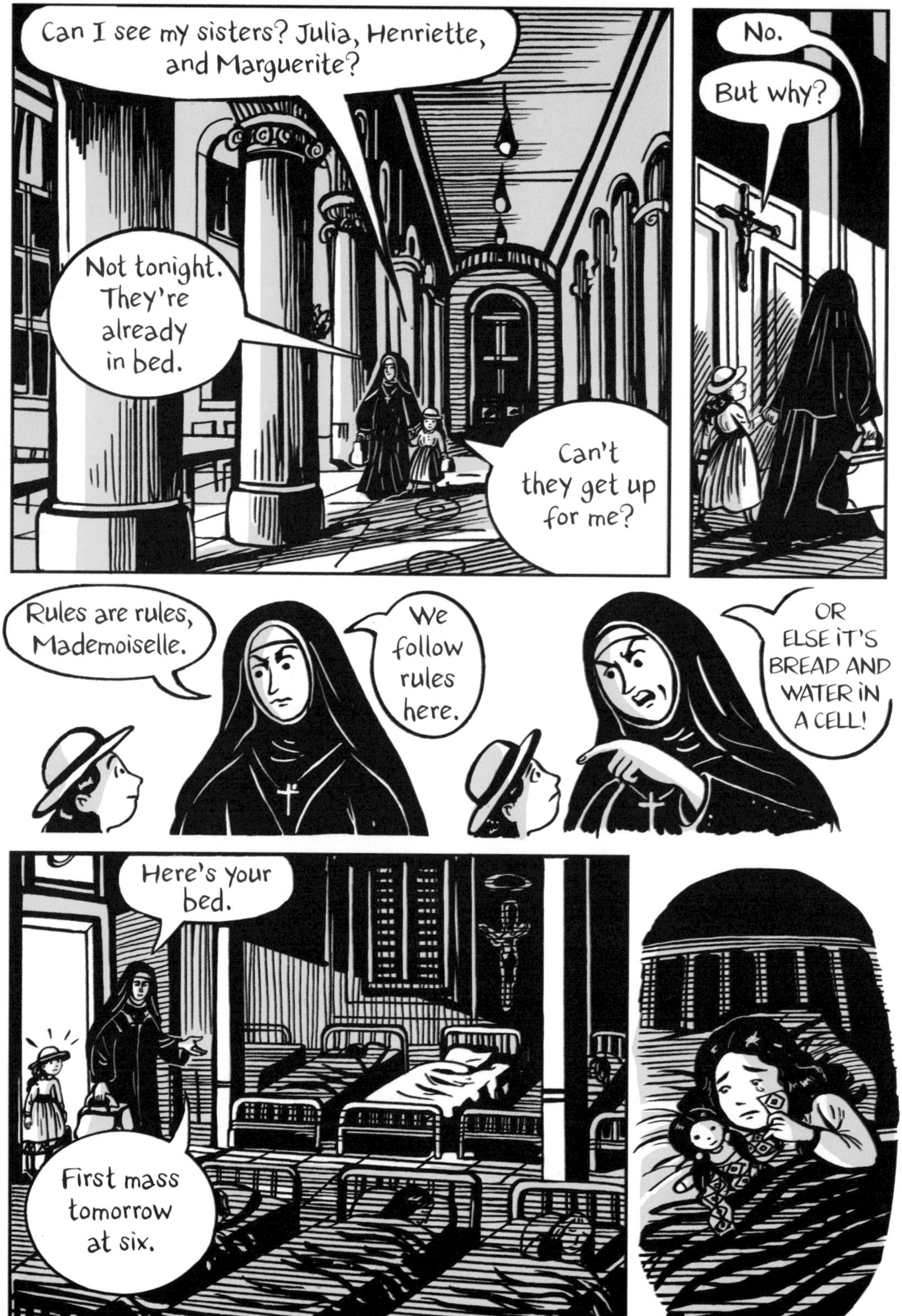
Can I see my sisters? Julia, Henriette, and Marguerite?
Not tonight. They're already in bed.
Can't they get up for me?
No.
But why?
Rules are rules, Mademoiselle.
We follow rules here.
OR ELSE IT'S BREAD AND WATER IN A CELL!
Here's your bed.
First mass tomorrow at six.

1885 – St. Joseph's Boarding School –
Ferney-Voltaire – France

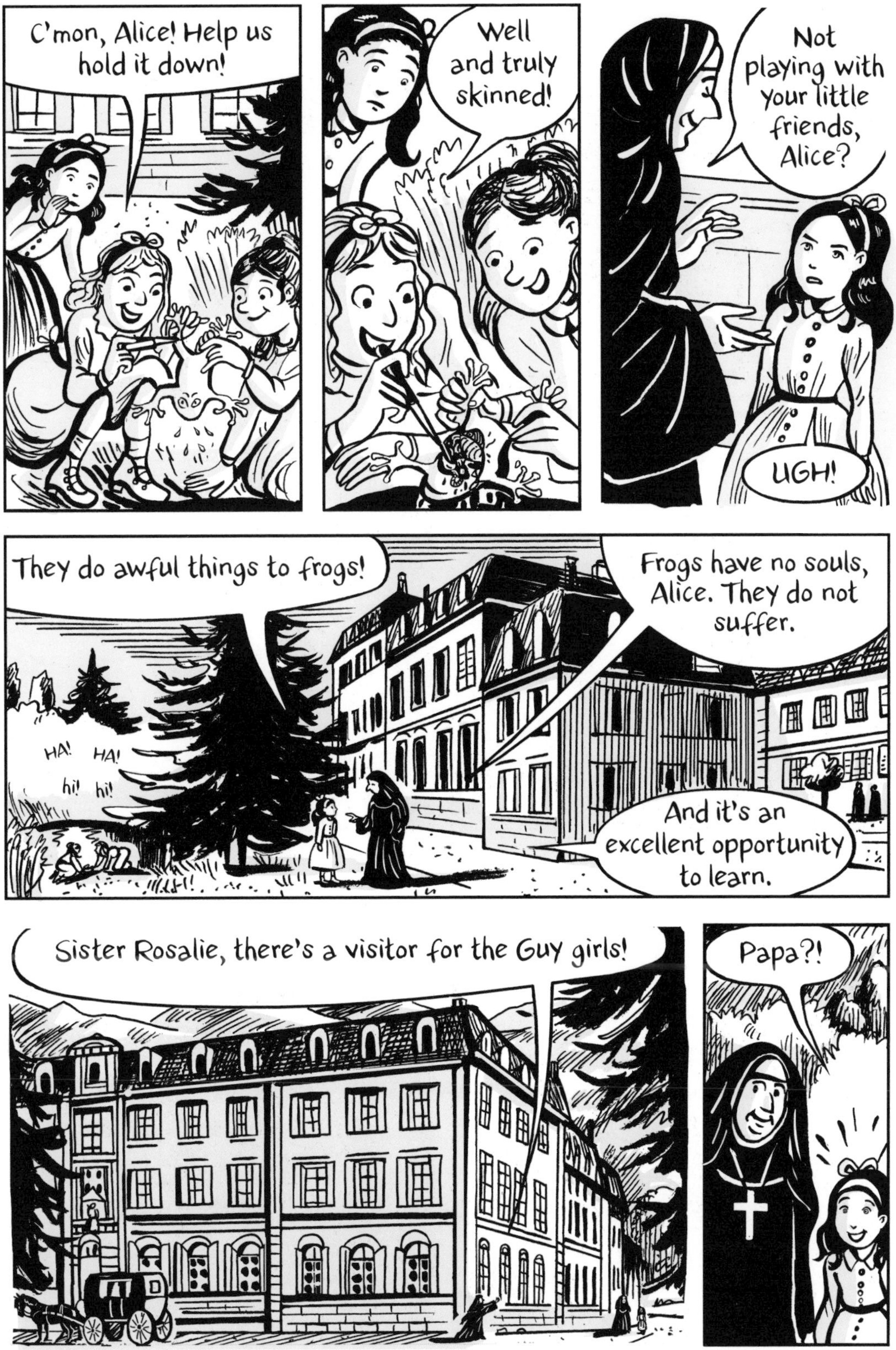
C'mon, Alice! Help us hold it down!
Well and truly skinned!
Not playing with your little friends, Alice?
UGH!
They do awful things to frogs!
Frogs have no souls, Alice. They do not suffer.
HA! HA!
hi! hi!
And it's an excellent opportunity to learn.
Sister Rosalie, there's a visitor for the Guy girls!
Papa?!

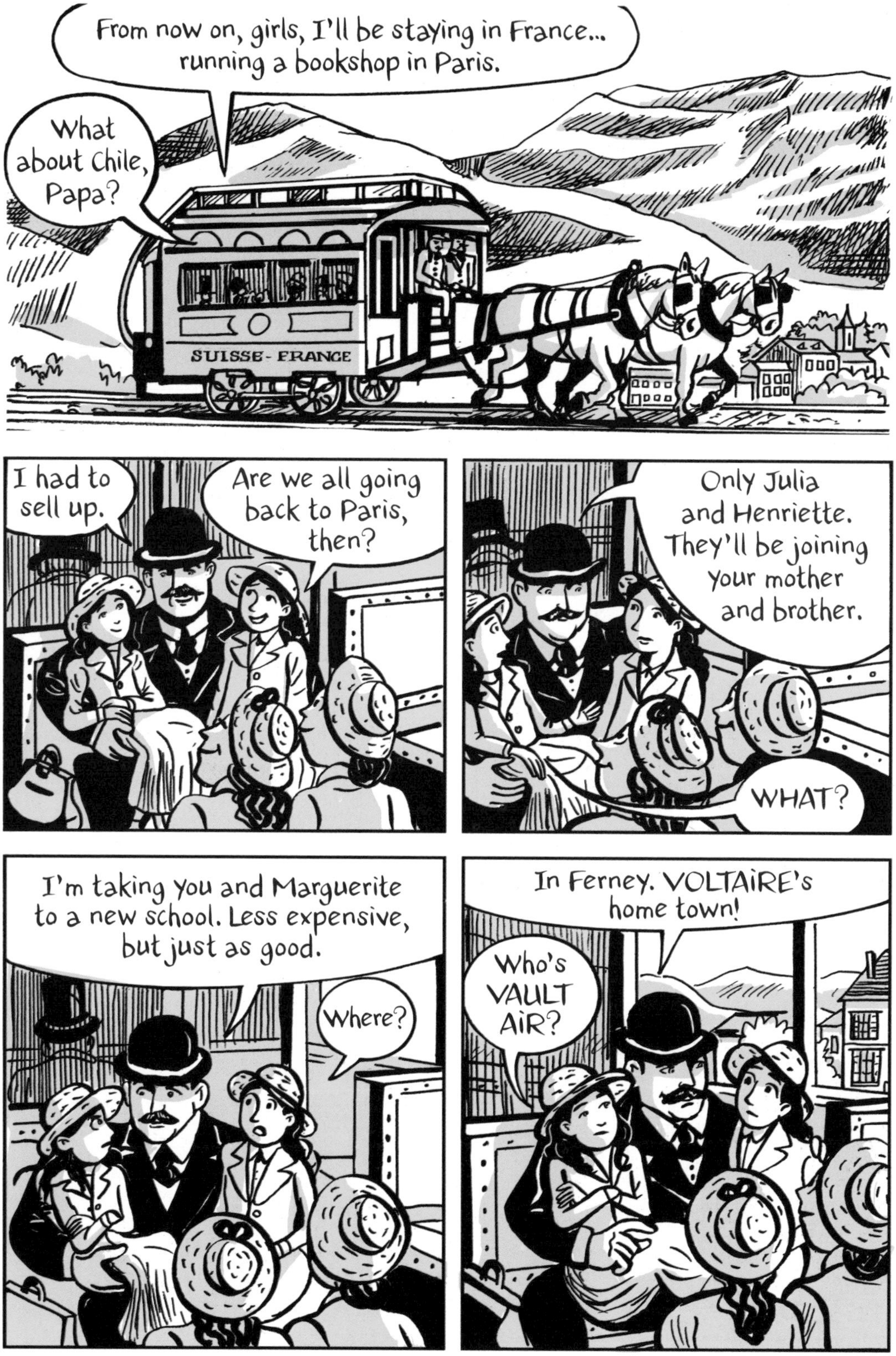
From now on, girls, I'll be staying in France... running a bookshop in Paris.
What about Chile, Papa?
SUISSE-FRANCE
I had to sell up.
Are we all going back to Paris, then?
Only Julia and Henriette. They'll be joining your mother and brother.
WHAT?
I'm taking you and Marguerite to a new school. Less expensive, but just as good.
Where?
In Ferney. VOLTAIRE's home town!
Who's VAULT AIR?

A philosopher whose ideas enlightened the French Revolution.

A bad man, then?

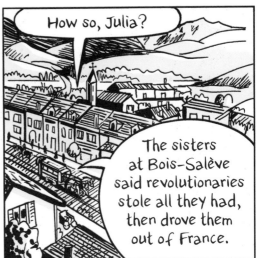

How so, Julia?

The sisters at Bois-Salève said revolutionaries stole all they had, then drove them out of France.

Is that VAULT AiR's fault?

Here we are!

SUISSE -FRANCE

VOLTAIRE

DEOCTIM MAKIMS

Papa, I want to stay with you!

Be reasonable, Alice.

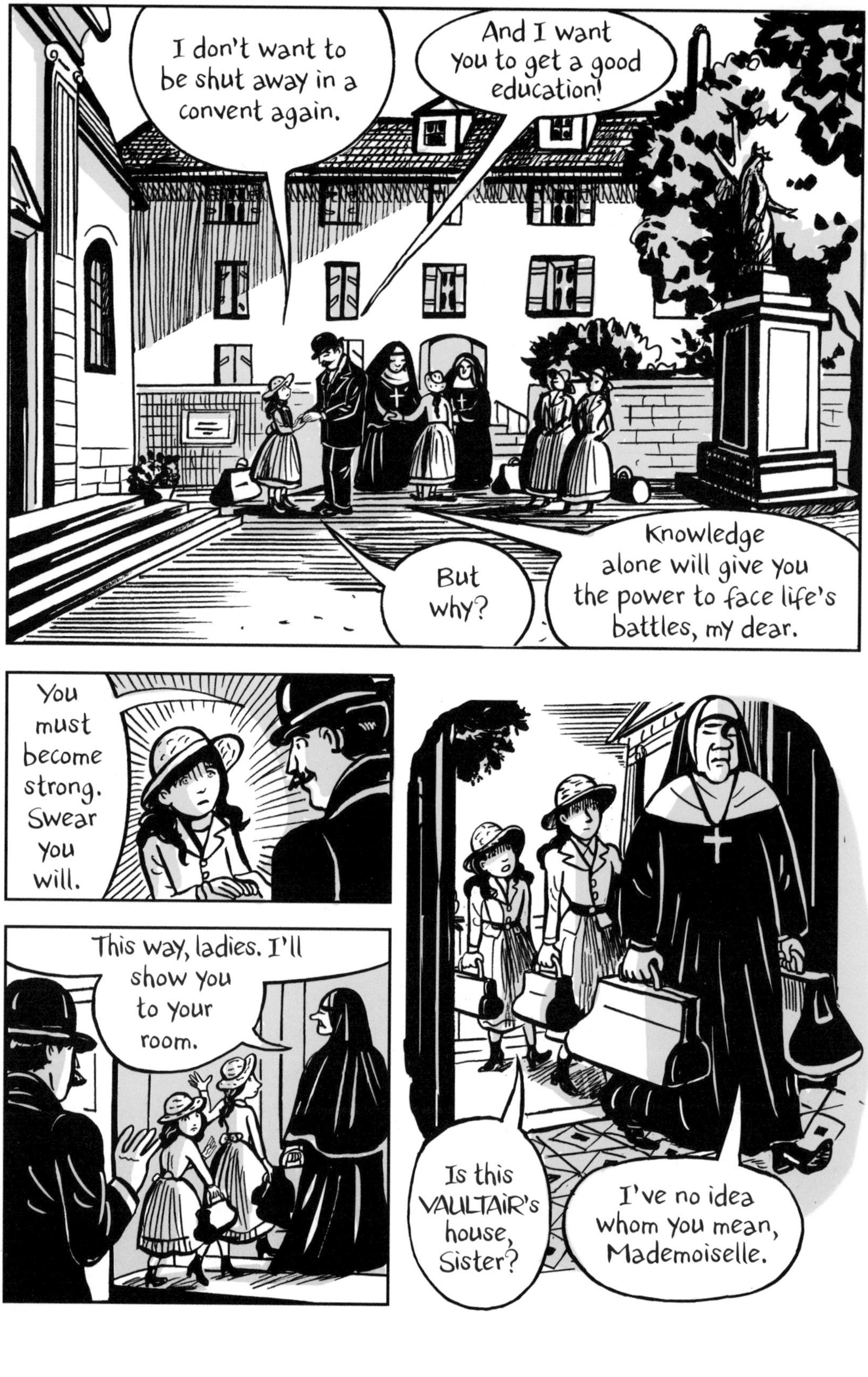
I don't want to be shut away in a convent again.
And I want you to get a good education!
But why?
Knowledge alone will give you the power to face life's battles, my dear.
You must become strong. Swear you will.
This way, ladies. I'll show you to your room.
Is this VAULTAIR's house, Sister?
I've no idea whom you mean, Mademoiselle.

1890 – 19, Rue Saint-Sulpice – Paris – France

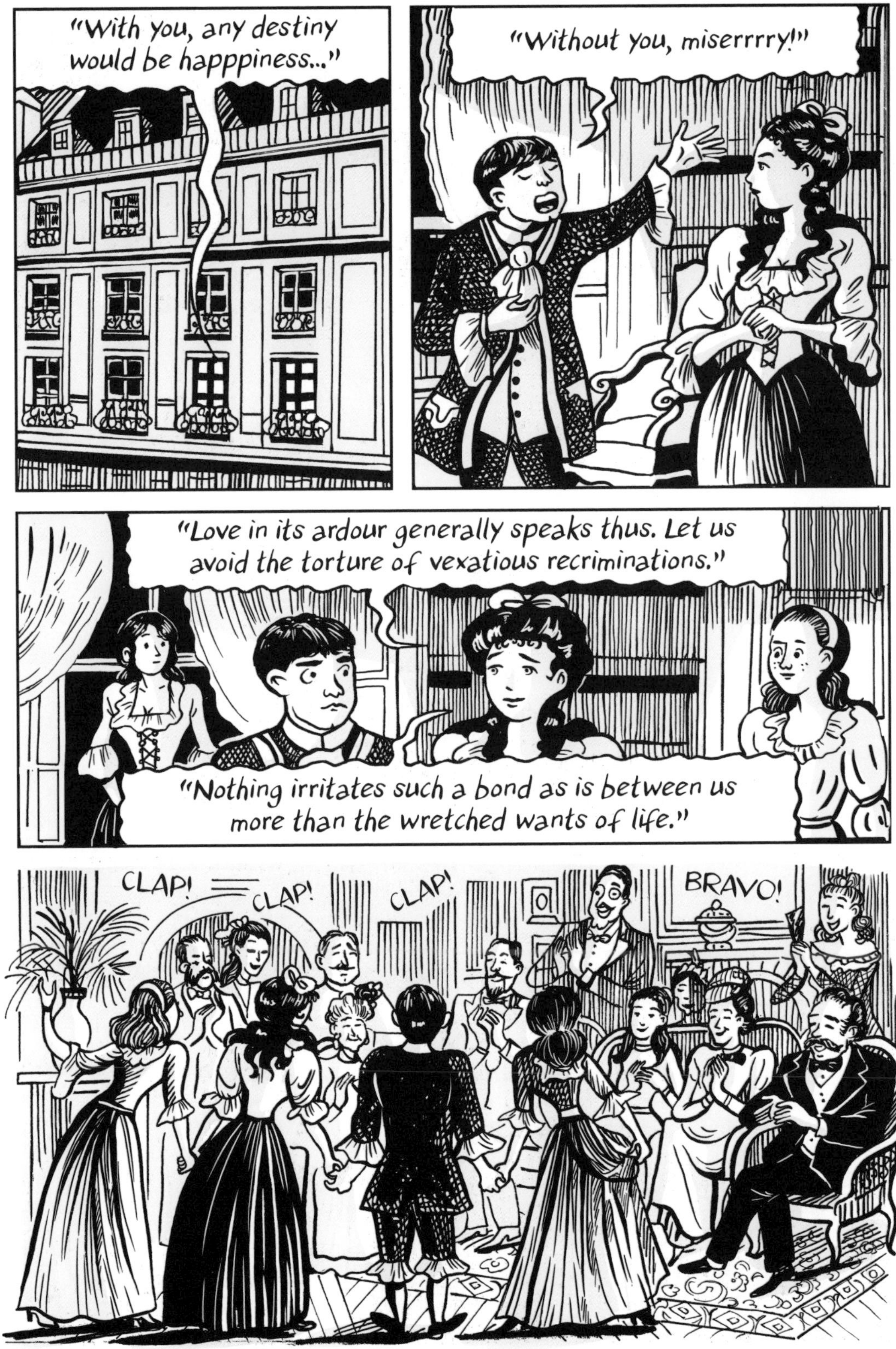
"With you, any destiny would be happppiness..."
"Without you, miserrrry!"
"Love in its ardour generally speaks thus. Let us avoid the torture of vexatious recriminations."
"Nothing irritates such a bond as is between us more than the wretched wants of life."
CLAP!
CLAP!
CLAP!
BRAVO!

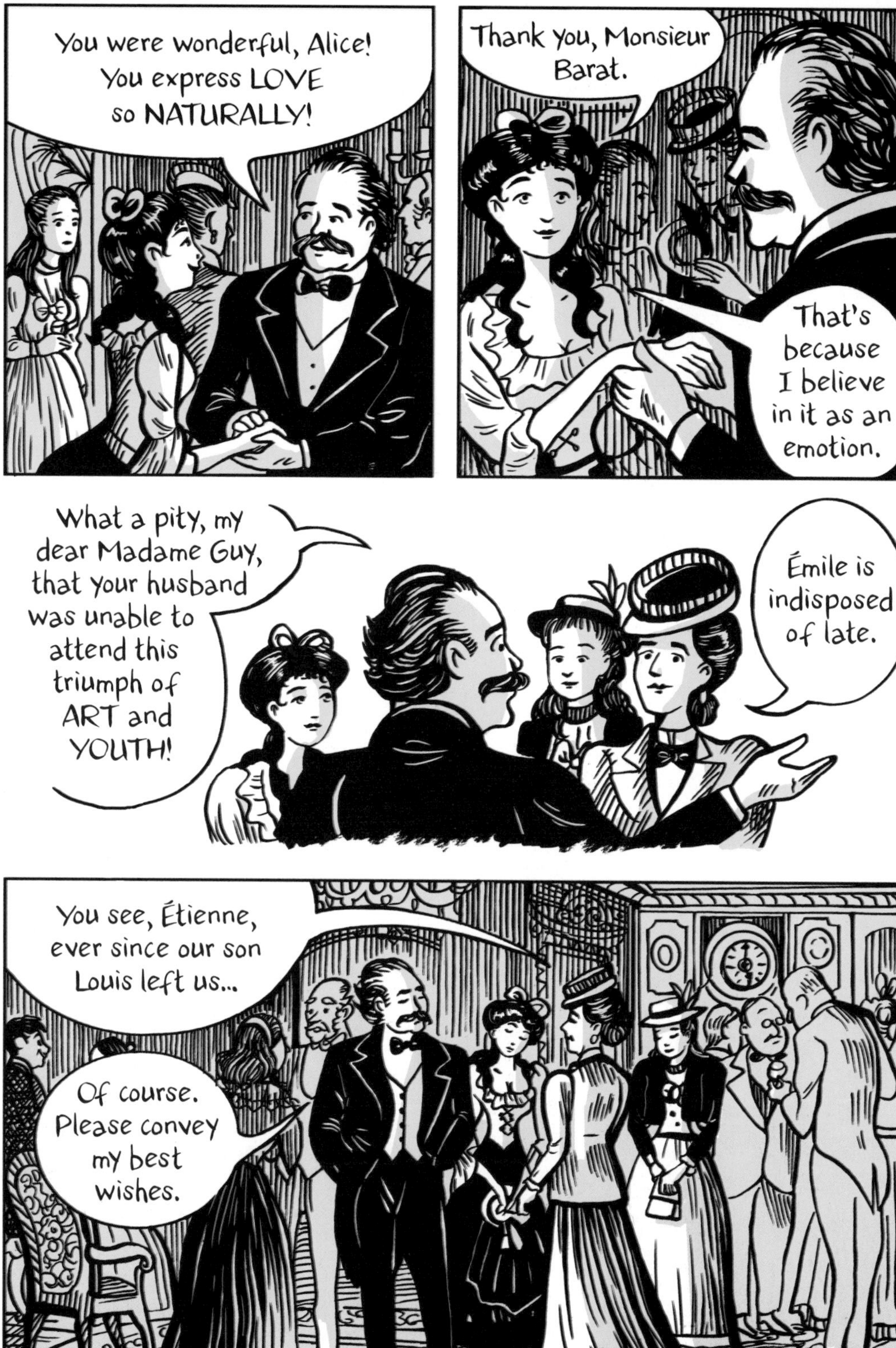
You were wonderful, Alice! You express LOVE so NATURALLY!
Thank you, Monsieur Barat.
That's because I believe in it as an emotion.
What a pity, my dear Madame Guy, that your husband was unable to attend this triumph of ART and YOUTH!
Émile is indisposed of late.
You see, Étienne, ever since our son Louis left us...
Of course. Please convey my best wishes.

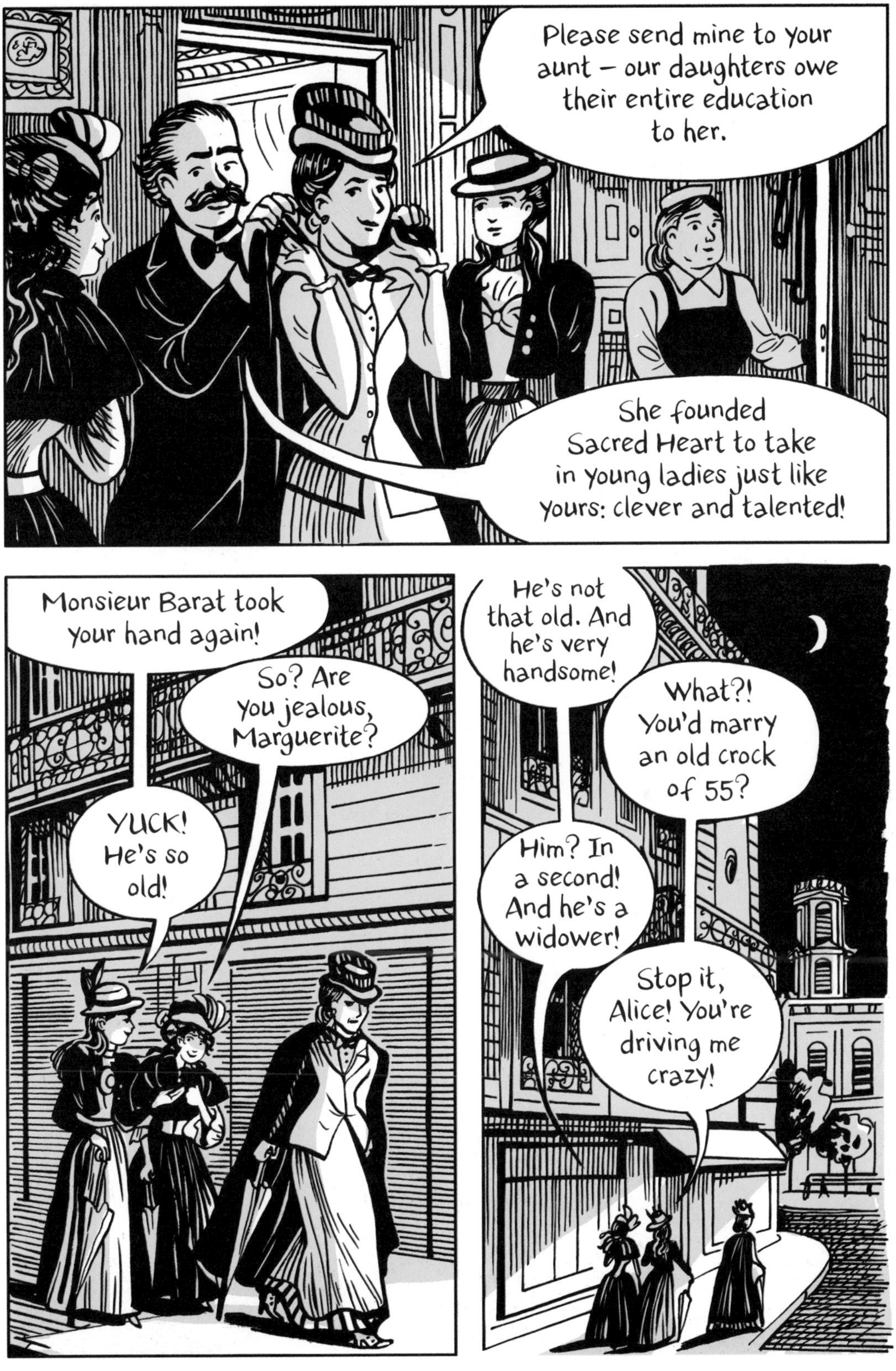
Please send mine to your aunt – our daughters owe their entire education to her.
She founded Sacred Heart to take in young ladies just like yours: clever and talented!
Monsieur Barat took your hand again!
So? Are you jealous, Marguerite?
YUCK! He's so old!
He's not that old. And he's very handsome!
What?! You'd marry an old crock of 55?
Him? In a second! And he's a widower!
Stop it, Alice! You're driving me crazy!

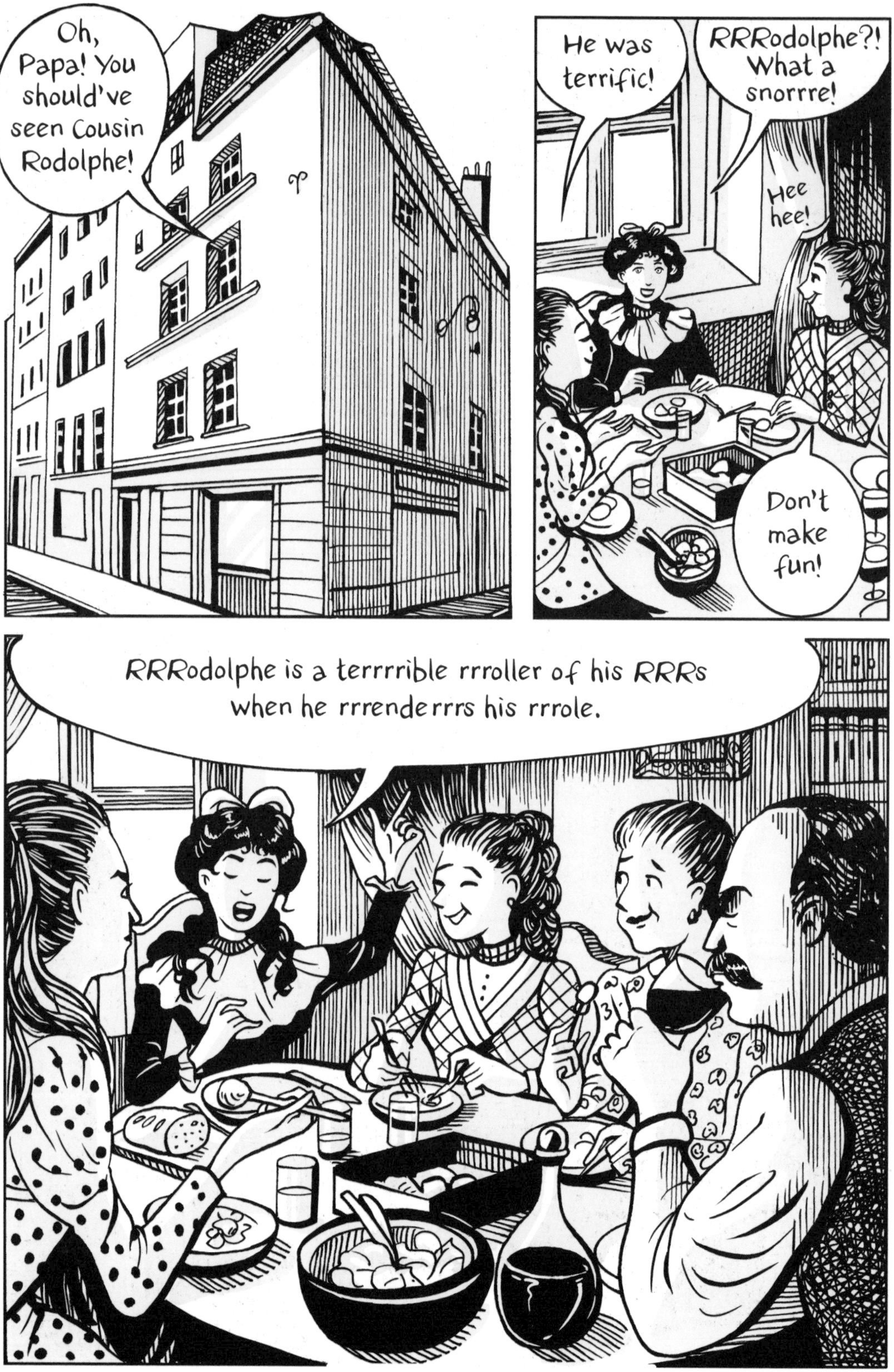

Oh, Papa! You should've seen Cousin Rodolphe!
He was terrific!
RRRodolphe?! What a snorrre!
Hee hee!
Don't make fun!
RRRodolphe is a terrrrible rrroller of his RRRs when he rrrenderrrs his rrrole.

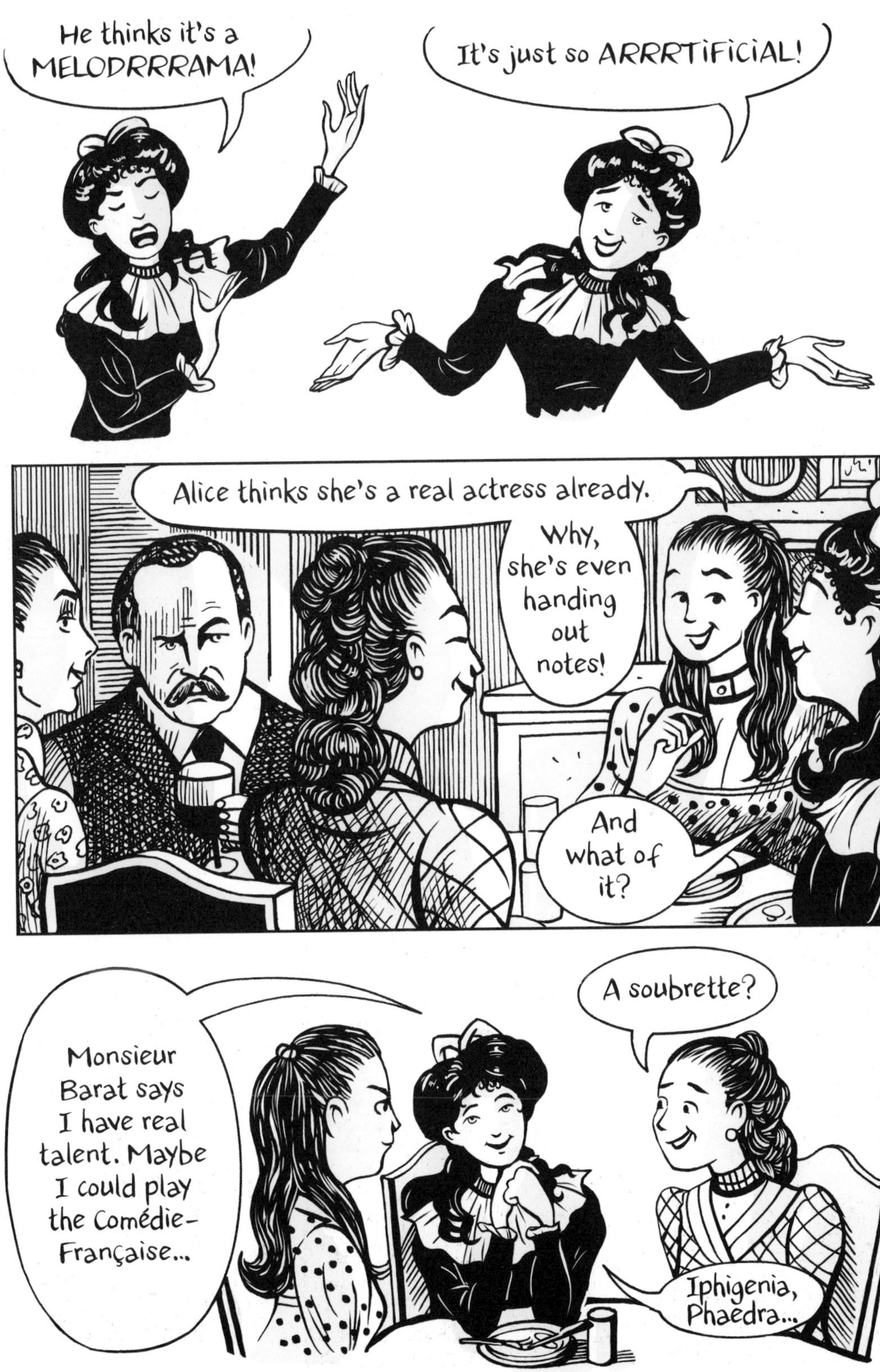
He thinks it's a MELODRRRAMA!
It's just so ARRRTIFICIAL!
Alice thinks she's a real actress already.
Why, she's even handing out notes!
And what of it?
Monsieur Barat says I have real talent. Maybe I could play the Comédie-Française...
A soubrette?
Iphigenia, Phaedra...

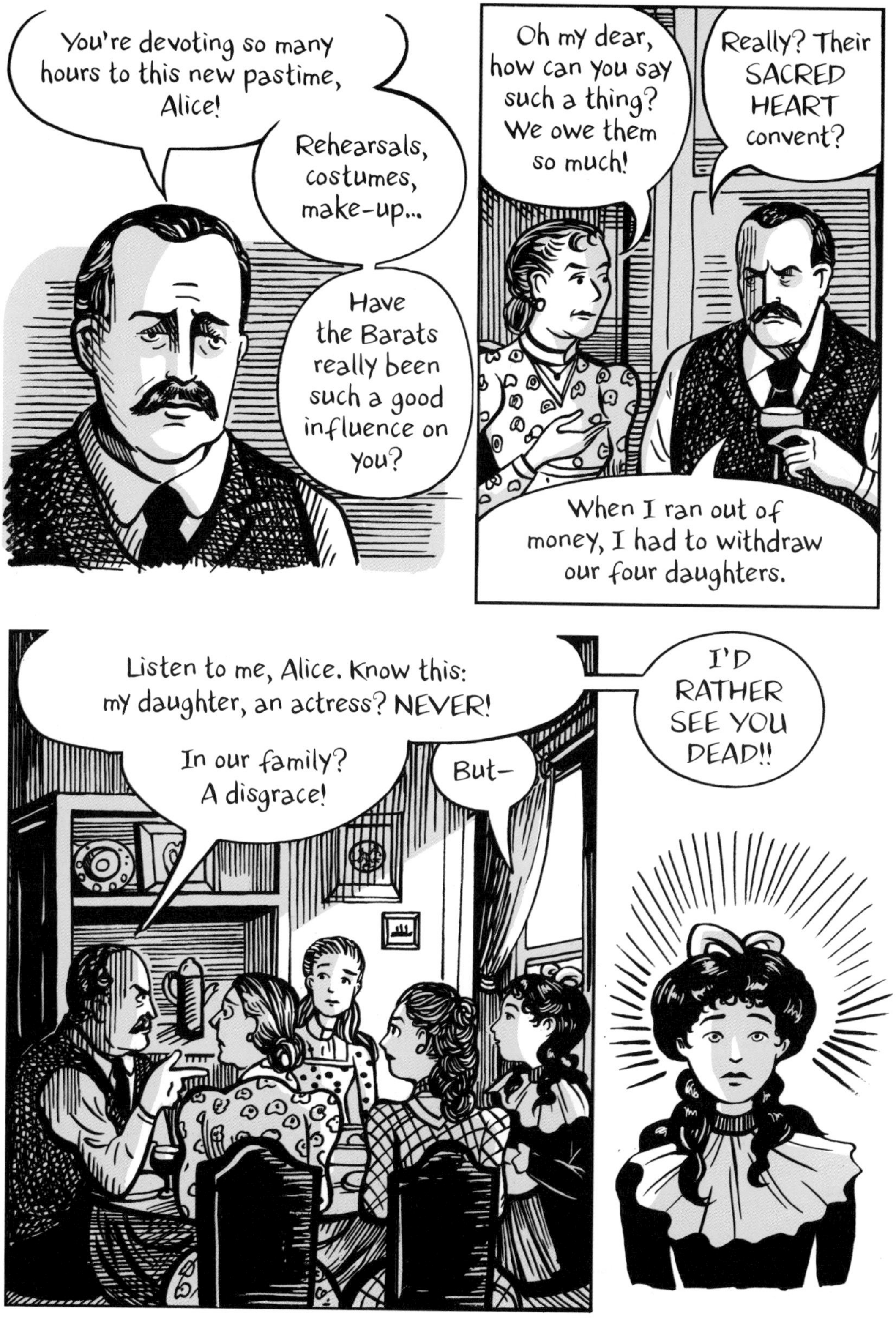
You're devoting so many hours to this new pastime, Alice!
Rehearsals, costumes, make-up...
Have the Barats really been such a good influence on you?
Oh my dear, how can you say such a thing? We owe them so much!
Really? Their SACRED HEART convent?
When I ran out of money, I had to withdraw our four daughters.
Listen to me, Alice. Know this: my daughter, an actress? NEVER!
In our family? A disgrace!
But–
I'D RATHER SEE YOU DEAD!!

January 1891 – Saint-Sulpice – Paris – France

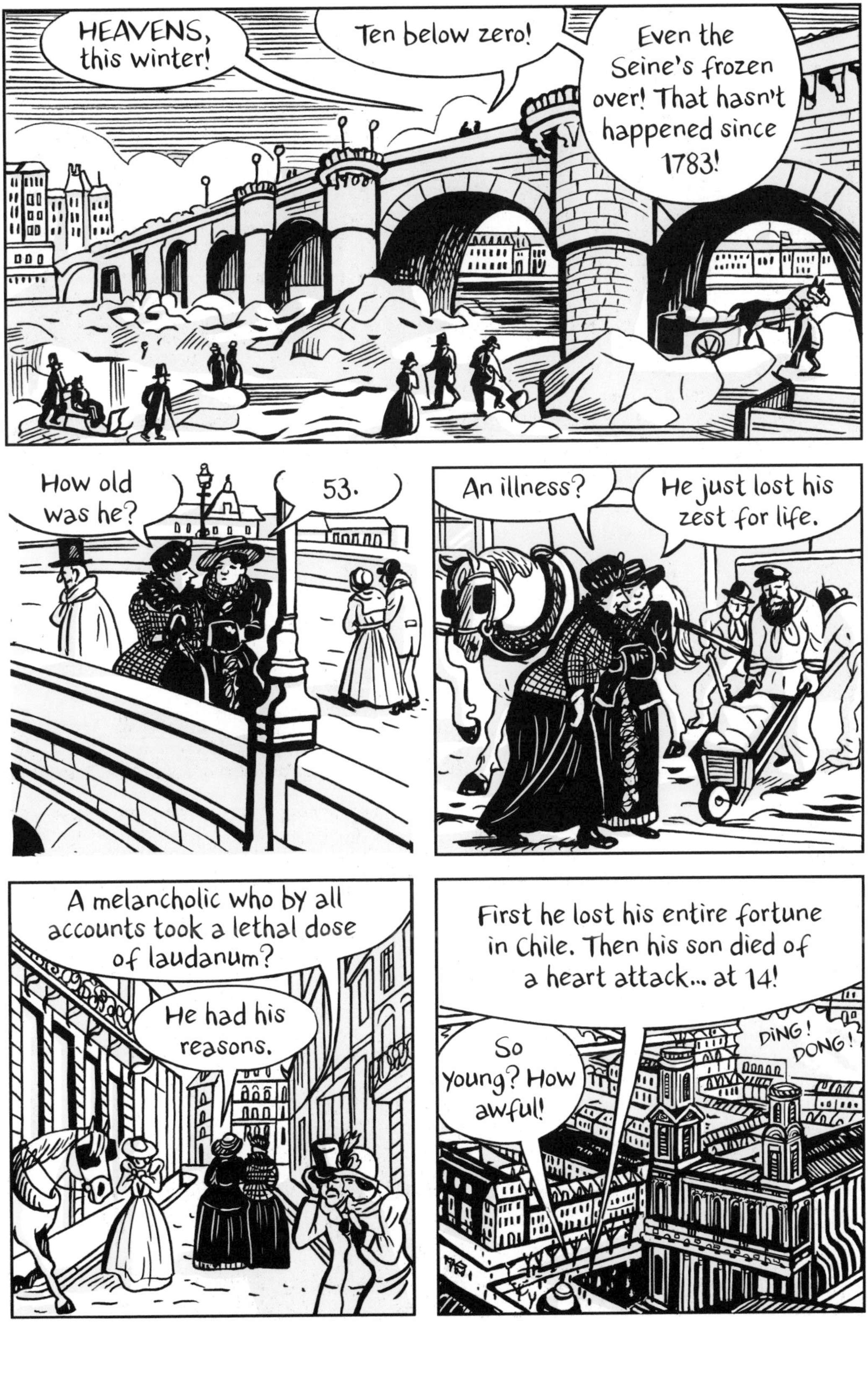
HEAVENS, this winter!
Ten below zero!
Even the Seine's frozen over! That hasn't happened since 1783!
How old was he?
53.
An illness?
He just lost his zest for life.
A melancholic who by all accounts took a lethal dose of laudanum?
He had his reasons.
First he lost his entire fortune in Chile. Then his son died of a heart attack... at 14!
So young? How awful!
DING! DONG!

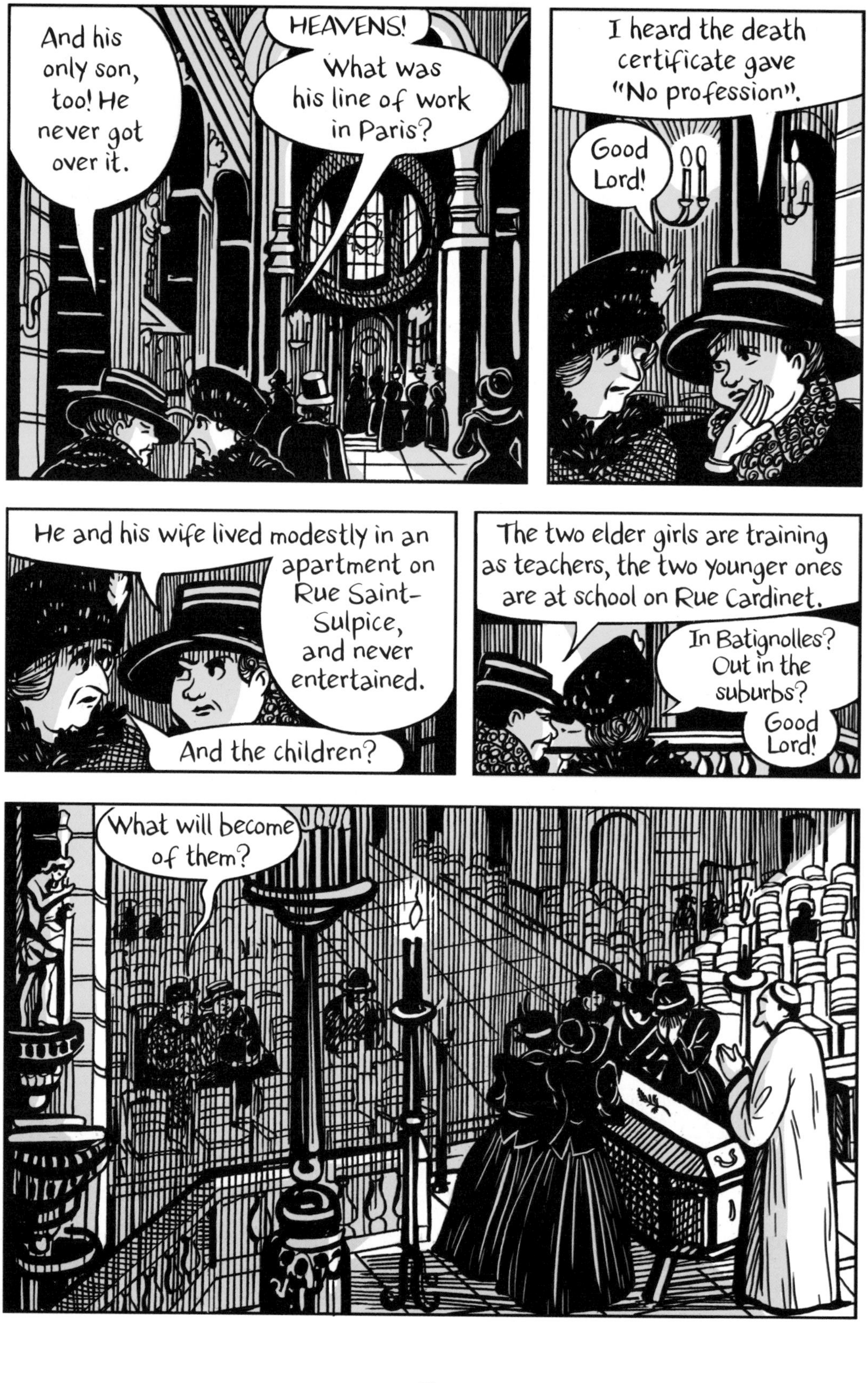
And his only son, too! He never got over it.
HEAVENS!
What was his line of work in Paris?
I heard the death certificate gave "No profession".
Good Lord!
He and his wife lived modestly in an apartment on Rue Saint-Sulpice, and never entertained.
And the children?
The two elder girls are training as teachers, the two younger ones are at school on Rue Cardinet.
In Batignolles? Out in the suburbs?
Good Lord!
What will become of them?

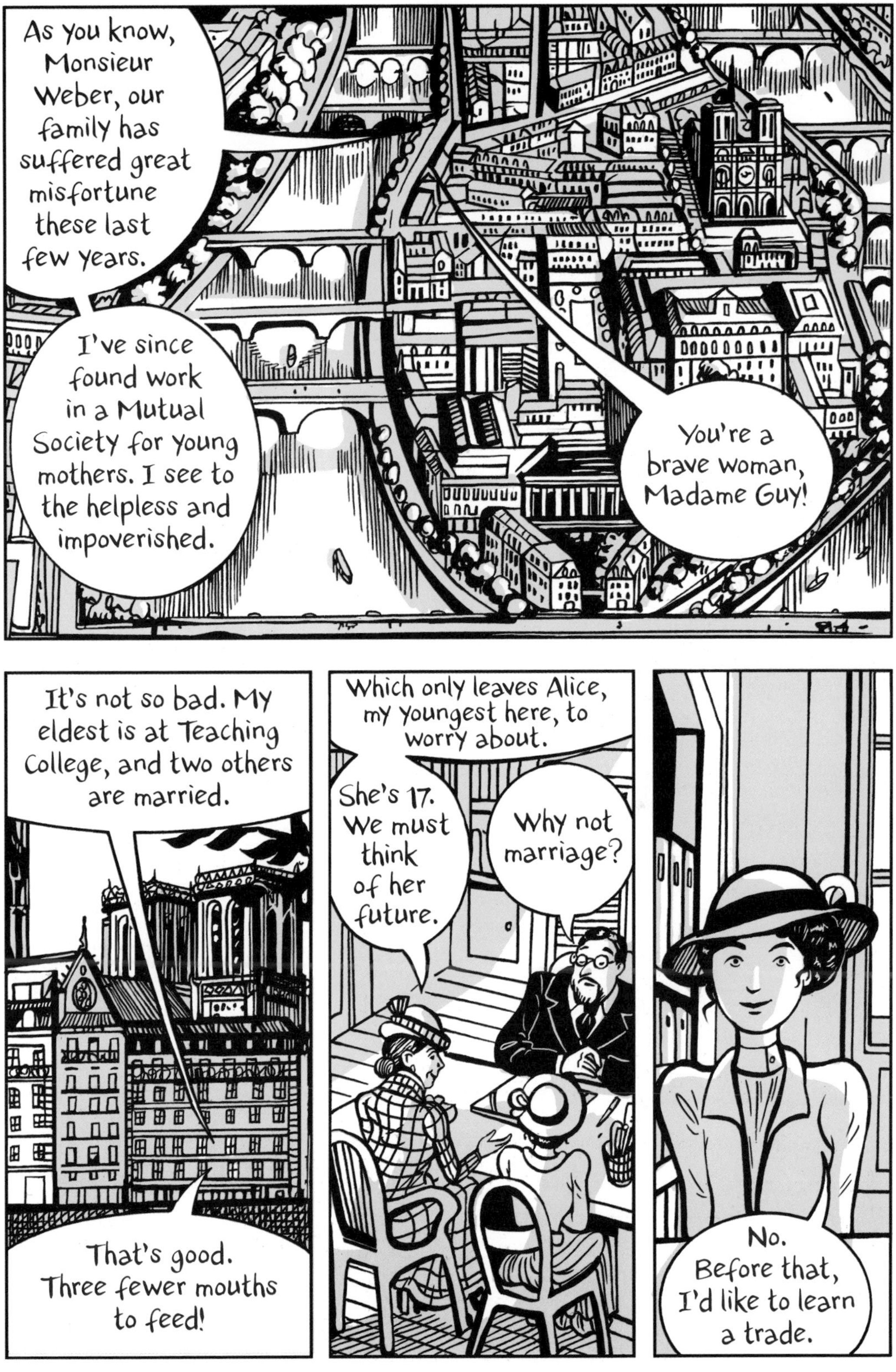
As you know, Monsieur Weber, our family has suffered great misfortune these last few years.
I've since found work in a Mutual Society for young mothers. I see to the helpless and impoverished.
You're a brave woman, Madame Guy!
It's not so bad. My eldest is at Teaching College, and two others are married.
That's good. Three fewer mouths to feed!
Which only leaves Alice, my youngest here, to worry about.
She's 17. We must think of her future.
Why not marriage?
No. Before that, I'd like to learn a trade.

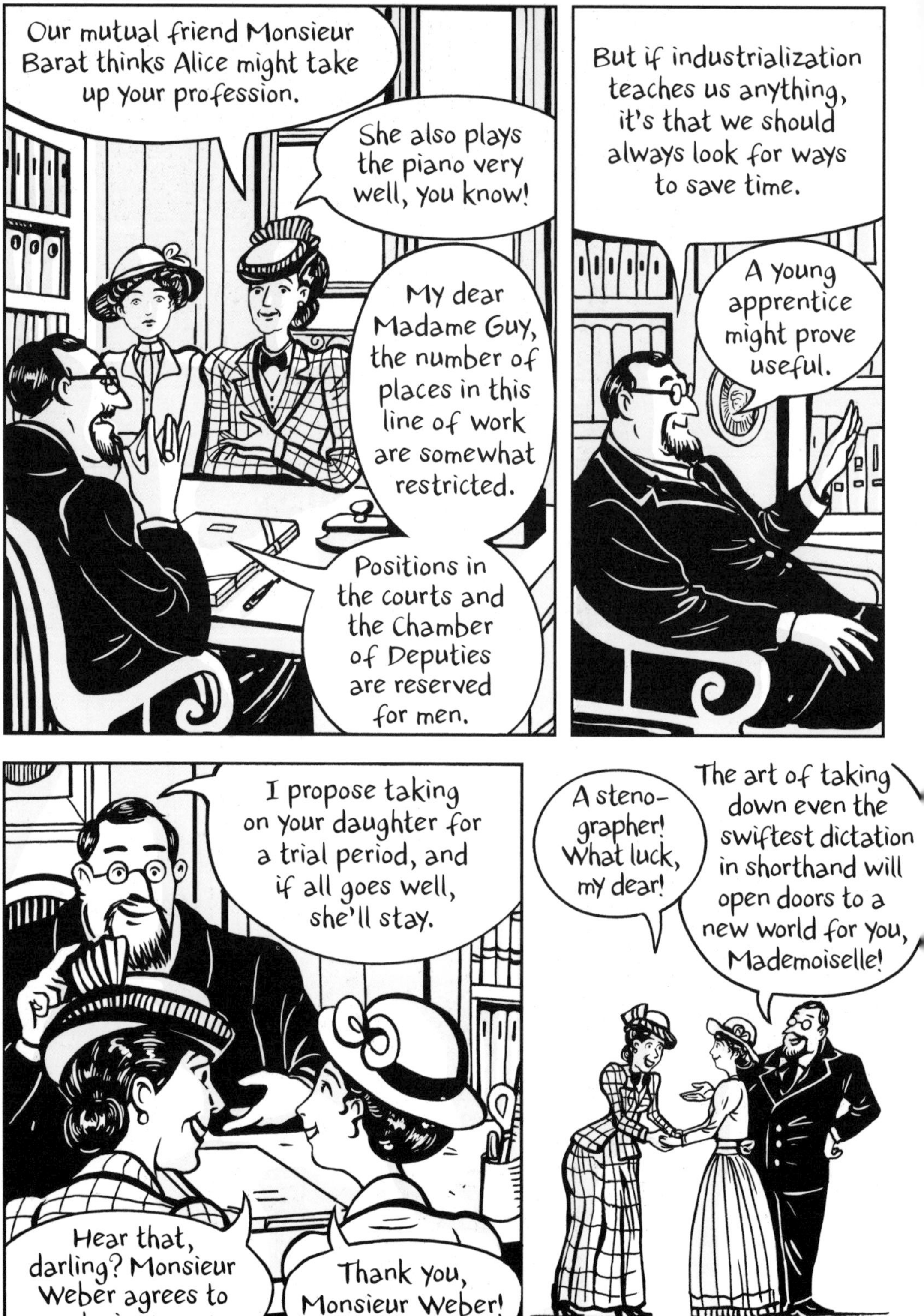
Our mutual friend Monsieur Barat thinks Alice might take up your profession.
She also plays the piano very well, you know!
My dear Madame Guy, the number of places in this line of work are somewhat restricted.
Positions in the courts and the Chamber of Deputies are reserved for men.
But if industrialization teaches us anything, it's that we should always look for ways to save time.
A young apprentice might prove useful.
I propose taking on your daughter for a trial period, and if all goes well, she'll stay.
Hear that, darling? Monsieur Weber agrees to train you.
Thank you, Monsieur Weber!
A stenographer! What luck, my dear!
The art of taking down even the swiftest dictation in shorthand will open doors to a new world for you, Mademoiselle!

1893 – Quai Malaquais – Paris – France

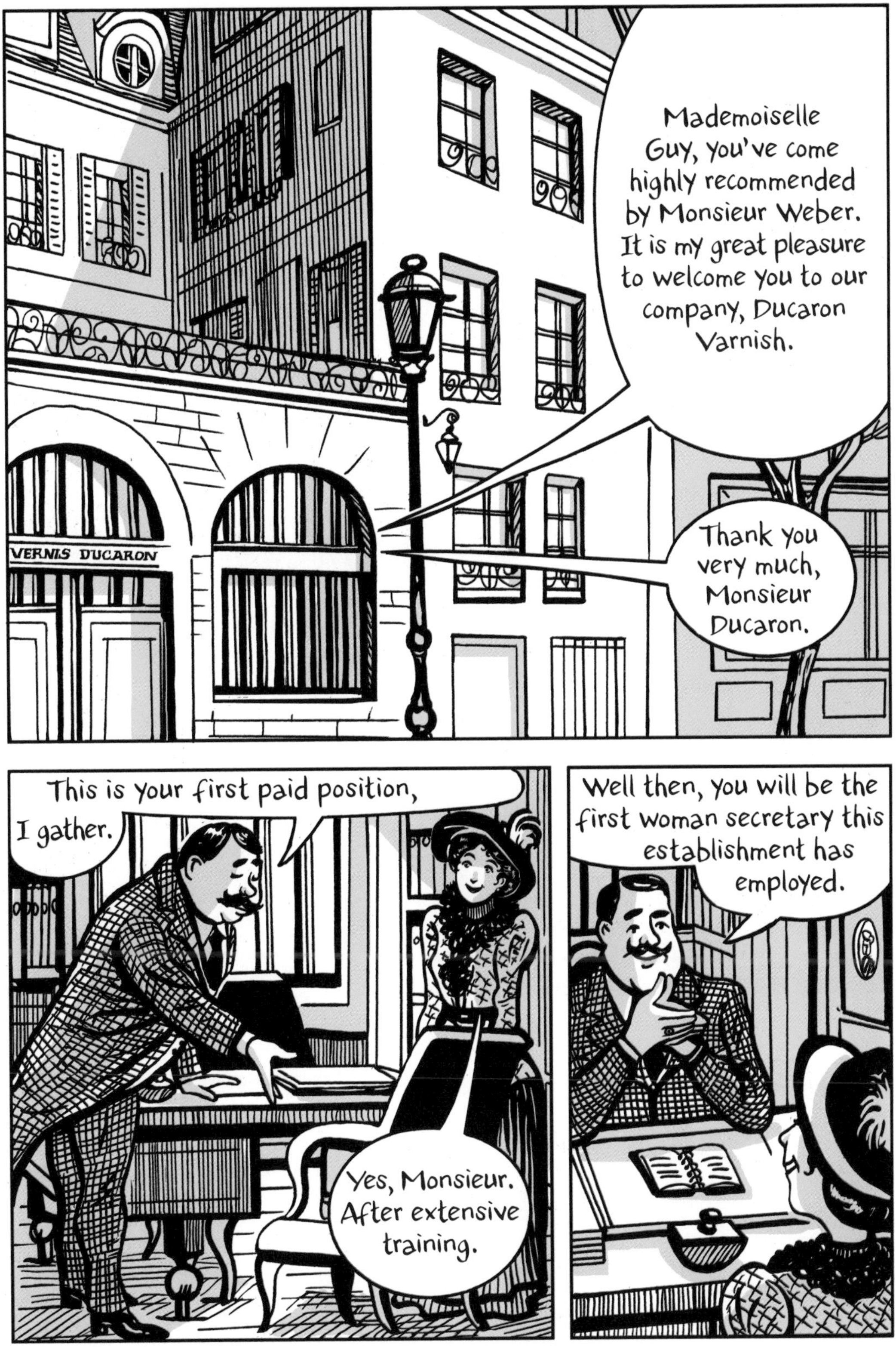
Mademoiselle Guy, you've come highly recommended by Monsieur Weber. It is my great pleasure to welcome you to our company, Ducaron Varnish.
VERNIS DUCARON
Thank you very much, Monsieur Ducaron.
This is your first paid position, I gather.
Yes, Monsieur. After extensive training.
Well then, you will be the first woman secretary this establishment has employed.

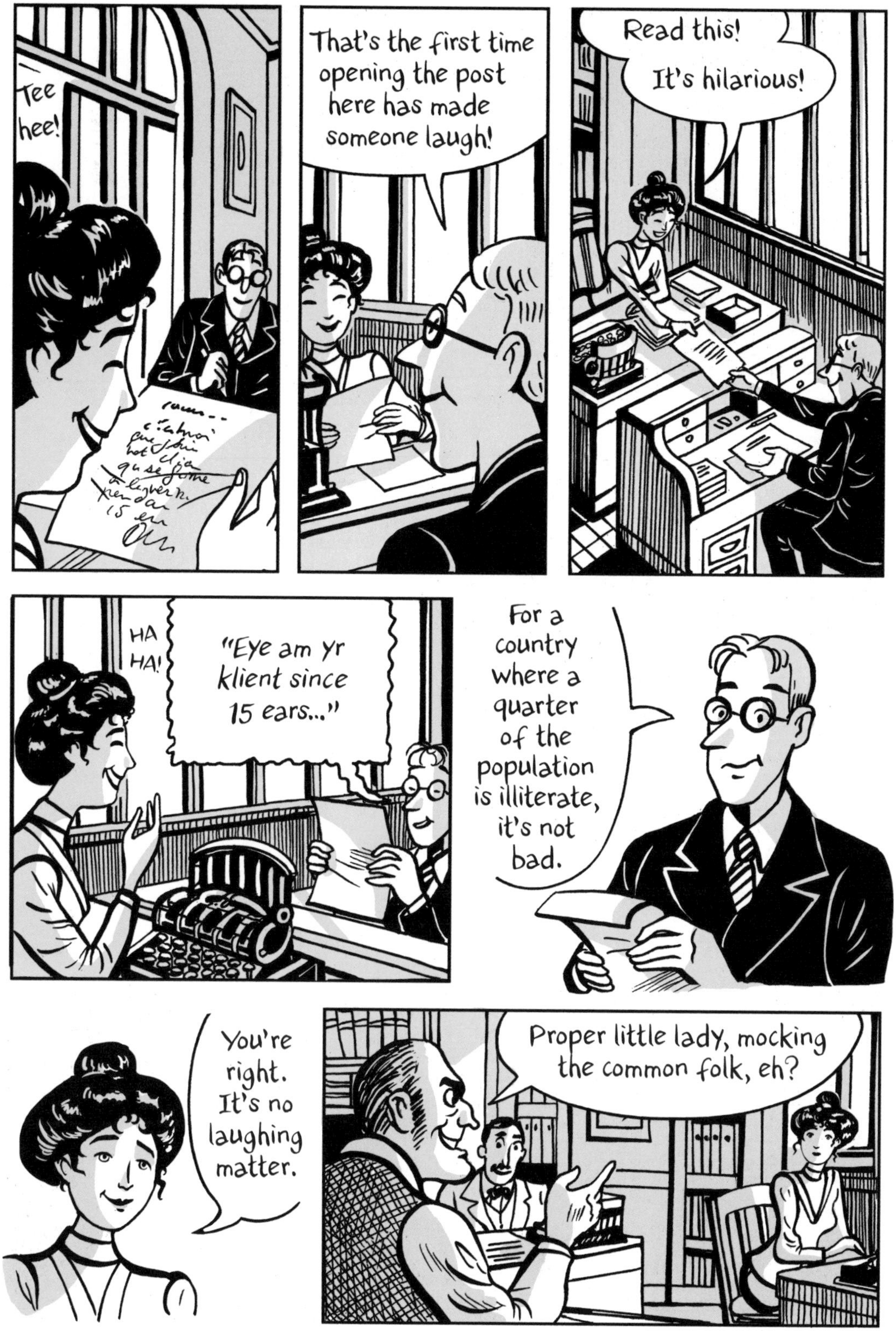
Tee hee!
That's the first time opening the post here has made someone laugh!
Read this!
It's hilarious!
HA HA!
"Eye am yr klient since 15 ears..."
For a country where a quarter of the population is illiterate, it's not bad.
You're right. It's no laughing matter.
Proper little lady, mocking the common folk, eh?

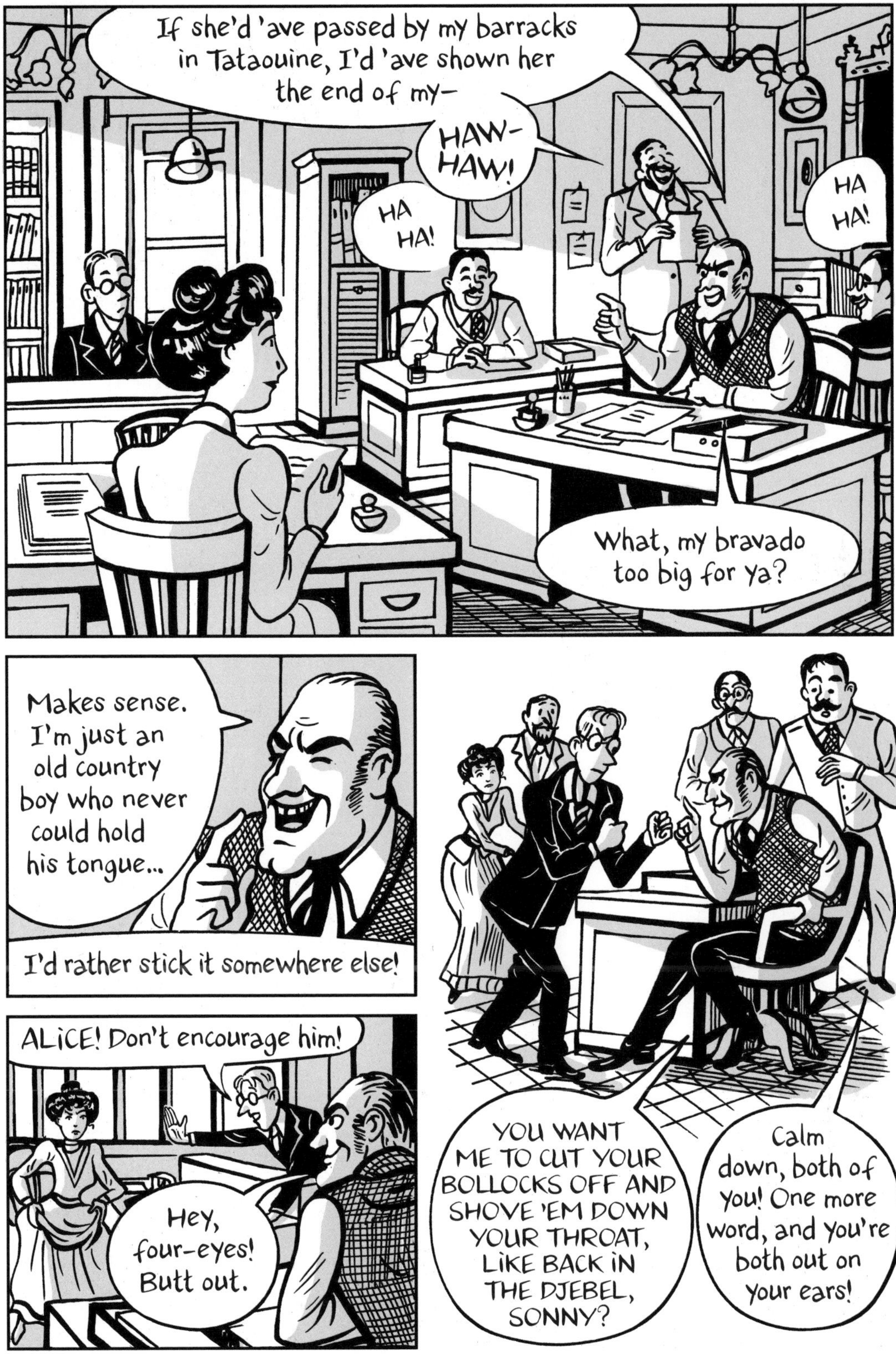
If she'd 'ave passed by my barracks in Tataouine, I'd 'ave shown her the end of my–
HAW-HAW!
HA HA!
HA HA!
What, my bravado too big for ya?
Makes sense. I'm just an old country boy who never could hold his tongue...
I'd rather stick it somewhere else!
ALICE! Don't encourage him!
Hey, four-eyes! Butt out.
YOU WANT ME TO CUT YOUR BOLLOCKS OFF AND SHOVE 'EM DOWN YOUR THROAT, LIKE BACK IN THE DJEBEL, SONNY?
Calm down, both of you! One more word, and you're both out on your ears!

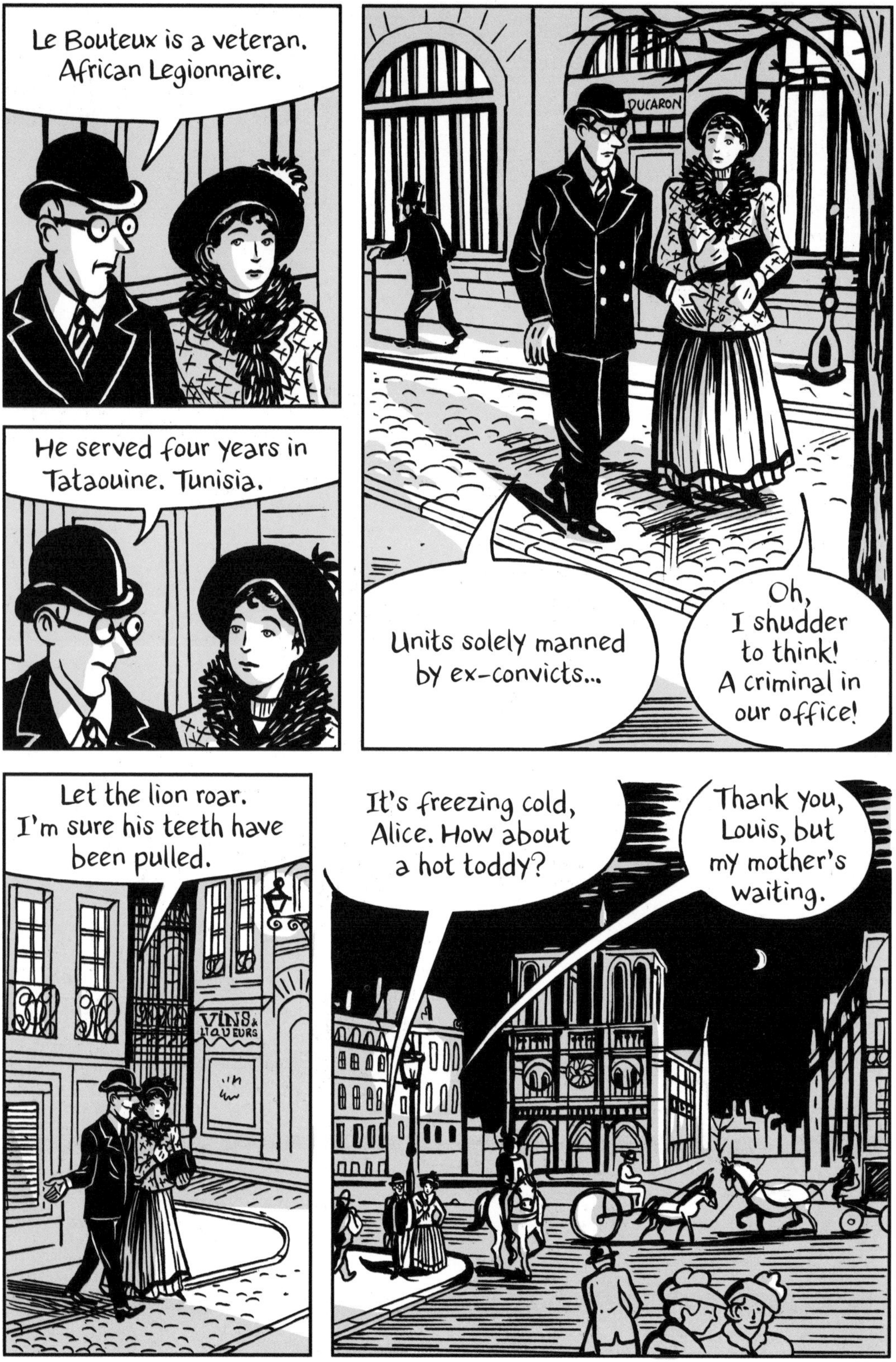
Le Bouteux is a veteran. African Legionnaire.
DUCARON
He served four years in Tataouine. Tunisia.
Units solely manned by ex-convicts...
Oh, I shudder to think! A criminal in our office!
Let the lion roar. I'm sure his teeth have been pulled.
VINS & LIQUEURS
It's freezing cold, Alice. How about a hot toddy?
Thank you, Louis, but my mother's waiting.

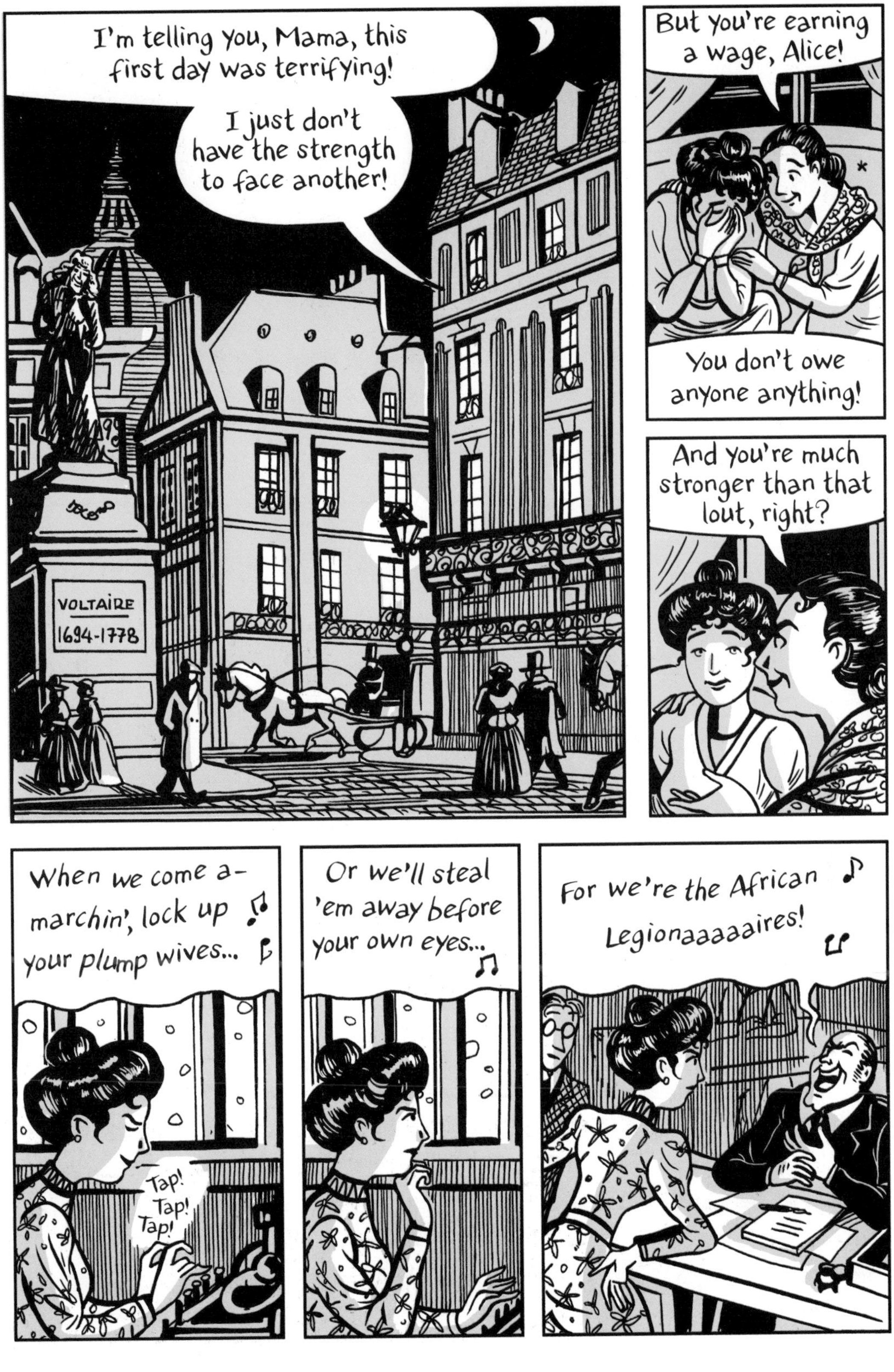
I'm telling you, Mama, this first day was terrifying!
I just don't have the strength to face another!
VOLTAIRE 1694-1778
But you're earning a wage, Alice!
You don't owe anyone anything!
And you're much stronger than that lout, right?
When we come a-marchin', lock up your plump wives...
Tap! Tap! Tap!
Or we'll steal 'em away before your own eyes...
For we're the African Legionaaaaaires!

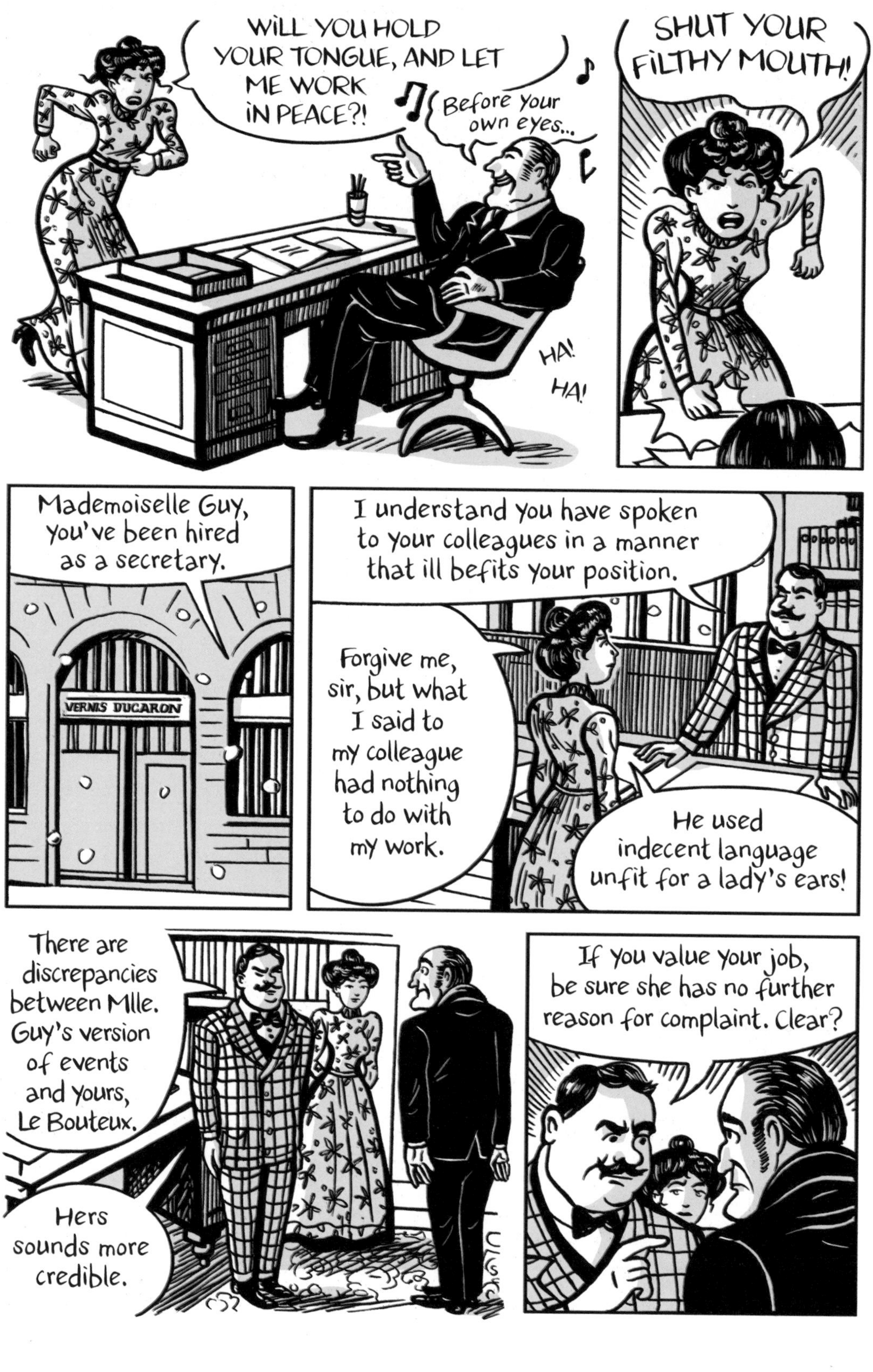
WILL YOU HOLD YOUR TONGUE, AND LET ME WORK IN PEACE?!
Before your own eyes...
HA! HA!
SHUT YOUR FILTHY MOUTH!
Mademoiselle Guy, you've been hired as a secretary.
VERNIS DUCARON
I understand you have spoken to your colleagues in a manner that ill befits your position.
Forgive me, sir, but what I said to my colleague had nothing to do with my work.
He used indecent language unfit for a lady's ears!
There are discrepancies between Mlle. Guy's version of events and yours, Le Bouteux.
Hers sounds more credible.
If you value your job, be sure she has no further reason for complaint. Clear?

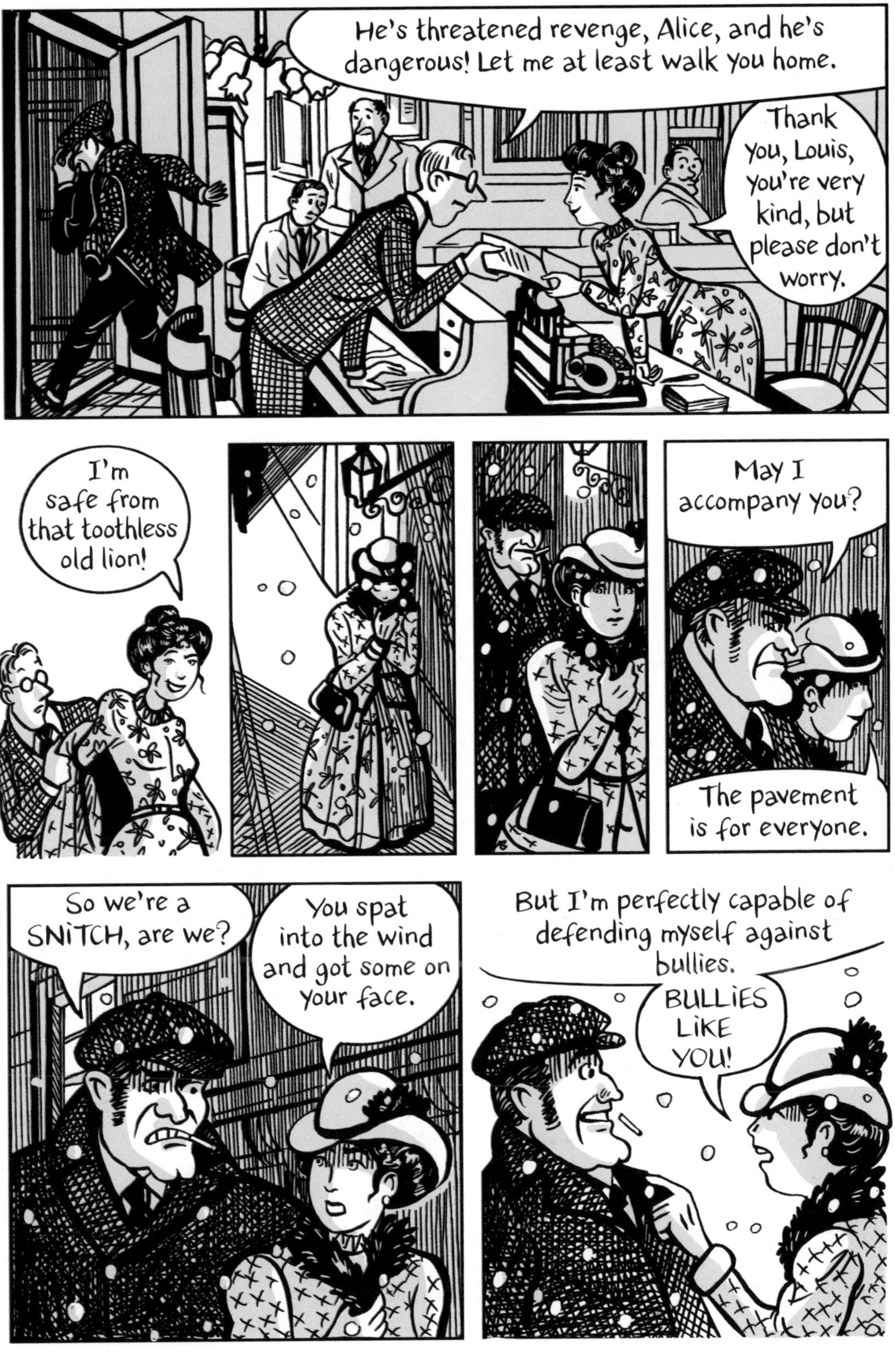
He's threatened revenge, Alice, and he's dangerous! Let me at least walk you home.
Thank you, Louis, you're very kind, but please don't worry.
I'm safe from that toothless old lion!
May I accompany you?
The pavement is for everyone.
So we're a SNITCH, are we?
You spat into the wind and got some on your face.
But I'm perfectly capable of defending myself against bullies.
BULLIES LIKE YOU!

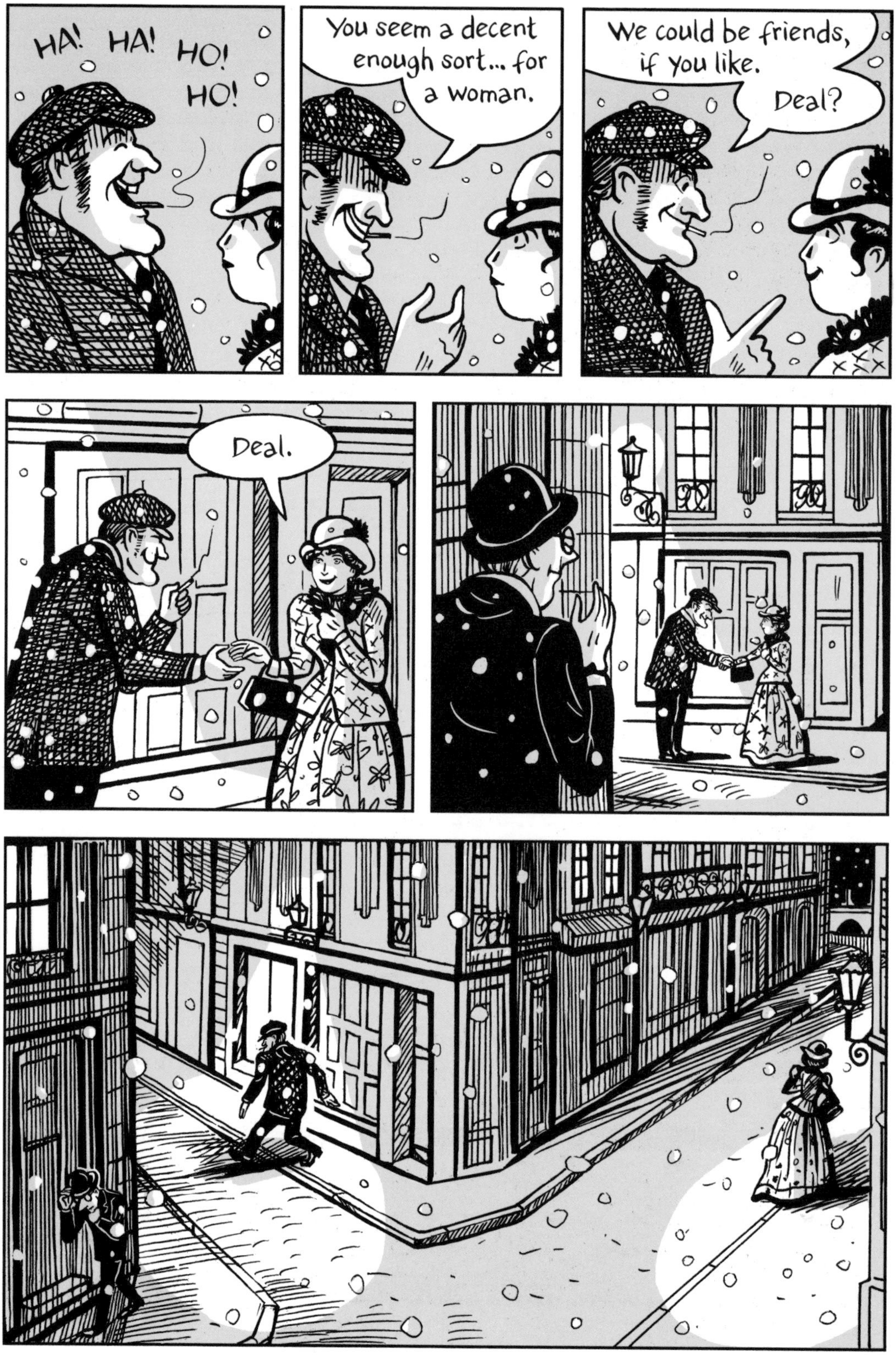
HA! HA! HO! HO!
You seem a decent enough sort... for a woman.
We could be friends, if you like.
Deal?
Deal.

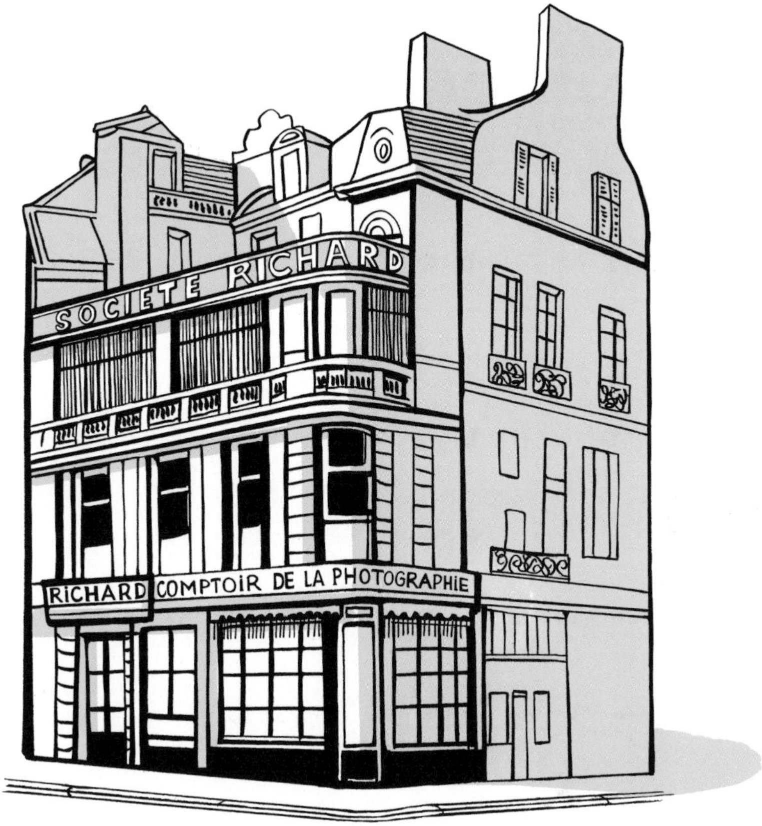
SOCIETE RICHARD
RICHARD
COMPTOIR DE LA PHOTOGRAPHIE

1894 – Rue Saint-Roch – Paris – France

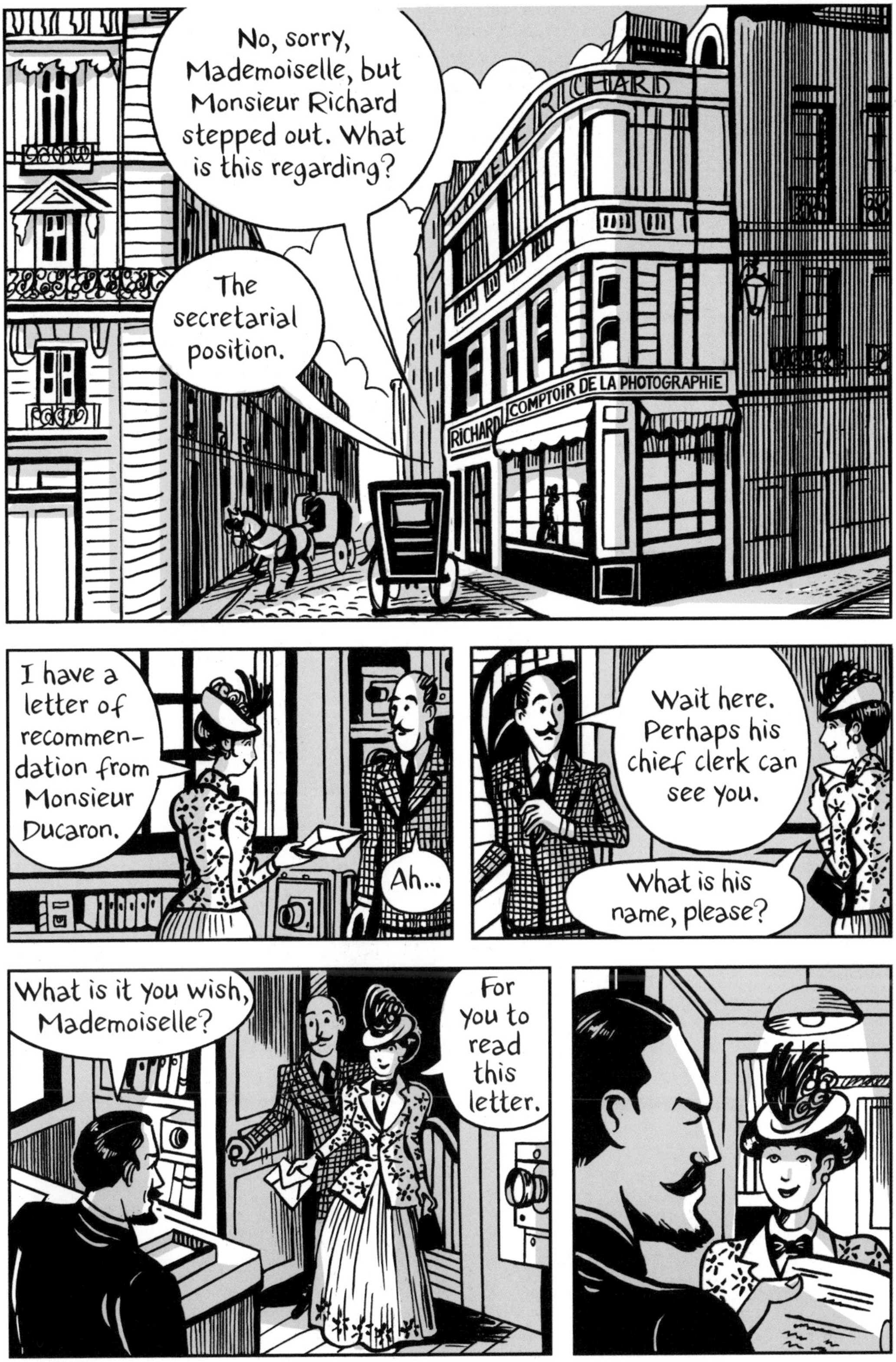

RICHARD
COMPTOIR DE LA PHOTOGRAPHIE
RICHARD
No, sorry, Mademoiselle, but Monsieur Richard stepped out. What is this regarding?
The secretarial position.
I have a letter of recommendation from Monsieur Ducaron.
Ah...
Wait here. Perhaps his chief clerk can see you.
What is his name, please?
What is it you wish, Mademoiselle?
For you to read this letter.

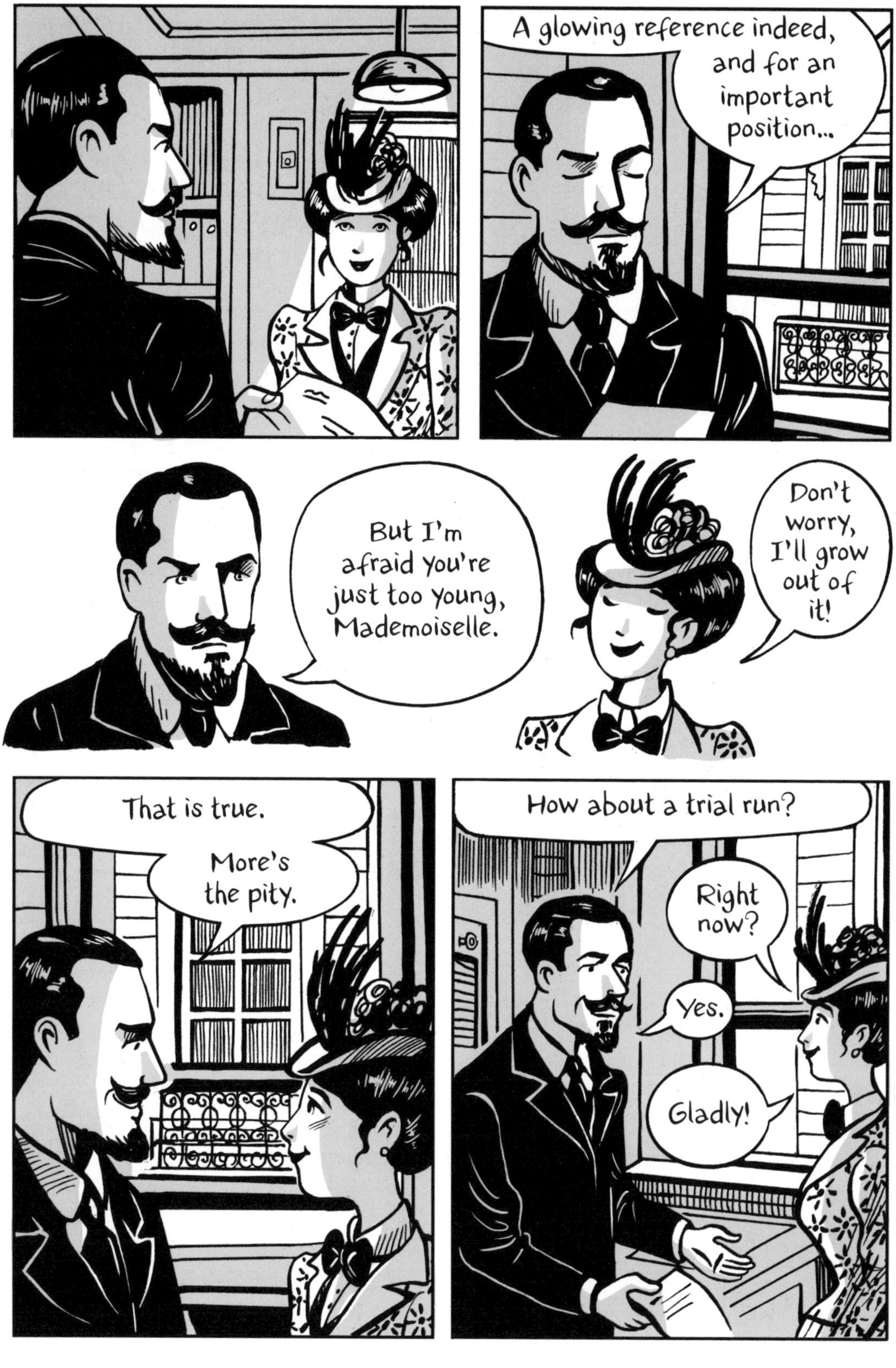
A glowing reference indeed, and for an important position...
But I'm afraid you're just too young, Mademoiselle.
Don't worry, I'll grow out of it!
That is true.
More's the pity.
How about a trial run?
Right now?
Yes.
Gladly!

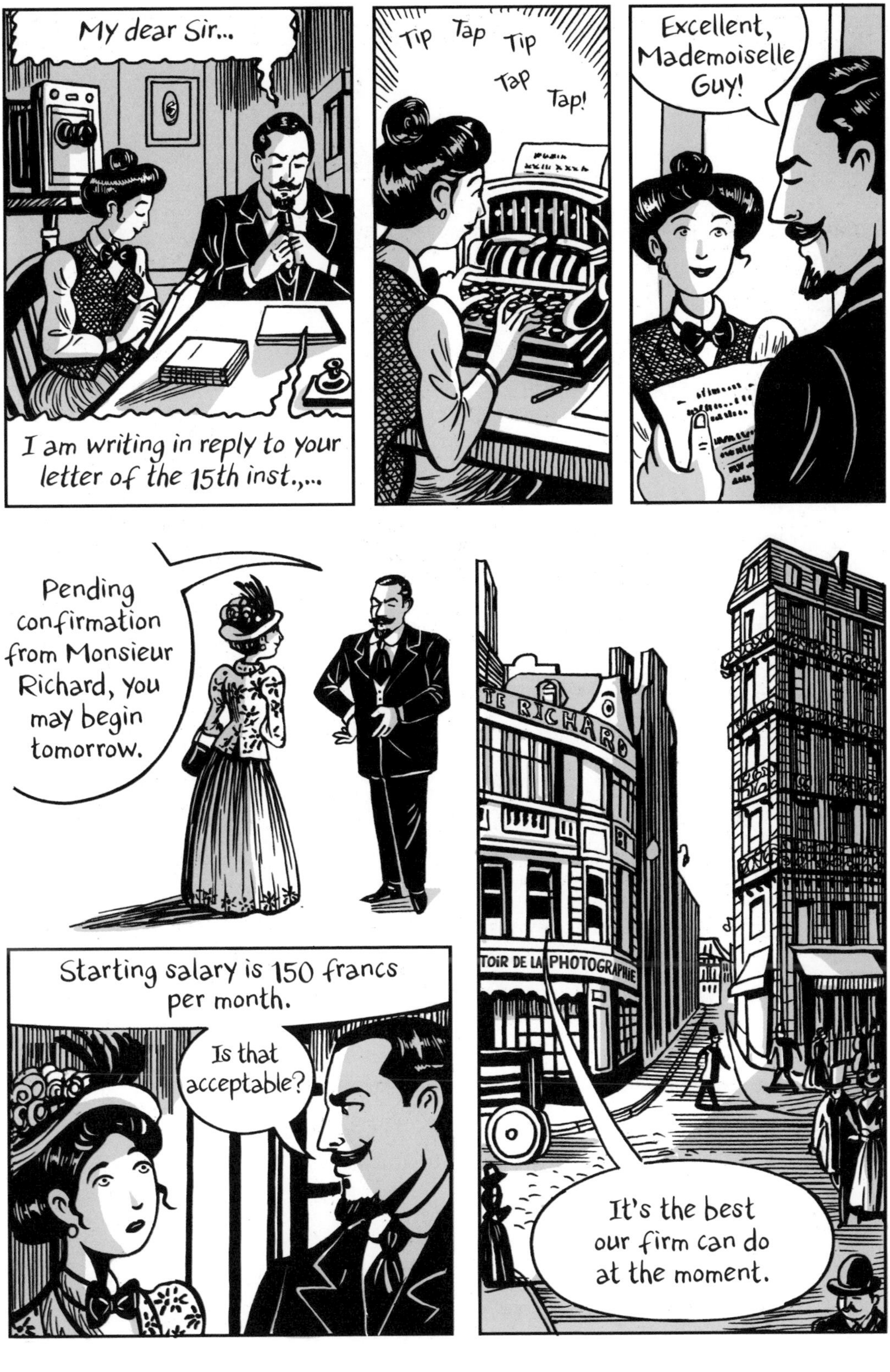
My dear Sir...
I am writing in reply to your letter of the 15th inst.,...
Tip Tap Tip Tap Tap!
Excellent, Mademoiselle Guy!
Pending confirmation from Monsieur Richard, you may begin tomorrow.
TE RICHARD
TOIR DE LA PHOTOGRAPHIE
Starting salary is 150 francs per month.
Is that acceptable?
It's the best our firm can do at the moment.

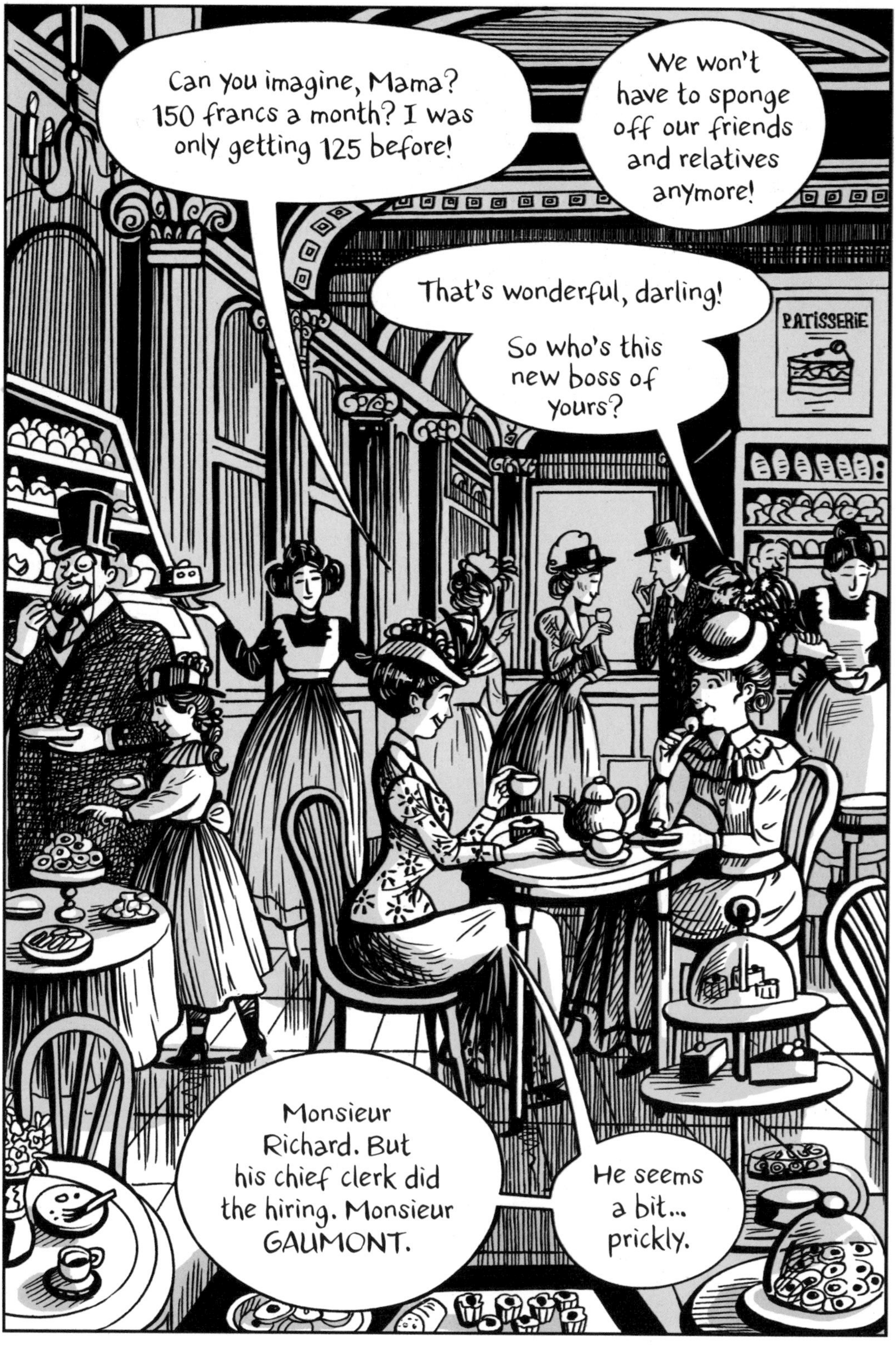
Can you imagine, Mama? 150 francs a month? I was only getting 125 before!
We won't have to sponge off our friends and relatives anymore!
That's wonderful, darling!
So who's this new boss of yours?
PATISSERIE
Monsieur Richard. But his chief clerk did the hiring. Monsieur GAUMONT.
He seems a bit... prickly.

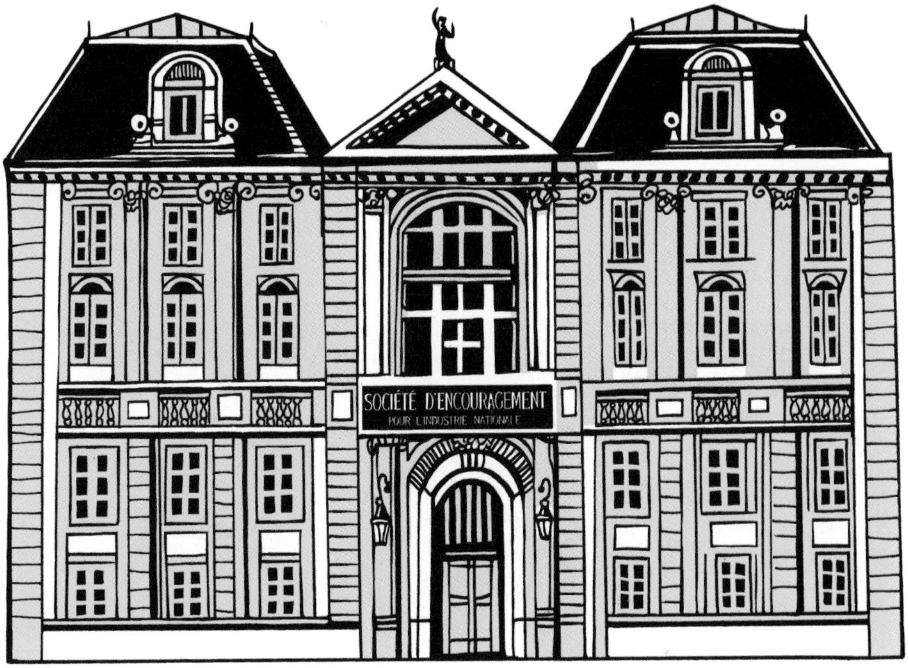
SOCIÉTÉ D'ENCOURAGEMENT
POUR L'INDUSTRIE NATIONALE

1895 – 4, Place Saint-Germain – Paris – France

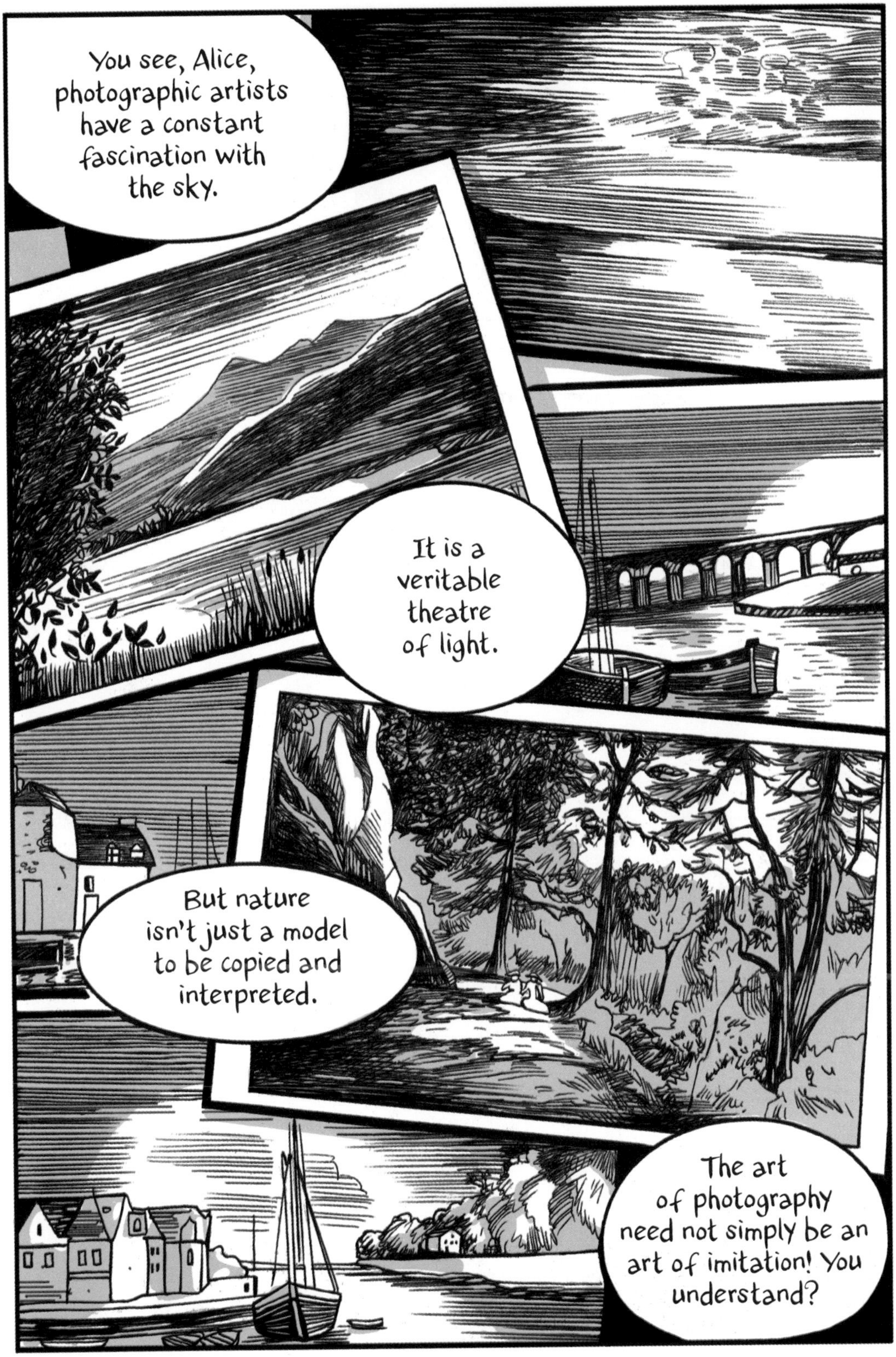
You see, Alice, photographic artists have a constant fascination with the sky.
It is a veritable theatre of light.
But nature isn't just a model to be copied and interpreted.
The art of photography need not simply be an art of imitation! You understand?

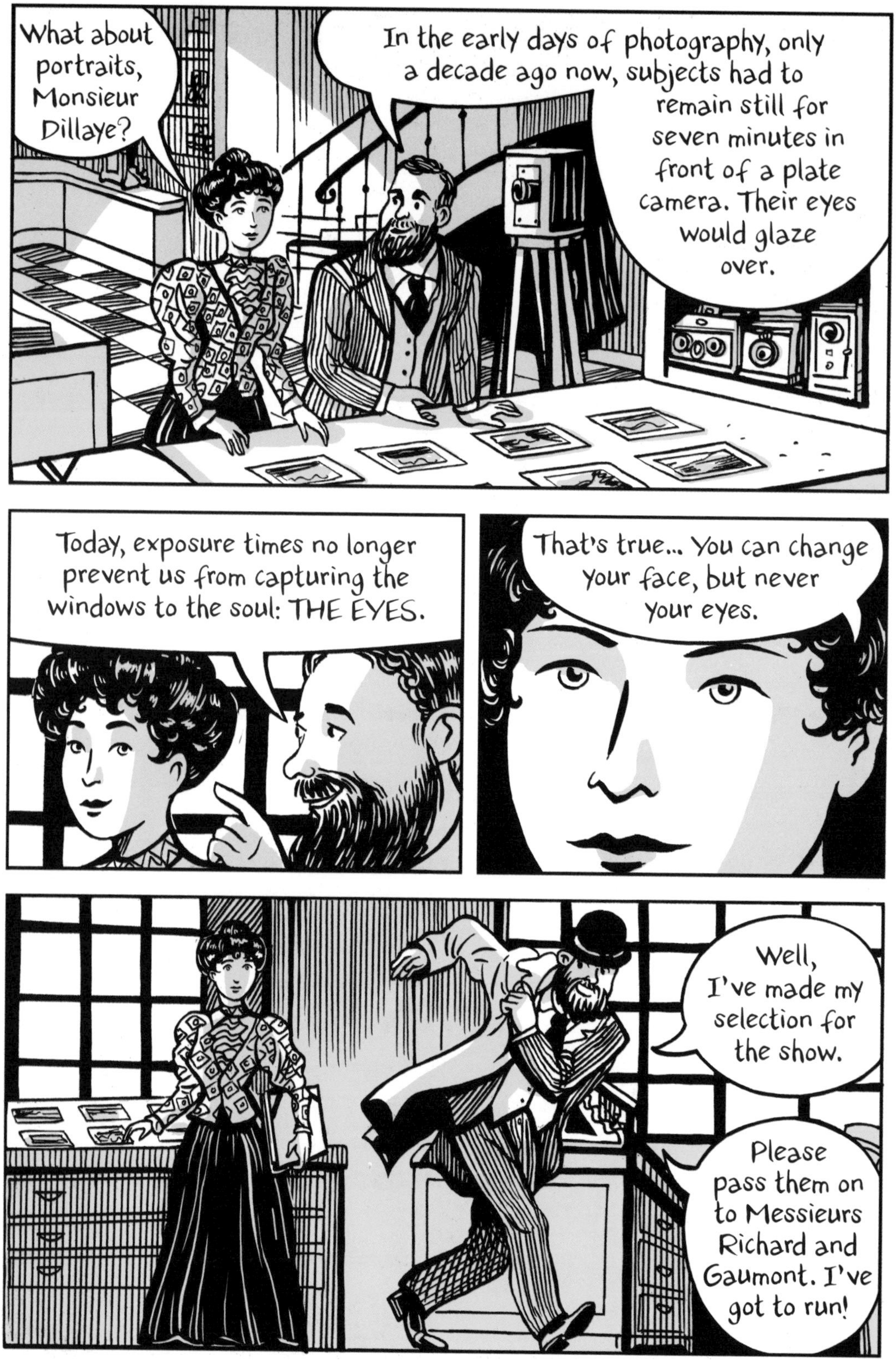
What about portraits, Monsieur Dillaye?
In the early days of photography, only a decade ago now, subjects had to remain still for seven minutes in front of a plate camera. Their eyes would glaze over.
Today, exposure times no longer prevent us from capturing the windows to the soul: THE EYES.
That's true... You can change your face, but never your eyes.
Well, I've made my selection for the show.
Please pass them on to Messieurs Richard and Gaumont. I've got to run!

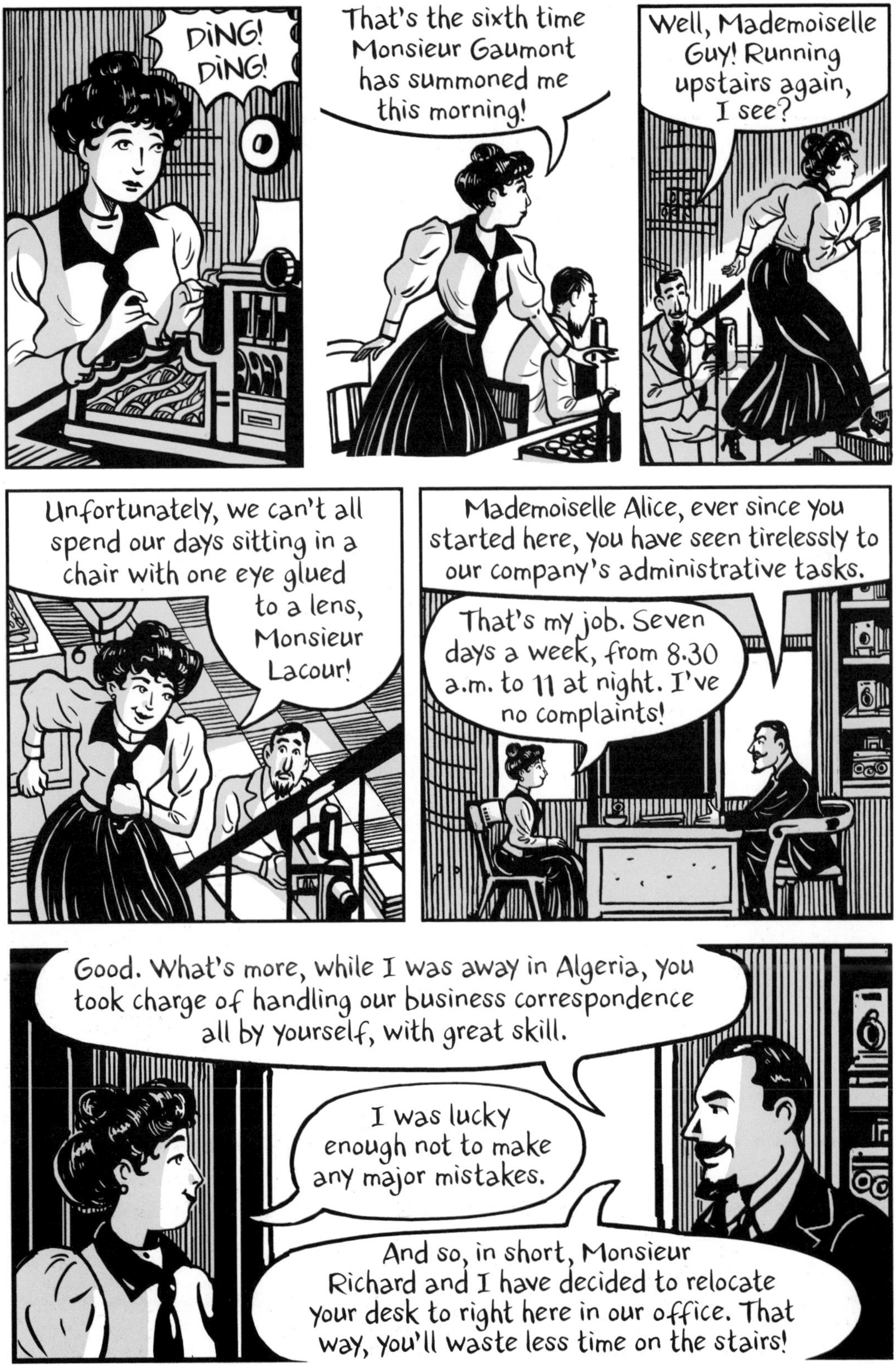
DING! DING!
That's the sixth time Monsieur Gaumont has summoned me this morning!
Well, Mademoiselle Guy! Running upstairs again, I see?
Unfortunately, we can't all spend our days sitting in a chair with one eye glued to a lens, Monsieur Lacour!
Mademoiselle Alice, ever since you started here, you have seen tirelessly to our company's administrative tasks.
That's my job. Seven days a week, from 8.30 a.m. to 11 at night. I've no complaints!
Good. What's more, while I was away in Algeria, you took charge of handling our business correspondence all by yourself, with great skill.
I was lucky enough not to make any major mistakes.
And so, in short, Monsieur Richard and I have decided to relocate your desk to right here in our office. That way, you'll waste less time on the stairs!

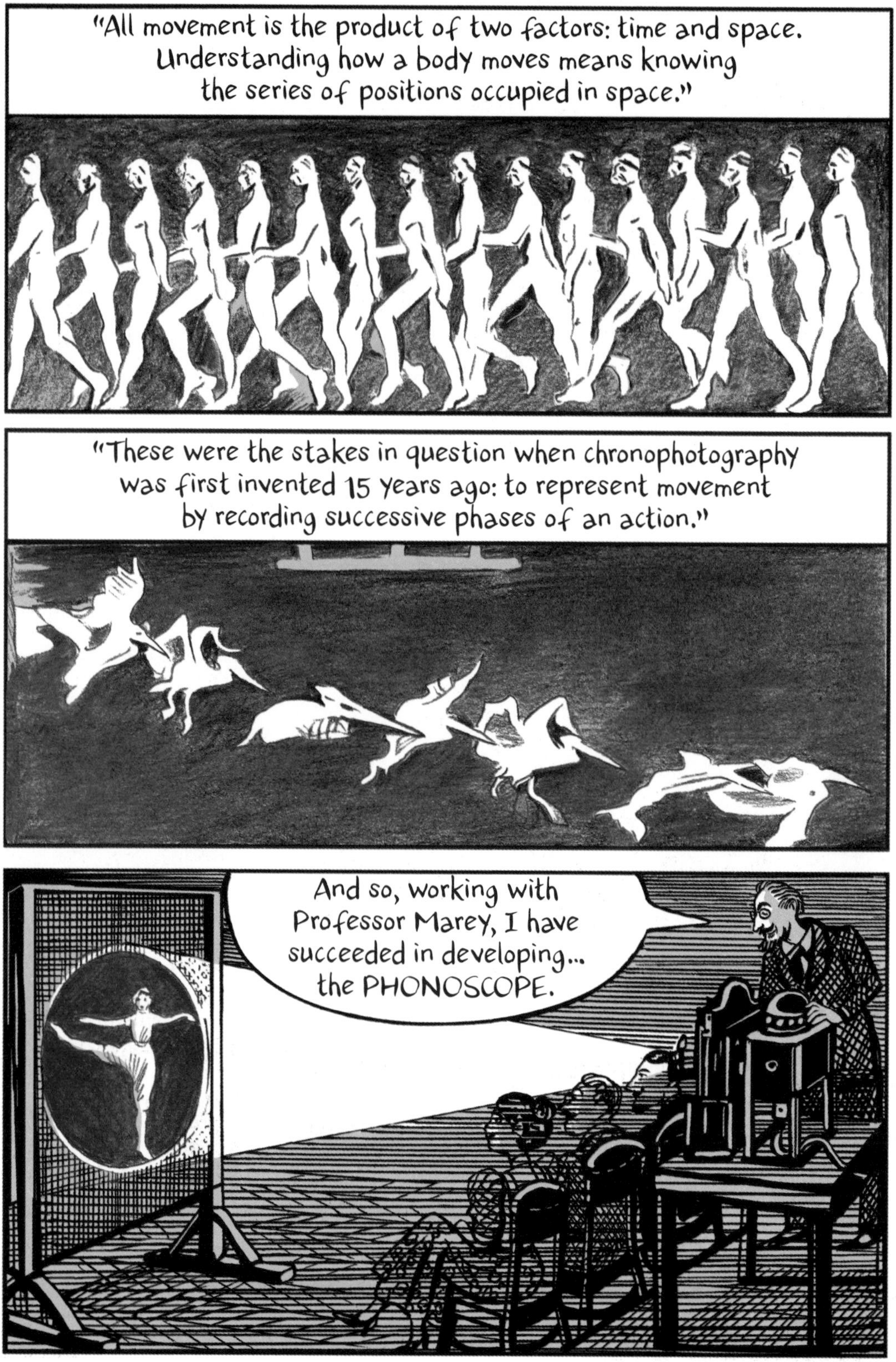
"All movement is the product of two factors: time and space. Understanding how a body moves means knowing the series of positions occupied in space."
"These were the stakes in question when chronophotography was first invented 15 years ago: to represent movement by recording successive phases of an action."
And so, working with Professor Marey, I have succeeded in developing... the PHONOSCOPE.

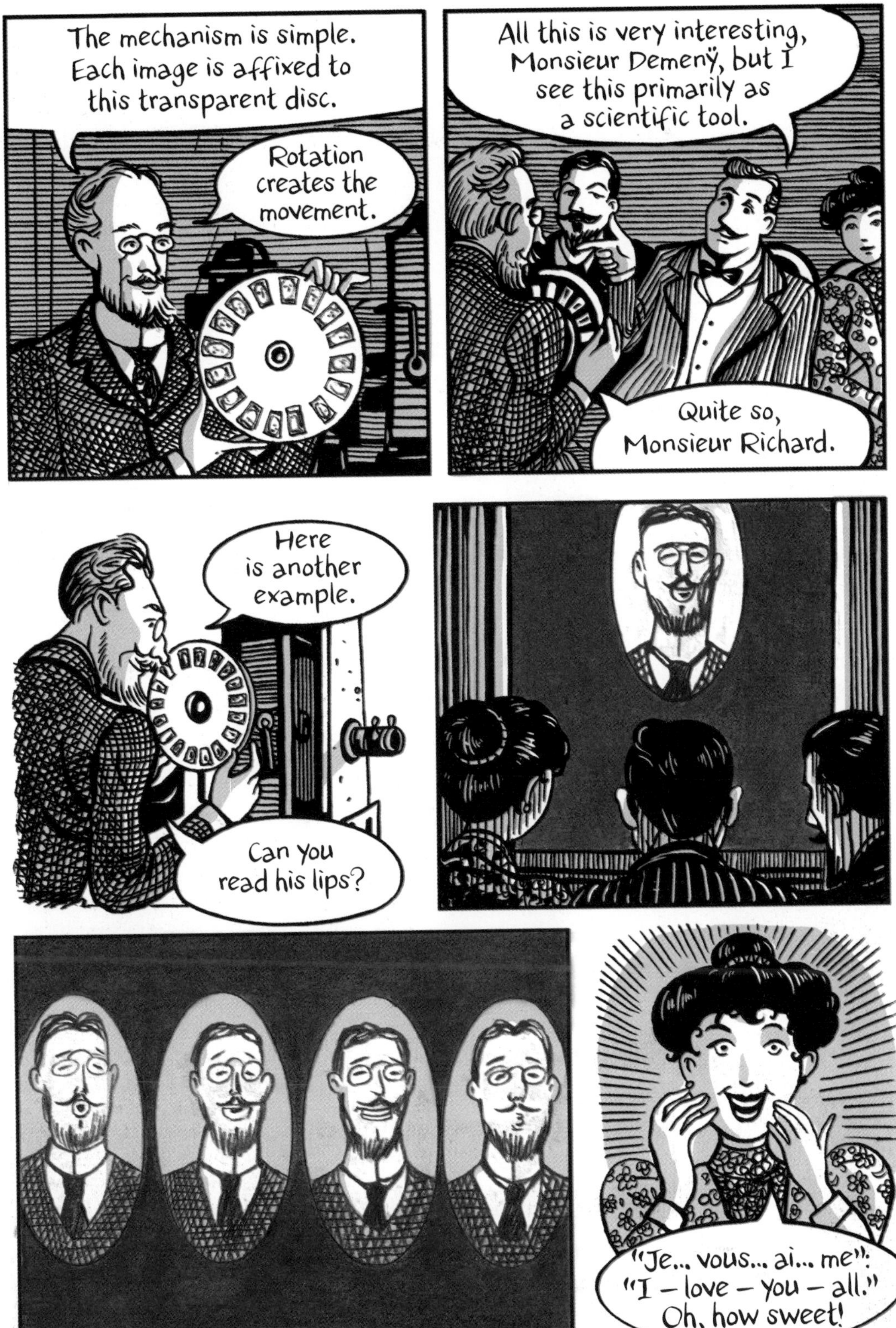
The mechanism is simple. Each image is affixed to this transparent disc.
Rotation creates the movement.
All this is very interesting, Monsieur Demenÿ, but I see this primarily as a scientific tool.
Quite so, Monsieur Richard.
Here is another example.
Can you read his lips?
"Je... vous... ai... me": "I – love – you – all." Oh, how sweet!

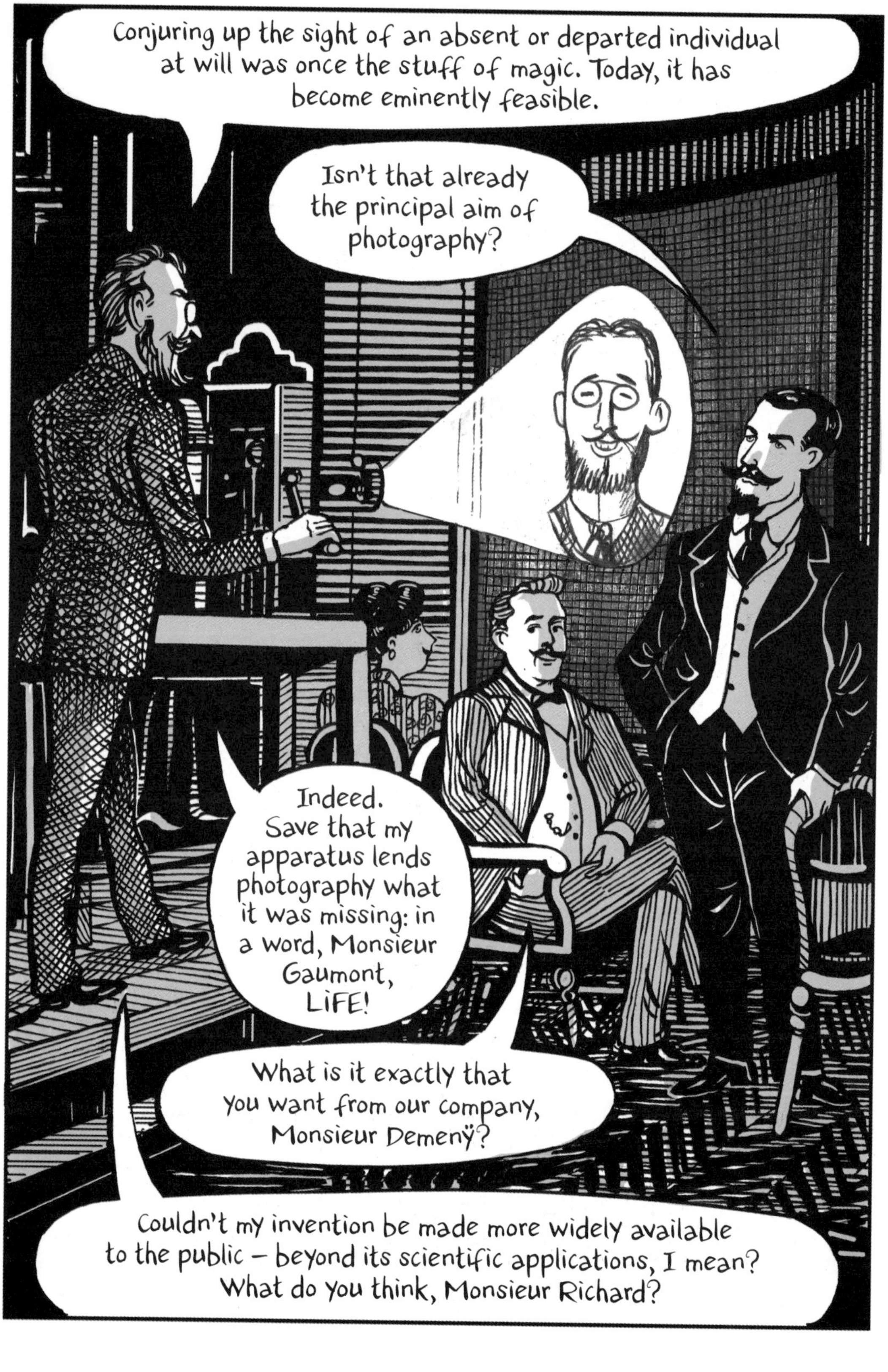
Conjuring up the sight of an absent or departed individual at will was once the stuff of magic. Today, it has become eminently feasible.
Isn't that already the principal aim of photography?
Indeed. Save that my apparatus lends photography what it was missing: in a word, Monsieur Gaumont, LIFE!
What is it exactly that you want from our company, Monsieur Demenÿ?
Couldn't my invention be made more widely available to the public – beyond its scientific applications, I mean? What do you think, Monsieur Richard?

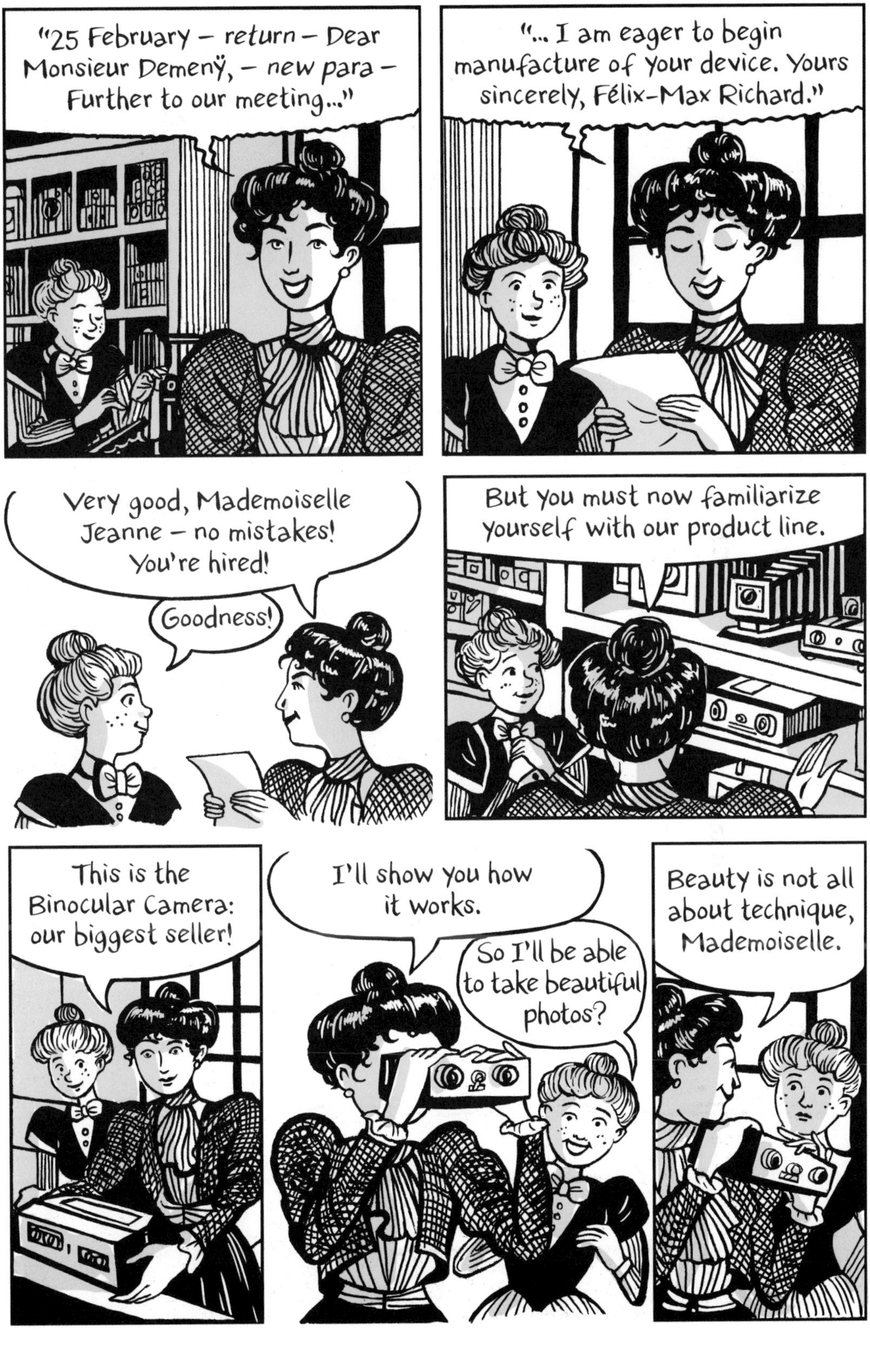
"25 February – return – Dear Monsieur Demenÿ, – new para – Further to our meeting..."
"... I am eager to begin manufacture of your device. Yours sincerely, Félix-Max Richard."
Very good, Mademoiselle Jeanne – no mistakes! You're hired!
Goodness!
But you must now familiarize yourself with our product line.
This is the Binocular Camera: our biggest seller!
I'll show you how it works.
So I'll be able to take beautiful photos?
Beauty is not all about technique, Mademoiselle.

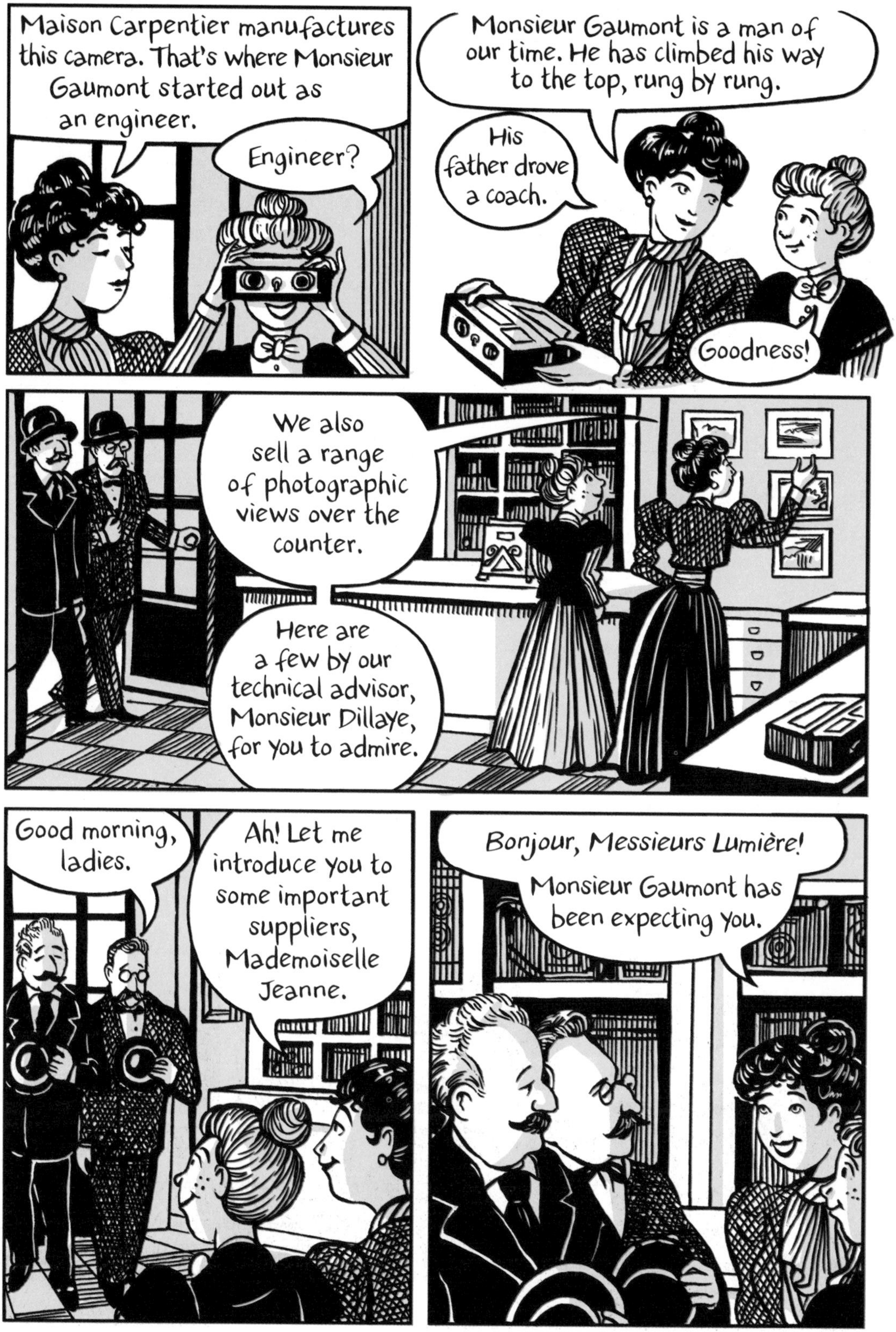
Maison Carpentier manufactures this camera. That's where Monsieur Gaumont started out as an engineer.
Engineer?
Monsieur Gaumont is a man of our time. He has climbed his way to the top, rung by rung.
His father drove a coach.
Goodness!
We also sell a range of photographic views over the counter.
Here are a few by our technical advisor, Monsieur Dillaye, for you to admire.
Good morning, ladies.
Ah! Let me introduce you to some important suppliers, Mademoiselle Jeanne.
Bonjour, Messieurs Lumière!
Monsieur Gaumont has been expecting you.

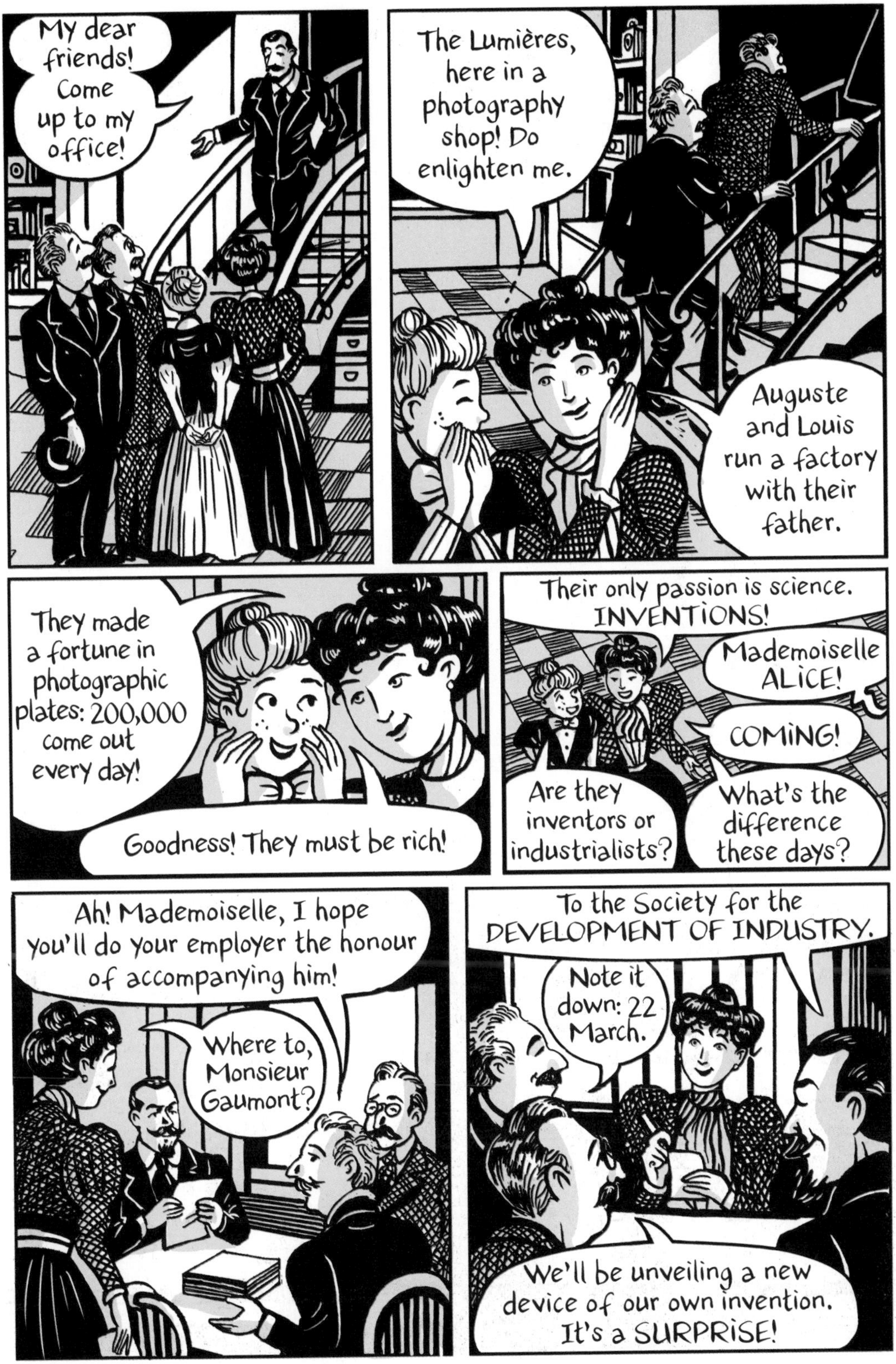
My dear friends! Come up to my office!
The Lumières, here in a photography shop! Do enlighten me.
Auguste and Louis run a factory with their father.
They made a fortune in photographic plates: 200,000 come out every day!
Goodness! They must be rich!
Their only passion is science. INVENTIONS!
Mademoiselle ALICE!
COMING!
Are they inventors or industrialists?
What's the difference these days?
Ah! Mademoiselle, I hope you'll do your employer the honour of accompanying him!
Where to, Monsieur Gaumont?
To the Society for the DEVELOPMENT OF INDUSTRY.
Note it down: 22 March.
We'll be unveiling a new device of our own invention. It's a SURPRISE!

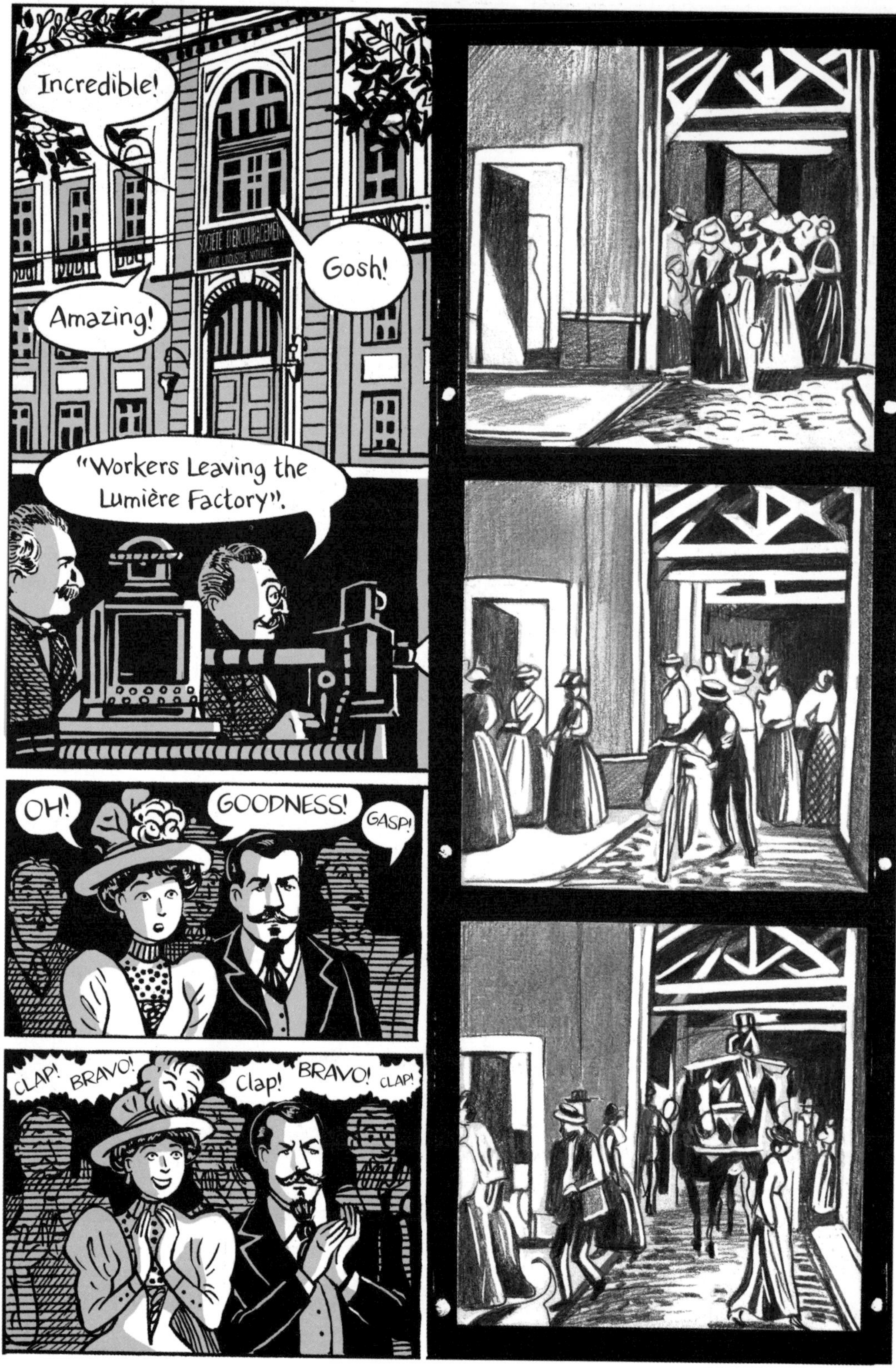
Incredible!
Gosh!
Amazing!
"Workers Leaving the Lumière Factory".
OH!
GOODNESS!
GASP!
CLAP!
BRAVO!
Clap!
BRAVO!
CLAP!

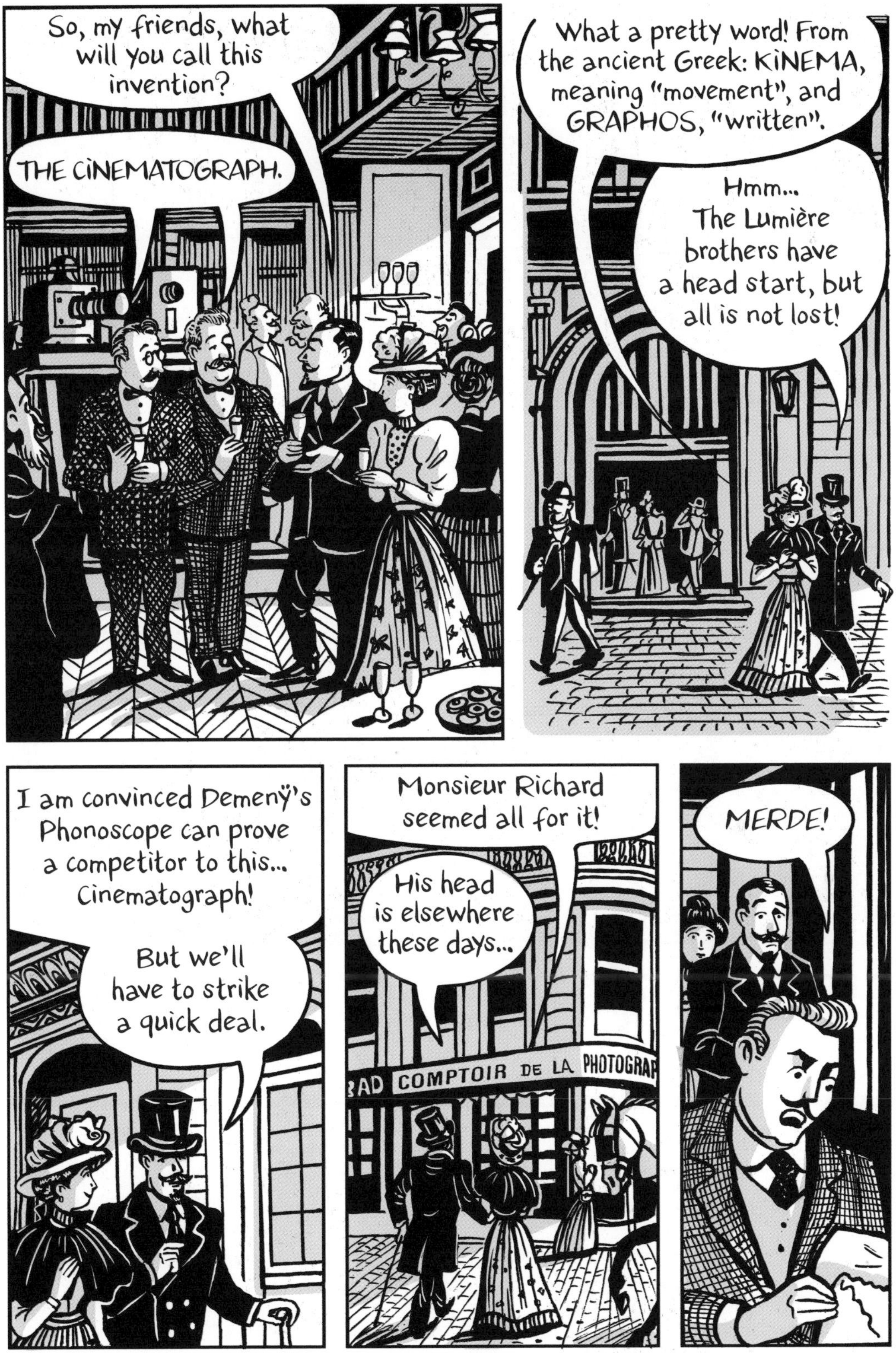
So, my friends, what will you call this invention?
THE CINEMATOGRAPH.
What a pretty word! From the ancient Greek: KINEMA, meaning "movement", and GRAPHOS, "written".
Hmm... The Lumière brothers have a head start, but all is not lost!
I am convinced Demenÿ's Phonoscope can prove a competitor to this... Cinematograph!
But we'll have to strike a quick deal.
Monsieur Richard seemed all for it!
His head is elsewhere these days...
COMPTOIR DE LA PHOTOGRAP
MERDE!

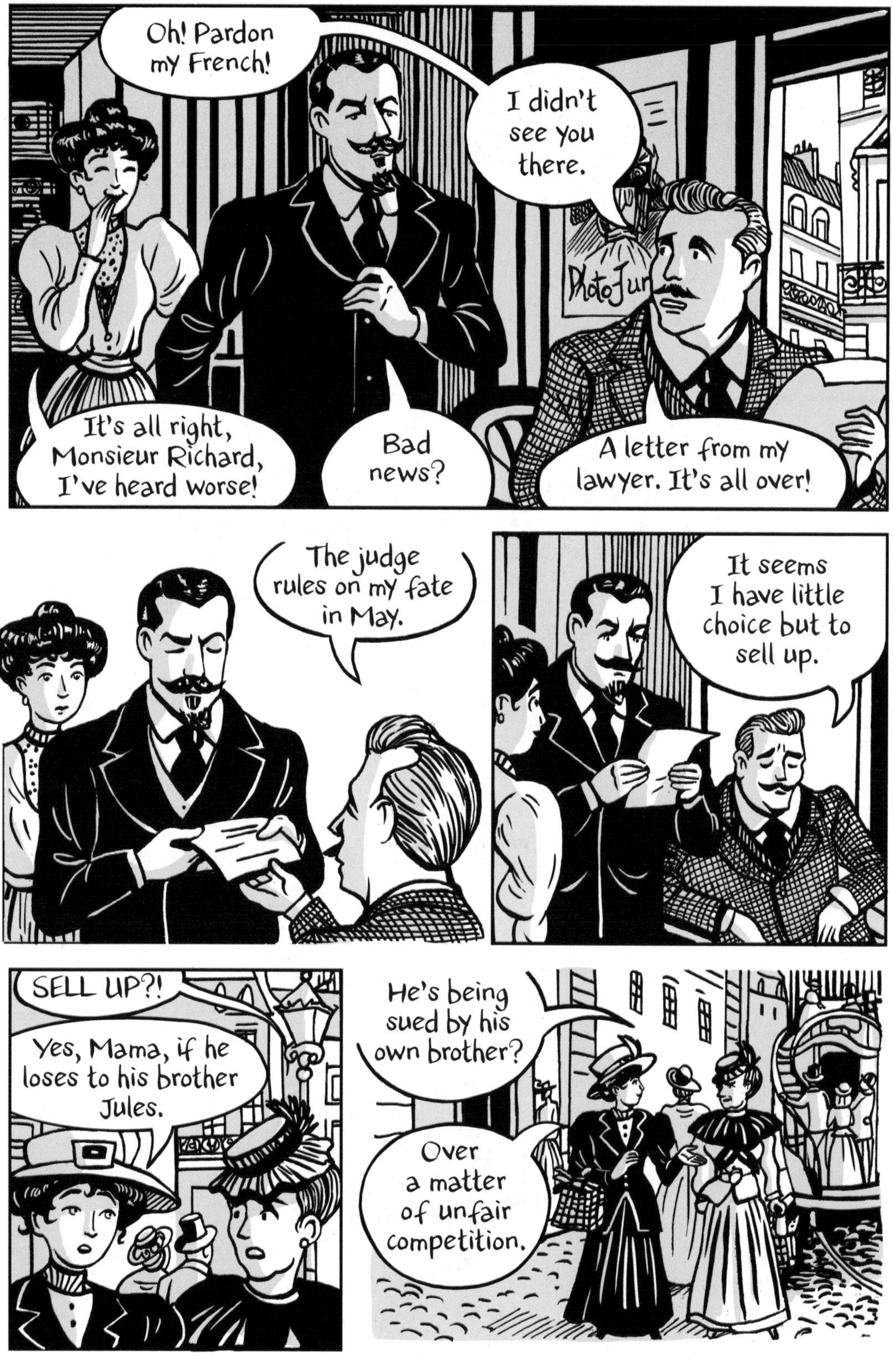
Oh! Pardon my French!
I didn't see you there.
It's all right, Monsieur Richard, I've heard worse!
Bad news?
A letter from my lawyer. It's all over!
The judge rules on my fate in May.
It seems I have little choice but to sell up.
SELL UP?!
Yes, Mama, if he loses to his brother Jules.
He's being sued by his own brother?
Over a matter of unfair competition.

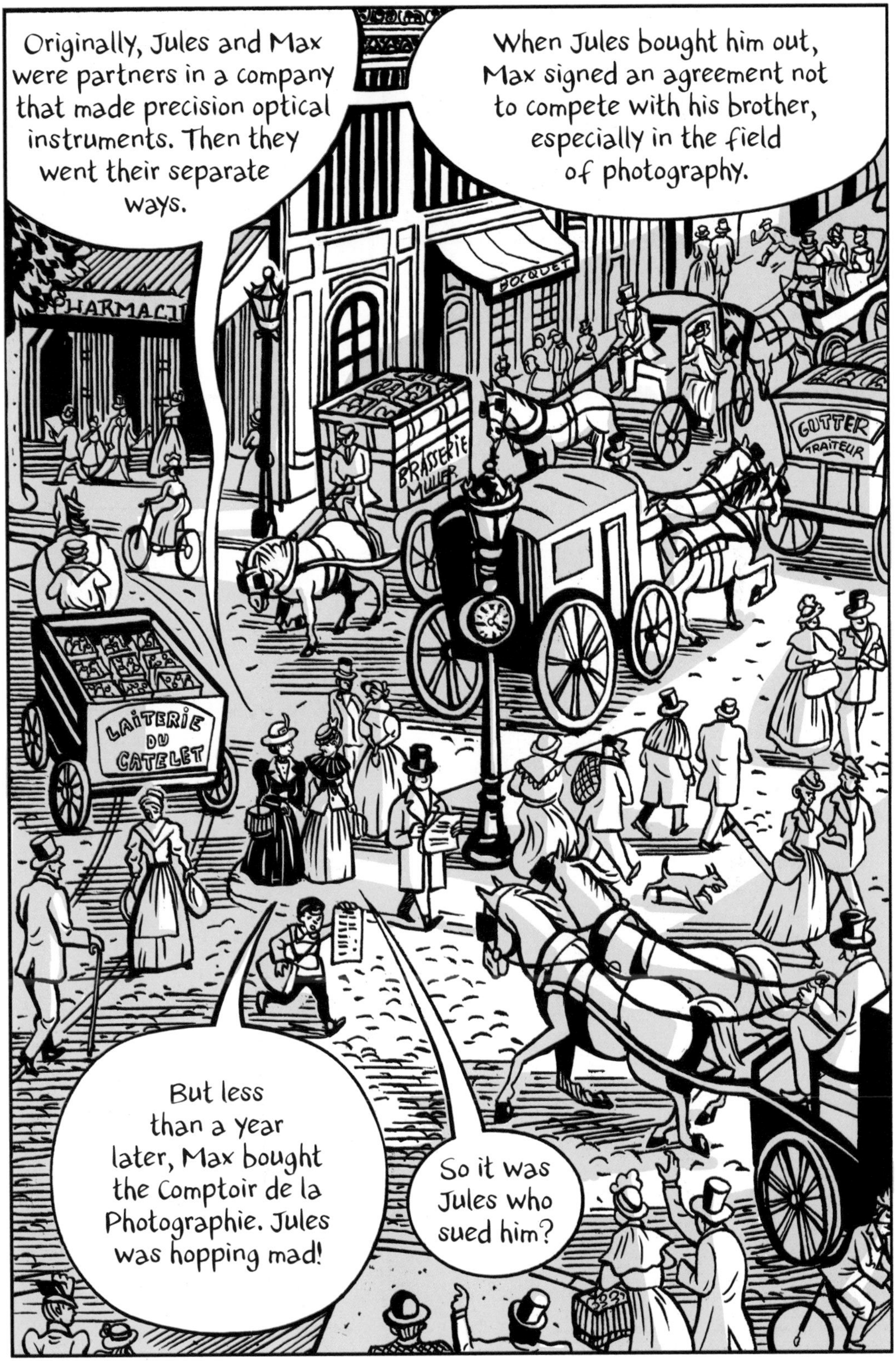
Originally, Jules and Max were partners in a company that made precision optical instruments. Then they went their separate ways.
When Jules bought him out, Max signed an agreement not to compete with his brother, especially in the field of photography.
PHARMACIE
BOCQUET
BRASSERIE MULLER
GUTTER TRAITEUR
LAITERIE DU CATELET
But less than a year later, Max bought the Comptoir de la Photographie. Jules was hopping mad!
So it was Jules who sued him?

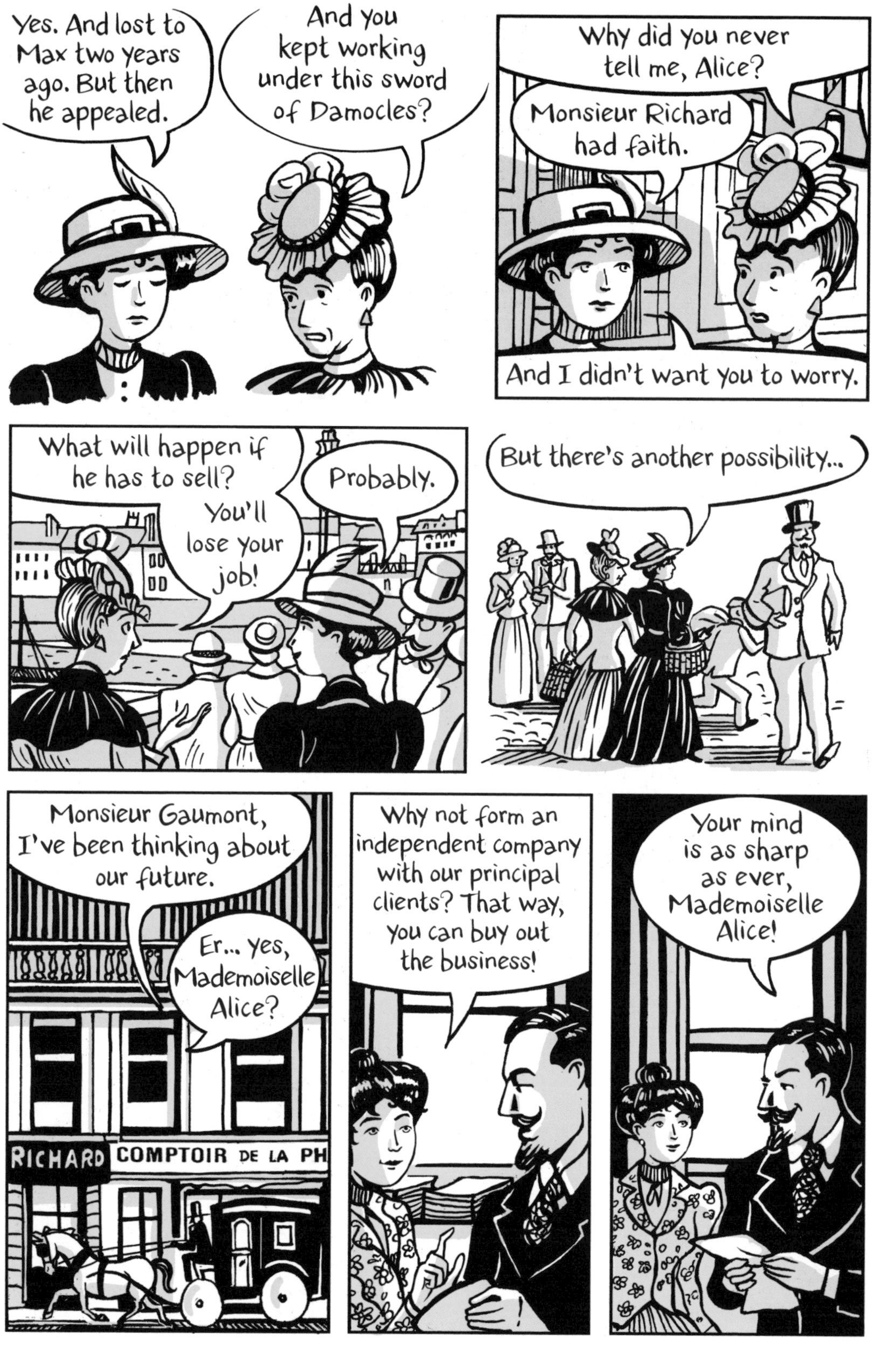
Yes. And lost to Max two years ago. But then he appealed.
And you kept working under this sword of Damocles?
Why did you never tell me, Alice?
Monsieur Richard had faith.
And I didn't want you to worry.
What will happen if he has to sell?
You'll lose your job!
Probably.
But there's another possibility...
Monsieur Gaumont, I've been thinking about our future.
Er... yes, Mademoiselle Alice?
RICHARD
COMPTOIR DE LA PH
Why not form an independent company with our principal clients? That way, you can buy out the business!
Your mind is as sharp as ever, Mademoiselle Alice!

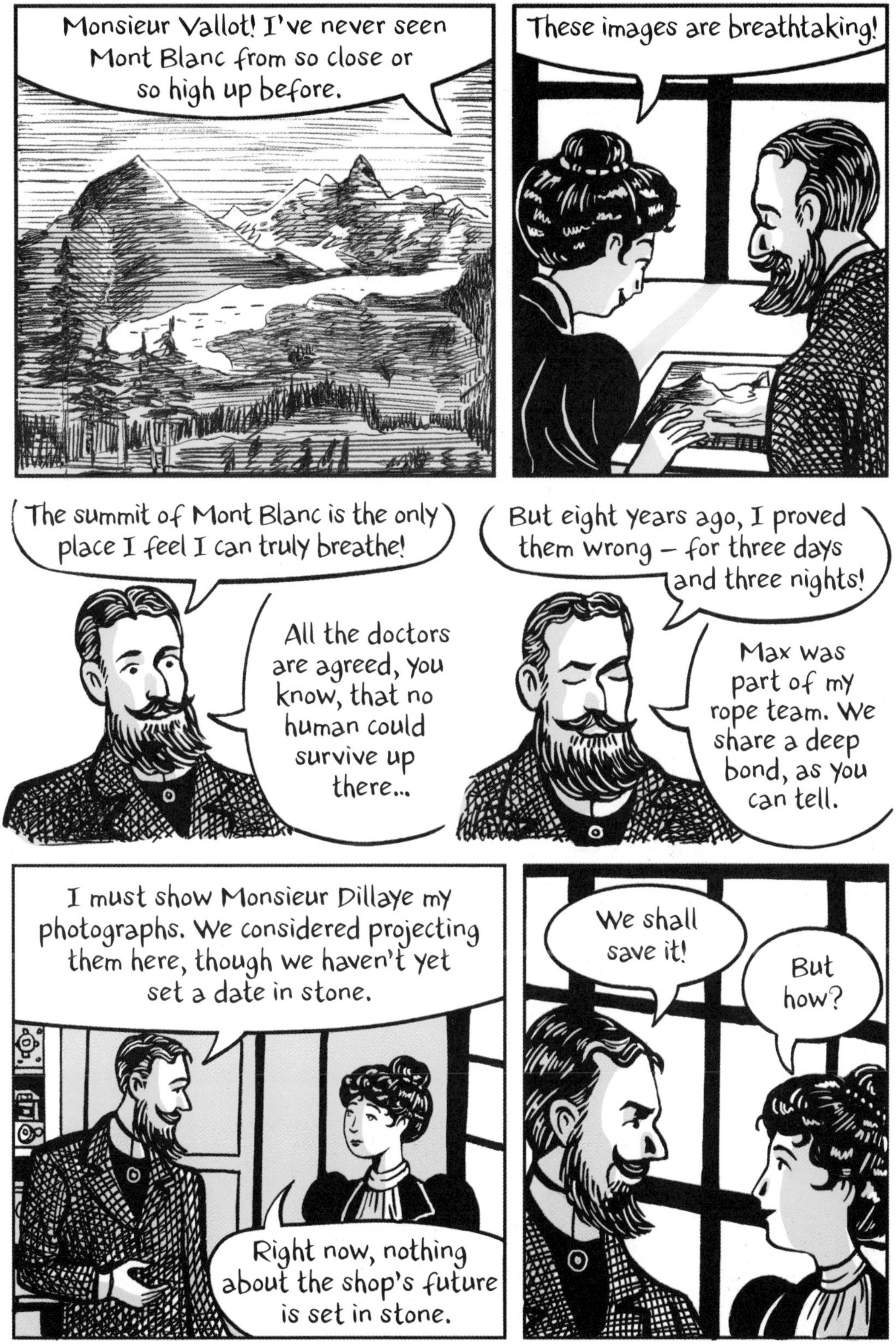
Monsieur Vallot! I've never seen Mont Blanc from so close or so high up before.
These images are breathtaking!
The summit of Mont Blanc is the only place I feel I can truly breathe!
All the doctors are agreed, you know, that no human could survive up there...
But eight years ago, I proved them wrong – for three days and three nights!
Max was part of my rope team. We share a deep bond, as you can tell.
I must show Monsieur Dillaye my photographs. We considered projecting them here, though we haven't yet set a date in stone.
Right now, nothing about the shop's future is set in stone.
We shall save it!
But how?

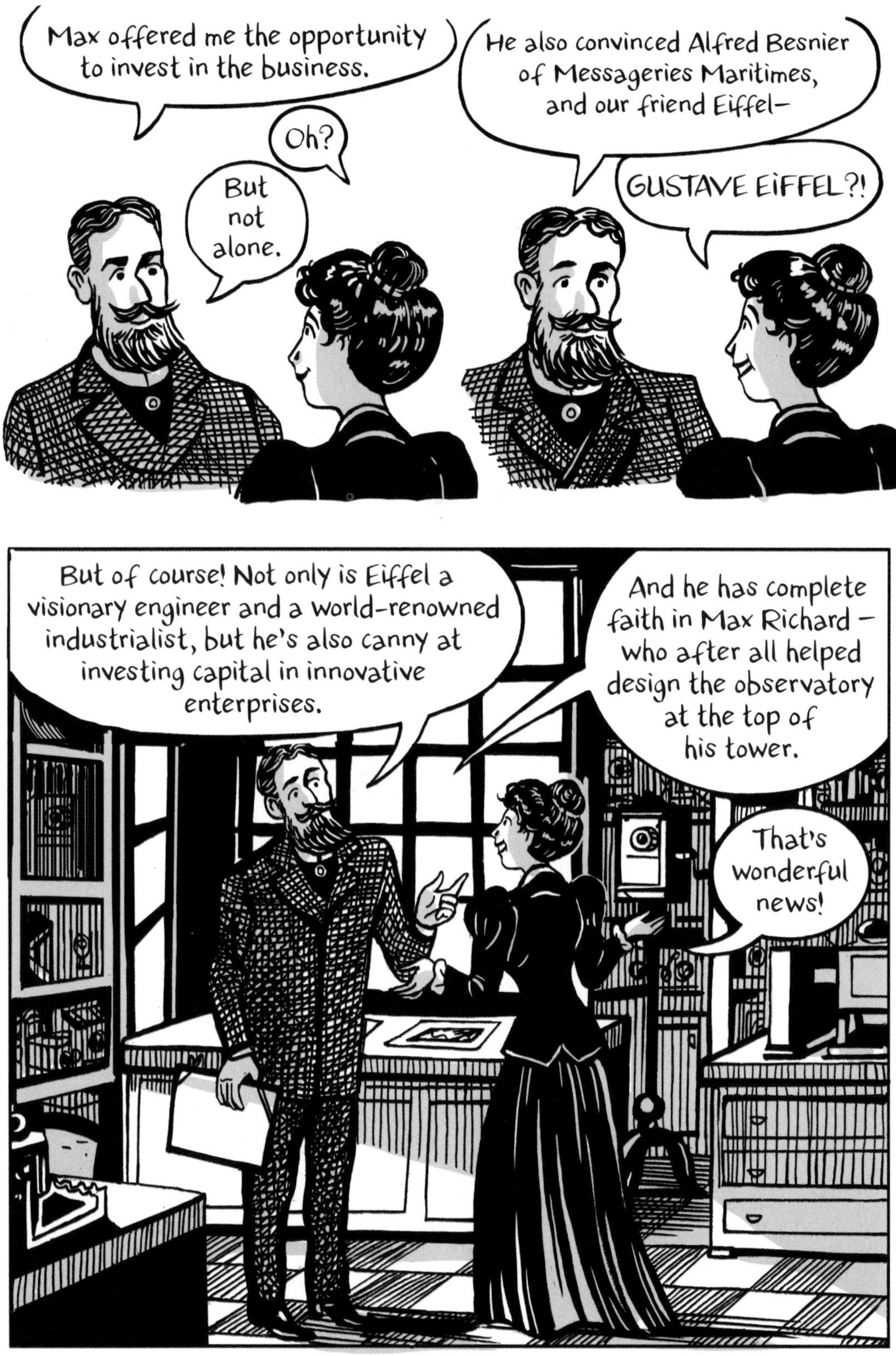
Max offered me the opportunity to invest in the business.
Oh?
But not alone.
He also convinced Alfred Besnier of Messageries Maritimes, and our friend Eiffel—
GUSTAVE EIFFEL?!
But of course! Not only is Eiffel a visionary engineer and a world-renowned industrialist, but he's also canny at investing capital in innovative enterprises.
And he has complete faith in Max Richard — who after all helped design the observatory at the top of his tower.
That's wonderful news!

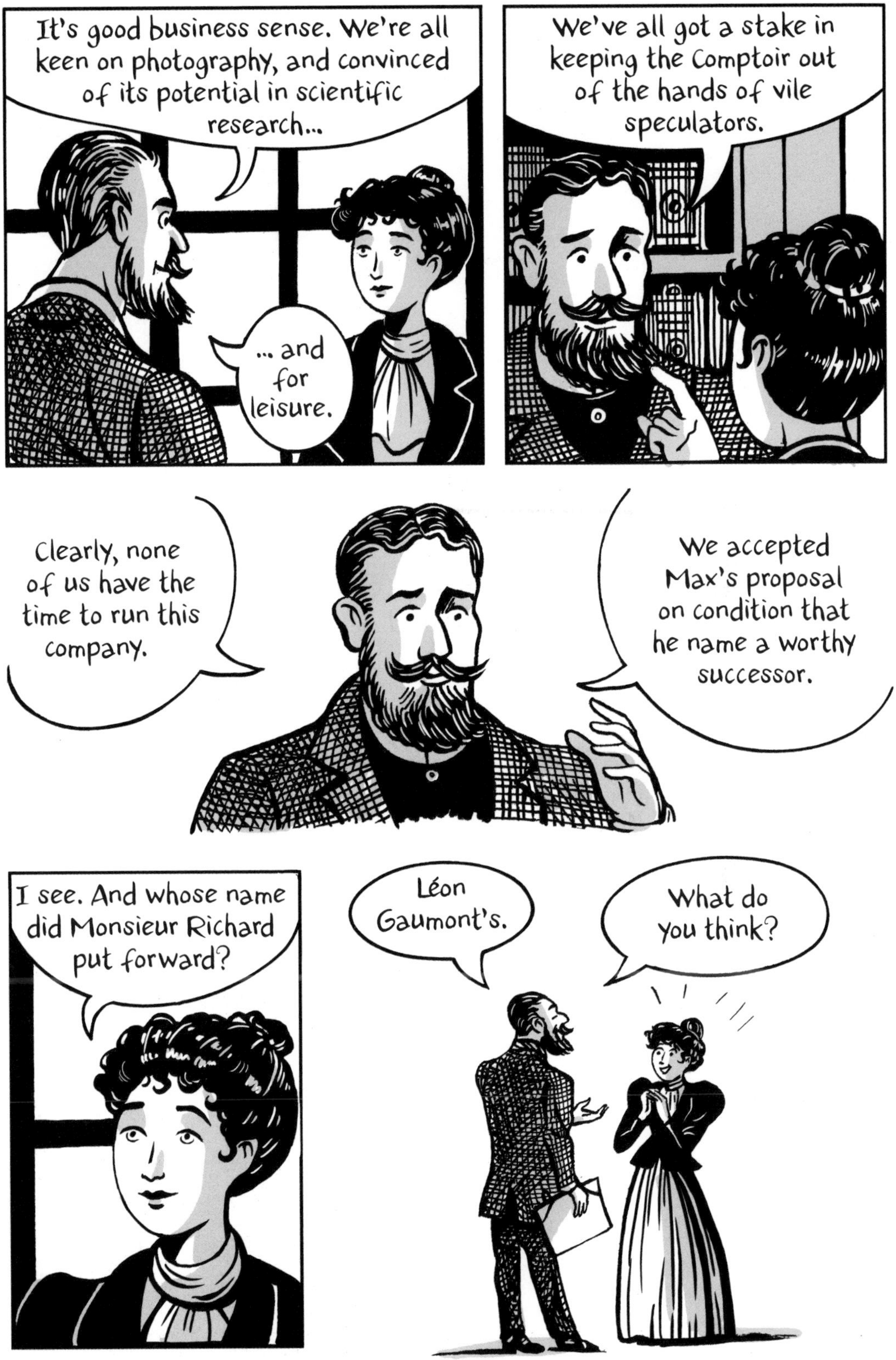
It's good business sense. We're all keen on photography, and convinced of its potential in scientific research...
... and for leisure.
We've all got a stake in keeping the Comptoir out of the hands of vile speculators.
Clearly, none of us have the time to run this company.
We accepted Max's proposal on condition that he name a worthy successor.
I see. And whose name did Monsieur Richard put forward?
Léon Gaumont's.
What do you think?

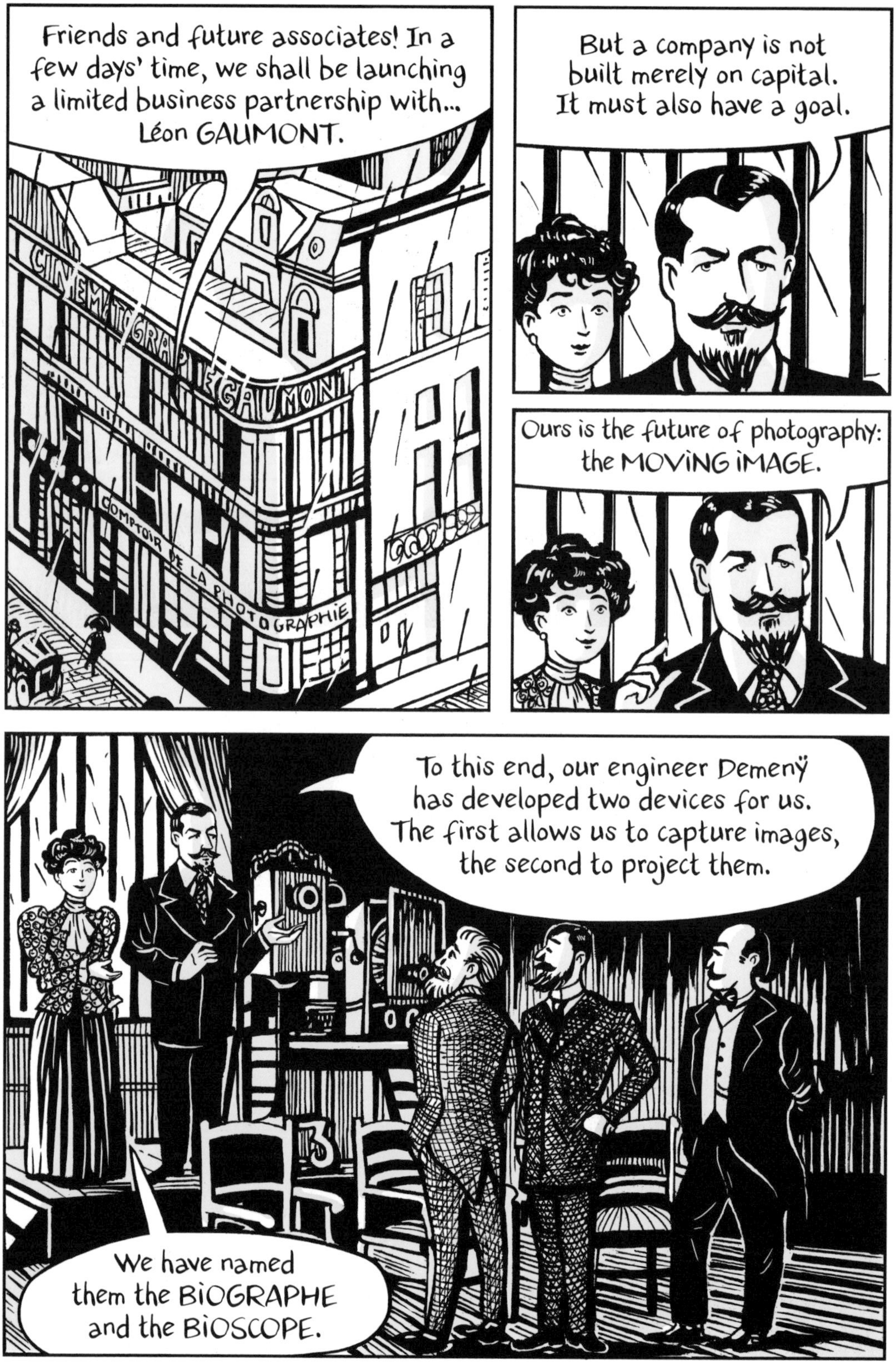
Friends and future associates! In a few days' time, we shall be launching a limited business partnership with... Léon GAUMONT.
CINEMATOGRAPHE GAUMONT
COMPTOIR DE LA PHOTOGRAPHIE
But a company is not built merely on capital. It must also have a goal.
Ours is the future of photography: the MOVING IMAGE.
To this end, our engineer Demenÿ has developed two devices for us. The first allows us to capture images, the second to project them.
We have named them the BIOGRAPHE and the BIOSCOPE.

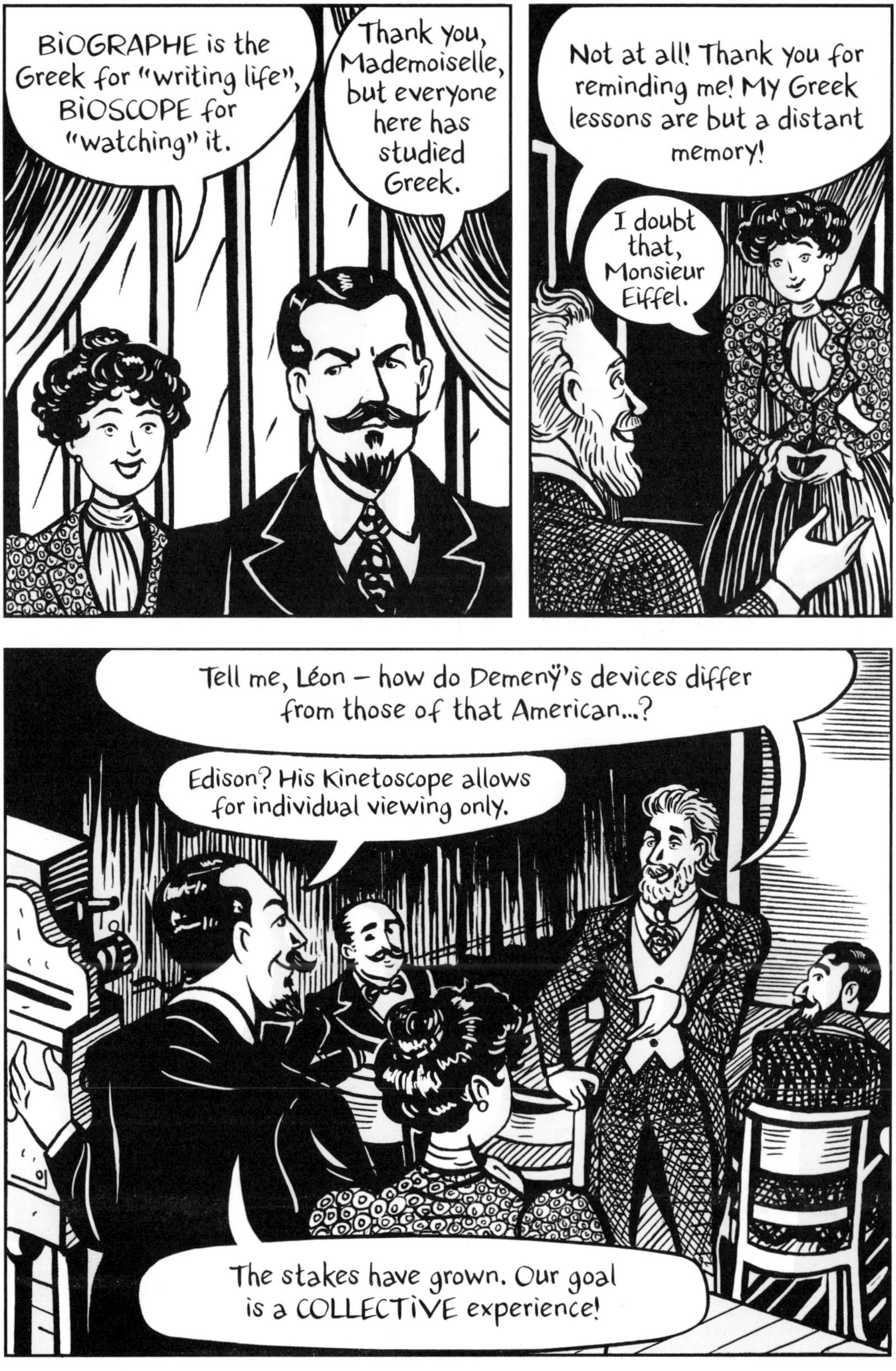
BIOGRAPHE is the Greek for "writing life", BIOSCOPE for "watching" it.
Thank you, Mademoiselle, but everyone here has studied Greek.
Not at all! Thank you for reminding me! My Greek lessons are but a distant memory!
I doubt that, Monsieur Eiffel.
Tell me, Léon – how do Demenÿ's devices differ from those of that American...?
Edison? His Kinetoscope allows for individual viewing only.
The stakes have grown. Our goal is a COLLECTIVE experience!

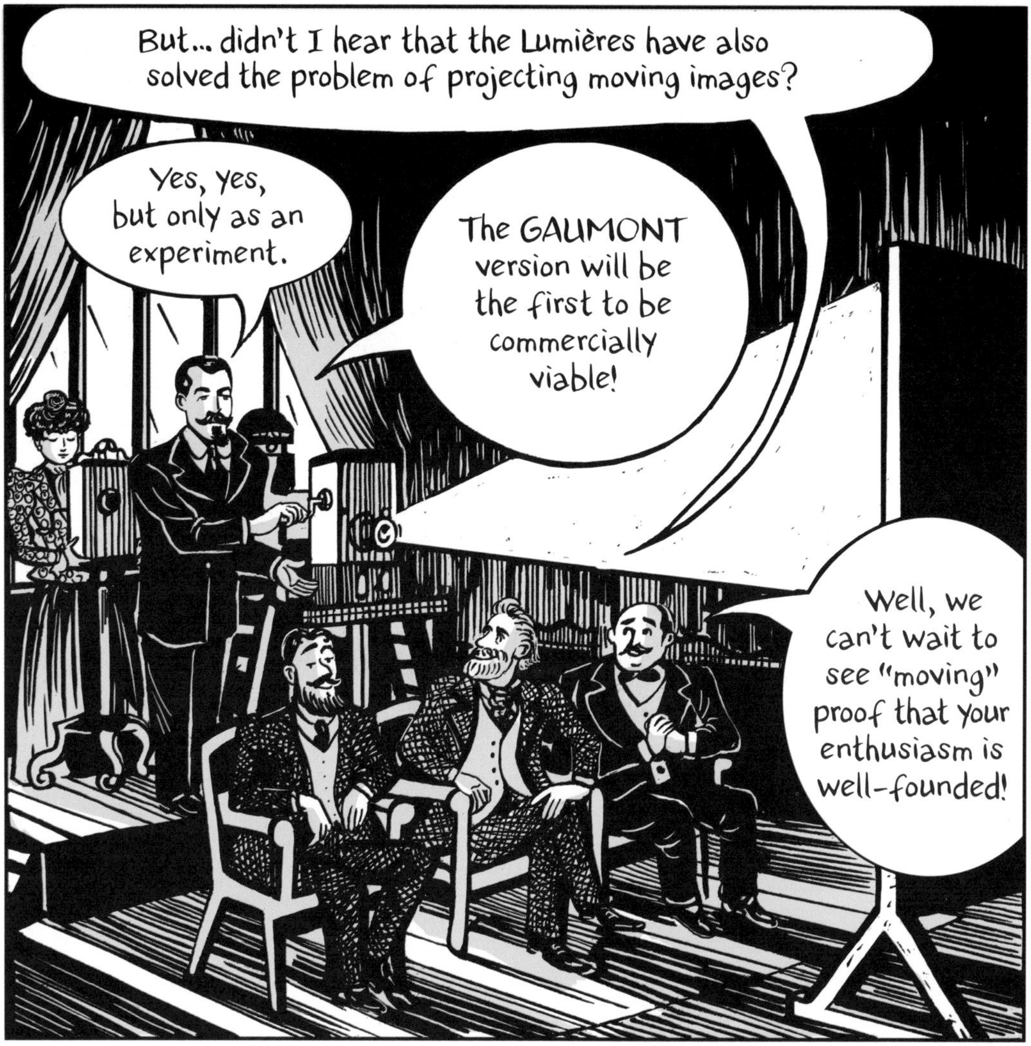
But... didn't I hear that the Lumières have also solved the problem of projecting moving images?
Yes, yes, but only as an experiment.
The GAUMONT version will be the first to be commercially viable!
Well, we can't wait to see "moving" proof that your enthusiasm is well-founded!

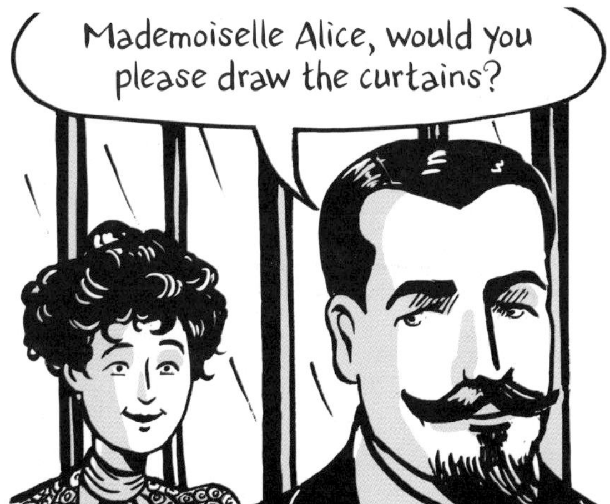
Mademoiselle Alice, would you please draw the curtains?

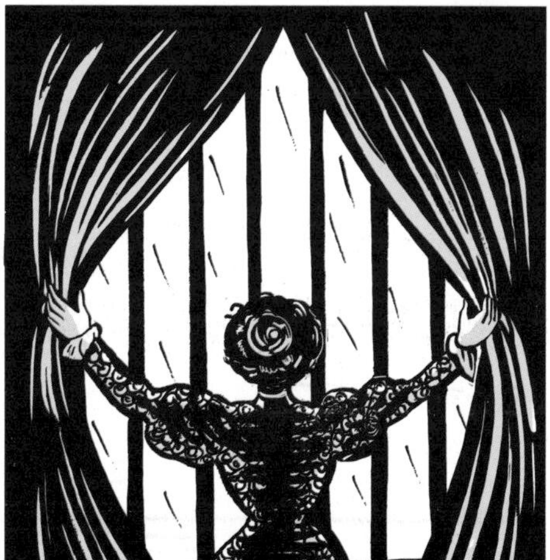

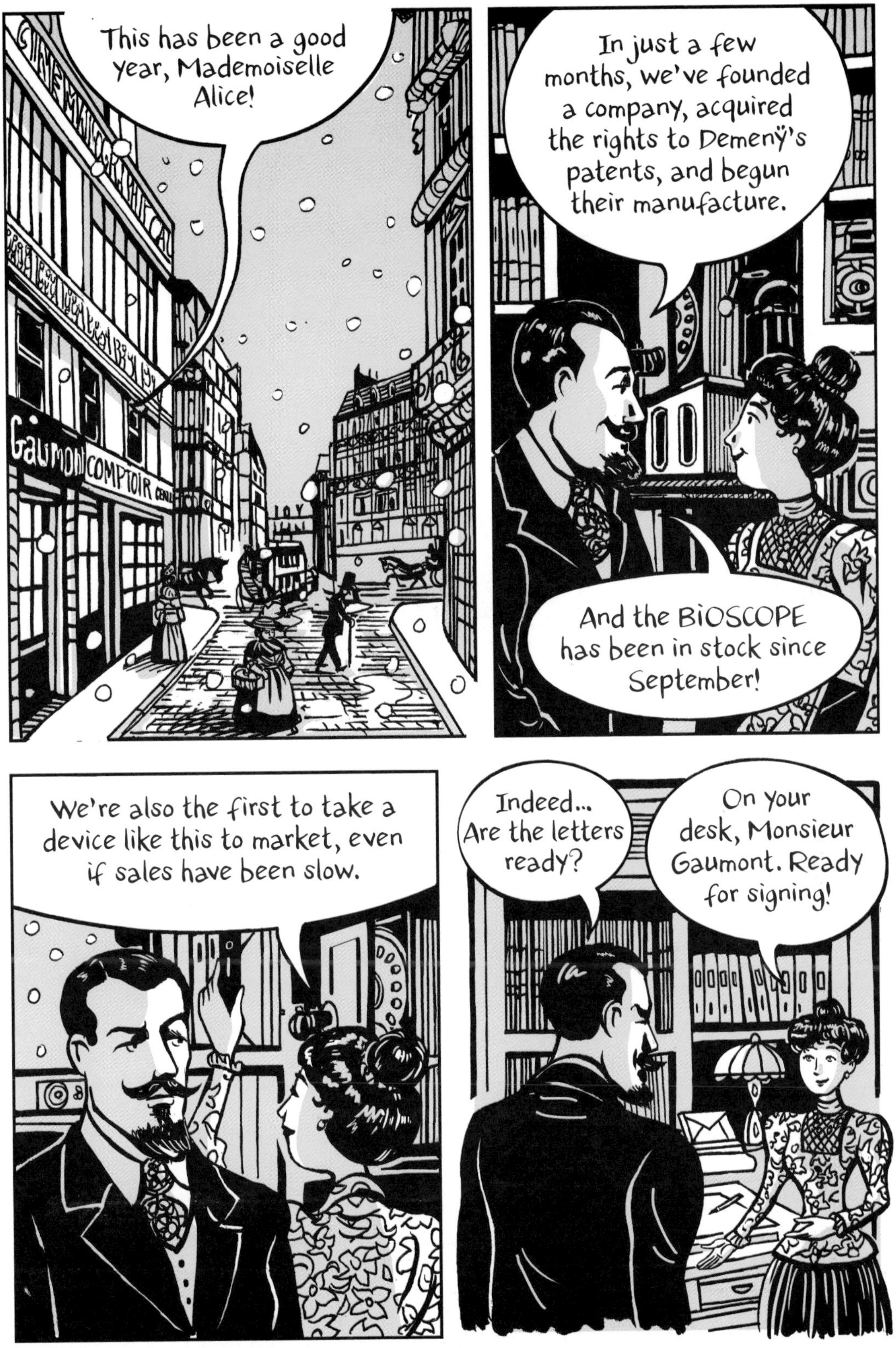
This has been a good year, Mademoiselle Alice!
In just a few months, we've founded a company, acquired the rights to Demenÿ's patents, and begun their manufacture.
And the BIOSCOPE has been in stock since September!
We're also the first to take a device like this to market, even if sales have been slow.
Indeed... Are the letters ready?
On your desk, Monsieur Gaumont. Ready for signing!

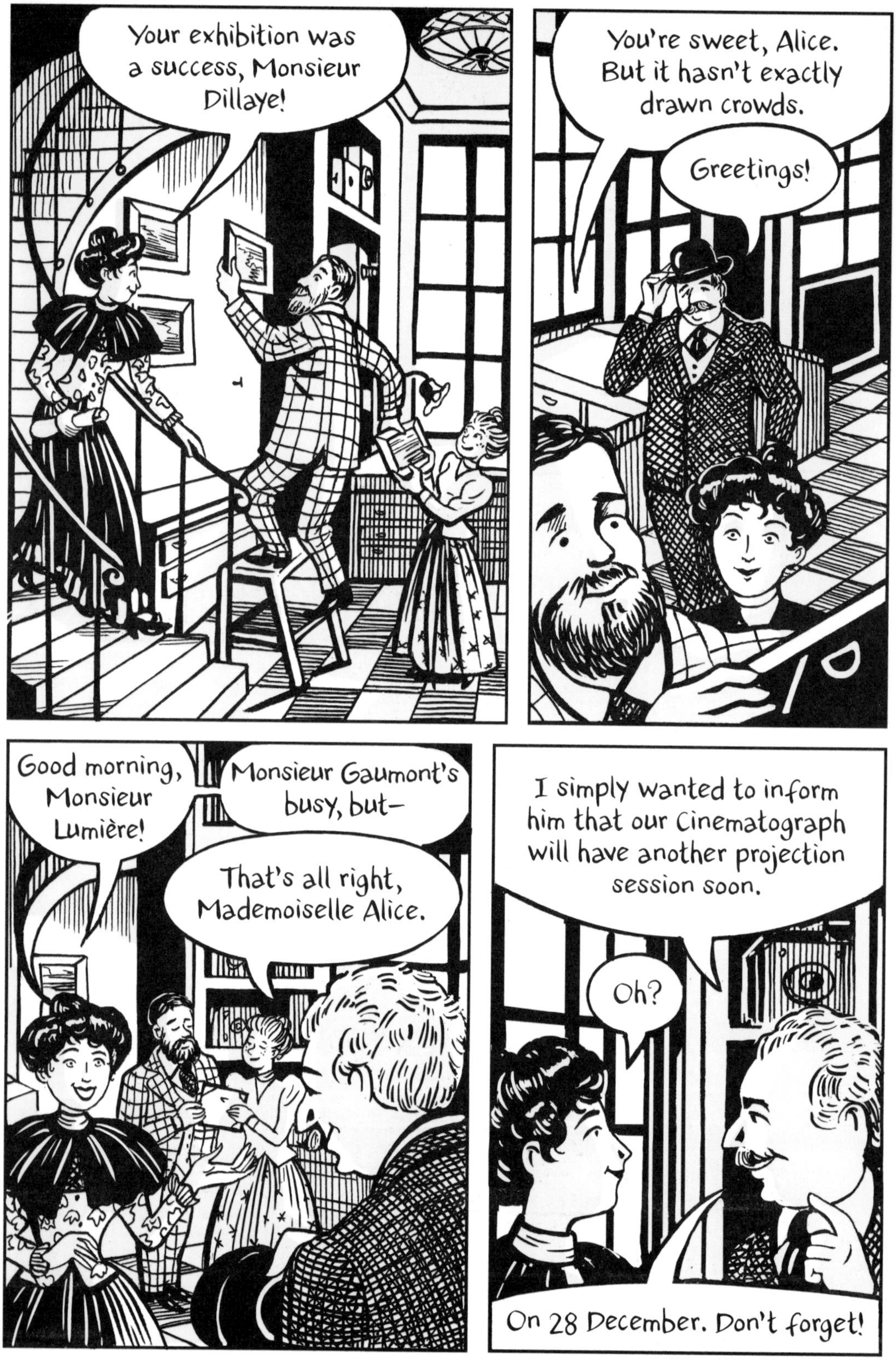
Your exhibition was a success, Monsieur Dillaye!
You're sweet, Alice. But it hasn't exactly drawn crowds.
Greetings!
Good morning, Monsieur Lumière!
Monsieur Gaumont's busy, but–
That's all right, Mademoiselle Alice.
I simply wanted to inform him that our Cinematograph will have another projection session soon.
Oh?
On 28 December. Don't forget!

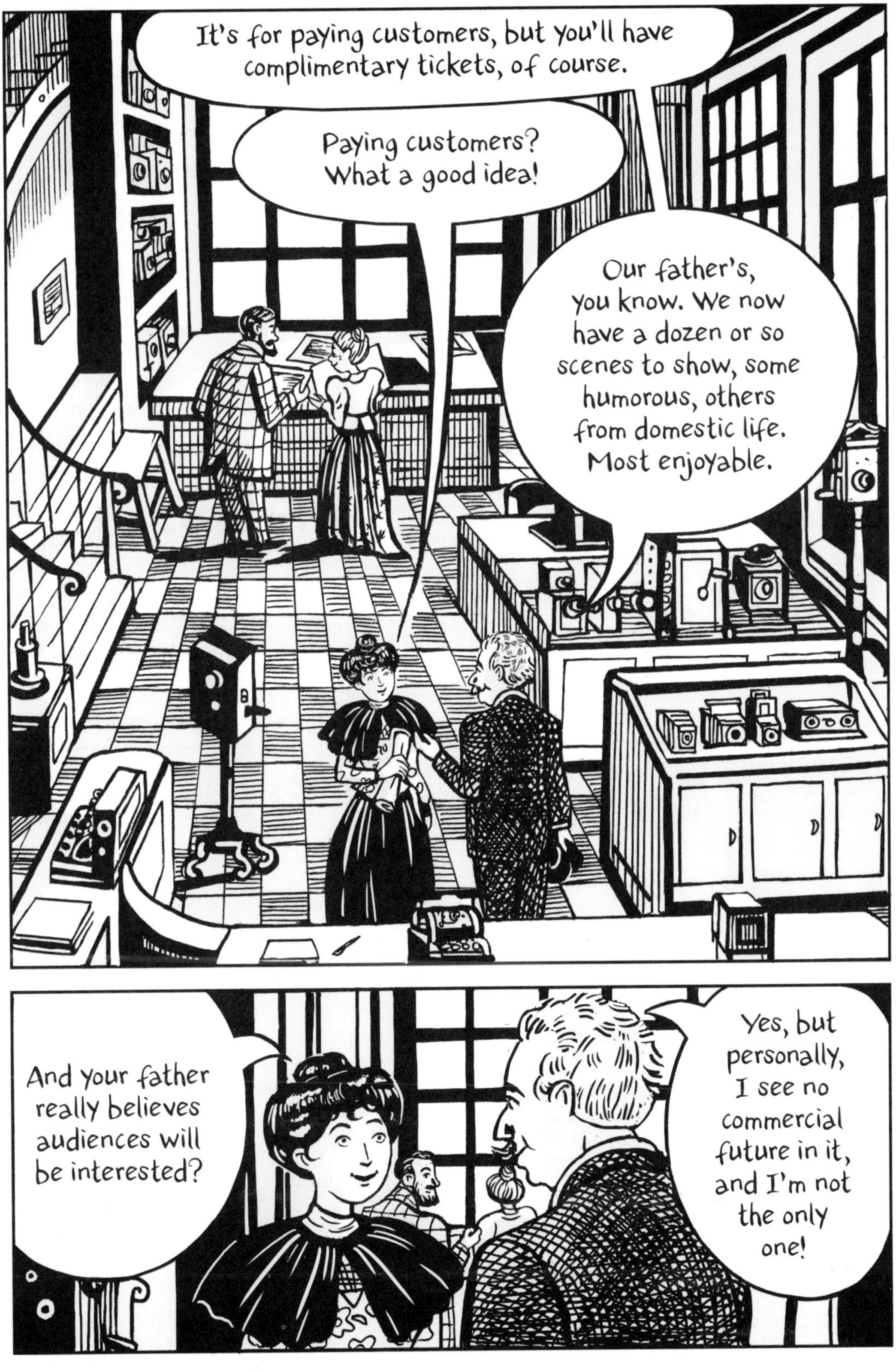
It's for paying customers, but you'll have complimentary tickets, of course.
Paying customers? What a good idea!
Our father's, you know. We now have a dozen or so scenes to show, some humorous, others from domestic life. Most enjoyable.
And your father really believes audiences will be interested?
Yes, but personally, I see no commercial future in it, and I'm not the only one!

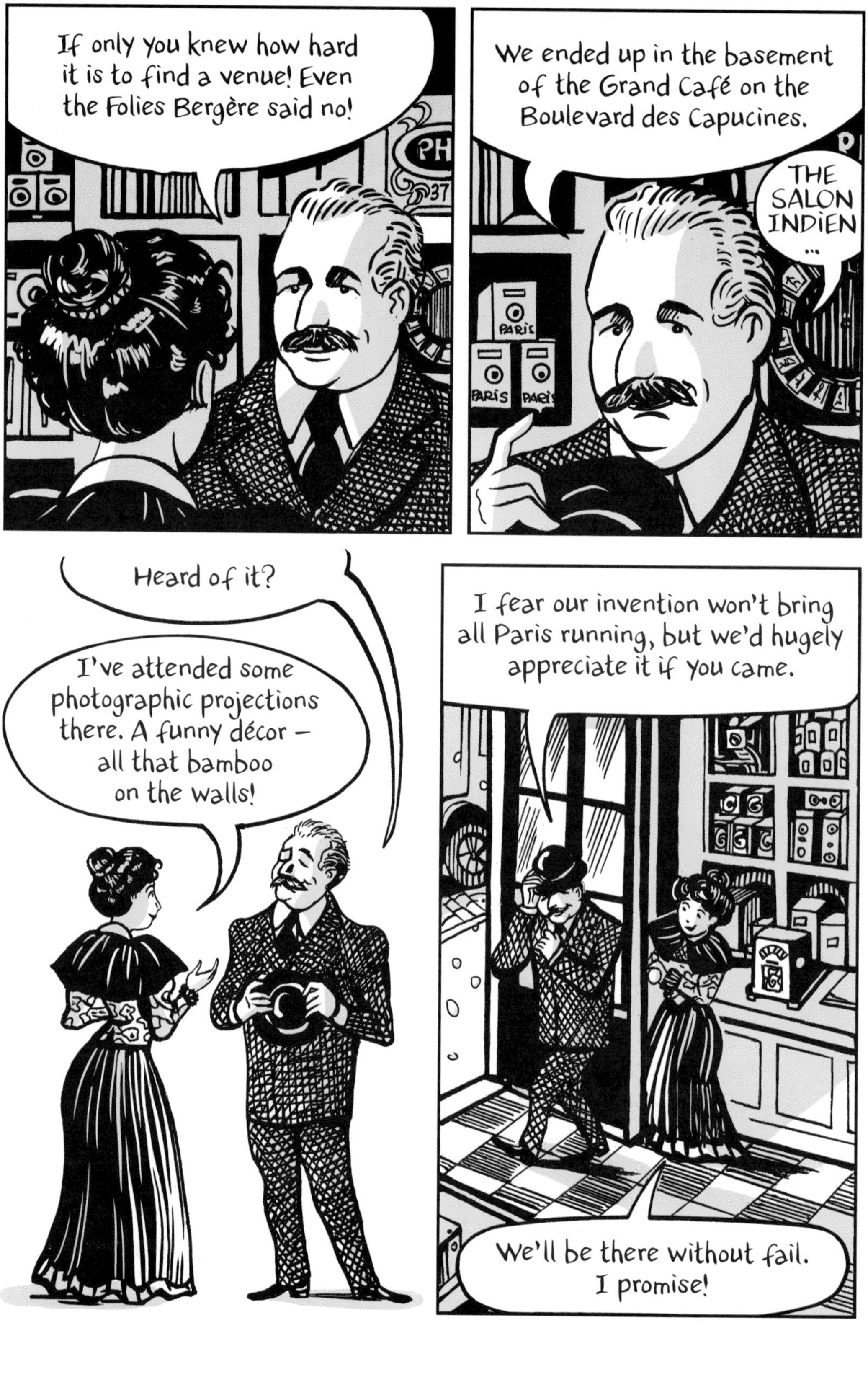
If only you knew how hard it is to find a venue! Even the Folies Bergère said no!
PH
37
We ended up in the basement of the Grand Café on the Boulevard des Capucines.
THE SALON INDIEN ...
PARIS
PARIS
PARIS
Heard of it?
I've attended some photographic projections there. A funny décor – all that bamboo on the walls!
I fear our invention won't bring all Paris running, but we'd hugely appreciate it if you came.
We'll be there without fail. I promise!

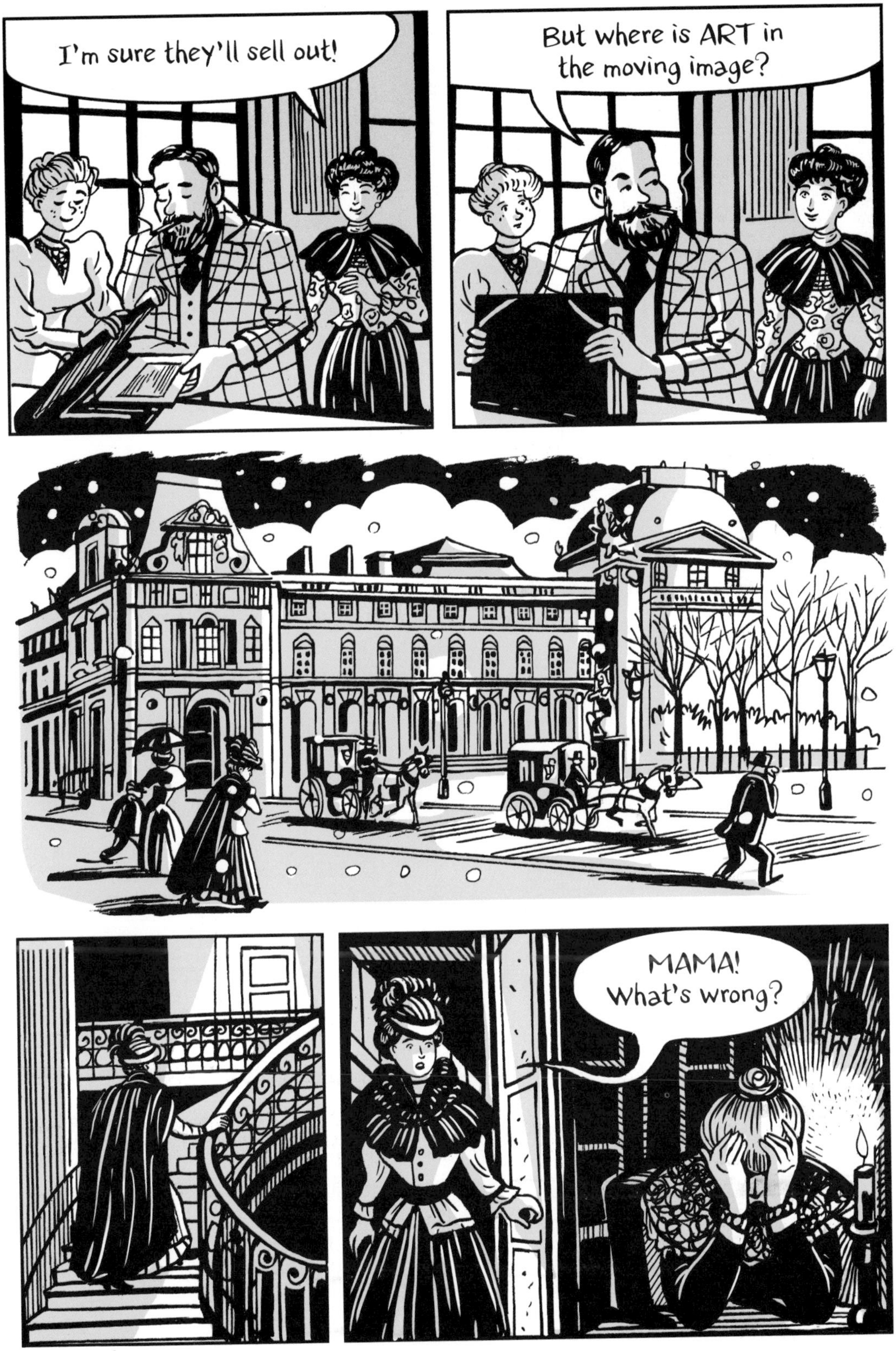
I'm sure they'll sell out!
But where is ART in the moving image?
MAMA! What's wrong?

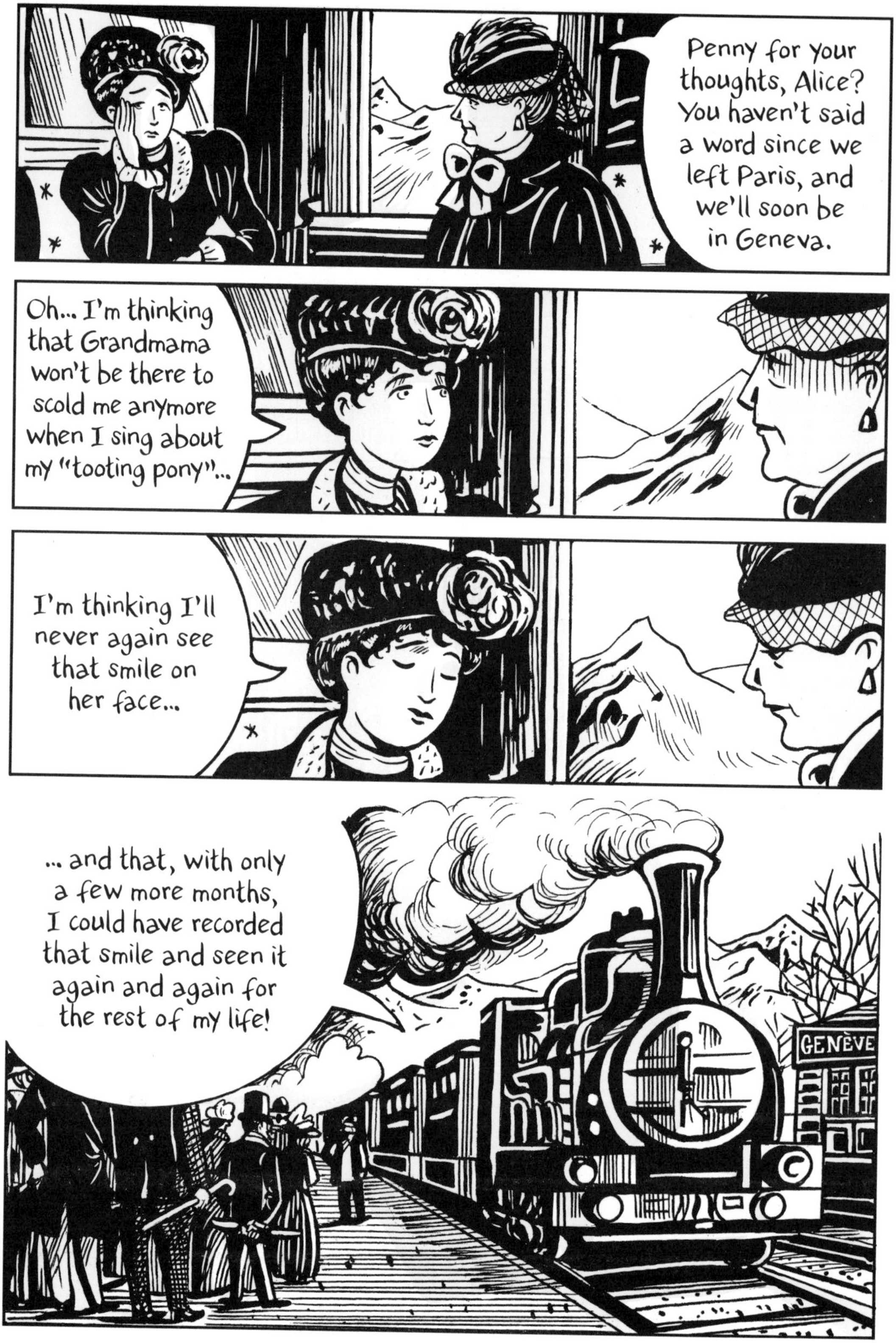
Penny for your thoughts, Alice? You haven't said a word since we left Paris, and we'll soon be in Geneva.
Oh... I'm thinking that Grandmama won't be there to scold me anymore when I sing about my "tooting pony"...
I'm thinking I'll never again see that smile on her face...
... and that, with only a few more months, I could have recorded that smile and seen it again and again for the rest of my life!
GENÈVE

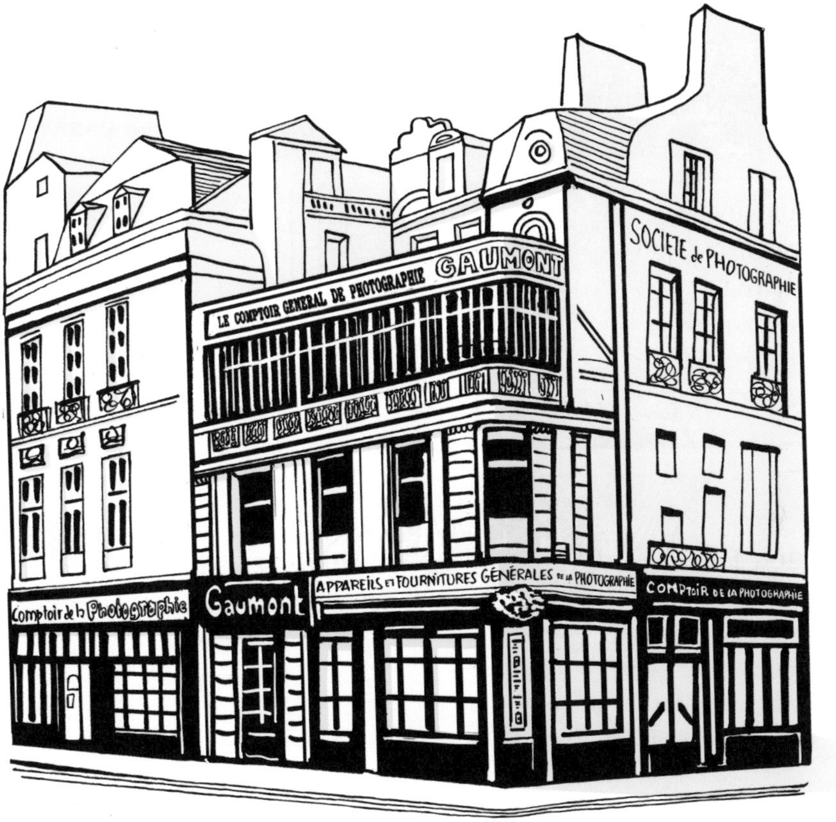

LE COMPTOIR GENERAL DE PHOTOGRAPHIE
GAUMONT
SOCIETE de PHOTOGRAPHIE
Comptoir de la Photographie
Gaumont
APPAREILS ET FOURNITURES GÉNÉRALES DE LA PHOTOGRAPHIE
COMPTOIR DE LA PHOTOGRAPHIE

1896 – Rue Saint-Roch – Paris – France

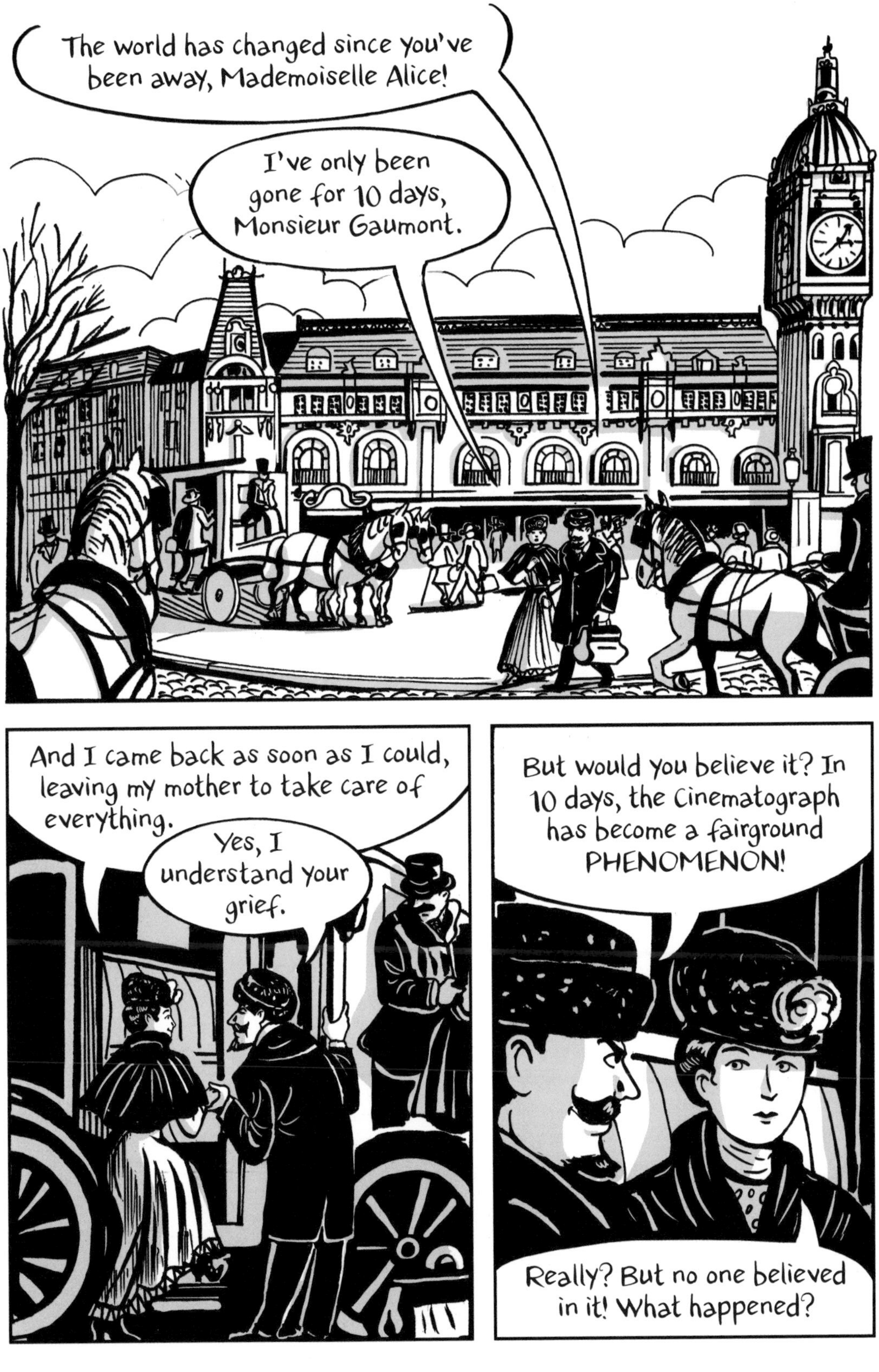
The world has changed since you've been away, Mademoiselle Alice!
I've only been gone for 10 days, Monsieur Gaumont.
And I came back as soon as I could, leaving my mother to take care of everything.
Yes, I understand your grief.
But would you believe it? In 10 days, the Cinematograph has become a fairground PHENOMENON!
Really? But no one believed in it! What happened?

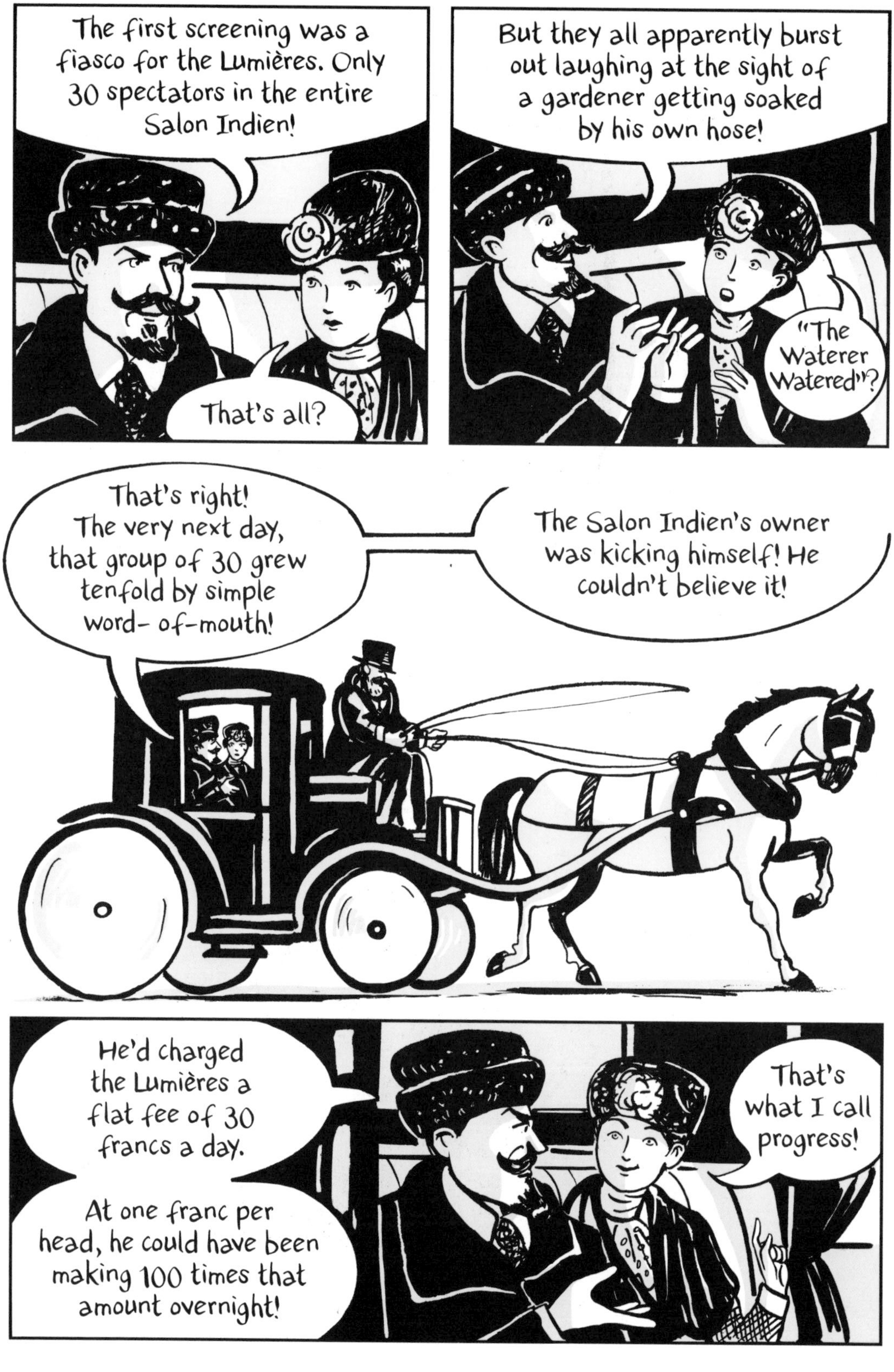

The first screening was a fiasco for the Lumières. Only 30 spectators in the entire Salon Indien!
That's all?
But they all apparently burst out laughing at the sight of a gardener getting soaked by his own hose!
"The Waterer Watered"?
That's right! The very next day, that group of 30 grew tenfold by simple word-of-mouth!
The Salon Indien's owner was kicking himself! He couldn't believe it!
He'd charged the Lumières a flat fee of 30 francs a day.
At one franc per head, he could have been making 100 times that amount overnight!
That's what I call progress!

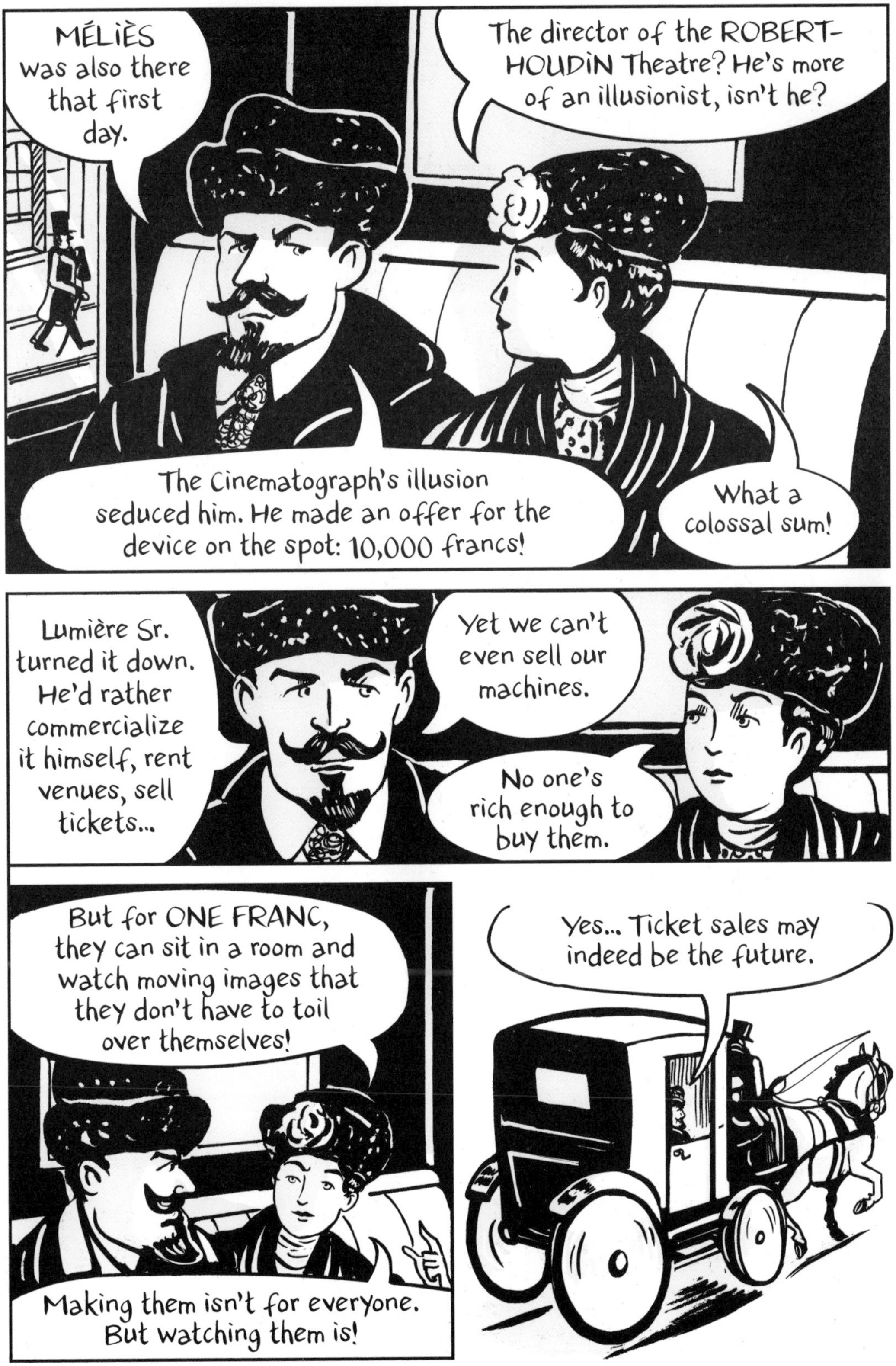
MÉLIÈS was also there that first day.
The director of the ROBERT-HOUDIN Theatre? He's more of an illusionist, isn't he?
The Cinematograph's illusion seduced him. He made an offer for the device on the spot: 10,000 francs!
What a colossal sum!
Lumière Sr. turned it down. He'd rather commercialize it himself, rent venues, sell tickets...
Yet we can't even sell our machines.
No one's rich enough to buy them.
But for ONE FRANC, they can sit in a room and watch moving images that they don't have to toil over themselves!
Making them isn't for everyone. But watching them is!
Yes... Ticket sales may indeed be the future.

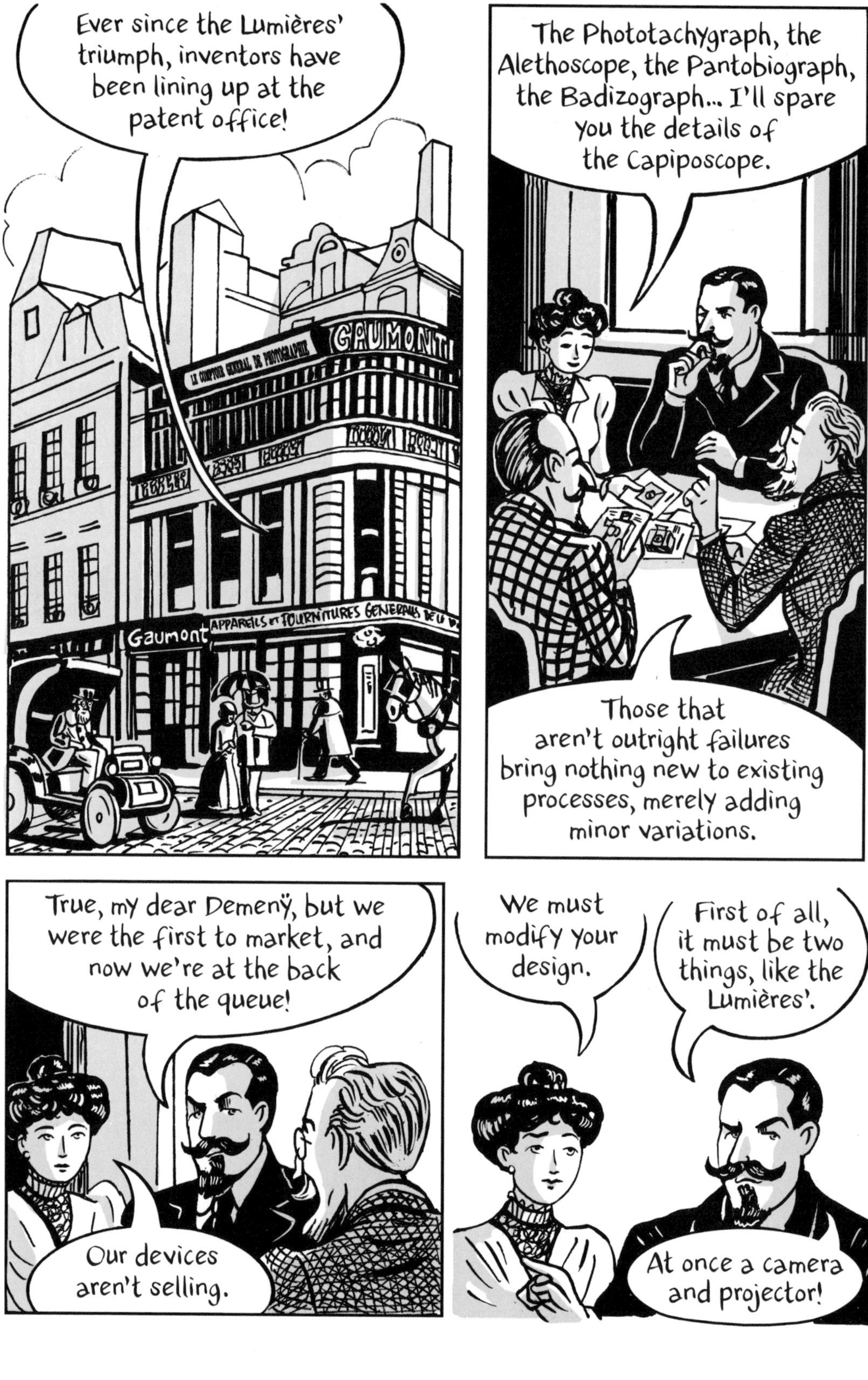
Ever since the Lumières' triumph, inventors have been lining up at the patent office!
GAUMONT
Gaumont
The Phototachygraph, the Alethoscope, the Pantobiograph, the Badizograph… I'll spare you the details of the Capiposcope.
Those that aren't outright failures bring nothing new to existing processes, merely adding minor variations.
True, my dear Demenÿ, but we were the first to market, and now we're at the back of the queue!
Our devices aren't selling.
We must modify your design.
First of all, it must be two things, like the Lumières'.
At once a camera and projector!

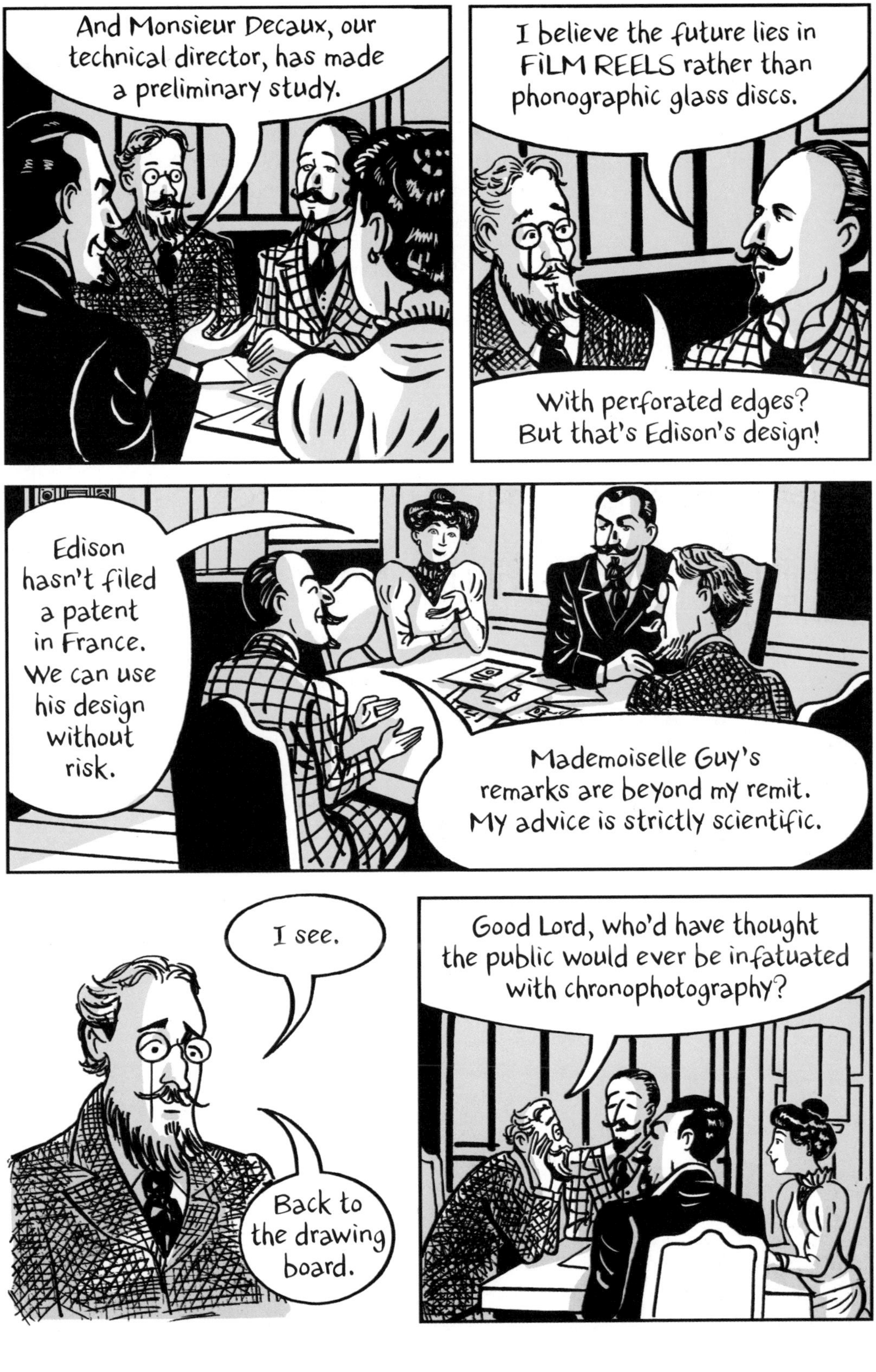
And Monsieur Decaux, our technical director, has made a preliminary study.
I believe the future lies in FILM REELS rather than phonographic glass discs.
With perforated edges? But that's Edison's design!
Edison hasn't filed a patent in France. We can use his design without risk.
Mademoiselle Guy's remarks are beyond my remit. My advice is strictly scientific.
I see.
Back to the drawing board.
Good Lord, who'd have thought the public would ever be infatuated with chronophotography?

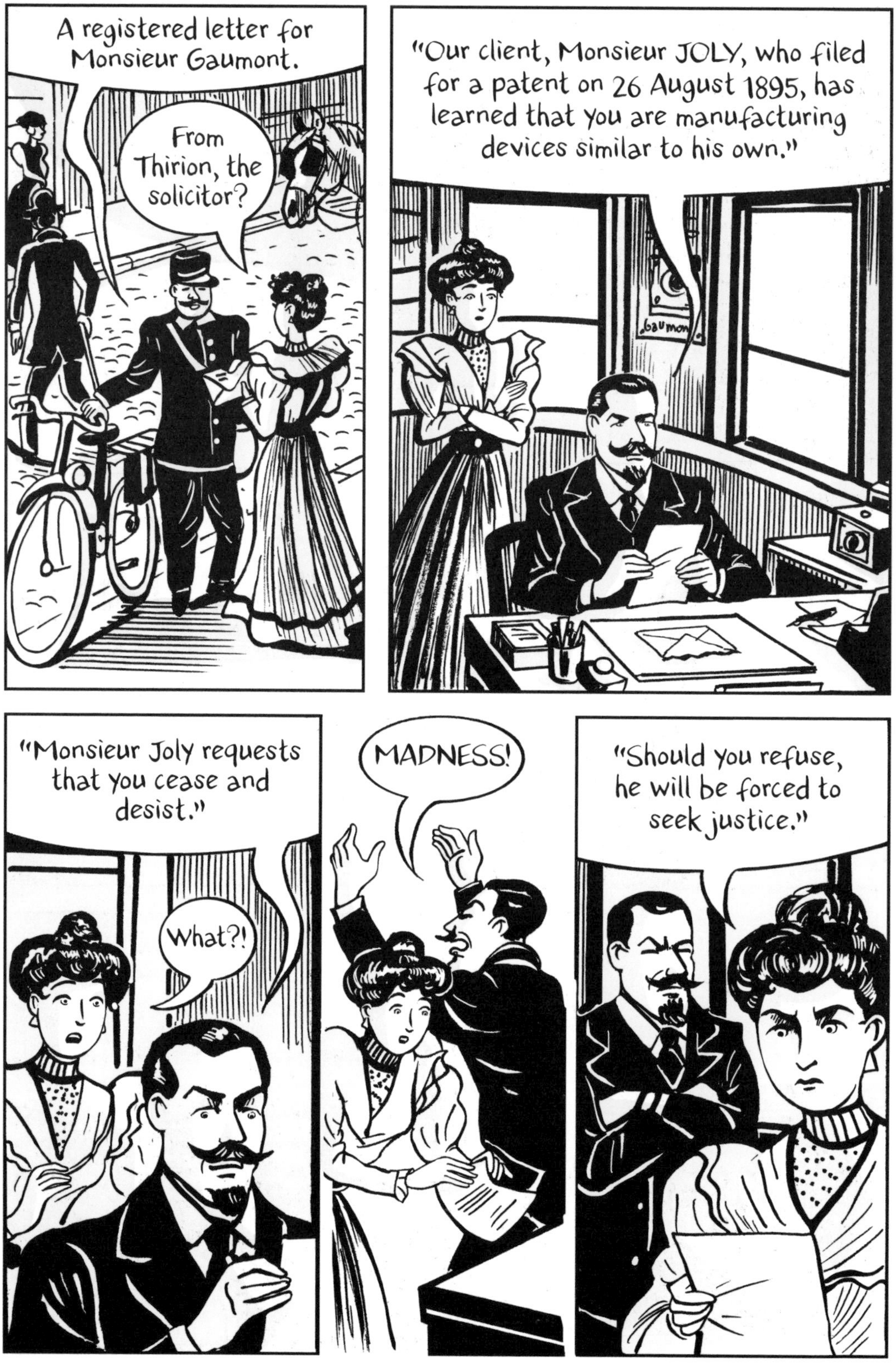
A registered letter for Monsieur Gaumont.
From Thirion, the solicitor?
"Our client, Monsieur JOLY, who filed for a patent on 26 August 1895, has learned that you are manufacturing devices similar to his own."
gaumon
"Monsieur Joly requests that you cease and desist."
What?!
MADNESS!
"Should you refuse, he will be forced to seek justice."

According to his lawyer, Monsieur Joly acknowledges that his work consisted in perfecting Demenÿ's system.

"Perfecting"! My eye!

Your expert opinion, Decaux?

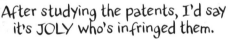

After studying the patents, I'd say it's JOLY who's infringed them.

HA!

What's he after?

A financial settlement.

To BLAZES with him!

We must find out what Demenÿ thinks.

I saw him this morning. He's completely shattered.

Poor Demenÿ.

He's panicking.

Business requires nerves of steel.

I think Demenÿ prefers science to business!

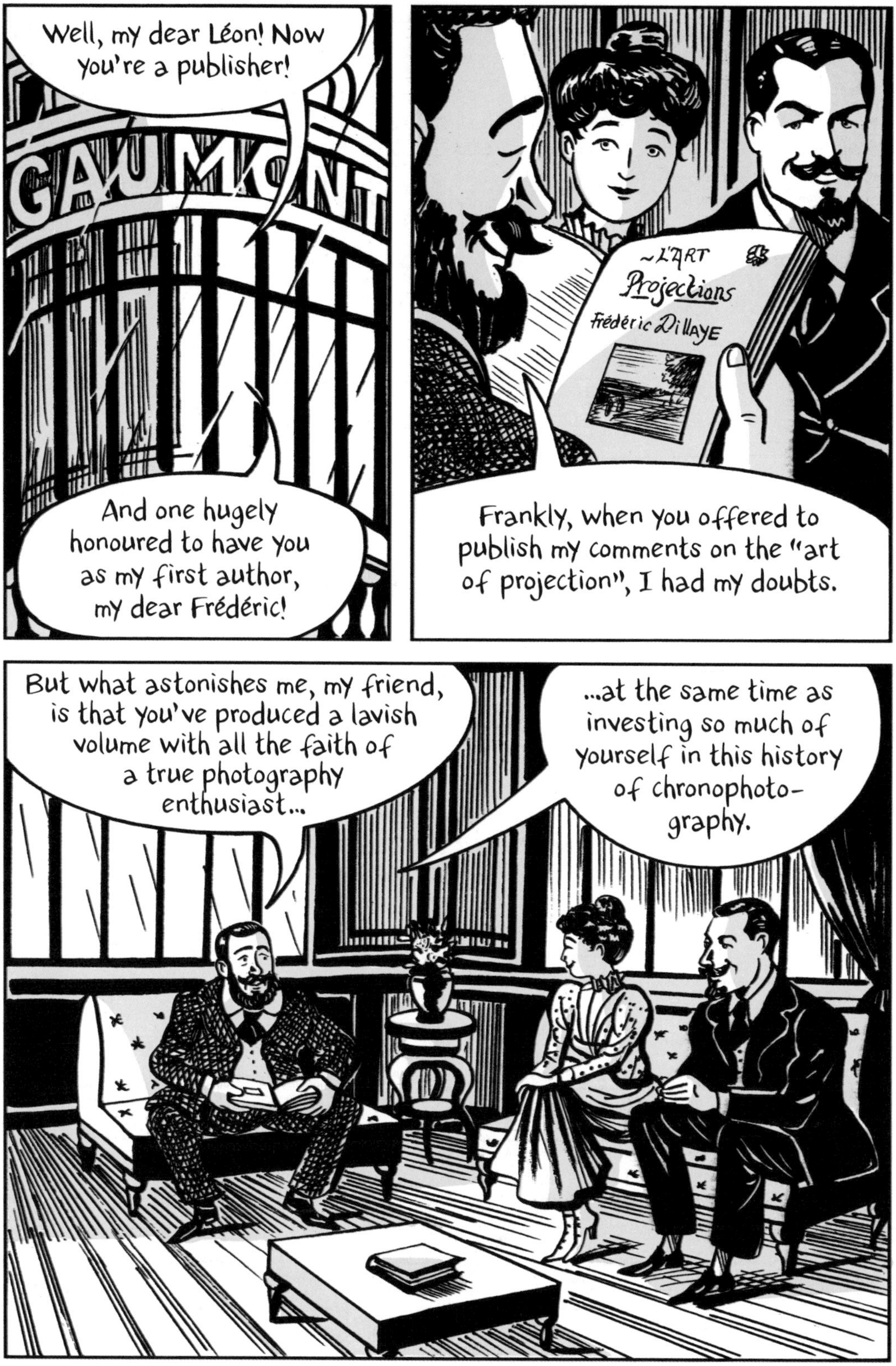
Well, my dear Léon! Now you're a publisher!
GAUMONT
And one hugely honoured to have you as my first author, my dear Frédéric!
L'ART Projections Frédéric Dillaye
Frankly, when you offered to publish my comments on the "art of projection", I had my doubts.
But what astonishes me, my friend, is that you've produced a lavish volume with all the faith of a true photography enthusiast...
...at the same time as investing so much of yourself in this history of chronophoto-graphy.

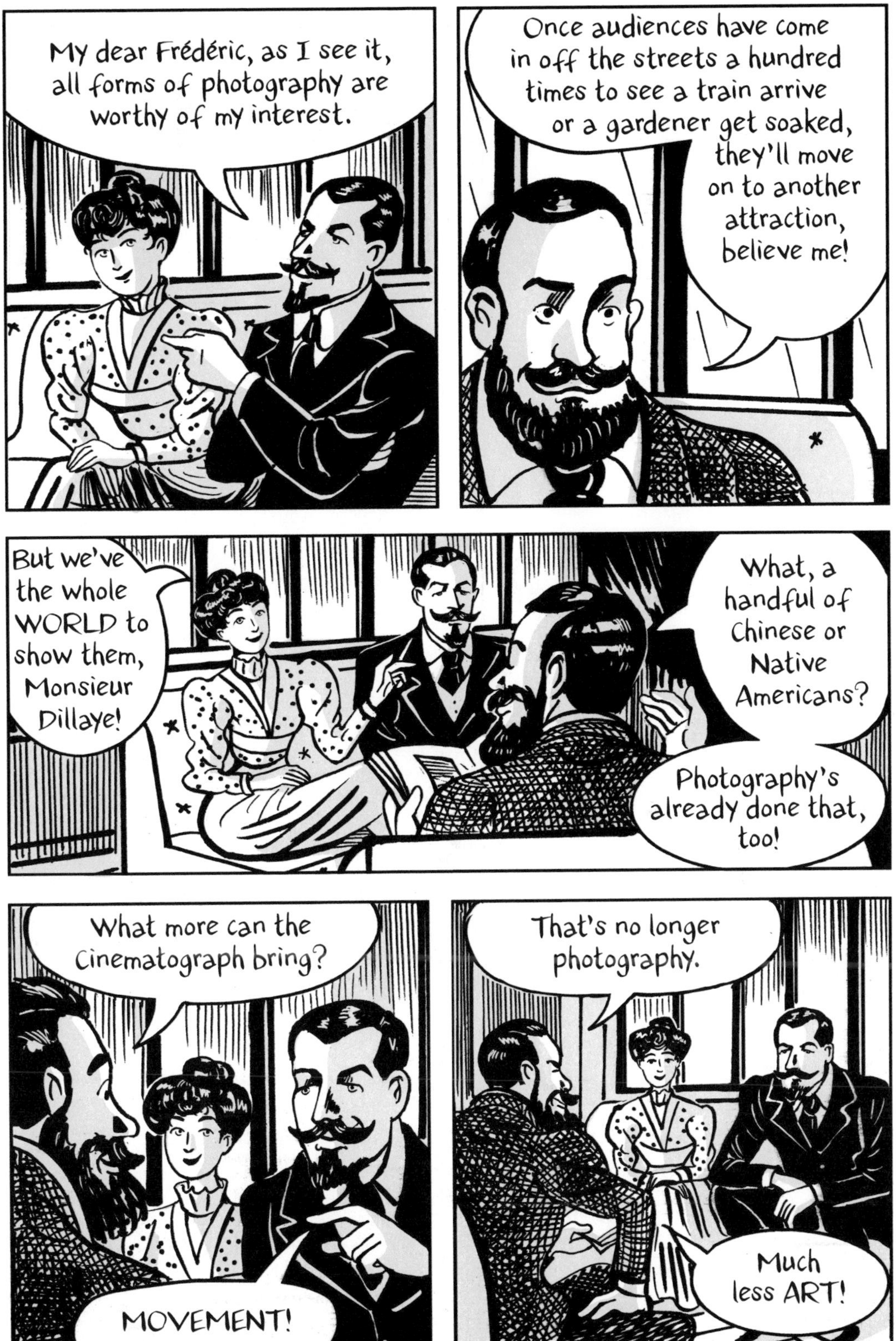
My dear Frédéric, as I see it, all forms of photography are worthy of my interest.
Once audiences have come in off the streets a hundred times to see a train arrive or a gardener get soaked, they'll move on to another attraction, believe me!
But we've the whole WORLD to show them, Monsieur Dillaye!
What, a handful of Chinese or Native Americans?
Photography's already done that, too!
What more can the Cinematograph bring?
MOVEMENT!
That's no longer photography.
Much less ART!

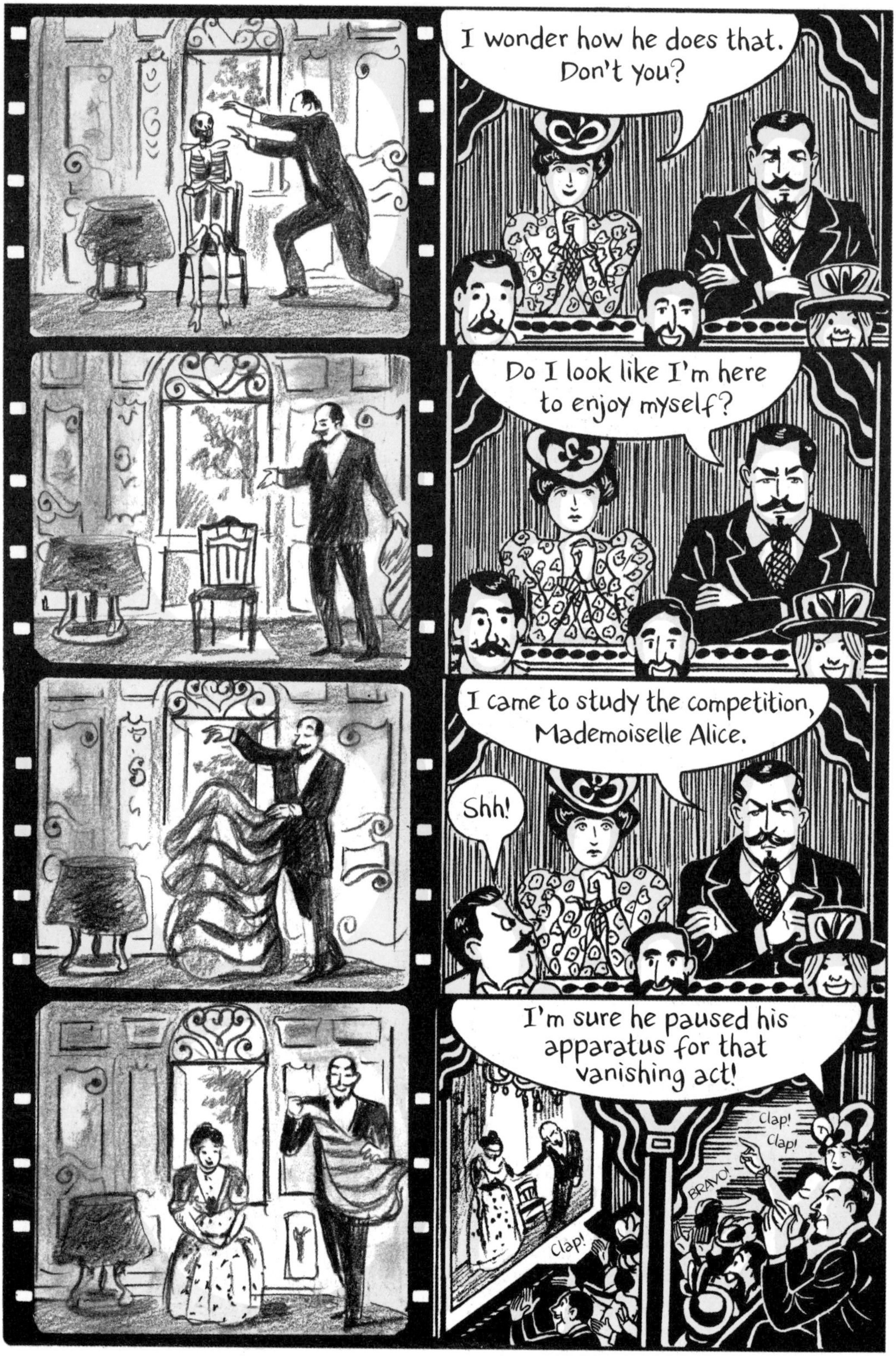

I wonder how he does that. Don't you?
Do I look like I'm here to enjoy myself?
I came to study the competition, Mademoiselle Alice.
Shh!
I'm sure he paused his apparatus for that vanishing act!
Clap!
Clap!
BRAVO!
Clap!

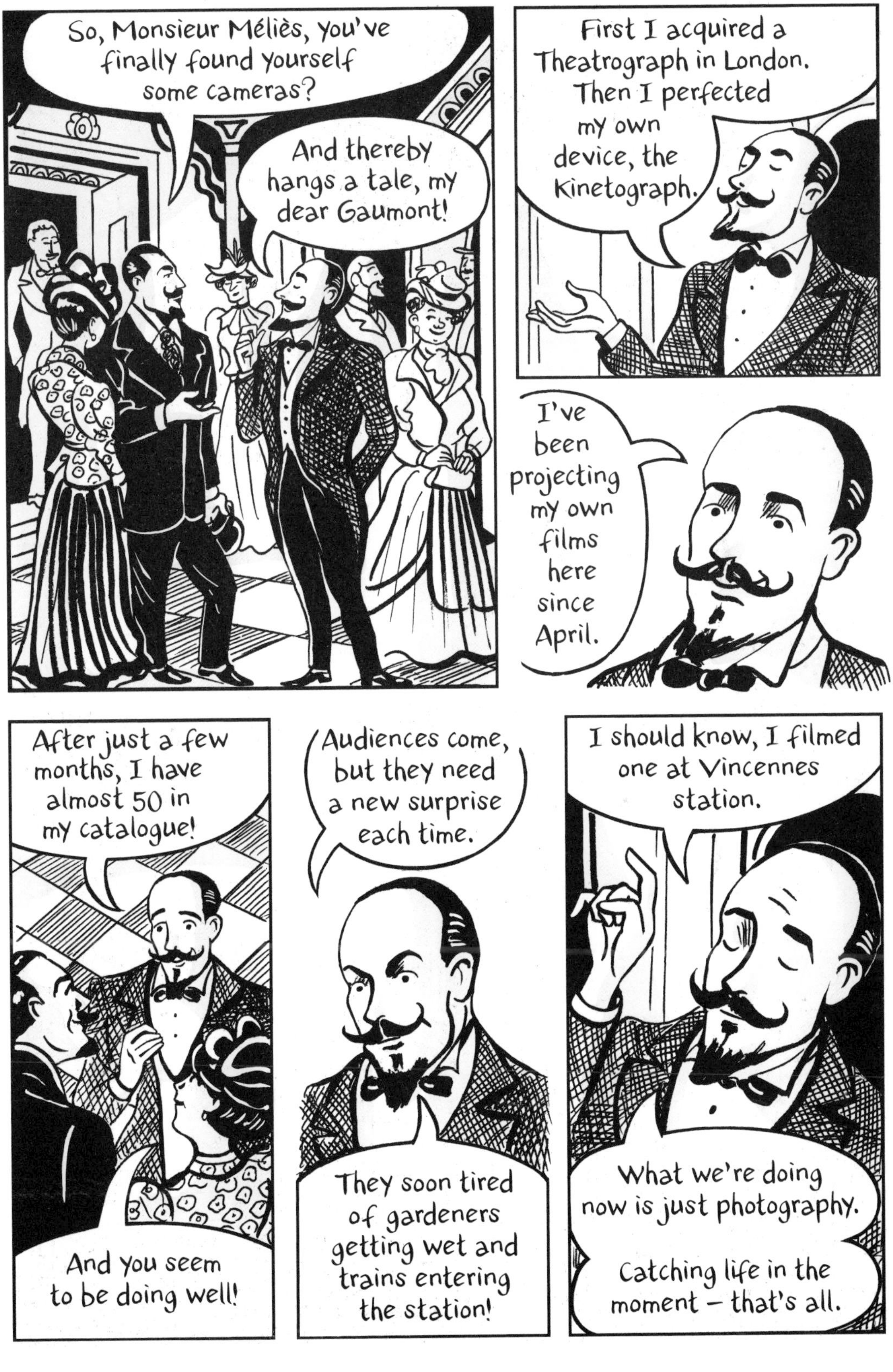

So, Monsieur Méliès, you've finally found yourself some cameras?
And thereby hangs a tale, my dear Gaumont!
First I acquired a Theatrograph in London. Then I perfected my own device, the Kinetograph.
I've been projecting my own films here since April.
After just a few months, I have almost 50 in my catalogue!
And you seem to be doing well!
Audiences come, but they need a new surprise each time.
They soon tired of gardeners getting wet and trains entering the station!
I should know, I filmed one at Vincennes station.
What we're doing now is just photography.
Catching life in the moment – that's all.

That's already extraordinary, isn't it?

Exactly the opposite. ORDINARY, not EXTRAORDINARY!

It's not enough to SHOW people things. We must make them DREAM, Mademoiselle!

You've just seen "The Vanishing Lady". MY first such attempt.

But then, first and foremost, I'm a magician.

And the camera is your new magic wand!

Méliès is an amateur — some sort of artiste! His father made a fortune in shoes, so the son can indulge his hobbies... He isn't accountable to anyone. But I am, Mademoiselle Alice...

Of course, Monsieur Gaumont. Still, his vanishing tricks are quite fun!

GEORGES MÉLIÈS

ROBERT HOUDIN

ROBERT HOUDIN THÉATRE

MAGIE

FILM ESCAMOTAGE

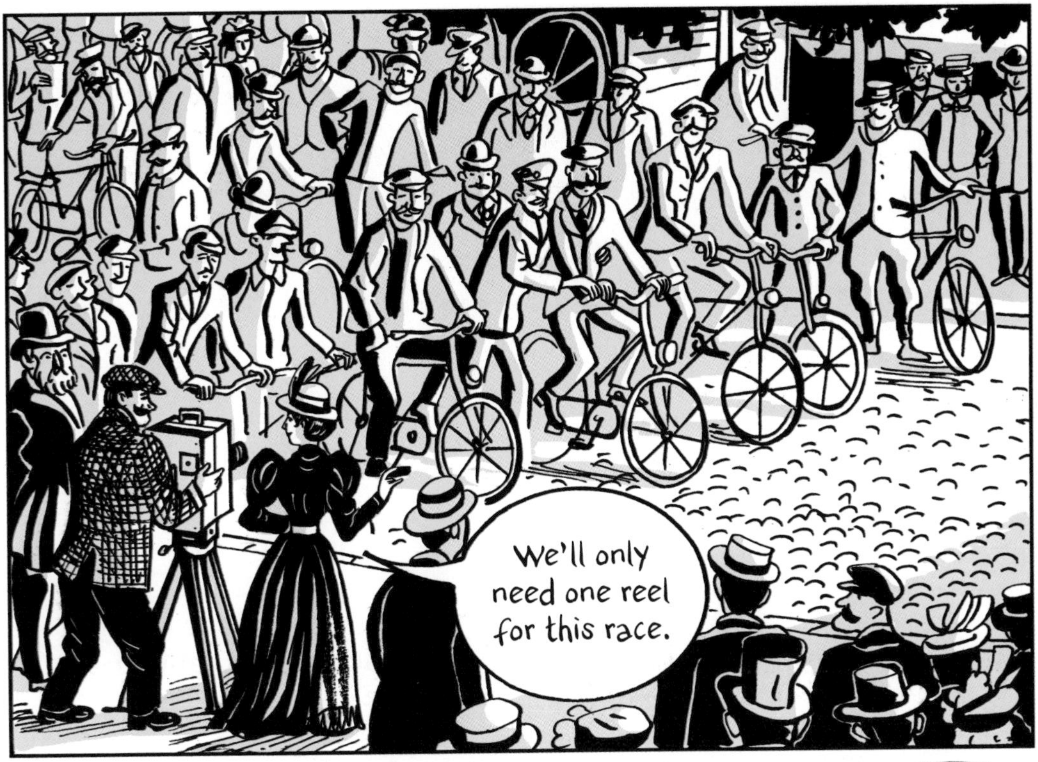
We'll only need one reel for this race.

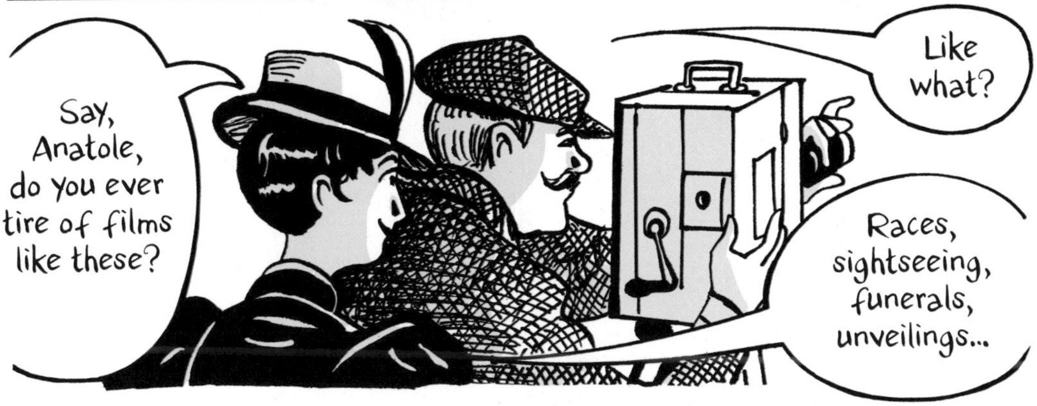
Say, Anatole, do you ever tire of films like these?
Like what?
Races, sightseeing, funerals, unveilings...

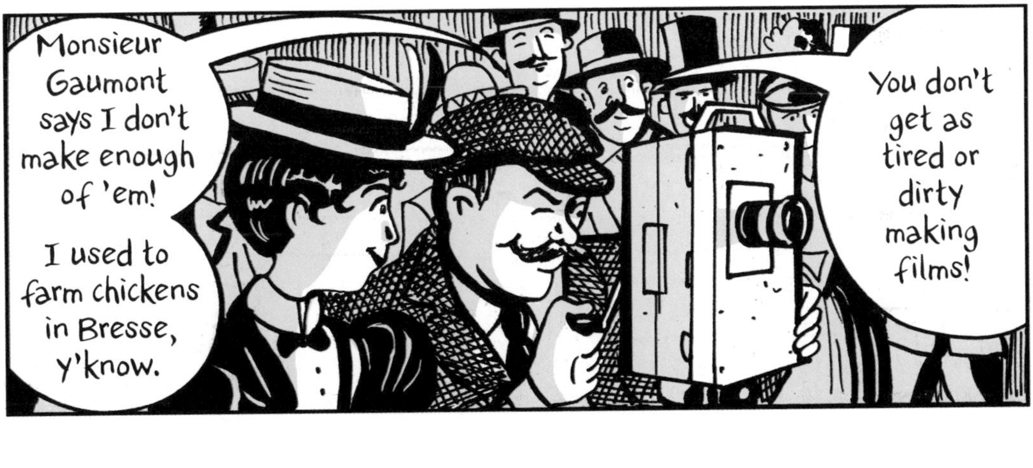
Monsieur Gaumont says I don't make enough of 'em!
I used to farm chickens in Bresse, y'know.
You don't get as tired or dirty making films!

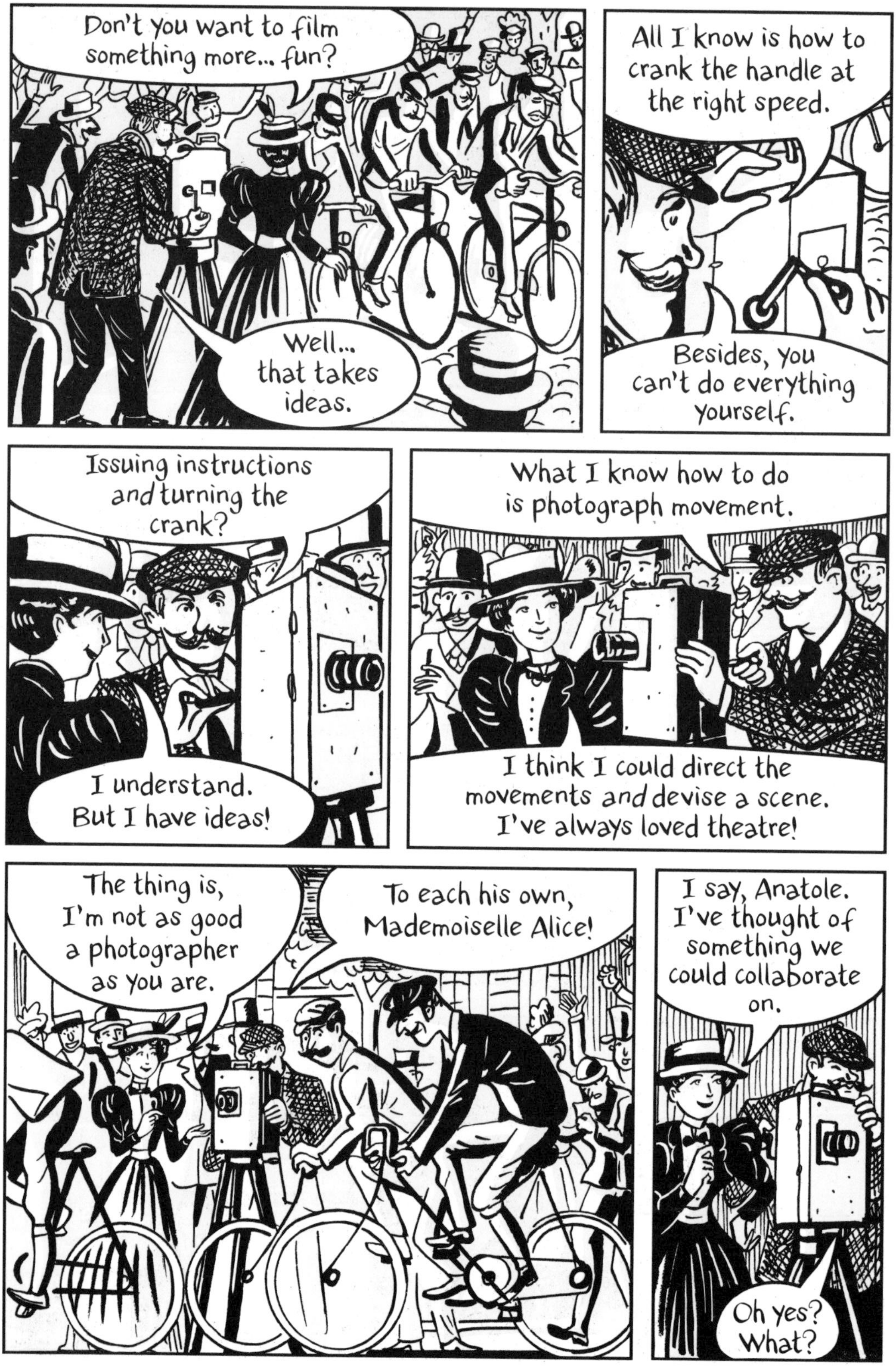
Don't you want to film something more... fun?
Well... that takes ideas.
All I know is how to crank the handle at the right speed.
Besides, you can't do everything yourself.
Issuing instructions *and* turning the crank?
I understand. But I have ideas!
What I know how to do is photograph movement.
I think I could direct the movements *and* devise a scene. I've always loved theatre!
The thing is, I'm not as good a photographer as you are.
To each his own, Mademoiselle Alice!
I say, Anatole. I've thought of something we could collaborate on.
Oh yes? What?

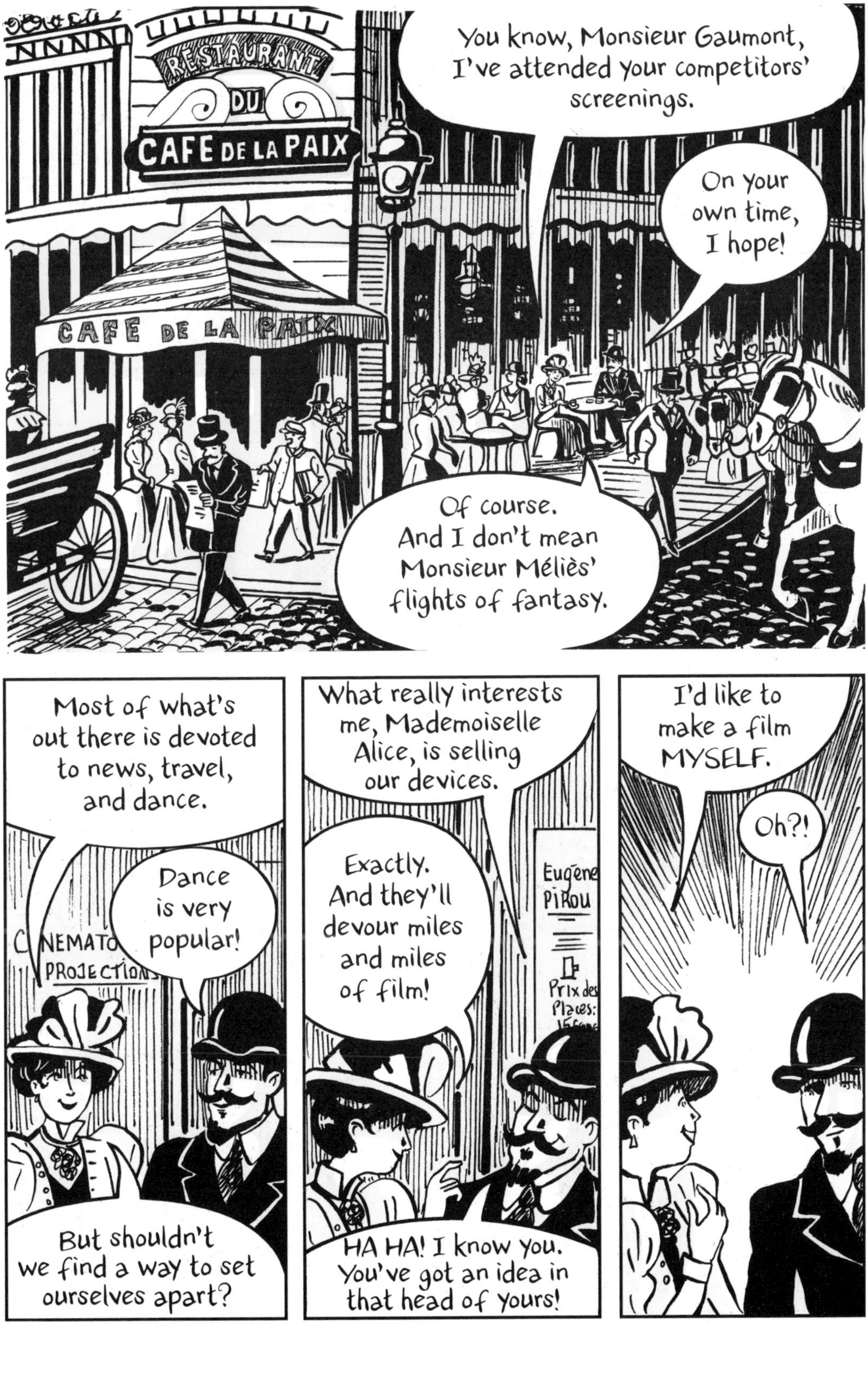
RESTAURANT DU
CAFE DE LA PAIX
You know, Monsieur Gaumont, I've attended your competitors' screenings.
On your own time, I hope!
CAFE DE LA PAIX
Of course. And I don't mean Monsieur Méliès' flights of fantasy.
Most of what's out there is devoted to news, travel, and dance.
Dance is very popular!
NEMATO
PROJECTIONS
But shouldn't we find a way to set ourselves apart?
What really interests me, Mademoiselle Alice, is selling our devices.
Exactly. And they'll devour miles and miles of film!
Eugène PIROU
Prix des Places:
HA HA! I know you. You've got an idea in that head of yours!
I'd like to make a film MYSELF.
Oh?!

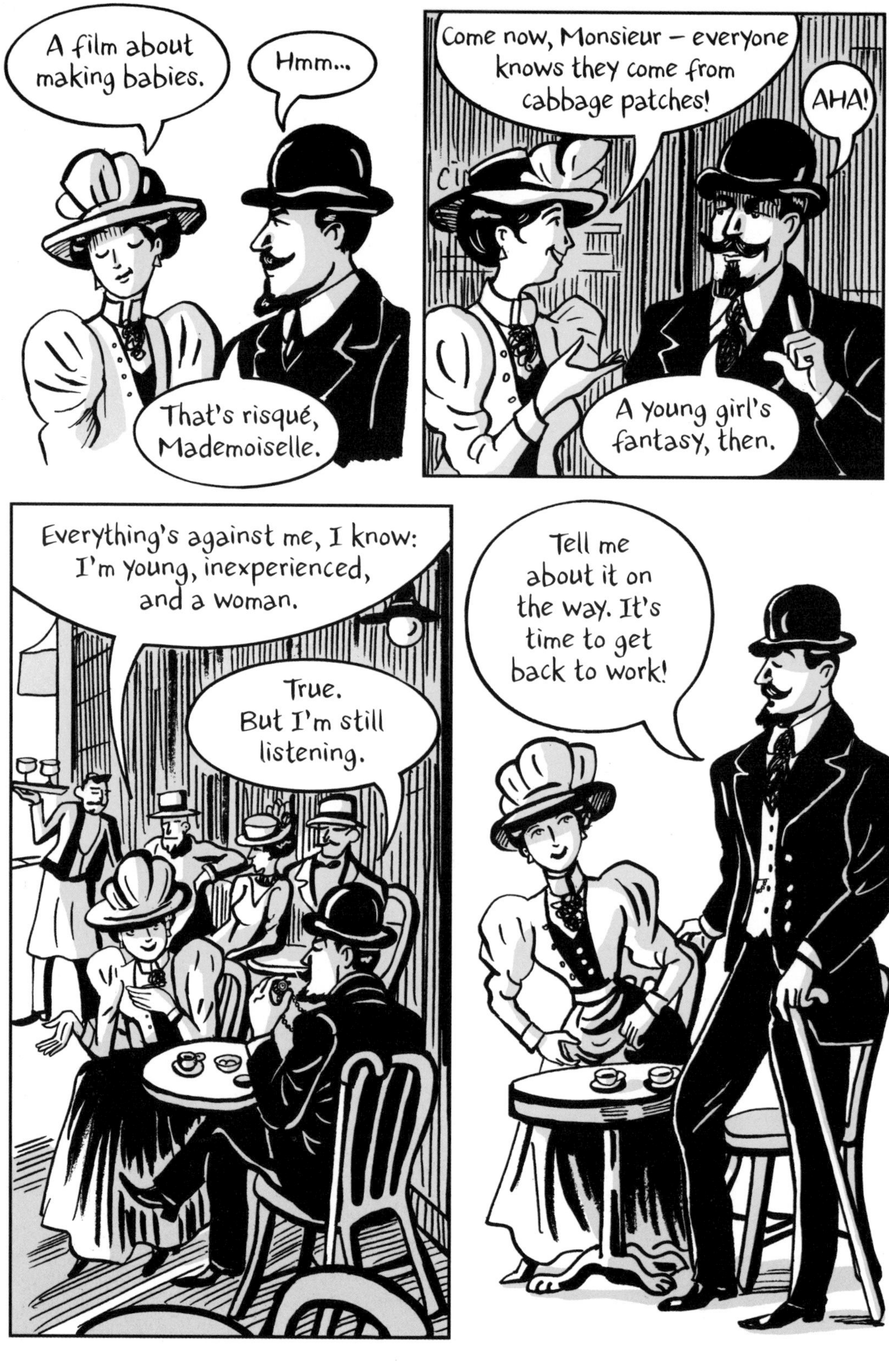
A film about making babies.
Hmm...
That's risqué, Mademoiselle.
Come now, Monsieur – everyone knows they come from cabbage patches!
AHA!
A young girl's fantasy, then.
Everything's against me, I know: I'm young, inexperienced, and a woman.
True. But I'm still listening.
Tell me about it on the way. It's time to get back to work!

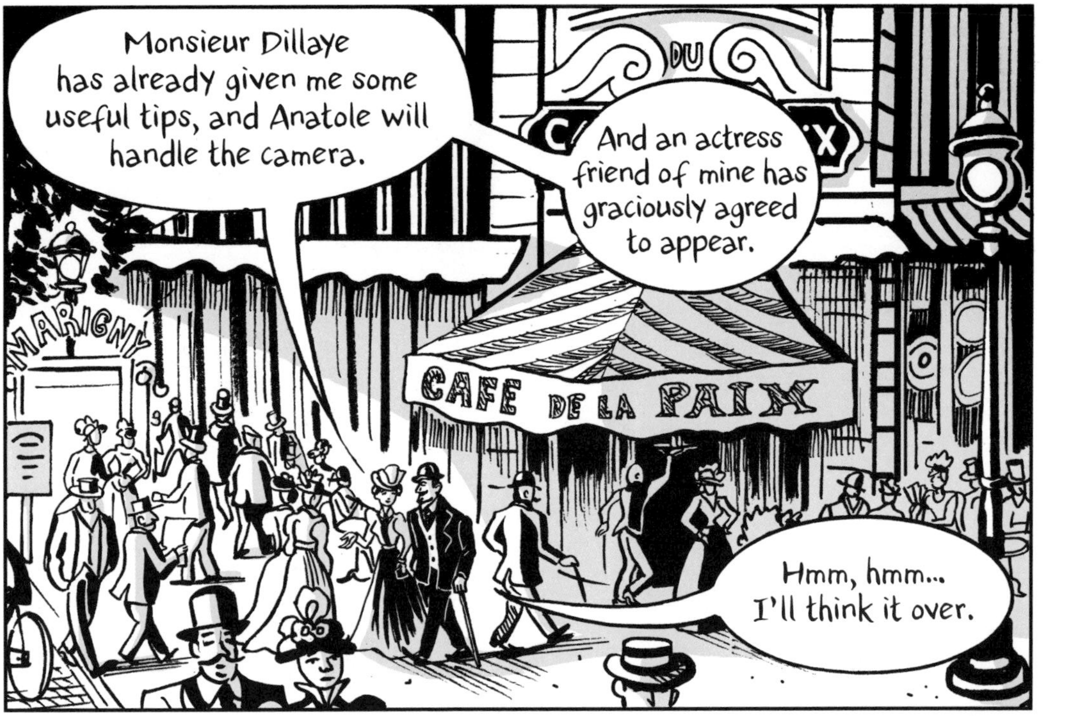
DU
CAFE DE LA PAIX
MARIGNY
Monsieur Dillaye has already given me some useful tips, and Anatole will handle the camera.
And an actress friend of mine has graciously agreed to appear.
Hmm, hmm... I'll think it over.

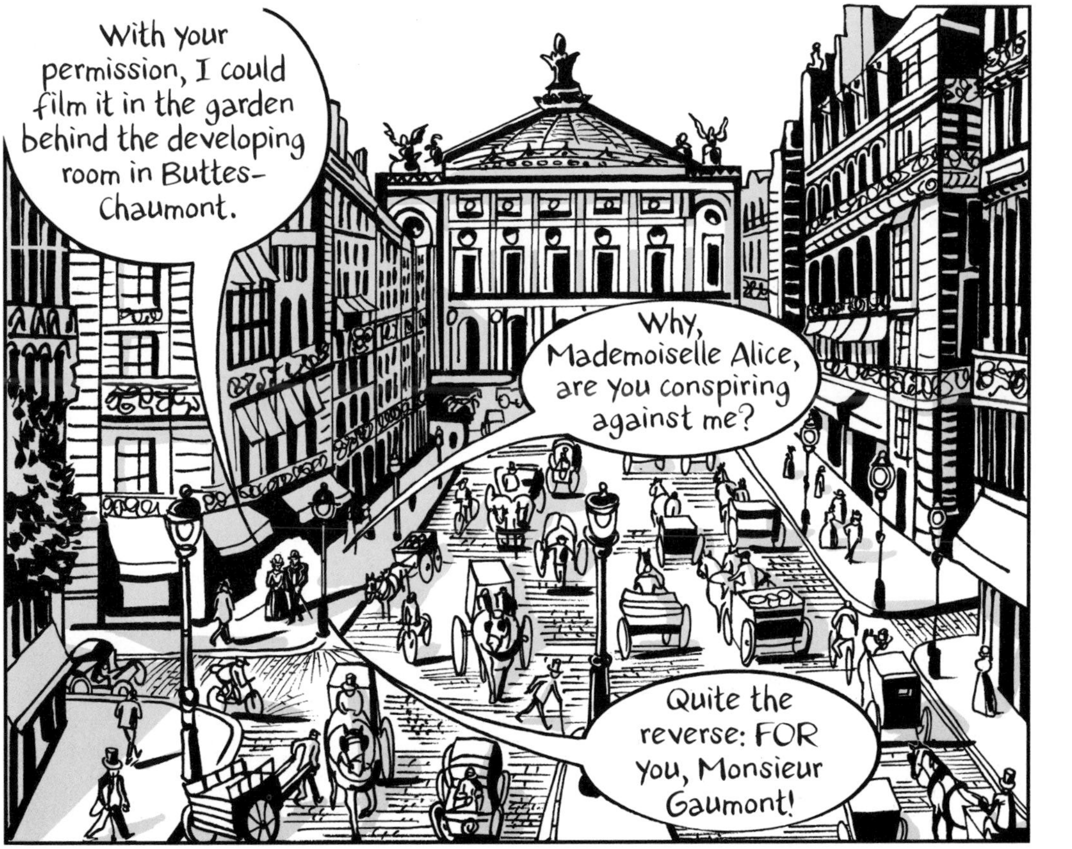
With your permission, I could film it in the garden behind the developing room in Buttes-Chaumont.
Why, Mademoiselle Alice, are you conspiring against me?
Quite the reverse: FOR you, Monsieur Gaumont!

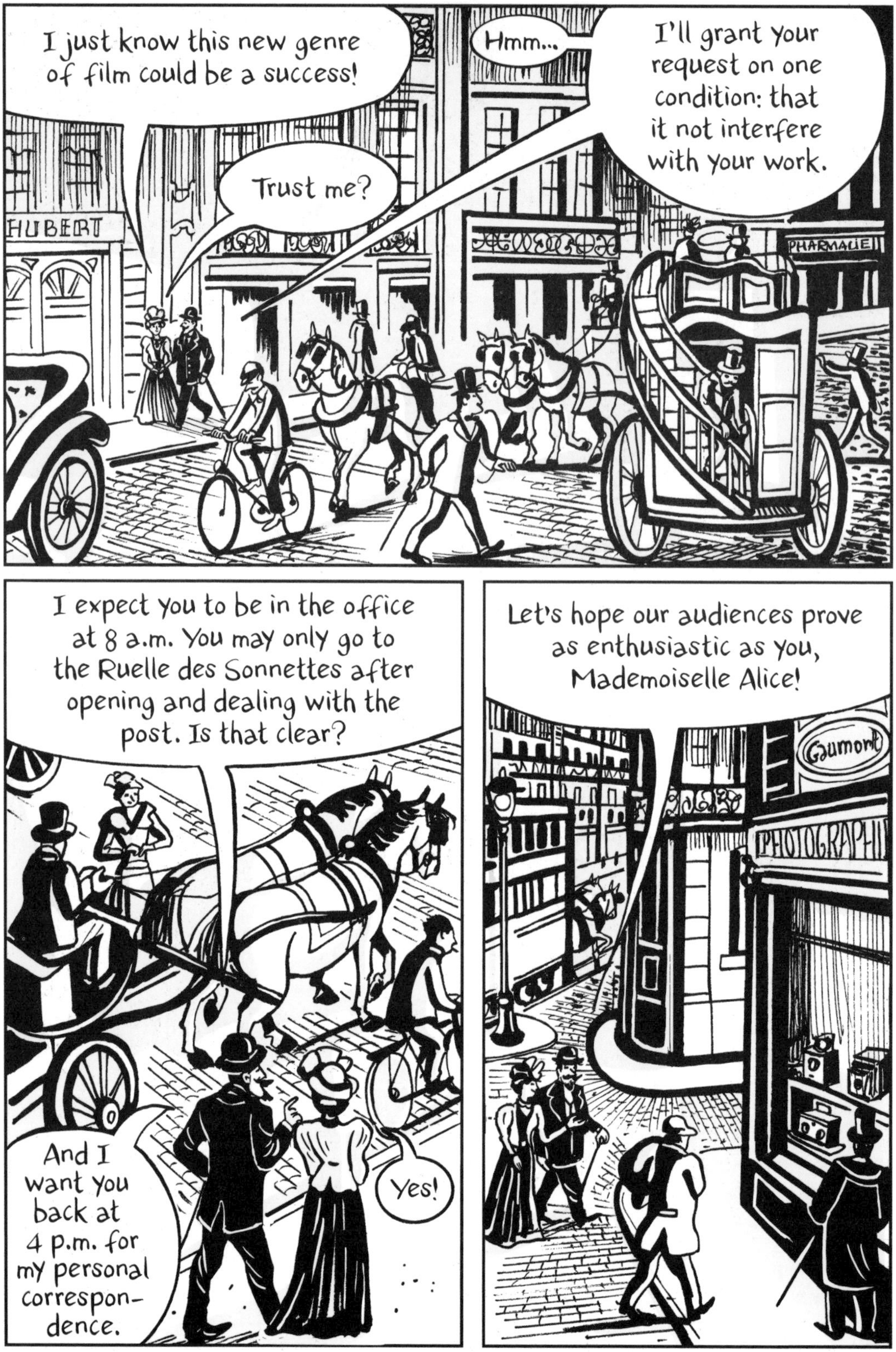
I just know this new genre of film could be a success!
Trust me?
Hmm...
I'll grant your request on one condition: that it not interfere with your work.
HUBERT
PHARMACIE
I expect you to be in the office at 8 a.m. You may only go to the Ruelle des Sonnettes after opening and dealing with the post. Is that clear?
Yes!
And I want you back at 4 p.m. for my personal correspondence.
Let's hope our audiences prove as enthusiastic as you, Mademoiselle Alice!
Gaumont
PHOTOGRAPHI

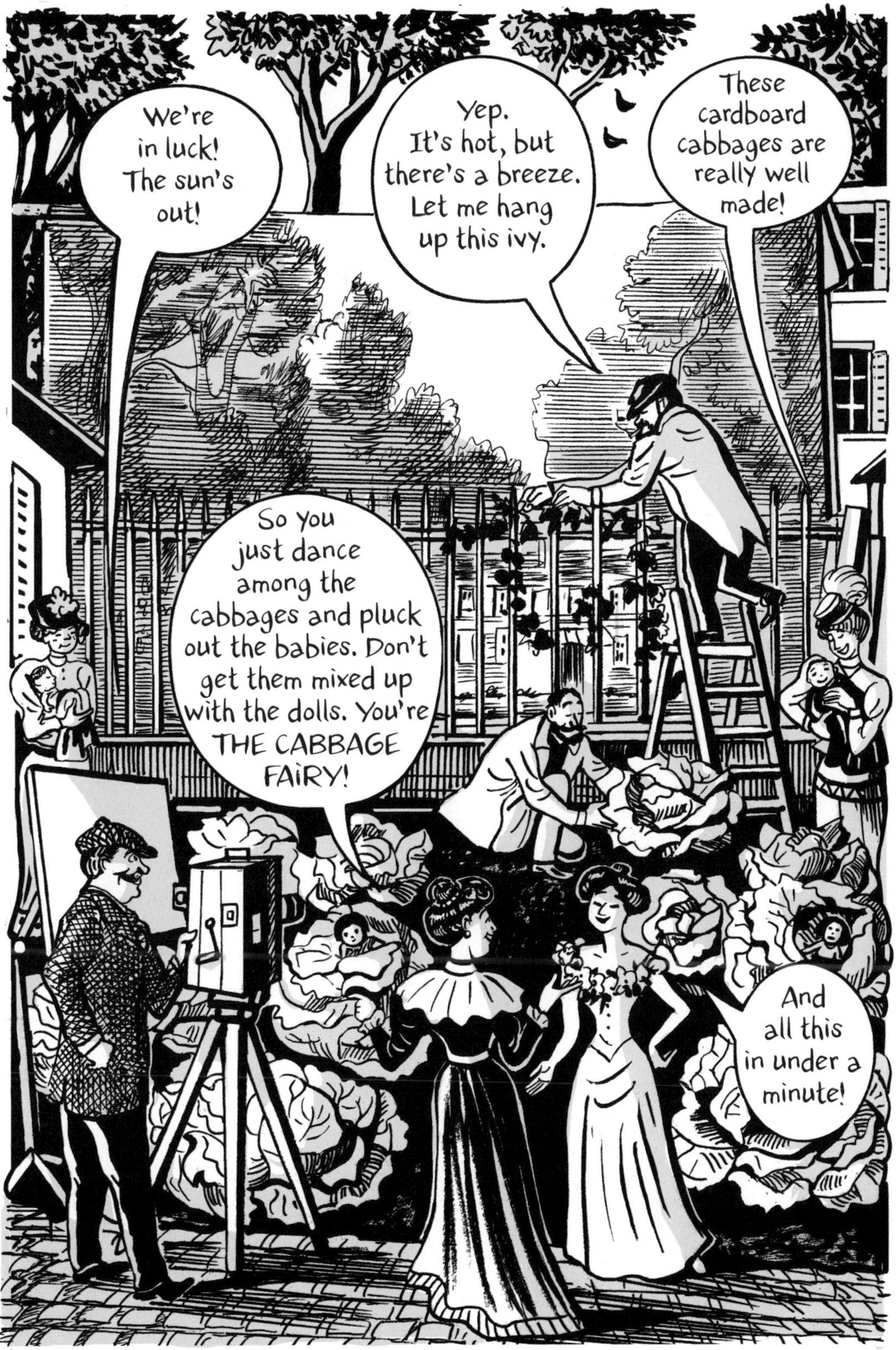
We're in luck! The sun's out!
Yep. It's hot, but there's a breeze. Let me hang up this ivy.
These cardboard cabbages are really well made!
So you just dance among the cabbages and pluck out the babies. Don't get them mixed up with the dolls. You're THE CABBAGE FAIRY!
And all this in under a minute!

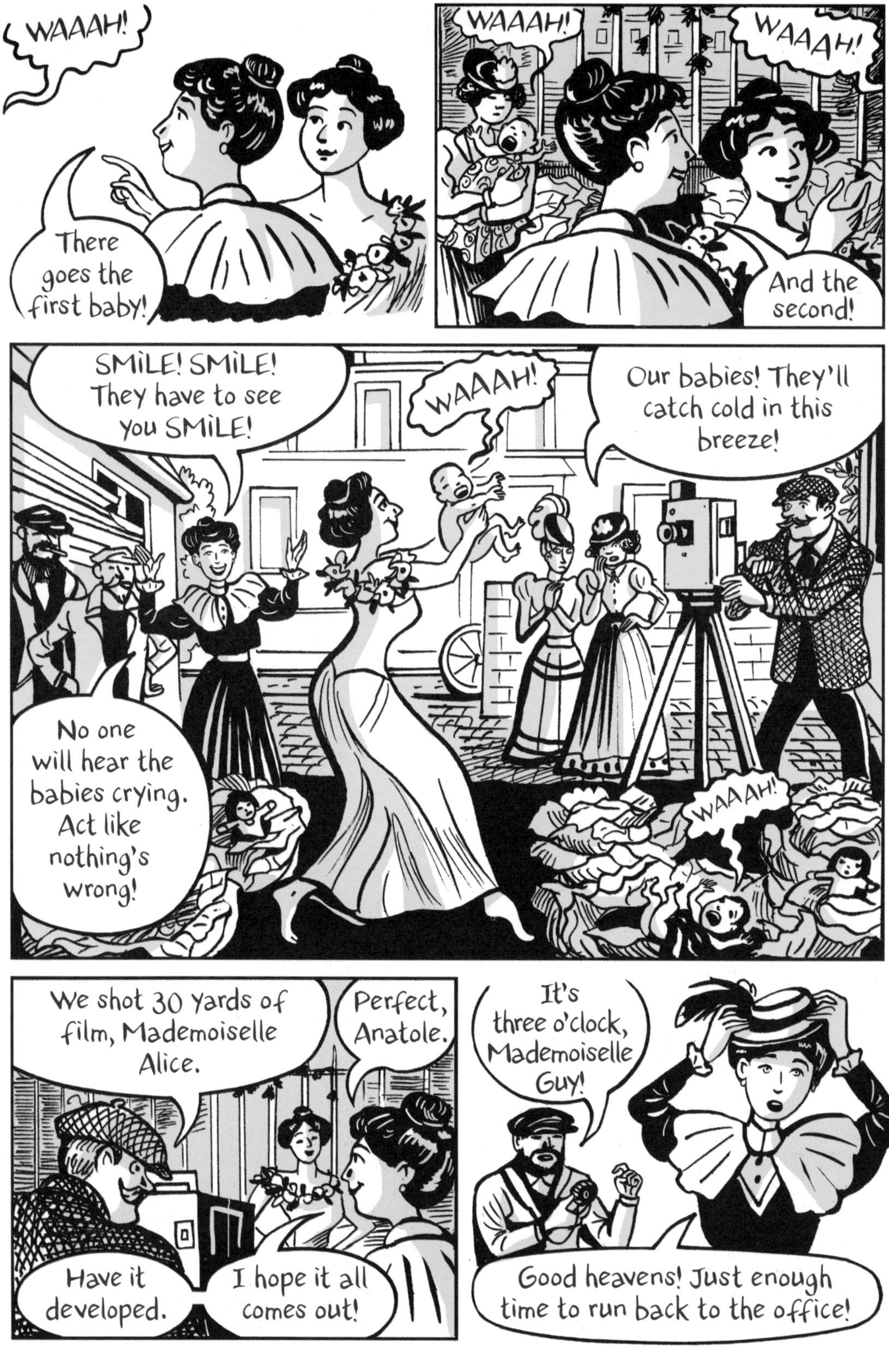

WAAAH!
There goes the first baby!
WAAAH!
WAAAH!
And the second!
SMILE! SMILE! They have to see you SMILE!
WAAAH!
Our babies! They'll catch cold in this breeze!
No one will hear the babies crying. Act like nothing's wrong!
WAAAH!
We shot 30 yards of film, Mademoiselle Alice.
Perfect, Anatole.
Have it developed.
I hope it all comes out!
It's three o'clock, Mademoiselle Guy!
Good heavens! Just enough time to run back to the office!

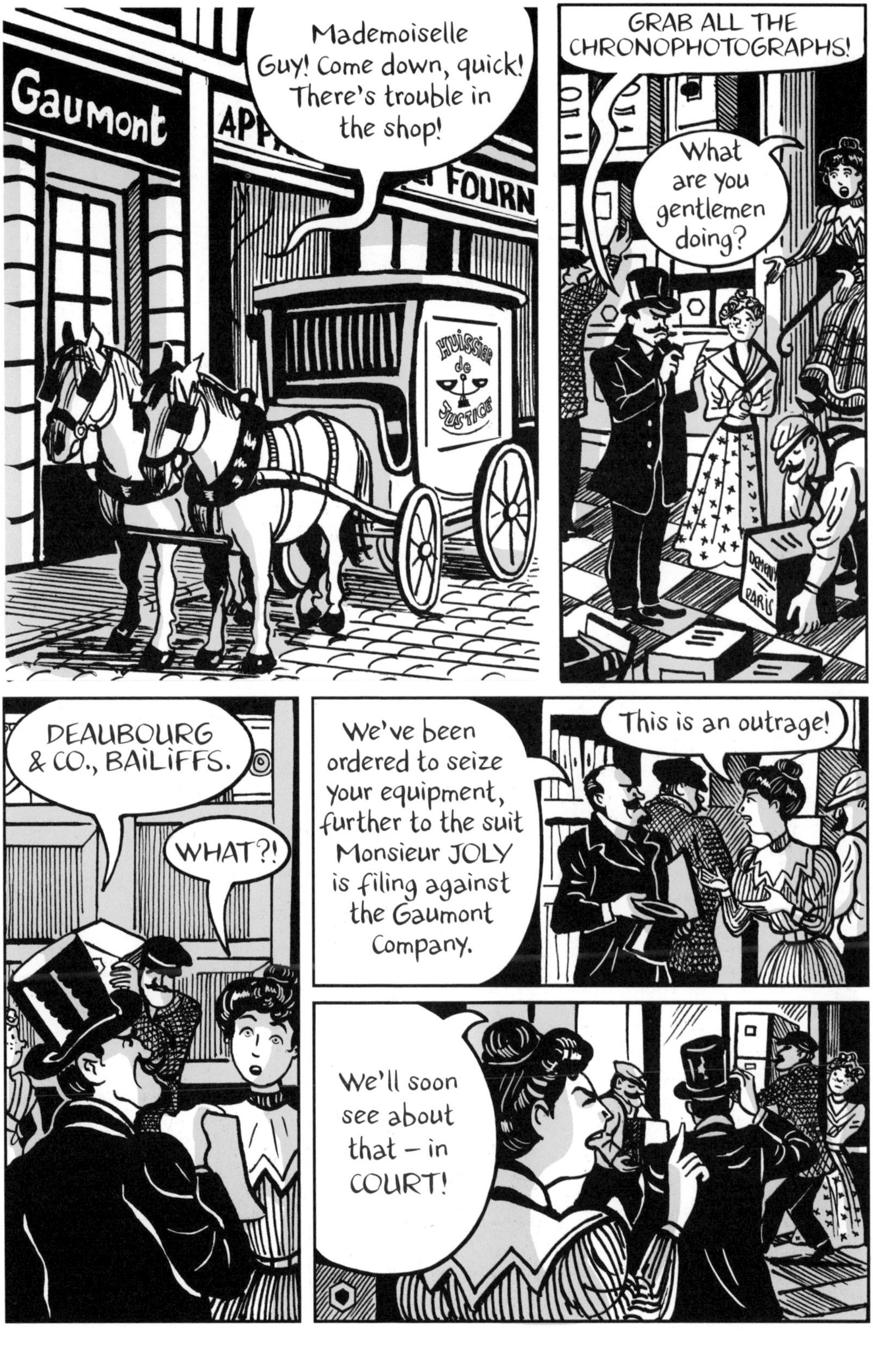
Gaumont
Mademoiselle Guy! Come down, quick! There's trouble in the shop!
Huissier de Justice
GRAB ALL THE CHRONOPHOTOGRAPHS!
What are you gentlemen doing?
DEAUBOURG & CO., BAILIFFS.
WHAT?!
We've been ordered to seize your equipment, further to the suit Monsieur JOLY is filing against the Gaumont Company.
This is an outrage!
We'll soon see about that – in COURT!

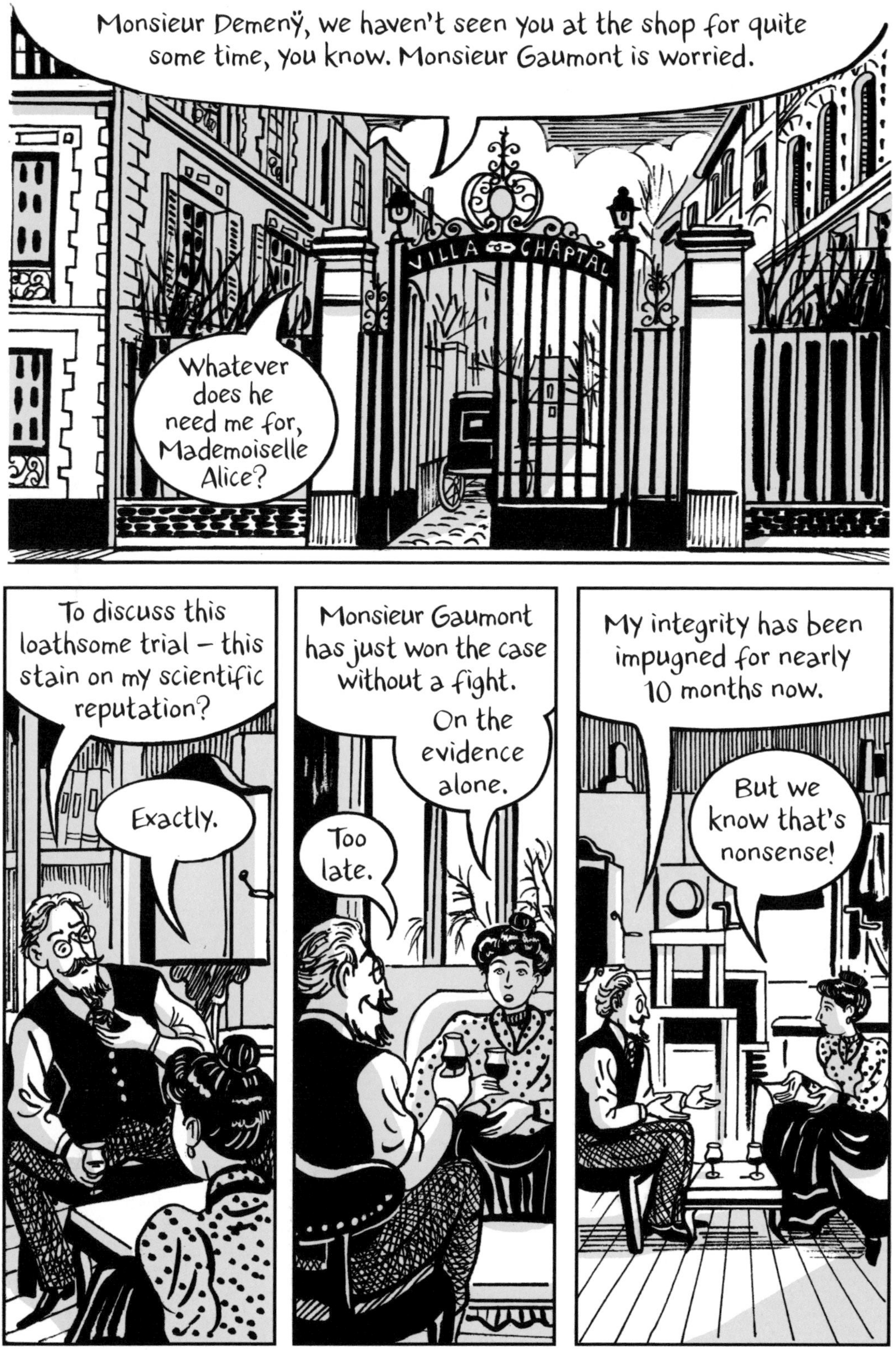

Monsieur Demenÿ, we haven't seen you at the shop for quite some time, you know. Monsieur Gaumont is worried.
VILLA CHAPTAL
Whatever does he need me for, Mademoiselle Alice?
To discuss this loathsome trial – this stain on my scientific reputation?
Exactly.
Monsieur Gaumont has just won the case without a fight.
On the evidence alone.
Too late.
My integrity has been impugned for nearly 10 months now.
But we know that's nonsense!

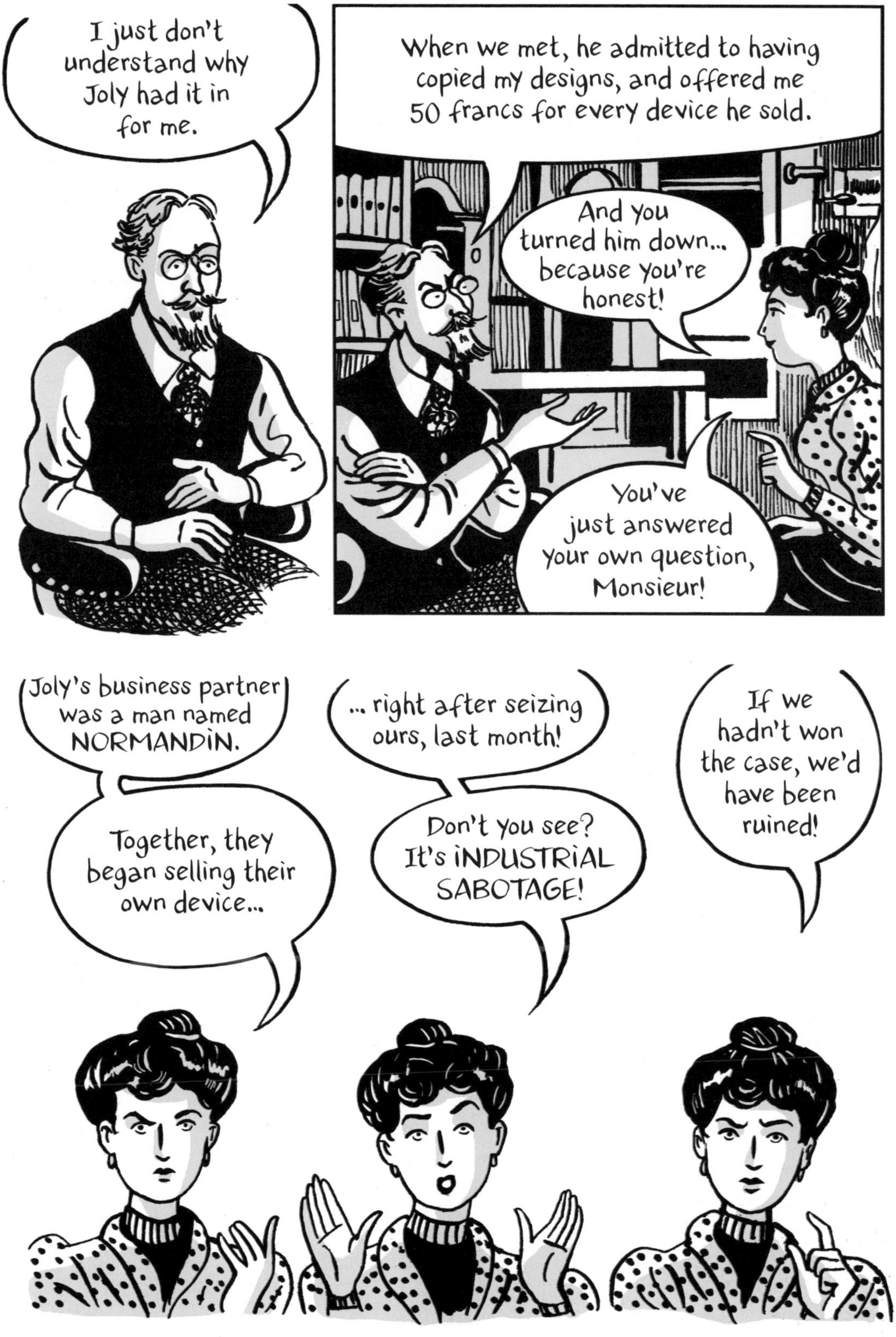
I just don't understand why Joly had it in for me.
When we met, he admitted to having copied my designs, and offered me 50 francs for every device he sold.
And you turned him down... because you're honest!
You've just answered your own question, Monsieur!
Joly's business partner was a man named NORMANDIN.
Together, they began selling their own device...
... right after seizing ours, last month!
Don't you see? It's INDUSTRIAL SABOTAGE!
If we hadn't won the case, we'd have been ruined!

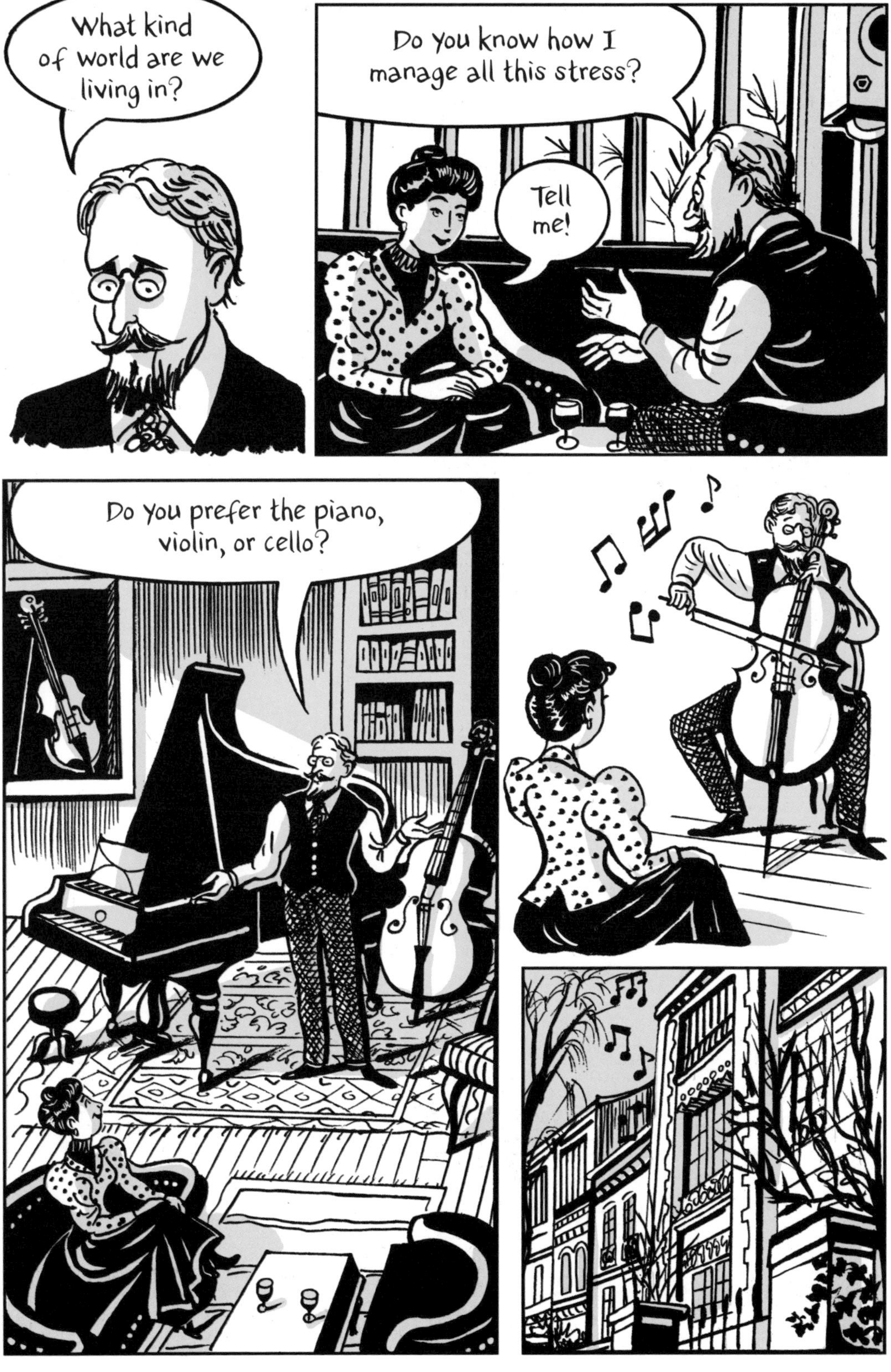
What kind of world are we living in?
Do you know how I manage all this stress?
Tell me!
Do you prefer the piano, violin, or cello?

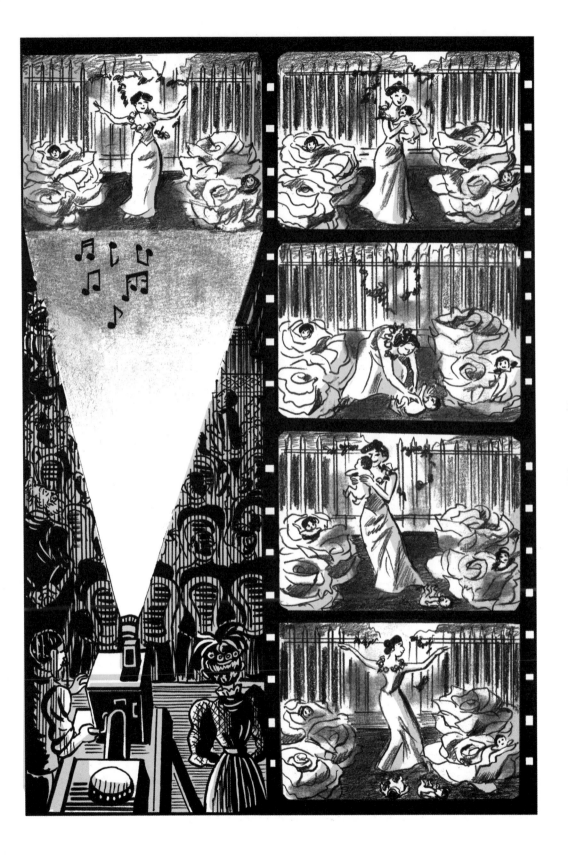

135

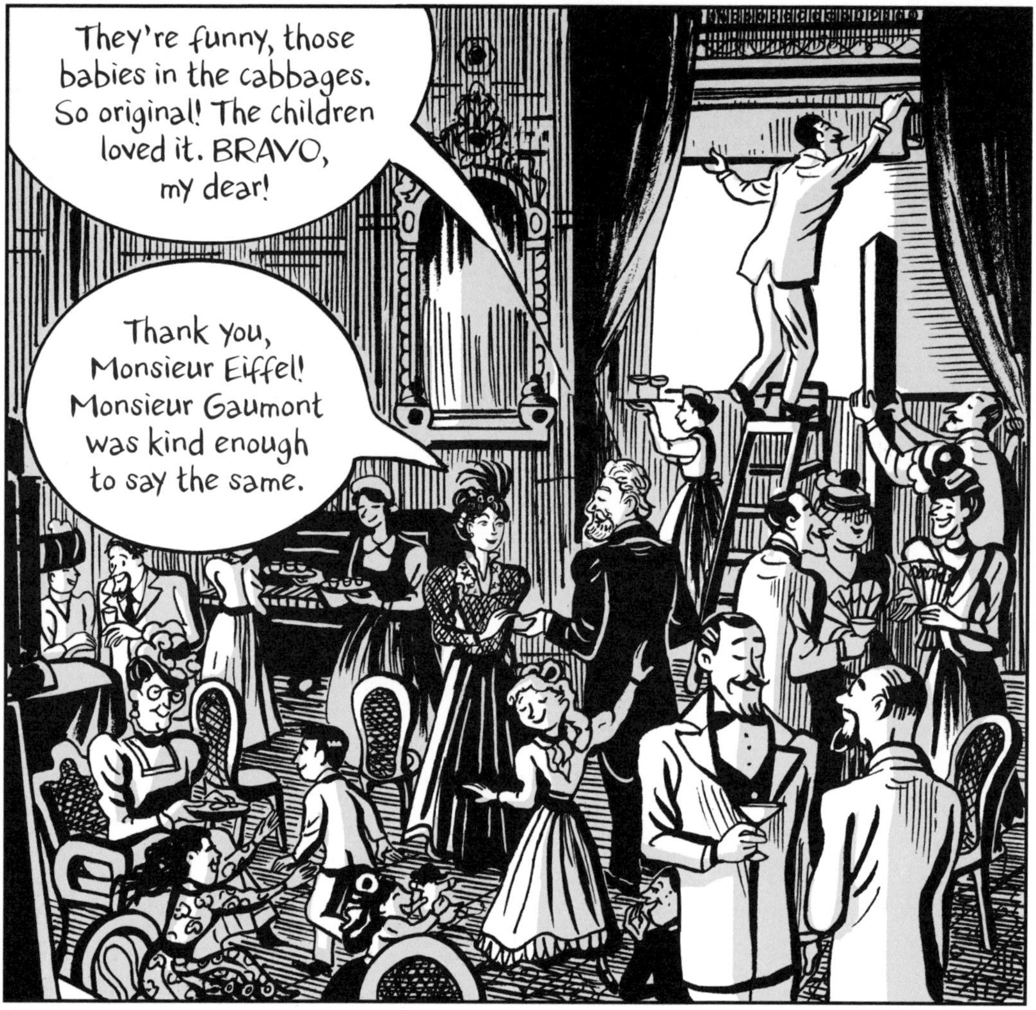
They're funny, those babies in the cabbages. So original! The children loved it. BRAVO, my dear!
Thank you, Monsieur Eiffel! Monsieur Gaumont was kind enough to say the same.

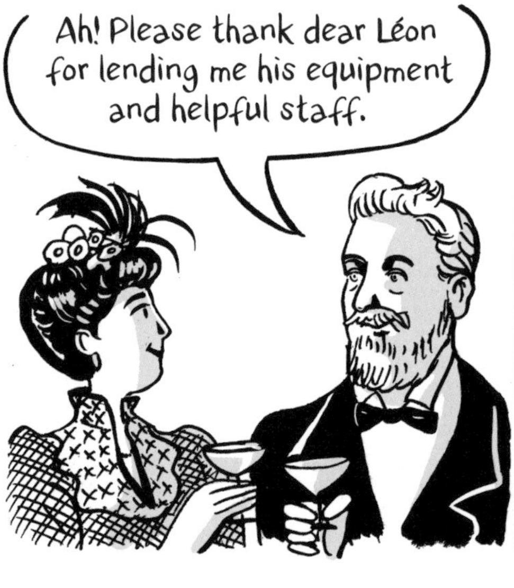
Ah! Please thank dear Léon for lending me his equipment and helpful staff.

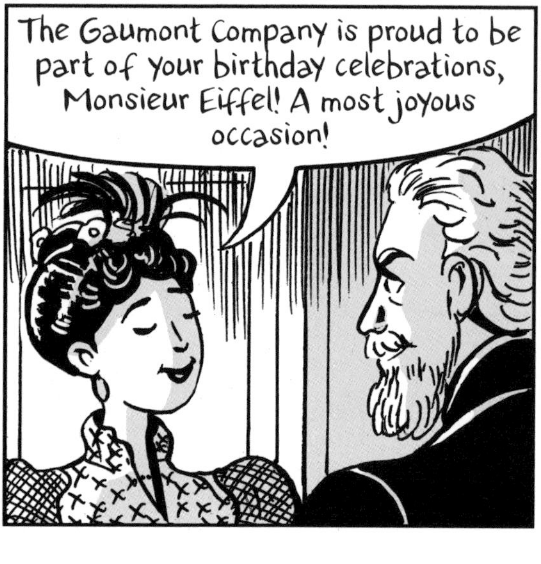
The Gaumont Company is proud to be part of your birthday celebrations, Monsieur Eiffel! A most joyous occasion!

Do forgive my boldness, but might I ask you a question? I've never dared...
Fire away!
You've probably forgotten that time I volunteered my etymology of "BIOSCOPE".
Monsieur Gaumont rebuked me, but you sprang to my defence...
When in fact you knew your Greek perfectly well!
Hmm...
Once again, you are right.
What a fool I was!
A woman giving lessons in ancient Greek in the boardroom is a rare sight!
You deserved encourage-ment.
Besides, I've always encouraged you, have I not?
Truly, Monsieur!

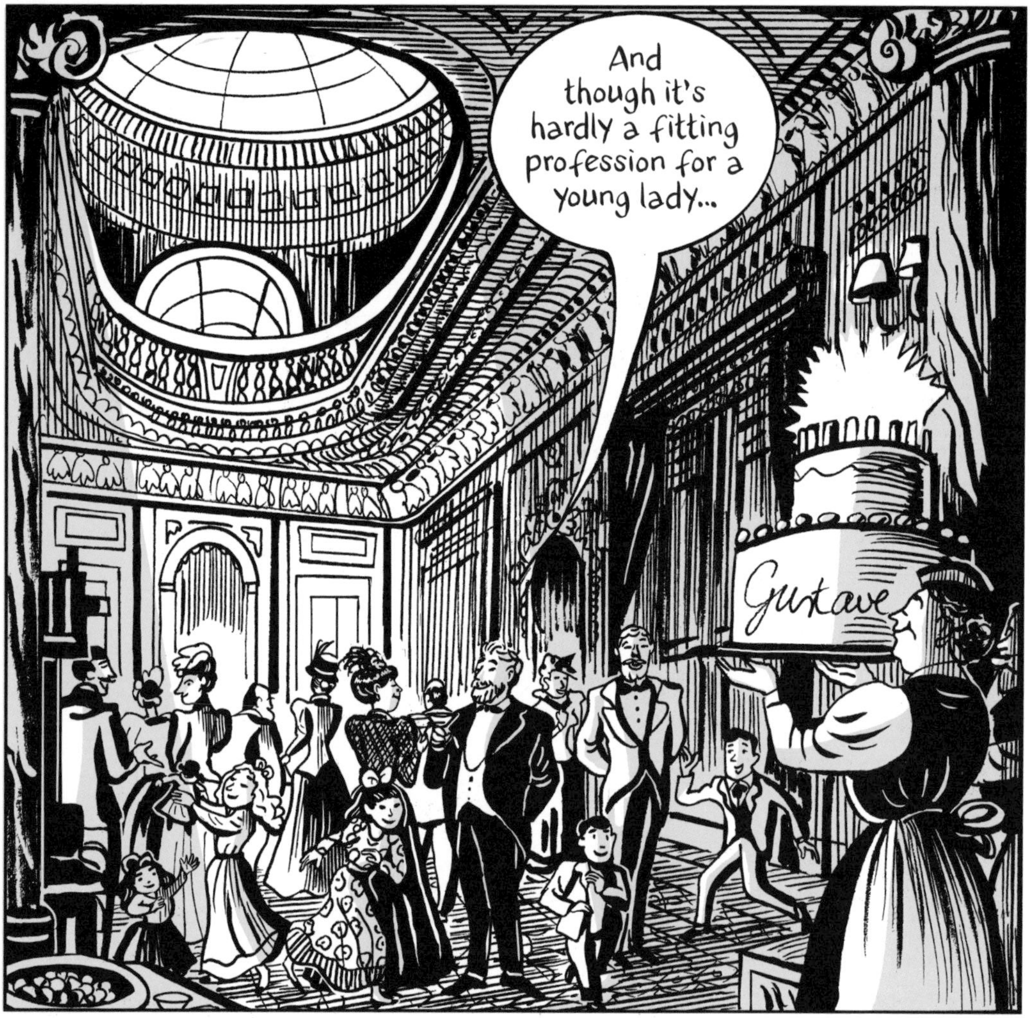
And though it's hardly a fitting profession for a young lady...
Gustave

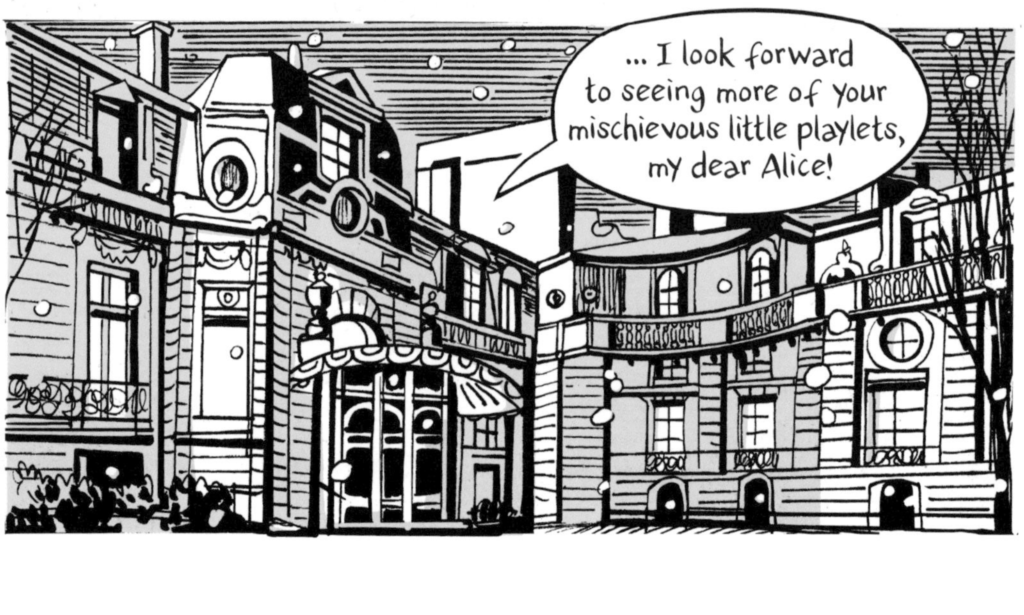
... I look forward to seeing more of your mischievous little playlets, my dear Alice!

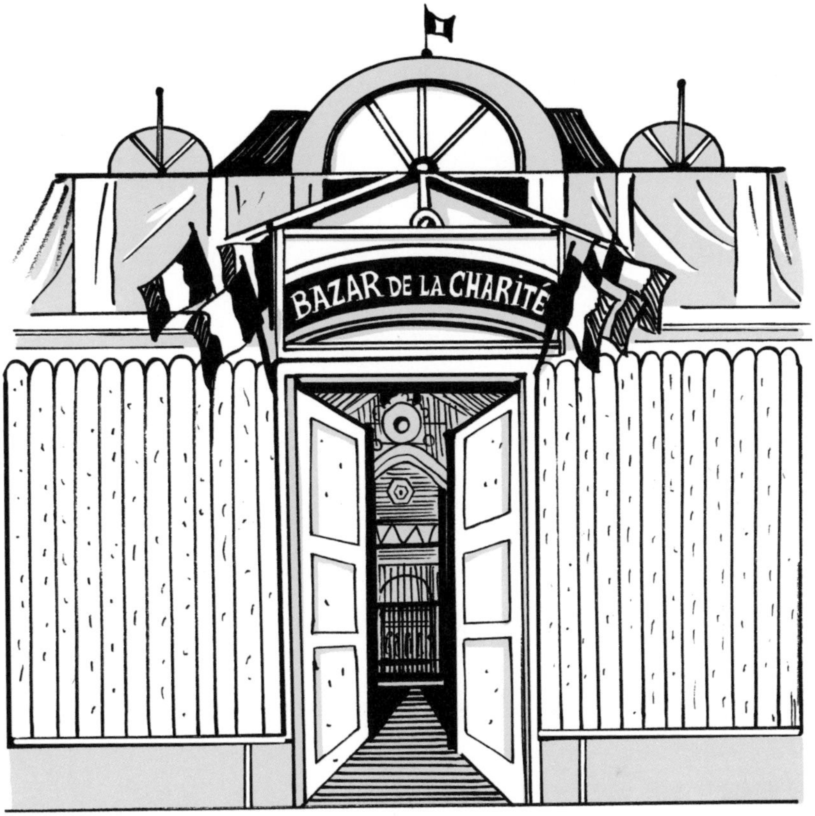
BAZAR DE LA CHARITÉ

4 May 1897 – Bazar de la Charité –
17, Rue Jean Goujon – Paris – France

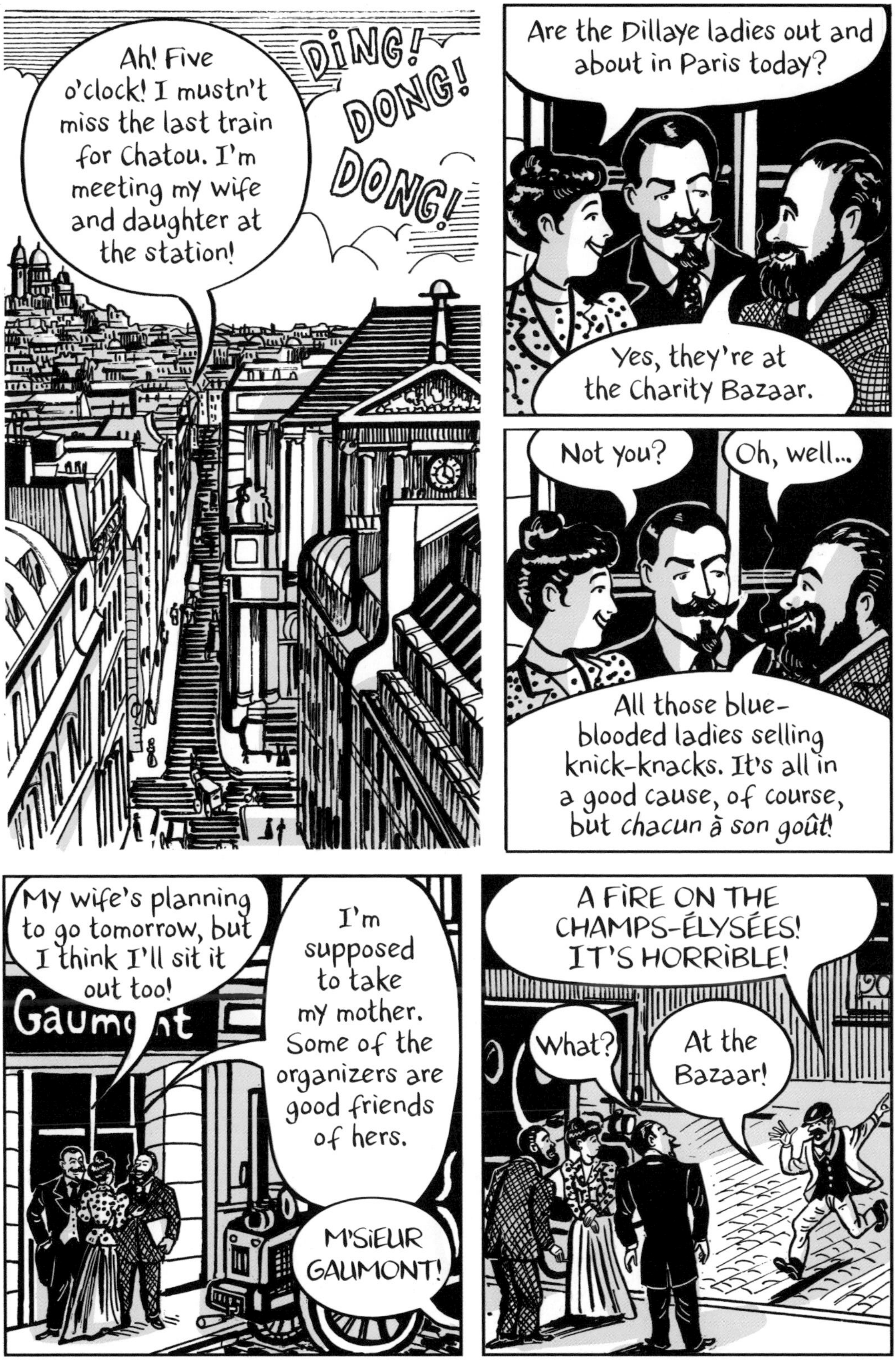
Ah! Five o'clock! I mustn't miss the last train for Chatou. I'm meeting my wife and daughter at the station!
DiNG! DONG! DONG!
Are the Dillaye ladies out and about in Paris today?
Yes, they're at the Charity Bazaar.
Not you?
Oh, well...
All those blue-blooded ladies selling knick-knacks. It's all in a good cause, of course, but *chacun à son goût!*
My wife's planning to go tomorrow, but I think I'll sit it out too!
Gaum nt
I'm supposed to take my mother. Some of the organizers are good friends of hers.
M'SIEUR GAUMONT!
A FIRE ON THE CHAMPS-ÉLYSÉES! IT'S HORRIBLE!
What?
At the Bazaar!

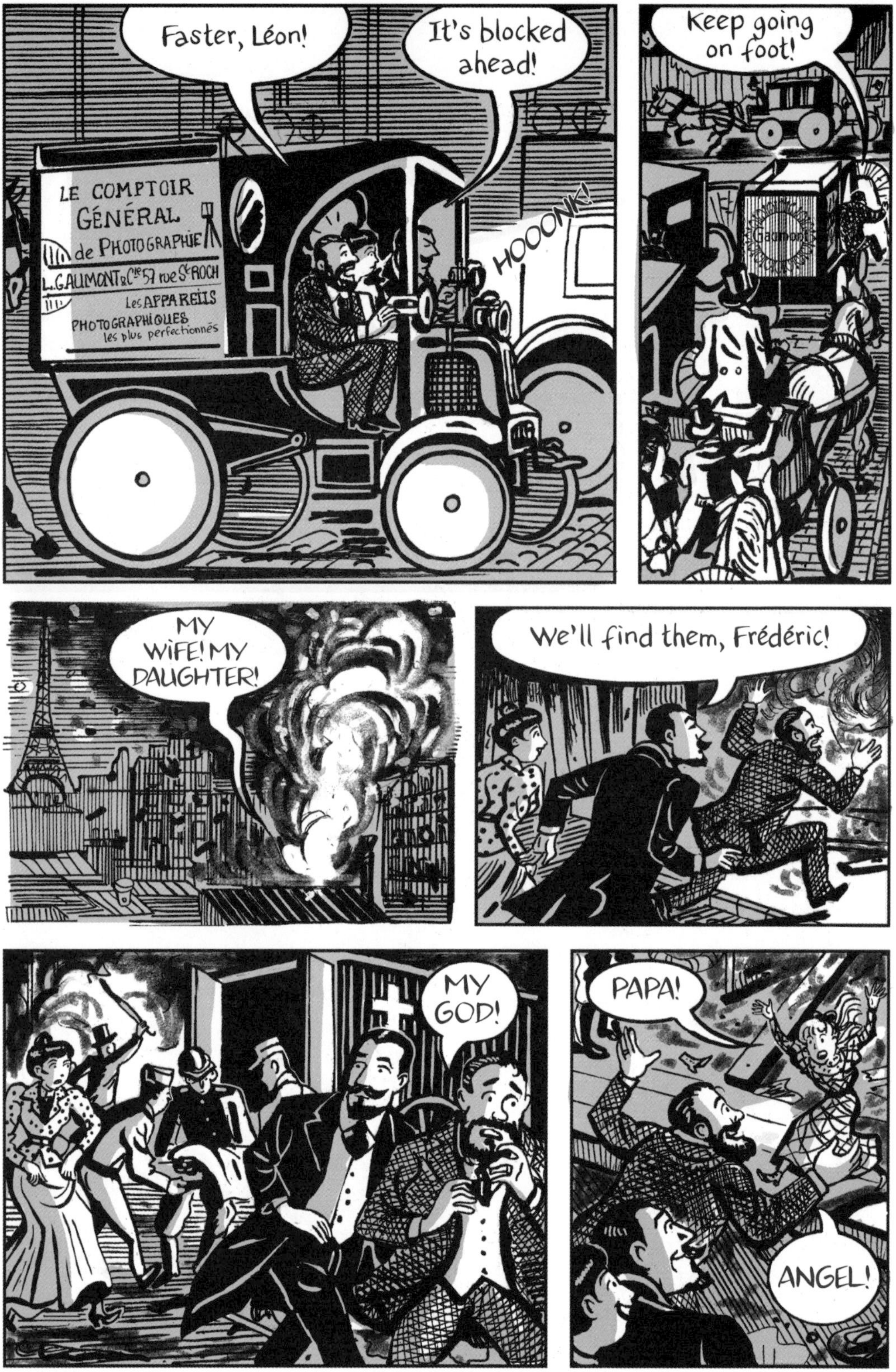
Faster, Léon!
It's blocked ahead!
LE COMPTOIR GÉNÉRAL de PHOTOGRAPHIE L. GAUMONT & Cie 57 rue St ROCH Les APPAREILS PHOTOGRAPHIQUES les plus perfectionnés
HOOONK!
Keep going on foot!
MY WIFE! MY DAUGHTER!
We'll find them, Frédéric!
MY GOD!
PAPA!
ANGEL!

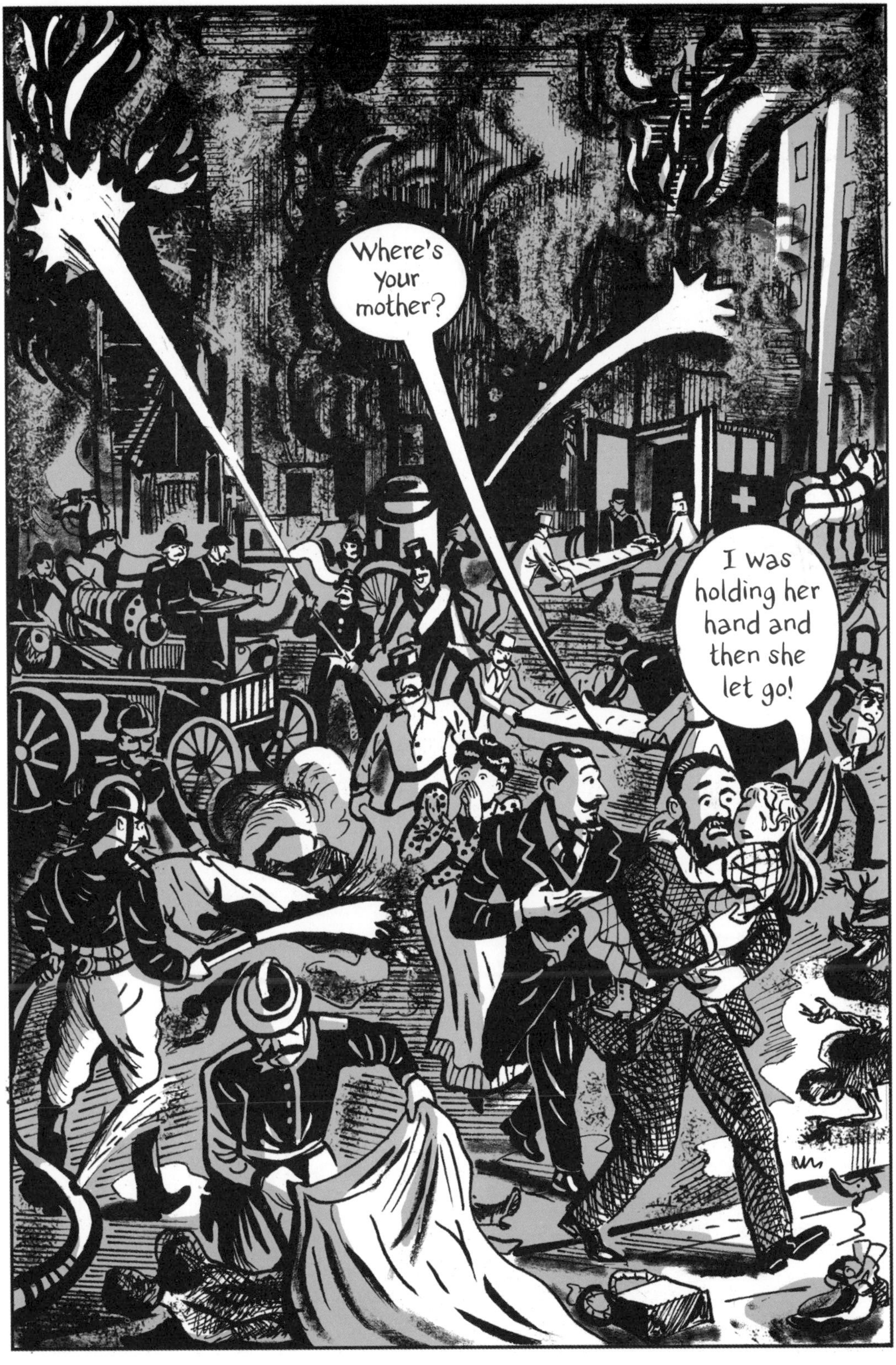
Where's your mother?
I was holding her hand and then she let go!

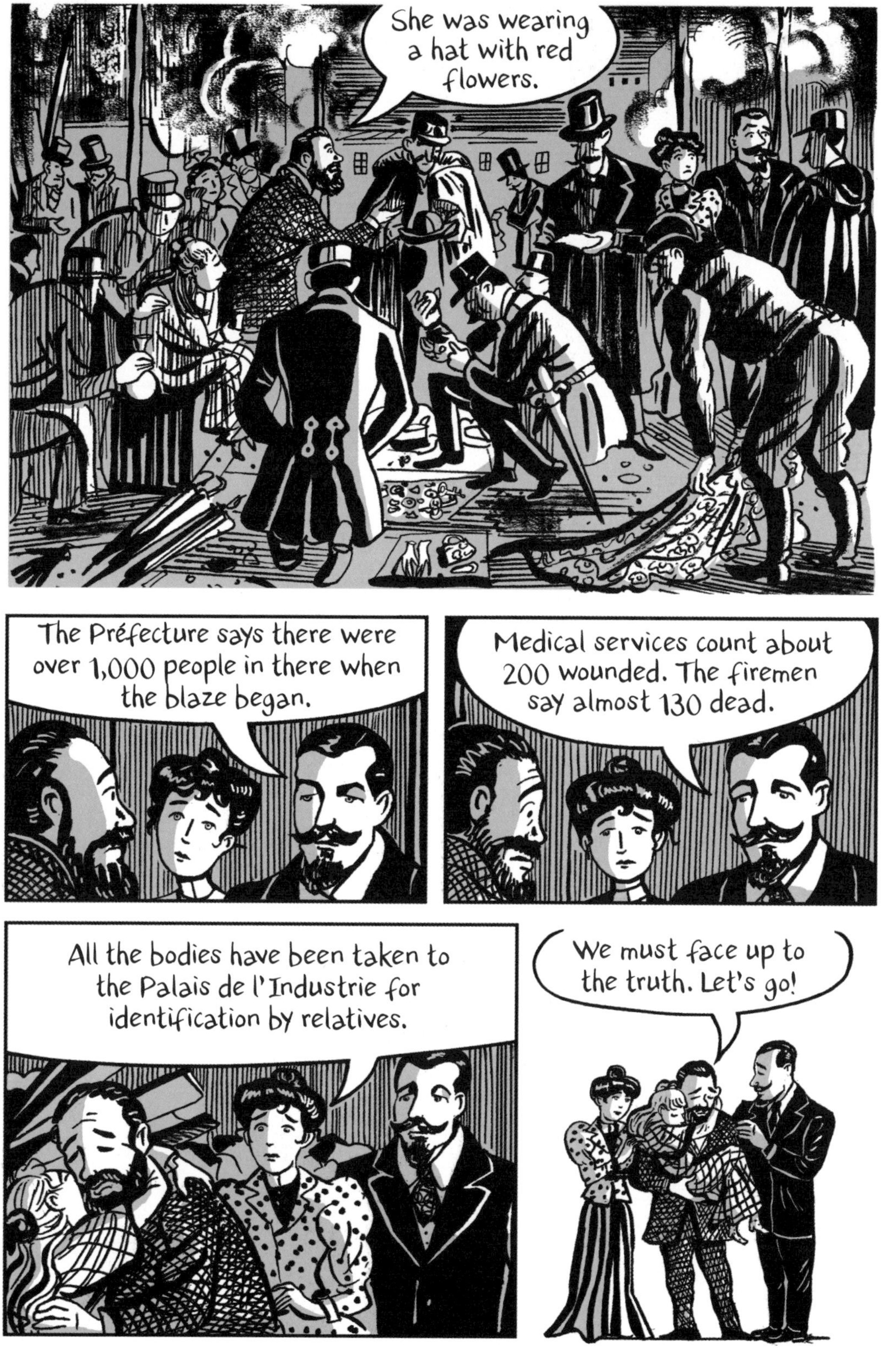
She was wearing a hat with red flowers.
The Préfecture says there were over 1,000 people in there when the blaze began.
Medical services count about 200 wounded. The firemen say almost 130 dead.
All the bodies have been taken to the Palais de l'Industrie for identification by relatives.
We must face up to the truth. Let's go!

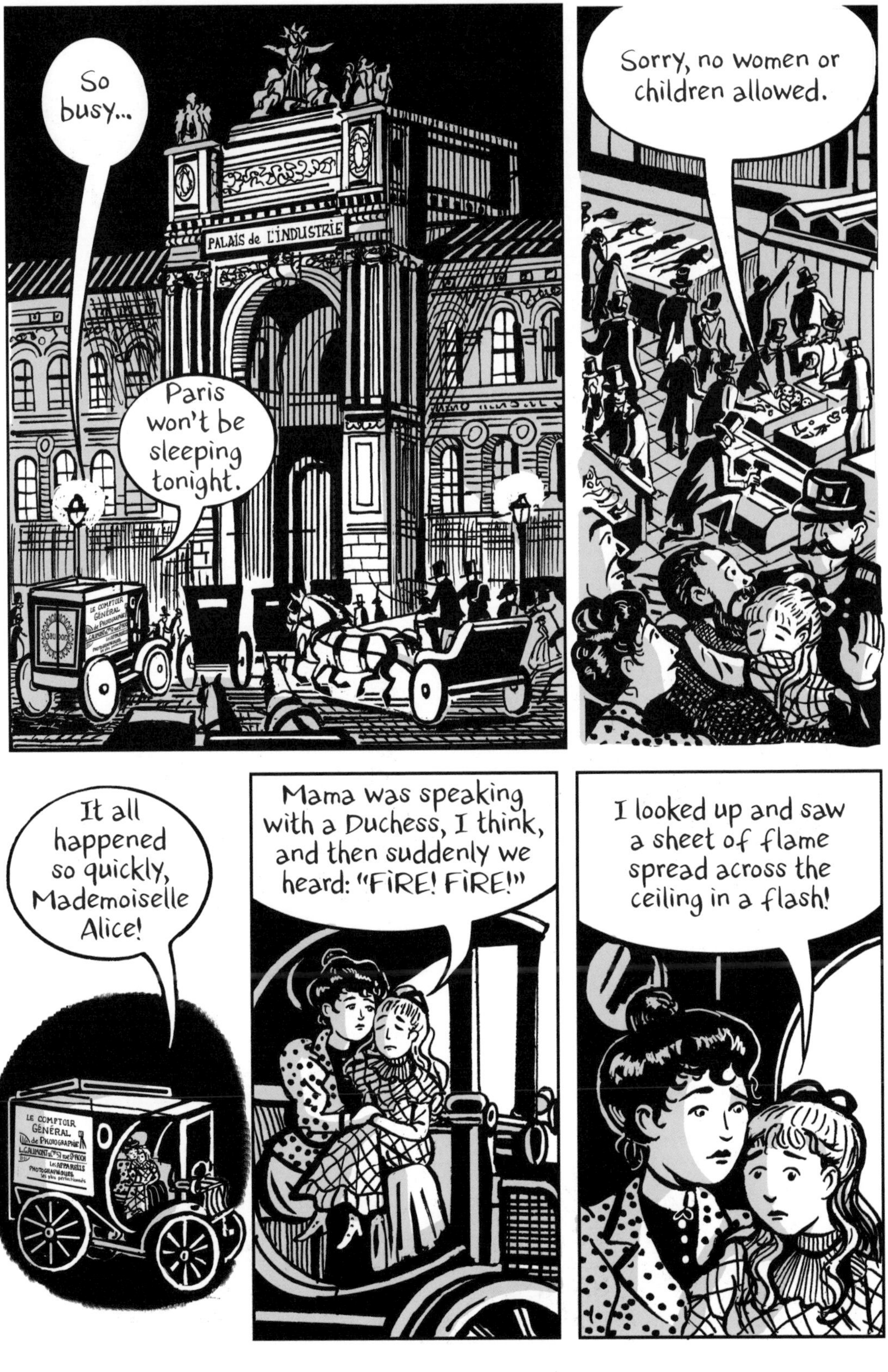
So busy...
PALAIS de L'INDUSTRIE
Paris won't be sleeping tonight.
LE COMPTOIR GÉNÉRAL de PHOTOGRAPHIE
Sorry, no women or children allowed.
It all happened so quickly, Mademoiselle Alice!
LE COMPTOIR GÉNÉRAL de PHOTOGRAPHIE
LES APPAREILS PHOTOGRAPHIQUES
Mama was speaking with a Duchess, I think, and then suddenly we heard: "FIRE! FIRE!"
I looked up and saw a sheet of flame spread across the ceiling in a flash!

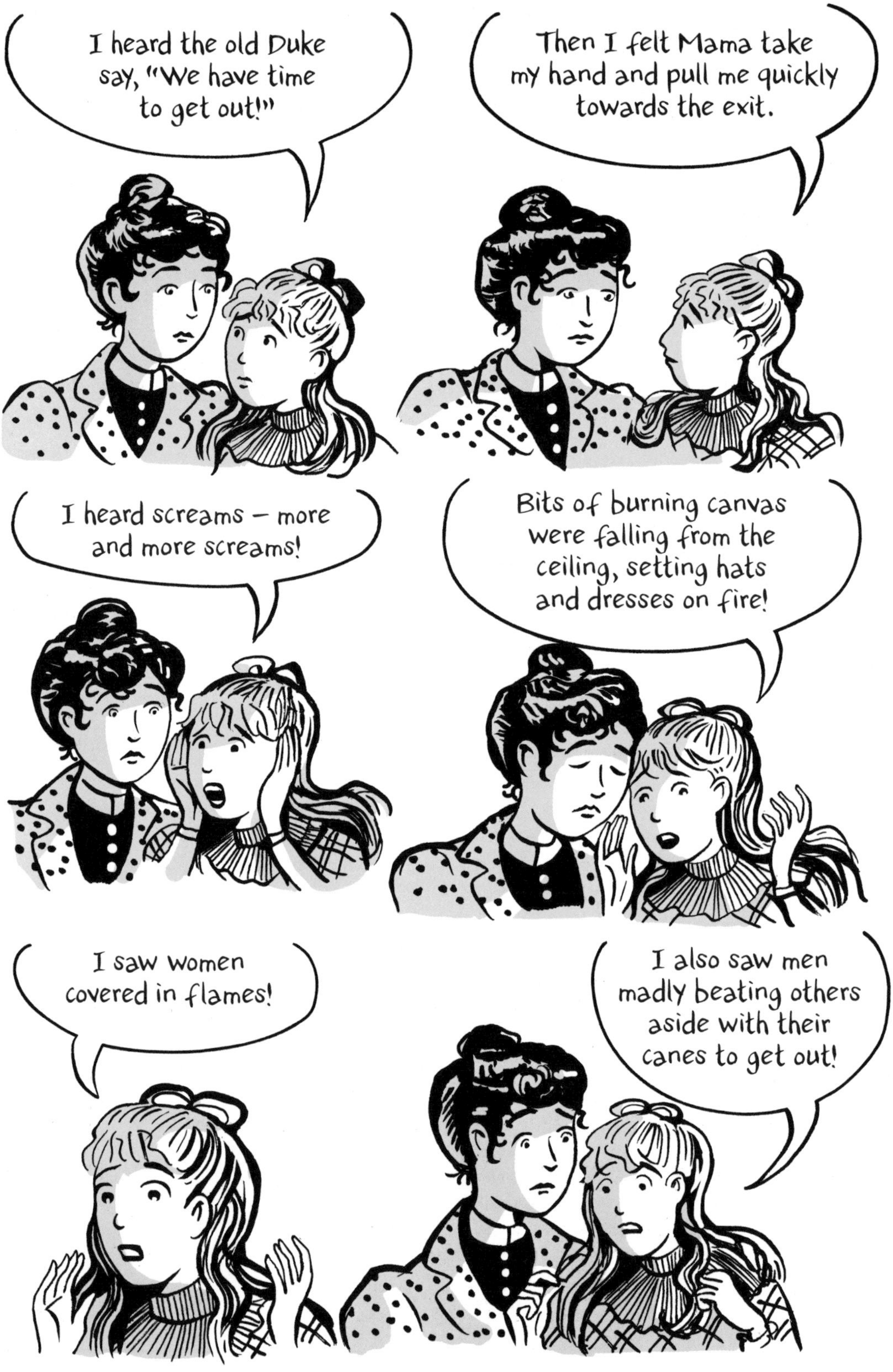
I heard the old Duke say, "We have time to get out!"
Then I felt Mama take my hand and pull me quickly towards the exit.
I heard screams – more and more screams!
Bits of burning canvas were falling from the ceiling, setting hats and dresses on fire!
I saw women covered in flames!
I also saw men madly beating others aside with their canes to get out!

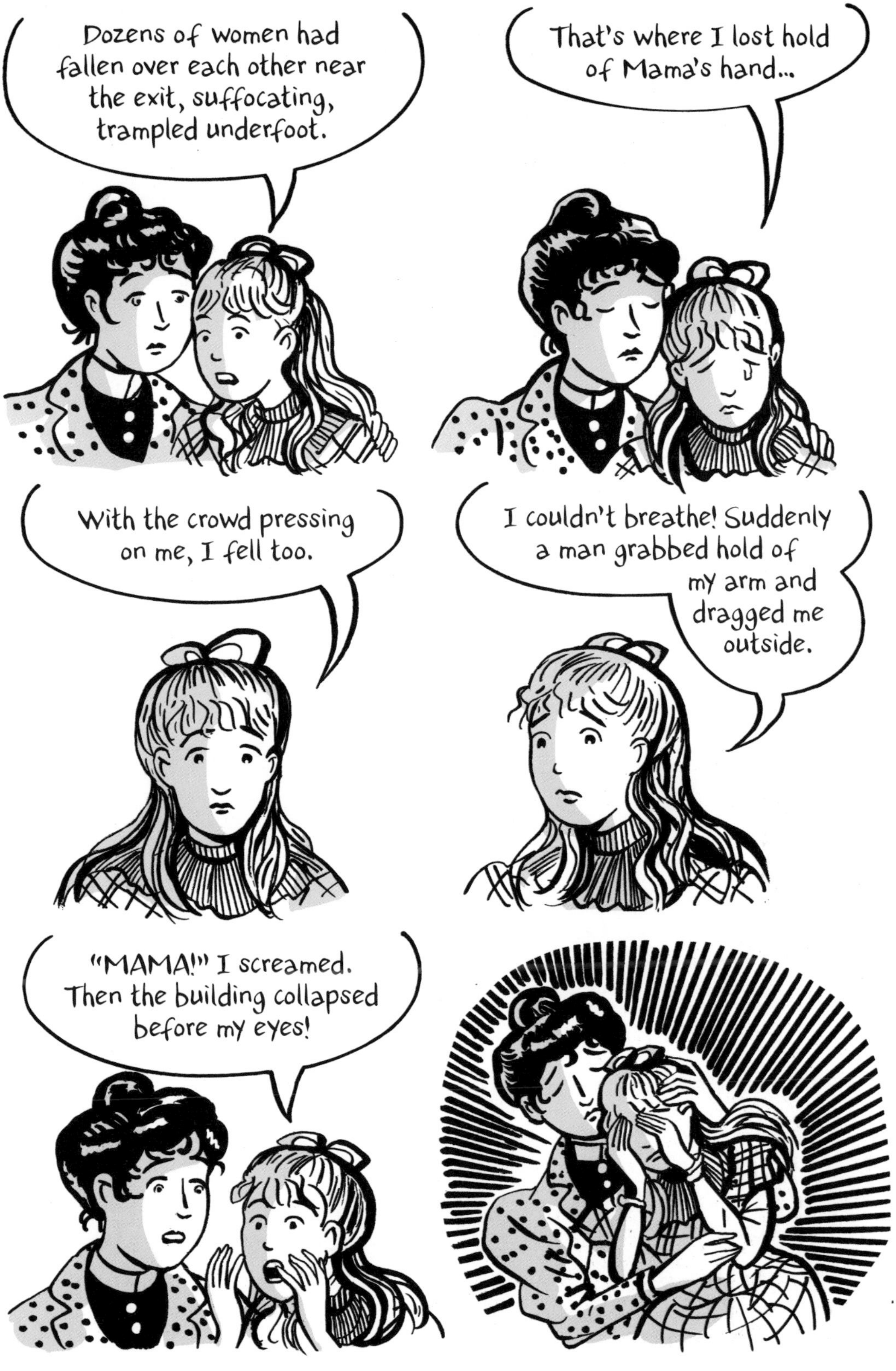
Dozens of women had fallen over each other near the exit, suffocating, trampled underfoot.
That's where I lost hold of Mama's hand...
With the crowd pressing on me, I fell too.
I couldn't breathe! Suddenly a man grabbed hold of my arm and dragged me outside.
"MAMA!" I screamed. Then the building collapsed before my eyes!

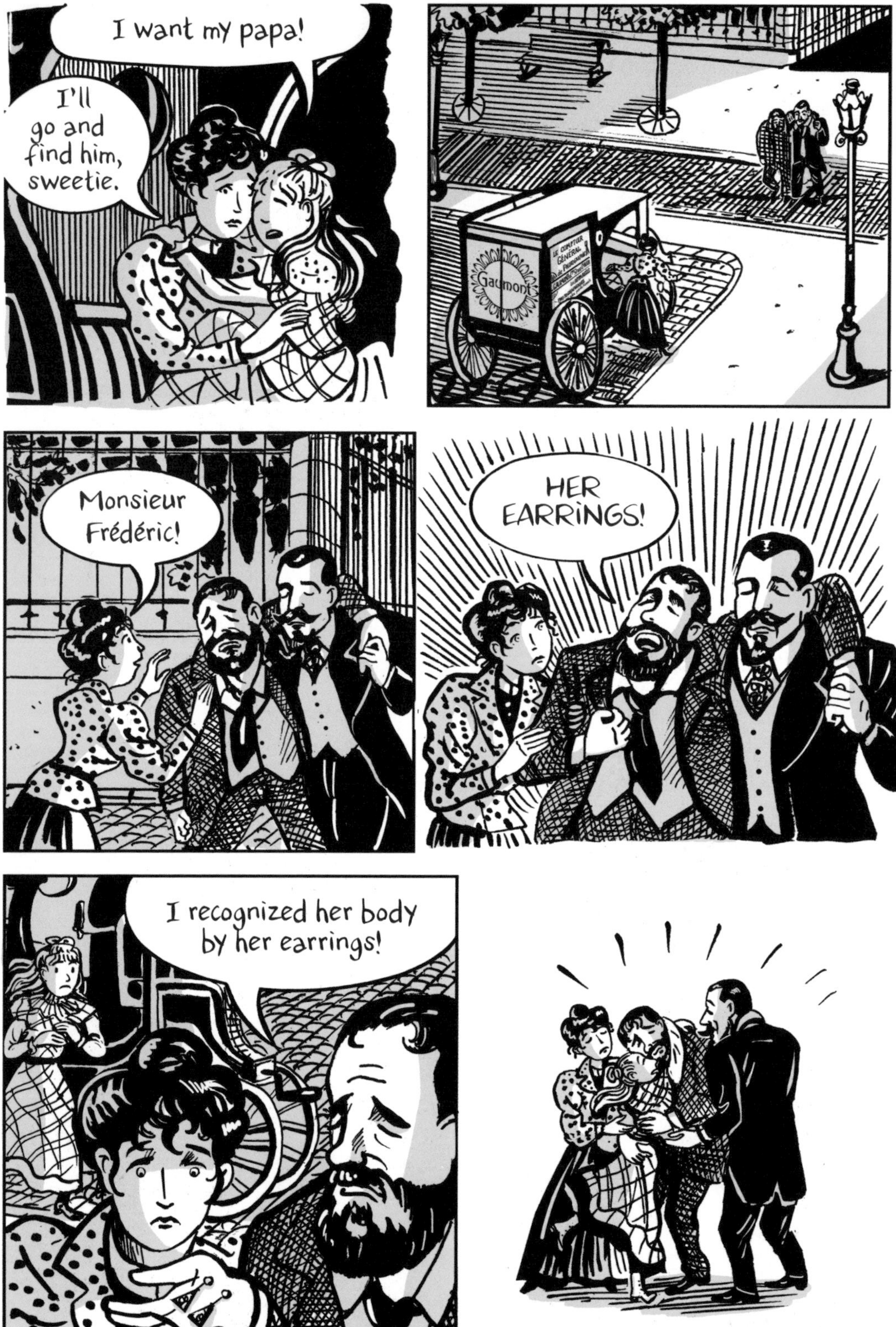

I want my papa!
I'll go and find him, sweetie.
Gaumont
Monsieur Frédéric!
HER EARRINGS!
I recognized her body by her earrings!

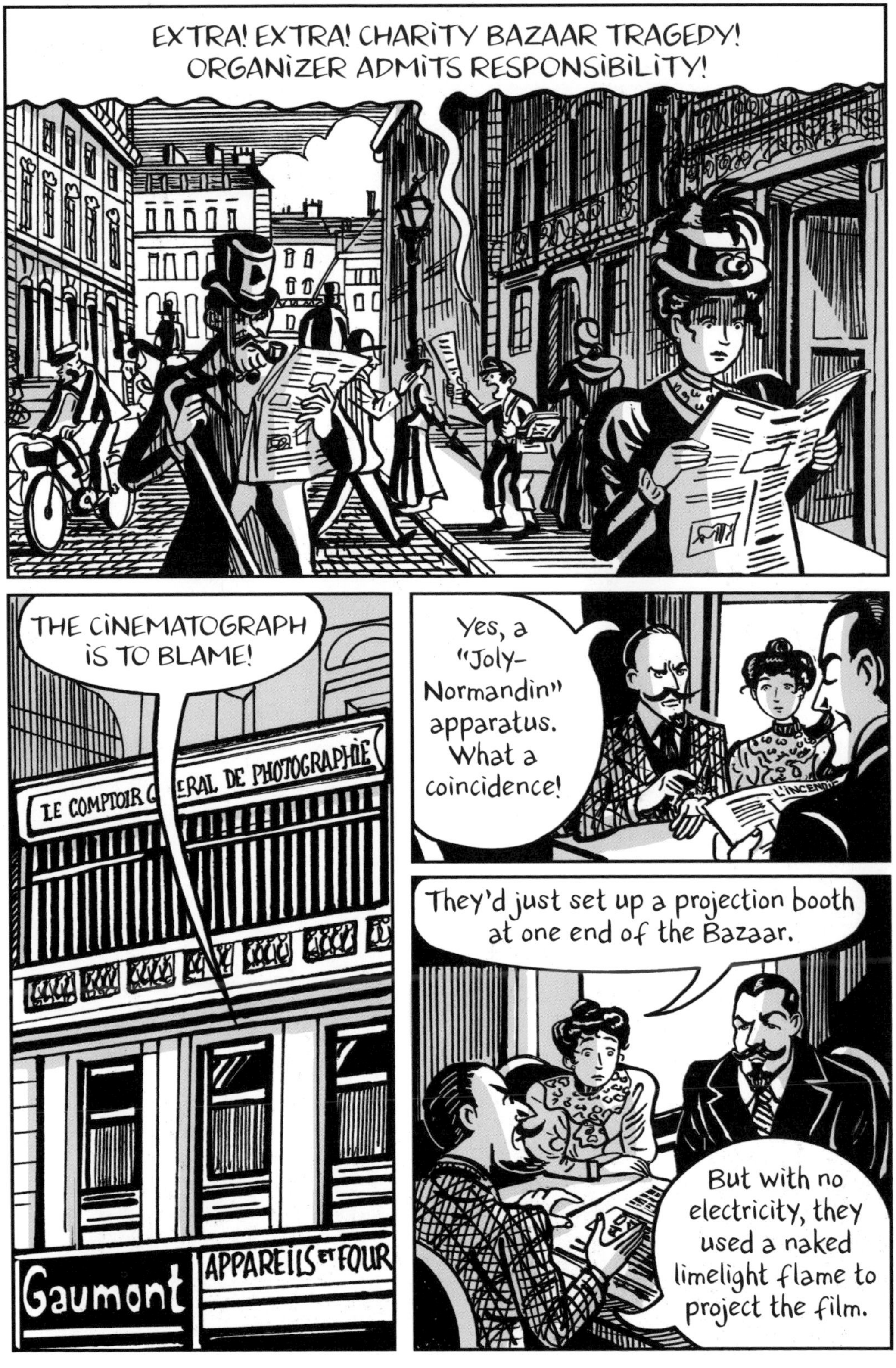
EXTRA! EXTRA! CHARITY BAZAAR TRAGEDY! ORGANIZER ADMITS RESPONSIBILITY!
THE CINEMATOGRAPH IS TO BLAME!
LE COMPTOIR G ERAL DE PHOTOGRAPHIE
Gaumont
APPAREILS ET FOUR
Yes, a "Joly-Normandin" apparatus. What a coincidence!
L'INCENDI
They'd just set up a projection booth at one end of the Bazaar.
But with no electricity, they used a naked limelight flame to project the film.

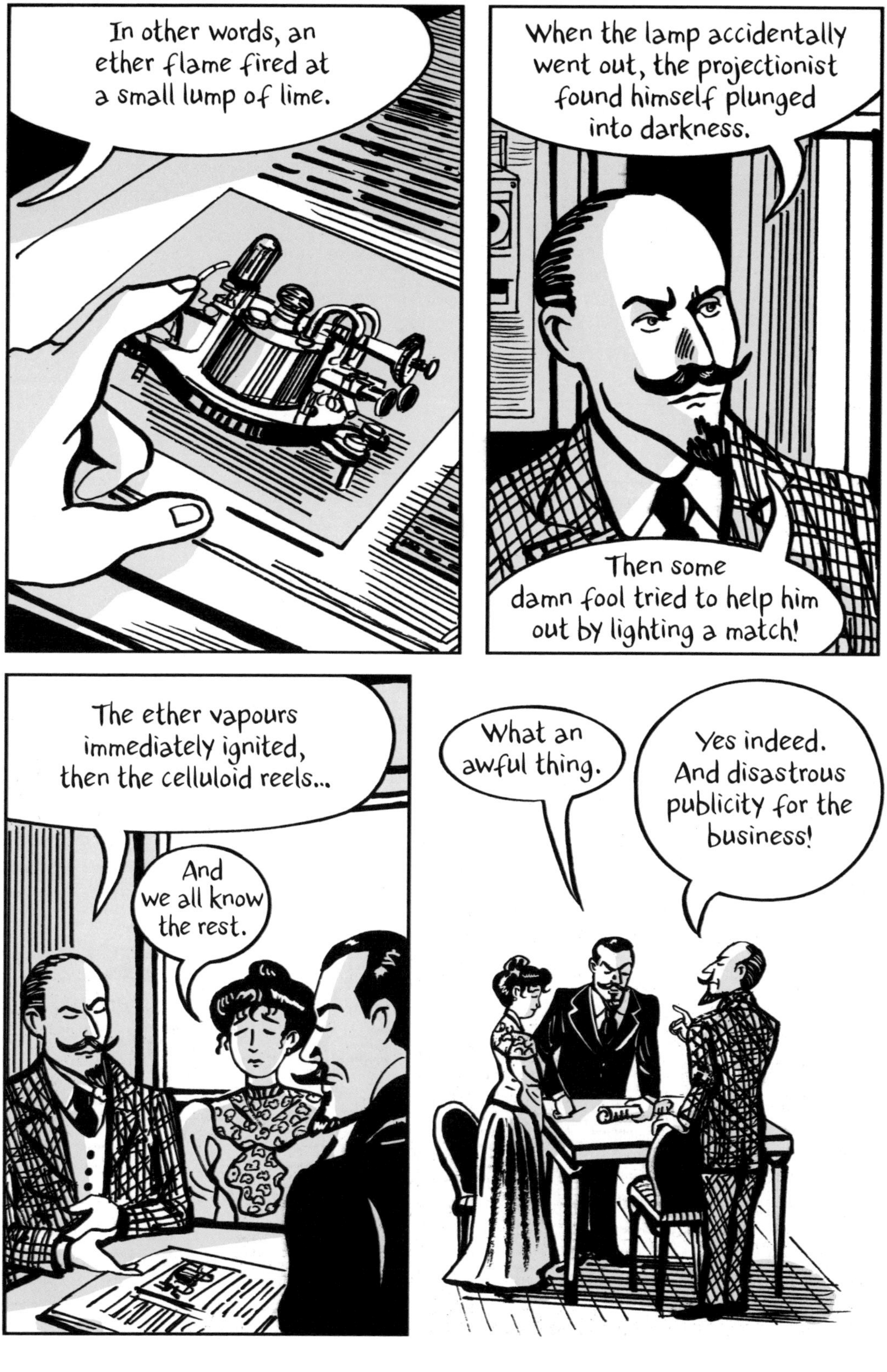
In other words, an ether flame fired at a small lump of lime.
When the lamp accidentally went out, the projectionist found himself plunged into darkness.
Then some damn fool tried to help him out by lighting a match!
The ether vapours immediately ignited, then the celluloid reels...
And we all know the rest.
What an awful thing.
Yes indeed. And disastrous publicity for the business!

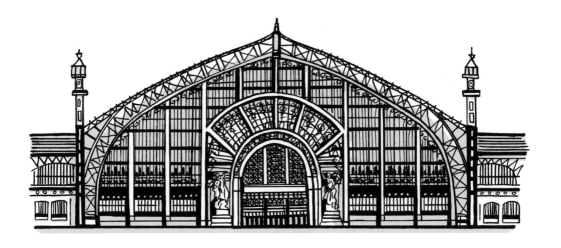

1900 – Great Hall, Galerie des Machines –
EXPOSITION UNIVERSELLE – Paris – France

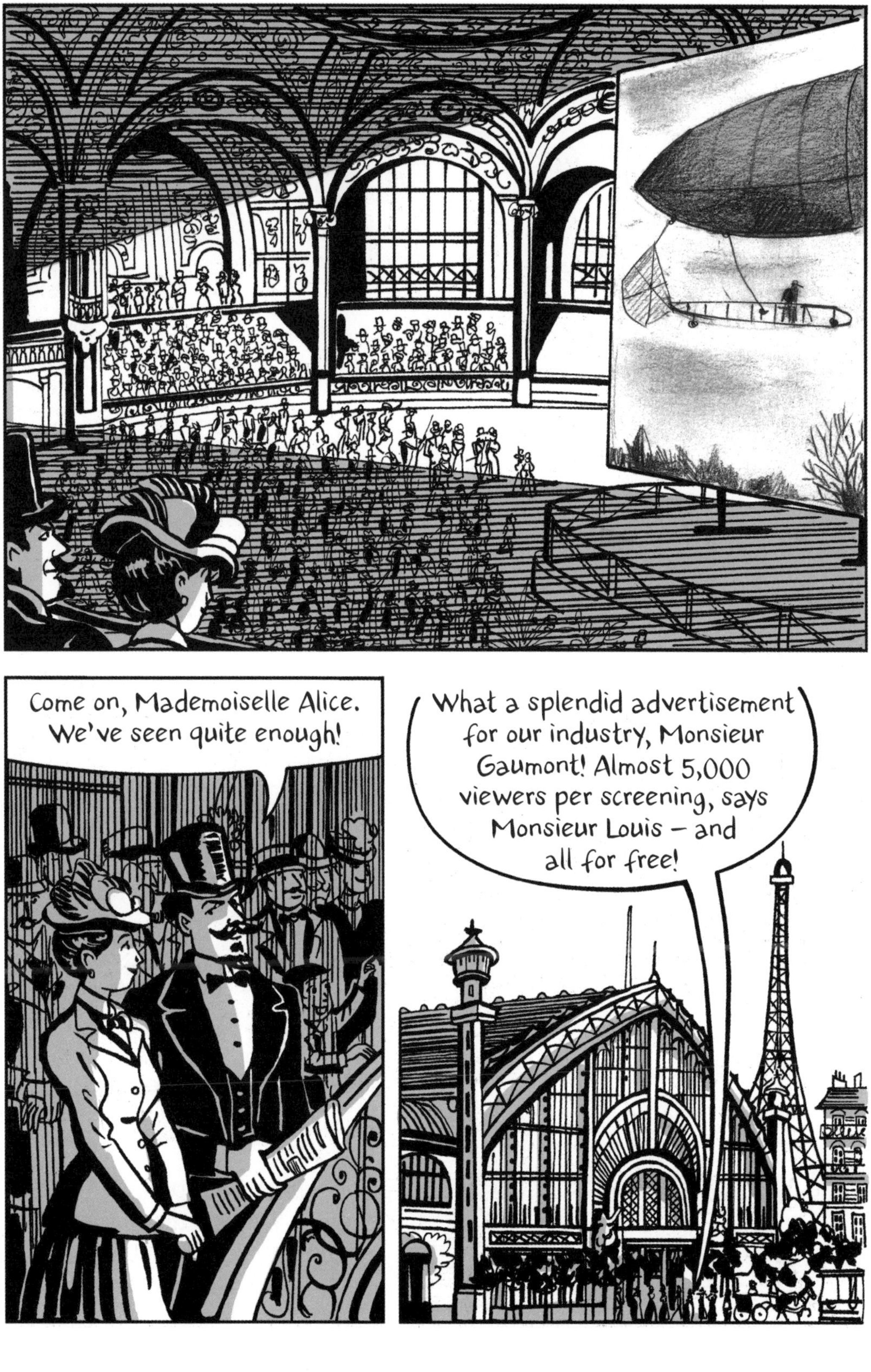
Come on, Mademoiselle Alice. We've seen quite enough!
What a splendid advertisement for our industry, Monsieur Gaumont! Almost 5,000 viewers per screening, says Monsieur Louis – and all for free!

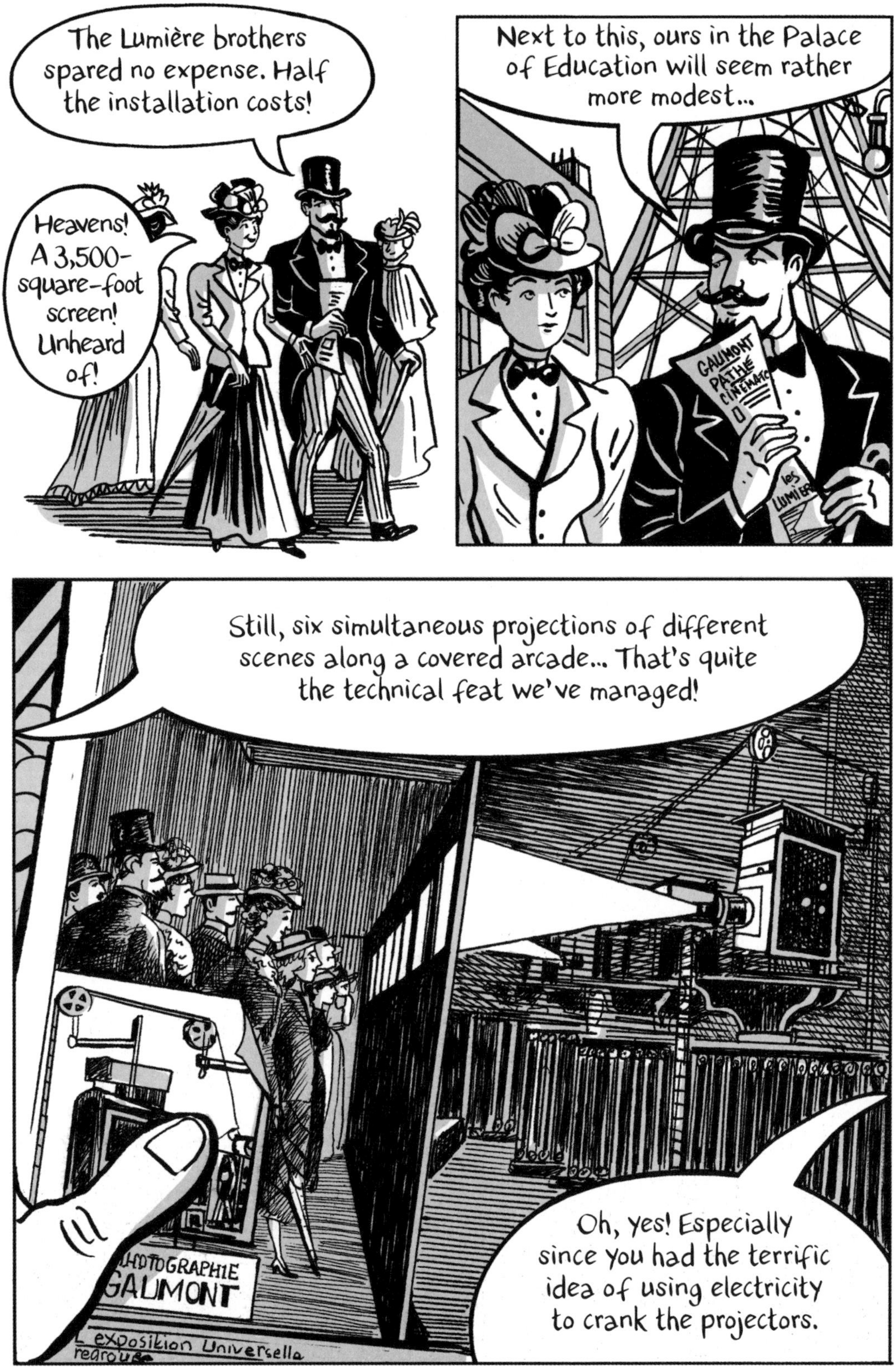
The Lumière brothers spared no expense. Half the installation costs!
Heavens! A 3,500-square-foot screen! Unheard of!
Next to this, ours in the Palace of Education will seem rather more modest...
GAUMONT
PATHÉ
Still, six simultaneous projections of different scenes along a covered arcade... That's quite the technical feat we've managed!
GAUMONT
Oh, yes! Especially since you had the terrific idea of using electricity to crank the projectors.

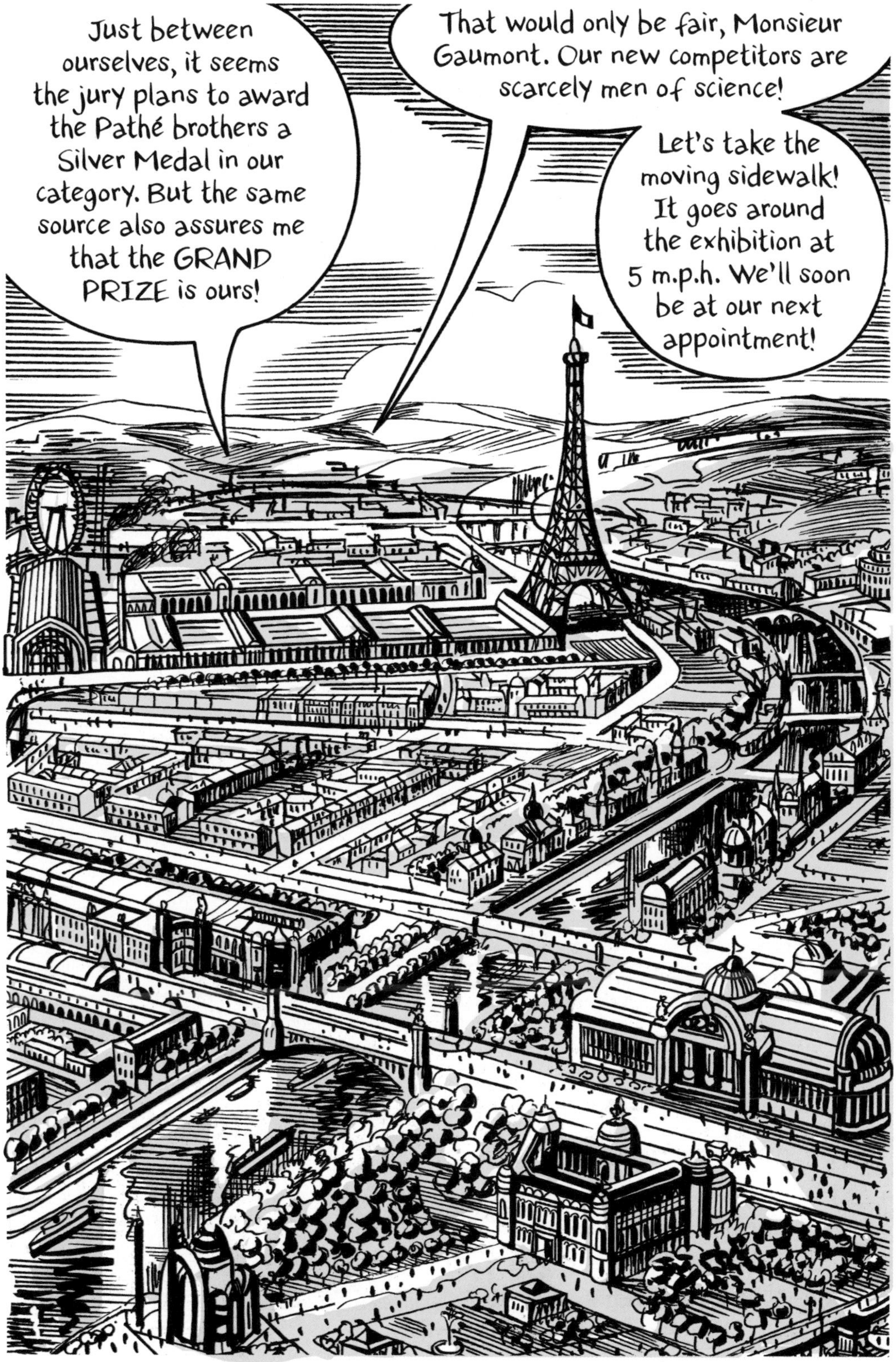
Just between ourselves, it seems the jury plans to award the Pathé brothers a Silver Medal in our category. But the same source also assures me that the GRAND PRIZE is ours!
That would only be fair, Monsieur Gaumont. Our new competitors are scarcely men of science!
Let's take the moving sidewalk! It goes around the exhibition at 5 m.p.h. We'll soon be at our next appointment!

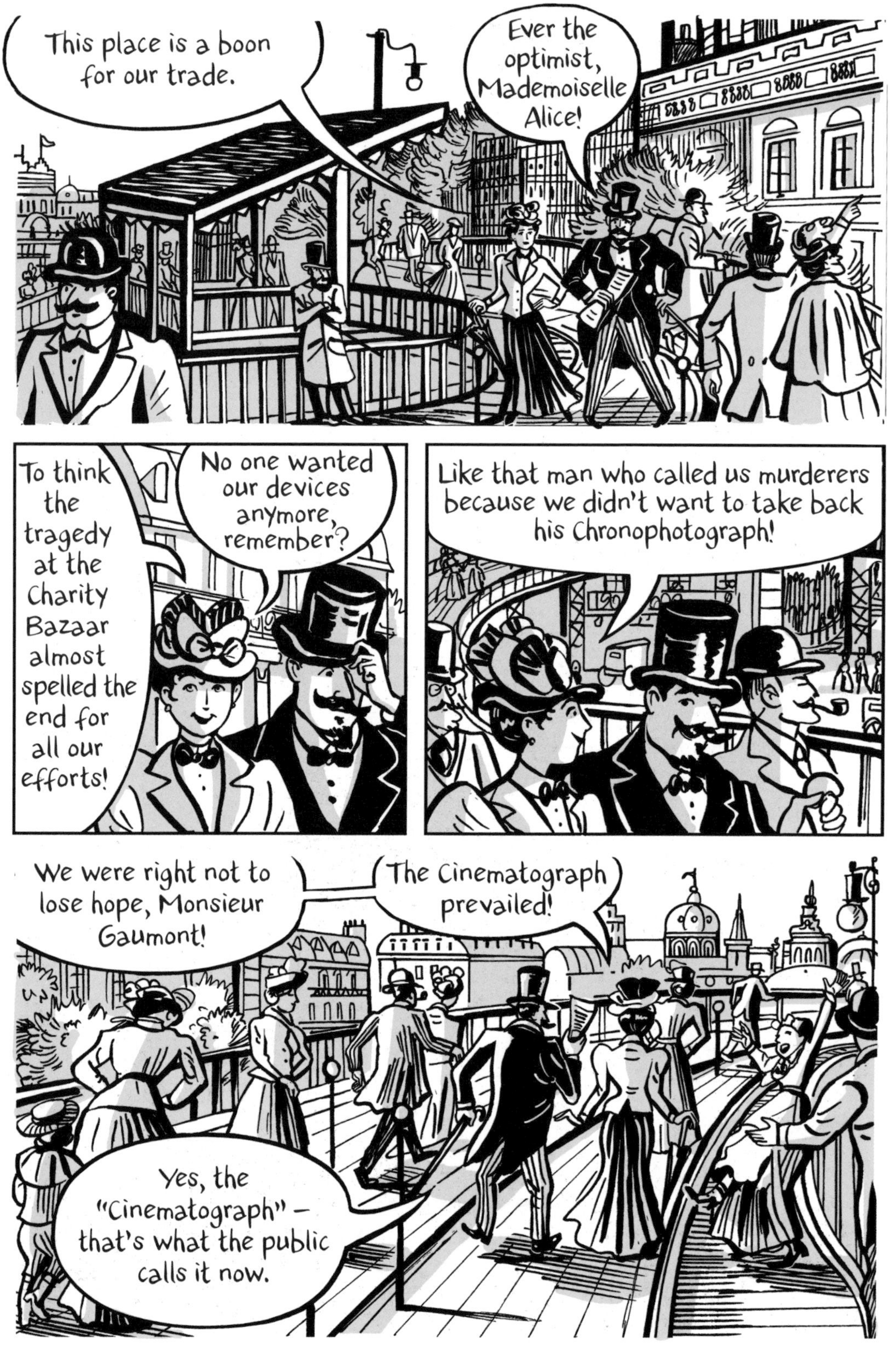
This place is a boon for our trade.
Ever the optimist, Mademoiselle Alice!
To think the tragedy at the Charity Bazaar almost spelled the end for all our efforts!
No one wanted our devices anymore, remember?
Like that man who called us murderers because we didn't want to take back his Chronophotograph!
We were right not to lose hope, Monsieur Gaumont!
The Cinematograph prevailed!
Yes, the "Cinematograph" – that's what the public calls it now.

1902 – Parc des Buttes-Chaumont – Paris – France

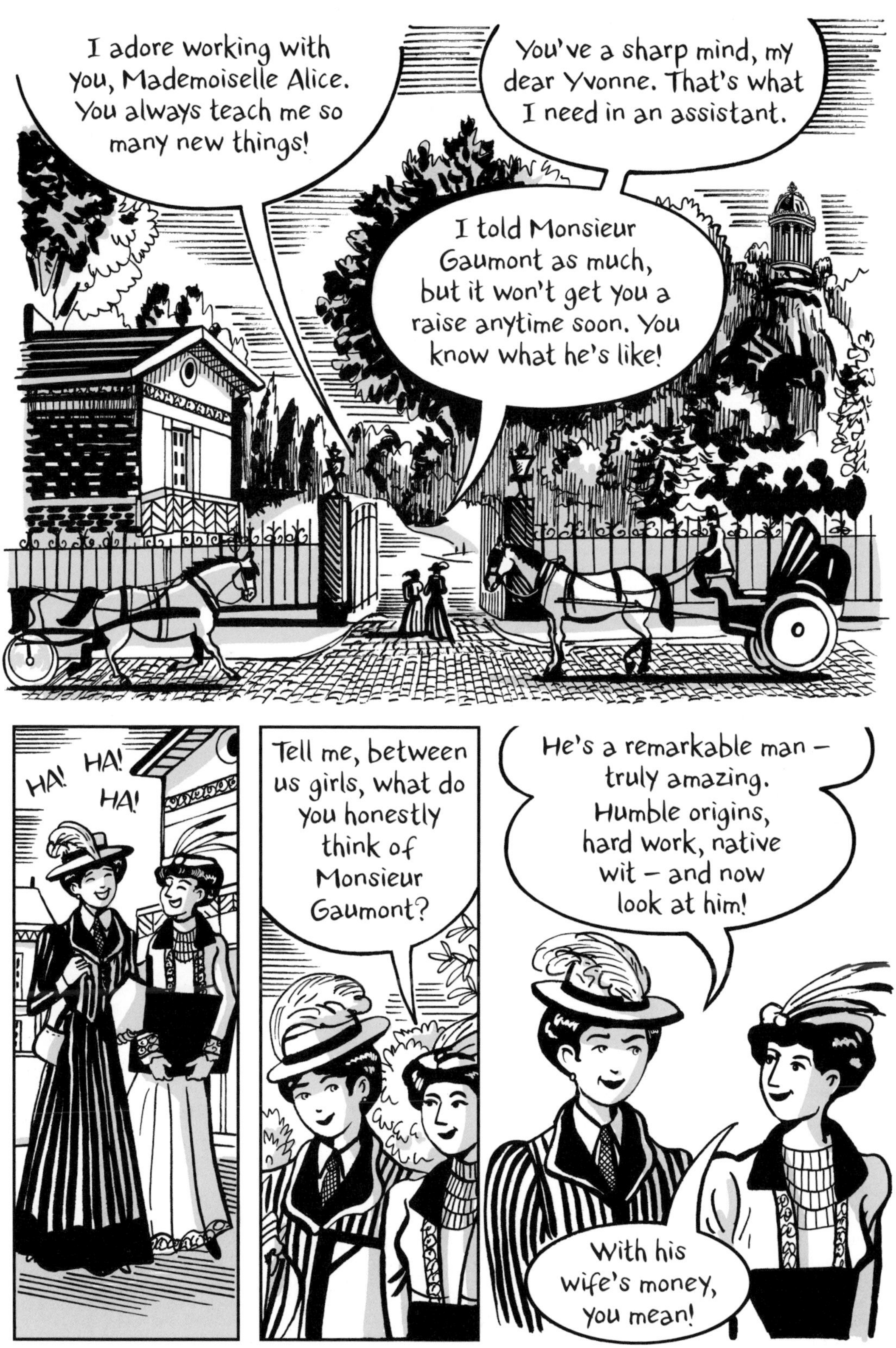
I adore working with you, Mademoiselle Alice. You always teach me so many new things!
You've a sharp mind, my dear Yvonne. That's what I need in an assistant.
I told Monsieur Gaumont as much, but it won't get you a raise anytime soon. You know what he's like!
HA! HA! HA!
Tell me, between us girls, what do you honestly think of Monsieur Gaumont?
He's a remarkable man – truly amazing. Humble origins, hard work, native wit – and now look at him!
With his wife's money, you mean!

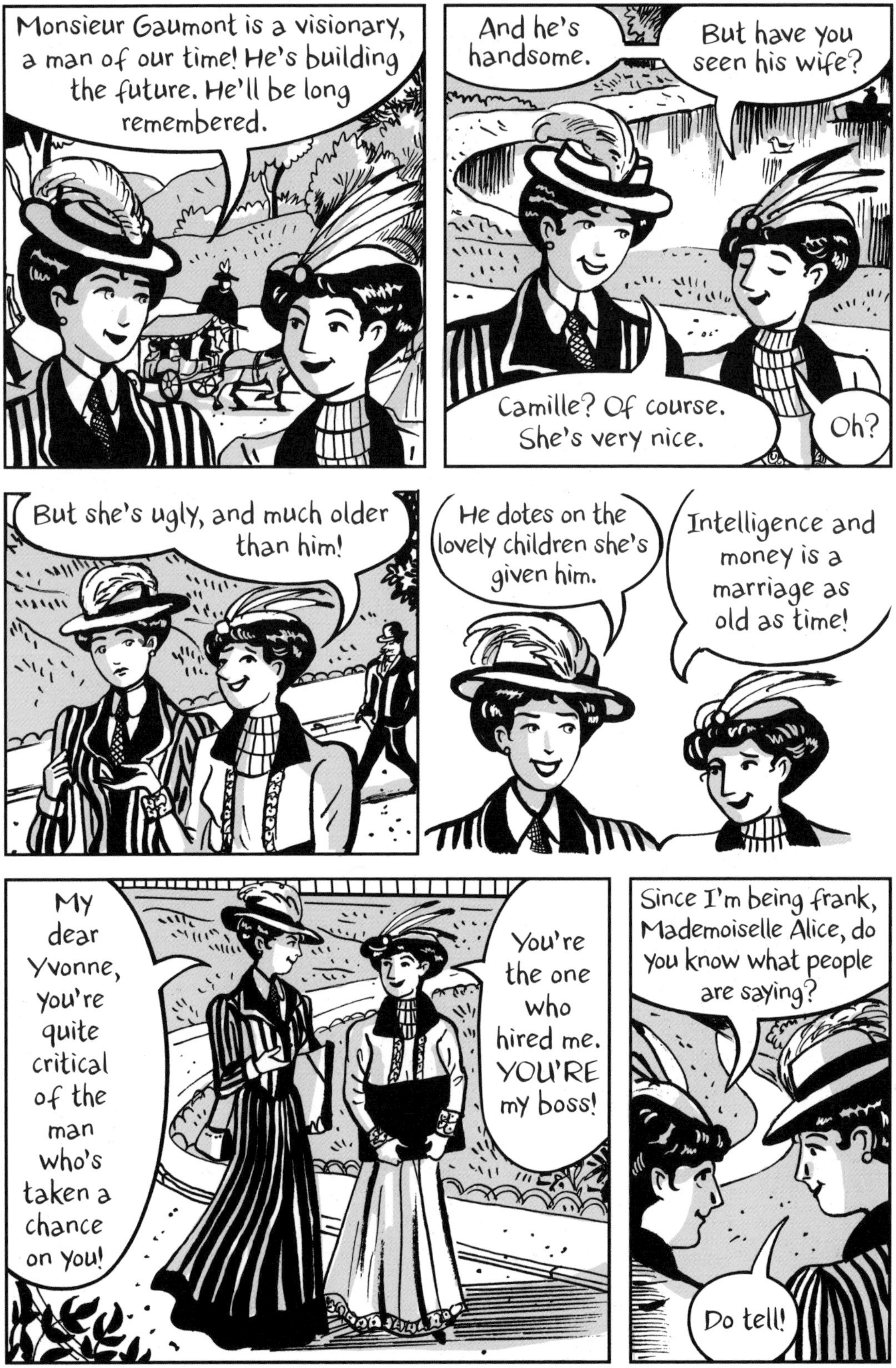
Monsieur Gaumont is a visionary, a man of our time! He's building the future. He'll be long remembered.
And he's handsome.
But have you seen his wife?
Camille? Of course. She's very nice.
Oh?
But she's ugly, and much older than him!
He dotes on the lovely children she's given him.
Intelligence and money is a marriage as old as time!
My dear Yvonne, you're quite critical of the man who's taken a chance on you!
You're the one who hired me. YOU'RE my boss!
Since I'm being frank, Mademoiselle Alice, do you know what people are saying?
Do tell!

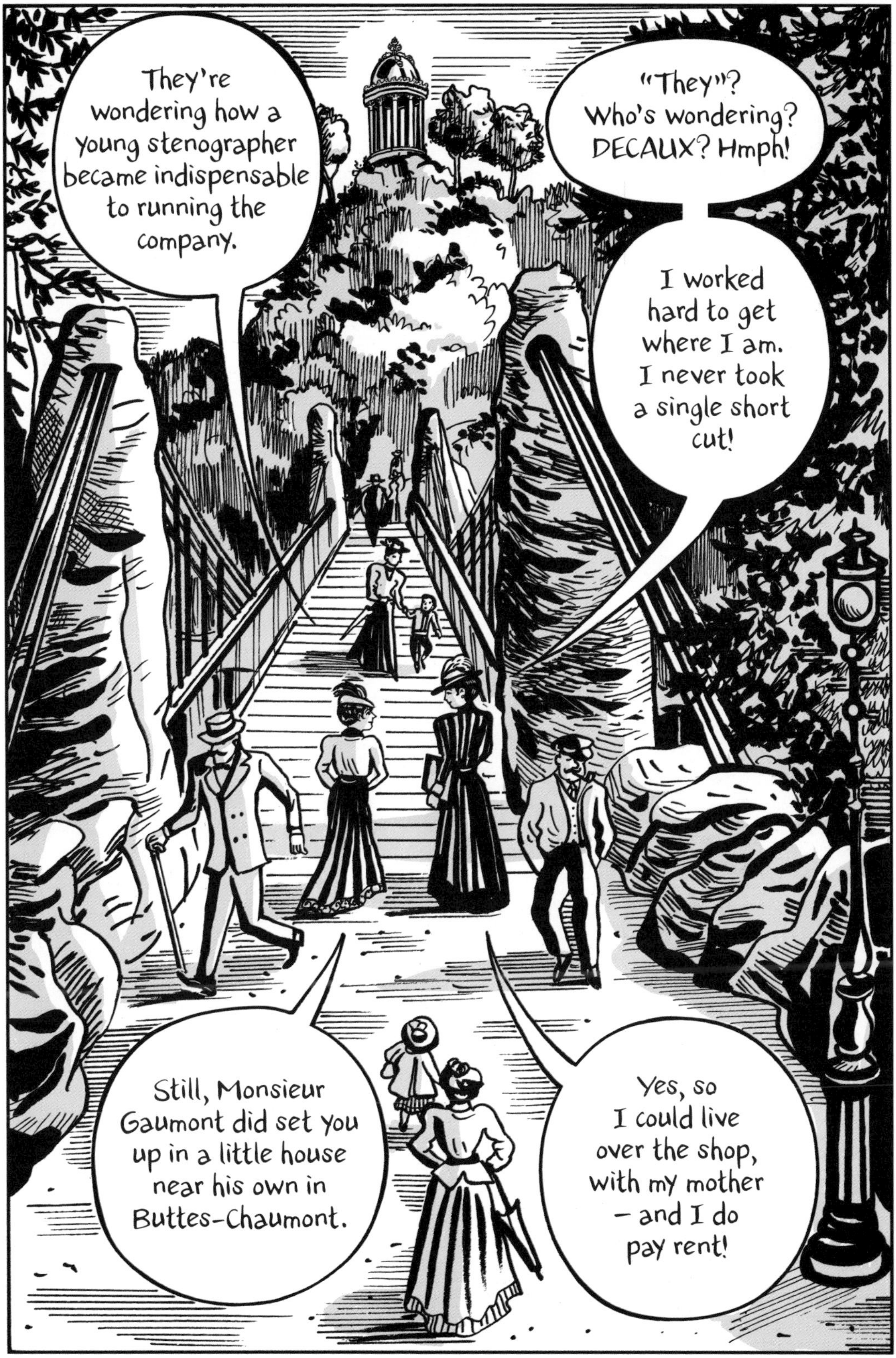
They're wondering how a young stenographer became indispensable to running the company.
"They"? Who's wondering? DECAUX? Hmph!
I worked hard to get where I am. I never took a single short cut!
Still, Monsieur Gaumont did set you up in a little house near his own in Buttes-Chaumont.
Yes, so I could live over the shop, with my mother – and I do pay rent!

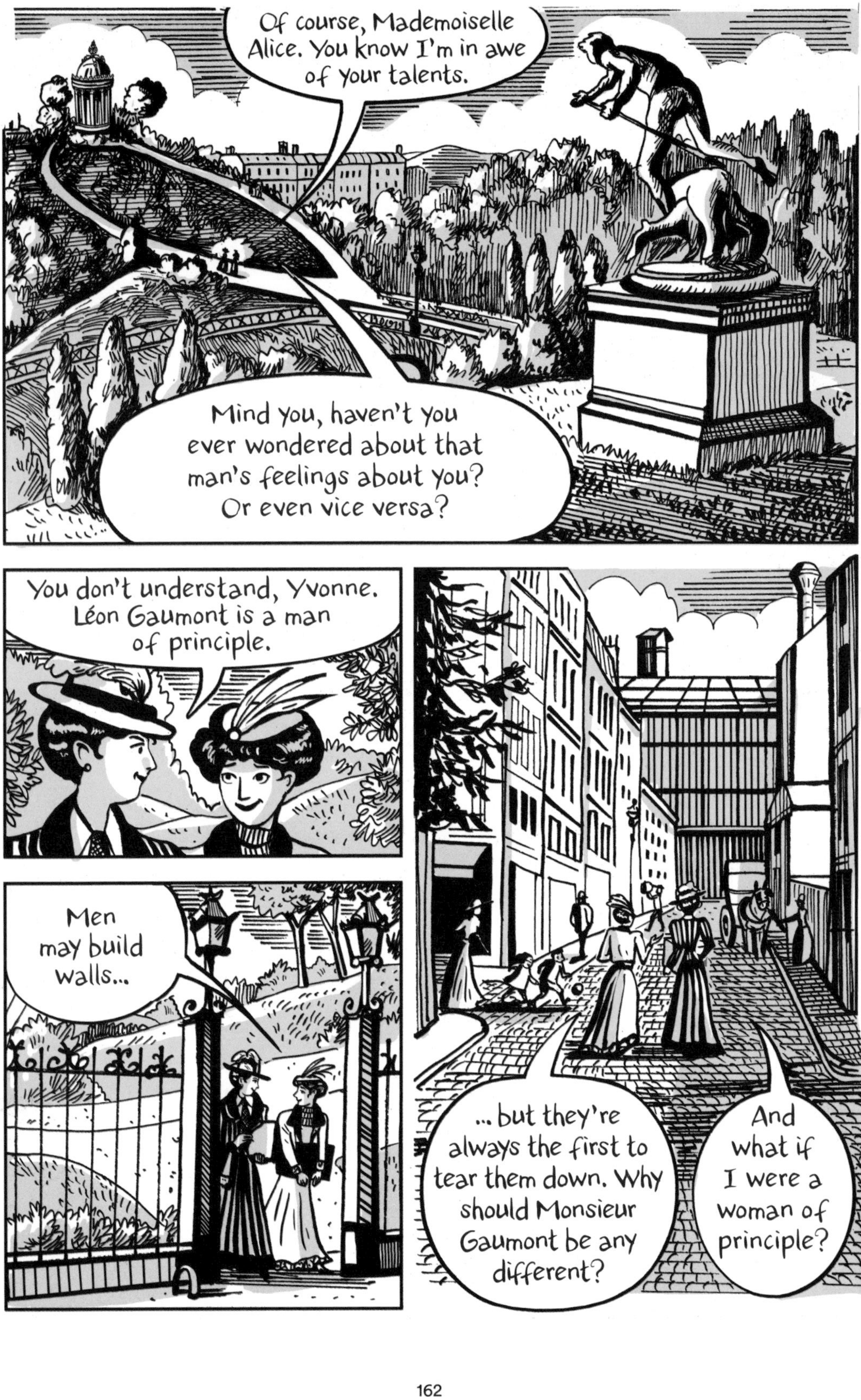
Of course, Mademoiselle Alice. You know I'm in awe of your talents.
Mind you, haven't you ever wondered about that man's feelings about you? Or even vice versa?
You don't understand, Yvonne. Léon Gaumont is a man of principle.
Men may build walls...
... but they're always the first to tear them down. Why should Monsieur Gaumont be any different?
And what if I were a woman of principle?

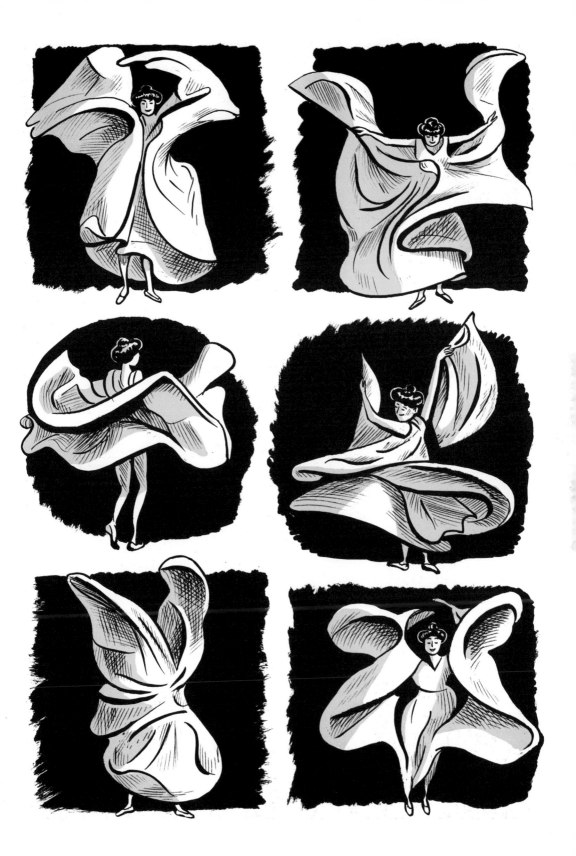

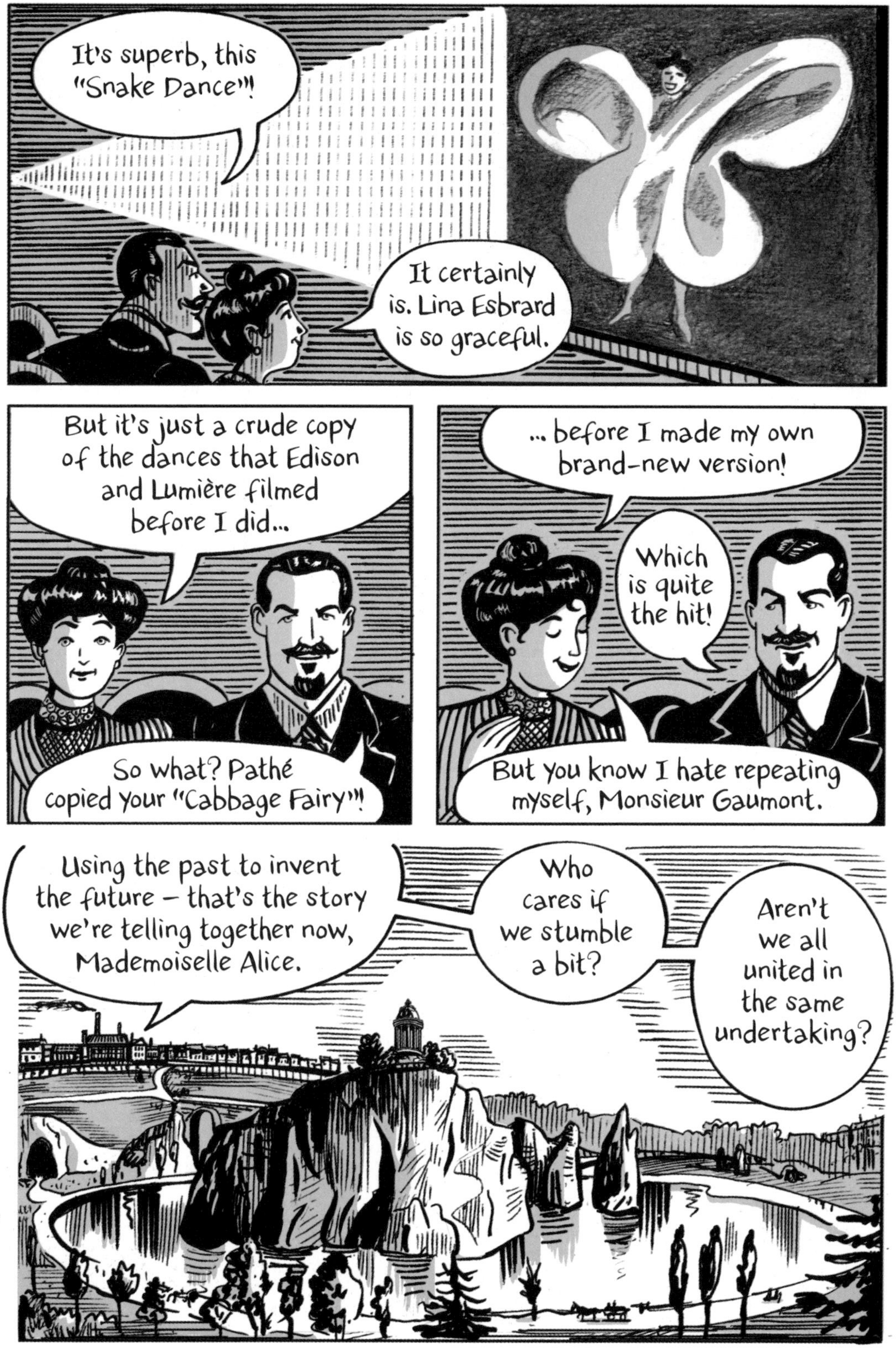

It's superb, this "Snake Dance"!
It certainly is. Lina Esbrard is so graceful.
But it's just a crude copy of the dances that Edison and Lumière filmed before I did...
So what? Pathé copied your "Cabbage Fairy"!
... before I made my own brand-new version!
Which is quite the hit!
But you know I hate repeating myself, Monsieur Gaumont.
Using the past to invent the future – that's the story we're telling together now, Mademoiselle Alice.
Who cares if we stumble a bit?
Aren't we all united in the same undertaking?

Société des Etablissements Gaumont
ELGÉ

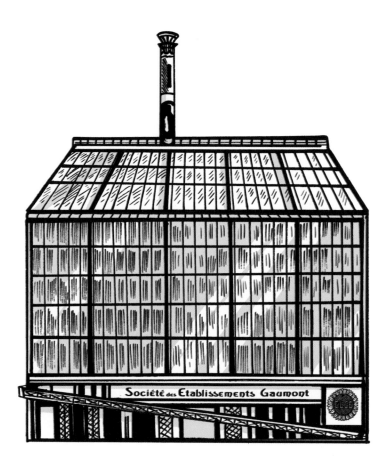

1905 – Cité ELGÉ, 55, Rue de la Villette – Paris – France

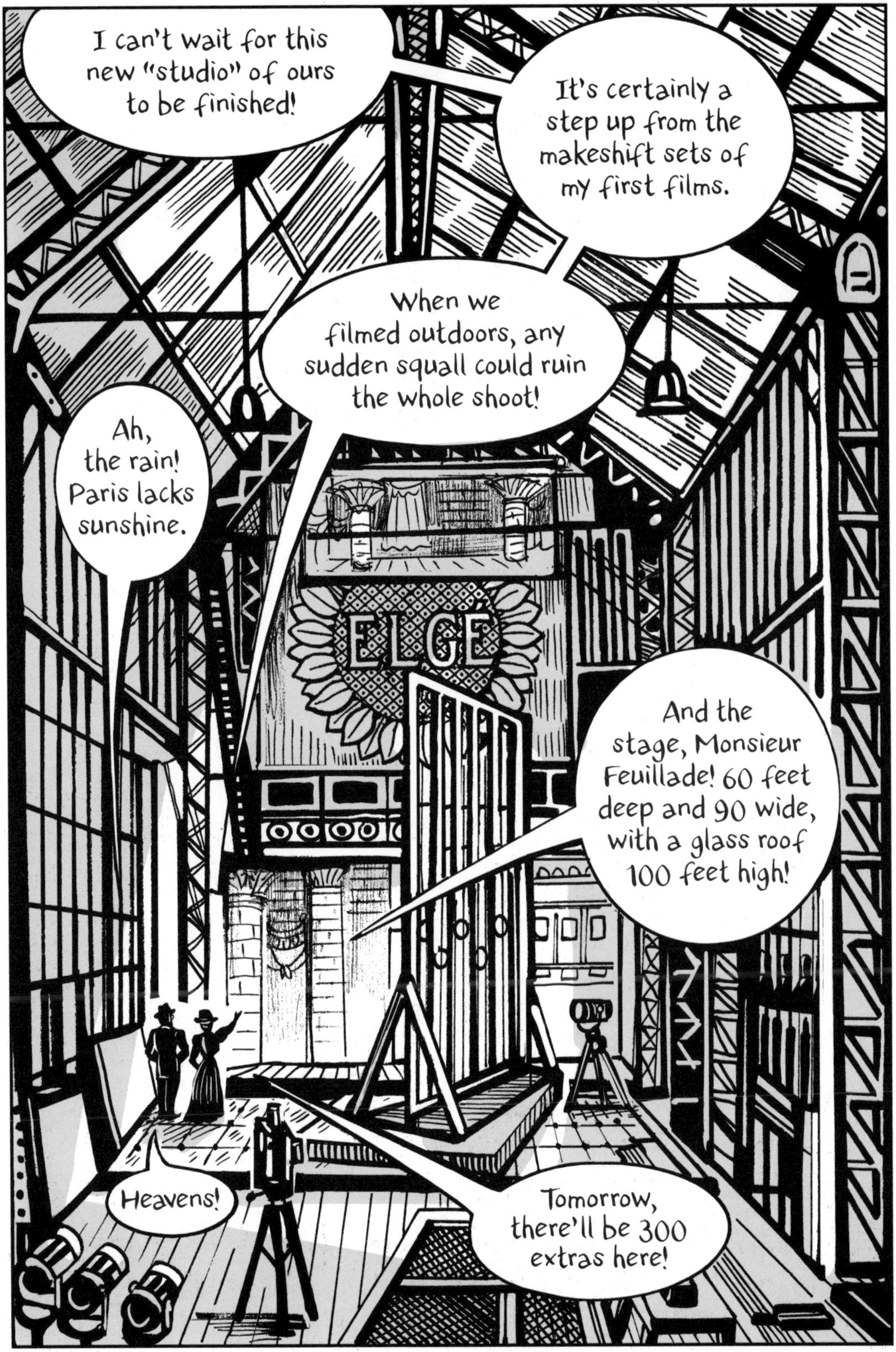
I can't wait for this new "studio" of ours to be finished!
It's certainly a step up from the makeshift sets of my first films.
When we filmed outdoors, any sudden squall could ruin the whole shoot!
Ah, the rain! Paris lacks sunshine.
ELGÉ
And the stage, Monsieur Feuillade! 60 feet deep and 90 wide, with a glass roof 100 feet high!
Heavens!
Tomorrow, there'll be 300 extras here!

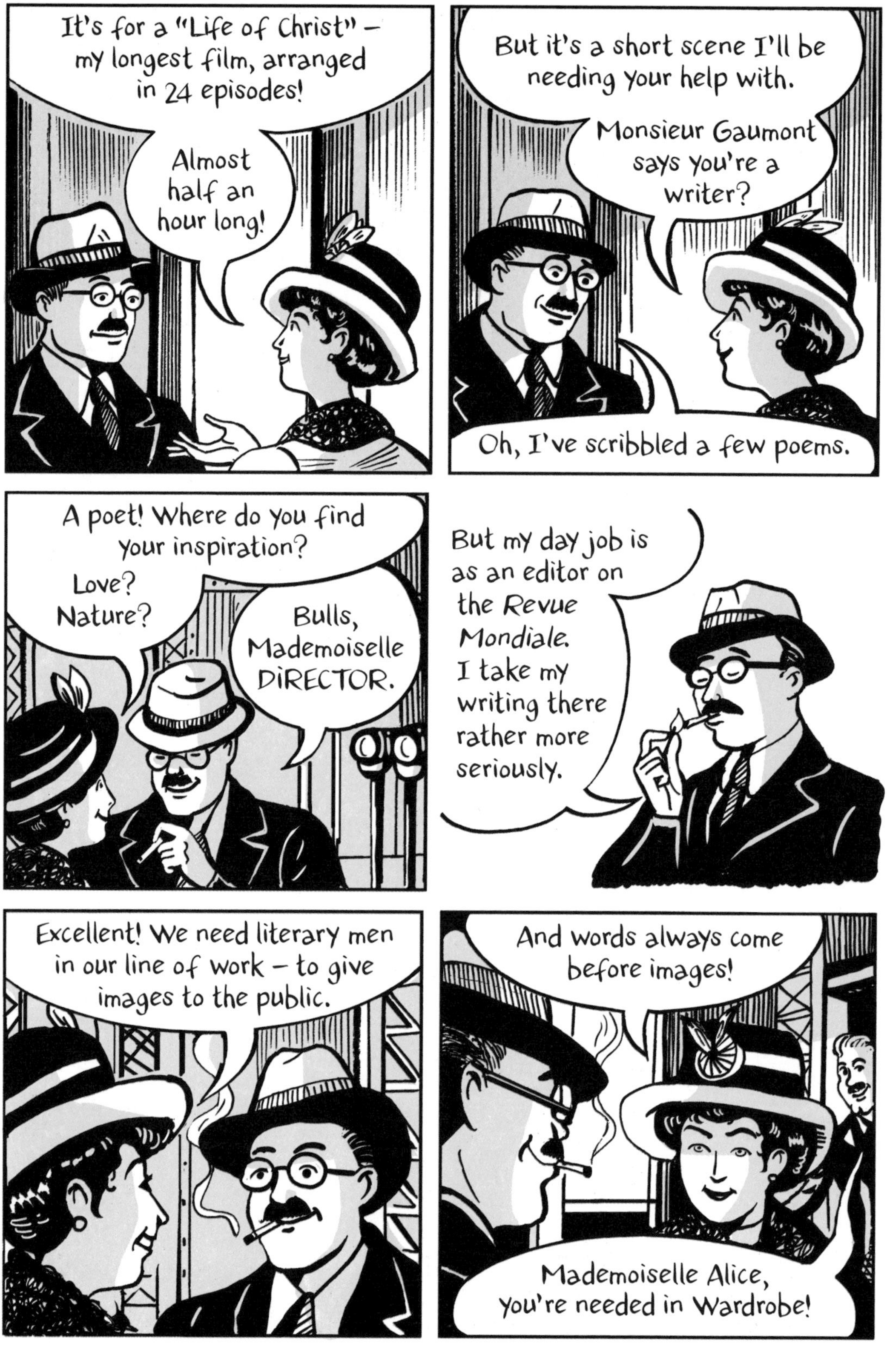
It's for a "Life of Christ" – my longest film, arranged in 24 episodes!
Almost half an hour long!
But it's a short scene I'll be needing your help with.
Monsieur Gaumont says you're a writer?
Oh, I've scribbled a few poems.
A poet! Where do you find your inspiration?
Love? Nature?
Bulls, Mademoiselle DIRECTOR.
But my day job is as an editor on the *Revue Mondiale*. I take my writing there rather more seriously.
Excellent! We need literary men in our line of work – to give images to the public.
And words always come before images!
Mademoiselle Alice, you're needed in Wardrobe!

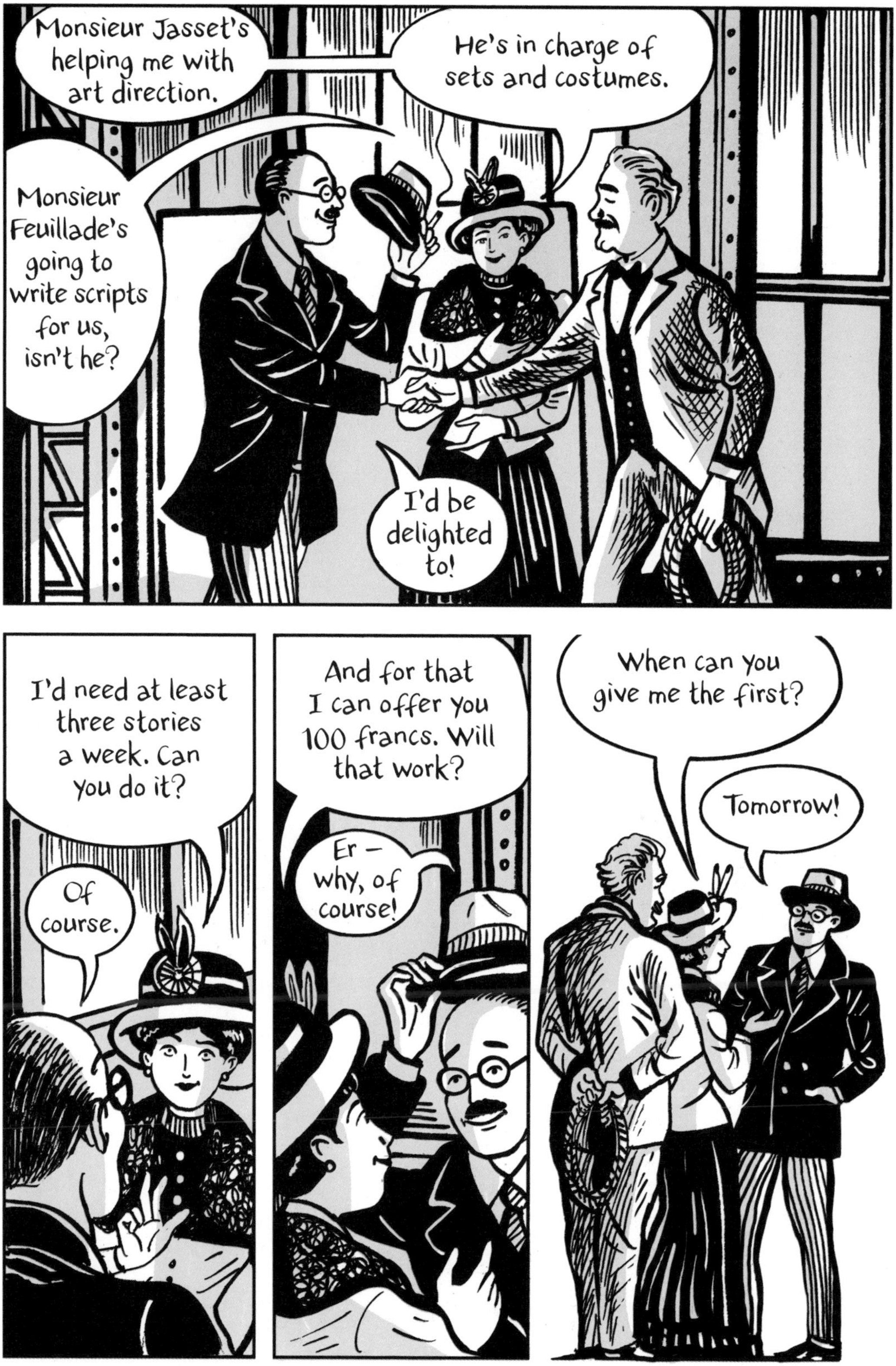
Monsieur Jasset's helping me with art direction.
He's in charge of sets and costumes.
Monsieur Feuillade's going to write scripts for us, isn't he?
I'd be delighted to!
I'd need at least three stories a week. Can you do it?
Of course.
And for that I can offer you 100 francs. Will that work?
Er – why, of course!
When can you give me the first?
Tomorrow!

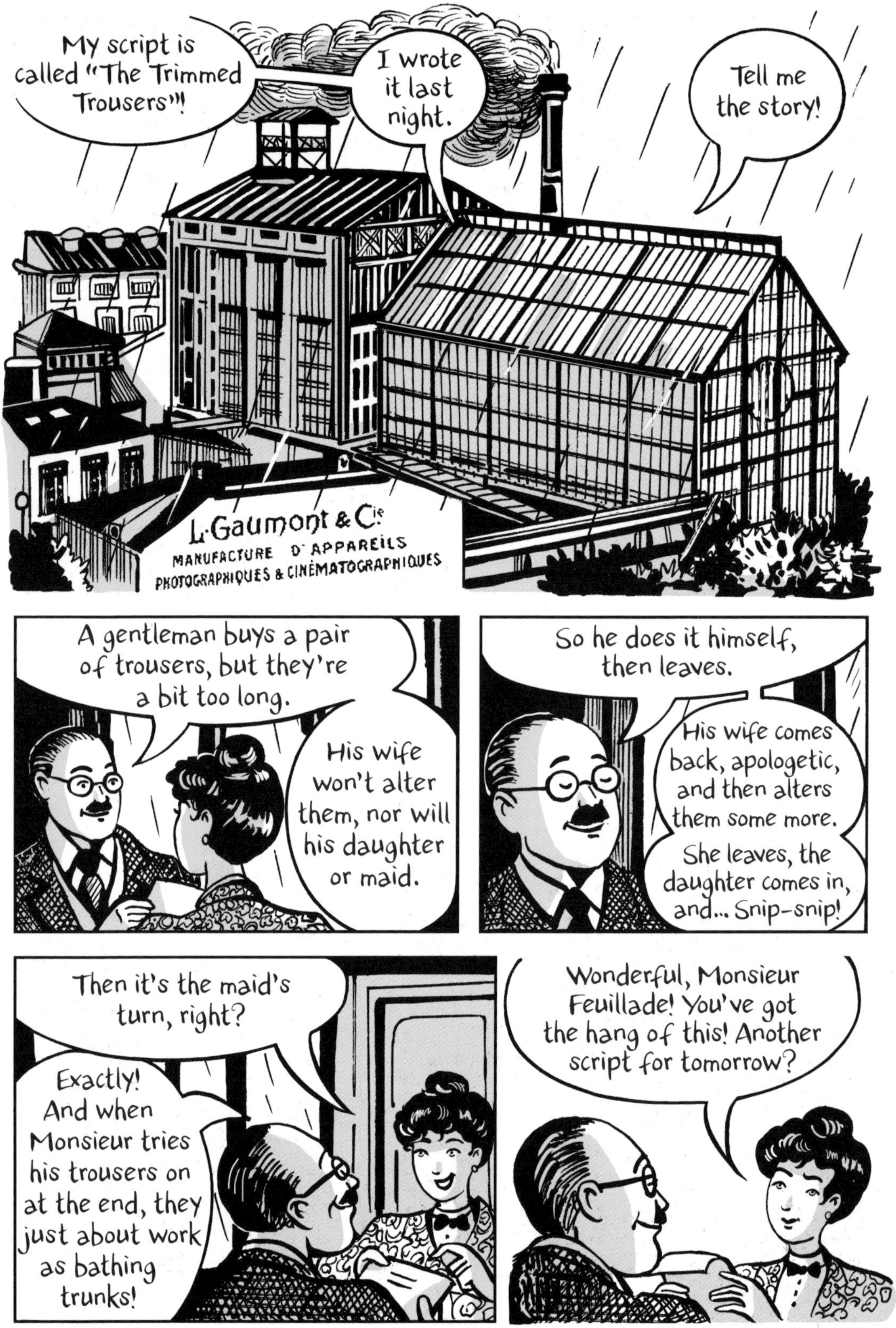
My script is called "The Trimmed Trousers"!
I wrote it last night.
Tell me the story!
L. Gaumont & Cie
MANUFACTURE D' APPAREILS PHOTOGRAPHIQUES & CINÉMATOGRAPHIQUES
A gentleman buys a pair of trousers, but they're a bit too long.
His wife won't alter them, nor will his daughter or maid.
So he does it himself, then leaves.
His wife comes back, apologetic, and then alters them some more.
She leaves, the daughter comes in, and... Snip-snip!
Then it's the maid's turn, right?
Exactly! And when Monsieur tries his trousers on at the end, they just about work as bathing trunks!
Wonderful, Monsieur Feuillade! You've got the hang of this! Another script for tomorrow?

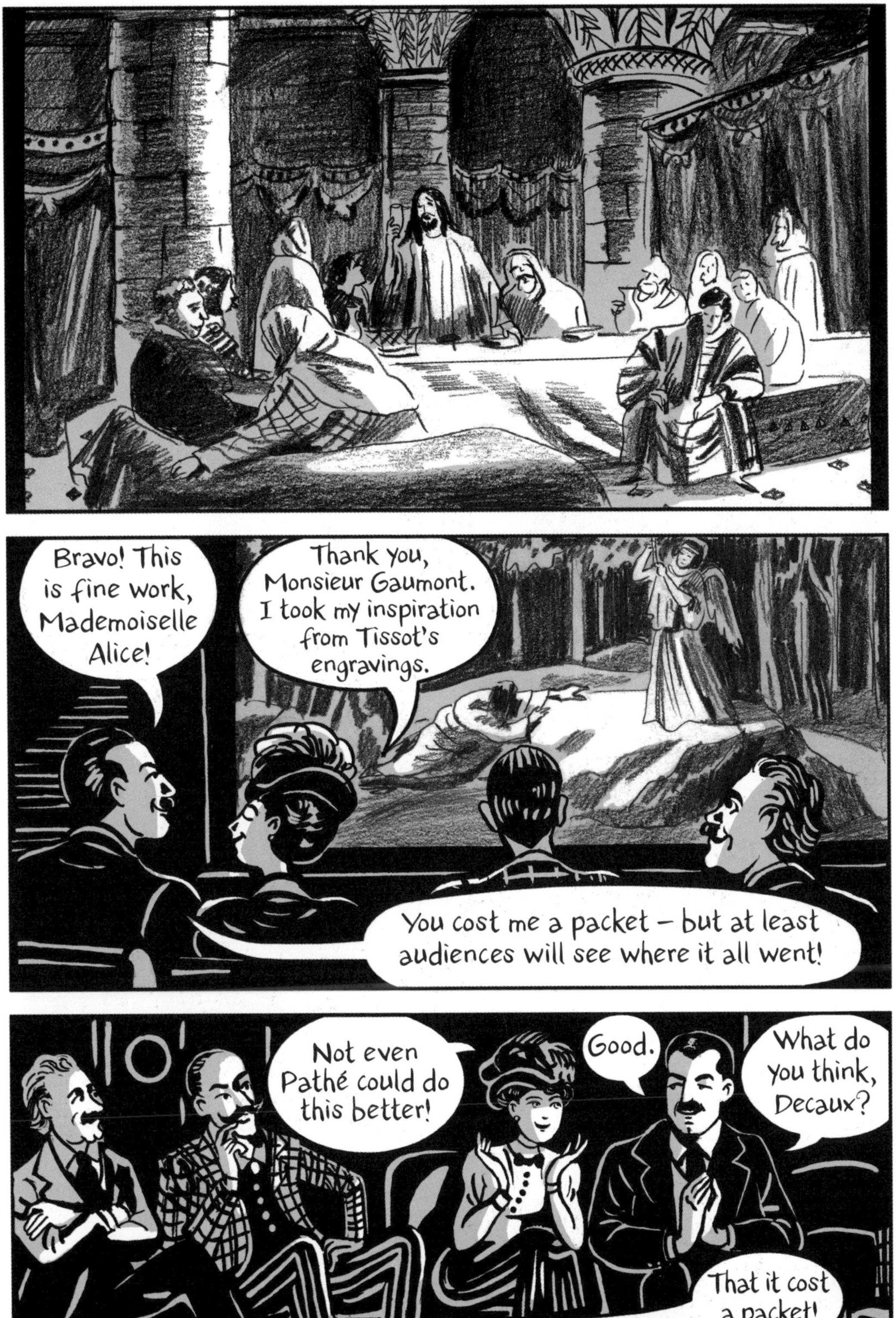

Bravo! This is fine work, Mademoiselle Alice!
Thank you, Monsieur Gaumont. I took my inspiration from Tissot's engravings.
You cost me a packet – but at least audiences will see where it all went!
Not even Pathé could do this better!
Good.
What do you think, Decaux?
That it cost a packet!

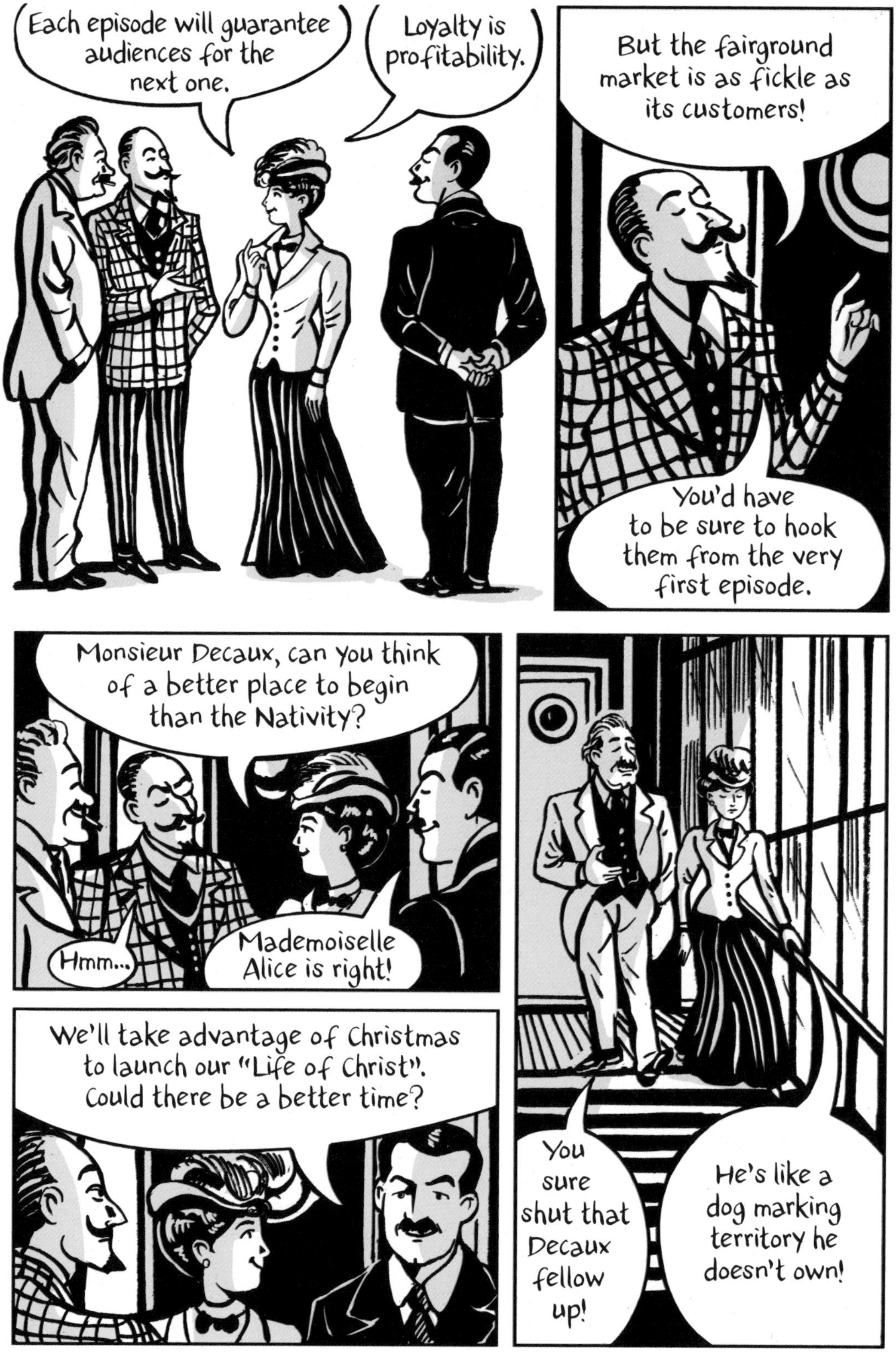
Each episode will guarantee audiences for the next one.
Loyalty is profitability.
But the fairground market is as fickle as its customers!
You'd have to be sure to hook them from the very first episode.
Monsieur Decaux, can you think of a better place to begin than the Nativity?
Hmm...
Mademoiselle Alice is right!
We'll take advantage of Christmas to launch our "Life of Christ". Could there be a better time?
You sure shut that Decaux fellow up!
He's like a dog marking territory he doesn't own!

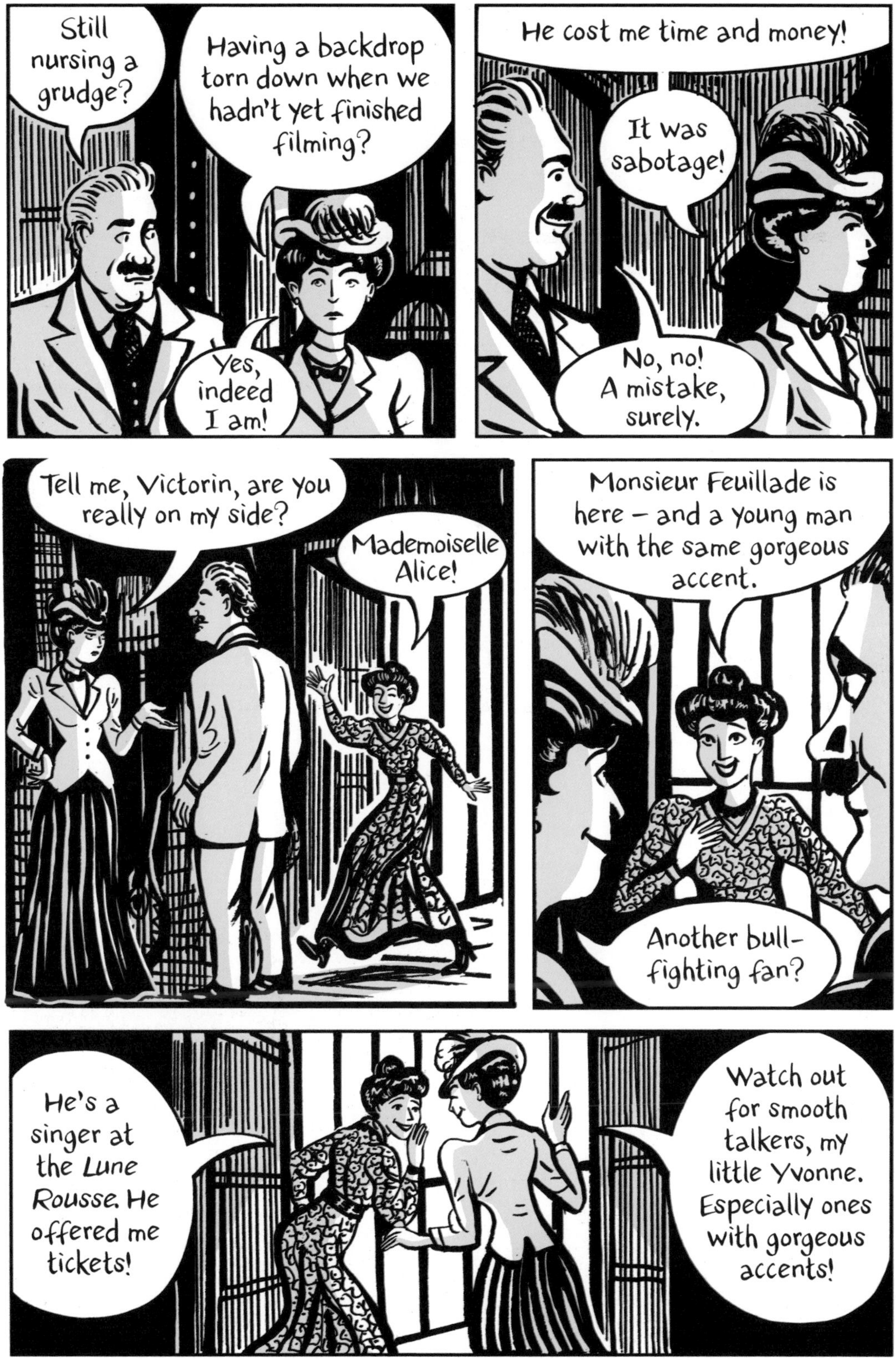
Still nursing a grudge?
Having a backdrop torn down when we hadn't yet finished filming?
Yes, indeed I am!
He cost me time and money!
It was sabotage!
No, no! A mistake, surely.
Tell me, Victorin, are you really on my side?
Mademoiselle Alice!
Monsieur Feuillade is here – and a young man with the same gorgeous accent.
Another bull-fighting fan?
He's a singer at the *Lune Rousse*. He offered me tickets!
Watch out for smooth talkers, my little Yvonne. Especially ones with gorgeous accents!

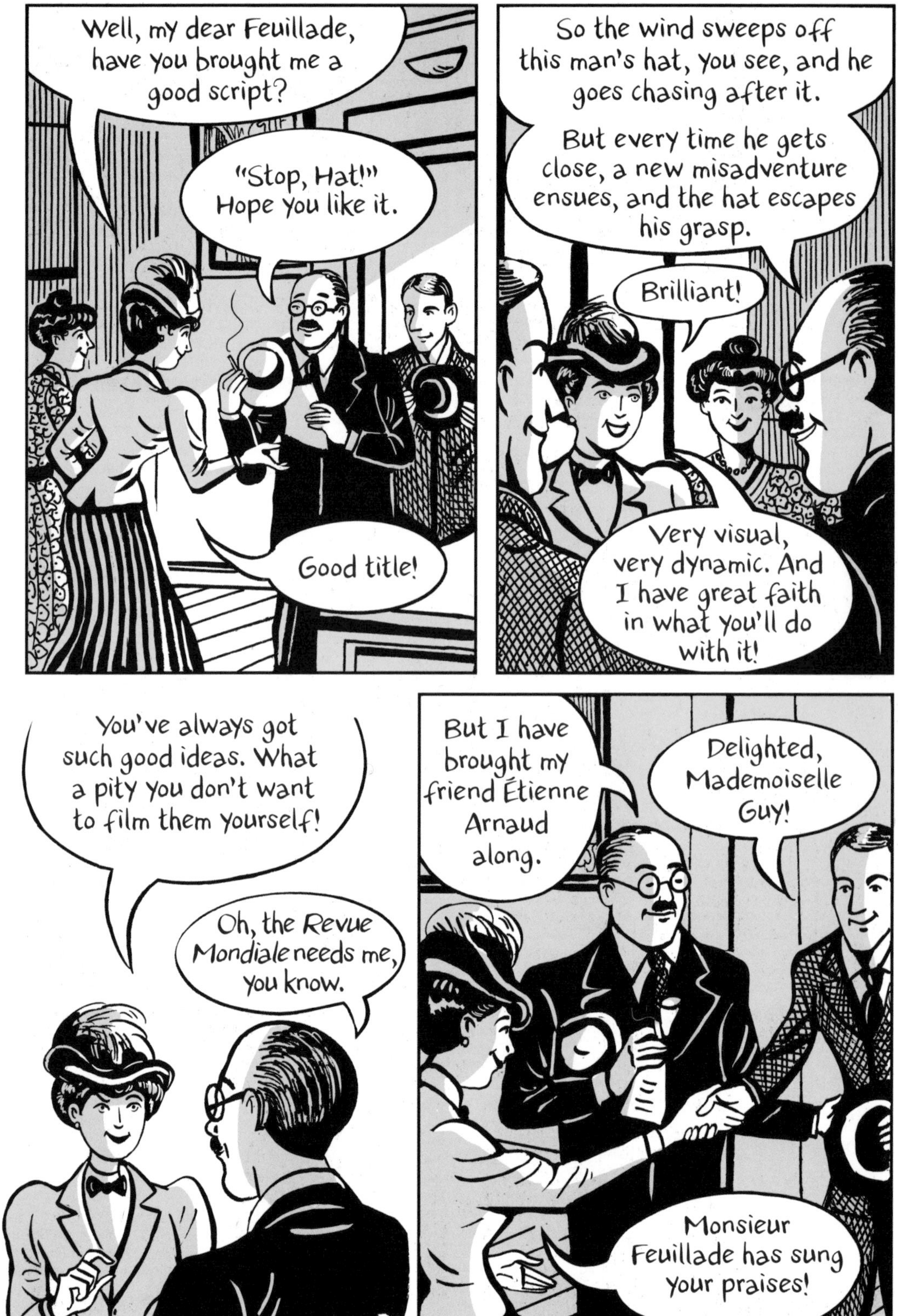
Well, my dear Feuillade, have you brought me a good script?
"Stop, Hat!" Hope you like it.
Good title!
So the wind sweeps off this man's hat, you see, and he goes chasing after it.
But every time he gets close, a new misadventure ensues, and the hat escapes his grasp.
Brilliant!
Very visual, very dynamic. And I have great faith in what you'll do with it!
You've always got such good ideas. What a pity you don't want to film them yourself!
Oh, the *Revue Mondiale* needs me, you know.
But I have brought my friend Étienne Arnaud along.
Delighted, Mademoiselle Guy!
Monsieur Feuillade has sung your praises!

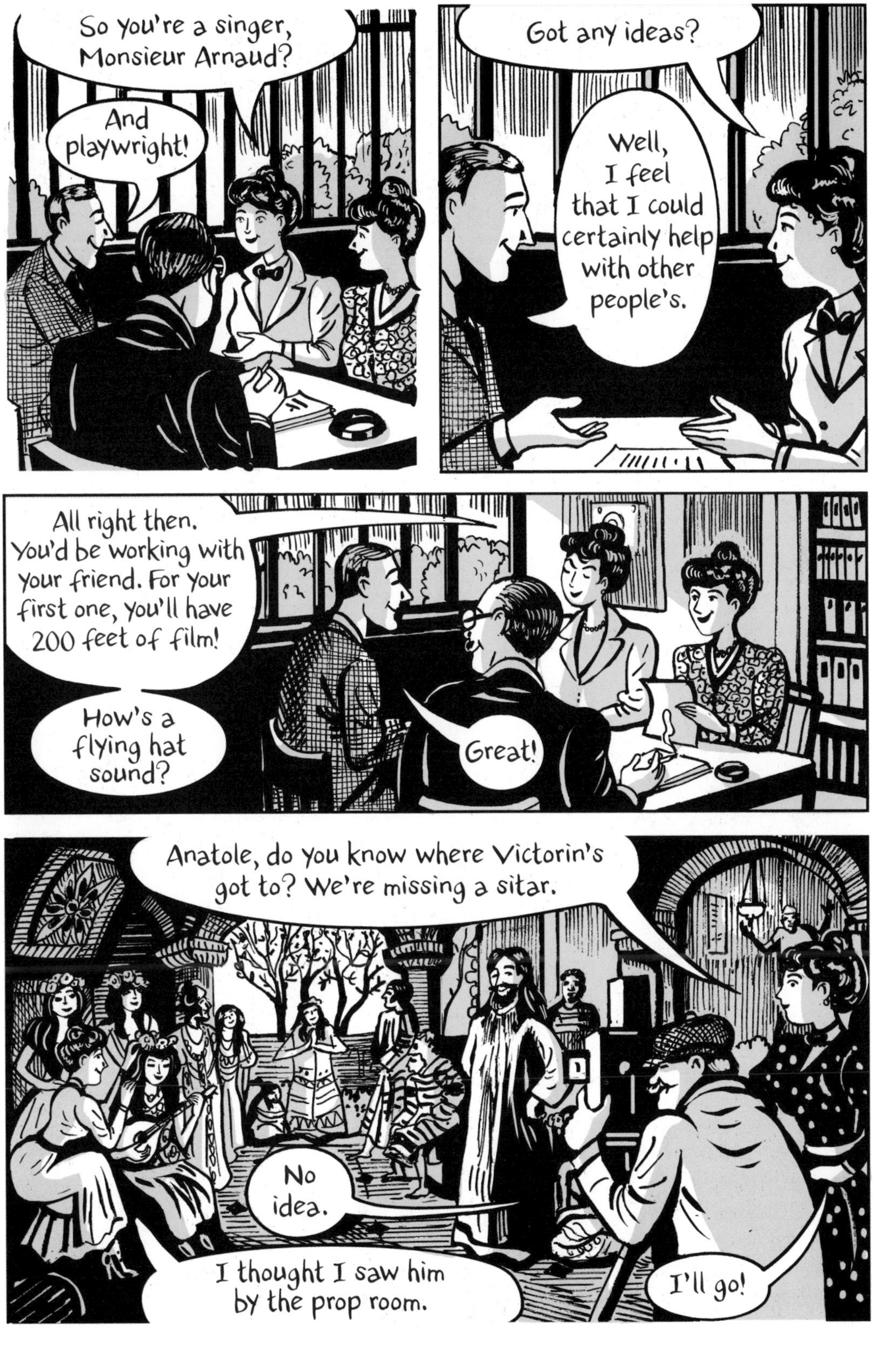
So you're a singer, Monsieur Arnaud?
And playwright!
Got any ideas?
Well, I feel that I could certainly help with other people's.
All right then. You'd be working with your friend. For your first one, you'll have 200 feet of film!
How's a flying hat sound?
Great!
Anatole, do you know where Victorin's got to? We're missing a sitar.
No idea.
I thought I saw him by the prop room.
I'll go!

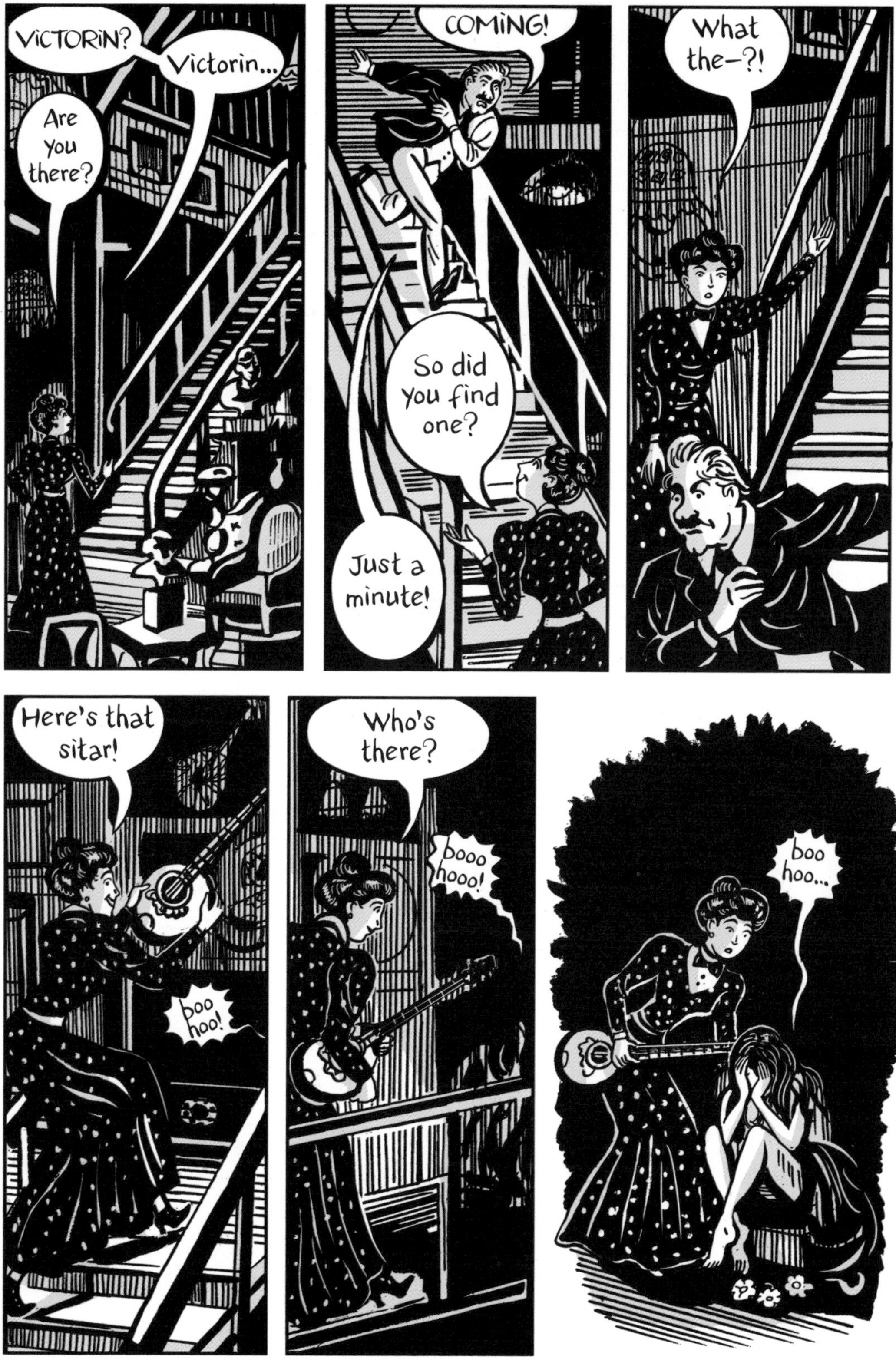
VICTORIN?
Victorin...
Are you there?
COMING!
So did you find one?
Just a minute!
What the–?!
Here's that sitar!
boo hoo!
Who's there?
booo hooo!
boo hoo...

1906 – L'Amarée – Saintes-Maries-de-la-Mer – France

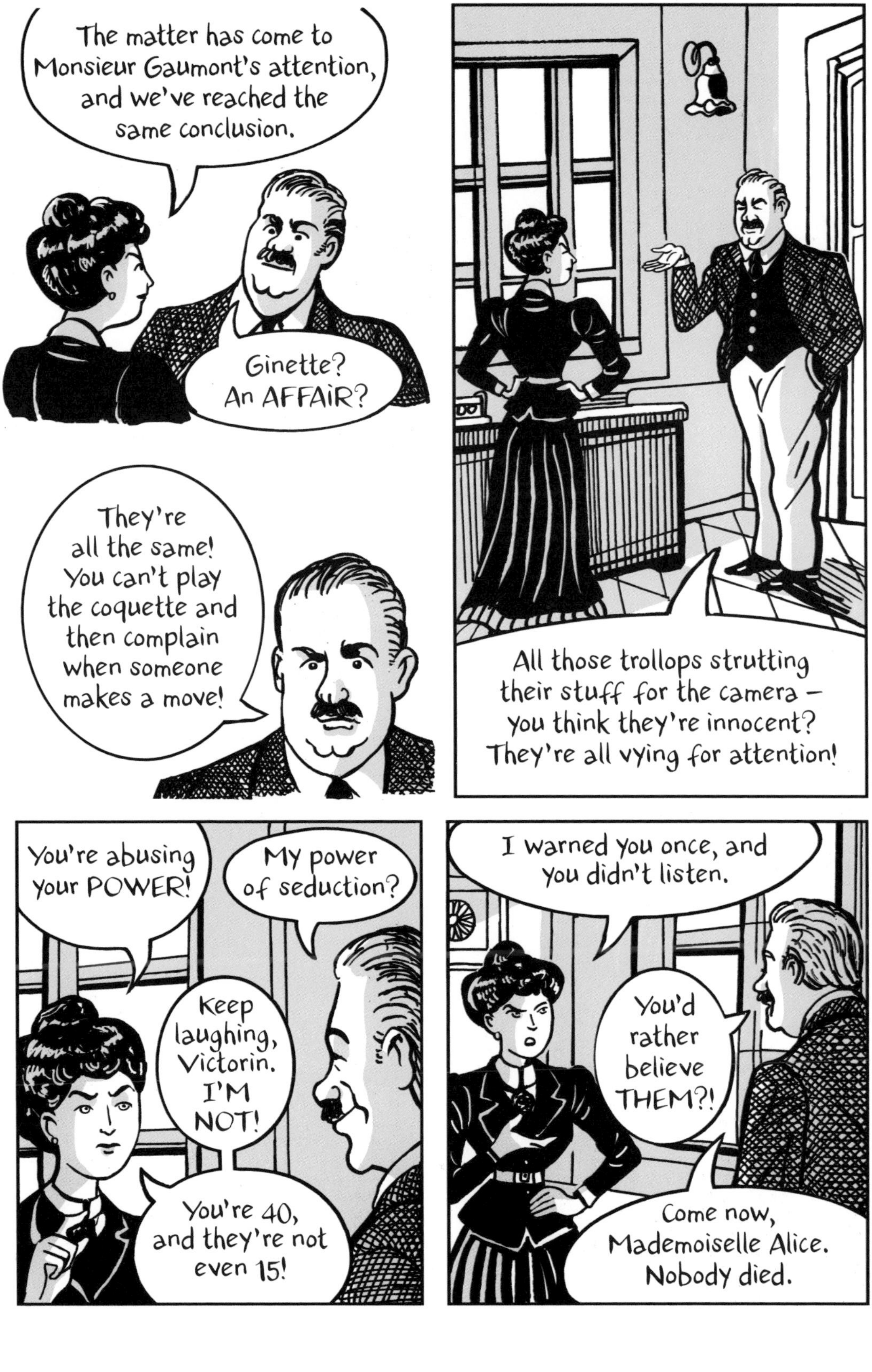
The matter has come to Monsieur Gaumont's attention, and we've reached the same conclusion.
Ginette? An AFFAIR?
They're all the same! You can't play the coquette and then complain when someone makes a move!
All those trollops strutting their stuff for the camera – you think they're innocent? They're all vying for attention!
You're abusing your POWER!
My power of seduction?
Keep laughing, Victorin. I'M NOT!
You're 40, and they're not even 15!
I warned you once, and you didn't listen.
You'd rather believe THEM?!
Come now, Mademoiselle Alice. Nobody died.

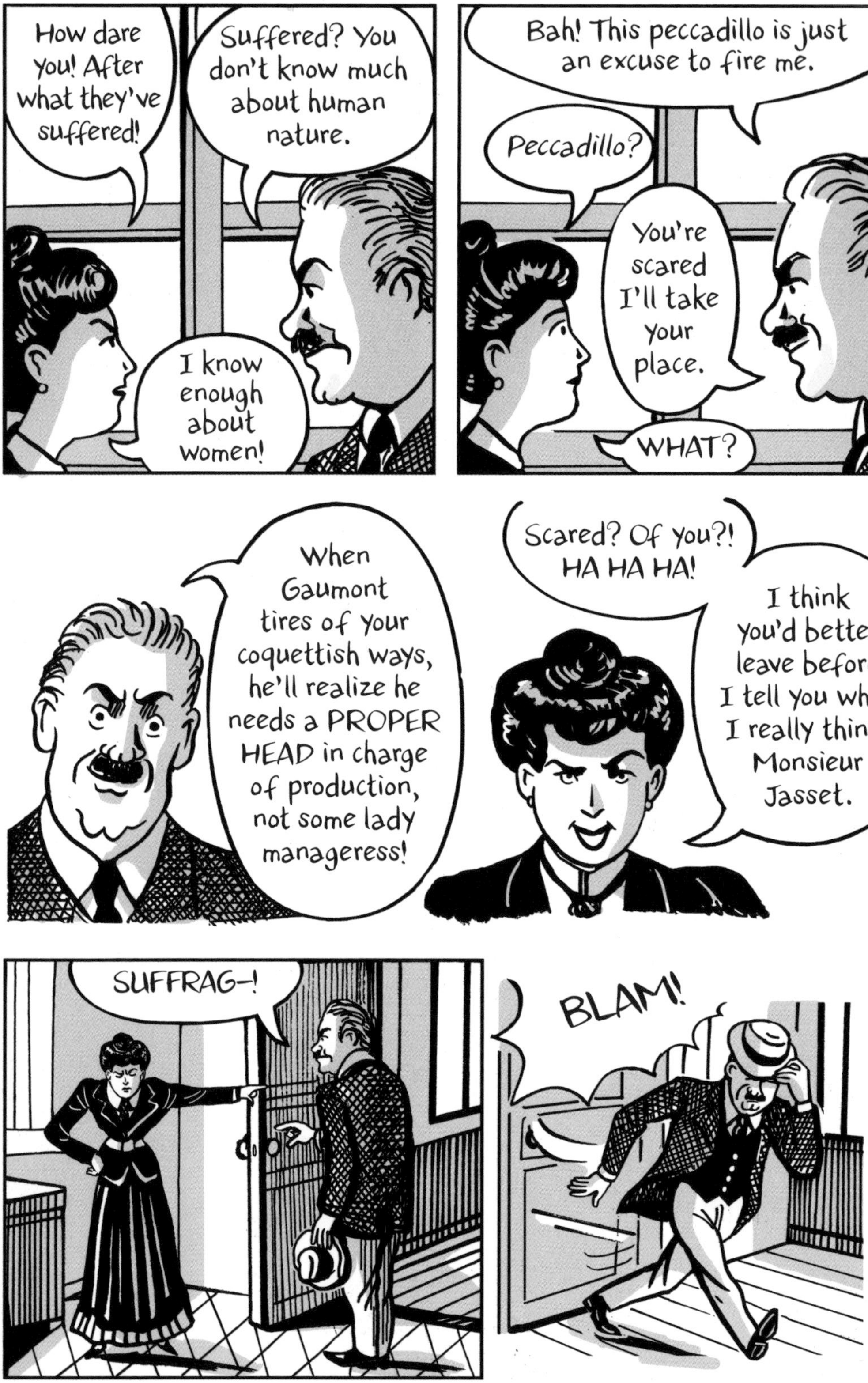
How dare you! After what they've suffered!
Suffered? You don't know much about human nature.
I know enough about women!
Bah! This peccadillo is just an excuse to fire me.
Peccadillo?
You're scared I'll take your place.
WHAT?
When Gaumont tires of your coquettish ways, he'll realize he needs a PROPER HEAD in charge of production, not some lady manageress!
Scared? Of you?! HA HA HA!
I think you'd better leave before I tell you what I really think, Monsieur Jasset.
SUFFRAG–!
BLAM!

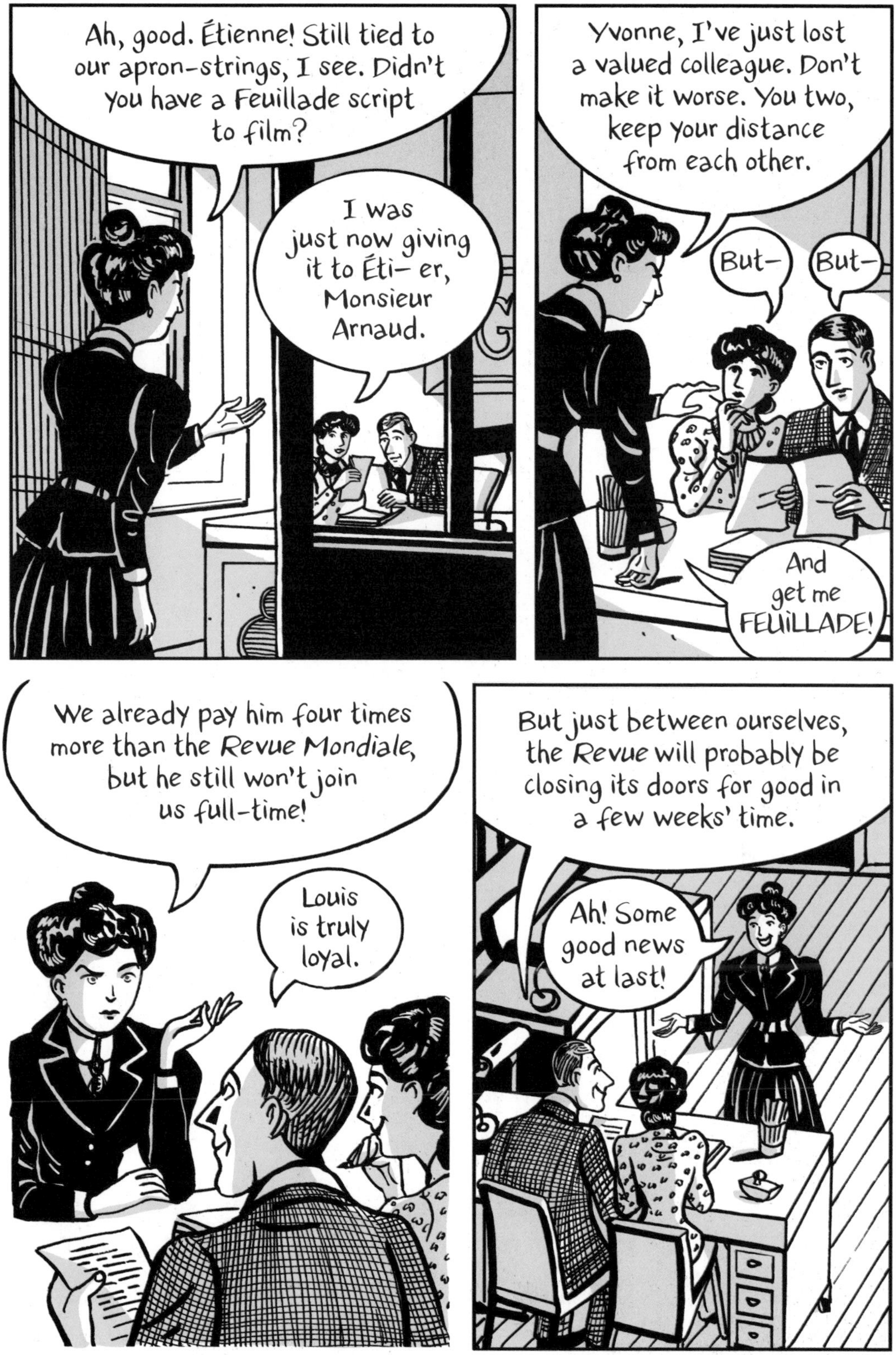

Ah, good. Étienne! Still tied to our apron-strings, I see. Didn't you have a Feuillade script to film?
I was just now giving it to Éti- er, Monsieur Arnaud.
Yvonne, I've just lost a valued colleague. Don't make it worse. You two, keep your distance from each other.
But-
But-
And get me FEUILLADE!
We already pay him four times more than the *Revue Mondiale*, but he still won't join us full-time!
Louis is truly loyal.
But just between ourselves, the *Revue* will probably be closing its doors for good in a few weeks' time.
Ah! Some good news at last!

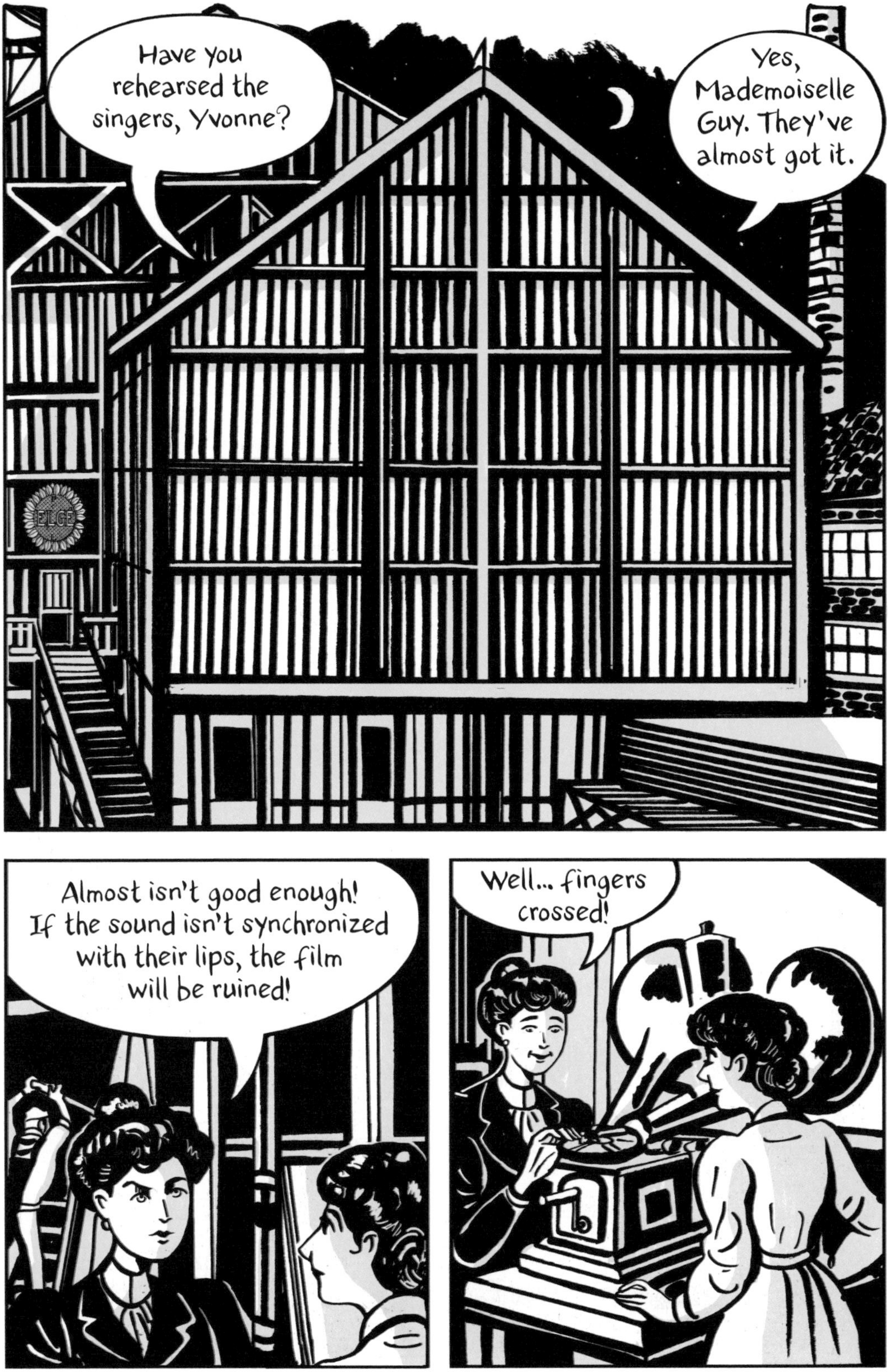
Have you rehearsed the singers, Yvonne?
Yes, Mademoiselle Guy. They've almost got it.
ELGE
Almost isn't good enough! If the sound isn't synchronized with their lips, the film will be ruined!
Well... fingers crossed!

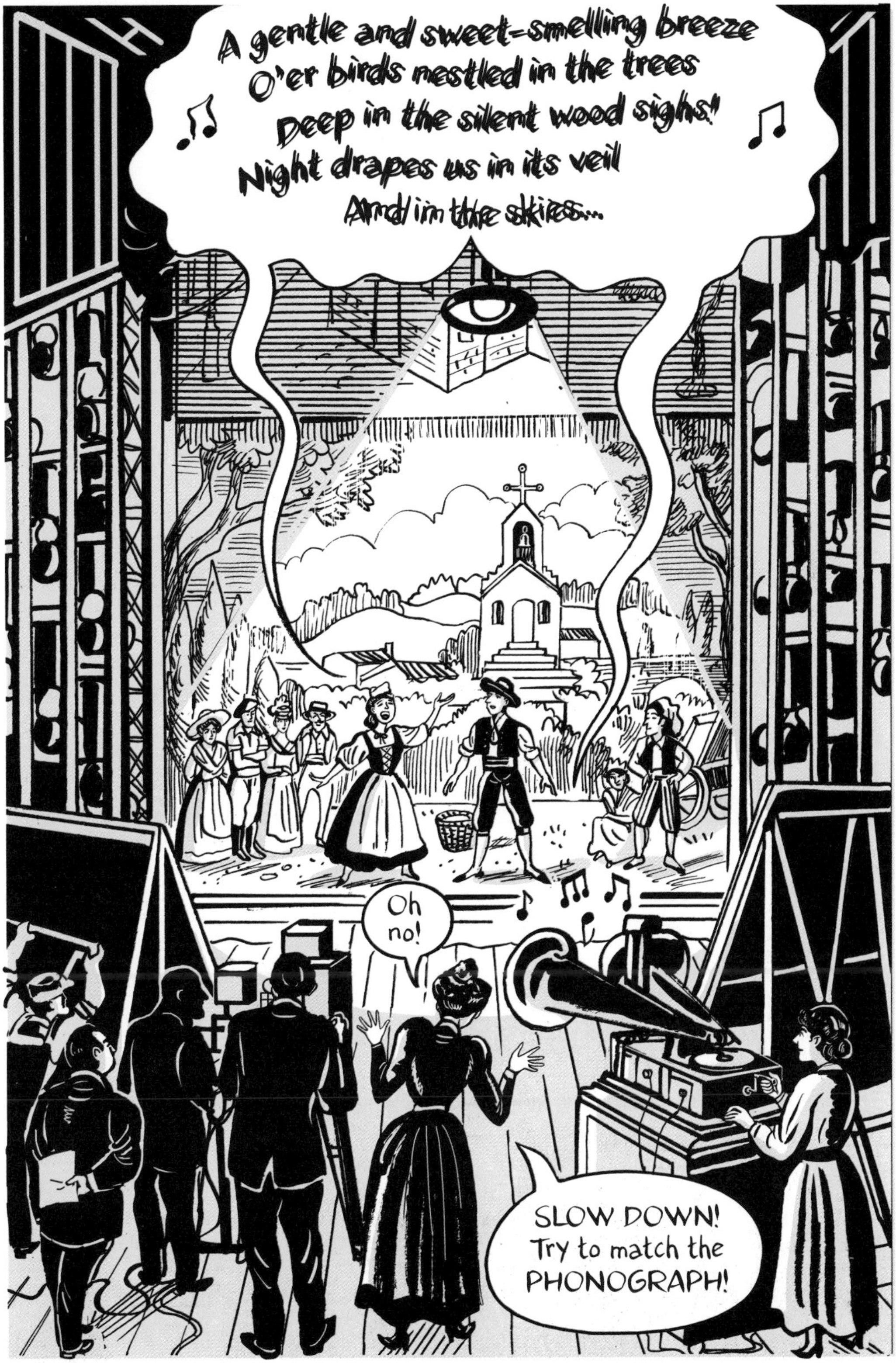
A gentle and sweet-smelling breeze
O'er birds nestled in the trees
Deep in the silent wood sighs!"
Night drapes us in its veil
And in the skies...
Oh no!
SLOW DOWN! Try to match the PHONOGRAPH!

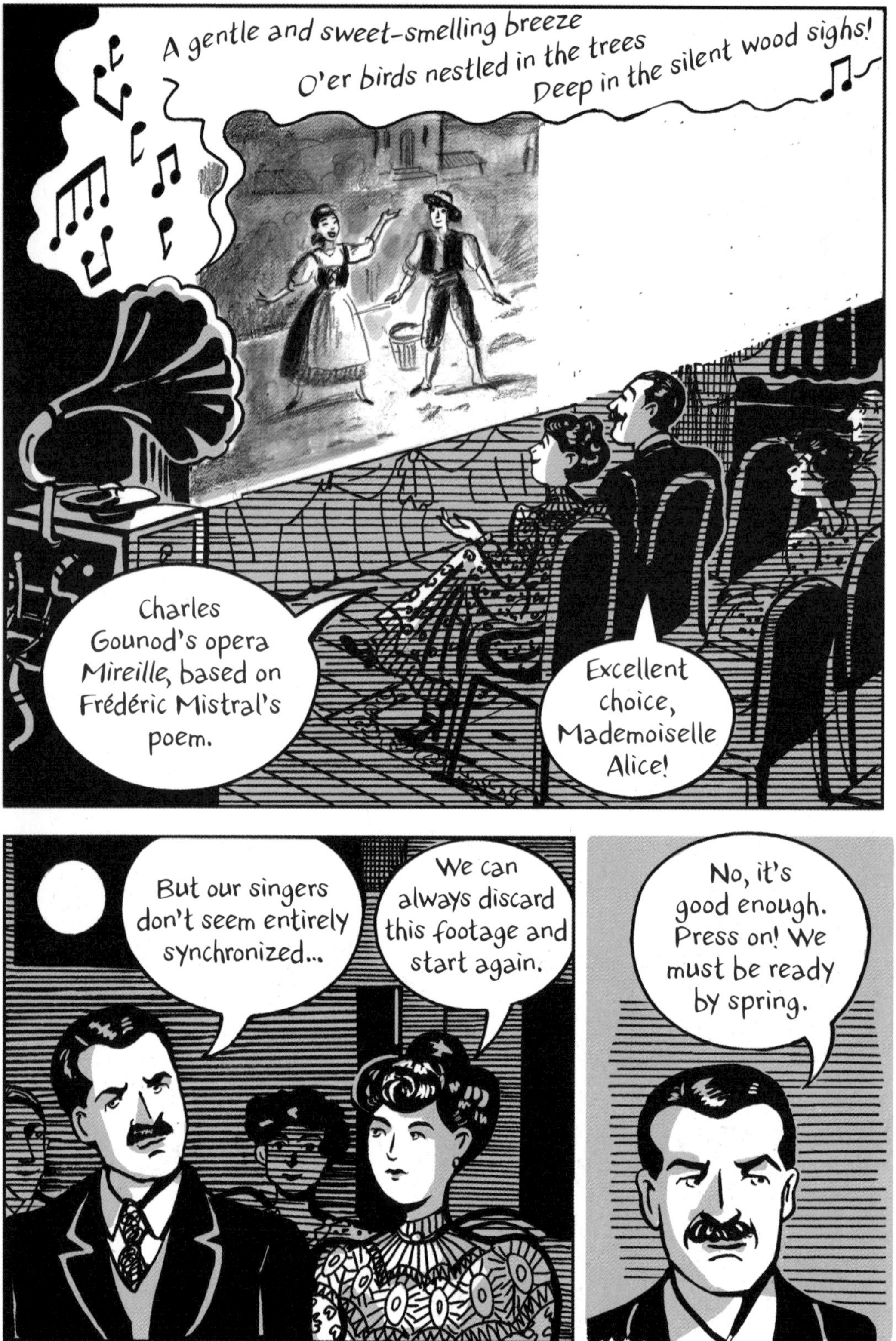
A gentle and sweet-smelling breeze
O'er birds nestled in the trees
Deep in the silent wood sighs!
Charles Gounod's opera Mireille, based on Frédéric Mistral's poem.
Excellent choice, Mademoiselle Alice!
But our singers don't seem entirely synchronized...
We can always discard this footage and start again.
No, it's good enough. Press on! We must be ready by spring.

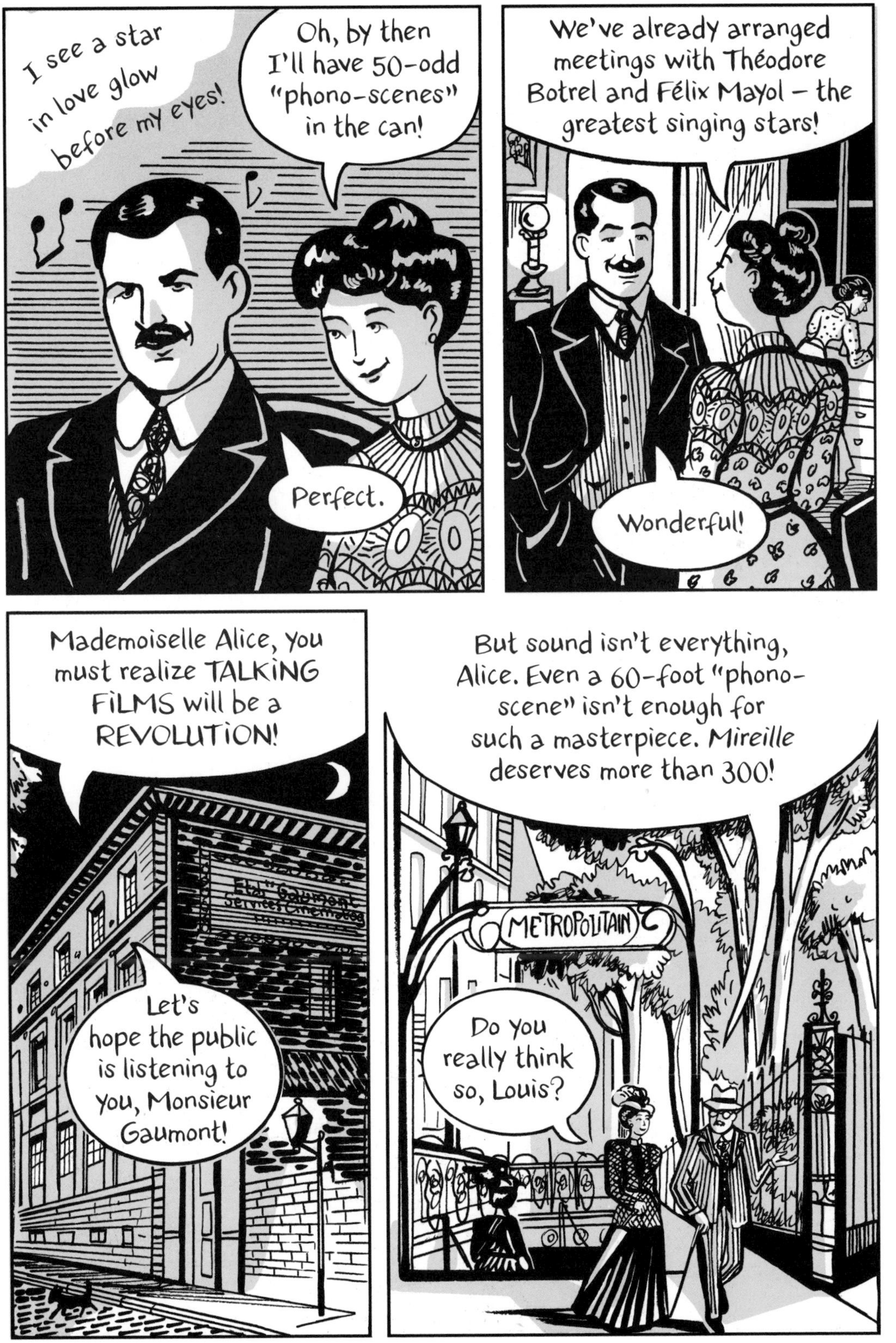
I see a star in love glow before my eyes!
Oh, by then I'll have 50-odd "phono-scenes" in the can!
Perfect.
We've already arranged meetings with Théodore Botrel and Félix Mayol – the greatest singing stars!
Wonderful!
Mademoiselle Alice, you must realize TALKING FILMS will be a REVOLUTION!
Let's hope the public is listening to you, Monsieur Gaumont!
But sound isn't everything, Alice. Even a 60-foot "phono-scene" isn't enough for such a masterpiece. Mireille deserves more than 300!
METROPOLITAIN
Do you really think so, Louis?

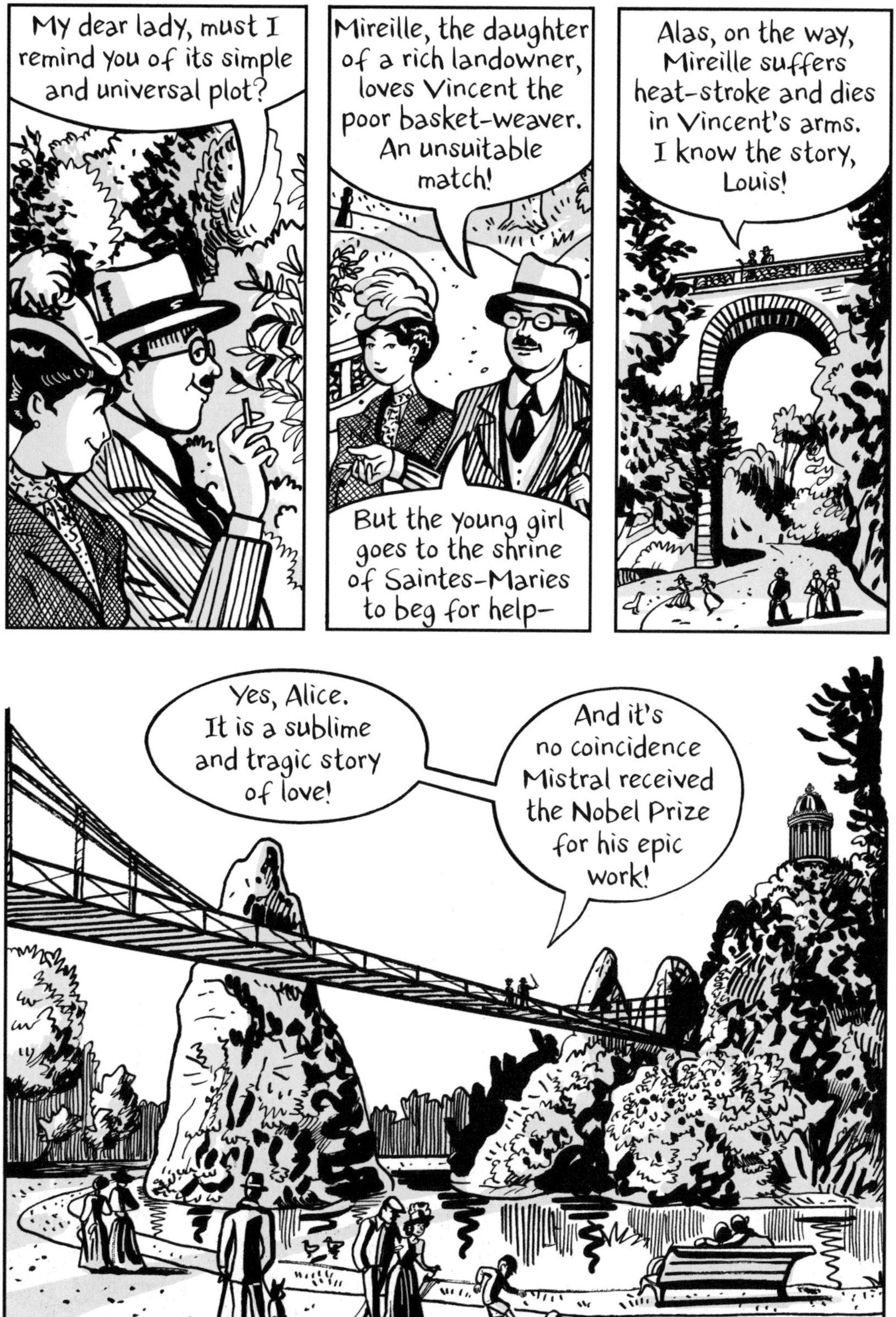
My dear lady, must I remind you of its simple and universal plot?
Mireille, the daughter of a rich landowner, loves Vincent the poor basket-weaver. An unsuitable match!
But the young girl goes to the shrine of Saintes-Maries to beg for help–
Alas, on the way, Mireille suffers heat-stroke and dies in Vincent's arms. I know the story, Louis!
Yes, Alice. It is a sublime and tragic story of love!
And it's no coincidence Mistral received the Nobel Prize for his epic work!

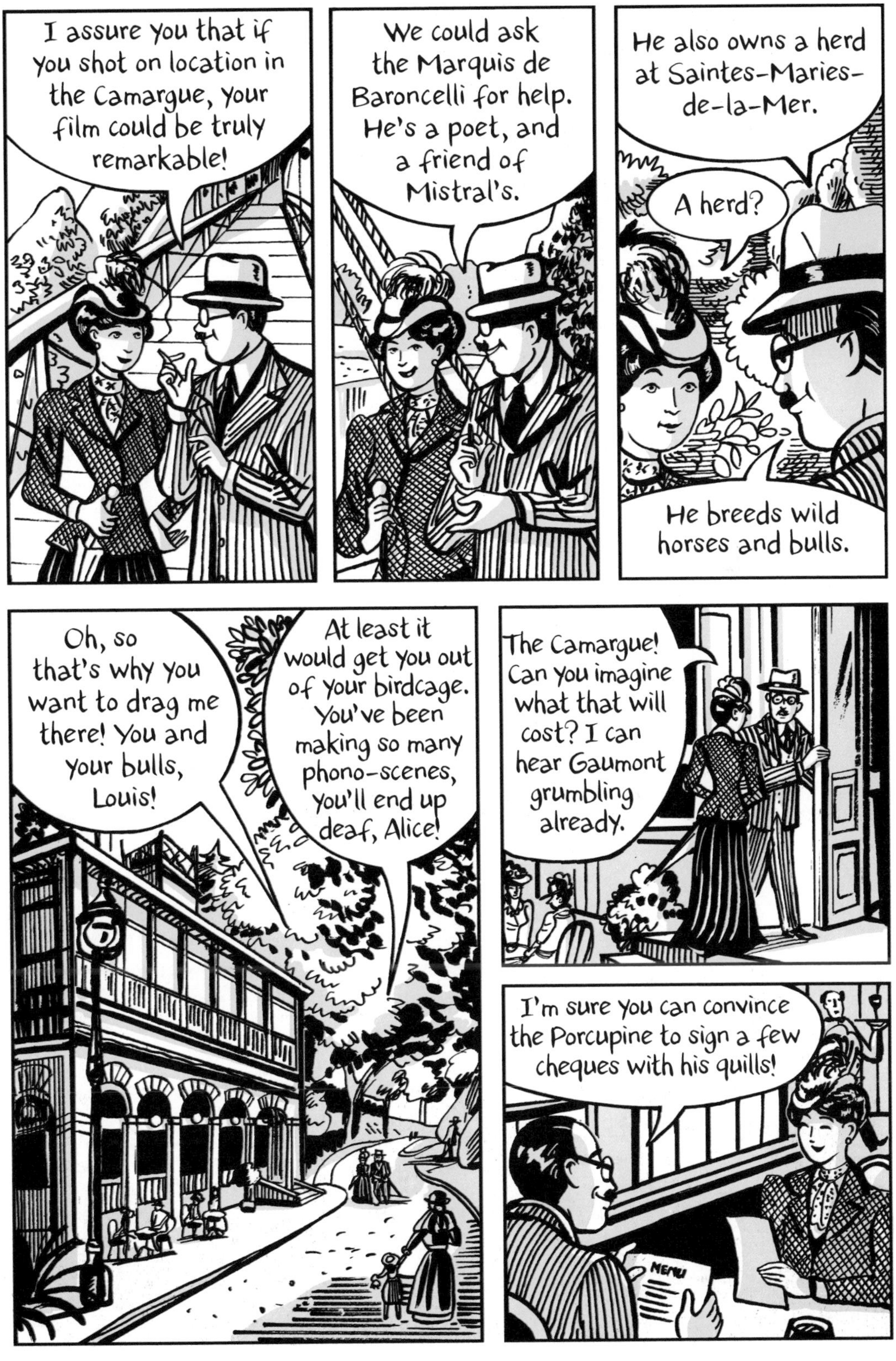
I assure you that if you shot on location in the Camargue, your film could be truly remarkable!
We could ask the Marquis de Baroncelli for help. He's a poet, and a friend of Mistral's.
He also owns a herd at Saintes-Maries-de-la-Mer.
A herd?
He breeds wild horses and bulls.
Oh, so that's why you want to drag me there! You and your bulls, Louis!
At least it would get you out of your birdcage. You've been making so many phono-scenes, you'll end up deaf, Alice!
The Camargue! Can you imagine what that will cost? I can hear Gaumont grumbling already.
I'm sure you can convince the Porcupine to sign a few cheques with his quills!
MENU

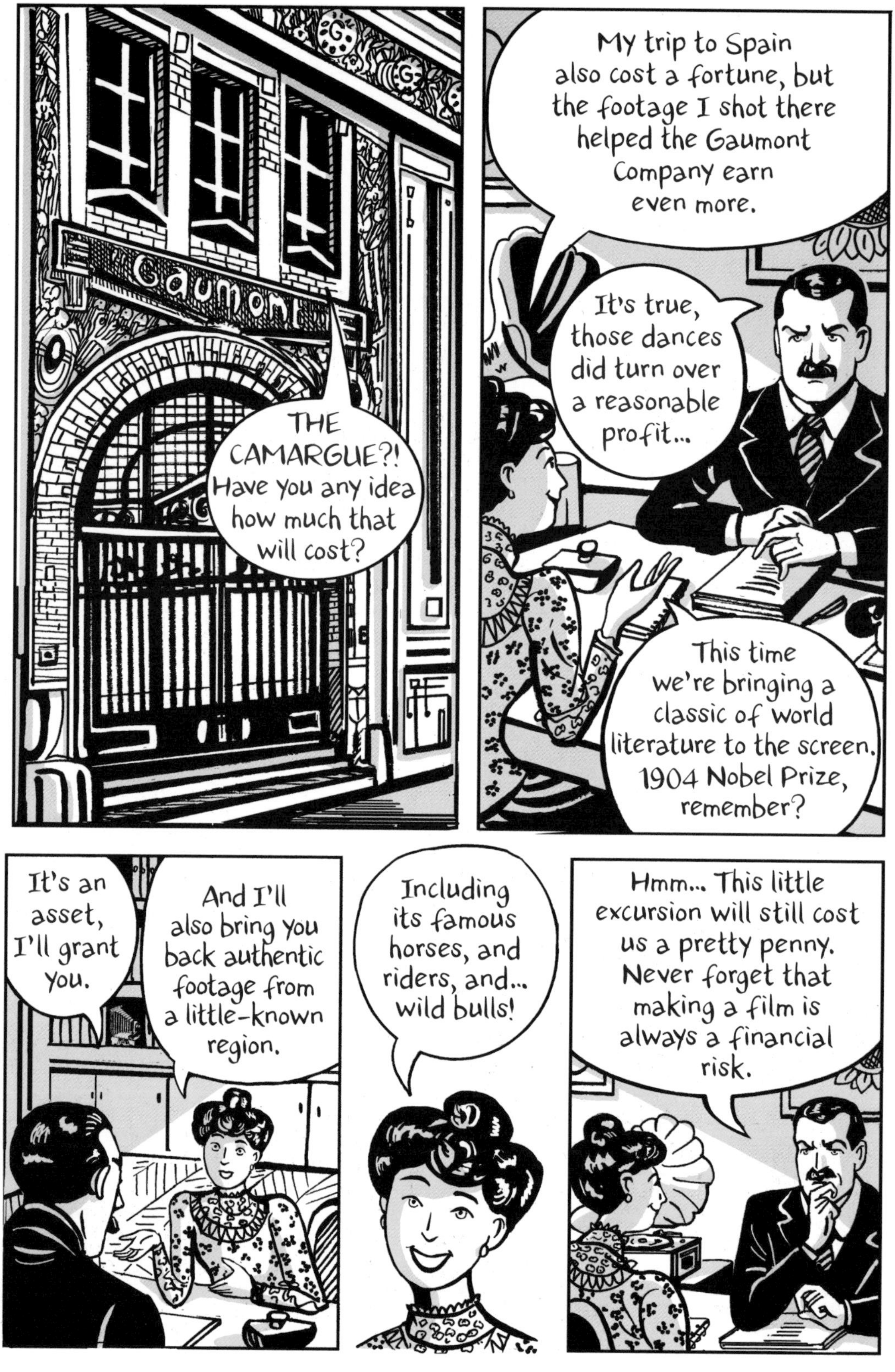
Gaumont
THE CAMARGUE?! Have you any idea how much that will cost?
My trip to Spain also cost a fortune, but the footage I shot there helped the Gaumont Company earn even more.
It's true, those dances did turn over a reasonable profit...
This time we're bringing a classic of world literature to the screen. 1904 Nobel Prize, remember?
It's an asset, I'll grant you.
And I'll also bring you back authentic footage from a little-known region.
Including its famous horses, and riders, and... wild bulls!
Hmm... This little excursion will still cost us a pretty penny. Never forget that making a film is always a financial risk.

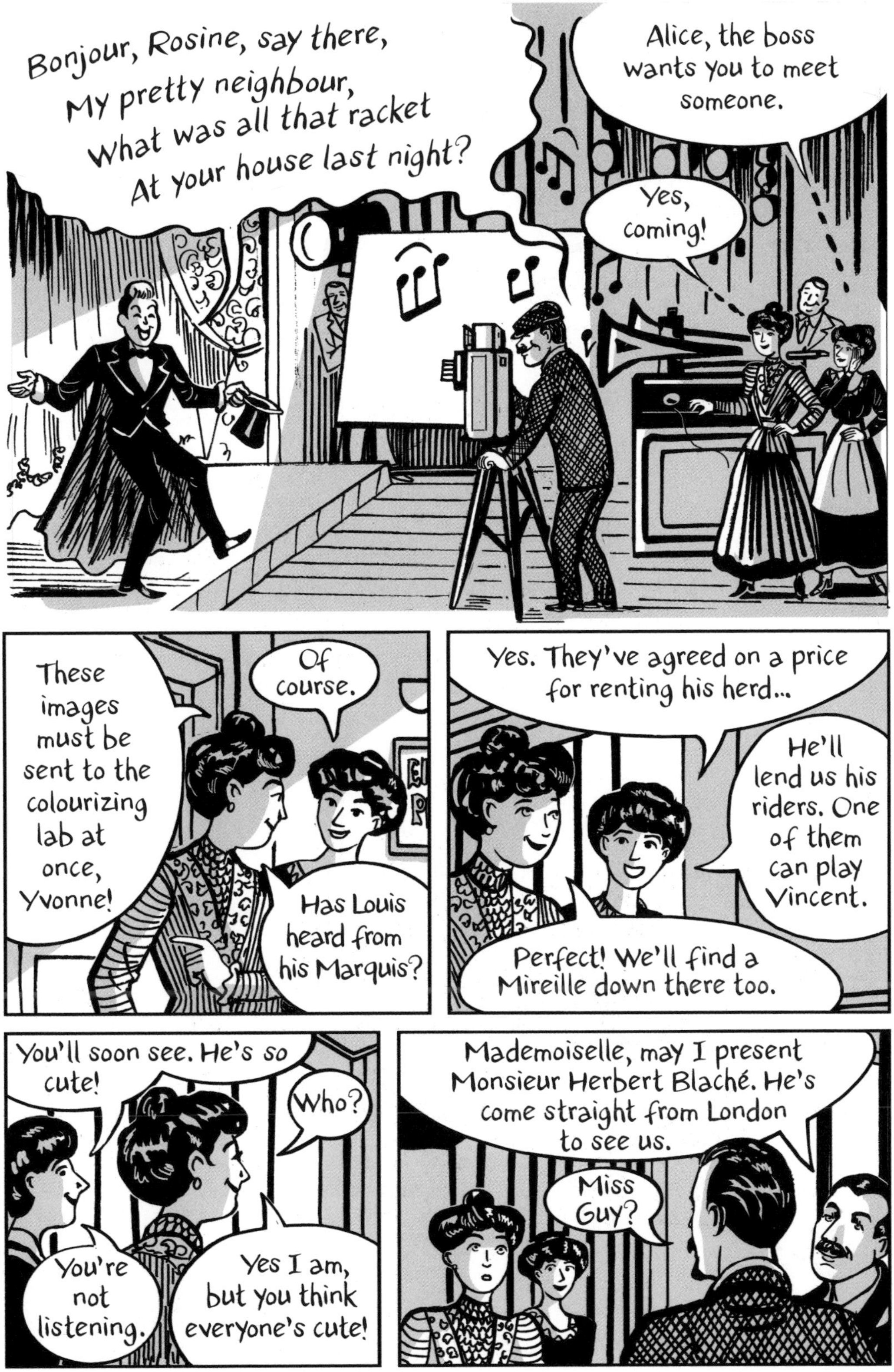

Bonjour, Rosine, say there, My pretty neighbour, What was all that racket At your house last night?
Alice, the boss wants you to meet someone.
Yes, coming!
These images must be sent to the colourizing lab at once, Yvonne!
Of course.
Has Louis heard from his Marquis?
Yes. They've agreed on a price for renting his herd...
He'll lend us his riders. One of them can play Vincent.
Perfect! We'll find a Mireille down there too.
You'll soon see. He's so cute!
Who?
You're not listening.
Yes I am, but you think everyone's cute!
Mademoiselle, may I present Monsieur Herbert Blaché. He's come straight from London to see us.
Miss Guy?

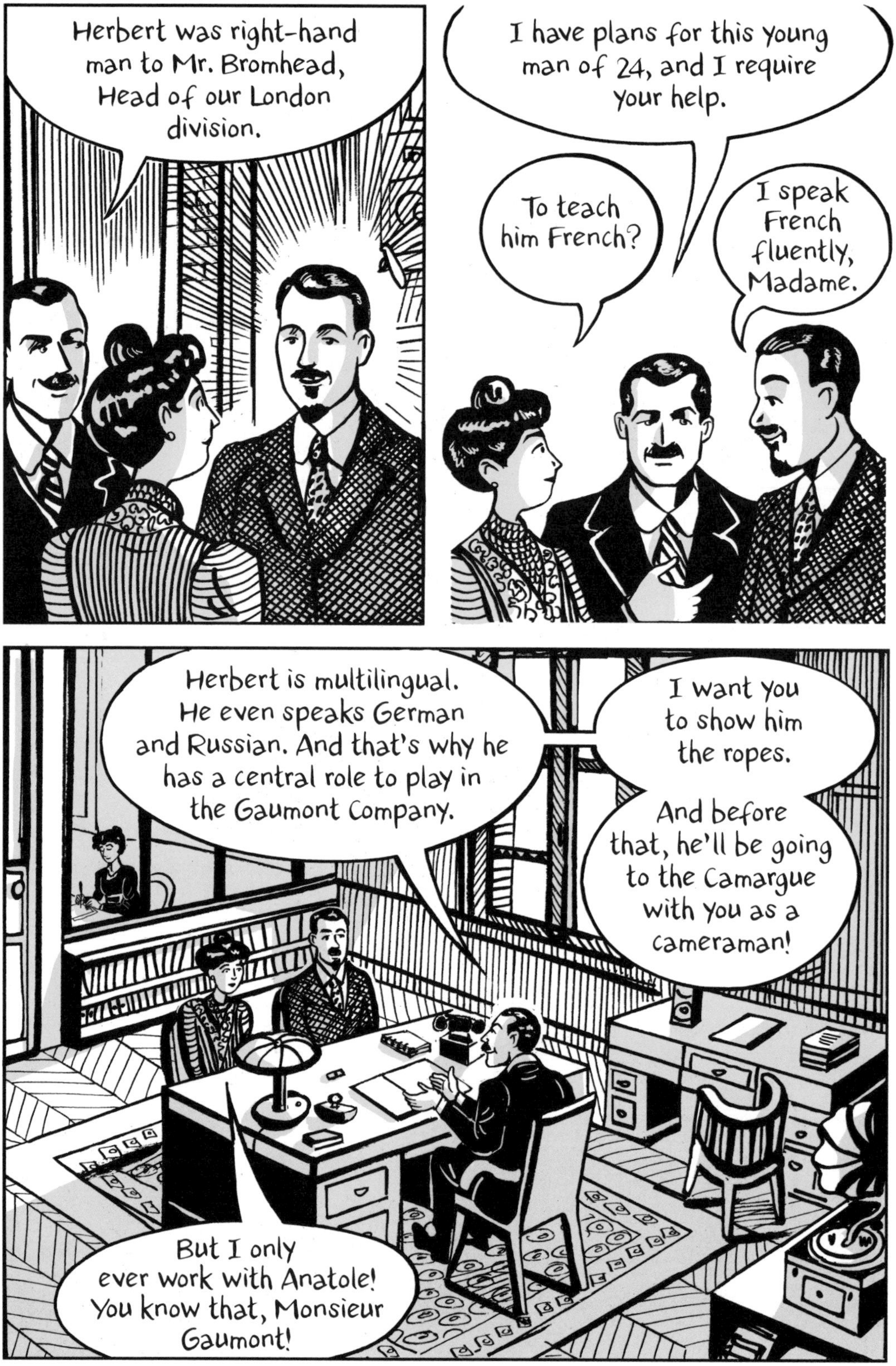
Herbert was right-hand man to Mr. Bromhead, Head of our London division.
I have plans for this young man of 24, and I require your help.
To teach him French?
I speak French fluently, Madame.
Herbert is multilingual. He even speaks German and Russian. And that's why he has a central role to play in the Gaumont Company.
I want you to show him the ropes.
And before that, he'll be going to the Camargue with you as a cameraman!
But I only ever work with Anatole! You know that, Monsieur Gaumont!

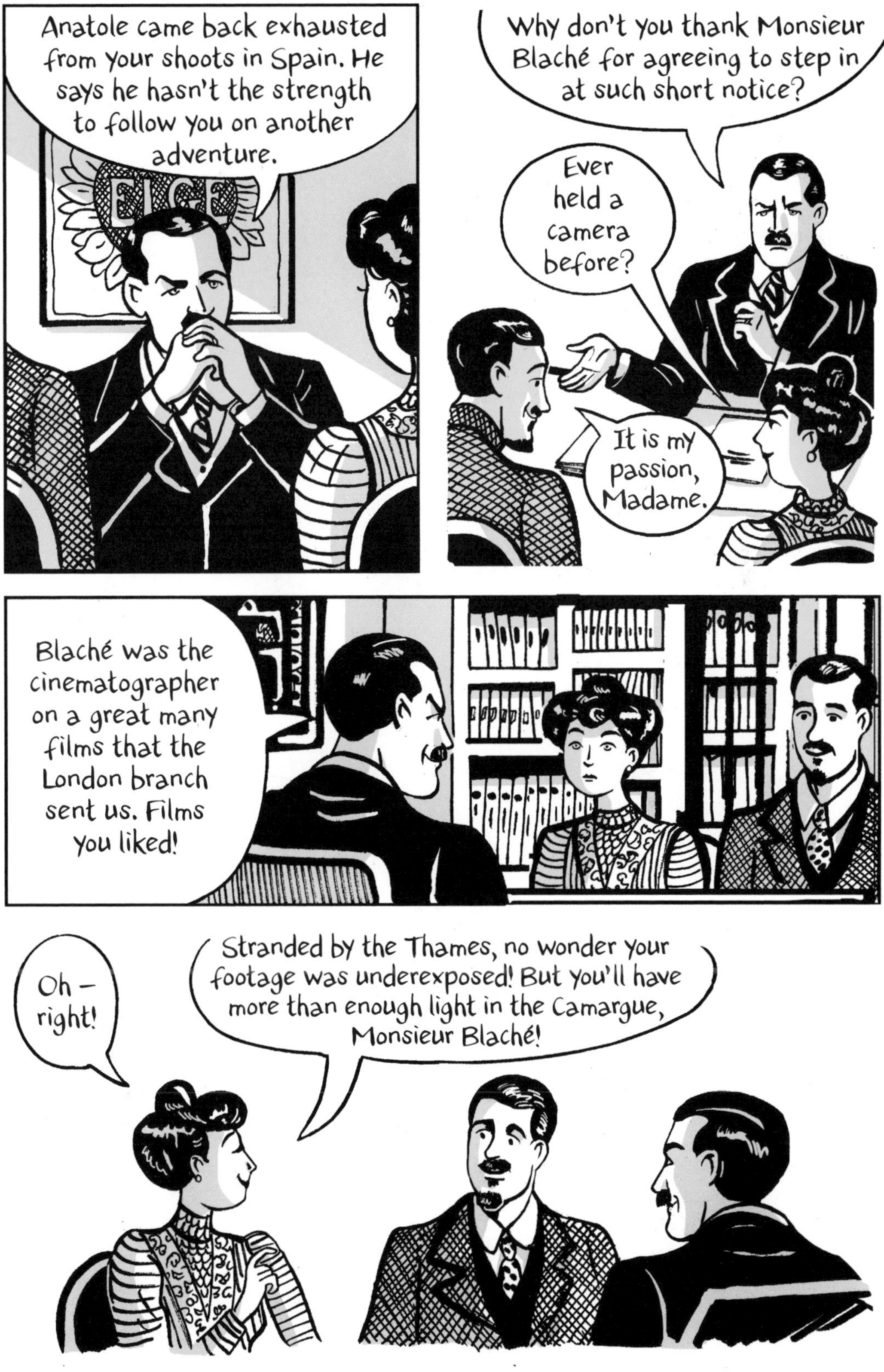
Anatole came back exhausted from your shoots in Spain. He says he hasn't the strength to follow you on another adventure.
Why don't you thank Monsieur Blaché for agreeing to step in at such short notice?
Ever held a camera before?
It is my passion, Madame.
Blaché was the cinematographer on a great many films that the London branch sent us. Films you liked!
Oh – right!
Stranded by the Thames, no wonder your footage was underexposed! But you'll have more than enough light in the Camargue, Monsieur Blaché!

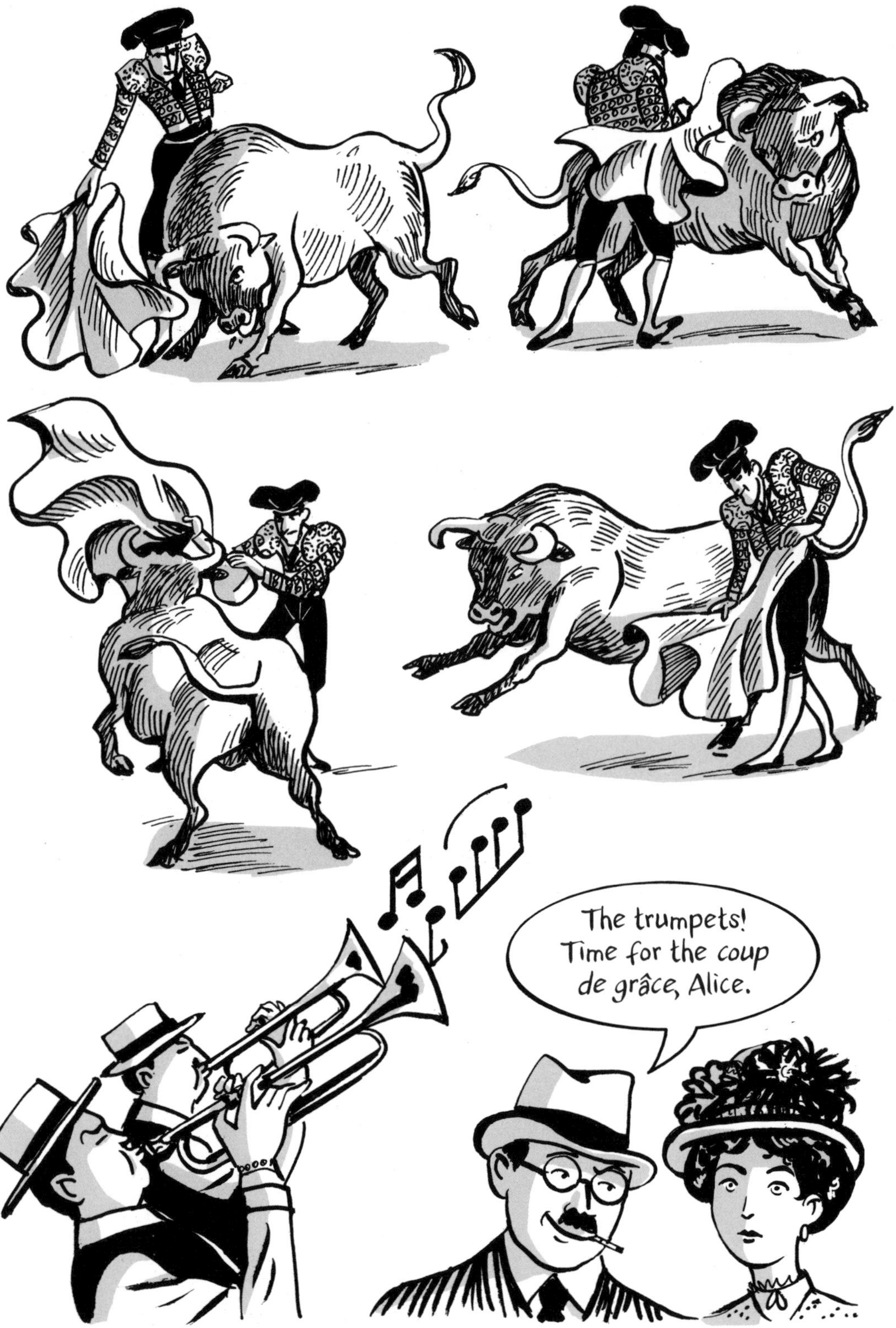
The trumpets! Time for the coup de grâce, Alice.

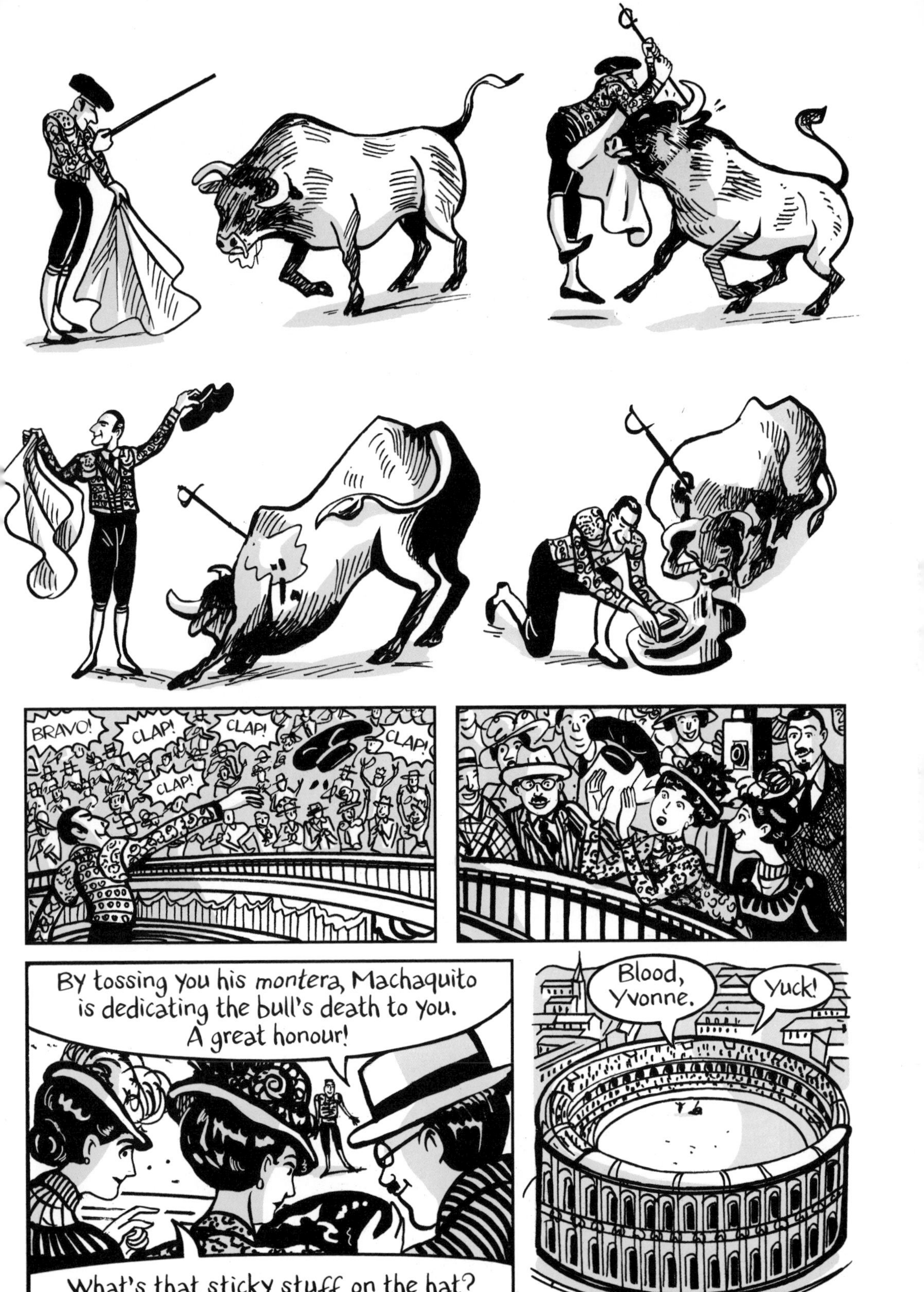
BRAVO!
CLAP!
CLAP!
CLAP!
CLAP!
By tossing you his *montera*, Machaquito is dedicating the bull's death to you. A great honour!
What's that sticky stuff on the hat?
Blood, Yvonne.
Yuck!

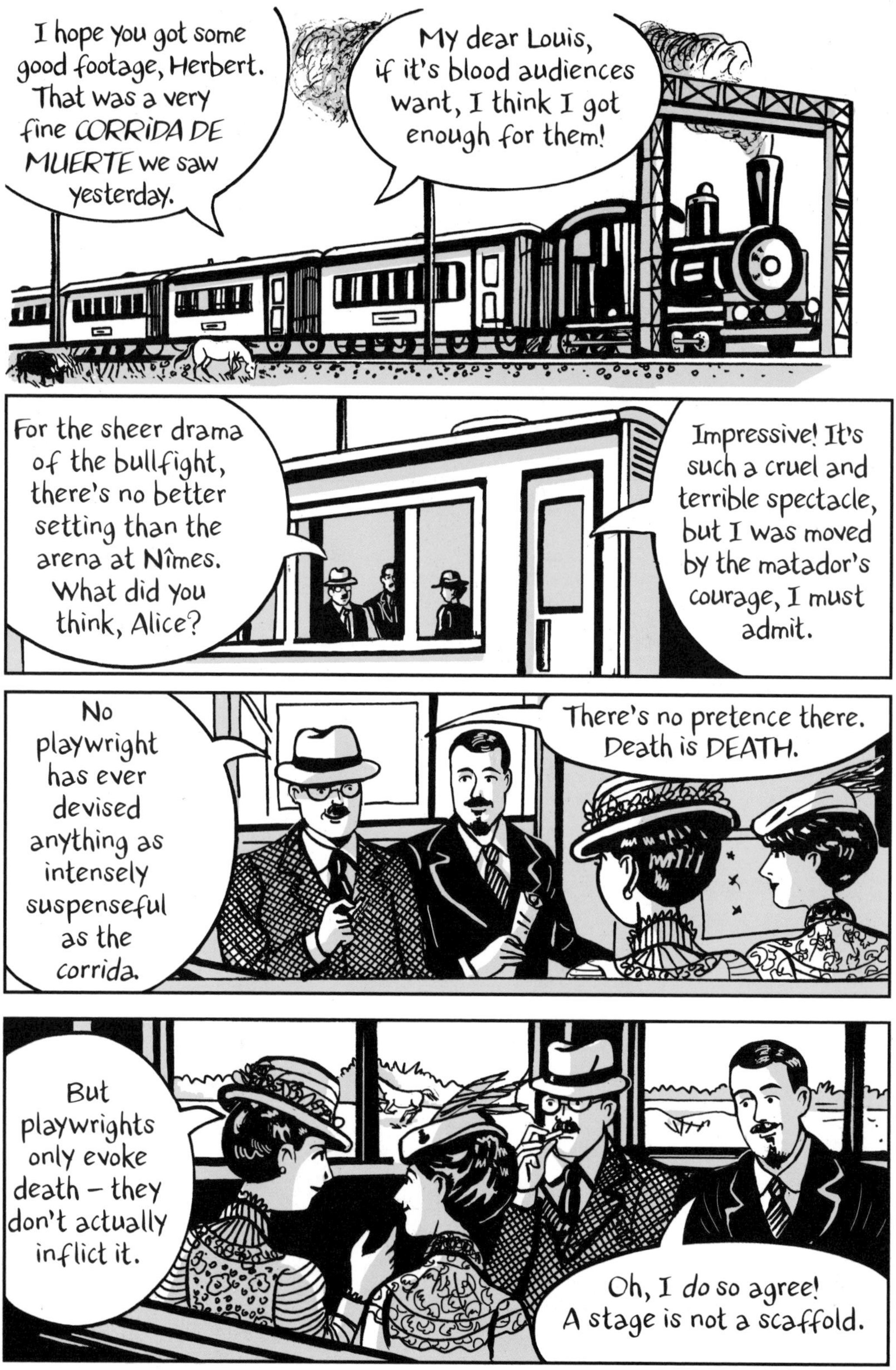
I hope you got some good footage, Herbert. That was a very fine CORRIDA DE MUERTE we saw yesterday.
My dear Louis, if it's blood audiences want, I think I got enough for them!
For the sheer drama of the bullfight, there's no better setting than the arena at Nîmes. What did you think, Alice?
Impressive! It's such a cruel and terrible spectacle, but I was moved by the matador's courage, I must admit.
No playwright has ever devised anything as intensely suspenseful as the corrida.
There's no pretence there. Death is DEATH.
But playwrights only evoke death – they don't actually inflict it.
Oh, I *do* so agree! A stage is not a scaffold.

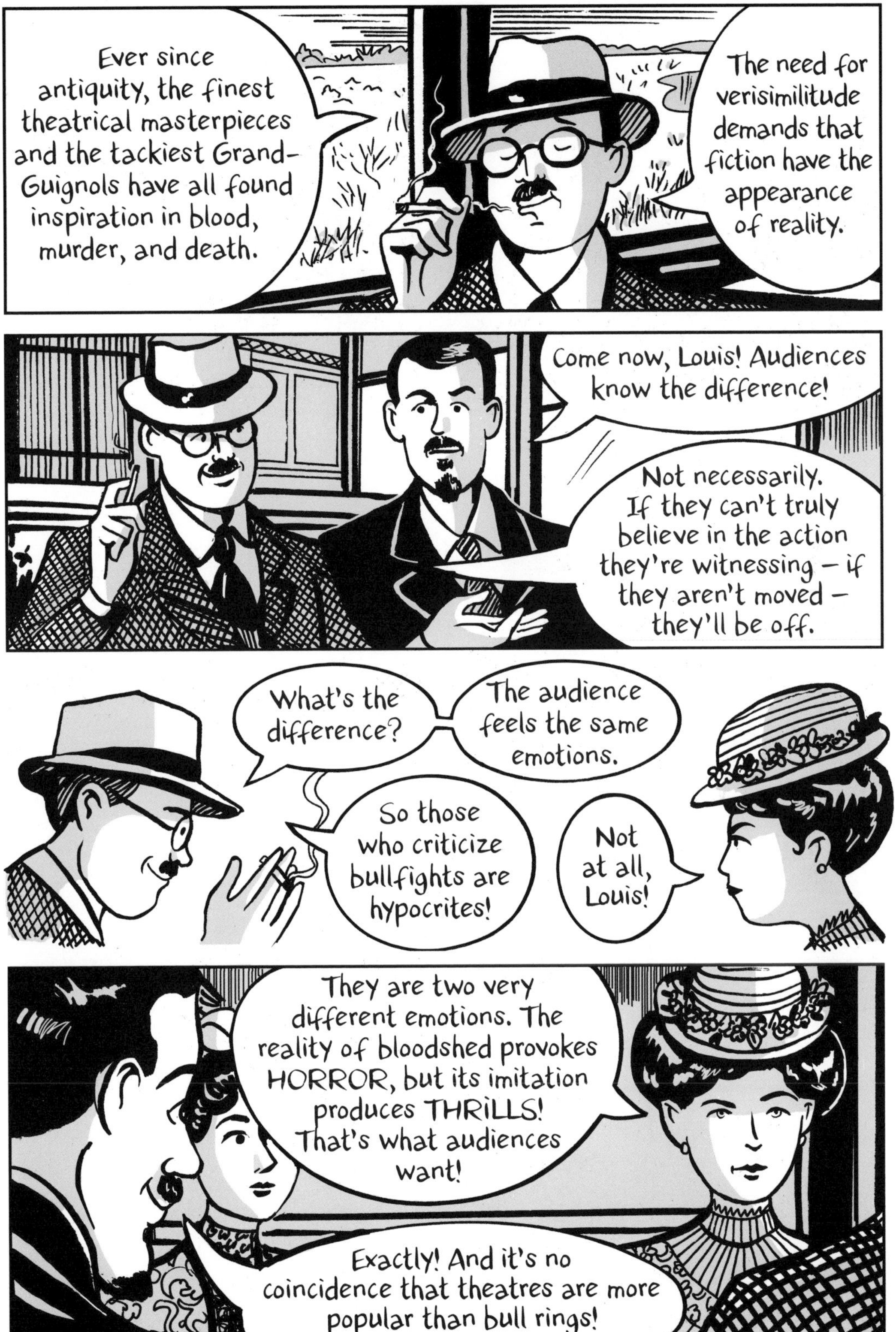

Ever since antiquity, the finest theatrical masterpieces and the tackiest Grand-Guignols have all found inspiration in blood, murder, and death.
The need for verisimilitude demands that fiction have the appearance of reality.
Come now, Louis! Audiences know the difference!
Not necessarily. If they can't truly believe in the action they're witnessing – if they aren't moved – they'll be off.
What's the difference?
The audience feels the same emotions.
So those who criticize bullfights are hypocrites!
Not at all, Louis!
They are two very different emotions. The reality of bloodshed provokes HORROR, but its imitation produces THRILLS! That's what audiences want!
Exactly! And it's no coincidence that theatres are more popular than bull rings!

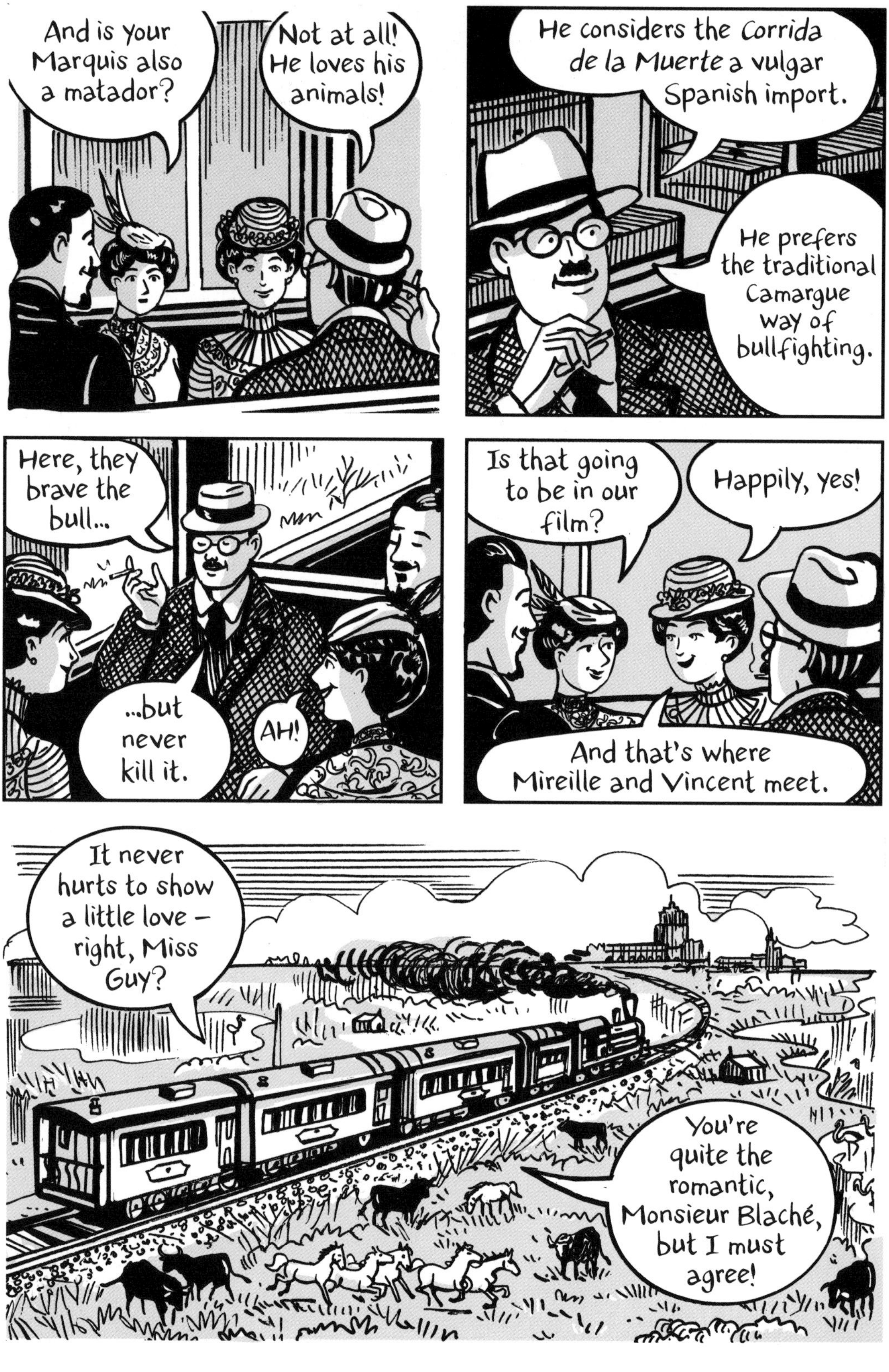
And is your Marquis also a matador?
Not at all! He loves his animals!
He considers the Corrida de la Muerte a vulgar Spanish import.
He prefers the traditional Camargue way of bullfighting.
Here, they brave the bull...
...but never kill it.
AH!
Is that going to be in our film?
Happily, yes!
And that's where Mireille and Vincent meet.
It never hurts to show a little love – right, Miss Guy?
You're quite the romantic, Monsieur Blaché, but I must agree!

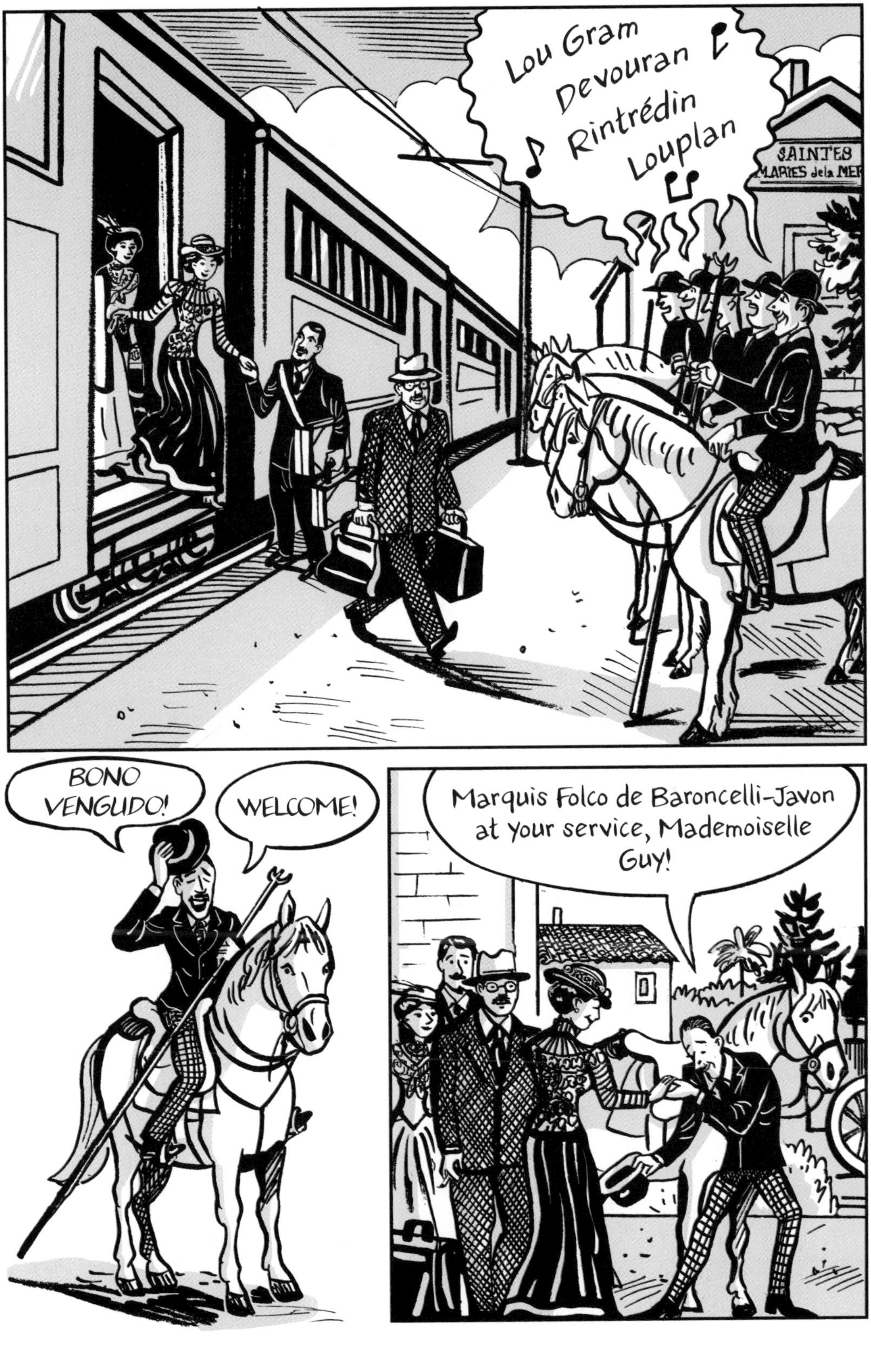
Lou Gram
Devouran
Rintrédin
Louplan
SAINTES MARIES de la MER
BONO VENGUDO!
WELCOME!
Marquis Folco de Baroncelli-Javon at your service, Mademoiselle Guy!

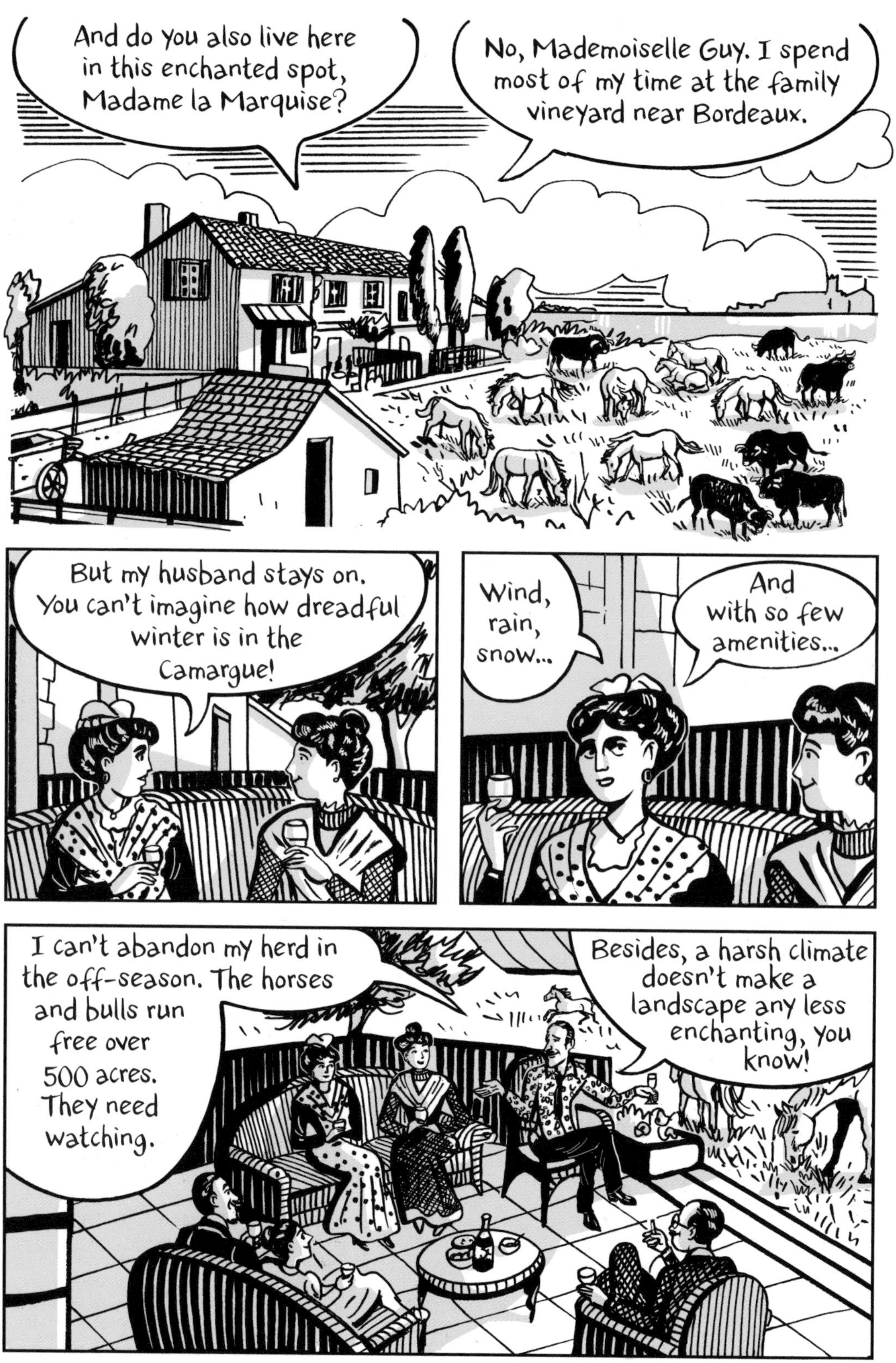
And do you also live here in this enchanted spot, Madame la Marquise?
No, Mademoiselle Guy. I spend most of my time at the family vineyard near Bordeaux.
But my husband stays on. You can't imagine how dreadful winter is in the Camargue!
Wind, rain, snow...
And with so few amenities...
I can't abandon my herd in the off-season. The horses and bulls run free over 500 acres. They need watching.
Besides, a harsh climate doesn't make a landscape any less enchanting, you know!

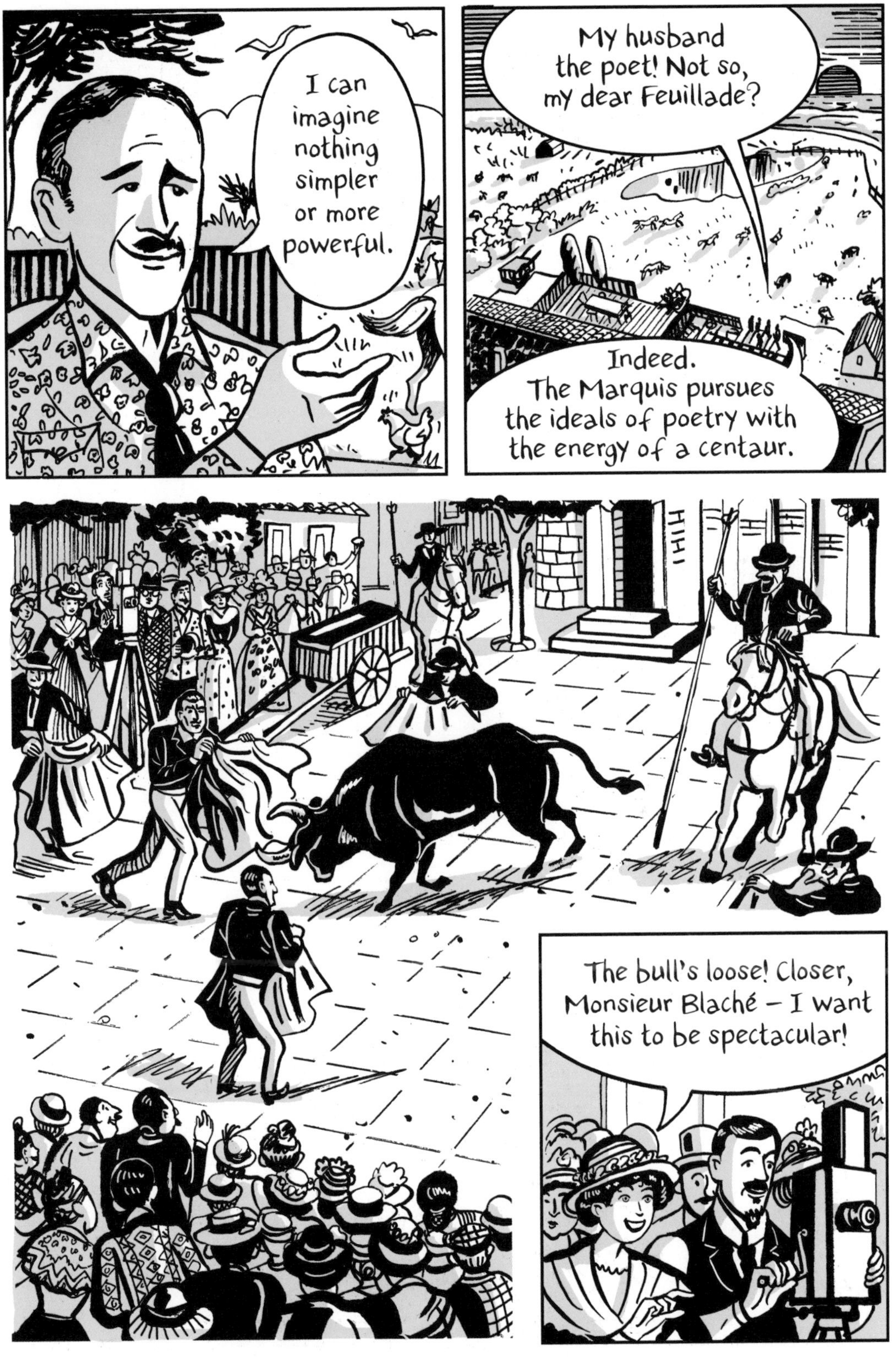
I can imagine nothing simpler or more powerful.
My husband the poet! Not so, my dear Feuillade?
Indeed. The Marquis pursues the ideals of poetry with the energy of a centaur.
The bull's loose! Closer, Monsieur Blaché – I want this to be spectacular!

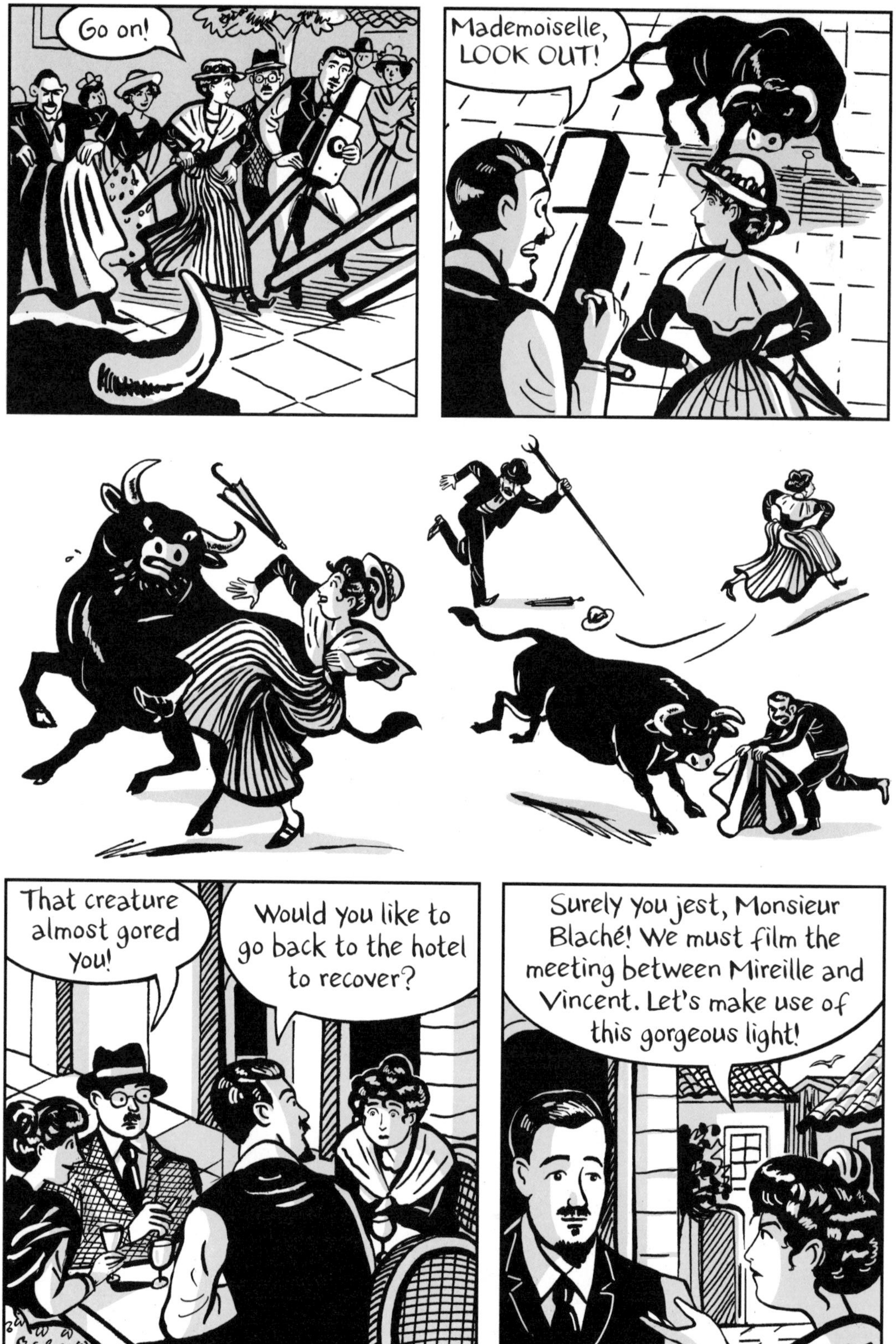
Go on!
Mademoiselle, LOOK OUT!
That creature almost gored you!
Would you like to go back to the hotel to recover?
Surely you jest, Monsieur Blaché! We must film the meeting between Mireille and Vincent. Let's make use of this gorgeous light!

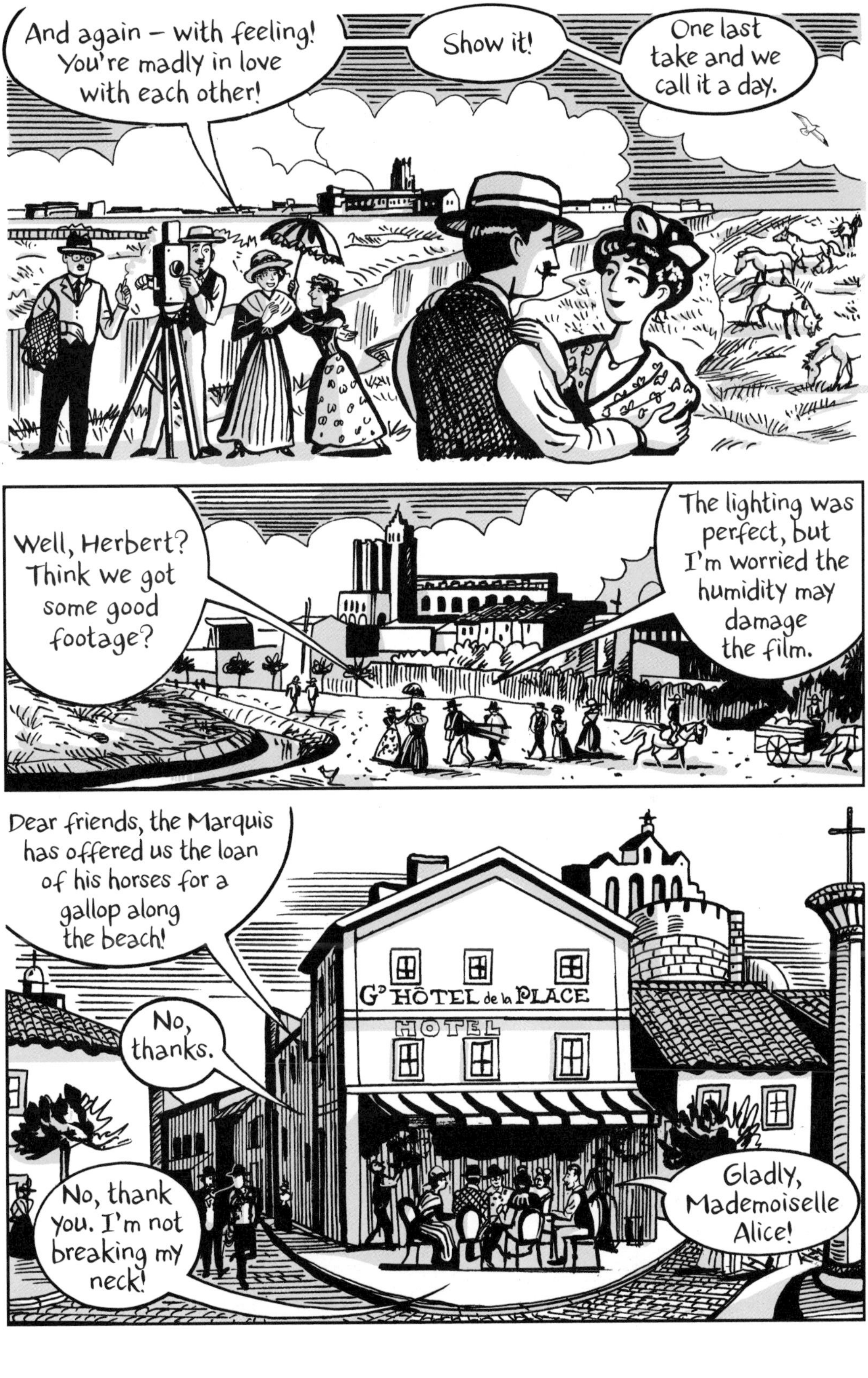
And again – with feeling! You're madly in love with each other!
Show it!
One last take and we call it a day.
Well, Herbert? Think we got some good footage?
The lighting was perfect, but I'm worried the humidity may damage the film.
Dear friends, the Marquis has offered us the loan of his horses for a gallop along the beach!
Gd HÔTEL de la PLACE
HOTEL
No, thanks.
No, thank you. I'm not breaking my neck!
Gladly, Mademoiselle Alice!

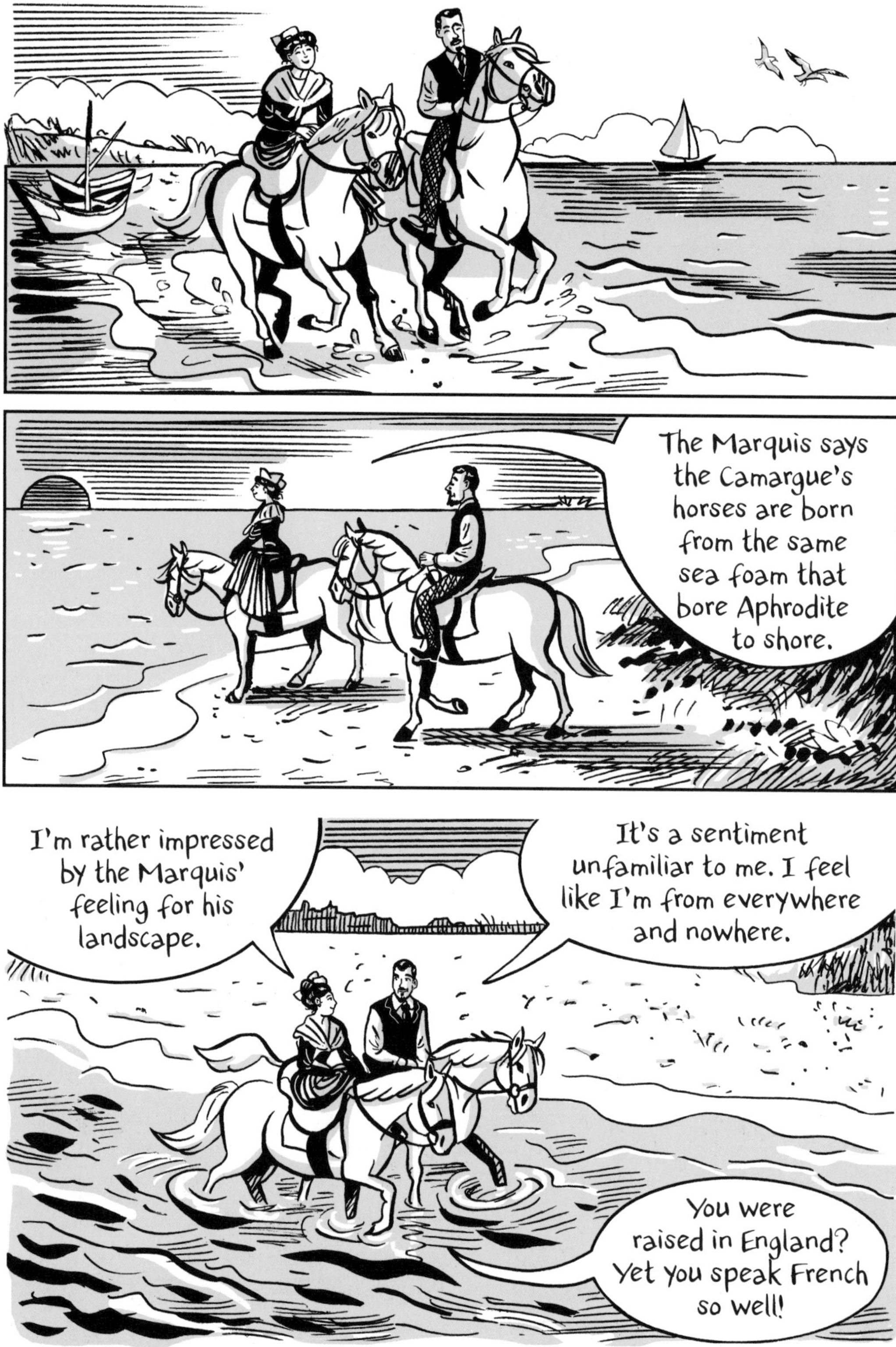
The Marquis says the Camargue's horses are born from the same sea foam that bore Aphrodite to shore.
I'm rather impressed by the Marquis' feeling for his landscape.
It's a sentiment unfamiliar to me. I feel like I'm from everywhere and nowhere.
You were raised in England? Yet you speak French so well!

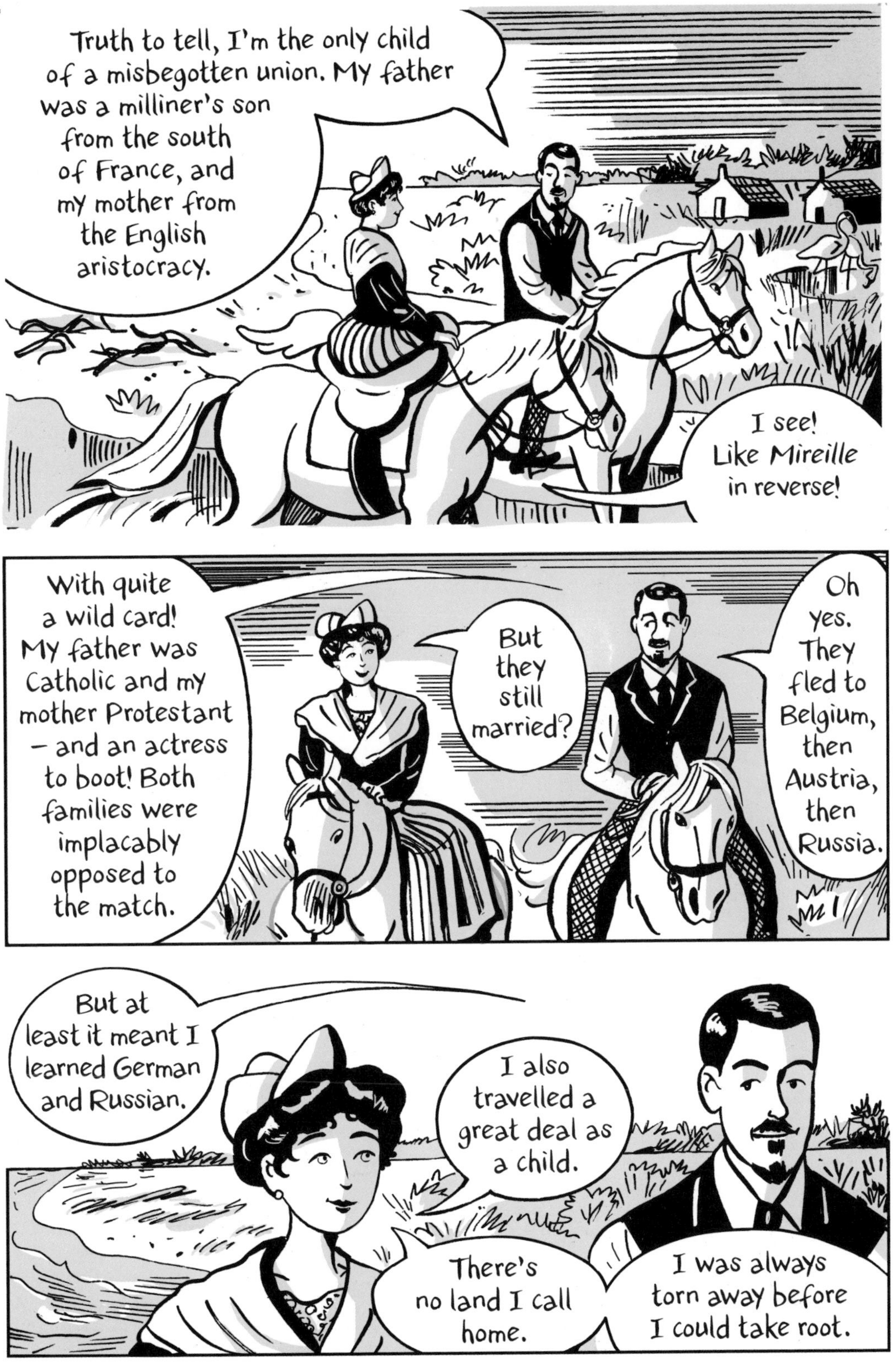
Truth to tell, I'm the only child of a misbegotten union. My father was a milliner's son from the south of France, and my mother from the English aristocracy.
I see! Like Mireille in reverse!
With quite a wild card! My father was Catholic and my mother Protestant – and an actress to boot! Both families were implacably opposed to the match.
But they still married?
Oh yes. They fled to Belgium, then Austria, then Russia.
But at least it meant I learned German and Russian.
I also travelled a great deal as a child.
There's no land I call home.
I was always torn away before I could take root.

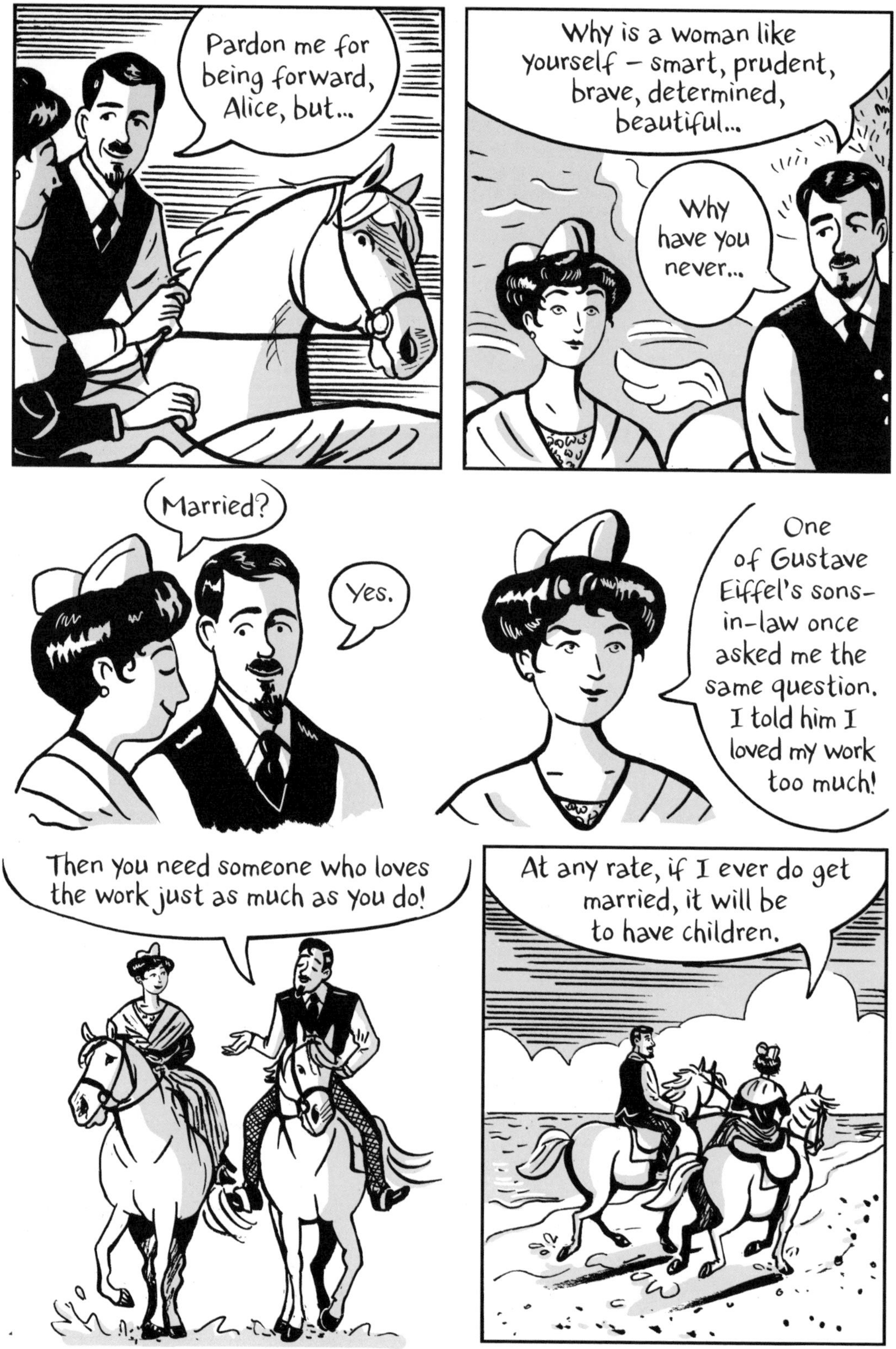
Pardon me for being forward, Alice, but...
Why is a woman like yourself – smart, prudent, brave, determined, beautiful...
Why have you never...
Married?
Yes.
One of Gustave Eiffel's sons-in-law once asked me the same question. I told him I loved my work too much!
Then you need someone who loves the work just as much as you do!
At any rate, if I ever do get married, it will be to have children.

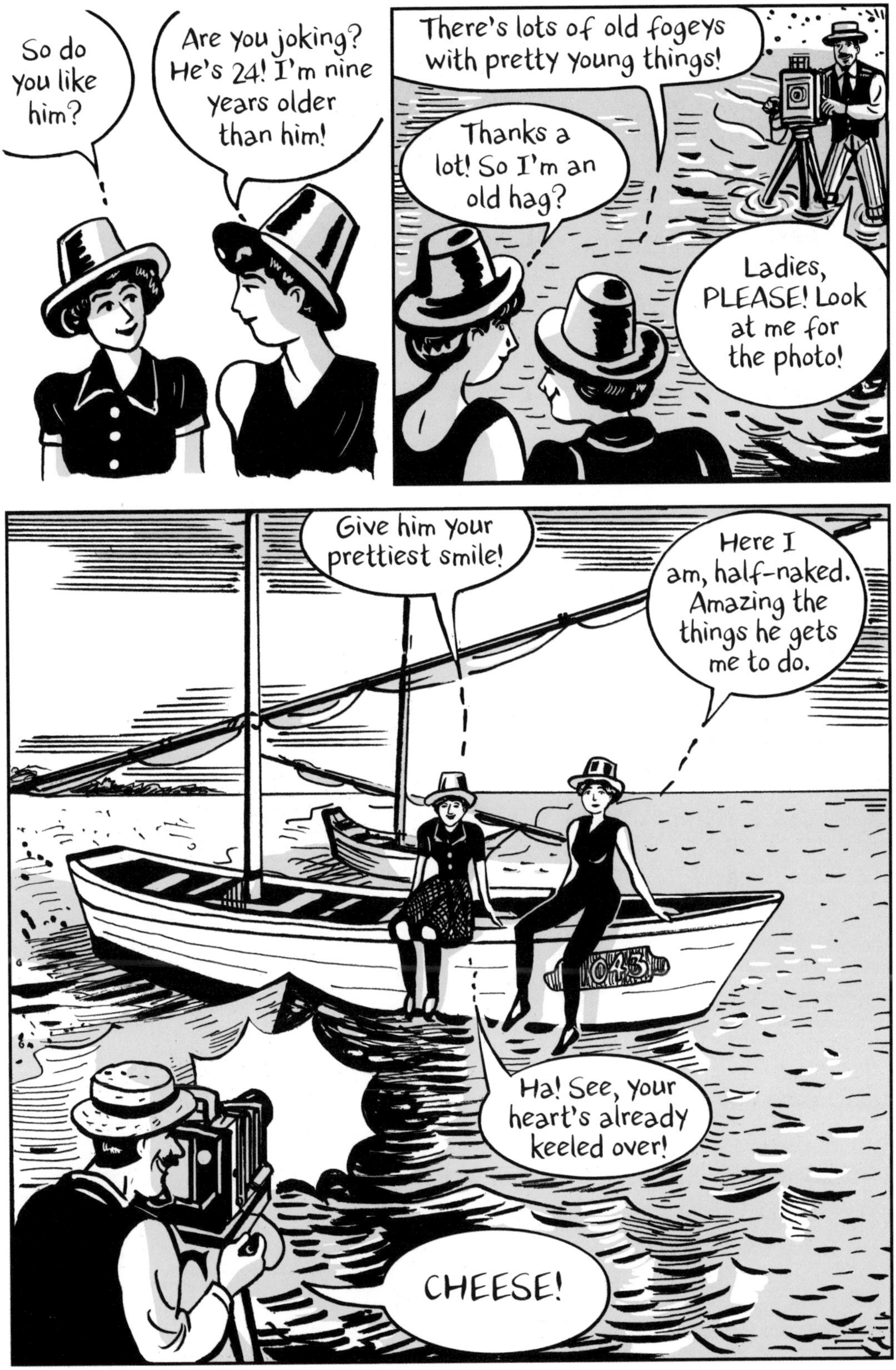
So do you like him?
Are you joking? He's 24! I'm nine years older than him!
There's lots of old fogeys with pretty young things!
Thanks a lot! So I'm an old hag?
Ladies, PLEASE! Look at me for the photo!
Give him your prettiest smile!
Here I am, half-naked. Amazing the things he gets me to do.
043
Ha! See, your heart's already keeled over!
CHEESE!

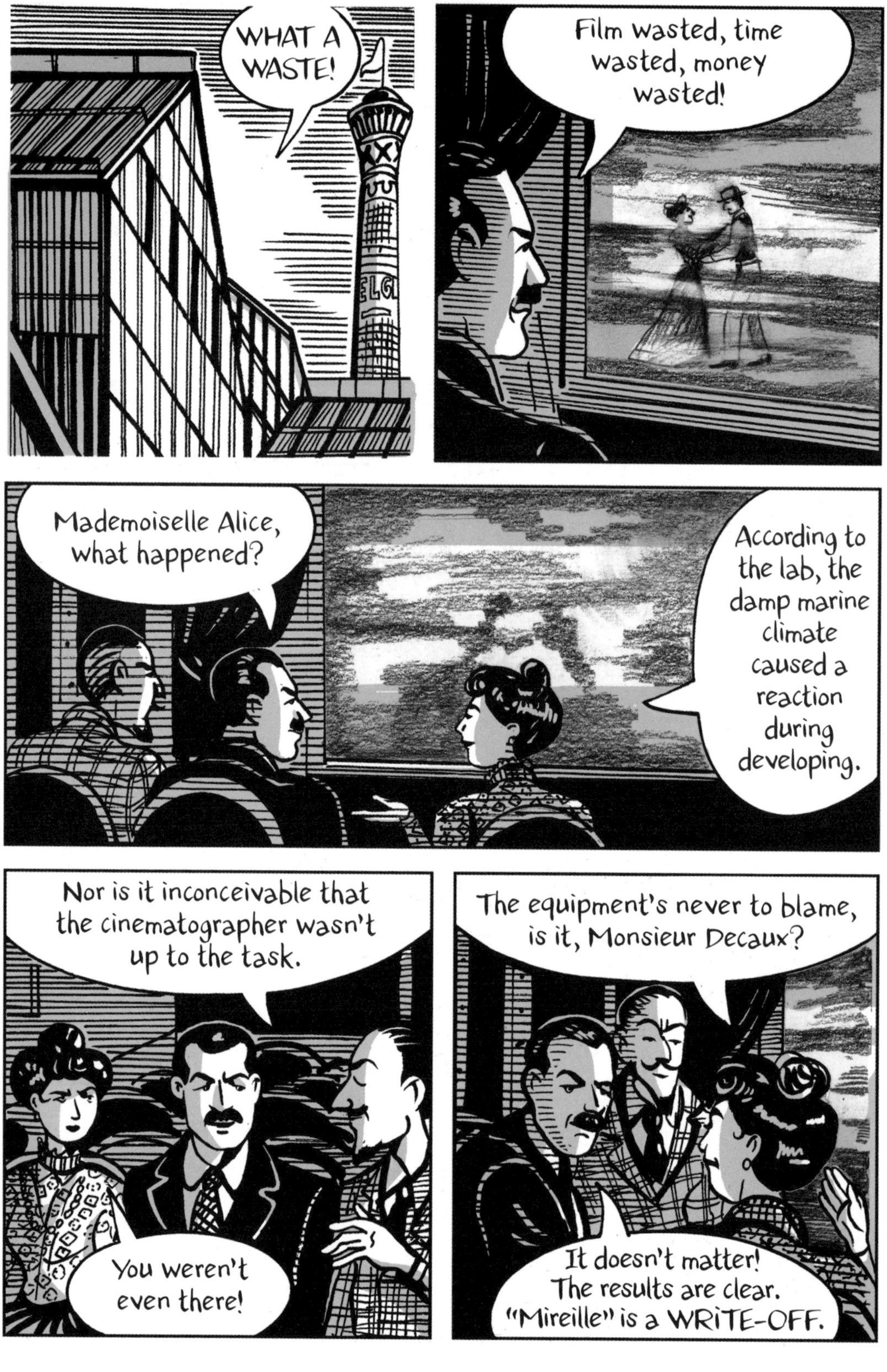
WHAT A WASTE!
Film wasted, time wasted, money wasted!
Mademoiselle Alice, what happened?
According to the lab, the damp marine climate caused a reaction during developing.
Nor is it inconceivable that the cinematographer wasn't up to the task.
You weren't even there!
The equipment's never to blame, is it, Monsieur Decaux?
It doesn't matter! The results are clear. "Mireille" is a WRITE-OFF.

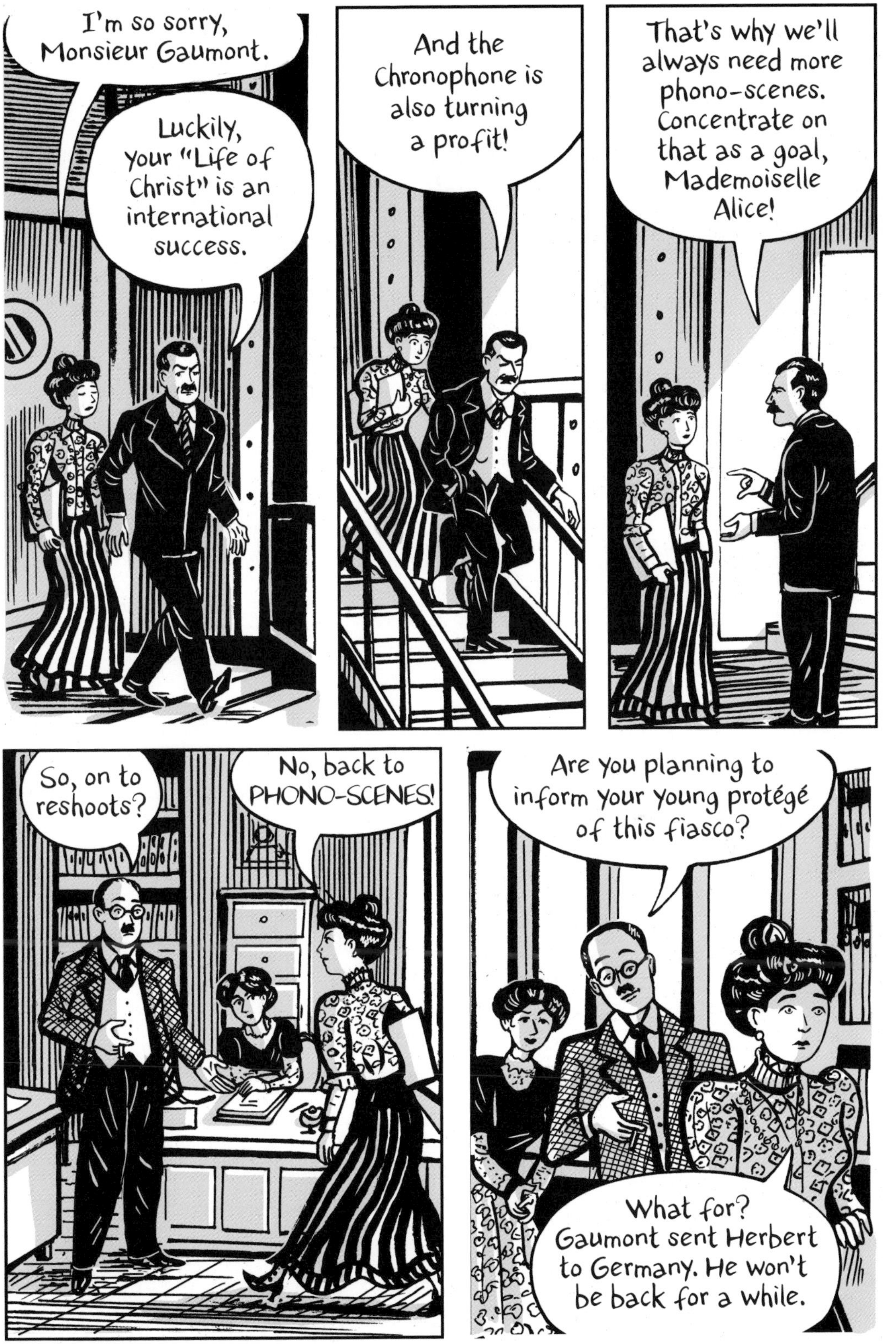
I'm so sorry, Monsieur Gaumont.
Luckily, your "Life of Christ" is an international success.
And the Chronophone is also turning a profit!
That's why we'll always need more phono-scenes. Concentrate on that as a goal, Mademoiselle Alice!
So, on to reshoots?
No, back to PHONO-SCENES!
Are you planning to inform your young protégé of this fiasco?
What for? Gaumont sent Herbert to Germany. He won't be back for a while.

It is to the newest shareholder in this limited partnership entity that I address these remarks, Mademoiselle Alice.

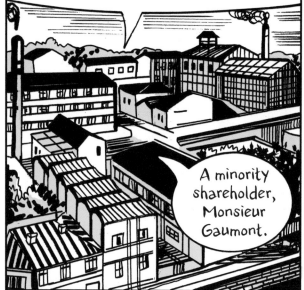

A minority shareholder, Monsieur Gaumont.

As you know, young Blaché has been in Germany five months now, and it's not going well!

I see...

Willkommen in Berlin, Fräulein Guy!

Bonjour, Monsieur Blaché.

I hadn't dared hope to see you so soon, Alice.

We are but playthings in the hands of fate, Herbert.

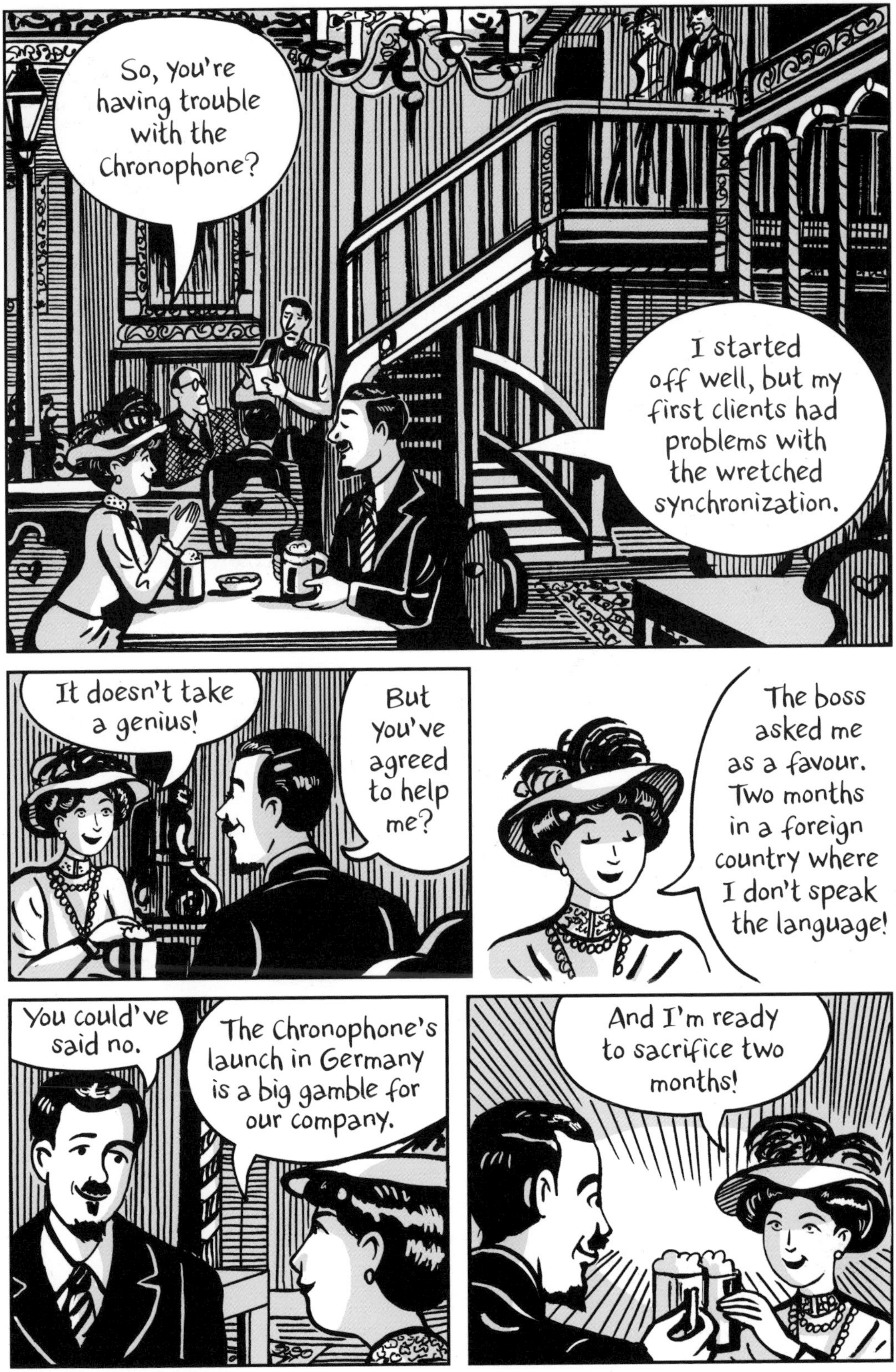
So, you're having trouble with the Chronophone?
I started off well, but my first clients had problems with the wretched synchronization.
It doesn't take a genius!
But you've agreed to help me?
The boss asked me as a favour. Two months in a foreign country where I don't speak the language!
You could've said no.
The Chronophone's launch in Germany is a big gamble for our company.
And I'm ready to sacrifice two months!

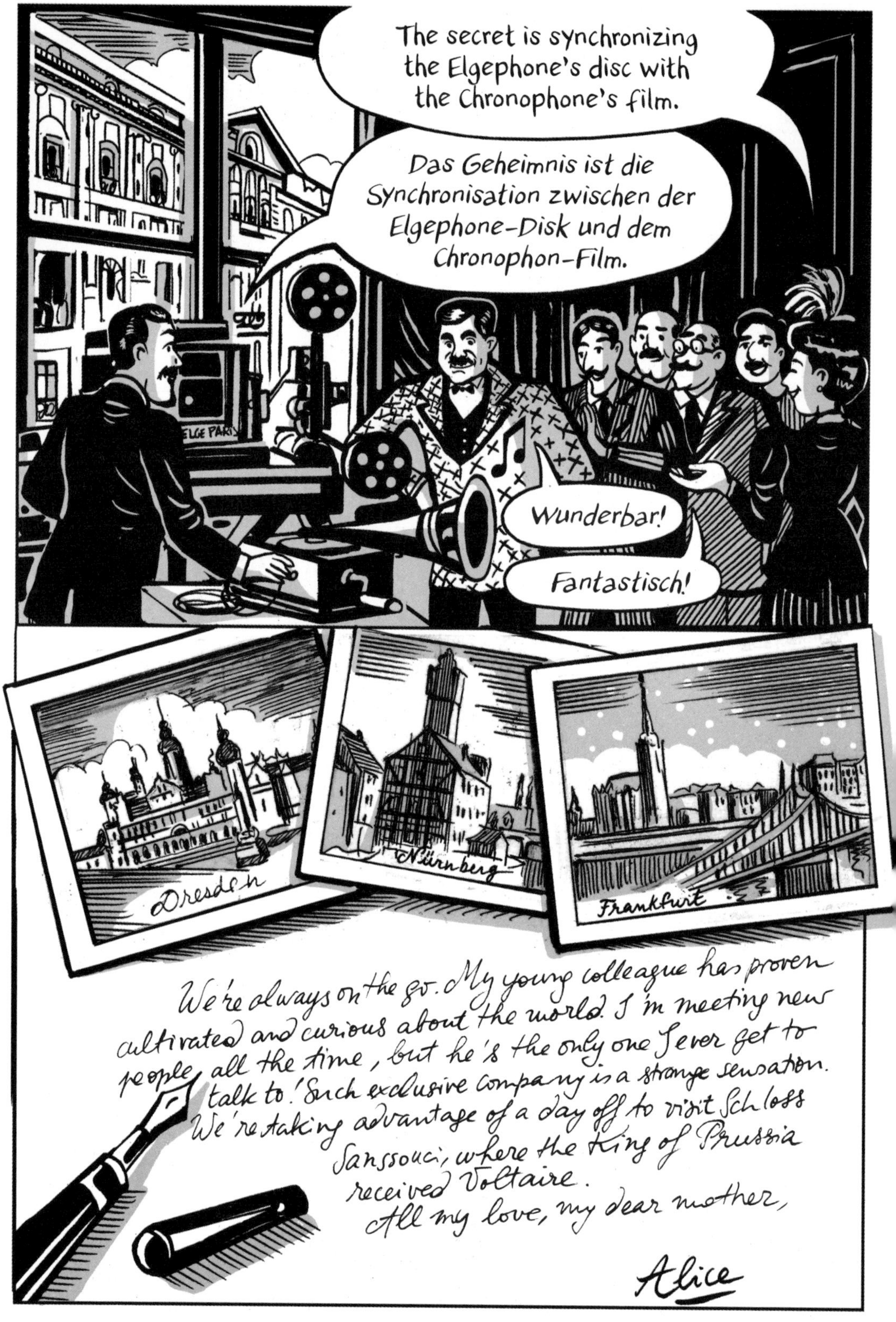
The secret is synchronizing the Elgephone's disc with the Chronophone's film.
Das Geheimnis ist die Synchronisation zwischen der Elgephone-Disk und dem Chronophon-Film.
ELGE PARIS
Wunderbar!
Fantastisch!
Dresden
Nürnberg
Frankfurt
We're always on the go. My young colleague has proven
cultivated and curious about the world. I'm meeting new
people all the time, but he's the only one I ever get to
talk to. Such exclusive company is a strange sensation.
We're taking advantage of a day off to visit Schloss
Sanssouci, where the King of Prussia
received Voltaire.
All my love, my dear mother,
Alice

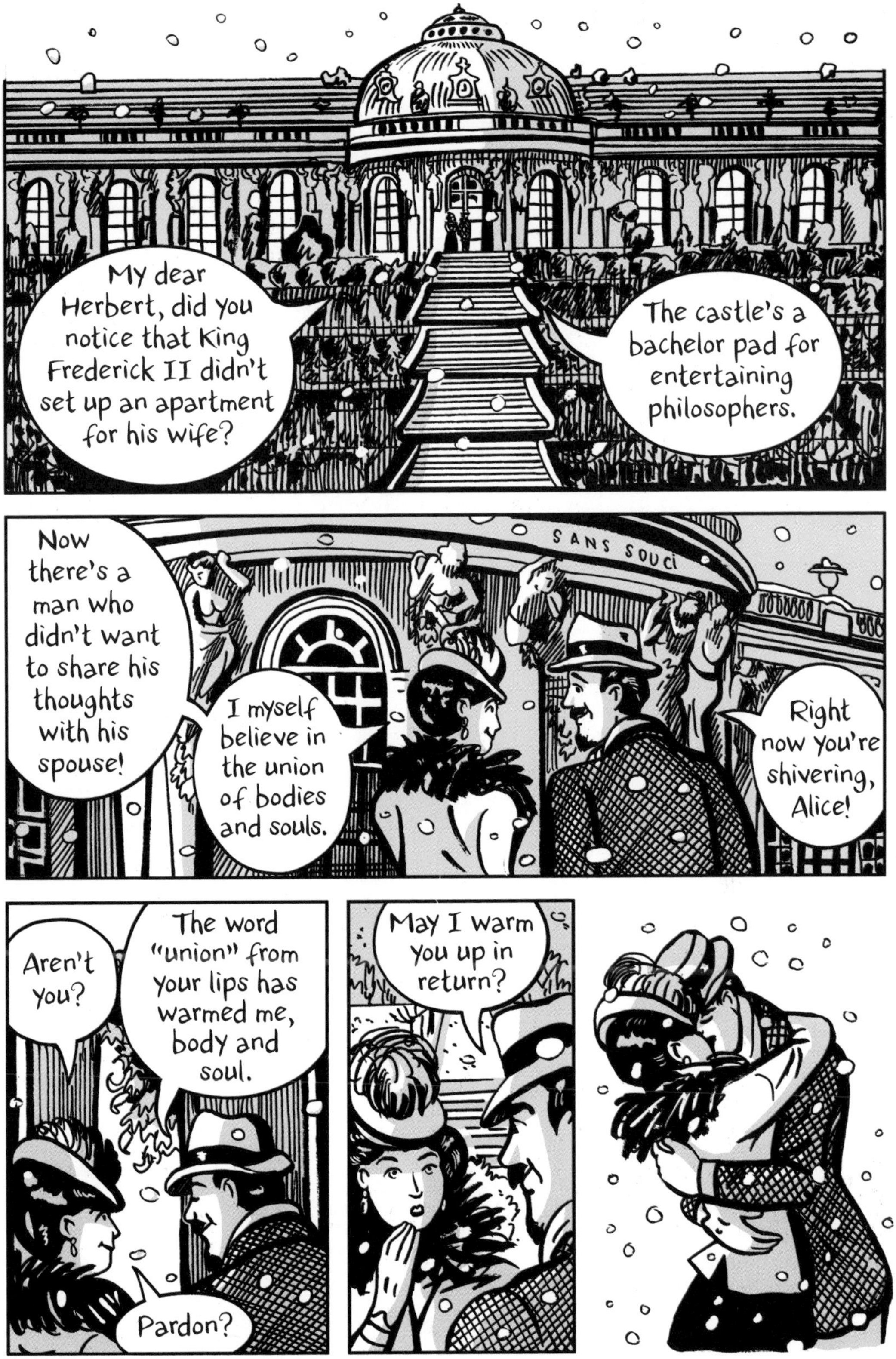
My dear Herbert, did you notice that King Frederick II didn't set up an apartment for his wife?
The castle's a bachelor pad for entertaining philosophers.
SANS SOUCI
Now there's a man who didn't want to share his thoughts with his spouse!
I myself believe in the union of bodies and souls.
Right now you're shivering, Alice!
Aren't you?
The word "union" from your lips has warmed me, body and soul.
Pardon?
May I warm you up in return?

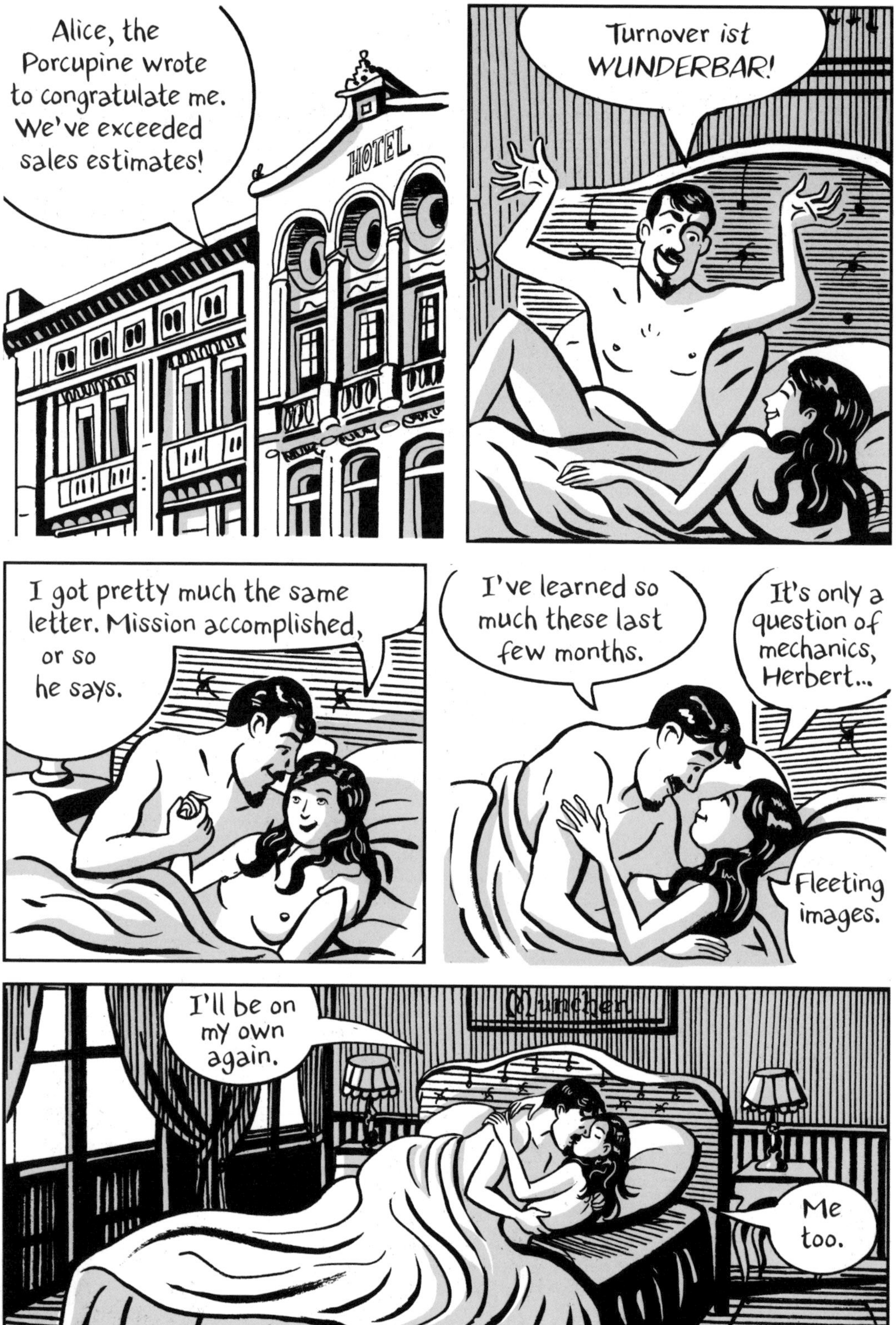
Alice, the Porcupine wrote to congratulate me. We've exceeded sales estimates!
HOTEL
Turnover ist WUNDERBAR!
I got pretty much the same letter. Mission accomplished, or so he says.
I've learned so much these last few months.
It's only a question of mechanics, Herbert...
Fleeting images.
I'll be on my own again.
Munchen
Me too.

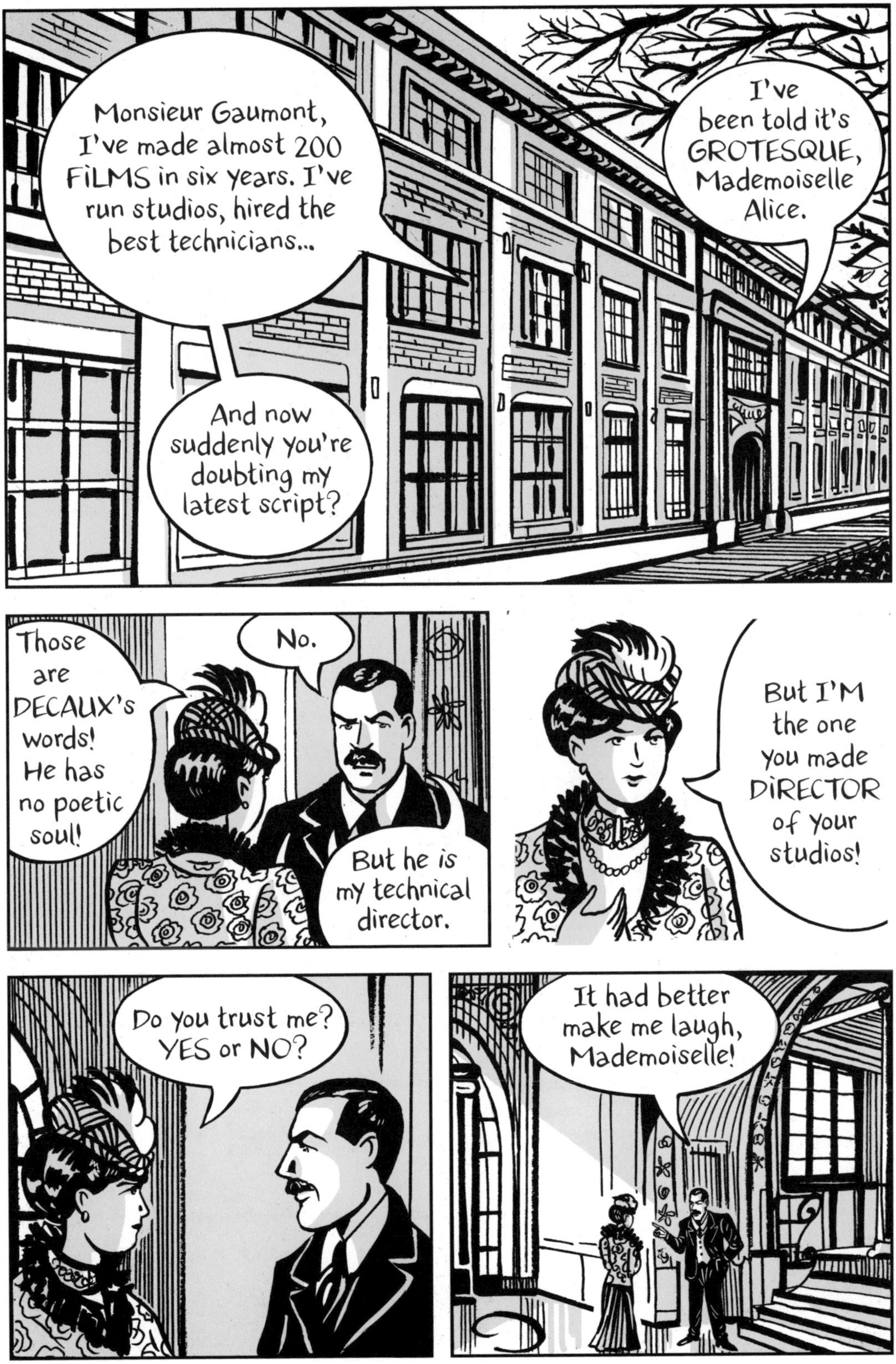
Monsieur Gaumont, I've made almost 200 FILMS in six years. I've run studios, hired the best technicians...
And now suddenly you're doubting my latest script?
I've been told it's GROTESQUE, Mademoiselle Alice.
Those are DECAUX's words! He has no poetic soul!
No.
But he is my technical director.
But I'M the one you made DIRECTOR of your studios!
Do you trust me? YES or NO?
It had better make me laugh, Mademoiselle!

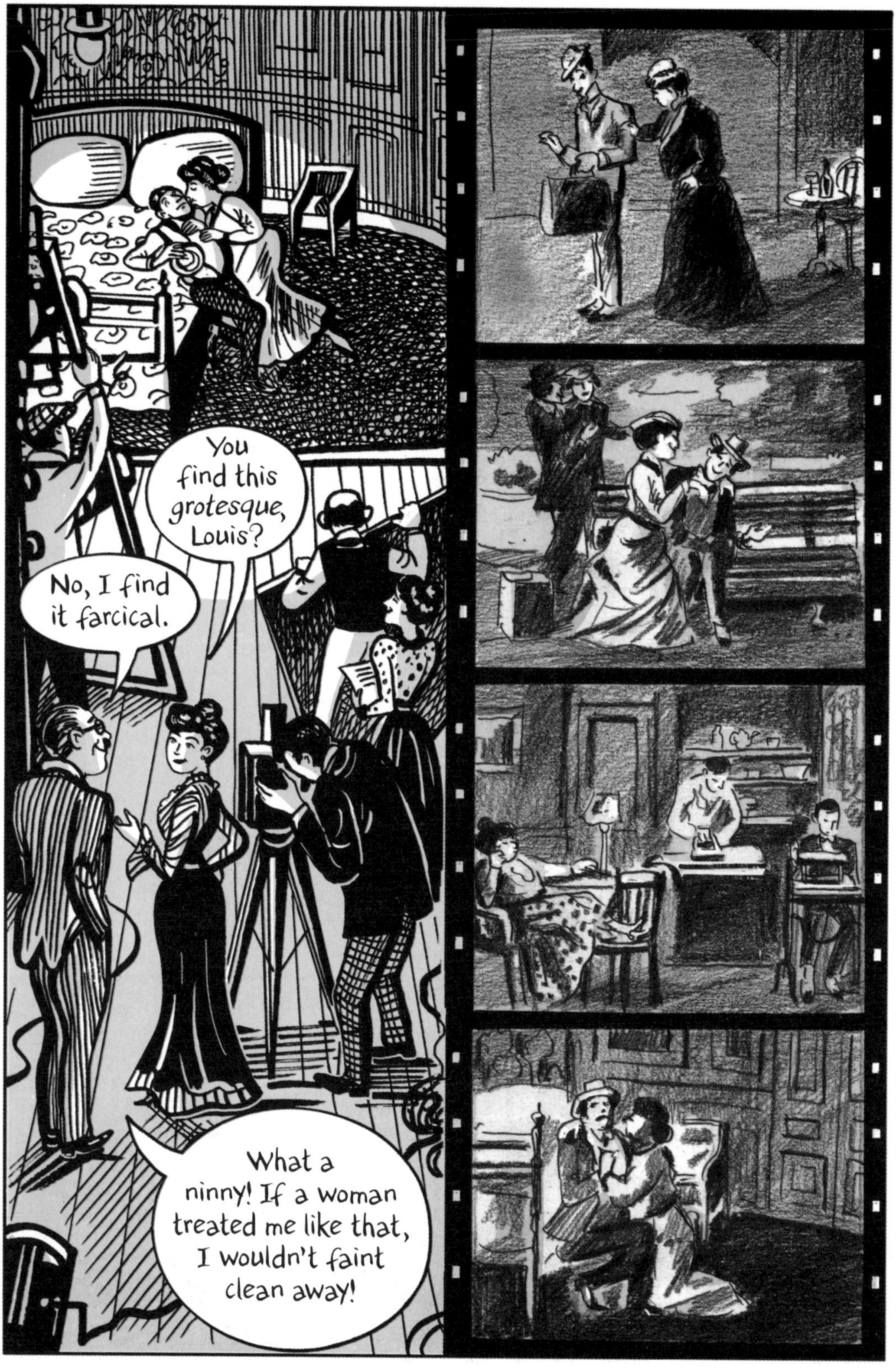

You find this grotesque, Louis?
No, I find it farcical.
What a ninny! If a woman treated me like that, I wouldn't faint clean away!

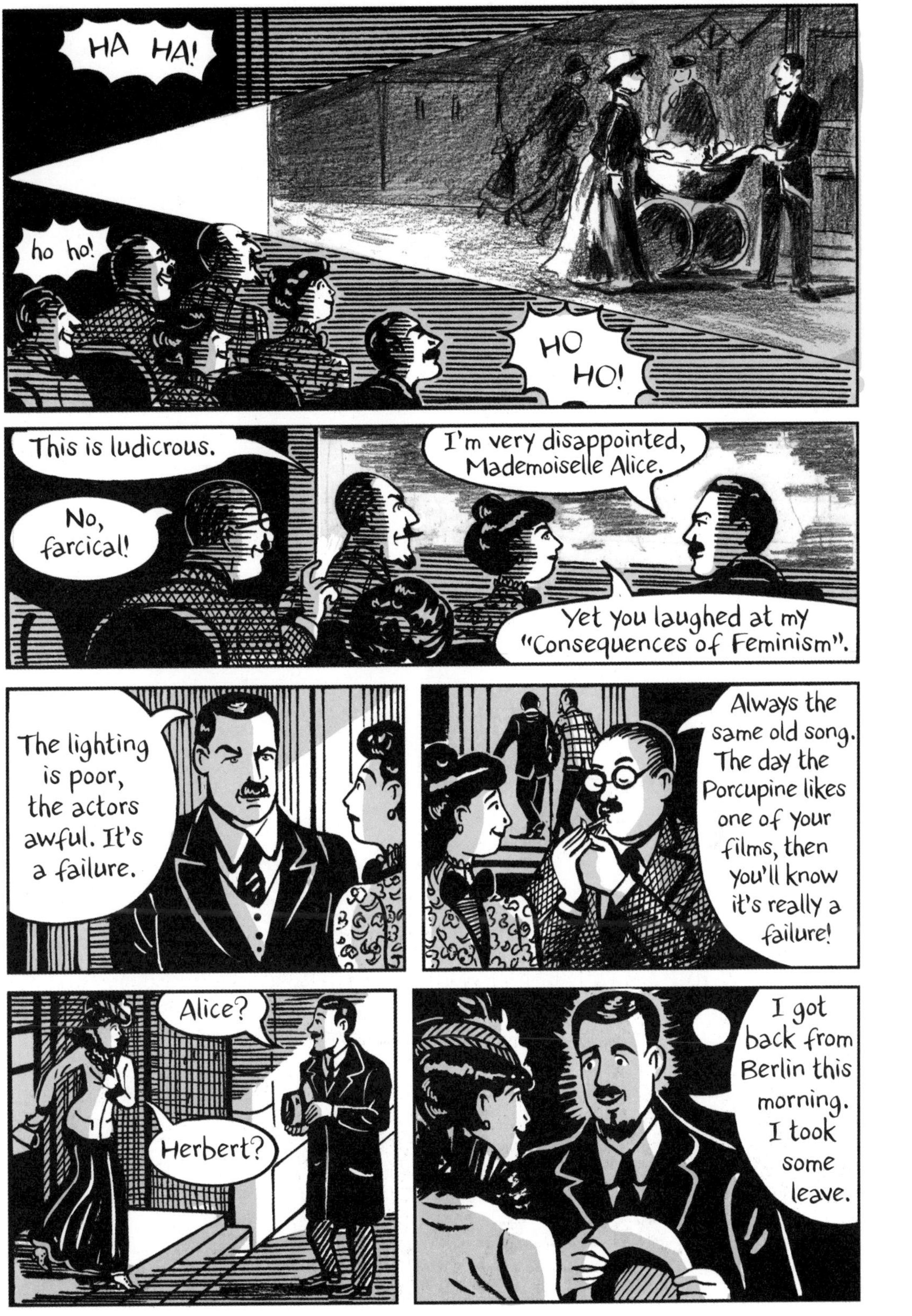
HA HA!
ho ho!
HO HO!
This is ludicrous.
No, farcical!
I'm very disappointed, Mademoiselle Alice.
Yet you laughed at my "Consequences of Feminism".
The lighting is poor, the actors awful. It's a failure.
Always the same old song. The day the Porcupine likes one of your films, then you'll know it's really a failure!
Alice?
Herbert?
I got back from Berlin this morning. I took some leave.

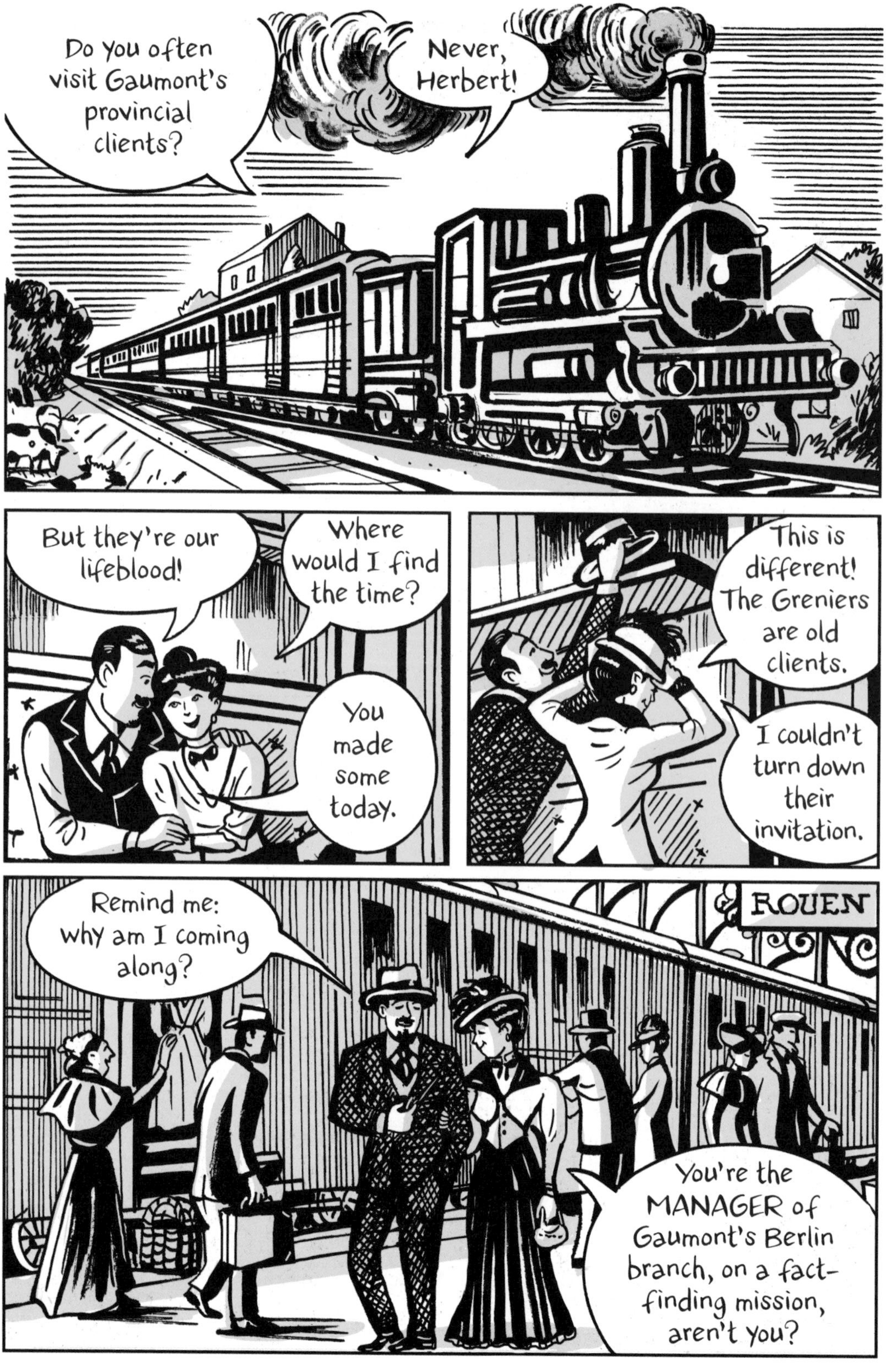
Do you often visit Gaumont's provincial clients?
Never, Herbert!
But they're our lifeblood!
Where would I find the time?
You made some today.
This is different! The Greniers are old clients.
I couldn't turn down their invitation.
Remind me: why am I coming along?
ROUEN
You're the MANAGER of Gaumont's Berlin branch, on a fact-finding mission, aren't you?

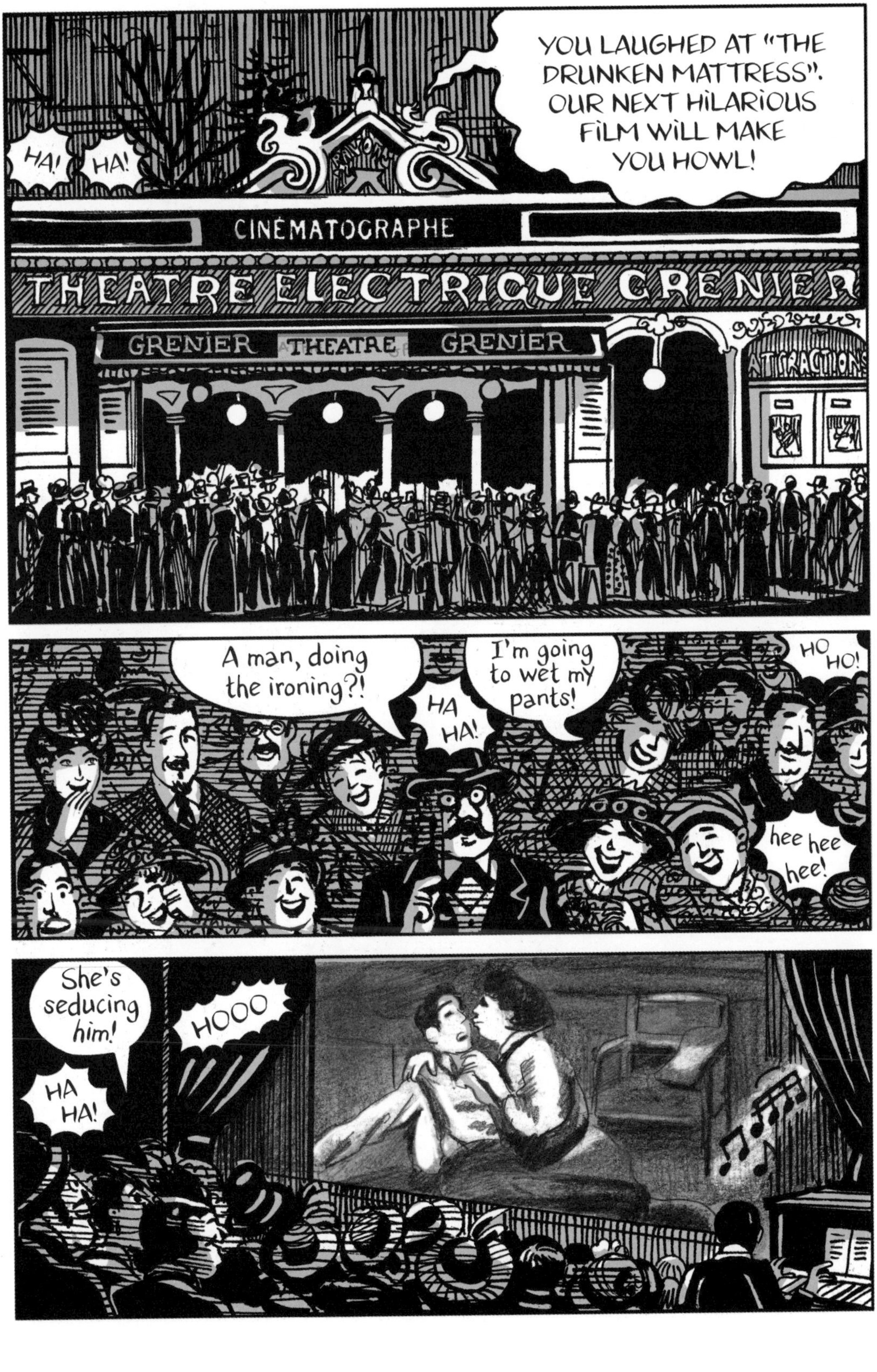
HA!
HA!
YOU LAUGHED AT "THE DRUNKEN MATTRESS". OUR NEXT HILARIOUS FILM WILL MAKE YOU HOWL!
CINÉMATOGRAPHE
THEATRE ELECTRIQUE GRENIER
GRENIER THEATRE GRENIER
ATTRACTIONS
A man, doing the ironing?!
HA HA!
I'm going to wet my pants!
HO HO!
hee hee hee!
She's seducing him!
HOOO
HA HA!

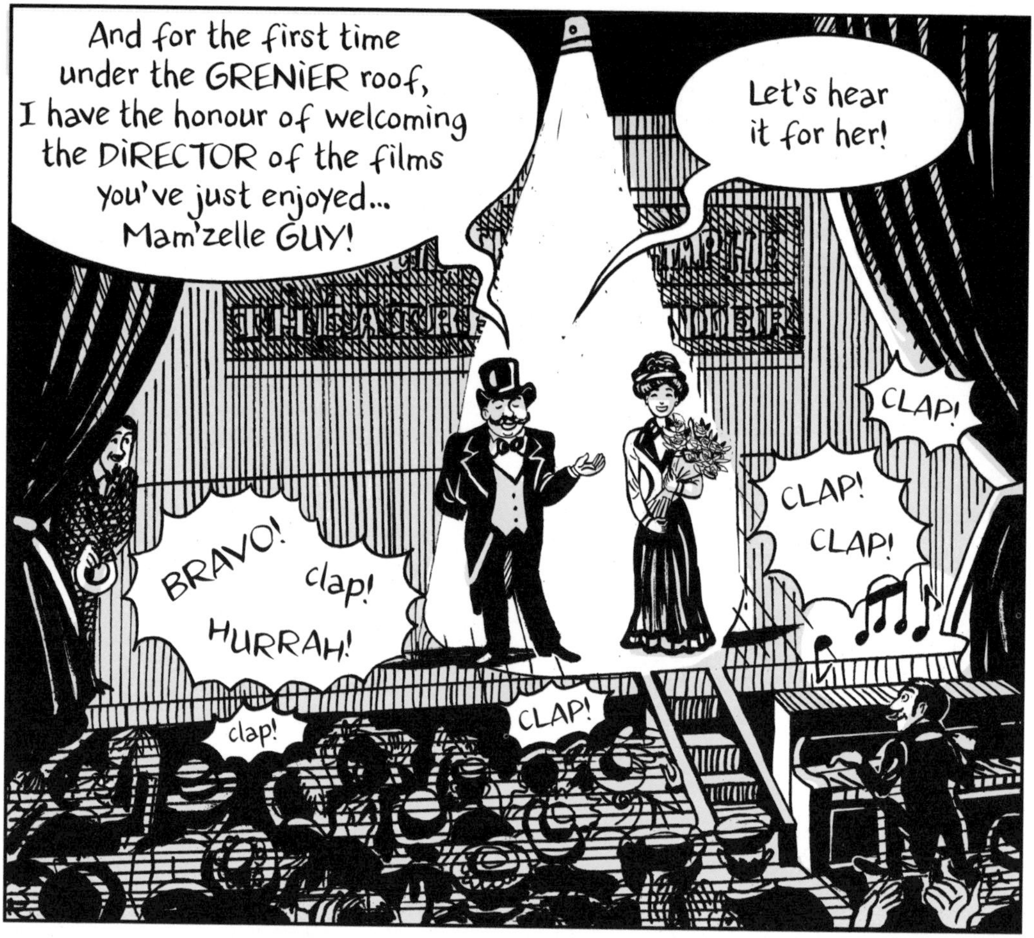
And for the first time under the GRENIER roof, I have the honour of welcoming the DIRECTOR of the films you've just enjoyed... Mam'zelle GUY!
Let's hear it for her!
CLAP!
CLAP! CLAP!
BRAVO! clap! HURRAH!
clap!
CLAP!

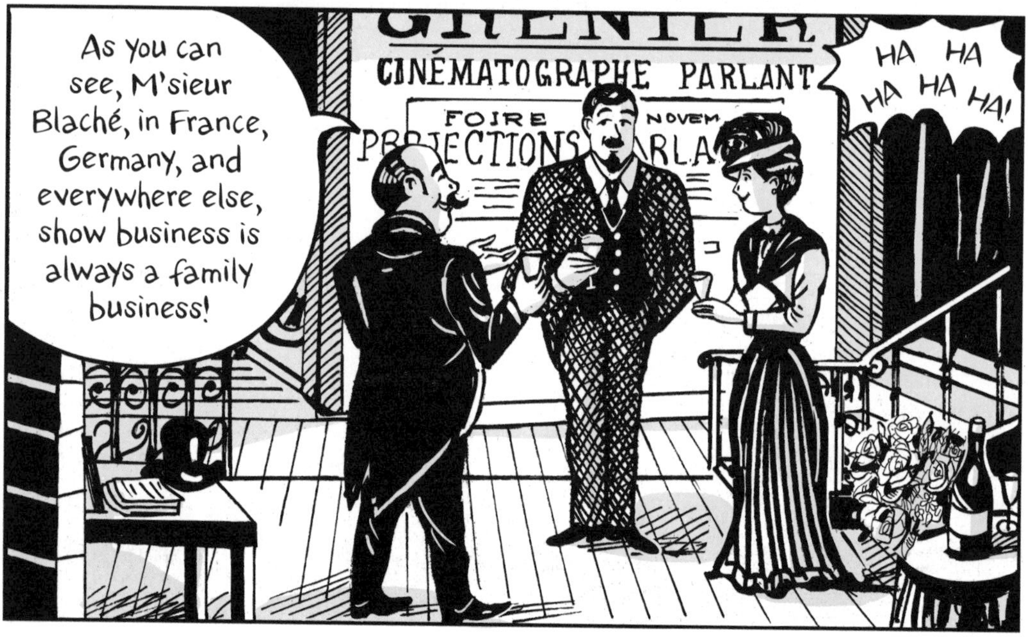
GRENIER
CINÉMATOGRAPHE PARLANT
FOIRE
NOVEM
PROJECTIONS PARLA
As you can see, M'sieur Blaché, in France, Germany, and everywhere else, show business is always a family business!
HA HA HA HA HA!

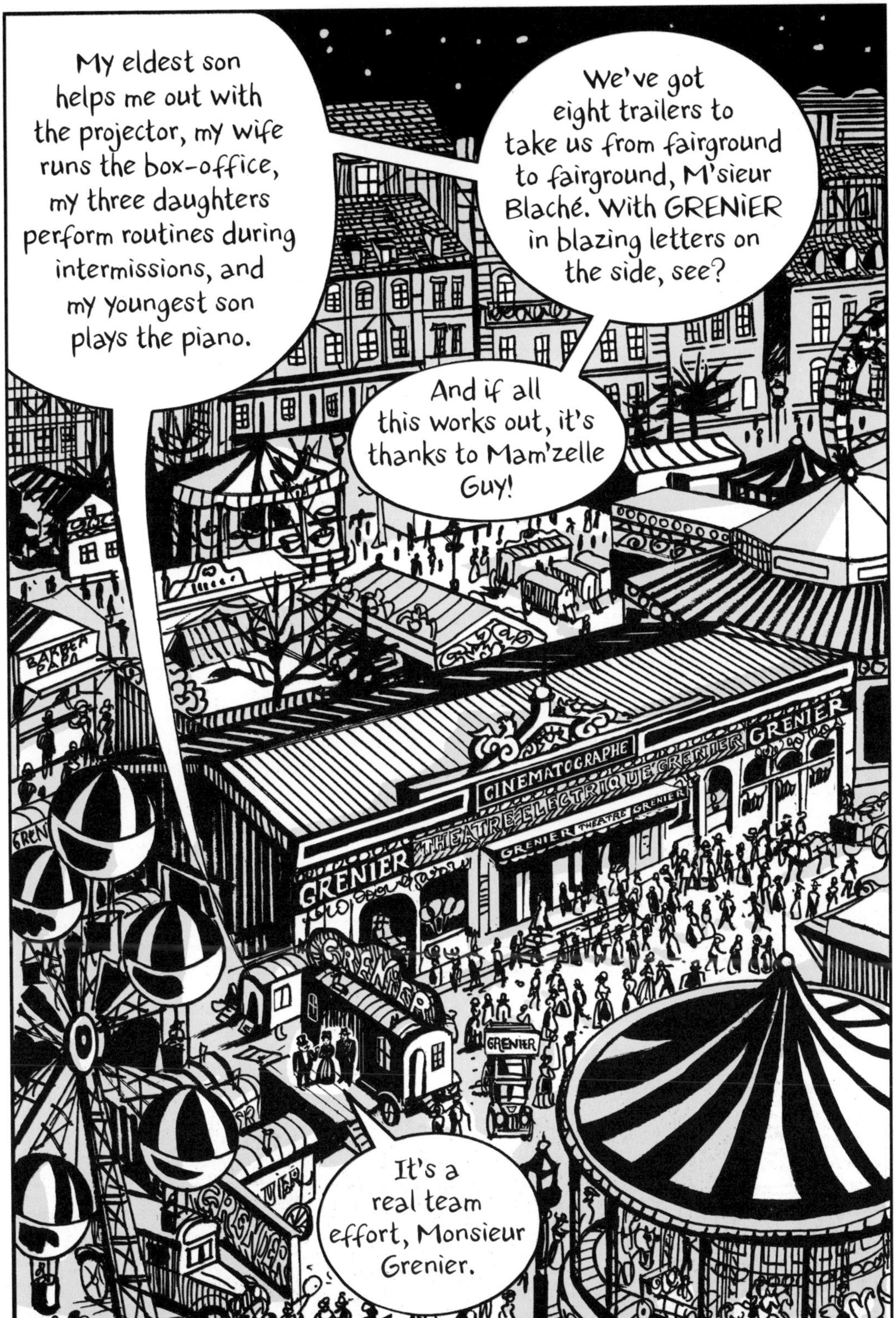
My eldest son helps me out with the projector, my wife runs the box-office, my three daughters perform routines during intermissions, and my youngest son plays the piano.
We've got eight trailers to take us from fairground to fairground, M'sieur Blaché. With GRENIER in blazing letters on the side, see?
And if all this works out, it's thanks to Mam'zelle Guy!
BARBE A PAPA
CINEMATOGRAPHE
GRENIER
THEATRE ELECTRIQUE GRENIER
GRENIER
GRENIER
It's a real team effort, Monsieur Grenier.

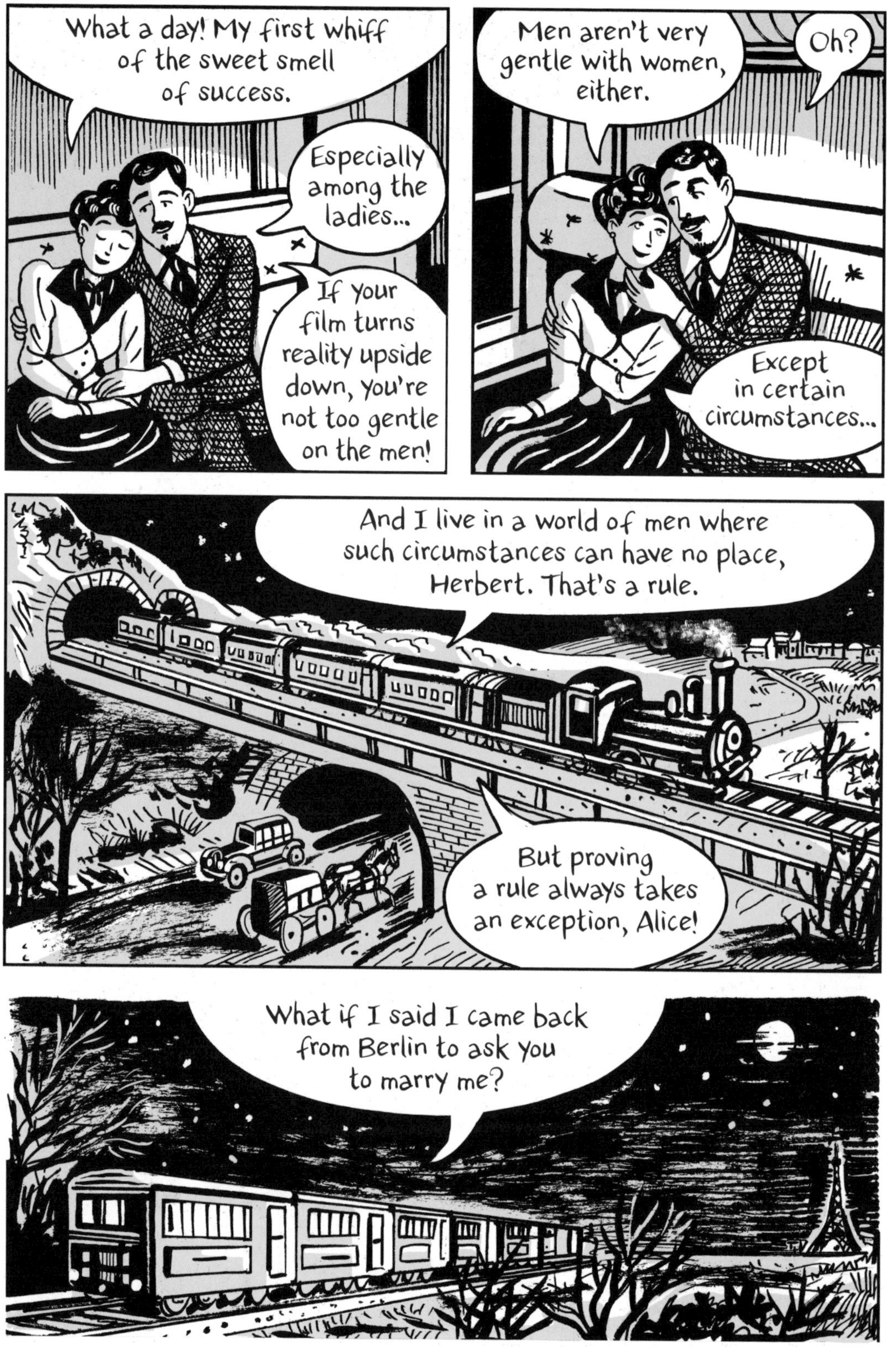
What a day! My first whiff of the sweet smell of success.
Especially among the ladies...
If your film turns reality upside down, you're not too gentle on the men!
Men aren't very gentle with women, either.
Oh?
Except in certain circumstances...
And I live in a world of men where such circumstances can have no place, Herbert. That's a rule.
But proving a rule always takes an exception, Alice!
What if I said I came back from Berlin to ask you to marry me?

March 1907 – Transatlantic Liner

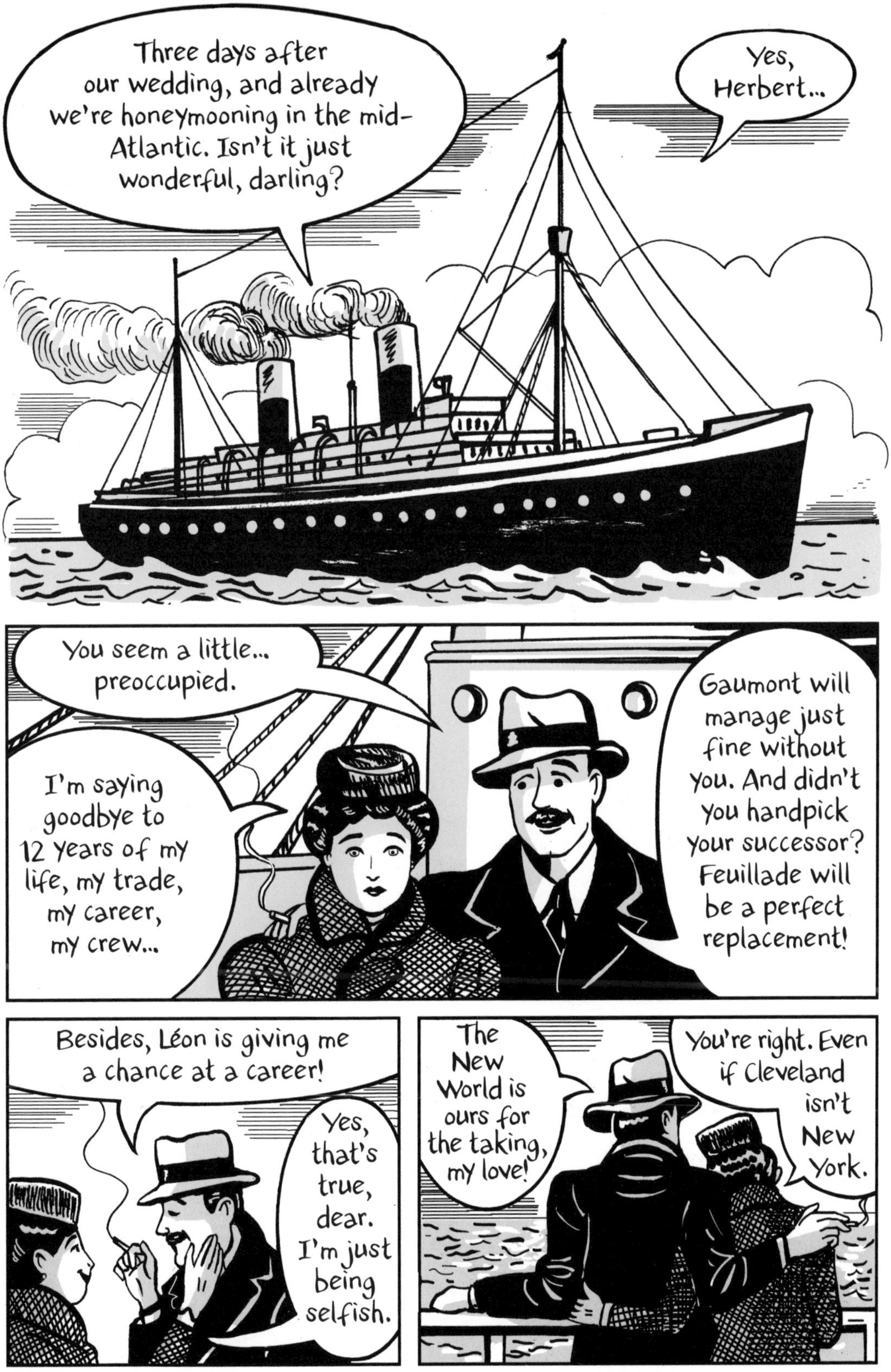
Three days after our wedding, and already we're honeymooning in the mid-Atlantic. Isn't it just wonderful, darling?
Yes, Herbert...
You seem a little... preoccupied.
I'm saying goodbye to 12 years of my life, my trade, my career, my crew...
Gaumont will manage just fine without you. And didn't you handpick your successor? Feuillade will be a perfect replacement!
Besides, Léon is giving me a chance at a career!
Yes, that's true, dear. I'm just being selfish.
The New World is ours for the taking, my love!
You're right. Even if Cleveland isn't New York.

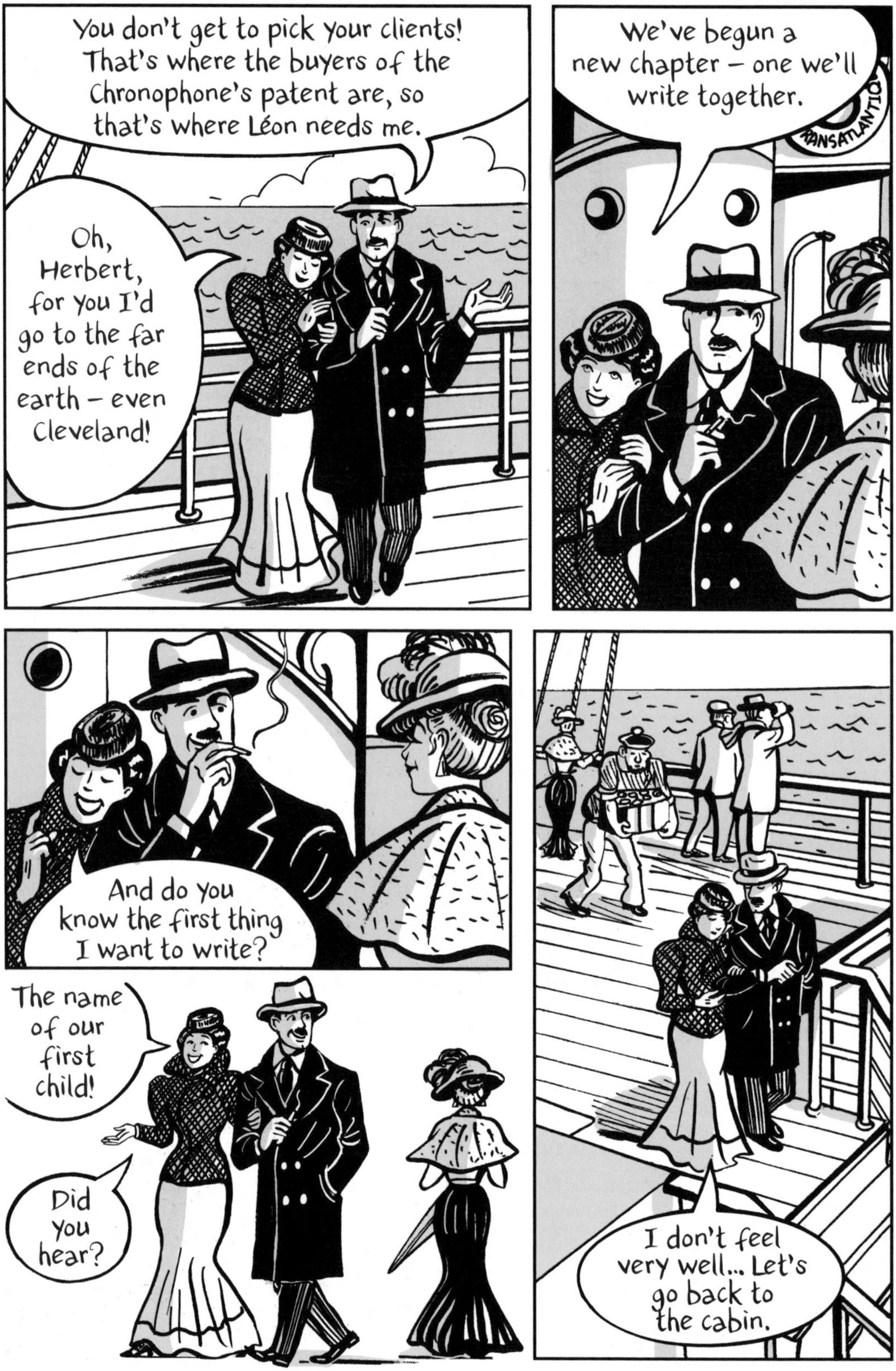
You don't get to pick your clients! That's where the buyers of the Chronophone's patent are, so that's where Léon needs me.
Oh, Herbert, for you I'd go to the far ends of the earth – even Cleveland!
We've begun a new chapter – one we'll write together.
And do you know the first thing I want to write?
The name of our first child!
Did you hear?
I don't feel very well... Let's go back to the cabin.

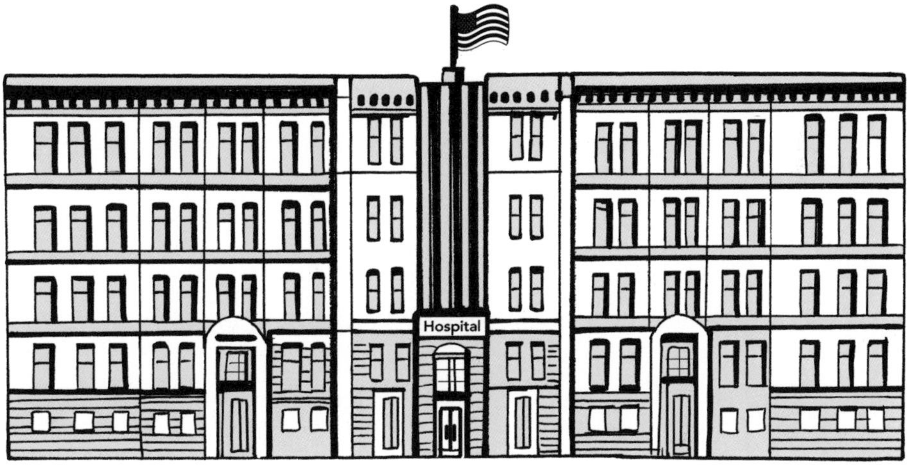
Hospital

1908 – Flushing Hospital – New York – U.S.A.

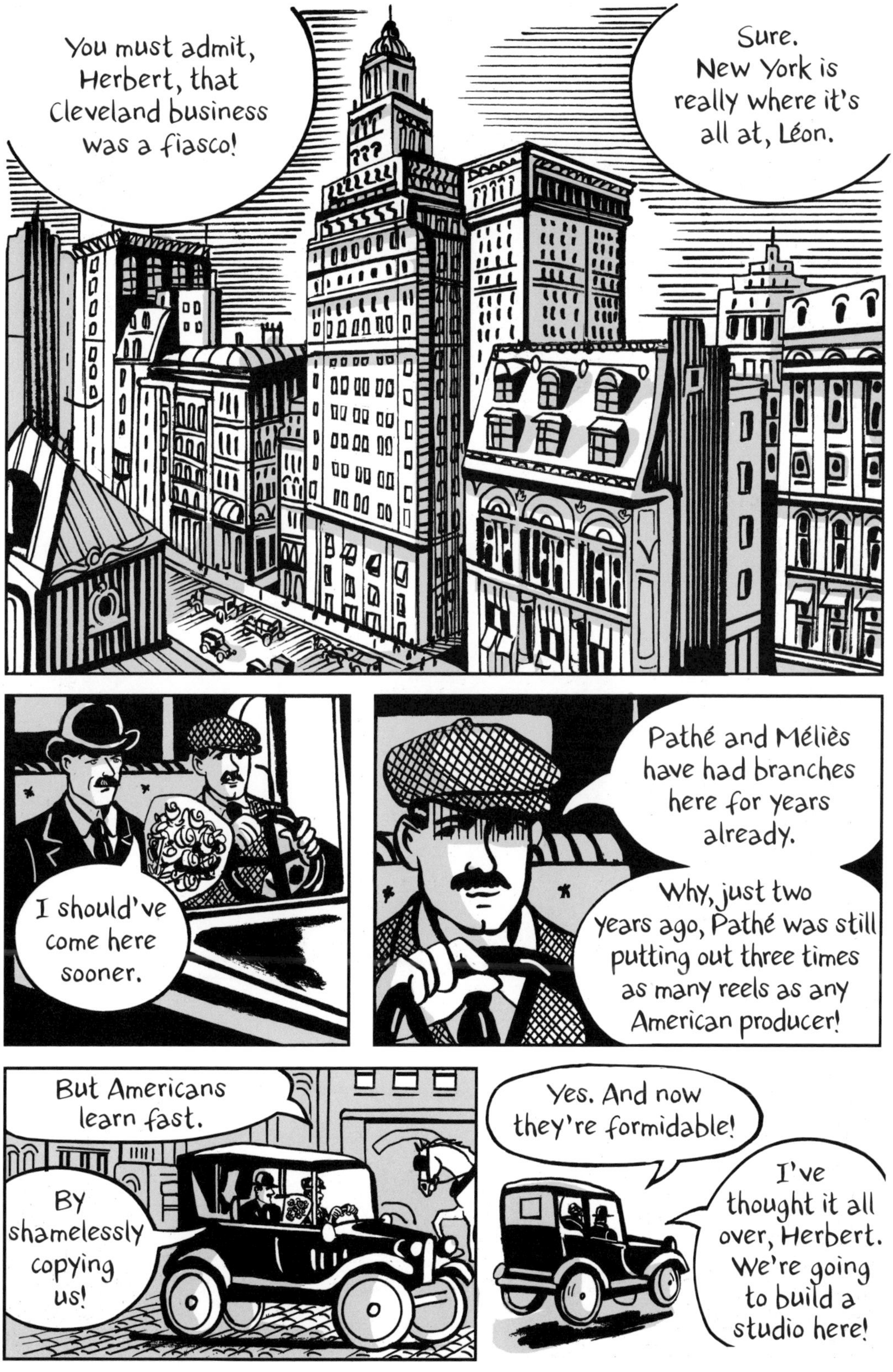
You must admit, Herbert, that Cleveland business was a fiasco!
Sure. New York is really where it's all at, Léon.
I should've come here sooner.
Pathé and Méliès have had branches here for years already.
Why, just two years ago, Pathé was still putting out three times as many reels as any American producer!
But Americans learn fast.
By shamelessly copying us!
Yes. And now they're formidable!
I've thought it all over, Herbert. We're going to build a studio here!

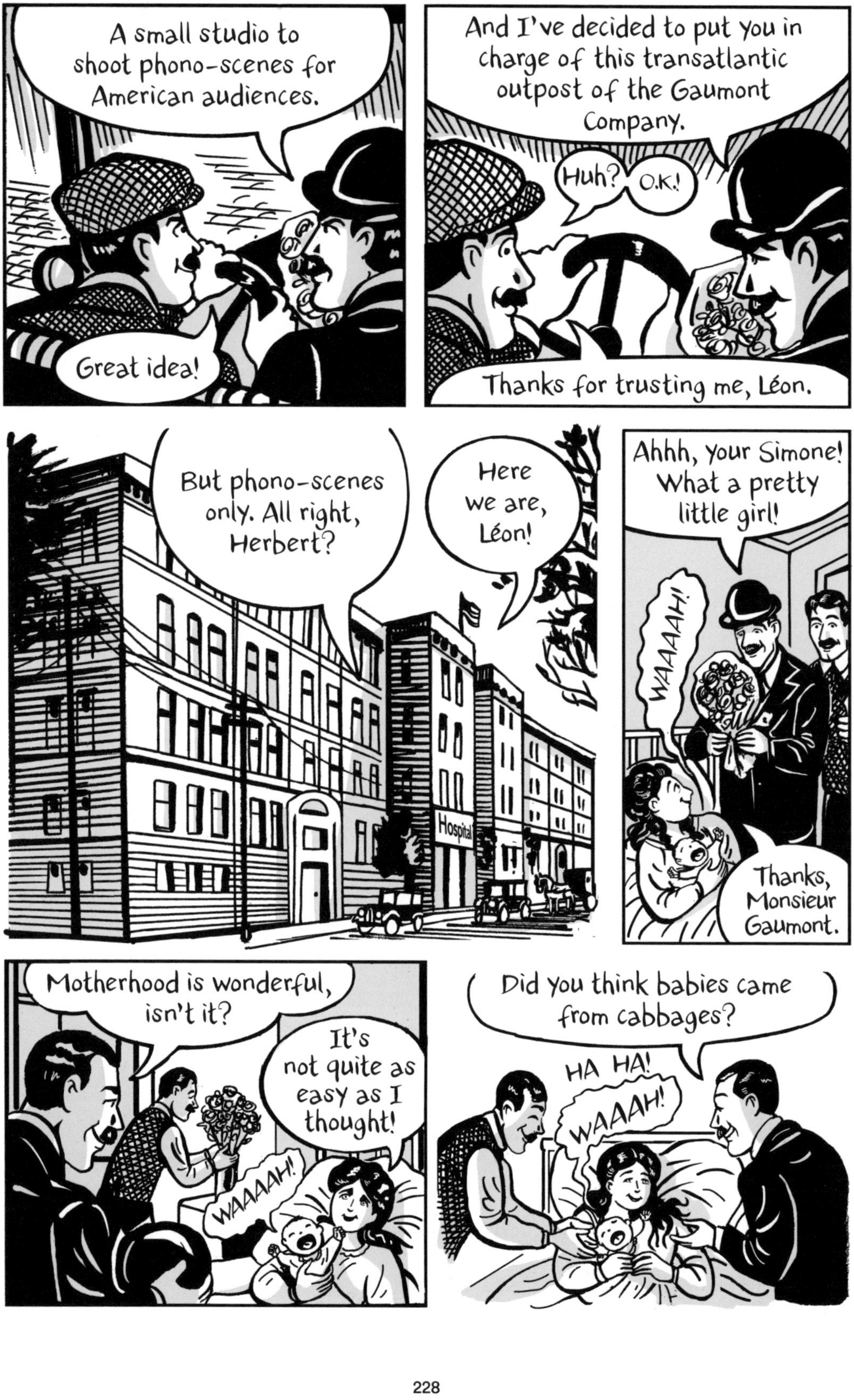
A small studio to shoot phono-scenes for American audiences.
Great idea!
And I've decided to put you in charge of this transatlantic outpost of the Gaumont Company.
Huh?
O.K.!
Thanks for trusting me, Léon.
But phono-scenes only. All right, Herbert?
Here we are, Léon!
Hospital
Ahhh, your Simone! What a pretty little girl!
WAAAAAH!
Thanks, Monsieur Gaumont.
Motherhood is wonderful, isn't it?
It's not quite as easy as I thought!
WAAAAH!
Did you think babies came from cabbages?
HA HA!
WAAAH!

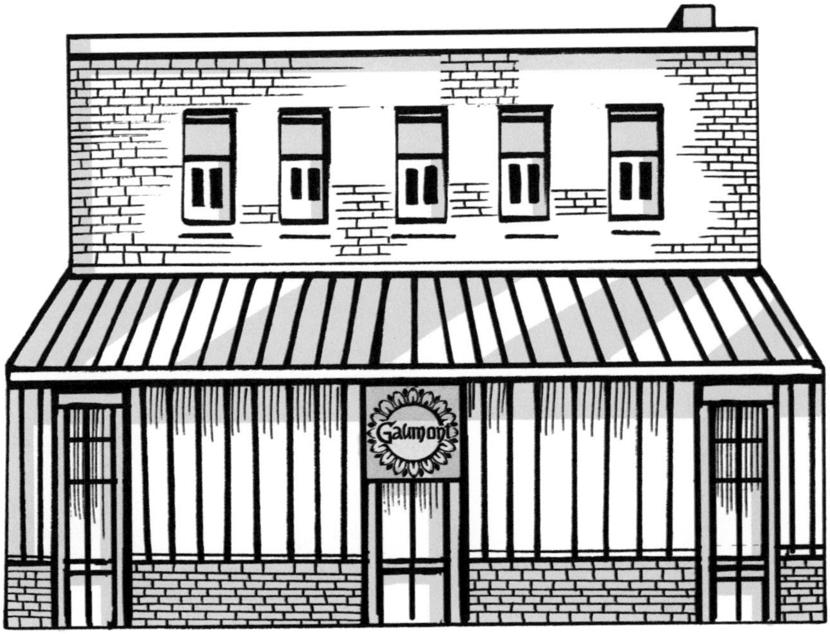
Gaumont

1910 – Laboratory – Gaumont Studios –
Flushing – U.S.A.

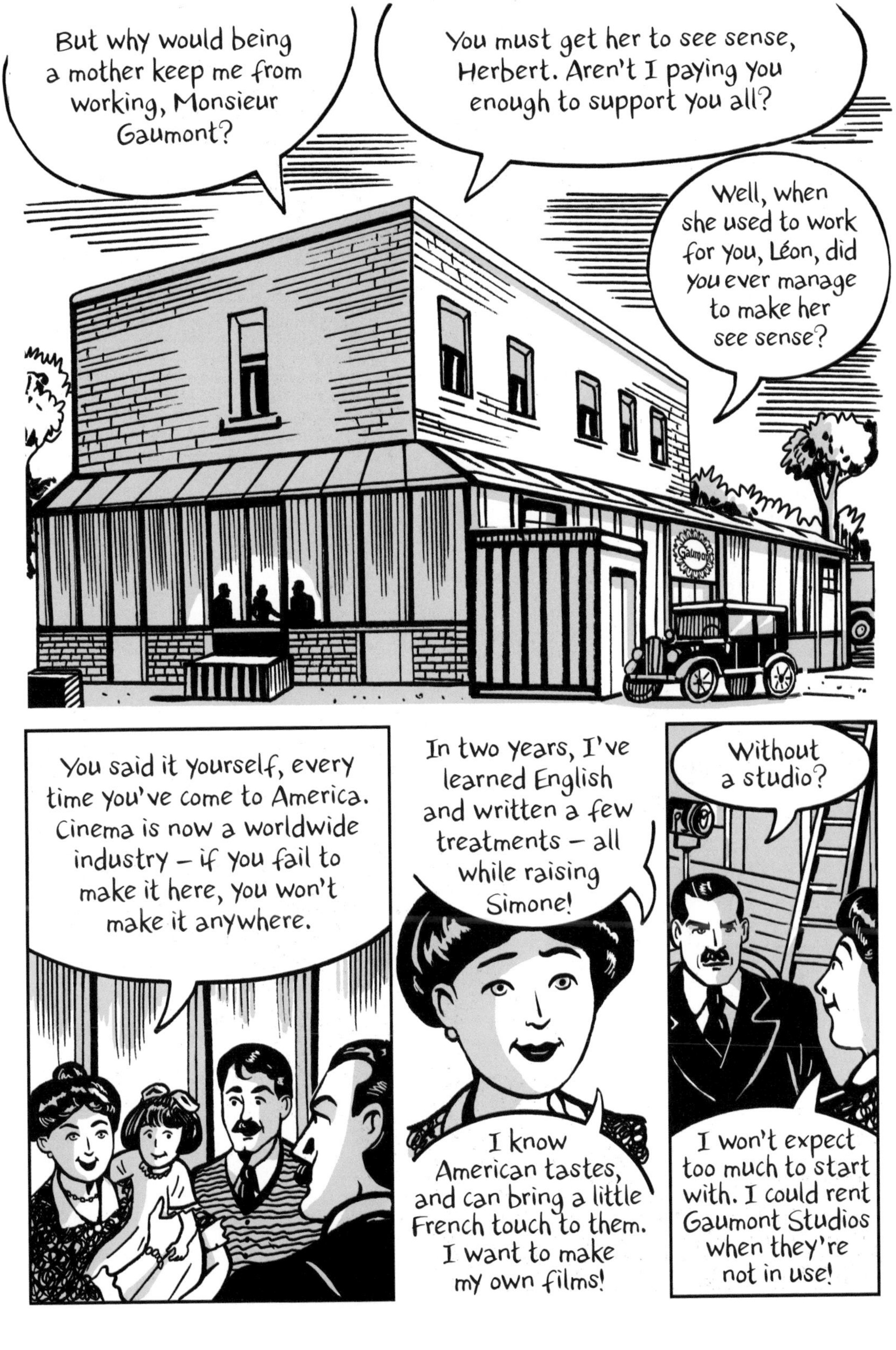
But why would being a mother keep me from working, Monsieur Gaumont?
You must get her to see sense, Herbert. Aren't I paying you enough to support you all?
Well, when she used to work for you, Léon, did you ever manage to make her see sense?
Gaumont
You said it yourself, every time you've come to America. Cinema is now a worldwide industry – if you fail to make it here, you won't make it anywhere.
In two years, I've learned English and written a few treatments – all while raising Simone!
I know American tastes, and can bring a little French touch to them. I want to make my own films!
Without a studio?
I won't expect too much to start with. I could rent Gaumont Studios when they're not in use!

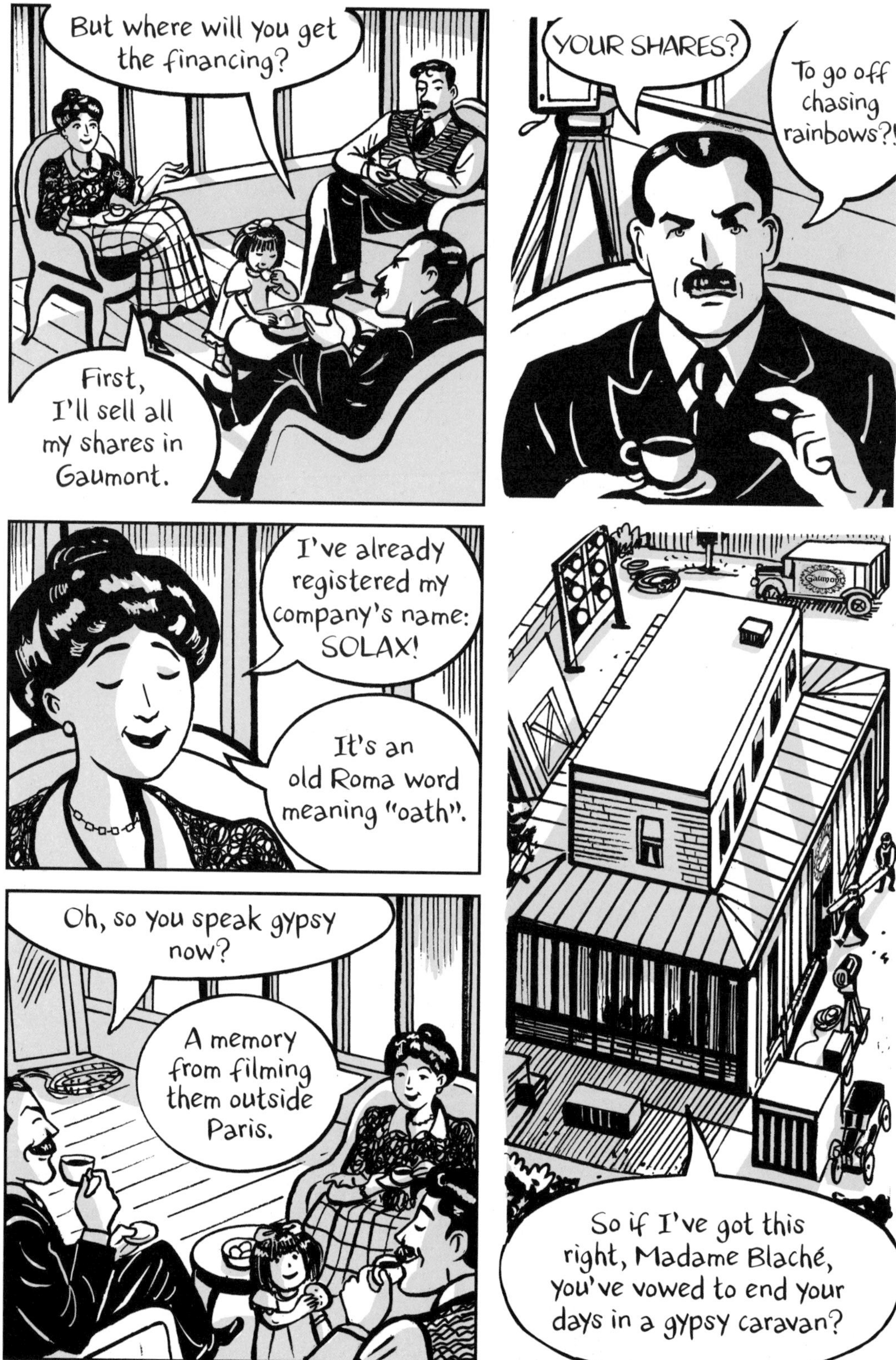
But where will you get the financing?
First, I'll sell all my shares in Gaumont.
YOUR SHARES?
To go off chasing rainbows?!
I've already registered my company's name: SOLAX!
It's an old Roma word meaning "oath".
Oh, so you speak gypsy now?
A memory from filming them outside Paris.
So if I've got this right, Madame Blaché, you've vowed to end your days in a gypsy caravan?

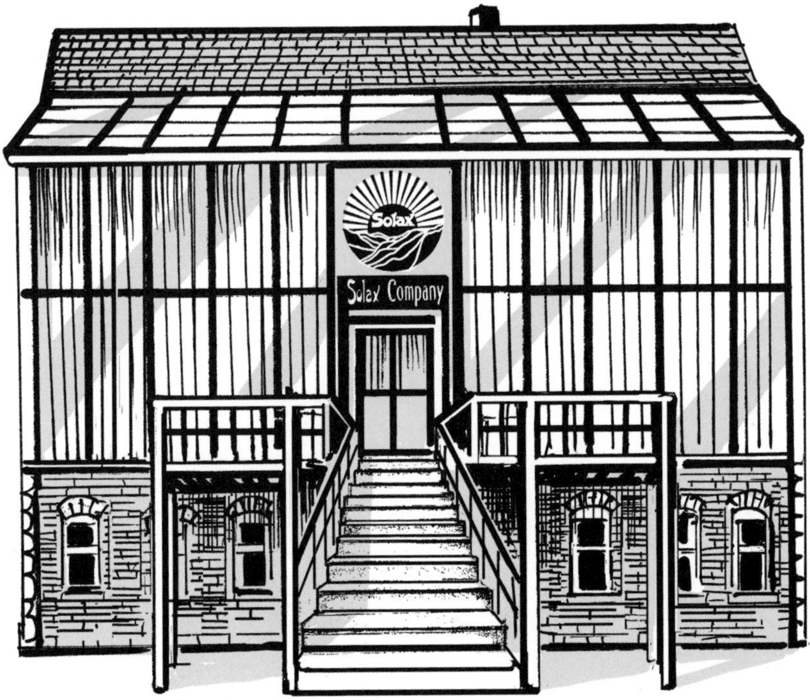
Solax
Solax Company

1912 – Solax Studios – Fort Lee – U.S.A.

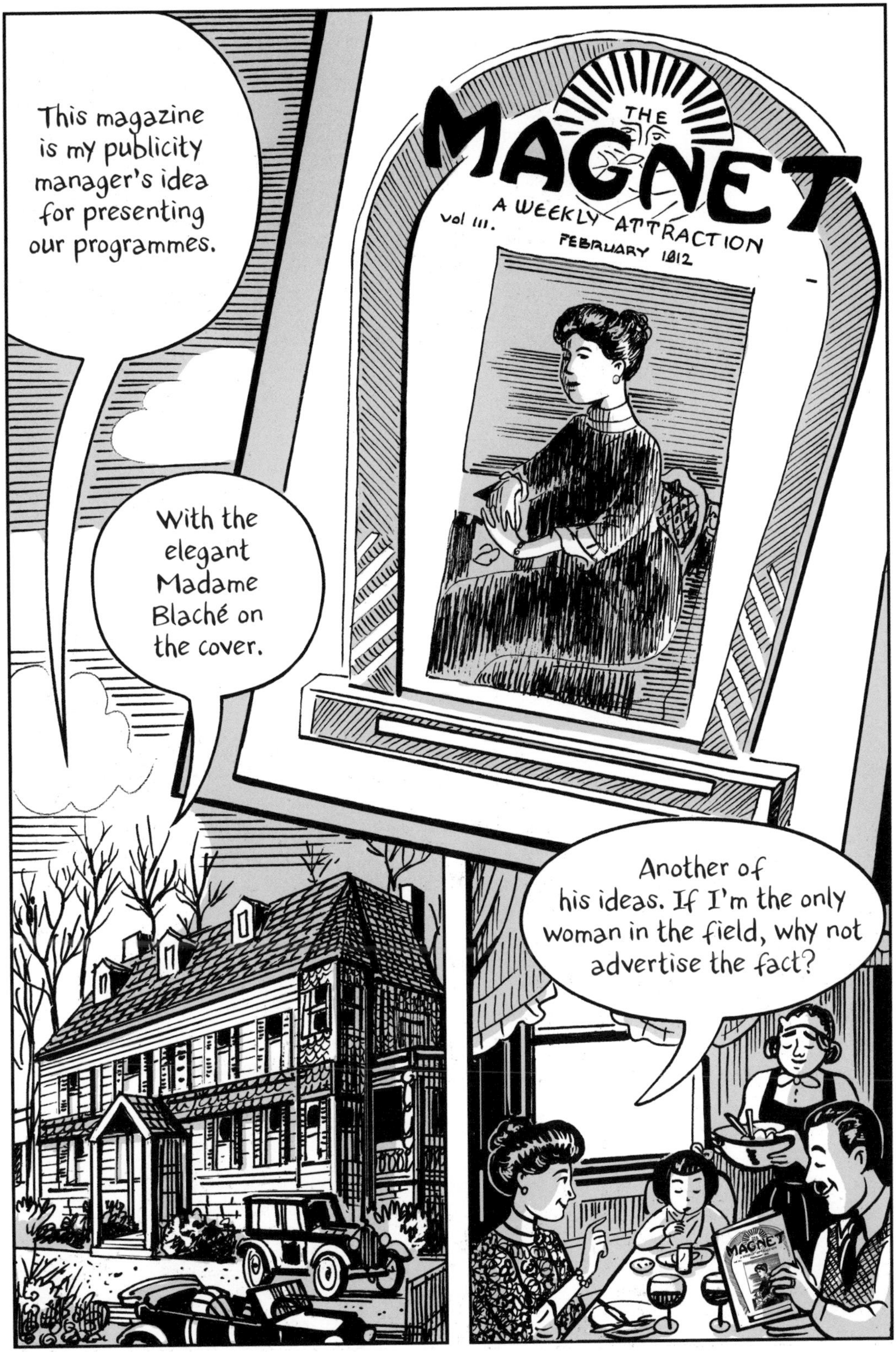
This magazine is my publicity manager's idea for presenting our programmes.
THE MAGNET
A WEEKLY ATTRACTION
Vol III.
FEBRUARY 1912
With the elegant Madame Blaché on the cover.
Another of his ideas. If I'm the only woman in the field, why not advertise the fact?

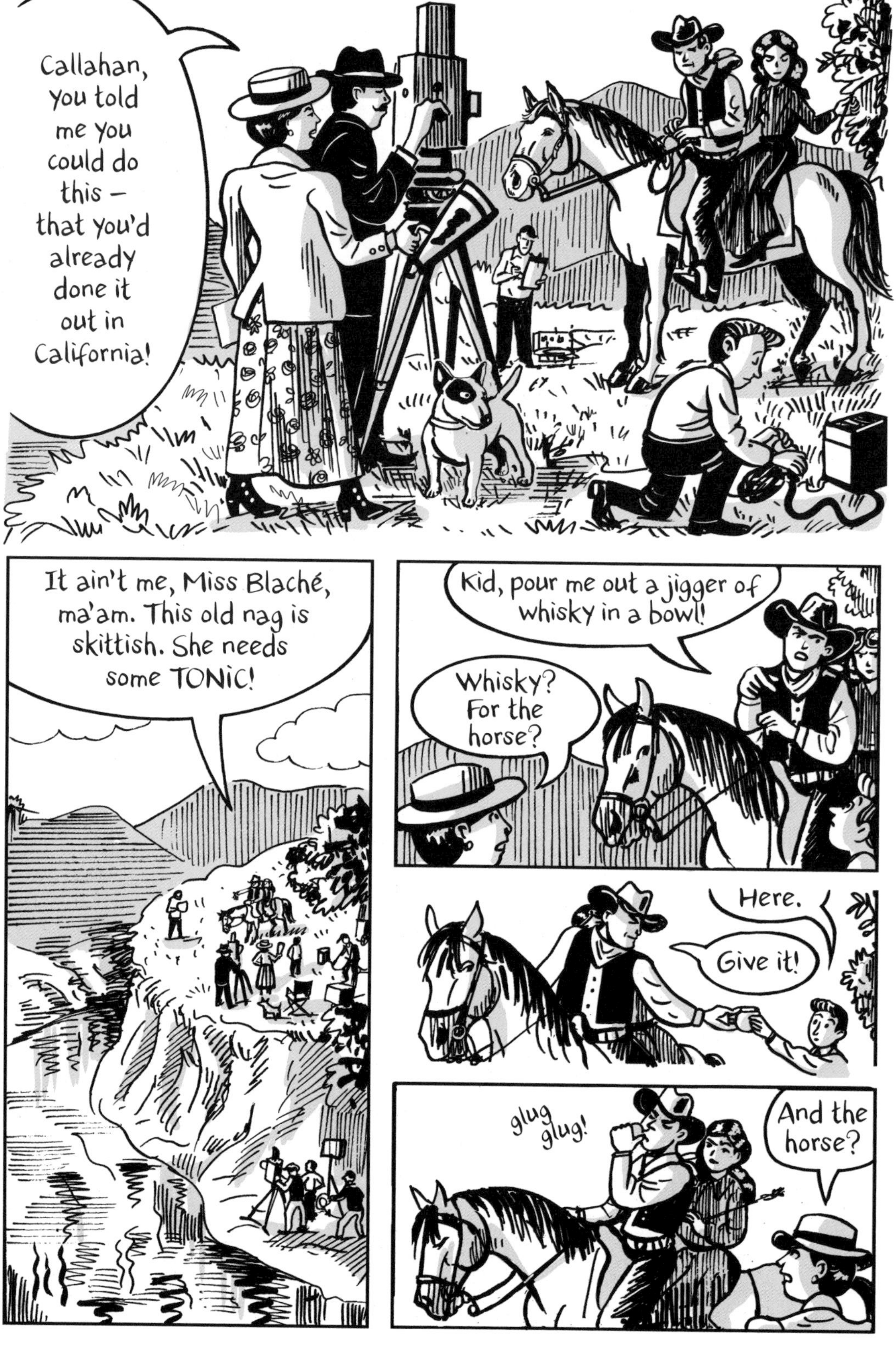
Callahan, you told me you could do this – that you'd already done it out in California!
It ain't me, Miss Blaché, ma'am. This old nag is skittish. She needs some TONIC!
Kid, pour me out a jigger of whisky in a bowl!
Whisky? For the horse?
Here.
Give it!
glug glug!
And the horse?

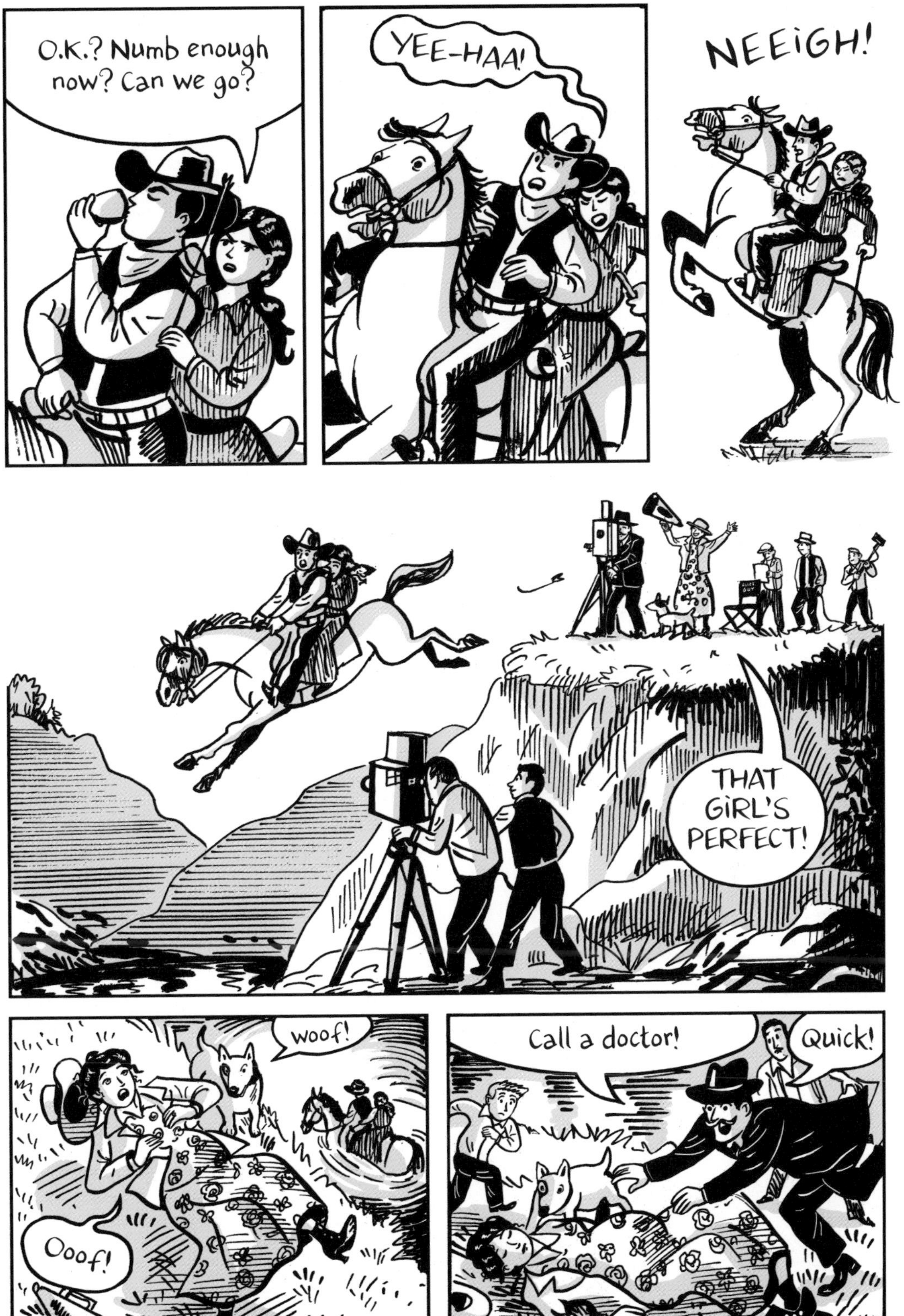
O.K.? Numb enough now? Can we go?
YEE-HAA!
NEEiGH!
THAT GiRL'S PERFECT!
woof!
Ooof!
Call a doctor!
Quick!

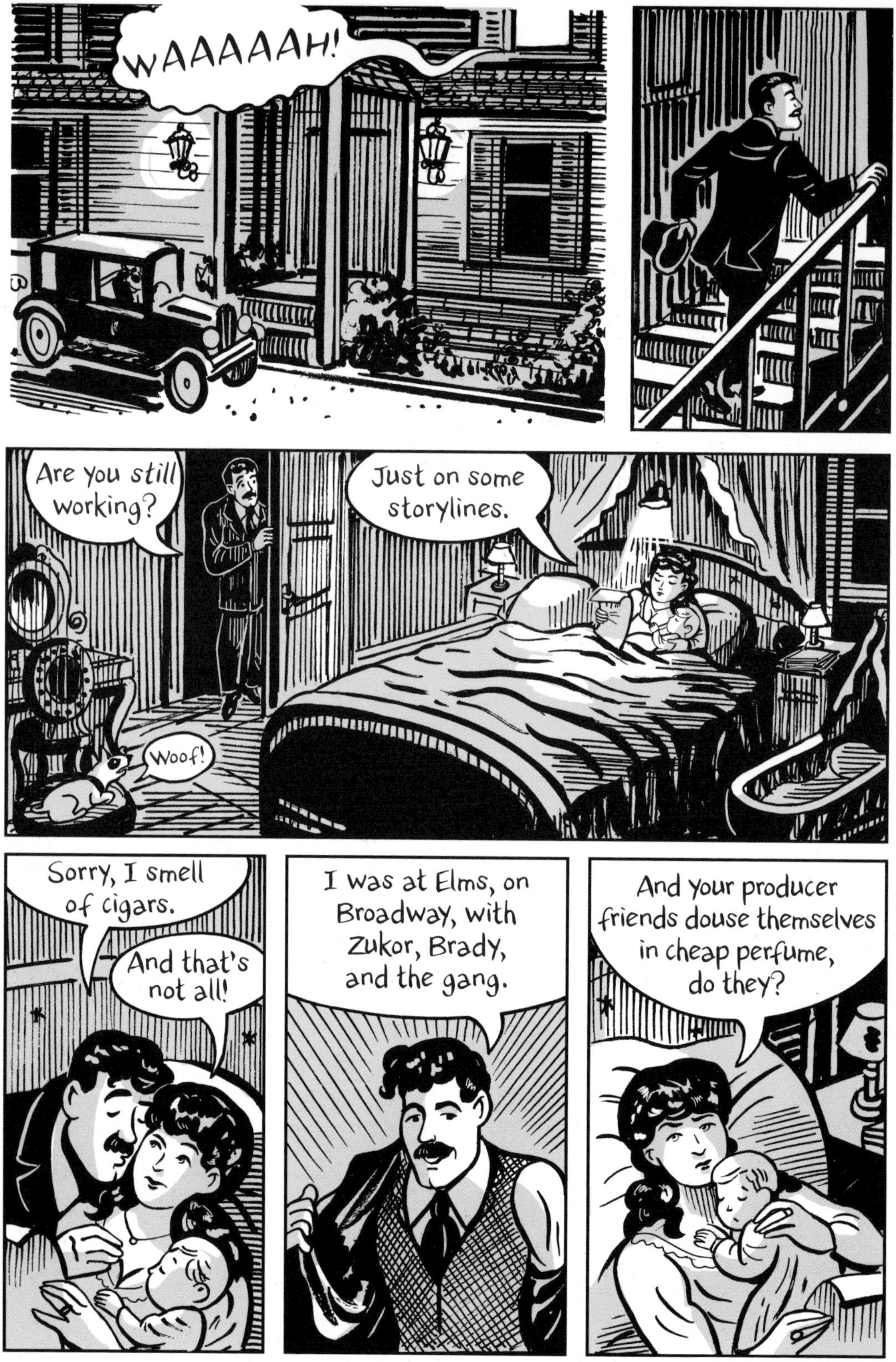
WAAAAAH!
Are you still working?
Just on some storylines.
Woof!
Sorry, I smell of cigars.
And that's not all!
I was at Elms, on Broadway, with Zukor, Brady, and the gang.
And your producer friends douse themselves in cheap perfume, do they?

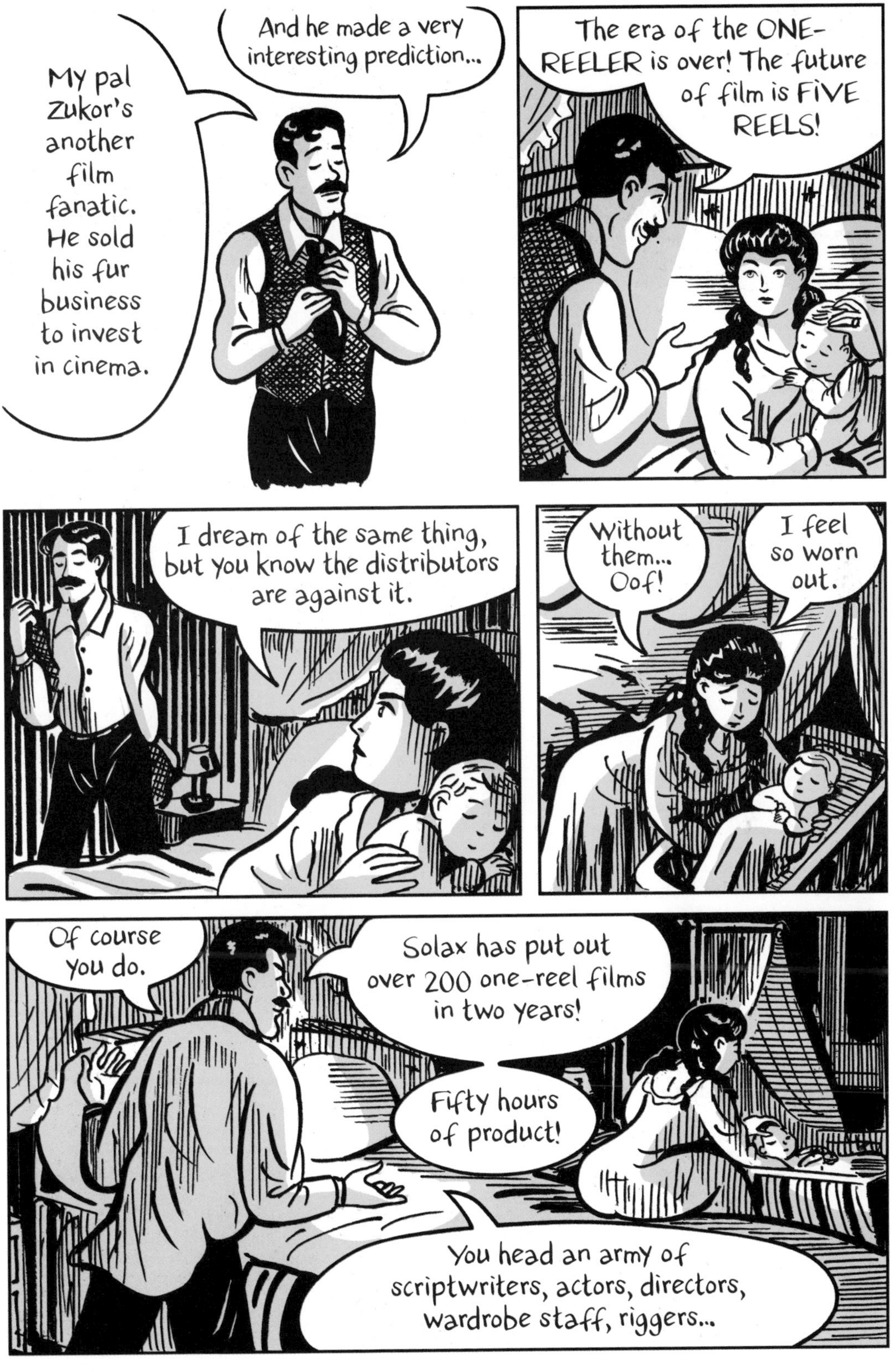
My pal Zukor's another film fanatic. He sold his fur business to invest in cinema.
And he made a very interesting prediction...
The era of the ONE-REELER is over! The future of film is FIVE REELS!
I dream of the same thing, but you know the distributors are against it.
Without them... Oof!
I feel so worn out.
Of course you do.
Solax has put out over 200 one-reel films in two years!
Fifty hours of product!
You head an army of scriptwriters, actors, directors, wardrobe staff, riggers...

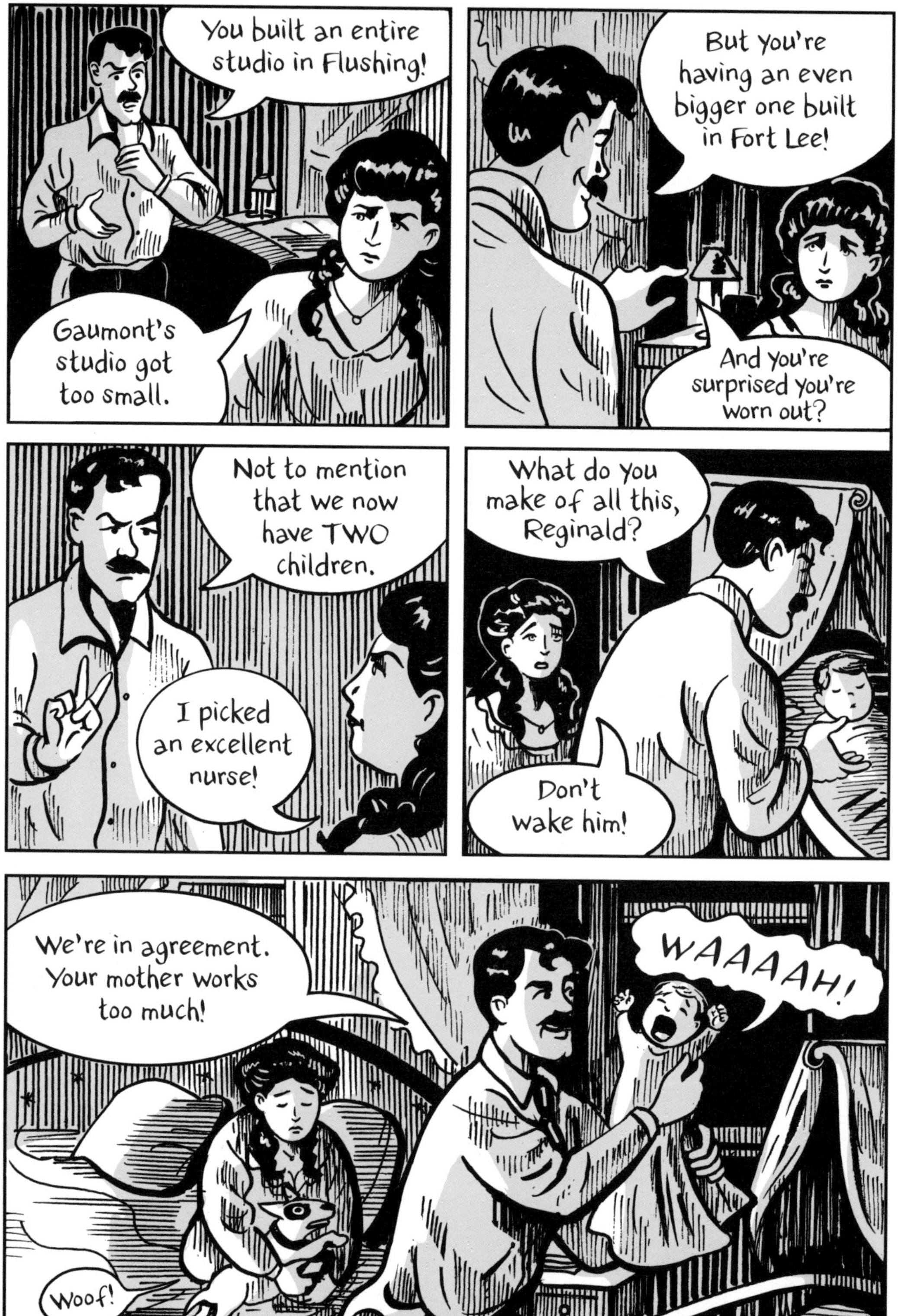
You built an entire studio in Flushing!
Gaumont's studio got too small.
But you're having an even bigger one built in Fort Lee!
And you're surprised you're worn out?
Not to mention that we now have TWO children.
I picked an excellent nurse!
What do you make of all this, Reginald?
Don't wake him!
We're in agreement. Your mother works too much!
WAAAAH!
Woof!

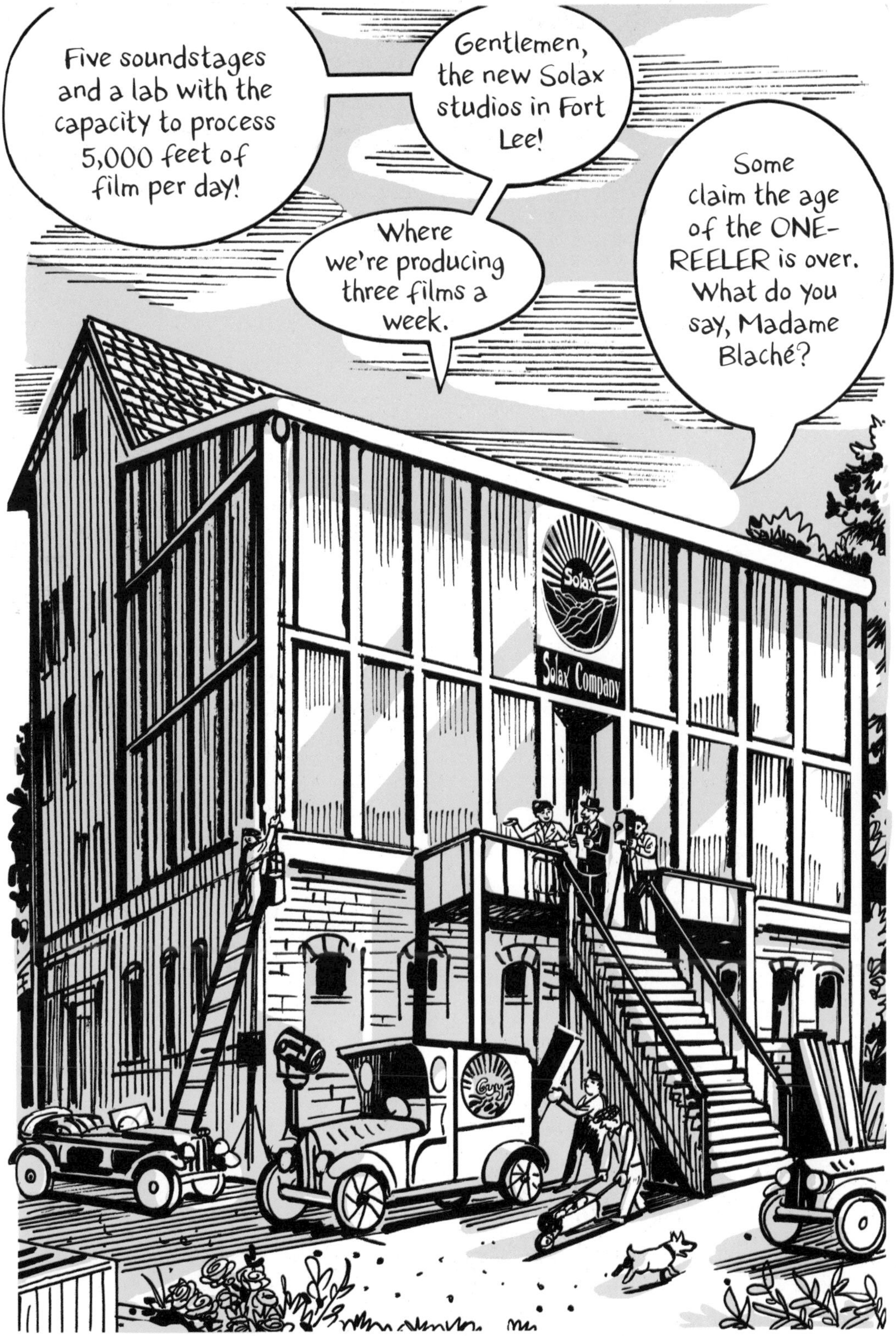
Gentlemen, the new Solax studios in Fort Lee!
Five soundstages and a lab with the capacity to process 5,000 feet of film per day!
Where we're producing three films a week.
Some claim the age of the ONE-REELER is over. What do you say, Madame Blaché?
Solax
Solax Company

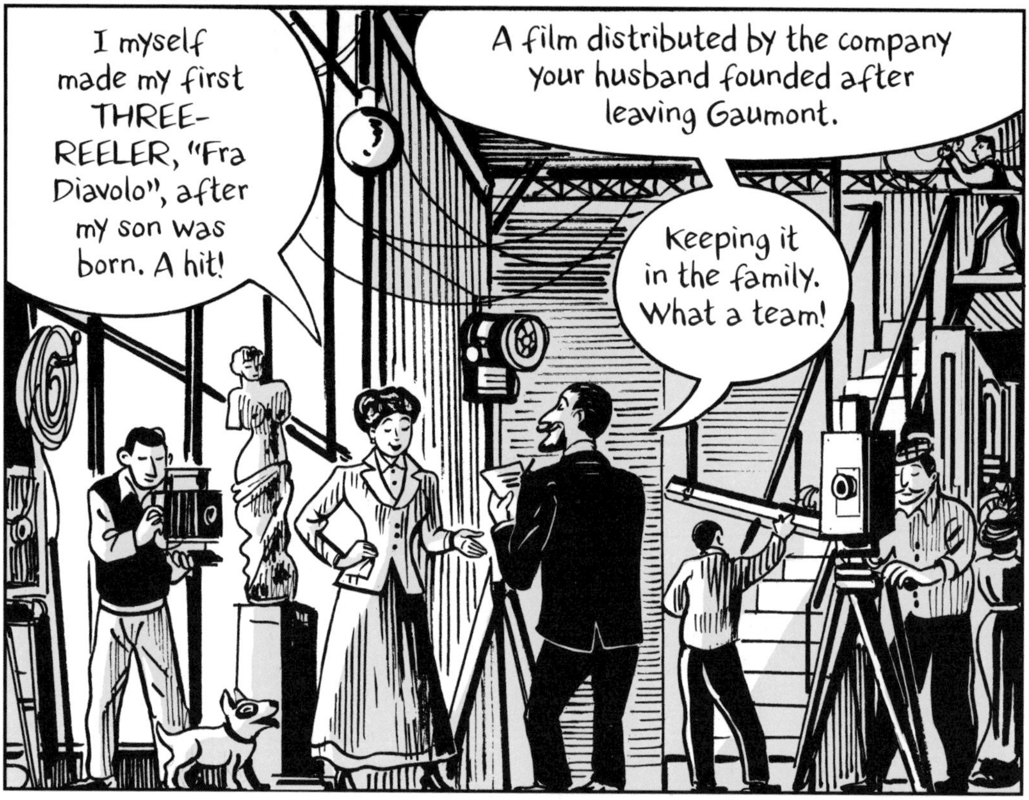
I myself made my first THREE-REELER, "Fra Diavolo", after my son was born. A hit!
A film distributed by the company your husband founded after leaving Gaumont.
Keeping it in the family. What a team!

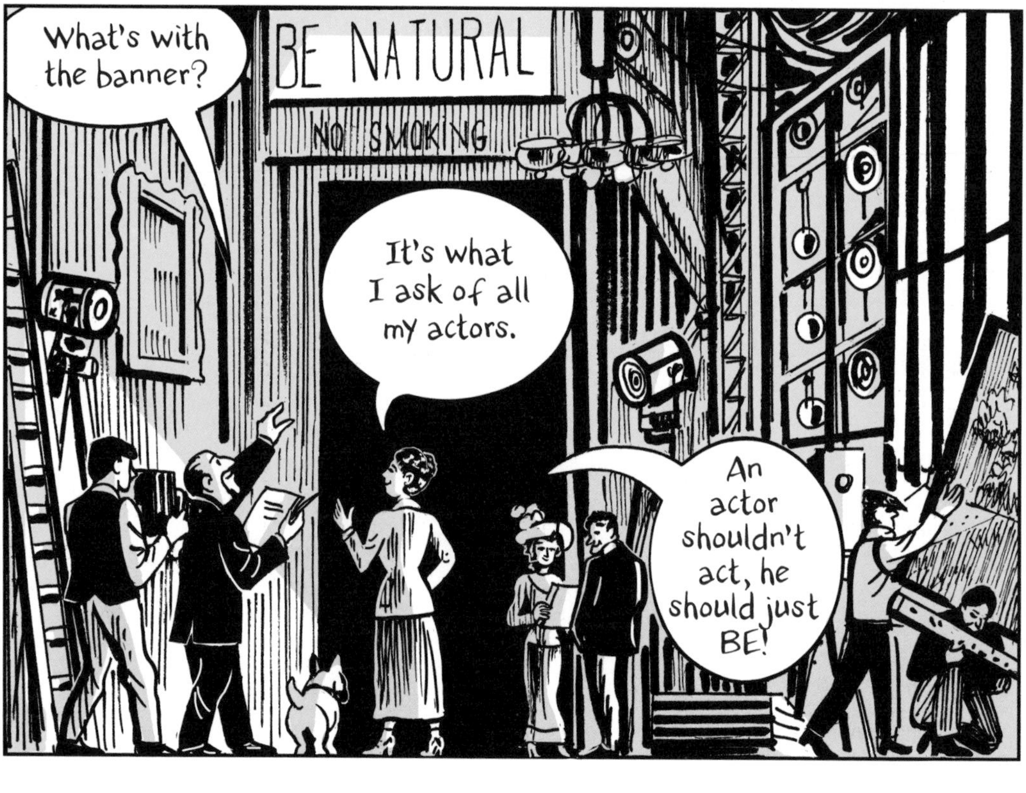
What's with the banner?
BE NATURAL
NO SMOKING
It's what I ask of all my actors.
An actor shouldn't act, he should just BE!

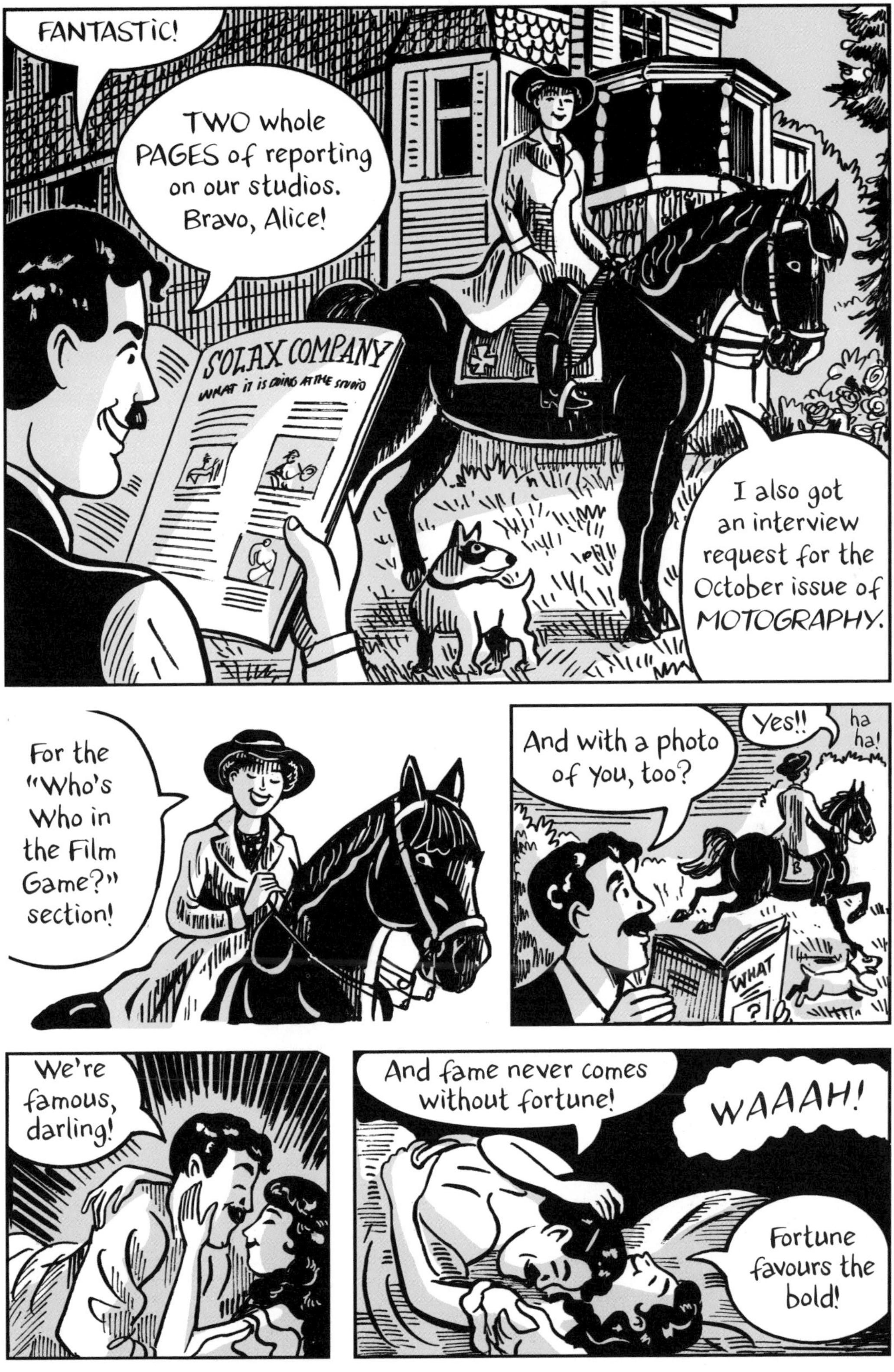

FANTASTIC!
TWO whole PAGES of reporting on our studios. Bravo, Alice!
SOLAX COMPANY
WHAT IT IS DOING AT THE STUDIO
I also got an interview request for the October issue of MOTOGRAPHY.
For the "Who's Who in the Film Game?" section!
And with a photo of you, too?
Yes!!
ha ha!
WHAT
We're famous, darling!
And fame never comes without fortune!
WAAAH!
Fortune favours the bold!

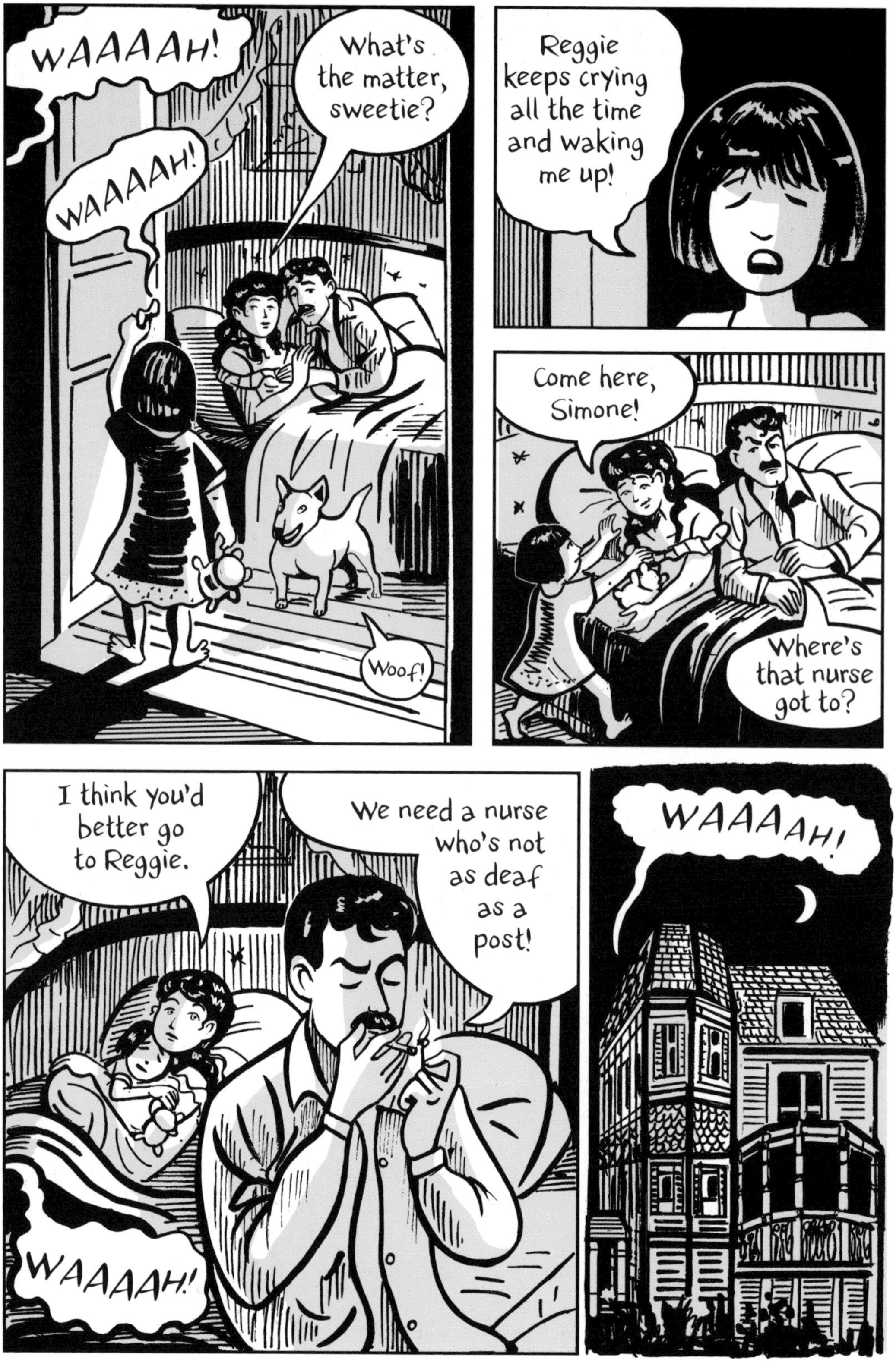
WAAAAH!
WAAAAH!
What's the matter, sweetie?
Woof!
Reggie keeps crying all the time and waking me up!
Come here, Simone!
Where's that nurse got to?
I think you'd better go to Reggie.
We need a nurse who's not as deaf as a post!
WAAAAH!
WAAAAH!

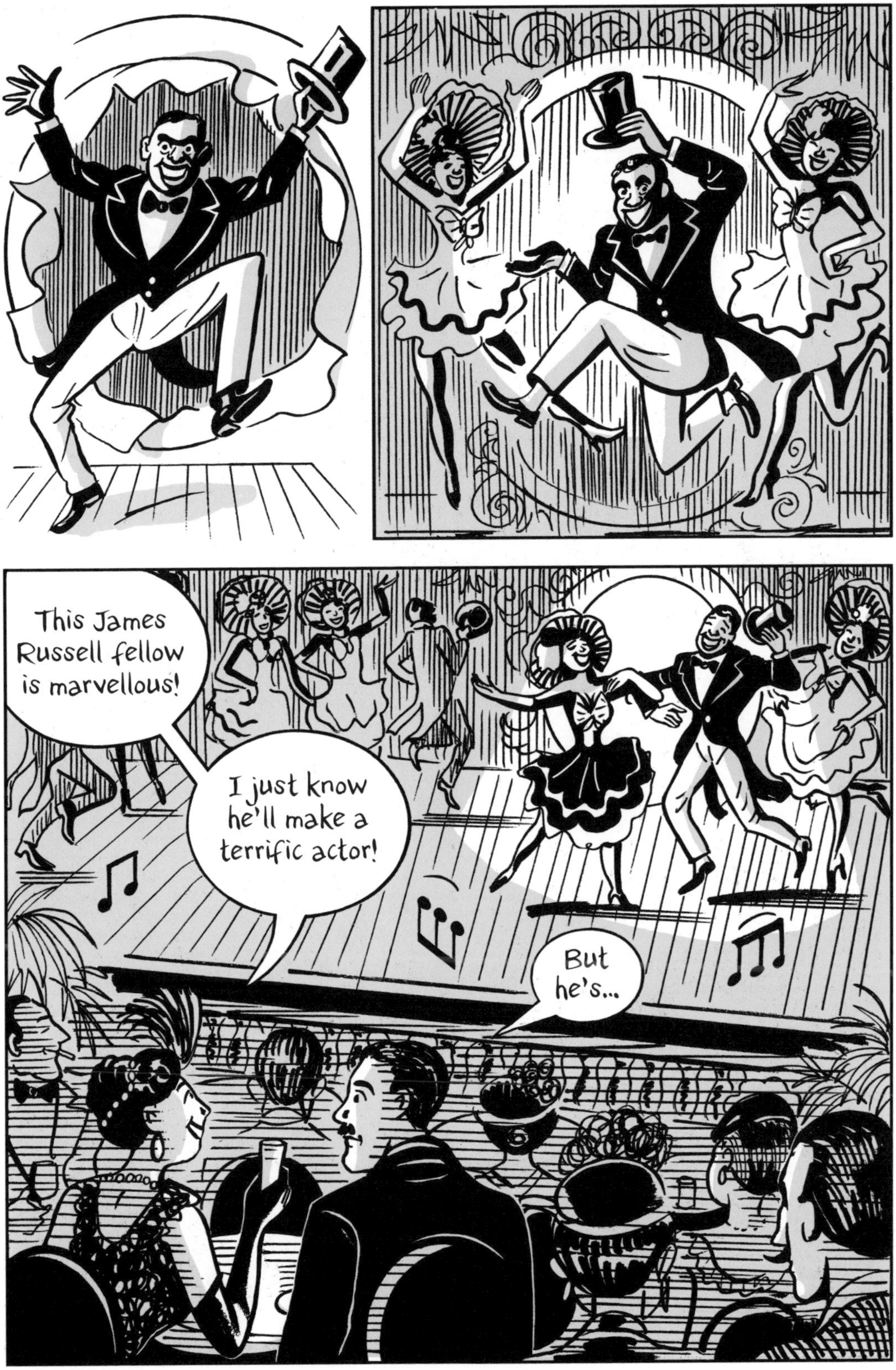
This James Russell fellow is marvellous!
I just know he'll make a terrific actor!
But he's...

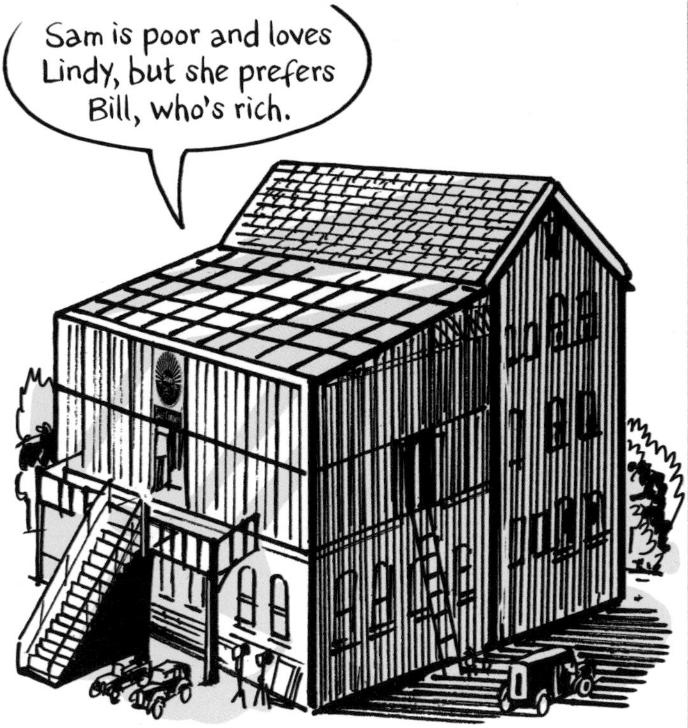
Sam is poor and loves Lindy, but she prefers Bill, who's rich.

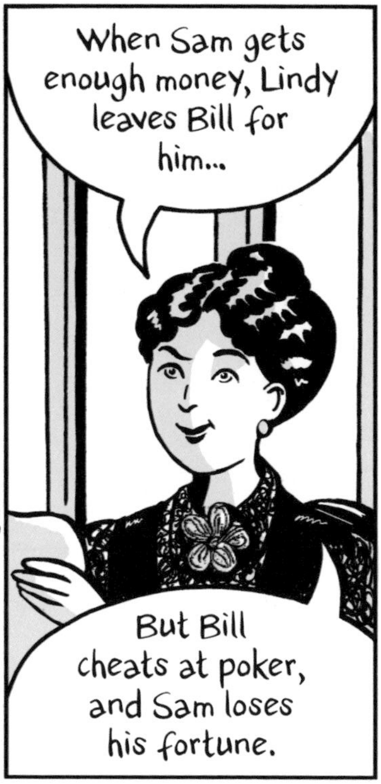
When Sam gets enough money, Lindy leaves Bill for him...
But Bill cheats at poker, and Sam loses his fortune.

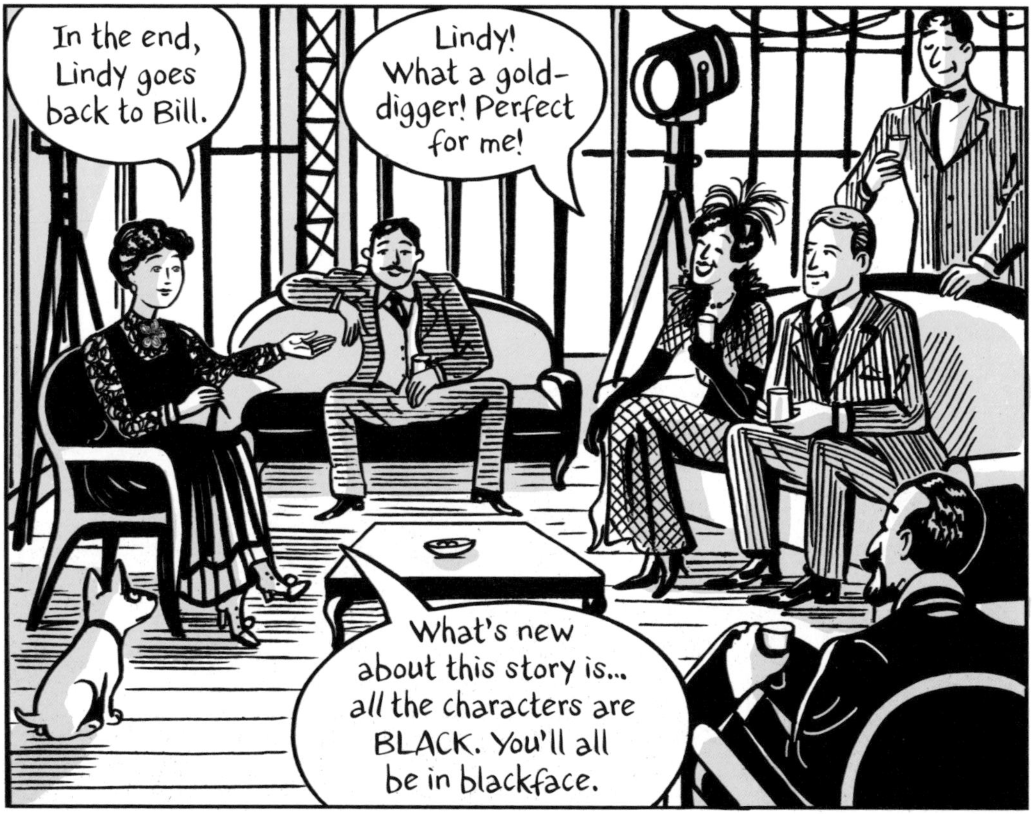
In the end, Lindy goes back to Bill.
Lindy! What a gold-digger! Perfect for me!
What's new about this story is... all the characters are BLACK. You'll all be in blackface.

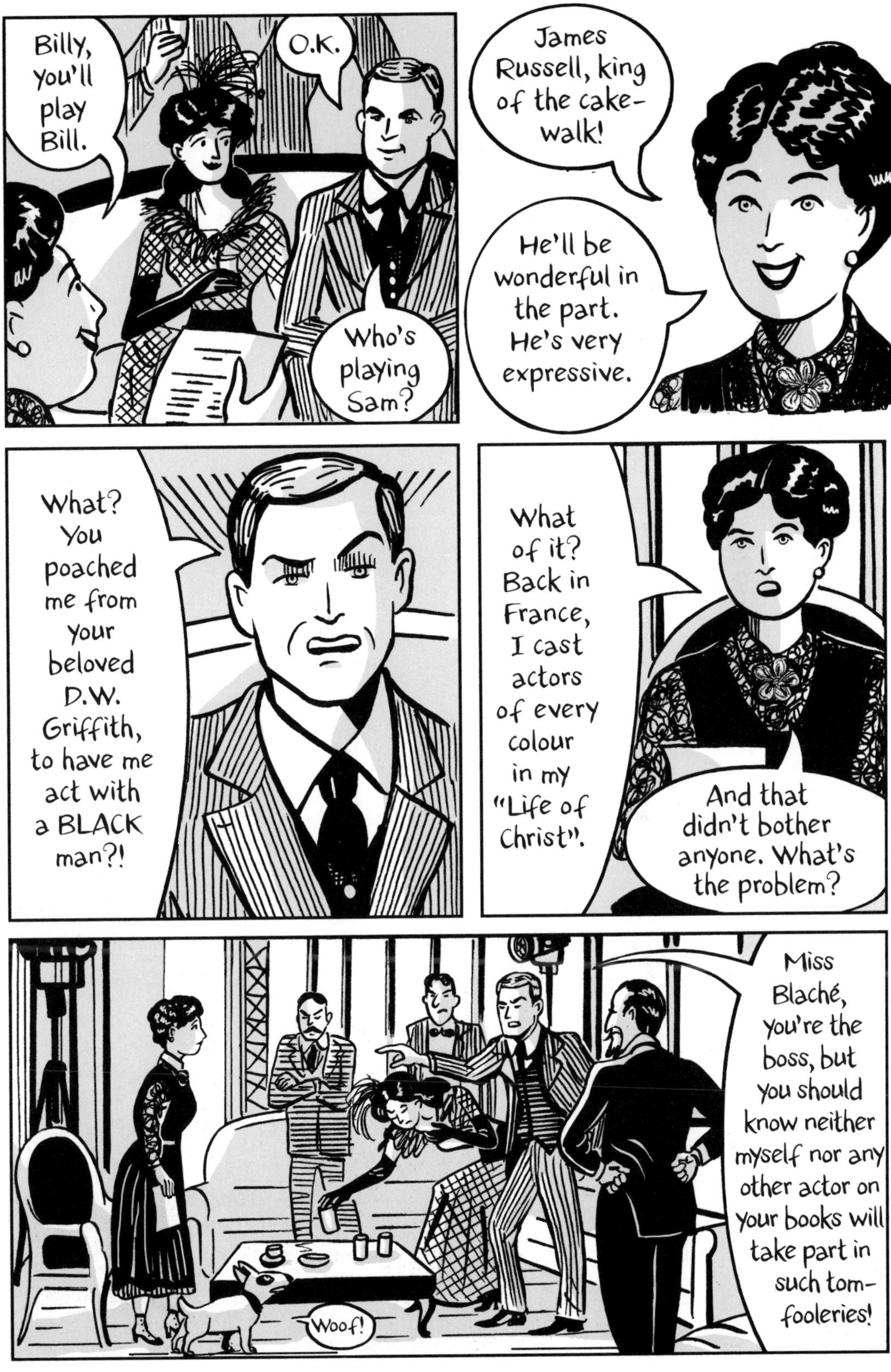
Billy, you'll play Bill.
O.K.
Who's playing Sam?
James Russell, king of the cake-walk!
He'll be wonderful in the part. He's very expressive.
What? You poached me from your beloved D.W. Griffith, to have me act with a BLACK man?!
What of it? Back in France, I cast actors of every colour in my "Life of Christ".
And that didn't bother anyone. What's the problem?
Miss Blaché, you're the boss, but you should know neither myself nor any other actor on your books will take part in such tom-fooleries!
Woof!

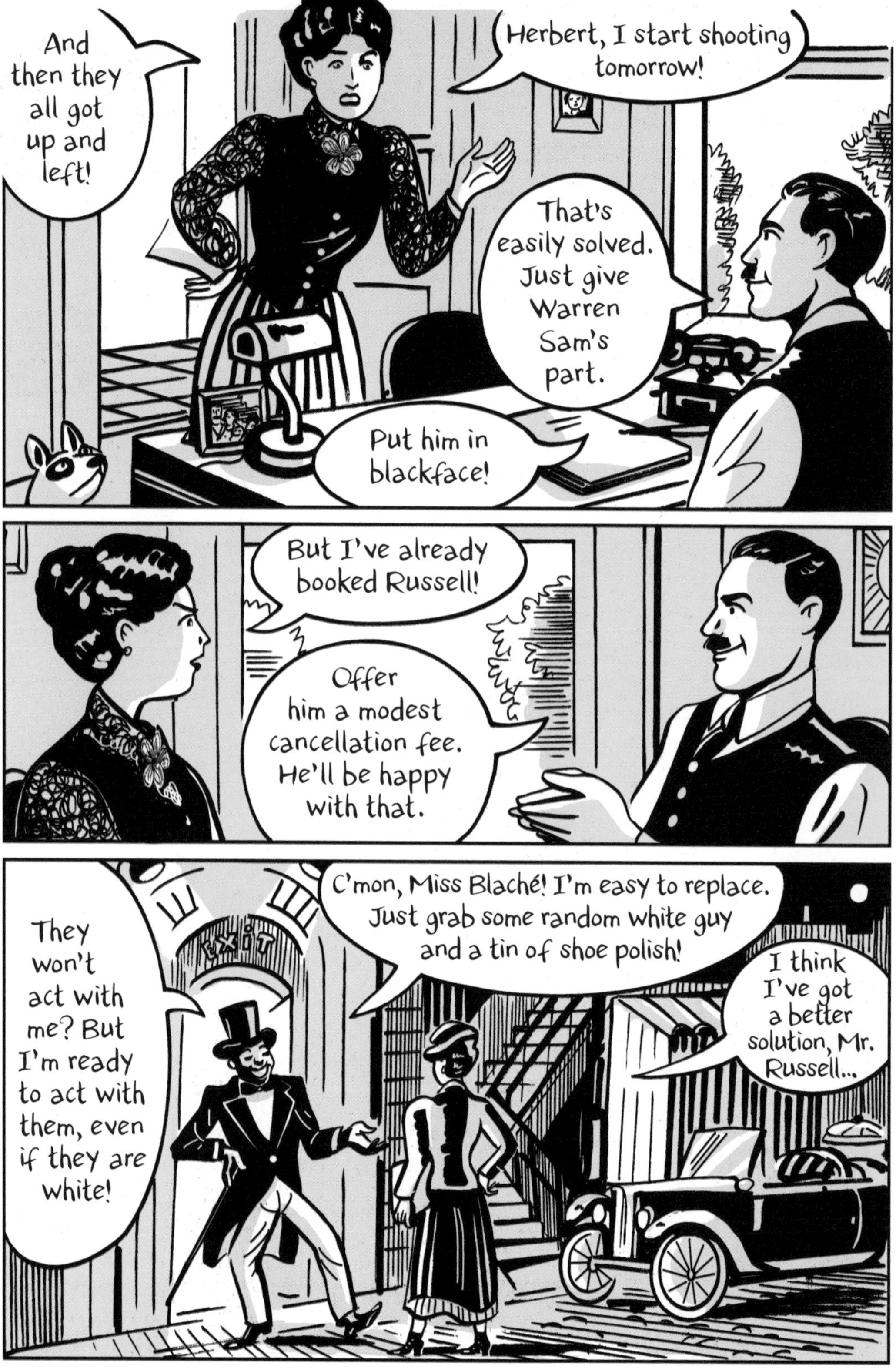
And then they all got up and left!
Herbert, I start shooting tomorrow!
That's easily solved. Just give Warren Sam's part.
Put him in blackface!
But I've already booked Russell!
Offer him a modest cancellation fee. He'll be happy with that.
They won't act with me? But I'm ready to act with them, even if they are white!
EXIT
C'mon, Miss Blaché! I'm easy to replace. Just grab some random white guy and a tin of shoe polish!
I think I've got a better solution, Mr. Russell...

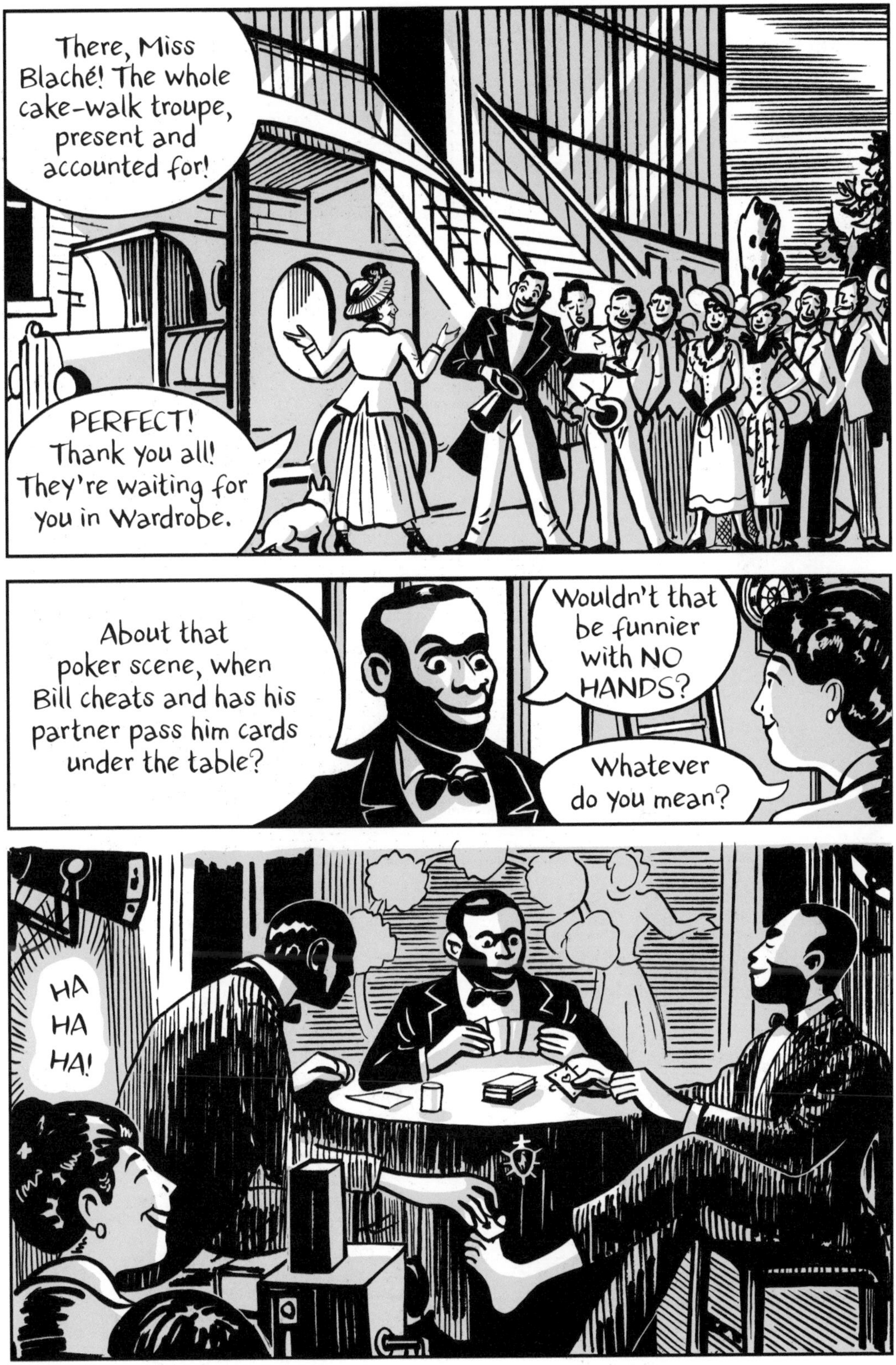
There, Miss Blaché! The whole cake-walk troupe, present and accounted for!
PERFECT! Thank you all! They're waiting for you in Wardrobe.
About that poker scene, when Bill cheats and has his partner pass him cards under the table?
Wouldn't that be funnier with NO HANDS?
Whatever do you mean?
HA HA HA!

No one wants to see a movie with a BLACK cast!

American box-office was disastrous!

Want white audiences to laugh? Put your actors in blackface! Now *that's* funny!

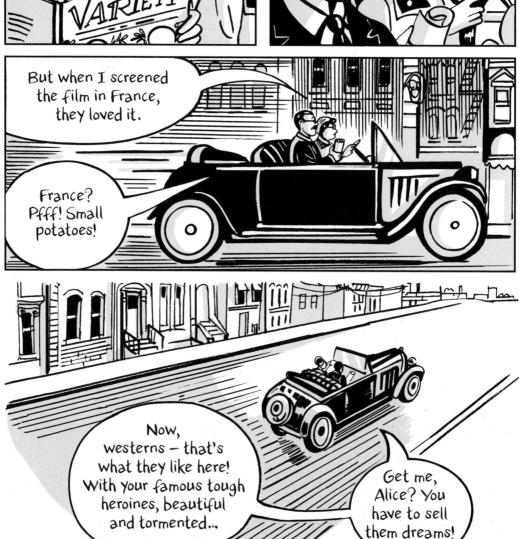

But when I screened the film in France, they loved it.

France? Pfff! Small potatoes!

Now, westerns — that's what they like here! With your famous tough heroines, beautiful and tormented...

Get me, Alice? You have to sell them dreams!

GRAND CENTRAL PALACE

THE PIT AND THE PENDULUM

1913 – Grand Central Palace – Lexington Avenue –
New York – U.S.A.

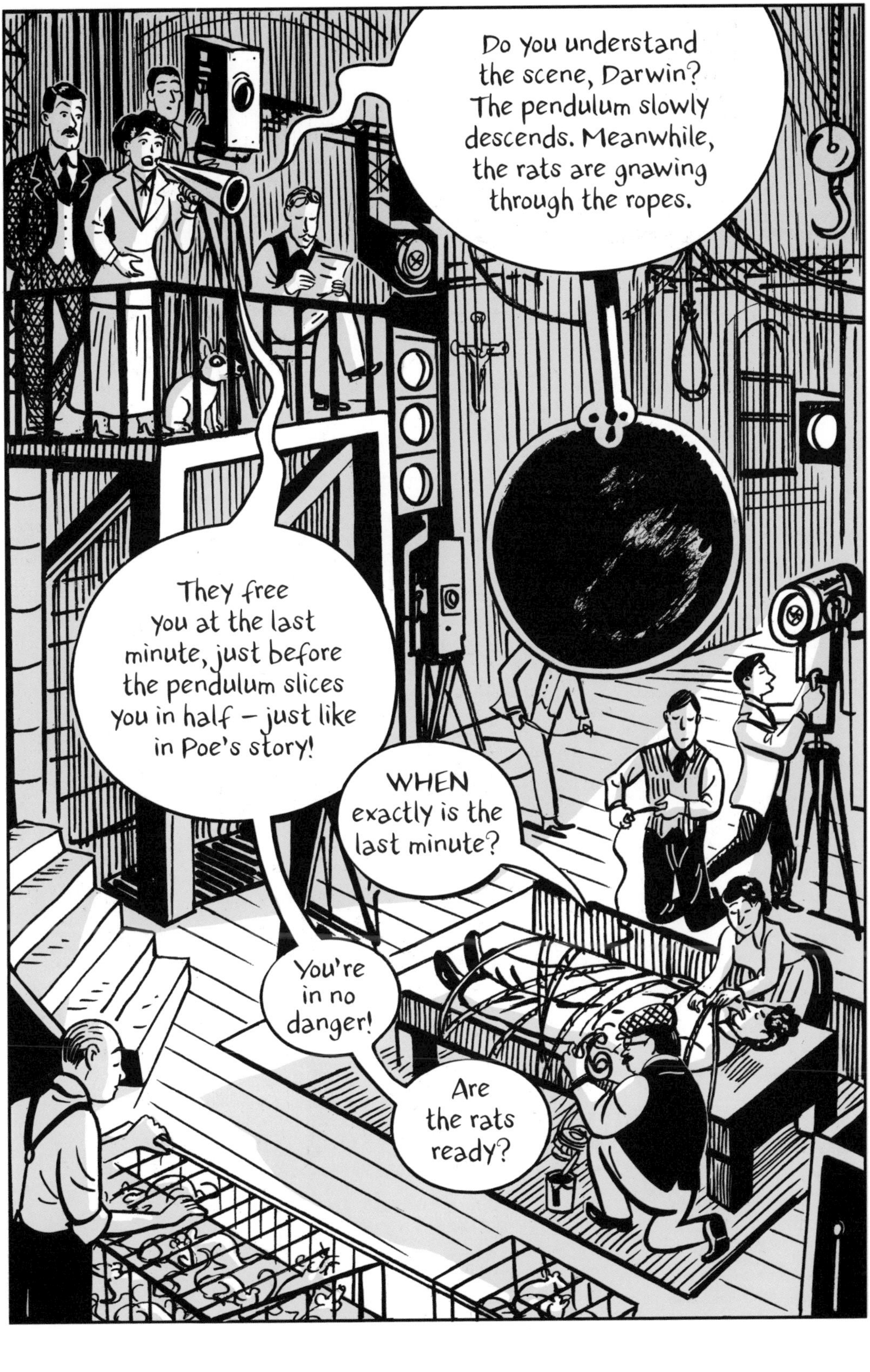
Do you understand the scene, Darwin? The pendulum slowly descends. Meanwhile, the rats are gnawing through the ropes.
They free you at the last minute, just before the pendulum slices you in half – just like in Poe's story!
WHEN exactly is the last minute?
You're in no danger!
Are the rats ready?

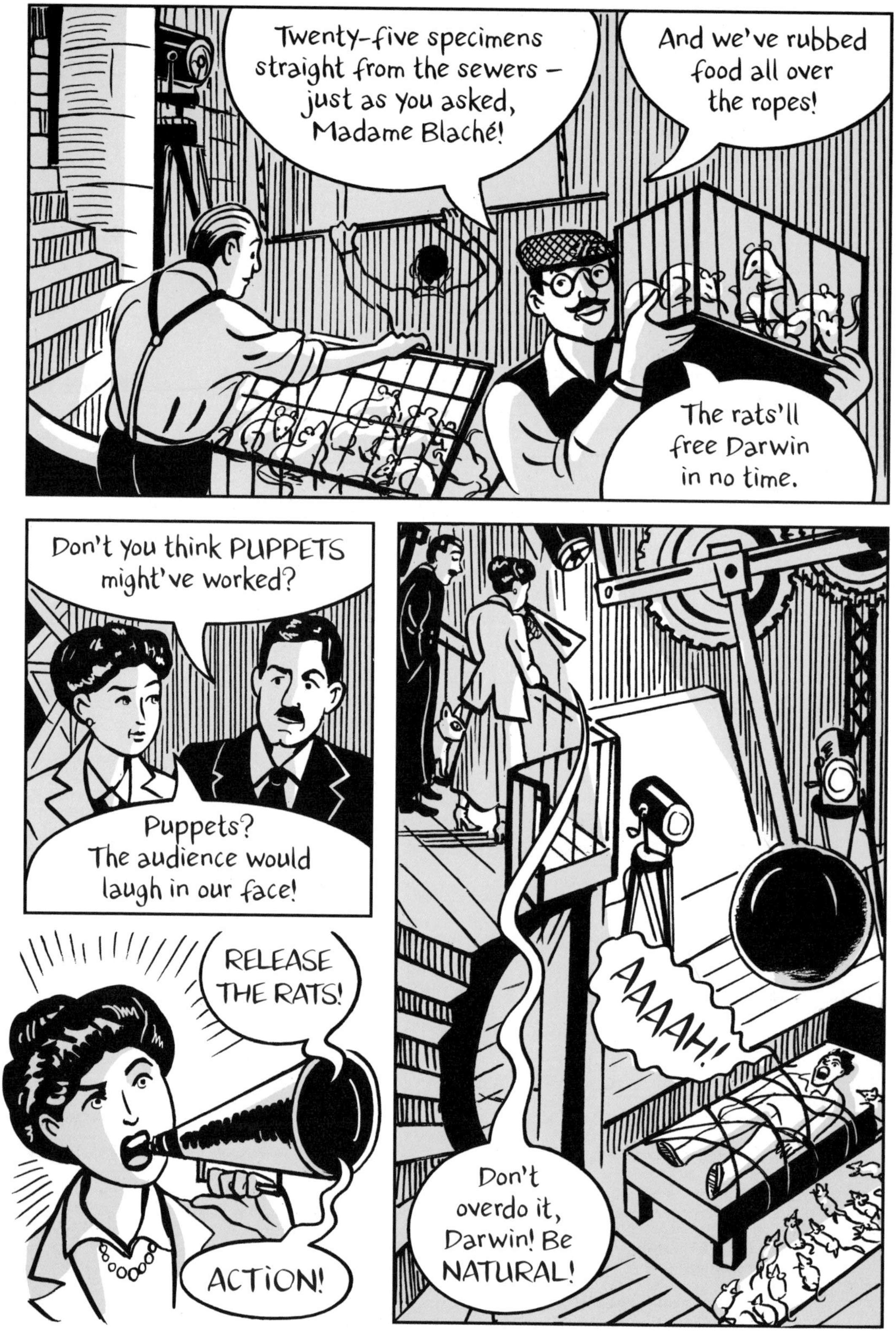
Twenty-five specimens straight from the sewers – just as you asked, Madame Blaché!
And we've rubbed food all over the ropes!
The rats'll free Darwin in no time.
Don't you think PUPPETS might've worked?
Puppets? The audience would laugh in our face!
RELEASE THE RATS!
ACTION!
AAAAH!
Don't overdo it, Darwin! Be NATURAL!

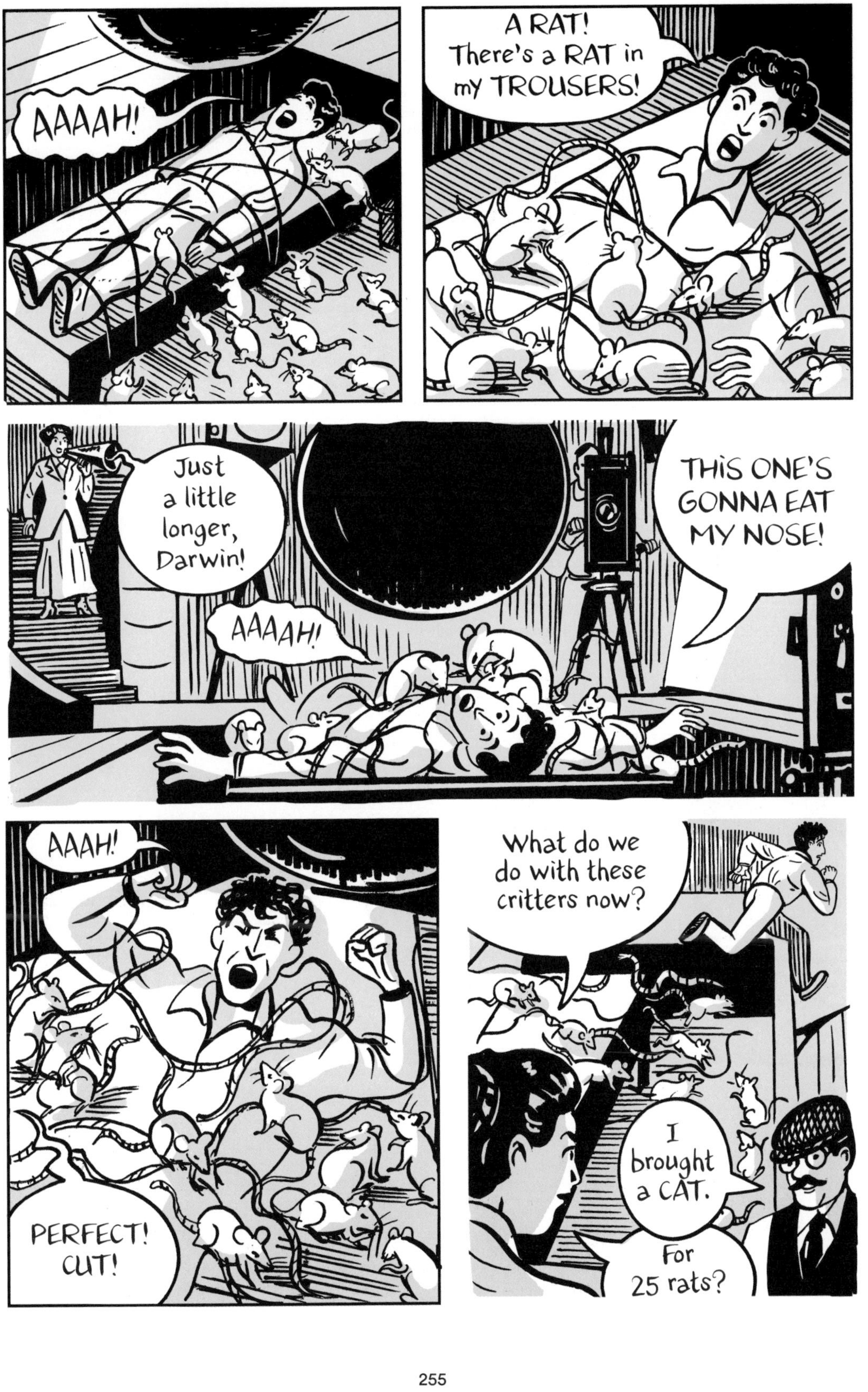
AAAAH!
A RAT! There's a RAT in my TROUSERS!
Just a little longer, Darwin!
THIS ONE'S GONNA EAT MY NOSE!
AAAAH!
AAAH!
PERFECT! CUT!
What do we do with these critters now?
I brought a CAT.
For 25 rats?

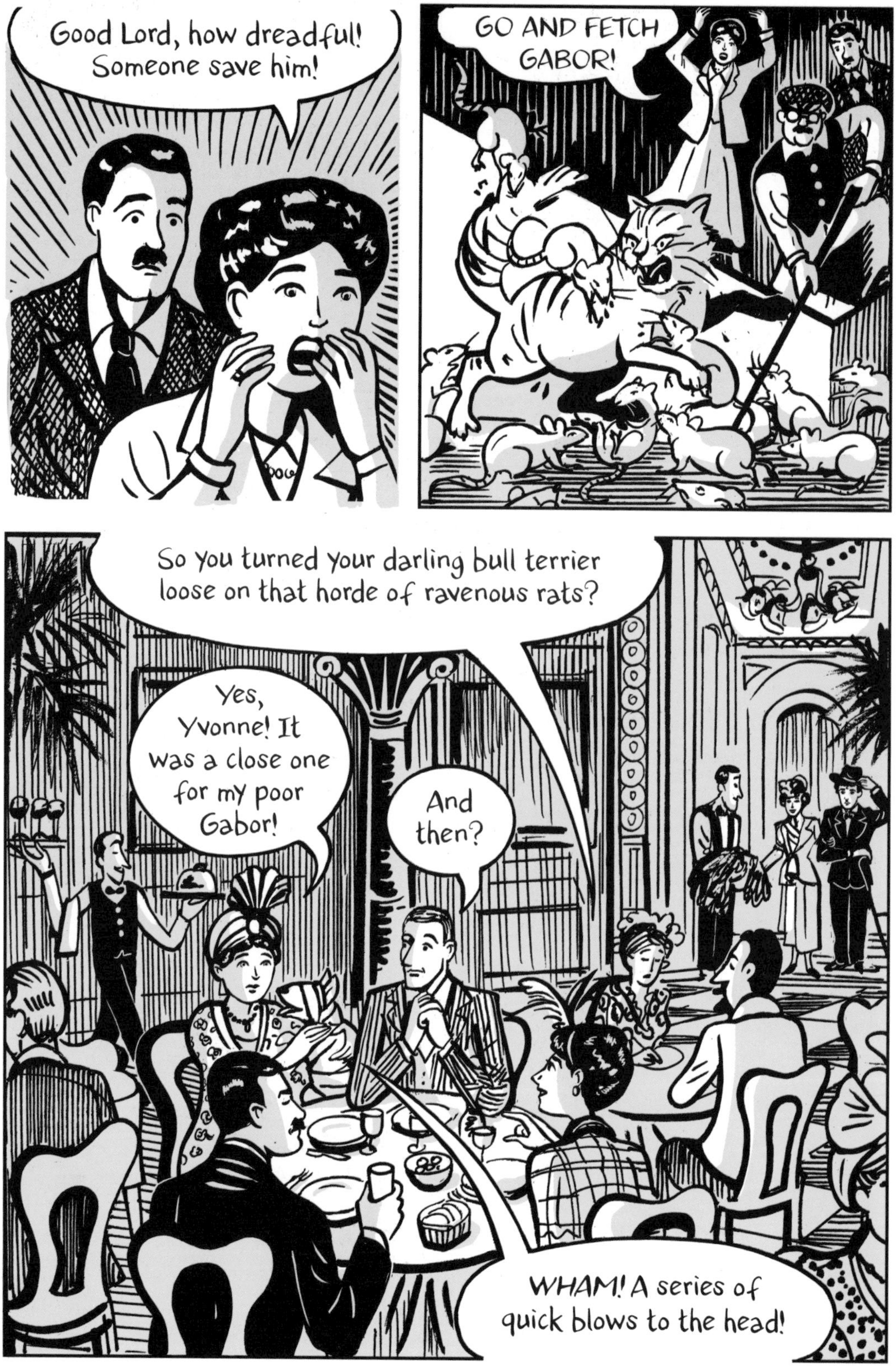
Good Lord, how dreadful! Someone save him!
GO AND FETCH GABOR!
So you turned your darling bull terrier loose on that horde of ravenous rats?
Yes, Yvonne! It was a close one for my poor Gabor!
And then?
WHAM! A series of quick blows to the head!

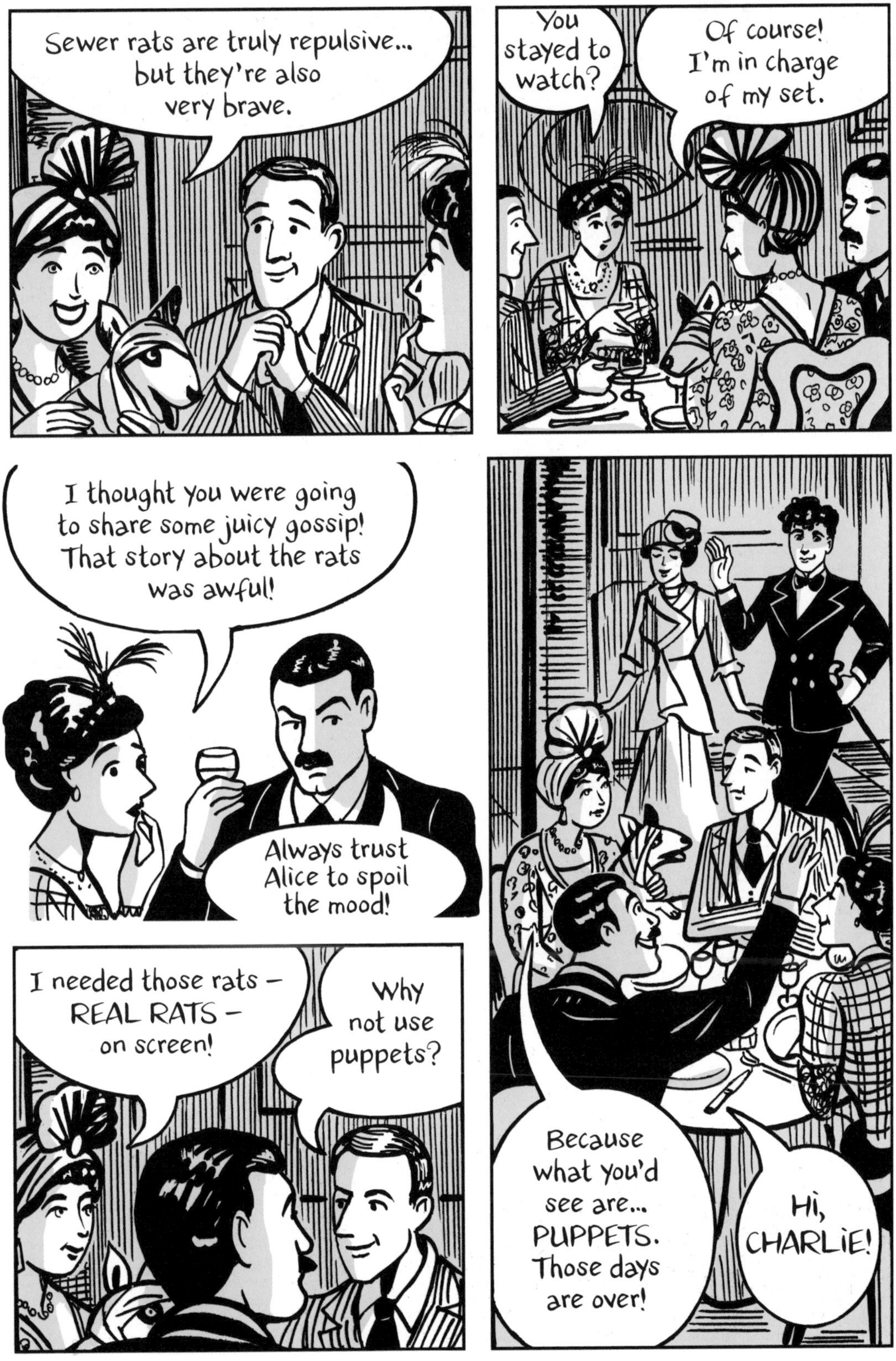
Sewer rats are truly repulsive... but they're also very brave.
You stayed to watch?
Of course! I'm in charge of my set.
I thought you were going to share some juicy gossip! That story about the rats was awful!
Always trust Alice to spoil the mood!
I needed those rats – REAL RATS – on screen!
Why not use puppets?
Because what you'd see are... PUPPETS. Those days are over!
Hi, CHARLIE!

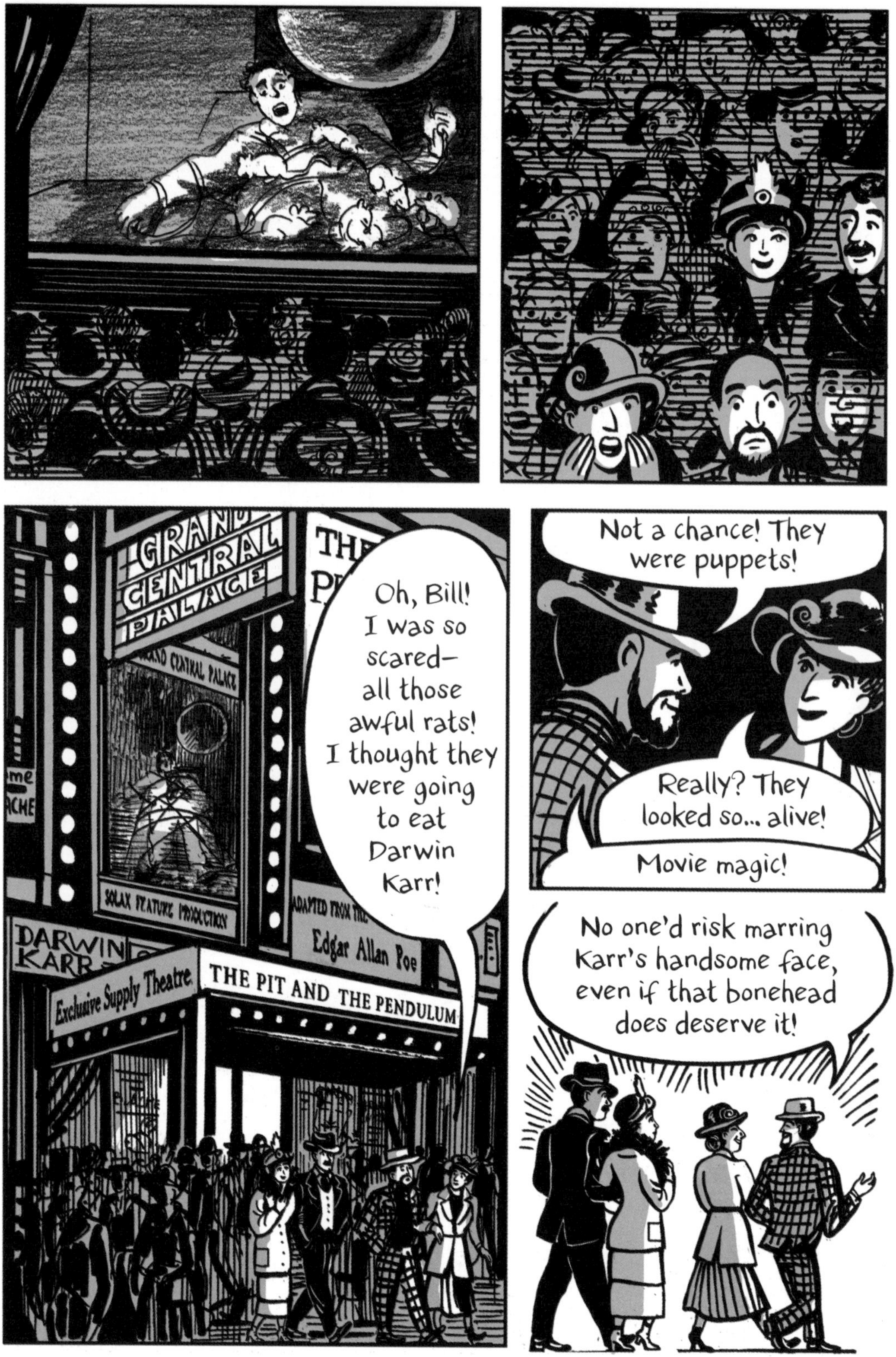
GRAND CENTRAL PALACE
GRAND CENTRAL PALACE
SOLAX FEATURE PRODUCTION
ADAPTED FROM THE
Edgar Allan Poe
DARWIN KARR
Exclusive Supply Theatre
THE PIT AND THE PENDULUM
Oh, Bill! I was so scared— all those awful rats! I thought they were going to eat Darwin Karr!
Not a chance! They were puppets!
Really? They looked so... alive!
Movie magic!
No one'd risk marring Karr's handsome face, even if that bonehead does deserve it!

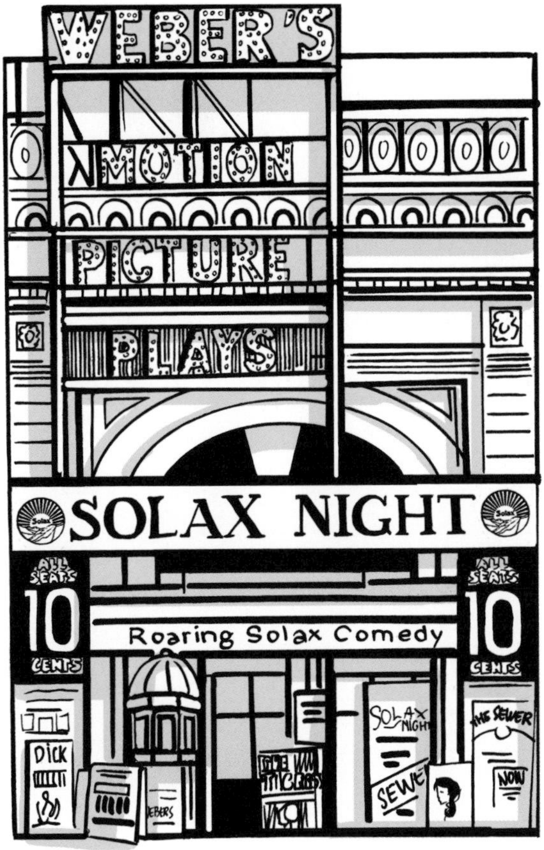
WEBER'S
MOTION
PICTURE
PLAYS
SOLAX NIGHT
ALL SEATS 10 CENTS
Roaring Solax Comedy
ALL SEATS 10 CENTS
DICK
SOLAX NIGHT
SEWE
THE SEWER
NOW

1913–1916 – Weber's Theatre – Broadway –
New York – U.S.A.

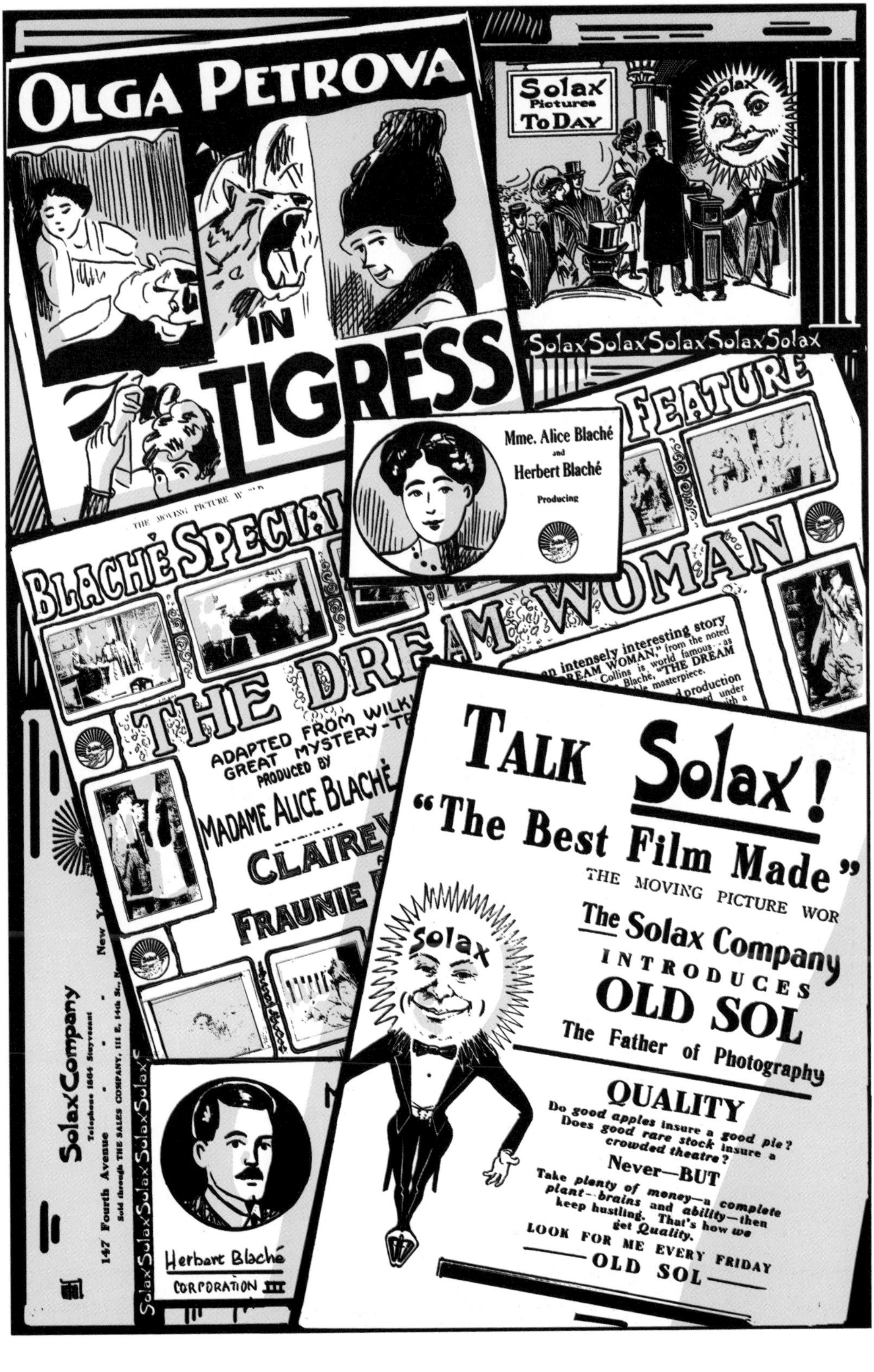
OLGA PETROVA
IN
TIGRESS
Solax Pictures ToDAY
Solax
Solax Solax Solax Solax Solax
FEATURE
Mme. Alice Blaché and Herbert Blaché Producing
BLACHÉ SPECIAL
THE DREAM WOMAN
ADAPTED FROM WILK
GREAT MYSTERY-T
PRODUCED BY
MADAME ALICE BLACHÉ
CLAIRE
FRAUNIE
TALK Solax!
"The Best Film Made"
THE MOVING PICTURE WOR
The Solax Company
INTRODUCES
OLD SOL
The Father of Photography
QUALITY
Do good apples insure a good pie? Does good rare stock insure a crowded theatre?
Never—BUT
Take plenty of money—a complete plant—brains and ability—then keep hustling. That's how we get Quality.
LOOK FOR ME EVERY FRIDAY
——OLD SOL——
Solax Company
Telephone 1864 Stuyvesant
147 Fourth Avenue
New York
Herbert Blaché
CORPORATION III
Solax Solax Solax Solax Solax

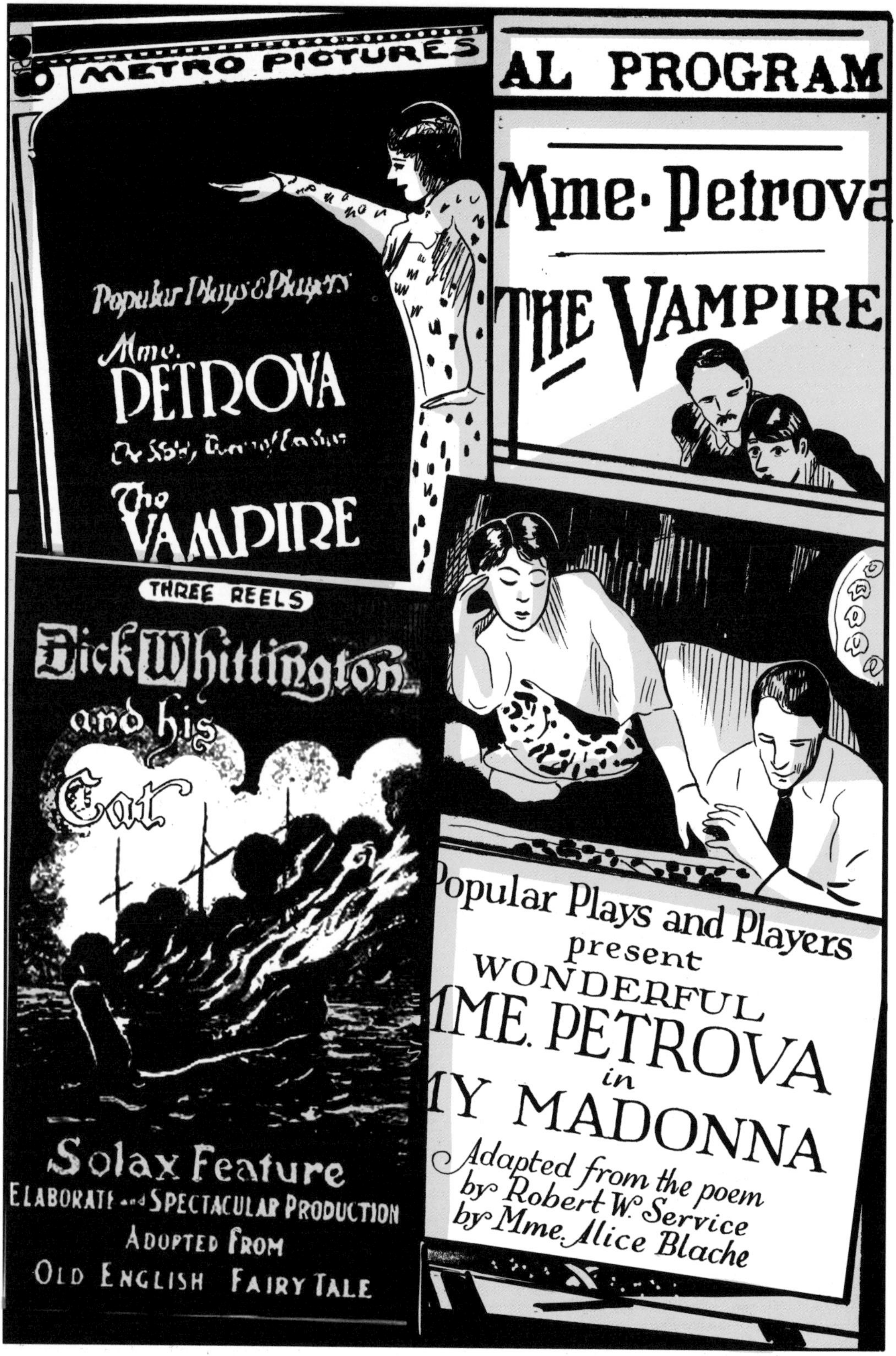
METRO PICTURES
AL PROGRAM
Mme· Petrova
THE VAMPIRE
Popular Plays & Players
Mme. PETROVA
The VAMPIRE
THREE REELS
Dick Whittington
and his
Cat
Solax Feature
ELABORATE and SPECTACULAR PRODUCTION
ADOPTED FROM
OLD ENGLISH FAIRY TALE
opular Plays and Players
present
WONDERFUL
ME. PETROVA
in
Y MADONNA
Adapted from the poem
by Robert W. Service
by Mme. Alice Blache

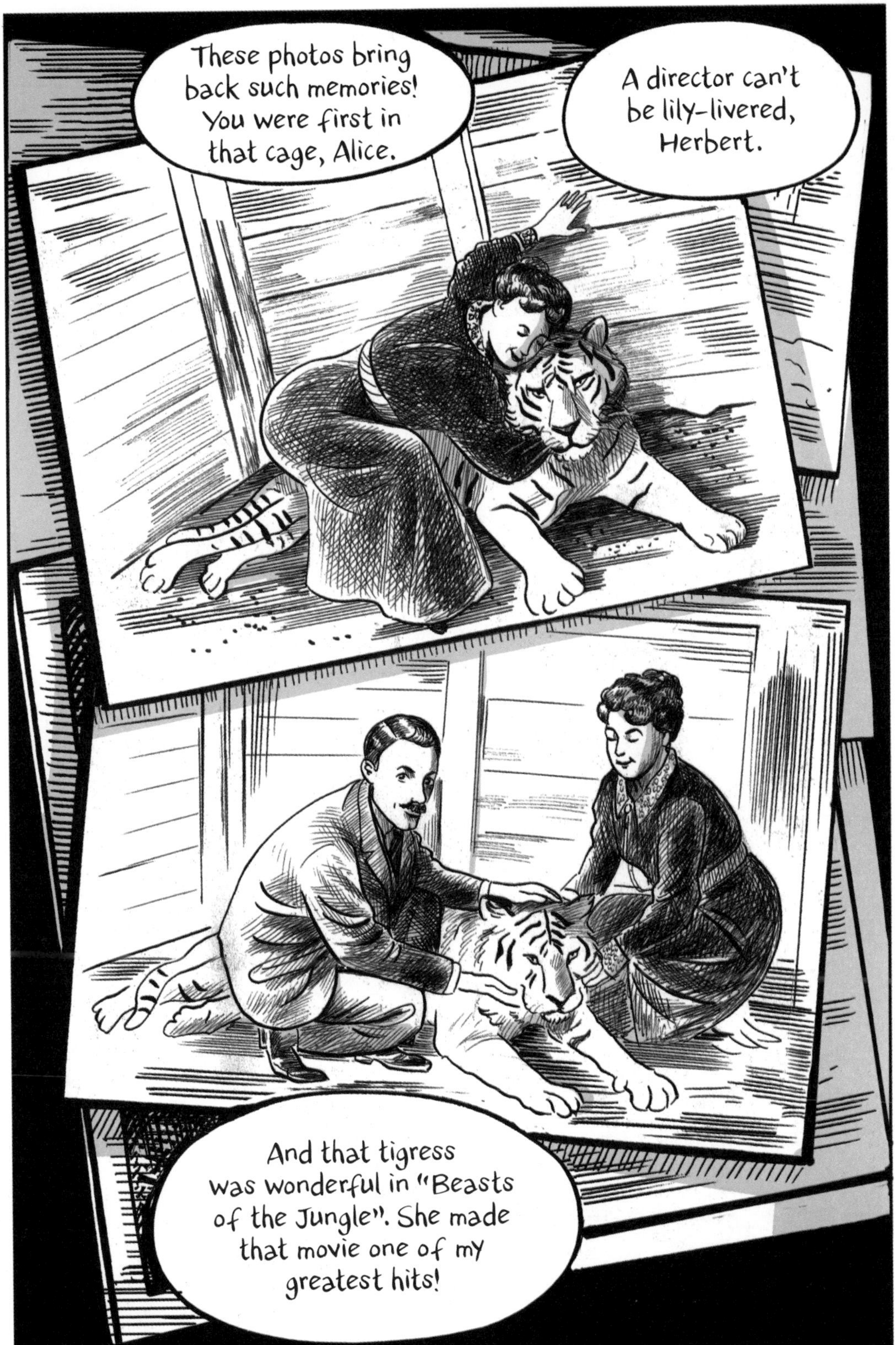
These photos bring back such memories! You were first in that cage, Alice.
A director can't be lily-livered, Herbert.
And that tigress was wonderful in "Beasts of the Jungle". She made that movie one of my greatest hits!

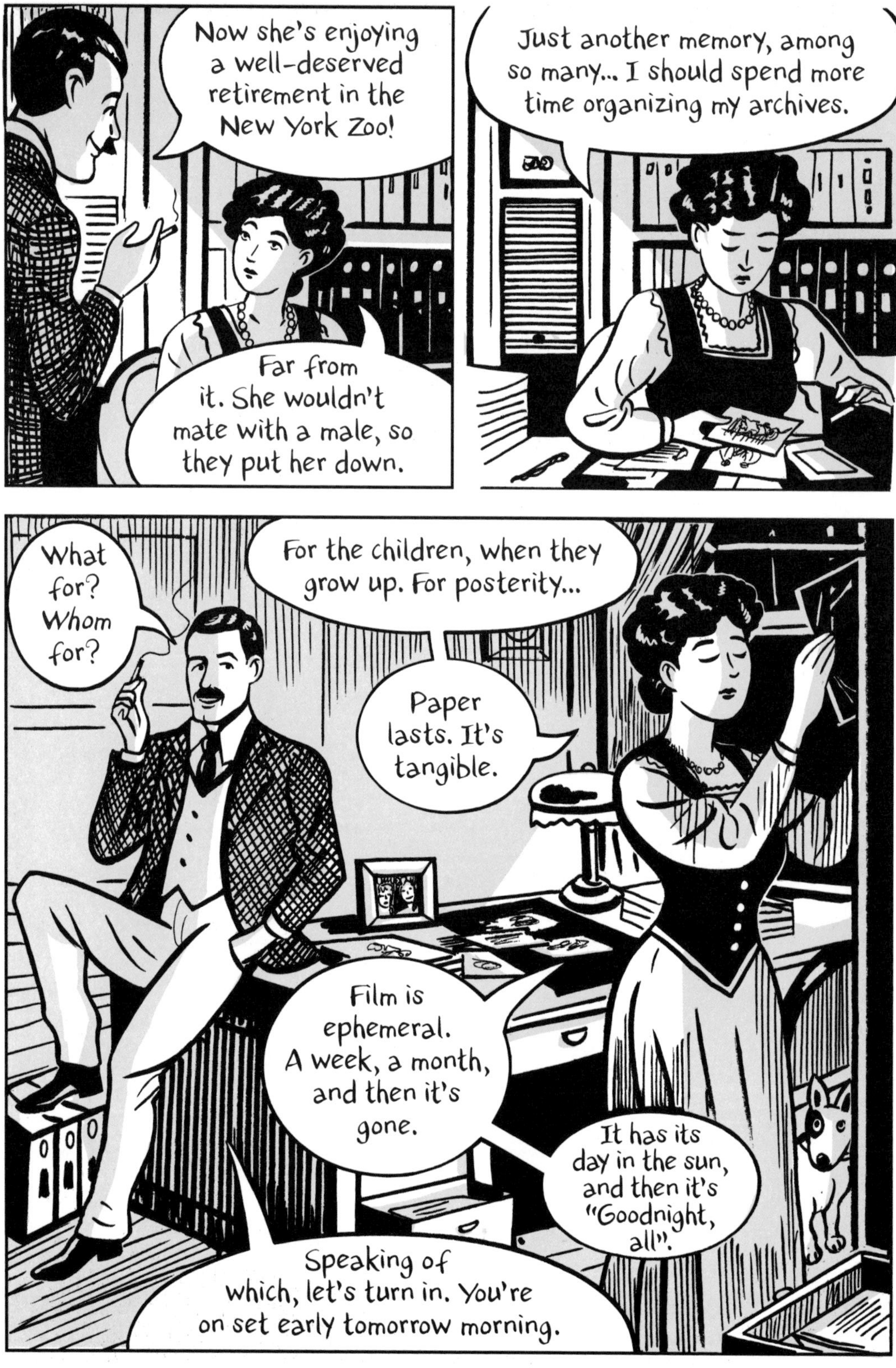
Now she's enjoying a well-deserved retirement in the New York Zoo!
Far from it. She wouldn't mate with a male, so they put her down.
Just another memory, among so many... I should spend more time organizing my archives.
What for? Whom for?
For the children, when they grow up. For posterity...
Paper lasts. It's tangible.
Film is ephemeral. A week, a month, and then it's gone.
It has its day in the sun, and then it's "Goodnight, all".
Speaking of which, let's turn in. You're on set early tomorrow morning.

1916 – Westport – Connecticut – U.S.A.

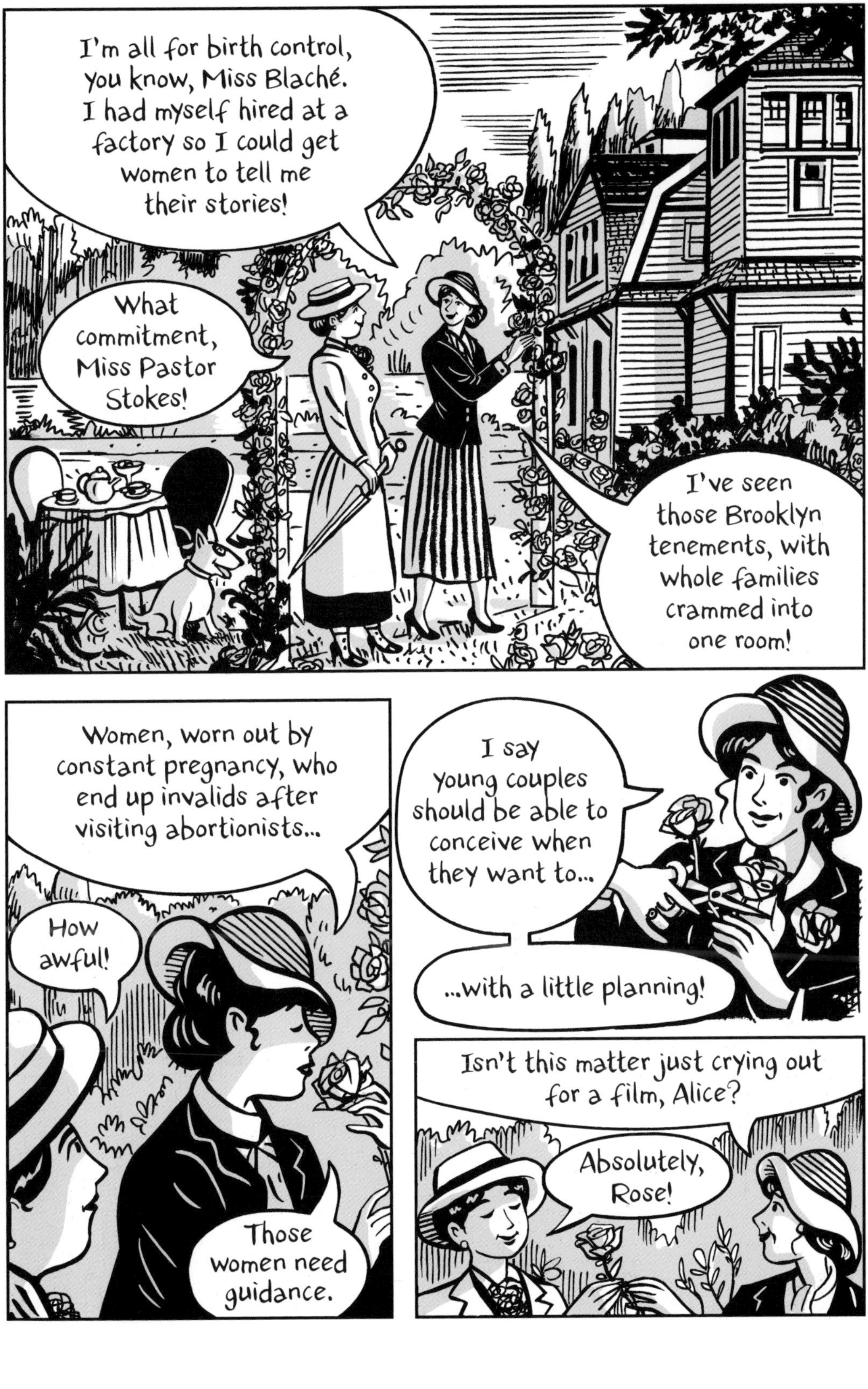
I'm all for birth control, you know, Miss Blaché. I had myself hired at a factory so I could get women to tell me their stories!
What commitment, Miss Pastor Stokes!
I've seen those Brooklyn tenements, with whole families crammed into one room!
Women, worn out by constant pregnancy, who end up invalids after visiting abortionists...
How awful!
Those women need guidance.
I say young couples should be able to conceive when they want to...
...with a little planning!
Isn't this matter just crying out for a film, Alice?
Absolutely, Rose!

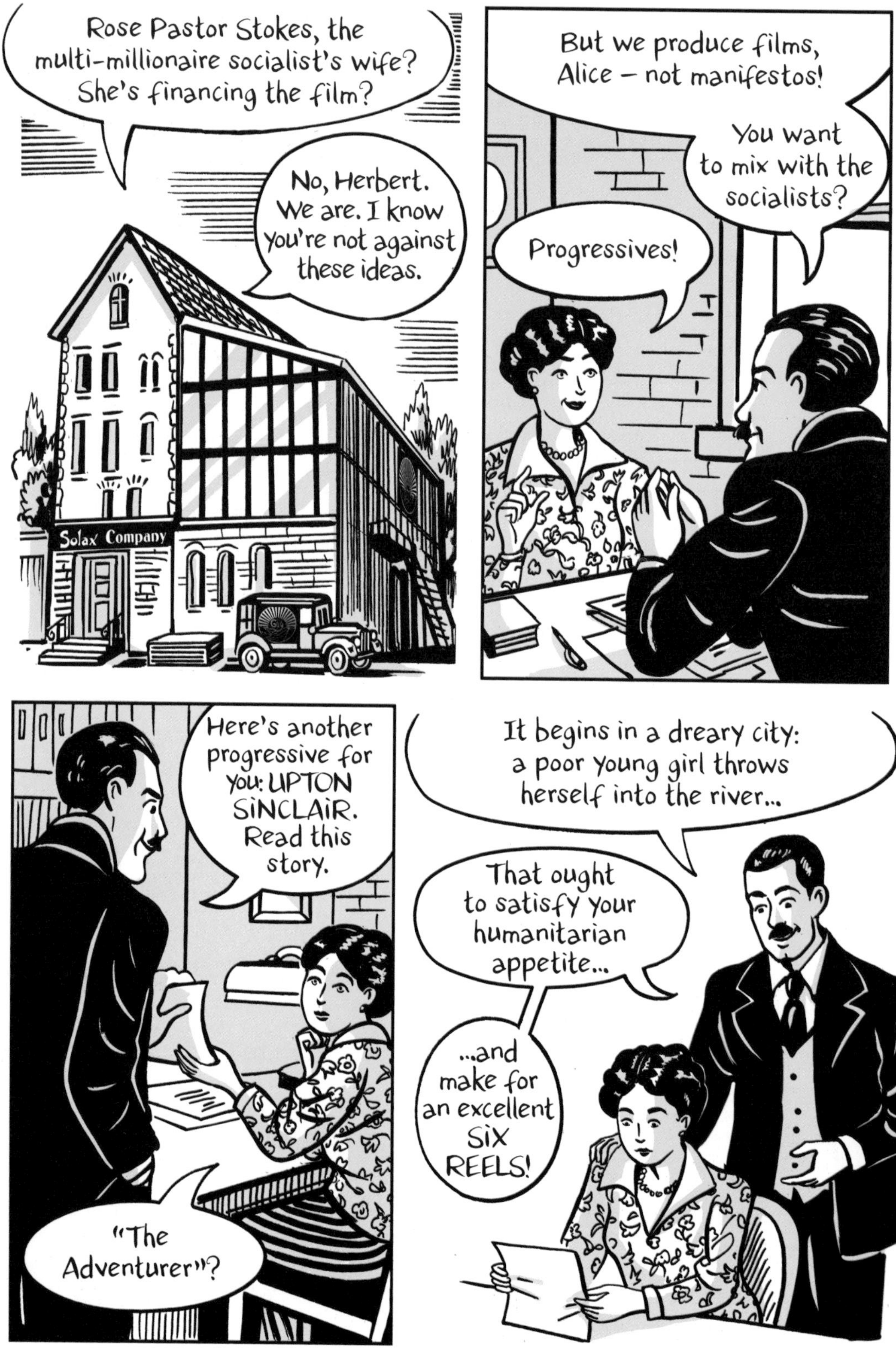
Rose Pastor Stokes, the multi-millionaire socialist's wife? She's financing the film?
No, Herbert. We are. I know you're not against these ideas.
Solax Company
But we produce films, Alice – not manifestos!
You want to mix with the socialists?
Progressives!
Here's another progressive for you: UPTON SINCLAIR. Read this story.
"The Adventurer"?
It begins in a dreary city: a poor young girl throws herself into the river...
That ought to satisfy your humanitarian appetite...
...and make for an excellent SIX REELS!

1917 – Columbia University – Buell Hall –
New York – U.S.A.

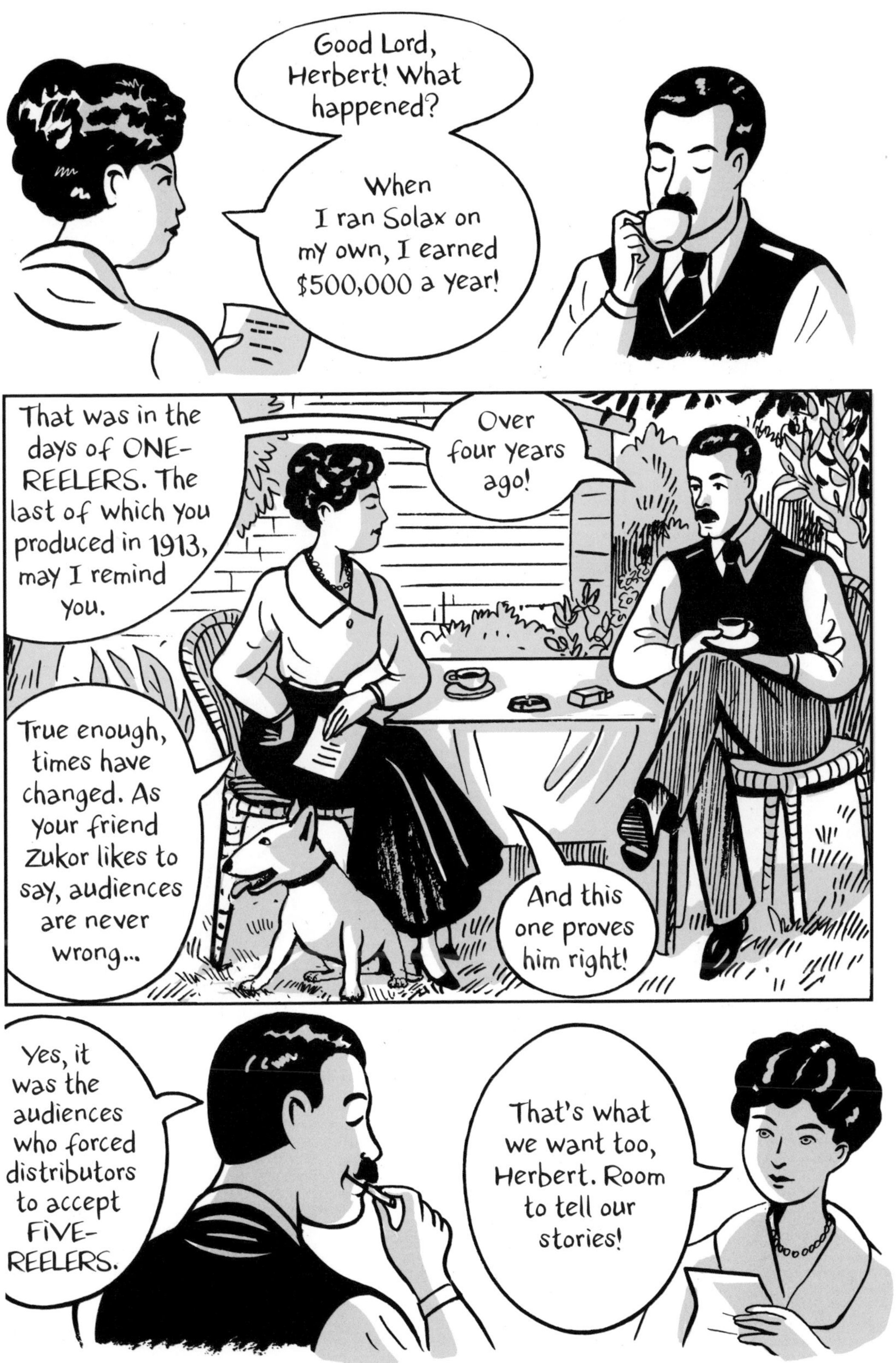
Good Lord, Herbert! What happened?
When I ran Solax on my own, I earned $500,000 a year!
That was in the days of ONE-REELERS. The last of which you produced in 1913, may I remind you.
Over four years ago!
True enough, times have changed. As your friend Zukor likes to say, audiences are never wrong...
And this one proves him right!
Yes, it was the audiences who forced distributors to accept FIVE-REELERS.
That's what we want too, Herbert. Room to tell our stories!

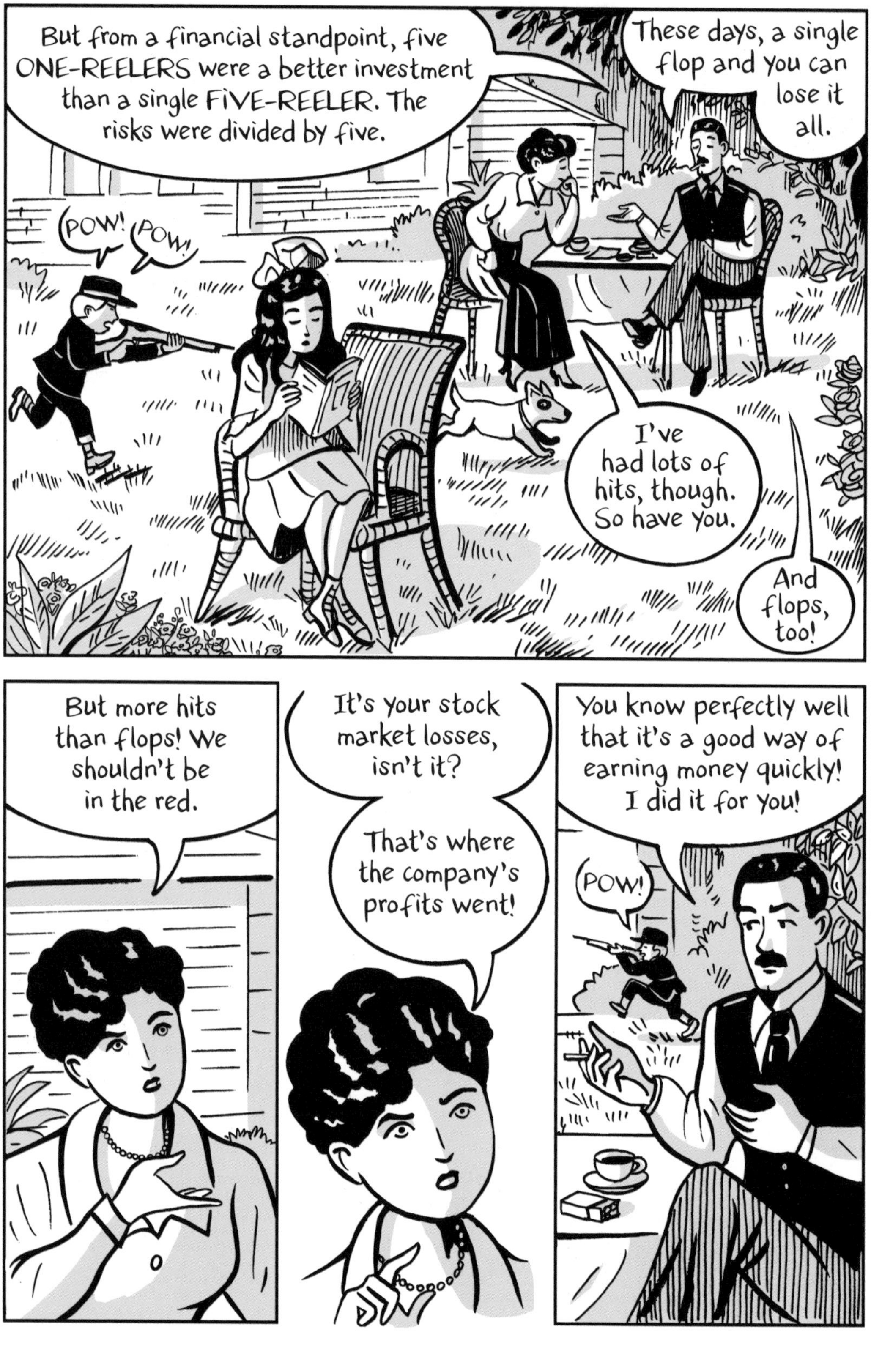
But from a financial standpoint, five ONE-REELERS were a better investment than a single FIVE-REELER. The risks were divided by five.
These days, a single flop and you can lose it all.
POW!
POW!
I've had lots of hits, though. So have you.
And flops, too!
But more hits than flops! We shouldn't be in the red.
It's your stock market losses, isn't it?
That's where the company's profits went!
You know perfectly well that it's a good way of earning money quickly! I did it for you!
POW!

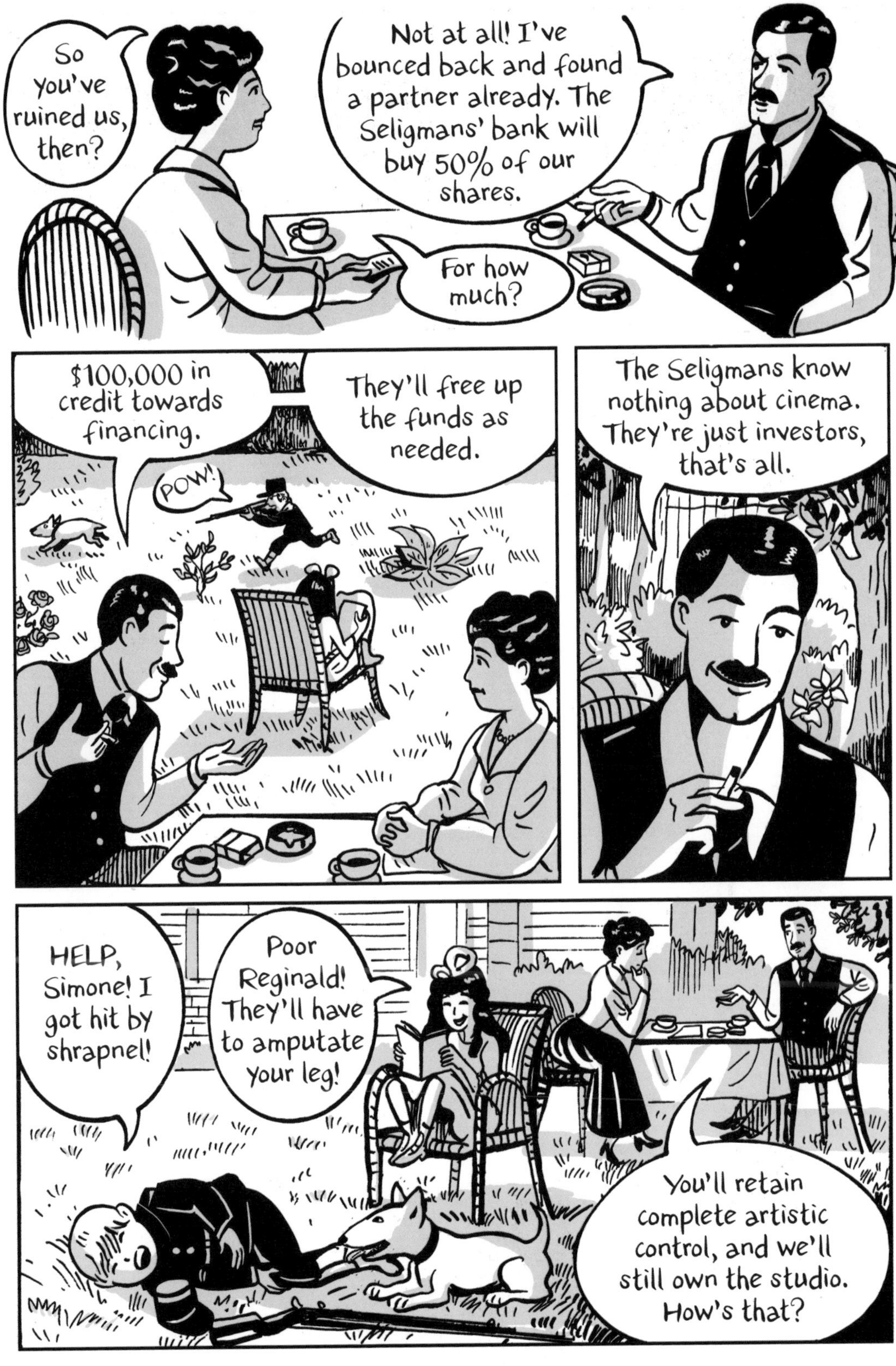
So you've ruined us, then?
Not at all! I've bounced back and found a partner already. The Seligmans' bank will buy 50% of our shares.
For how much?
$100,000 in credit towards financing.
They'll free up the funds as needed.
POW!
The Seligmans know nothing about cinema. They're just investors, that's all.
HELP, Simone! I got hit by shrapnel!
Poor Reginald! They'll have to amputate your leg!
You'll retain complete artistic control, and we'll still own the studio. How's that?

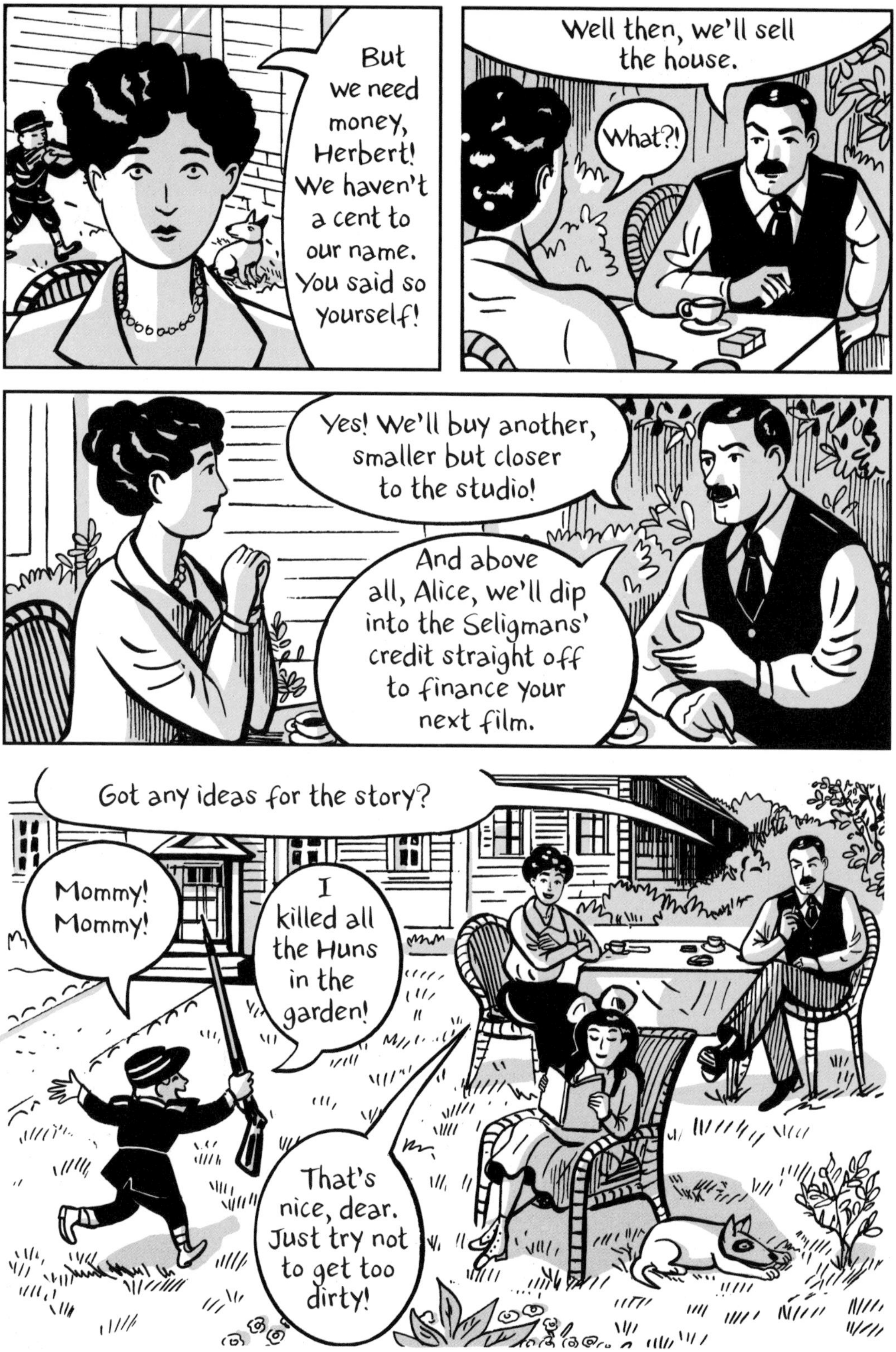
But we need money, Herbert! We haven't a cent to our name. You said so yourself!
Well then, we'll sell the house.
What?!
Yes! We'll buy another, smaller but closer to the studio!
And above all, Alice, we'll dip into the Seligmans' credit straight off to finance your next film.
Got any ideas for the story?
Mommy! Mommy!
I killed all the Huns in the garden!
That's nice, dear. Just try not to get too dirty!

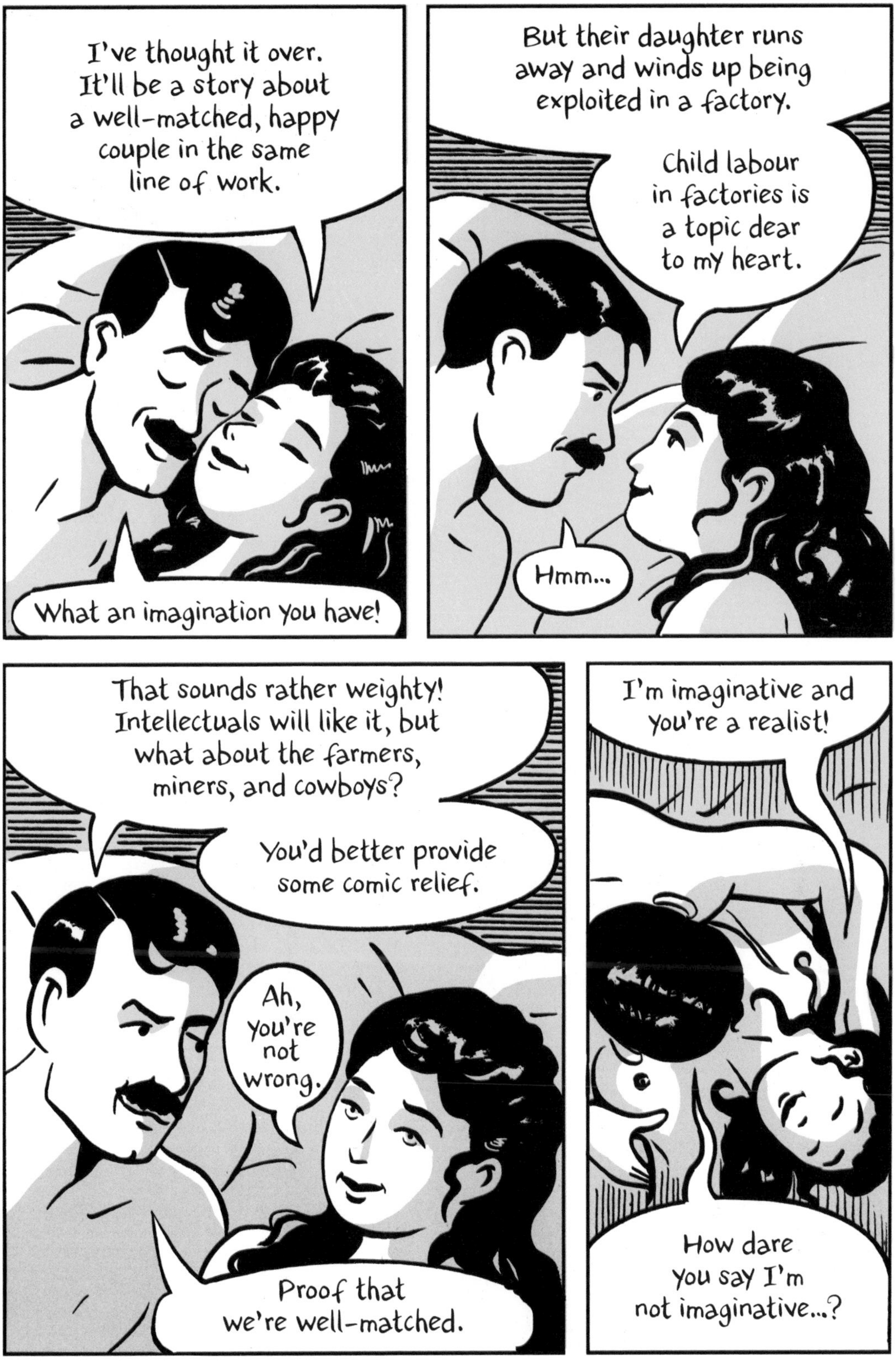

I've thought it over. It'll be a story about a well-matched, happy couple in the same line of work.
What an imagination you have!
But their daughter runs away and winds up being exploited in a factory.
Child labour in factories is a topic dear to my heart.
Hmm...
That sounds rather weighty! Intellectuals will like it, but what about the farmers, miners, and cowboys?
You'd better provide some comic relief.
Ah, you're not wrong.
Proof that we're well-matched.
I'm imaginative and you're a realist!
How dare you say I'm not imaginative...?

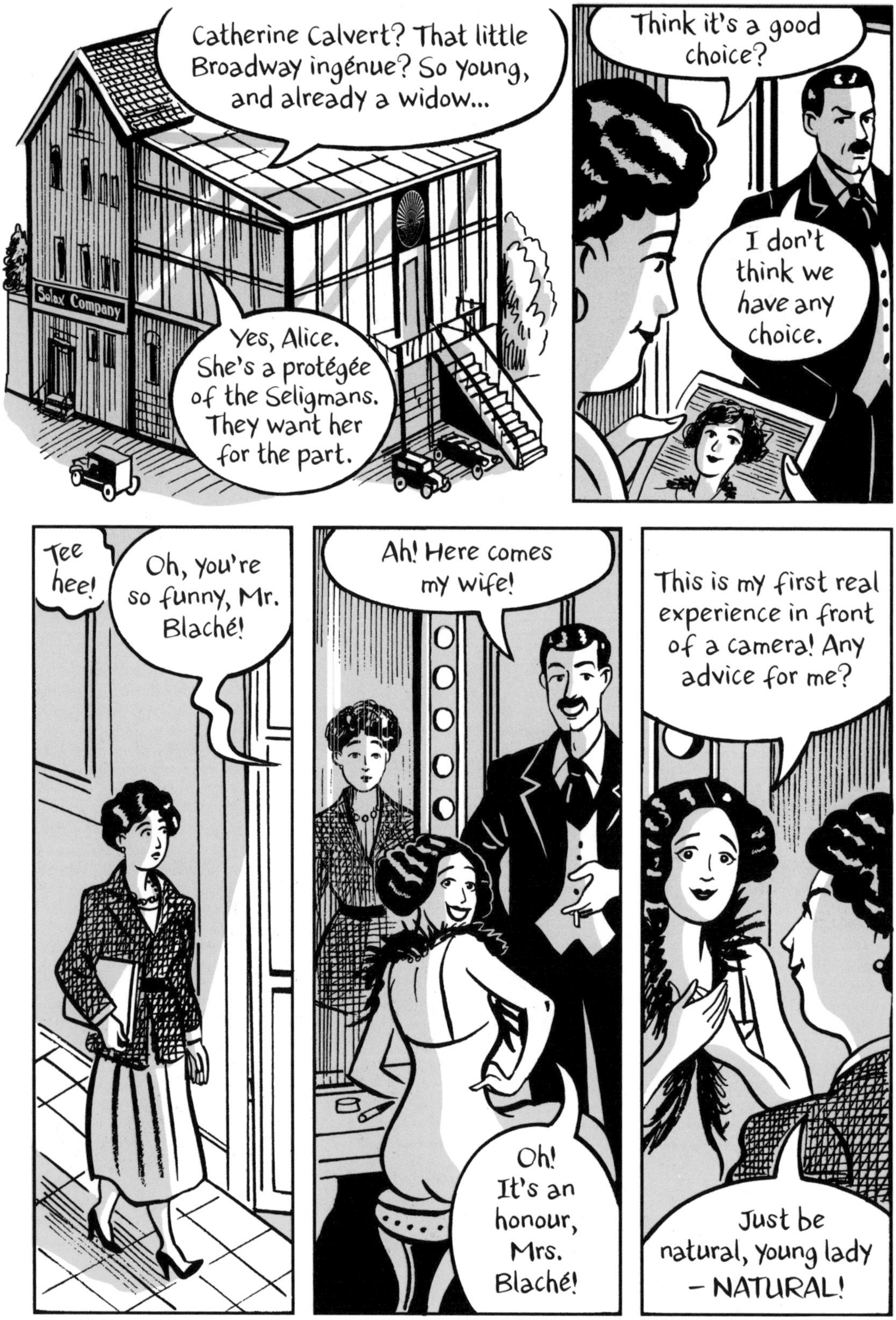
Catherine Calvert? That little Broadway ingénue? So young, and already a widow...
Solax Company
Yes, Alice. She's a protégée of the Seligmans. They want her for the part.
Think it's a good choice?
I don't think we have any choice.
Tee hee!
Oh, you're so funny, Mr. Blaché!
Ah! Here comes my wife!
Oh! It's an honour, Mrs. Blaché!
This is my first real experience in front of a camera! Any advice for me?
Just be natural, young lady – NATURAL!

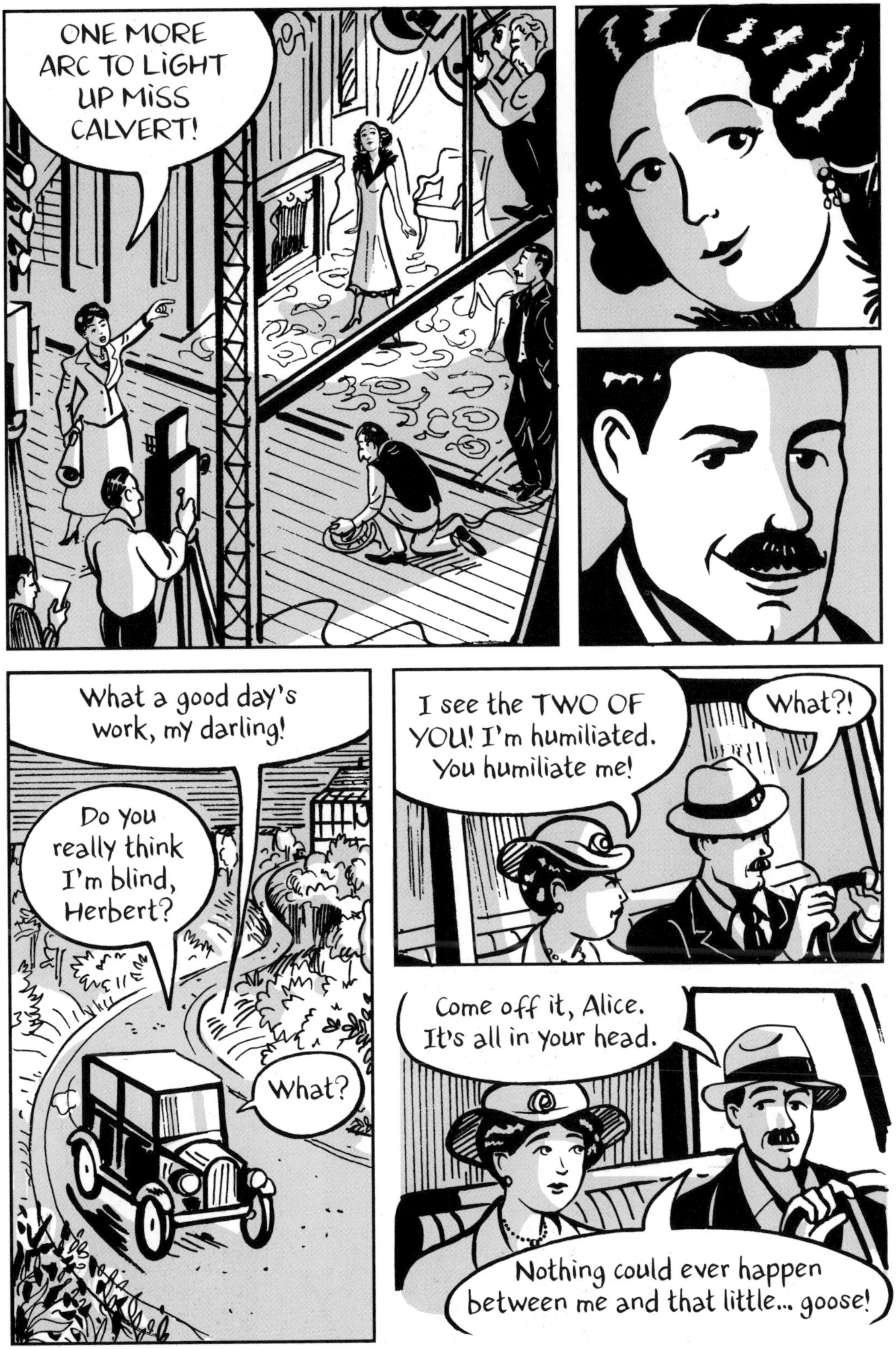
ONE MORE ARC TO LIGHT UP MISS CALVERT!
What a good day's work, my darling!
Do you really think I'm blind, Herbert?
What?
I see the TWO OF YOU! I'm humiliated. You humiliate me!
What?!
Come off it, Alice. It's all in your head.
Nothing could ever happen between me and that little... goose!

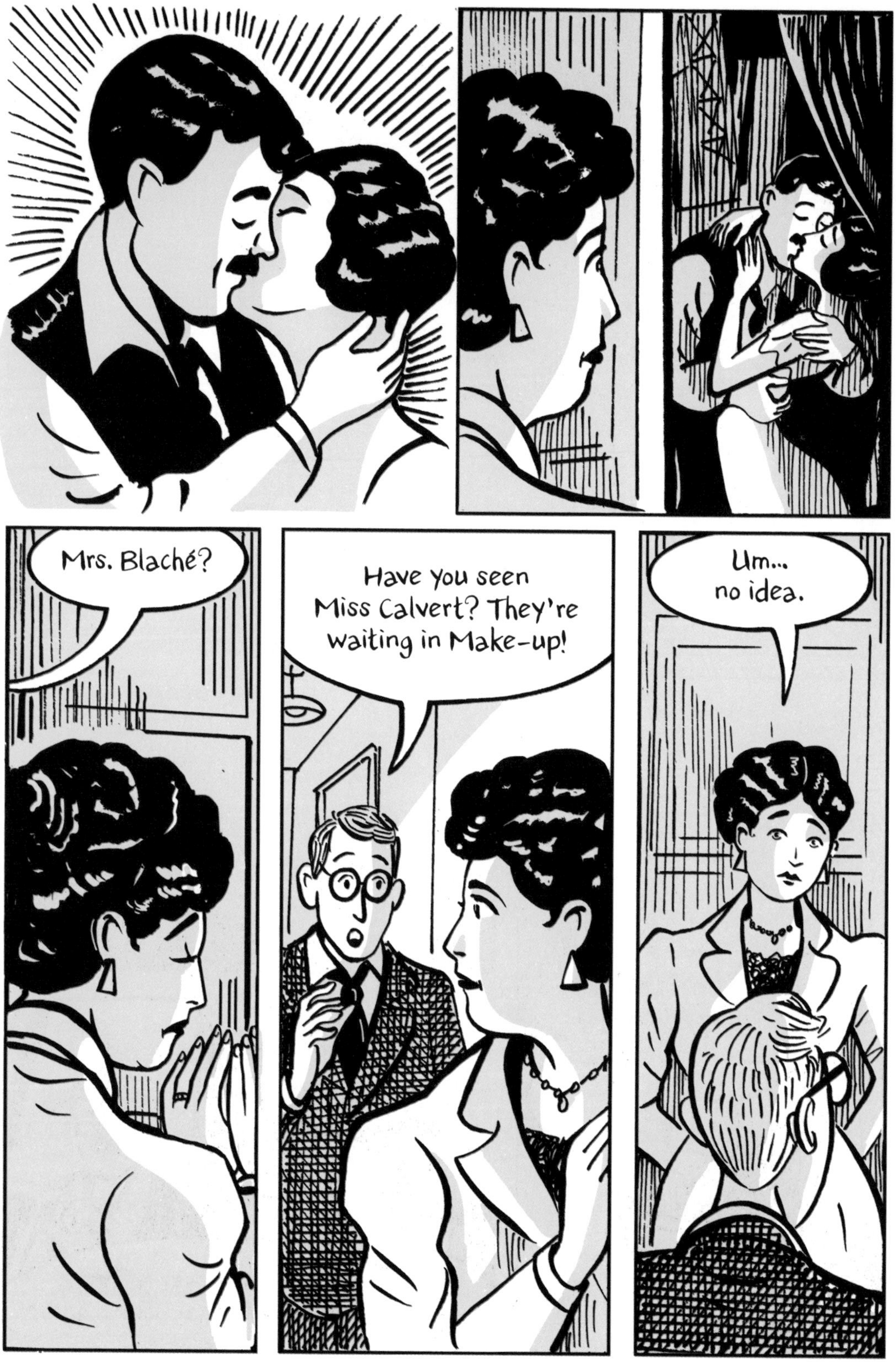
Mrs. Blaché?
Have you seen Miss Calvert? They're waiting in Make-up!
Um... no idea.

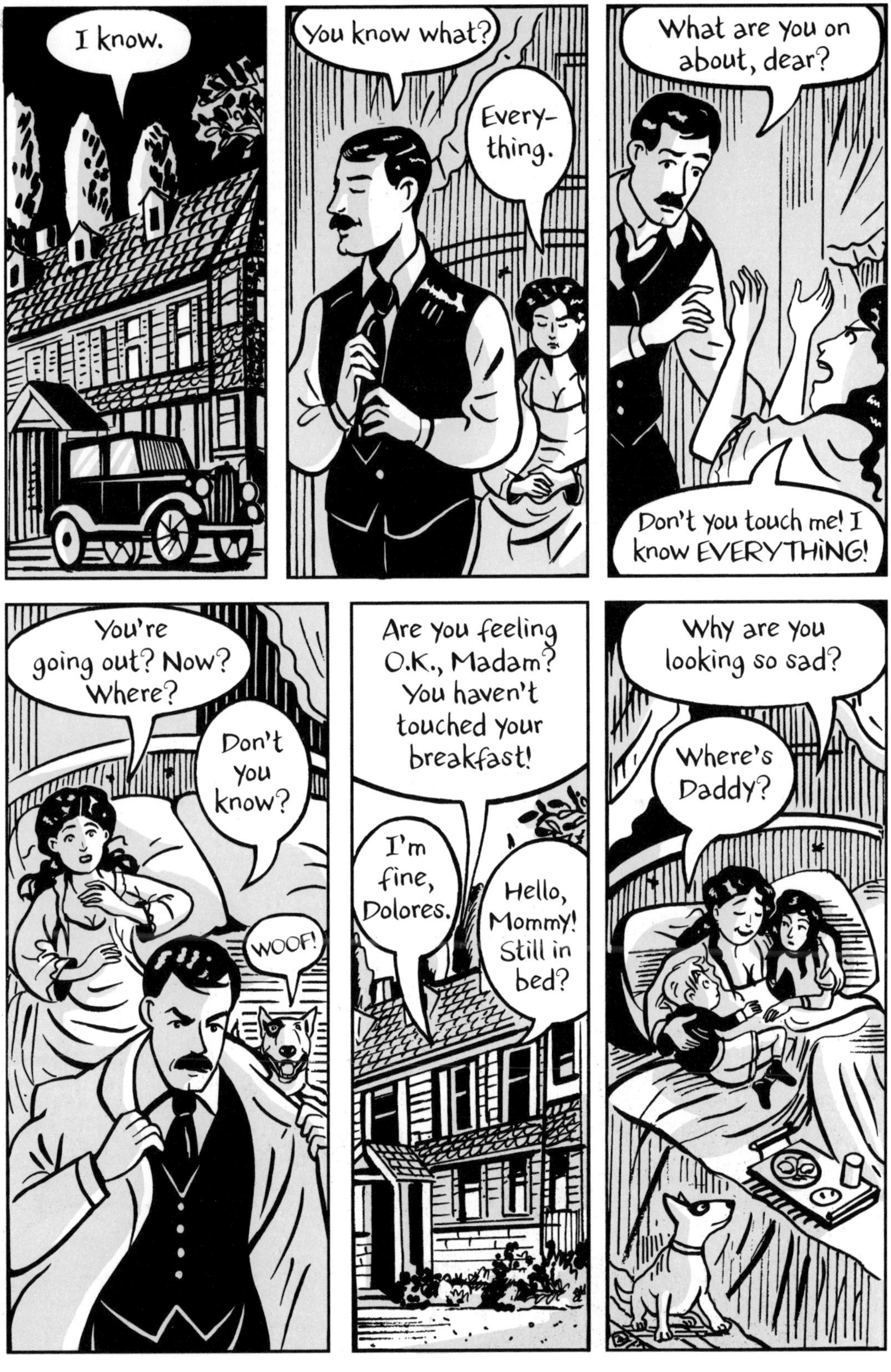

I know.
You know what?
Every-thing.
What are you on about, dear?
Don't you touch me! I know EVERYTHING!
You're going out? Now? Where?
Don't you know?
WOOF!
Are you feeling O.K., Madam? You haven't touched your breakfast!
I'm fine, Dolores.
Hello, Mommy! Still in bed?
Why are you looking so sad?
Where's Daddy?

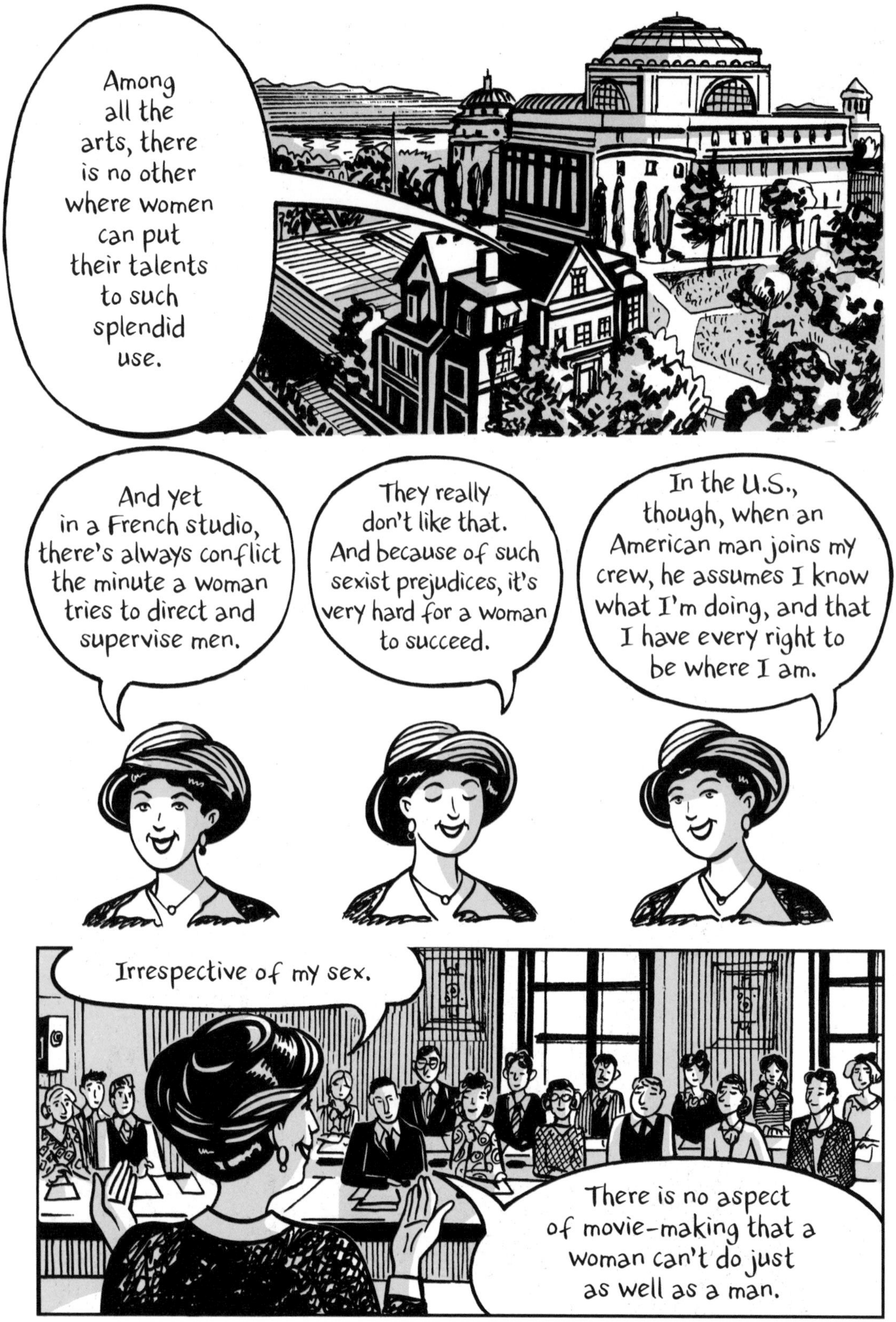
Among all the arts, there is no other where women can put their talents to such splendid use.
And yet in a French studio, there's always conflict the minute a woman tries to direct and supervise men.
They really don't like that. And because of such sexist prejudices, it's very hard for a woman to succeed.
In the U.S., though, when an American man joins my crew, he assumes I know what I'm doing, and that I have every right to be where I am.
Irrespective of my sex.
There is no aspect of movie-making that a woman can't do just as well as a man.

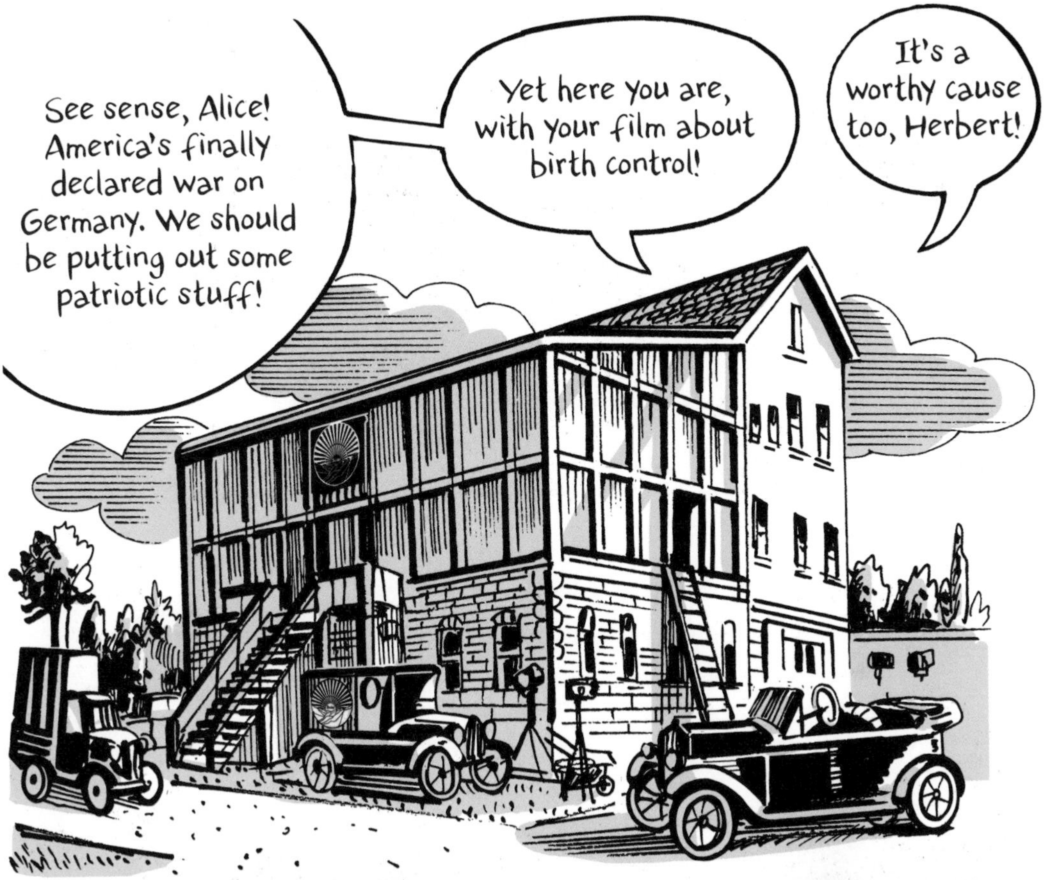
See sense, Alice! America's finally declared war on Germany. We should be putting out some patriotic stuff!
Yet here you are, with your film about birth control!
It's a worthy cause too, Herbert!

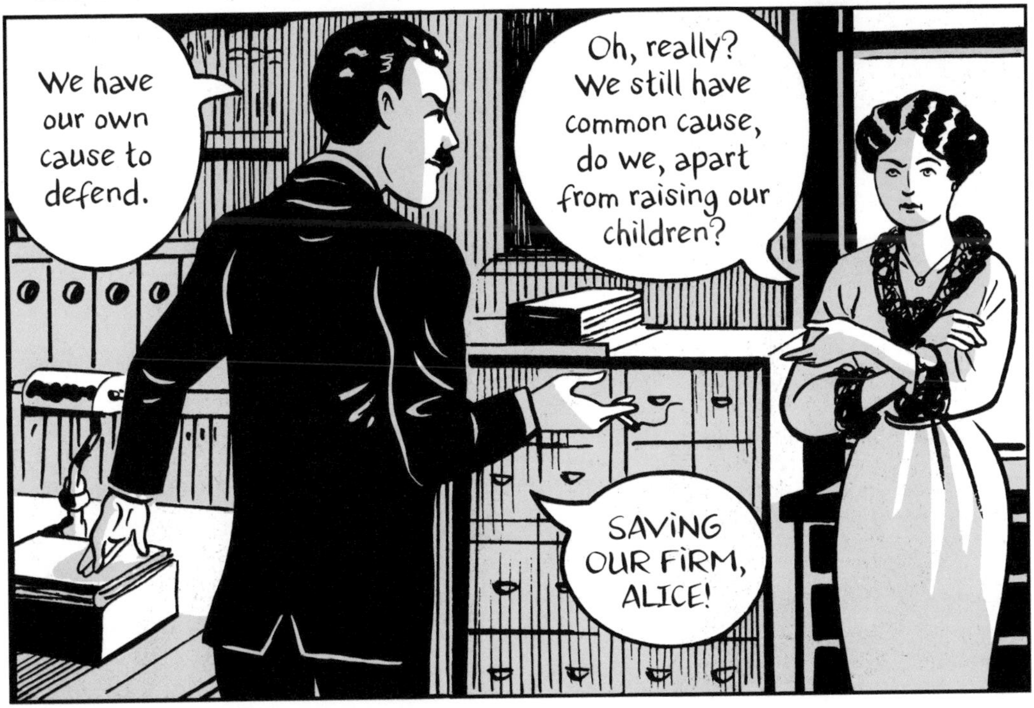
We have our own cause to defend.
Oh, really? We still have common cause, do we, apart from raising our children?
SAVING OUR FIRM, ALICE!

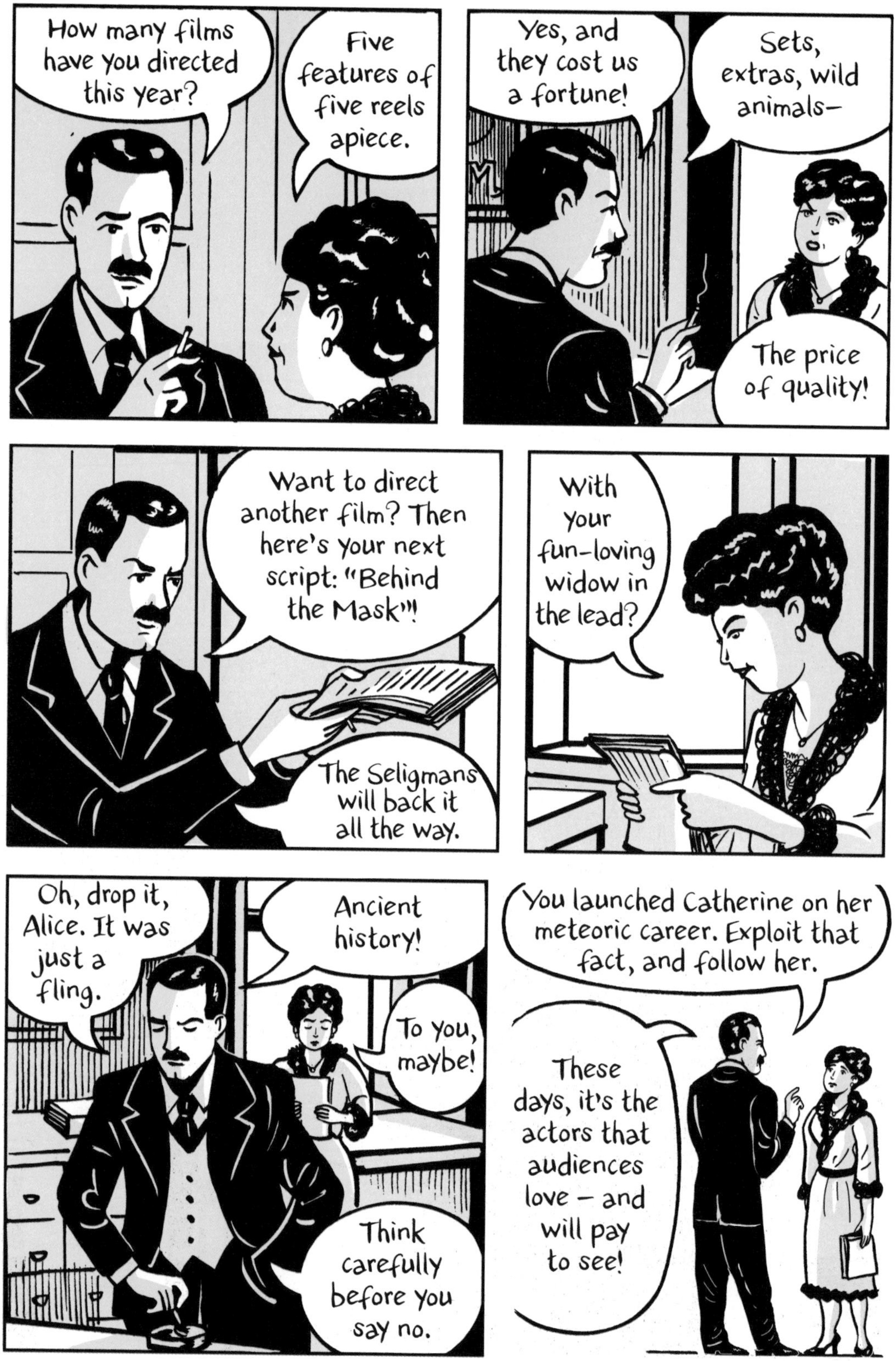
How many films have you directed this year?
Five features of five reels apiece.
Yes, and they cost us a fortune!
Sets, extras, wild animals—
The price of quality!
Want to direct another film? Then here's your next script: "Behind the Mask"!
The Seligmans will back it all the way.
With your fun-loving widow in the lead?
Oh, drop it, Alice. It was just a fling.
Ancient history!
To you, maybe!
Think carefully before you say no.
You launched Catherine on her meteoric career. Exploit that fact, and follow her.
These days, it's the actors that audiences love — and will pay to see!

1918 – Bretton Hall Hotel – 2350, Broadway –
New York – U.S.A.

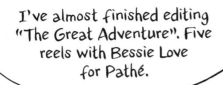

I've almost finished editing "The Great Adventure". Five reels with Bessie Love for Pathé.

Heavens! Gaumont's oldest competitor! Was it a commission?

Yes, since I no longer have the means to finance my own films.

We had to shut our company down, you know, Léonce.

But cinema is booming!

We lost a lot on the stock market.

But we still own the studio and, luckily, it's always being hired.

Even if Herbert thinks Hollywood is the future.

He's just moved us out here to keep a closer eye on his, er... starlet's career. Miss Calvert!

I saw "Behind the Mask". Wonderful!

I prefer the films I made with Olga Petrova.

285

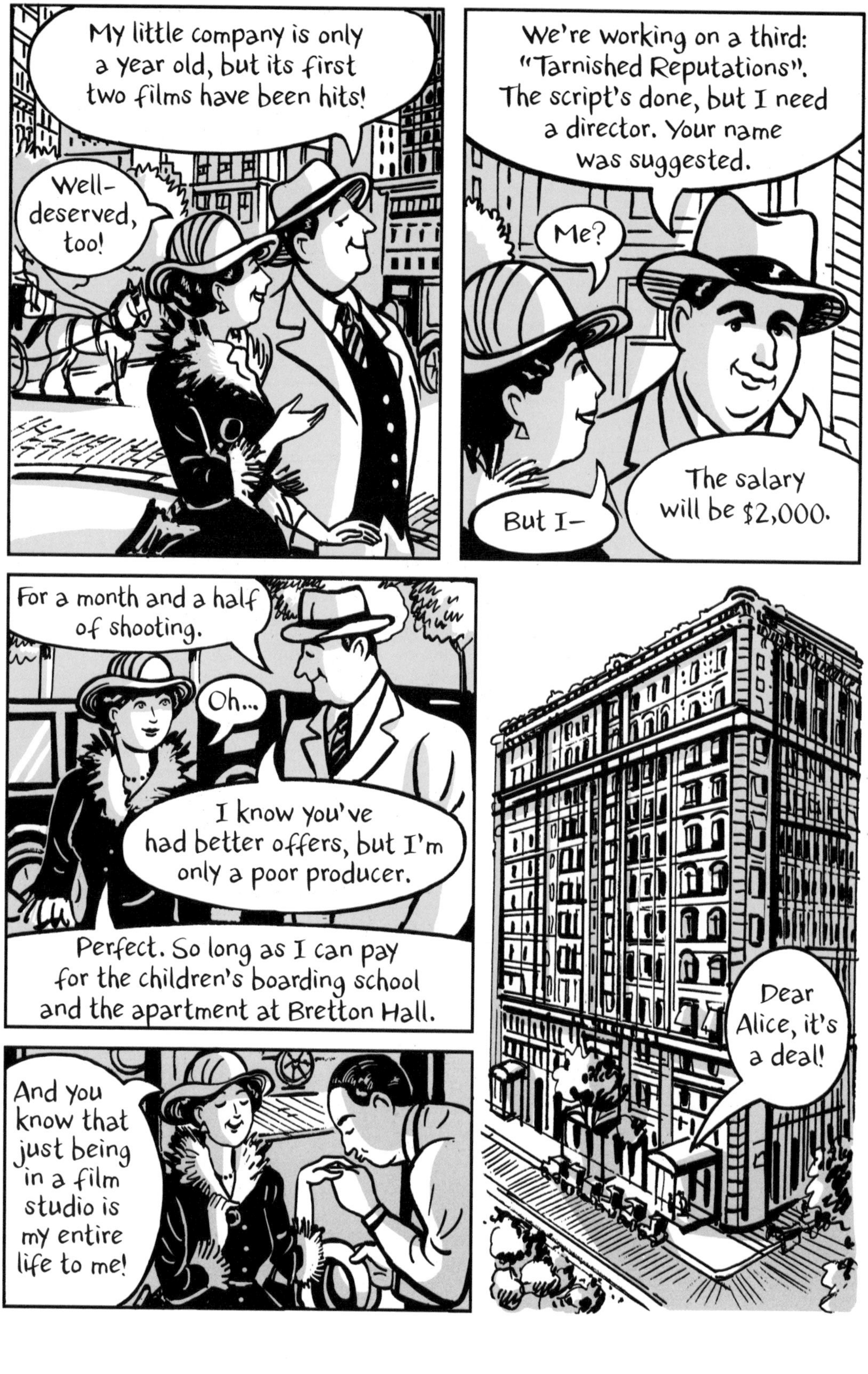
My little company is only a year old, but its first two films have been hits!
Well-deserved, too!
We're working on a third: "Tarnished Reputations". The script's done, but I need a director. Your name was suggested.
Me?
But I–
The salary will be $2,000.
For a month and a half of shooting.
Oh...
I know you've had better offers, but I'm only a poor producer.
Perfect. So long as I can pay for the children's boarding school and the apartment at Bretton Hall.
And you know that just being in a film studio is my entire life to me!
Dear Alice, it's a deal!

1920 – Chaplin Studios – La Brea Avenue – Hollywood –
Los Angeles – U.S.A.

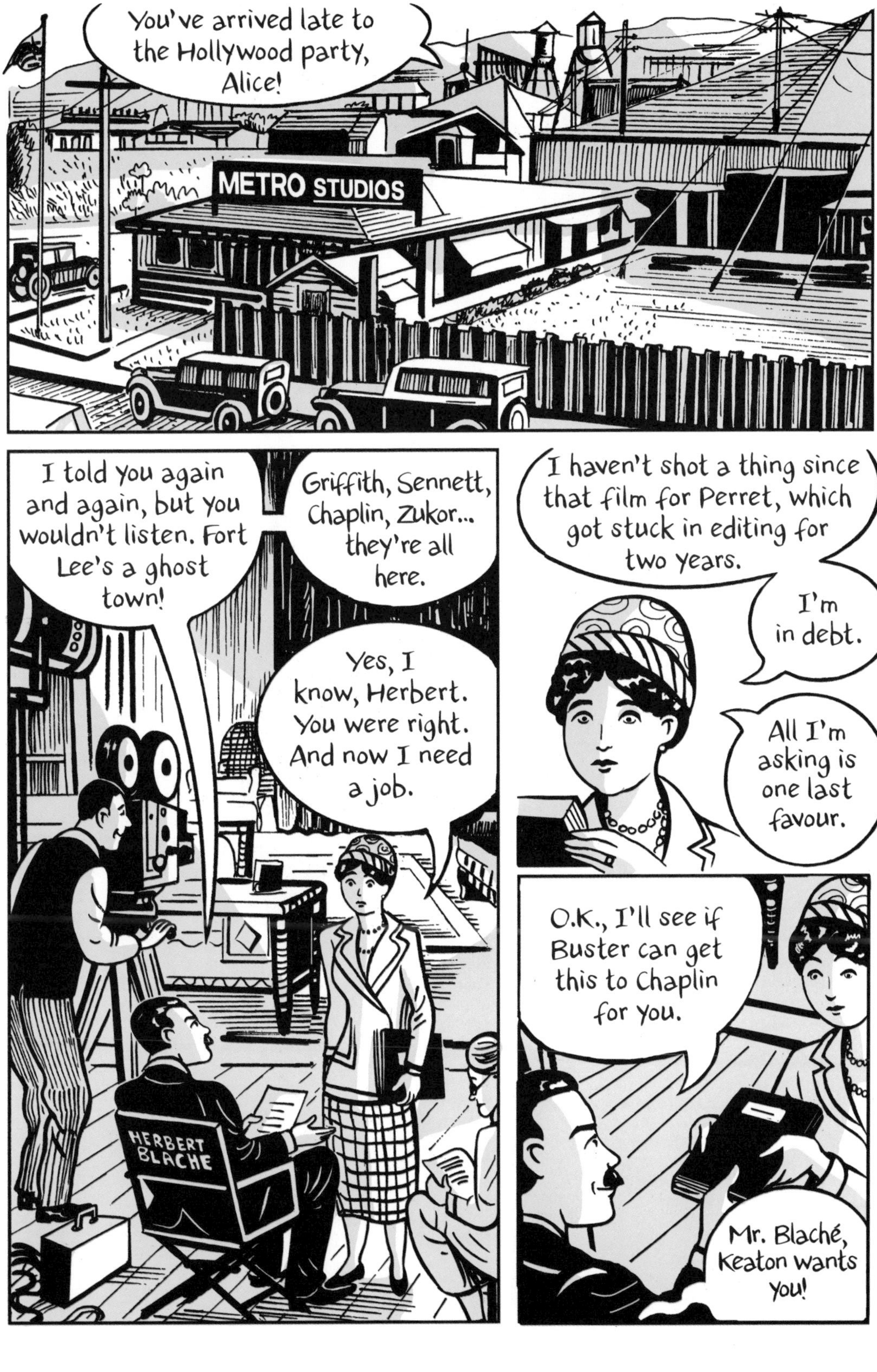
You've arrived late to the Hollywood party, Alice!
METRO STUDIOS
I told you again and again, but you wouldn't listen. Fort Lee's a ghost town!
Griffith, Sennett, Chaplin, Zukor... they're all here.
Yes, I know, Herbert. You were right. And now I need a job.
HERBERT BLACHE
I haven't shot a thing since that film for Perret, which got stuck in editing for two years.
I'm in debt.
All I'm asking is one last favour.
O.K., I'll see if Buster can get this to Chaplin for you.
Mr. Blaché, Keaton wants you!

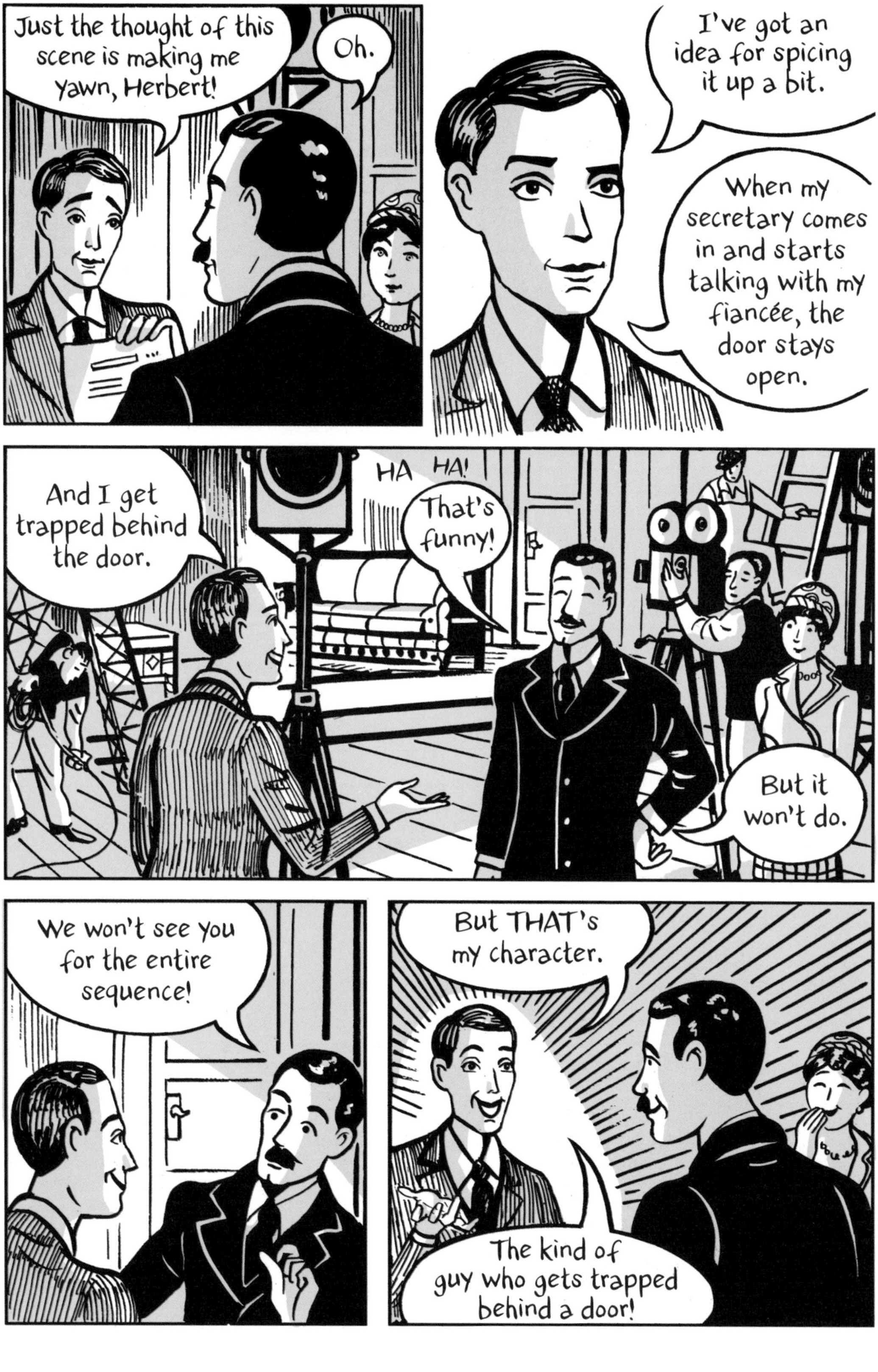
Just the thought of this scene is making me yawn, Herbert!
Oh.
I've got an idea for spicing it up a bit.
When my secretary comes in and starts talking with my fiancée, the door stays open.
And I get trapped behind the door.
HA HA!
That's funny!
But it won't do.
We won't see you for the entire sequence!
But THAT's my character.
The kind of guy who gets trapped behind a door!

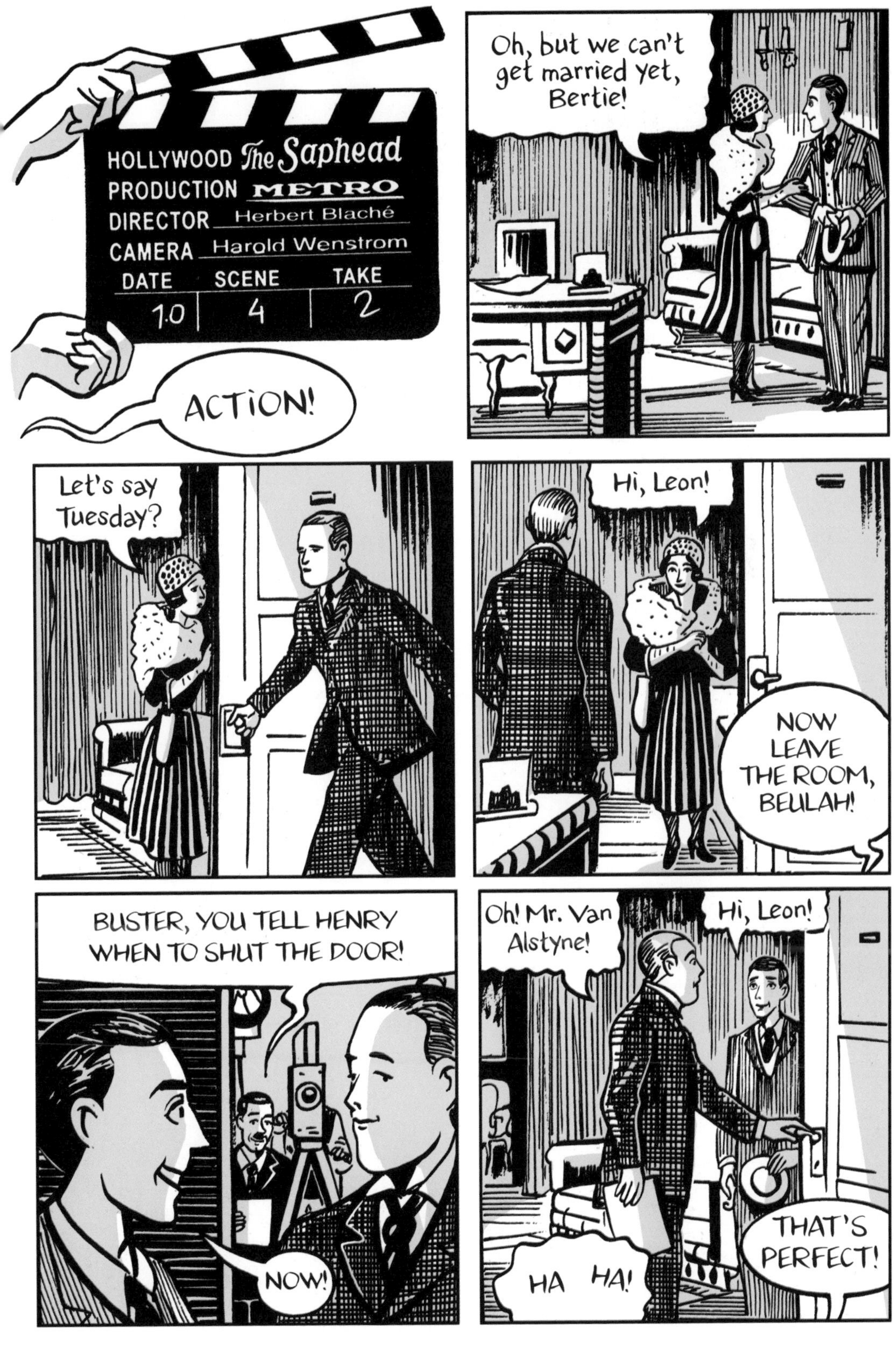
HOLLYWOOD The Saphead
PRODUCTION METRO
DIRECTOR Herbert Blaché
CAMERA Harold Wenstrom
DATE SCENE TAKE
1.0 4 2
ACTION!
Oh, but we can't get married yet, Bertie!
Let's say Tuesday?
Hi, Leon!
NOW LEAVE THE ROOM, BEULAH!
BUSTER, YOU TELL HENRY WHEN TO SHUT THE DOOR!
NOW!
Oh! Mr. Van Alstyne!
Hi, Leon!
THAT'S PERFECT!
HA HA!

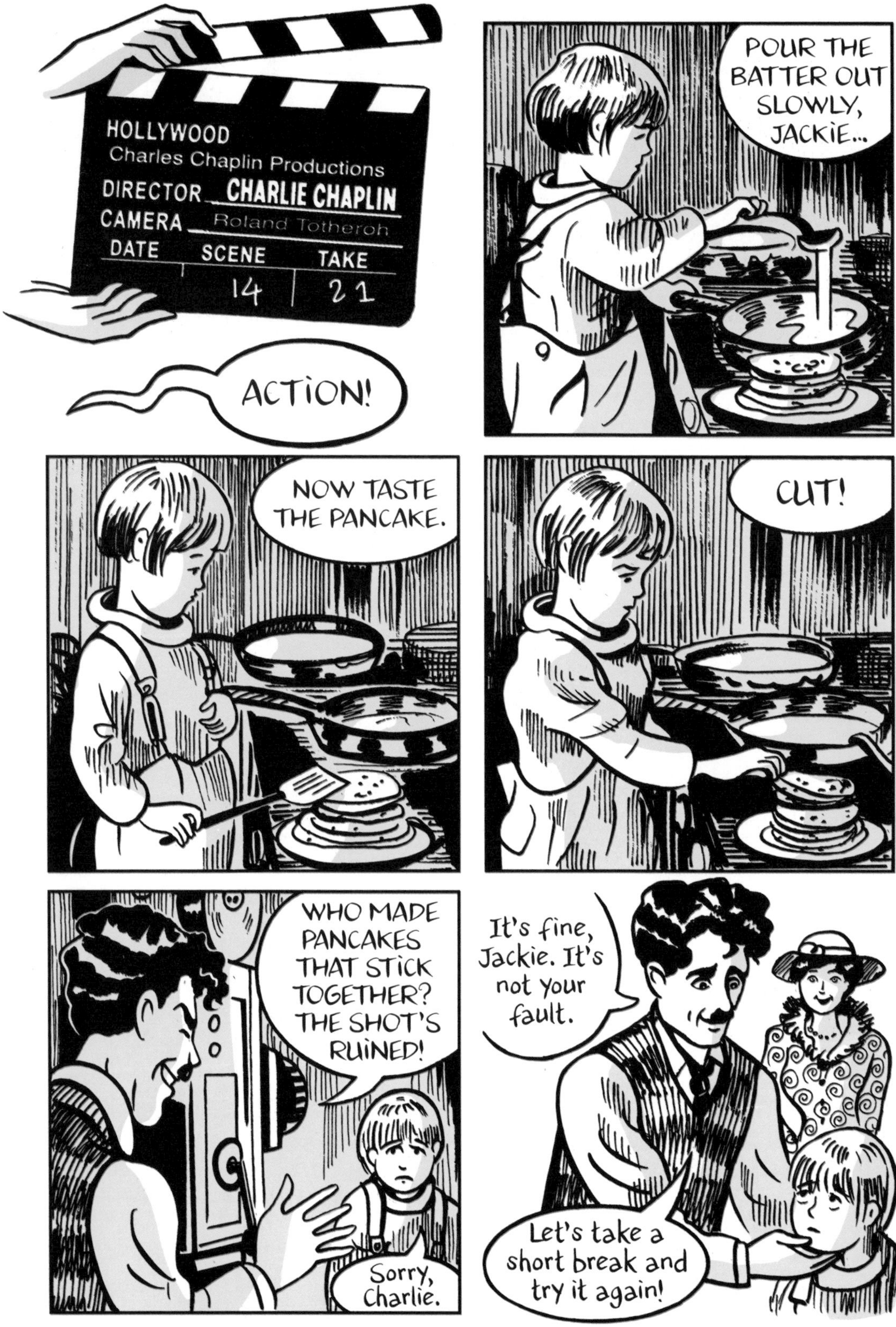
HOLLYWOOD
Charles Chaplin Productions
DIRECTOR CHARLIE CHAPLIN
CAMERA Roland Totheroh
DATE SCENE TAKE
14 21
ACTION!
POUR THE BATTER OUT SLOWLY, JACKIE...
NOW TASTE THE PANCAKE.
CUT!
WHO MADE PANCAKES THAT STICK TOGETHER? THE SHOT'S RUINED!
Sorry, Charlie.
It's fine, Jackie. It's not your fault.
Let's take a short break and try it again!

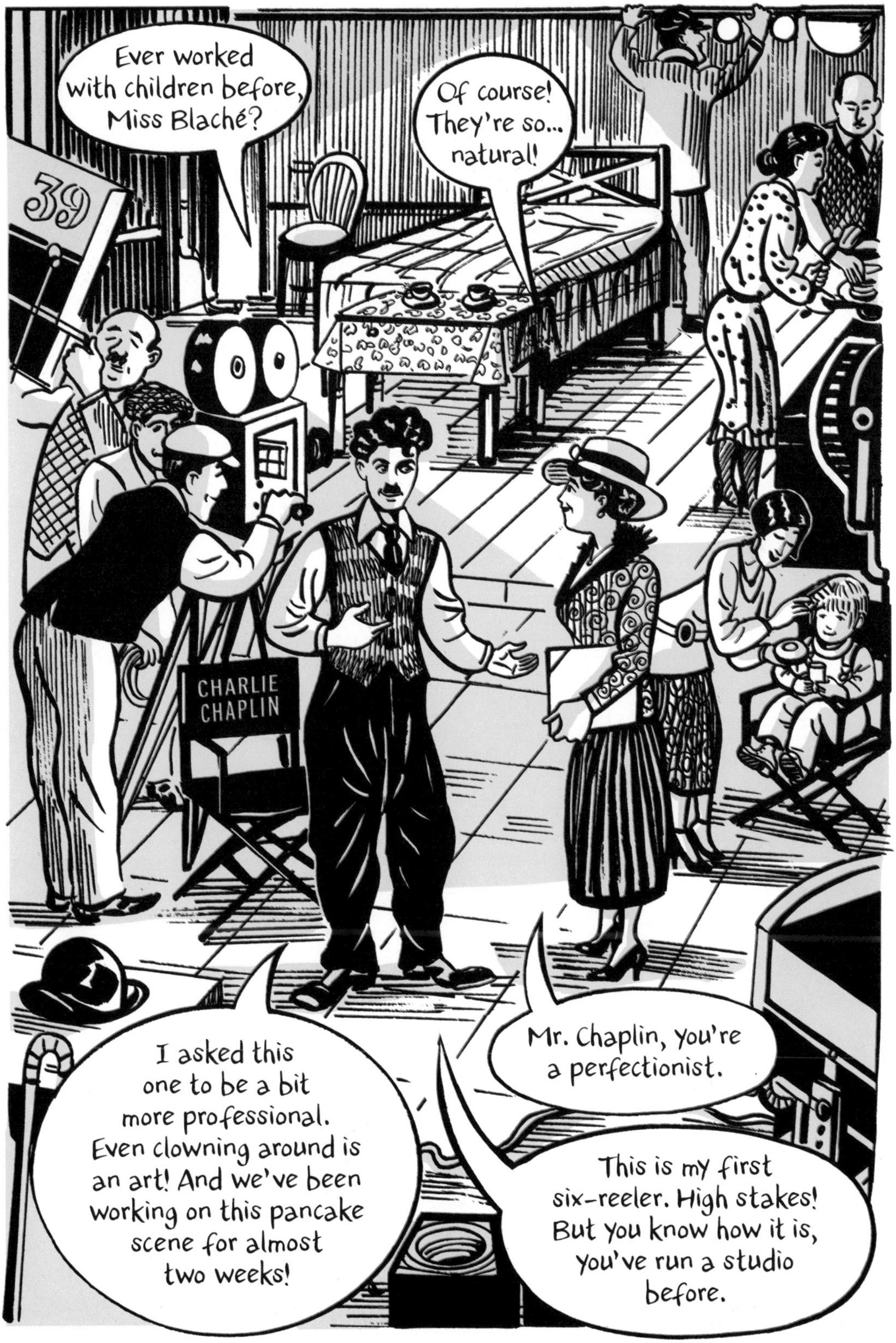
Ever worked with children before, Miss Blaché?
Of course! They're so... natural!
39
CHARLIE CHAPLIN
I asked this one to be a bit more professional. Even clowning around is an art! And we've been working on this pancake scene for almost two weeks!
Mr. Chaplin, you're a perfectionist.
This is my first six-reeler. High stakes! But you know how it is, you've run a studio before.

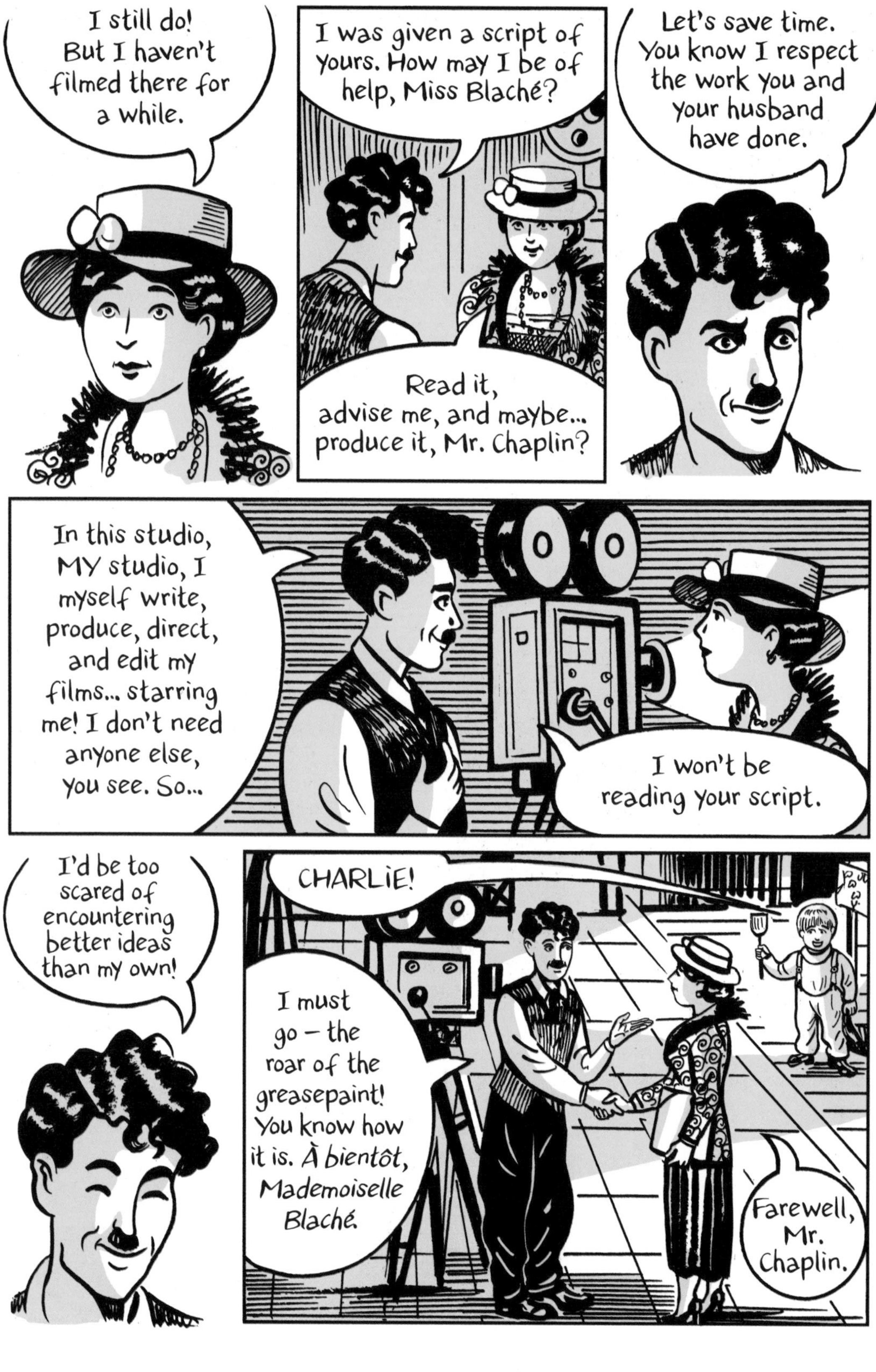

I still do! But I haven't filmed there for a while.
I was given a script of yours. How may I be of help, Miss Blaché?
Read it, advise me, and maybe... produce it, Mr. Chaplin?
Let's save time. You know I respect the work you and your husband have done.
In this studio, MY studio, I myself write, produce, direct, and edit my films... starring me! I don't need anyone else, you see. So...
I won't be reading your script.
I'd be too scared of encountering better ideas than my own!
CHARLIE!
I must go – the roar of the greasepaint! You know how it is. *À bientôt*, Mademoiselle Blaché.
Farewell, Mr. Chaplin.

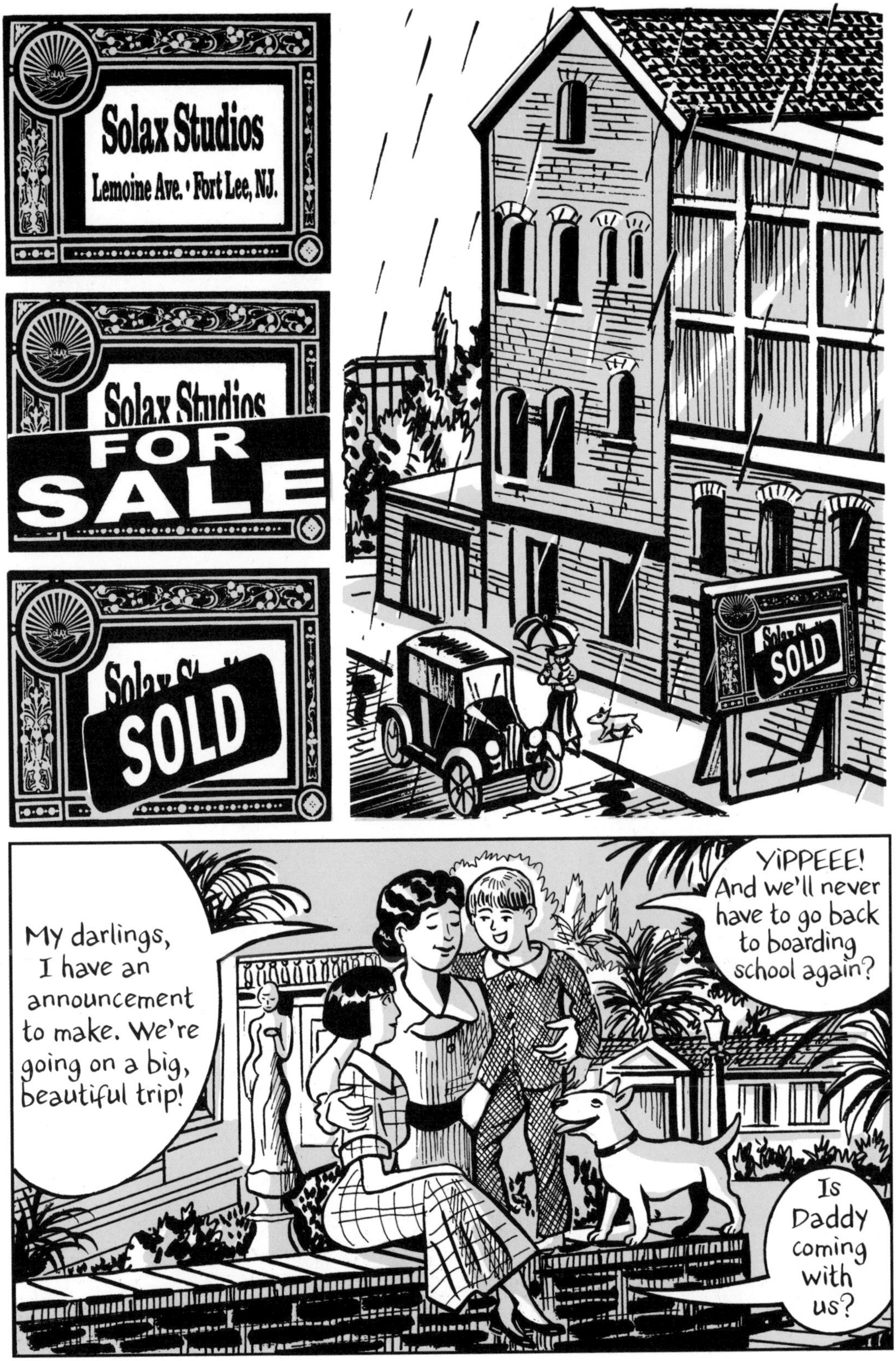
Solax Studios
Lemoine Ave. • Fort Lee, NJ.
Solax Studios
FOR SALE
SOLD
SOLD
My darlings, I have an announcement to make. We're going on a big, beautiful trip!
YiPPEEE! And we'll never have to go back to boarding school again?
Is Daddy coming with us?

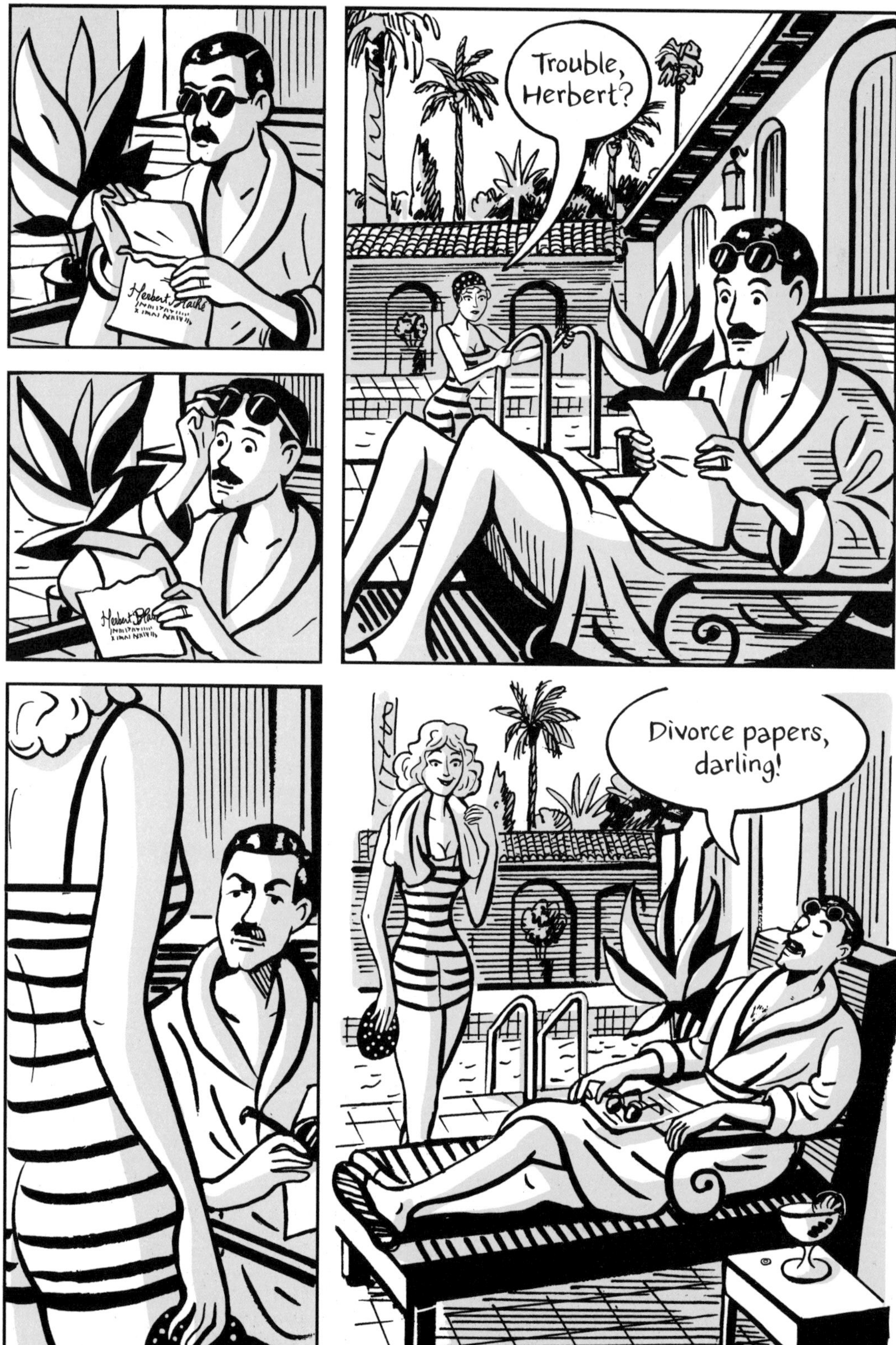
Trouble, Herbert?
Divorce papers, darling!

1922 – Studios de la Victorine – Nice – France

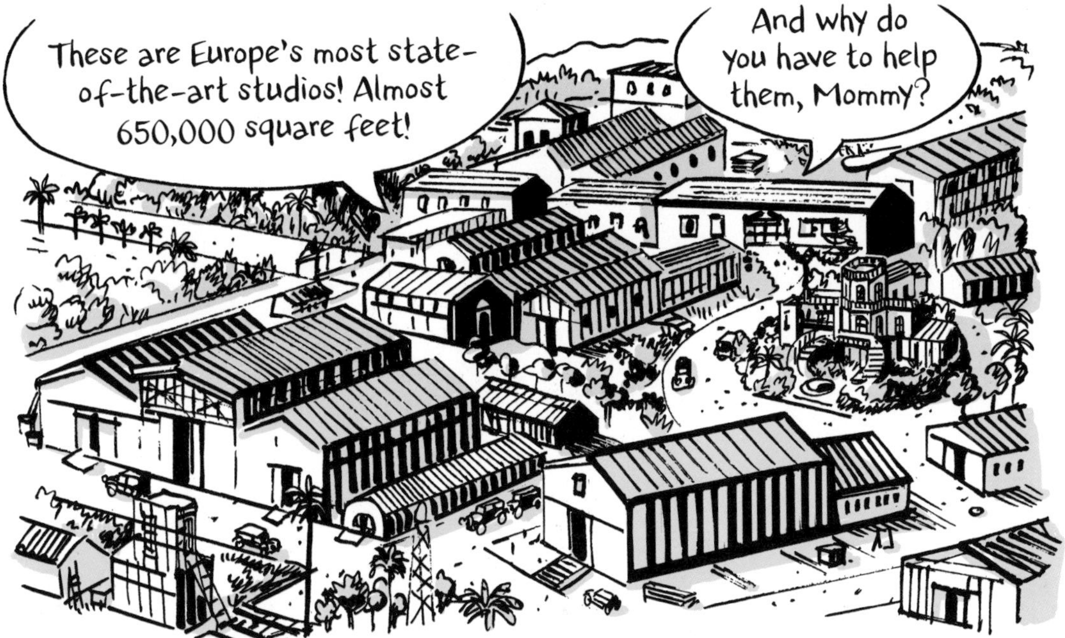
These are Europe's most state-of-the-art studios! Almost 650,000 square feet!
And why do you have to help them, Mommy?

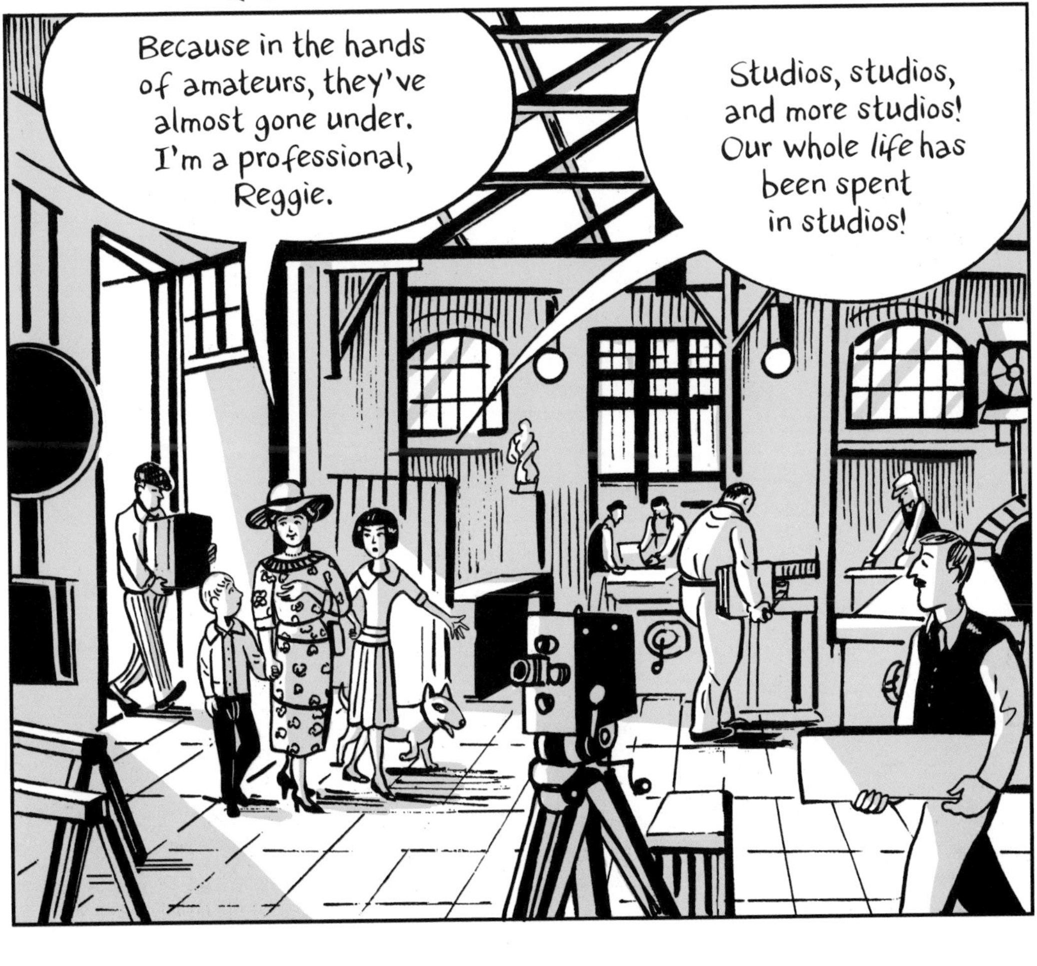
Because in the hands of amateurs, they've almost gone under. I'm a professional, Reggie.
Studios, studios, and more studios! Our whole *life* has been spent in studios!

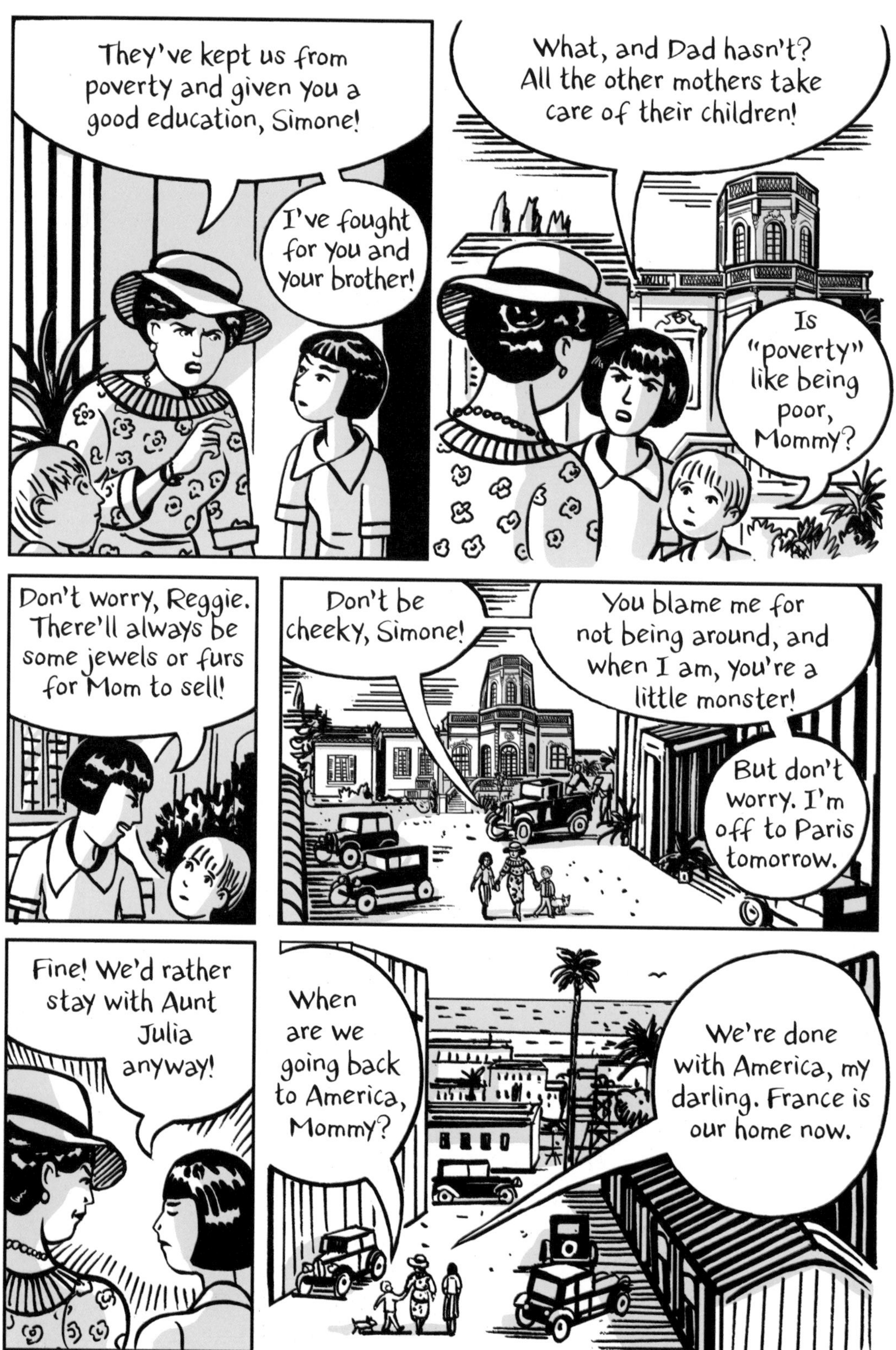
They've kept us from poverty and given you a good education, Simone!
I've fought for you and your brother!
What, and Dad hasn't? All the other mothers take care of their children!
Is "poverty" like being poor, Mommy?
Don't worry, Reggie. There'll always be some jewels or furs for Mom to sell!
Don't be cheeky, Simone!
You blame me for not being around, and when I am, you're a little monster!
But don't worry. I'm off to Paris tomorrow.
Fine! We'd rather stay with Aunt Julia anyway!
When are we going back to America, Mommy?
We're done with America, my darling. France is our home now.

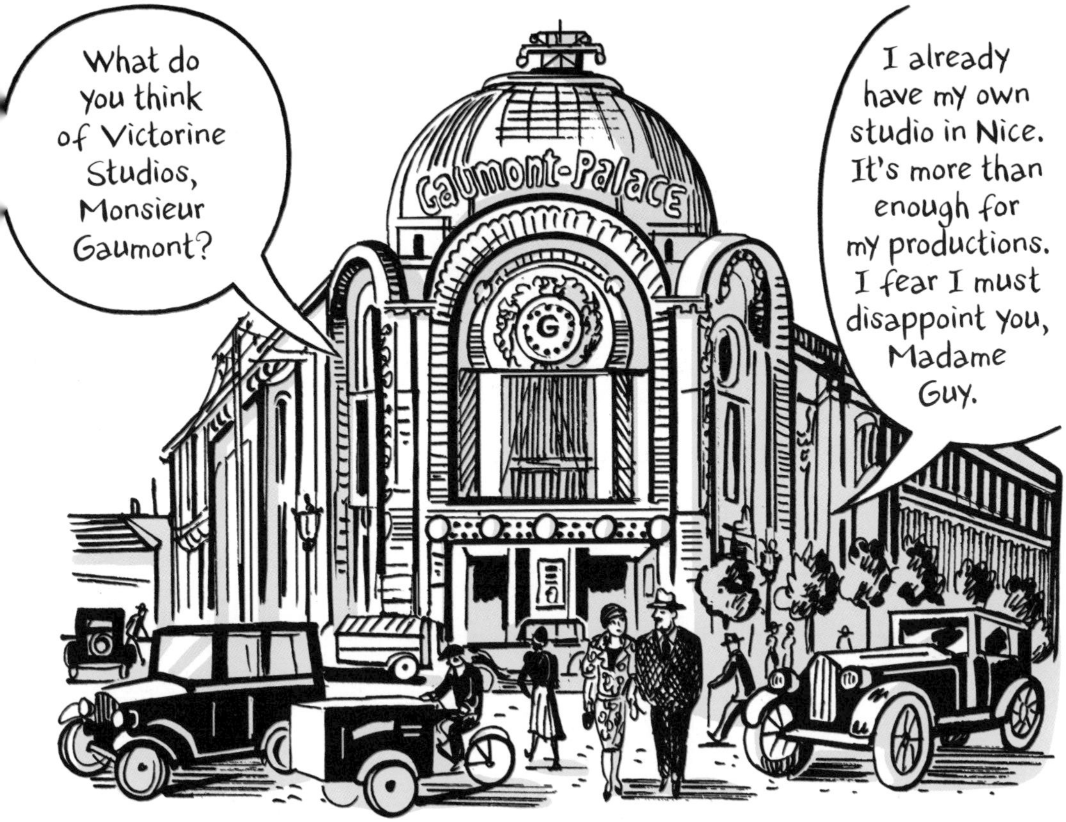
What do you think of Victorine Studios, Monsieur Gaumont?
Gaumont-Palace
I already have my own studio in Nice. It's more than enough for my productions. I fear I must disappoint you, Madame Guy.

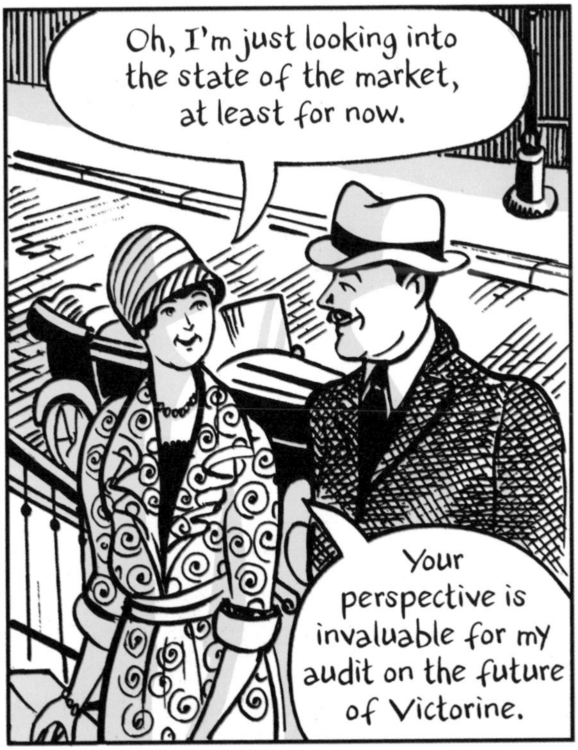
Oh, I'm just looking into the state of the market, at least for now.
Your perspective is invaluable for my audit on the future of Victorine.

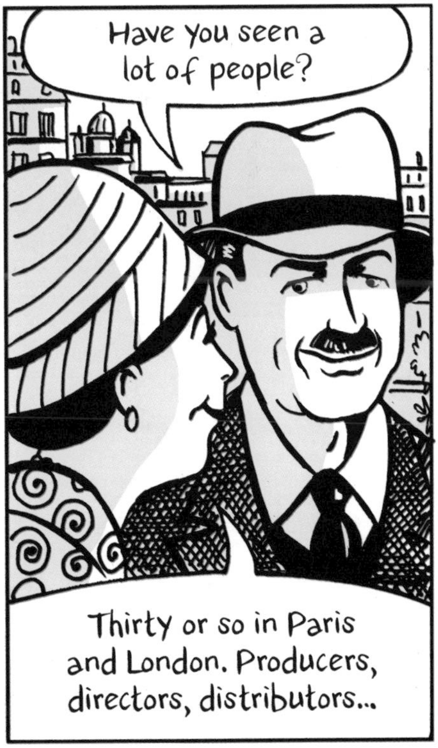
Have you seen a lot of people?
Thirty or so in Paris and London. Producers, directors, distributors...

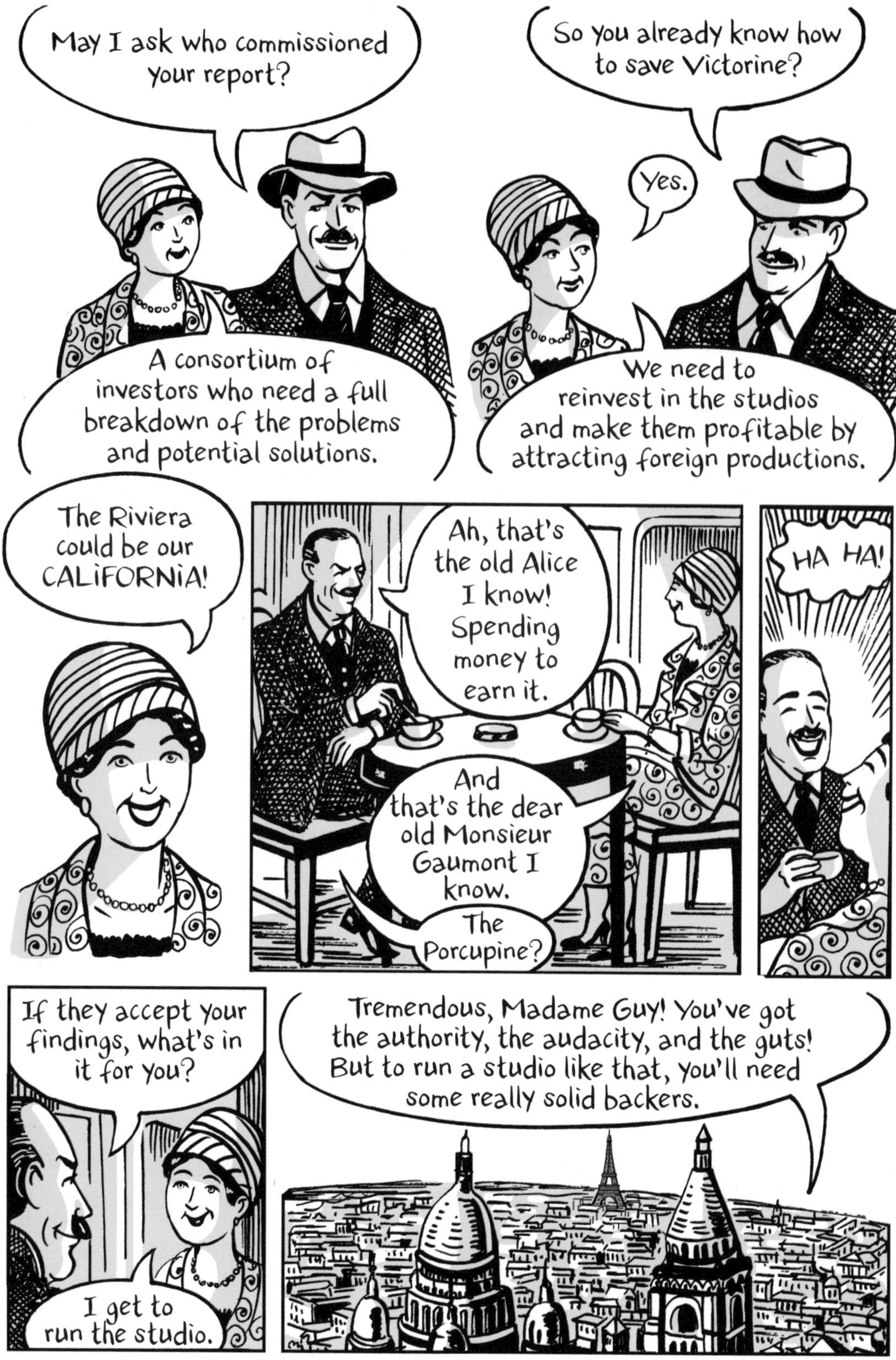
May I ask who commissioned your report?
A consortium of investors who need a full breakdown of the problems and potential solutions.
So you already know how to save Victorine?
Yes.
We need to reinvest in the studios and make them profitable by attracting foreign productions.
The Riviera could be our CALIFORNIA!
Ah, that's the old Alice I know! Spending money to earn it.
And that's the dear old Monsieur Gaumont I know.
The Porcupine?
HA HA!
If they accept your findings, what's in it for you?
I get to run the studio.
Tremendous, Madame Guy! You've got the authority, the audacity, and the guts! But to run a studio like that, you'll need some really solid backers.

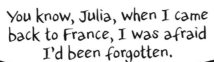

You know, Julia, when I came back to France, I was afraid I'd been forgotten.

But... well, I was wrong.

What do you mean, Alice?

I'm not forgotten.

It's just that, in the eyes of French cinema, I never existed.

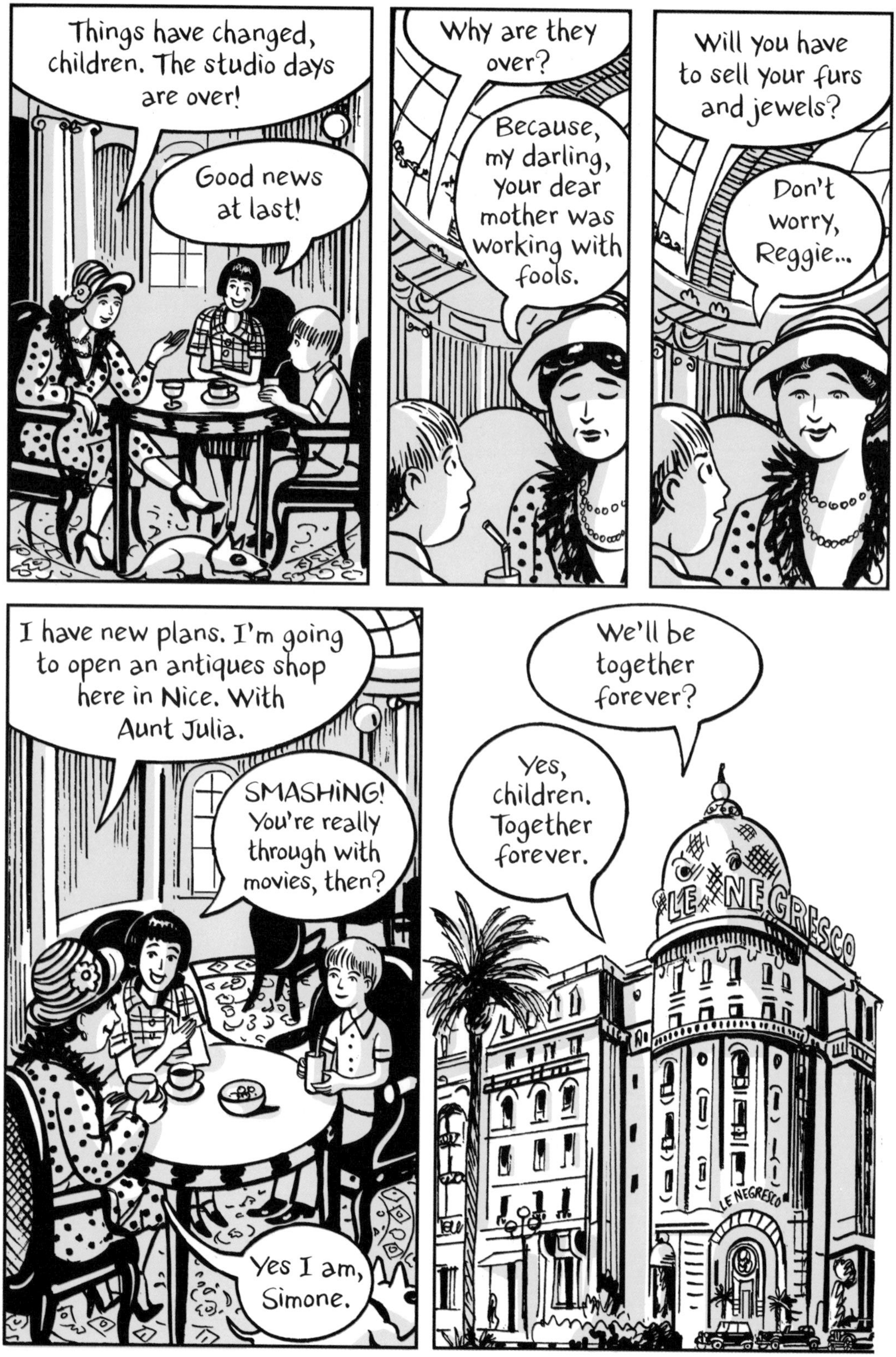
Things have changed, children. The studio days are over!
Good news at last!
Why are they over?
Because, my darling, your dear mother was working with fools.
Will you have to sell your furs and jewels?
Don't worry, Reggie...
I have new plans. I'm going to open an antiques shop here in Nice. With Aunt Julia.
SMASHING! You're really through with movies, then?
Yes I am, Simone.
We'll be together forever?
Yes, children. Together forever.
LE NEGRESCO
LE NEGRESCO

1933 – 19, Rue de l'Atlas – Paris – France

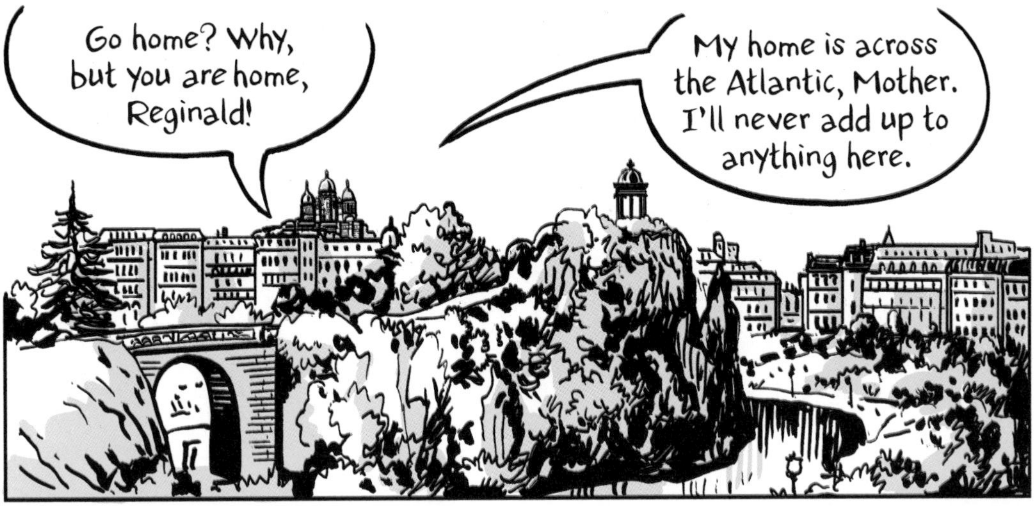

Go home? Why, but you are home, Reginald!
My home is across the Atlantic, Mother. I'll never add up to anything here.

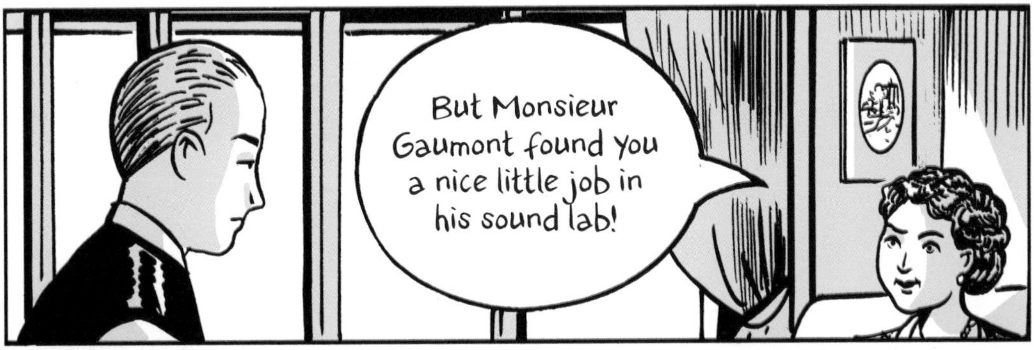

But Monsieur Gaumont found you a nice little job in his sound lab!

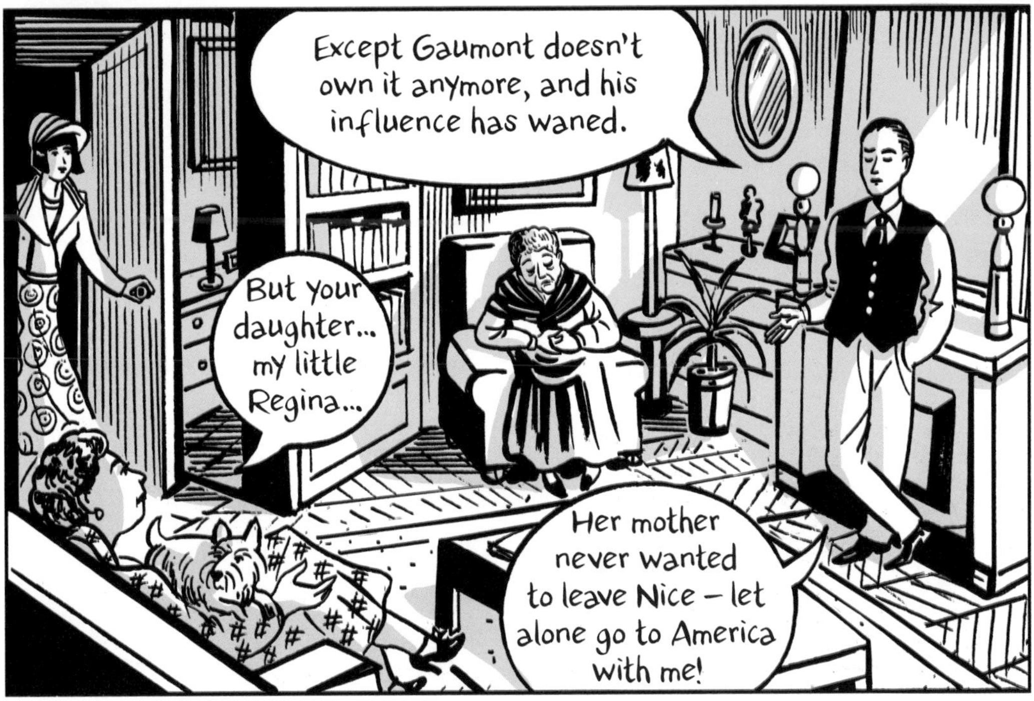

Except Gaumont doesn't own it anymore, and his influence has waned.
But your daughter... my little Regina...
Her mother never wanted to leave Nice – let alone go to America with me!

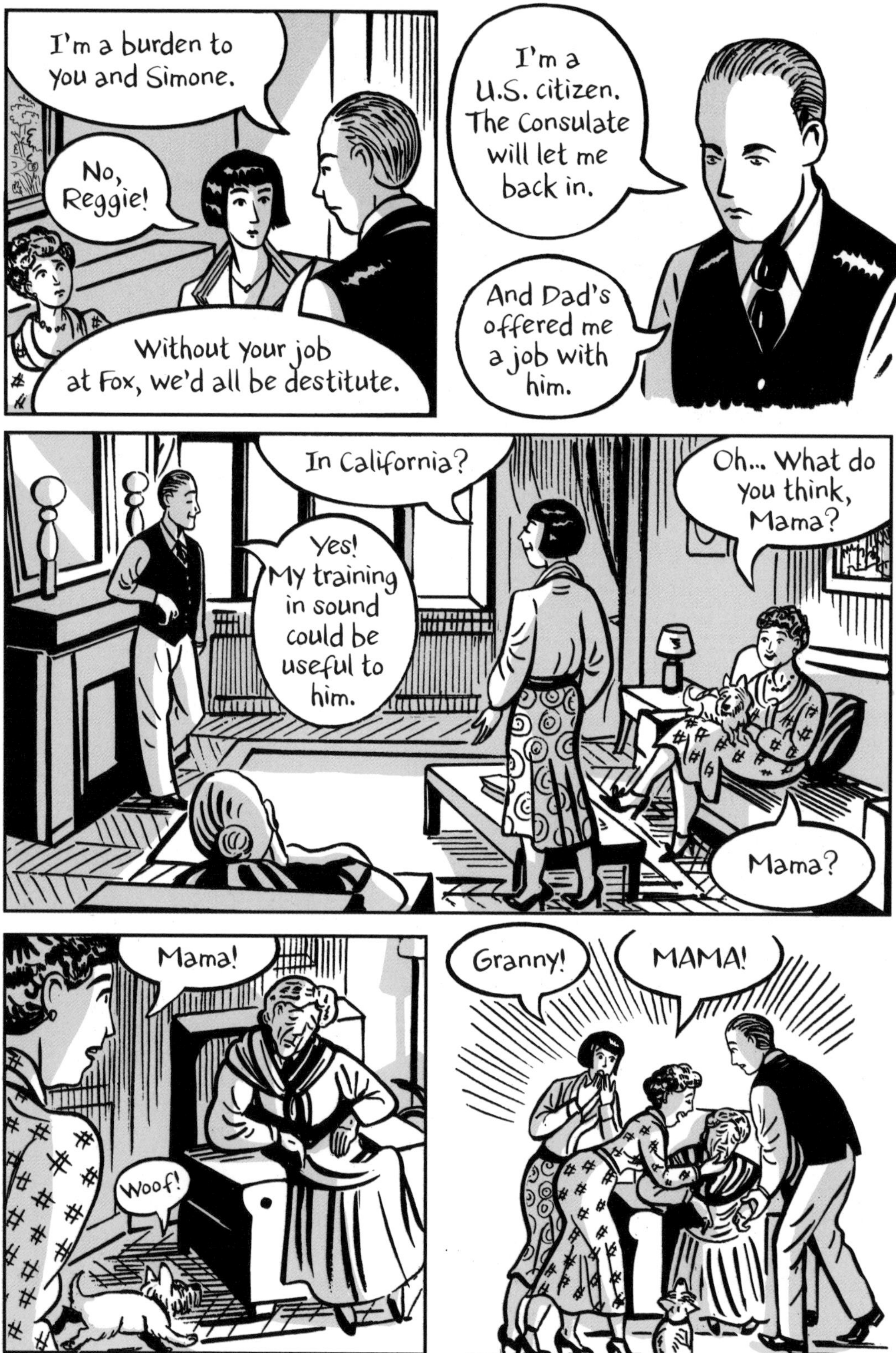

I'm a burden to you and Simone.
No, Reggie!
Without your job at Fox, we'd all be destitute.
I'm a U.S. citizen. The Consulate will let me back in.
And Dad's offered me a job with him.
In California?
Yes! My training in sound could be useful to him.
Oh... What do you think, Mama?
Mama?
Mama!
Woof!
Granny!
MAMA!

1963 – Avenue de Tervueren – Brussels – Belgium

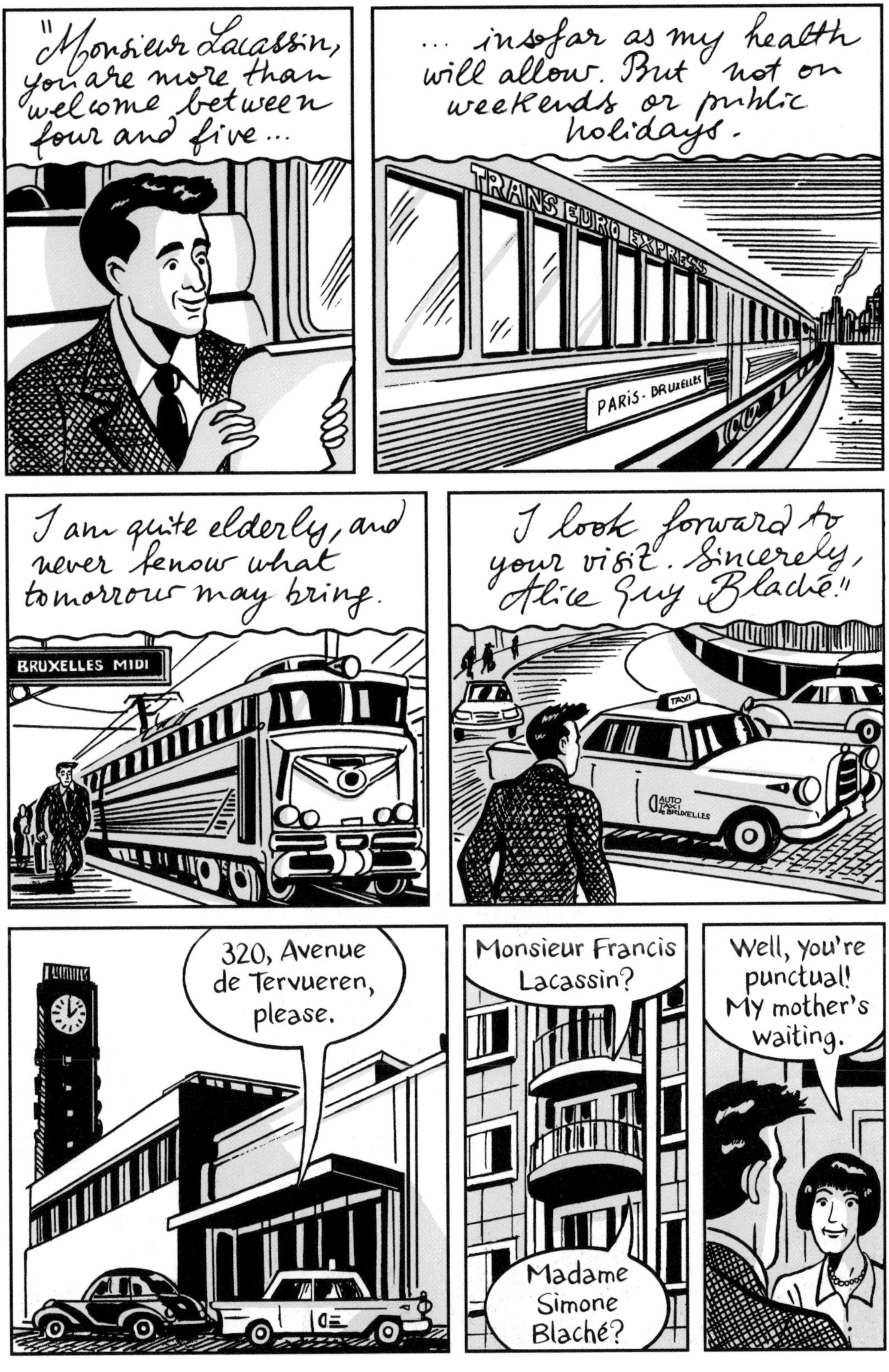
"Monsieur Lacassin, you are more than welcome between four and five...
... insofar as my health will allow. But not on weekends or public holidays.
TRANS EURO EXPRESS
PARIS - BRUXELLES
I am quite elderly, and never know what tomorrow may bring.
BRUXELLES MIDI
I look forward to your visit. Sincerely, Alice Guy Blaché!"
TAXI
AUTO TAXI de BRUXELLES
320, Avenue de Tervueren, please.
Monsieur Francis Lacassin?
Madame Simone Blaché?
Well, you're punctual! My mother's waiting.

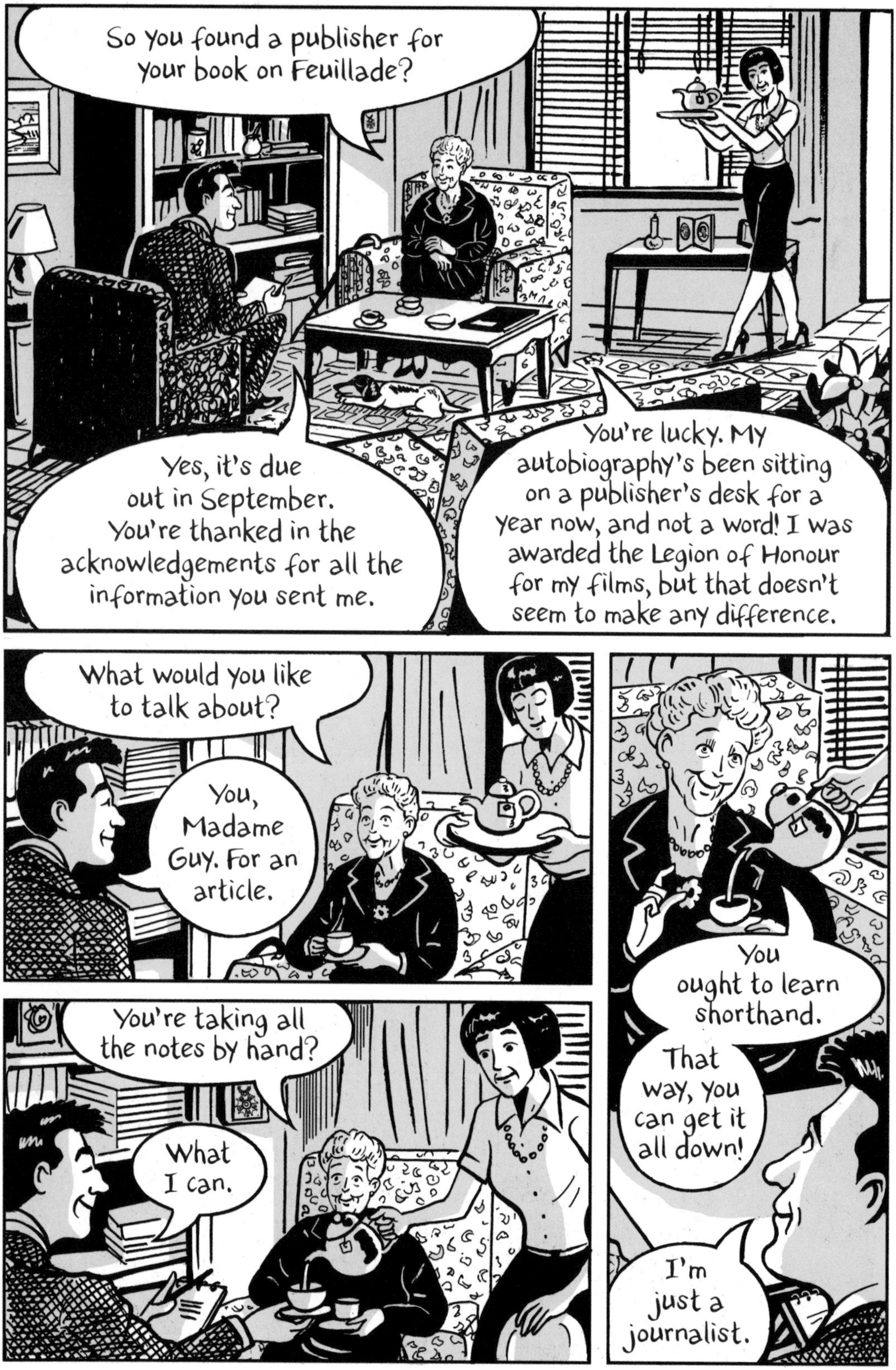
So you found a publisher for your book on Feuillade?
Yes, it's due out in September. You're thanked in the acknowledgements for all the information you sent me.
You're lucky. My autobiography's been sitting on a publisher's desk for a year now, and not a word! I was awarded the Legion of Honour for my films, but that doesn't seem to make any difference.
What would you like to talk about?
You, Madame Guy. For an article.
You're taking all the notes by hand?
What I can.
You ought to learn shorthand.
That way, you can get it all down!
I'm just a journalist.

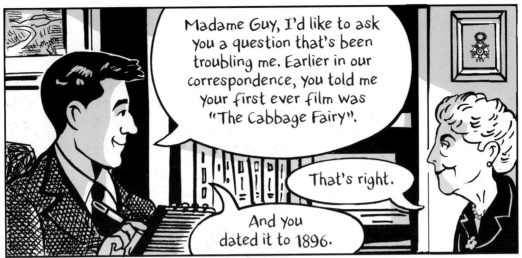

Madame Guy, I'd like to ask you a question that's been troubling me. Earlier in our correspondence, you told me your first ever film was "The Cabbage Fairy".

That's right.

And you dated it to 1896.

Indeed.

But I checked Gaumont's catalogue, and that film is listed for 1900, under another title.

Gaumont's youngest son asked me the same question. The 1900 film is a remake.

I ought to know what I did!

But what does it matter? The history of cinema has completely forgotten about me.

And to add insult to injury, Georges Sadoul's book attributed all my films to Henri Gallet!

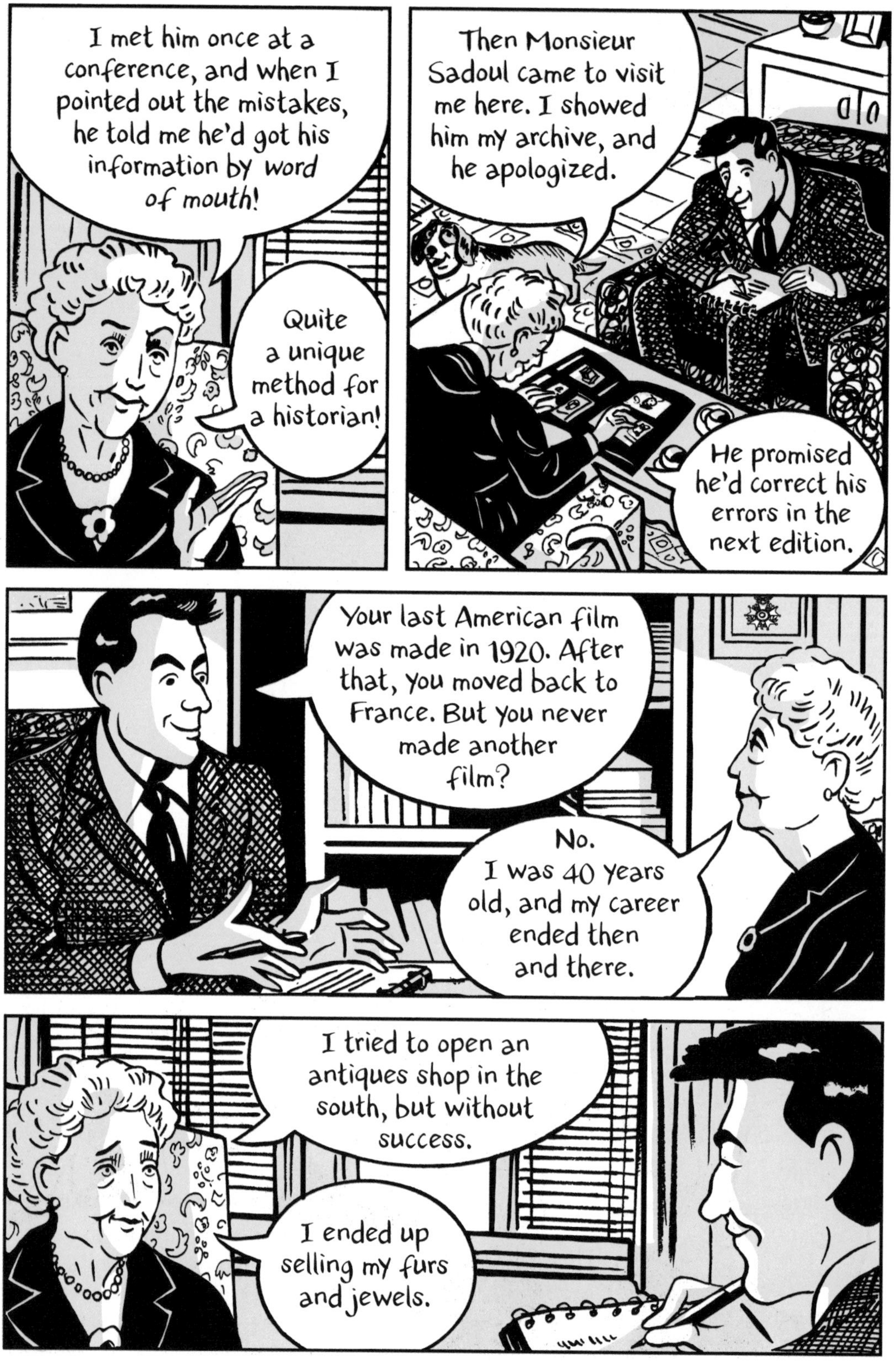
I met him once at a conference, and when I pointed out the mistakes, he told me he'd got his information by word of mouth!
Quite a unique method for a historian!
Then Monsieur Sadoul came to visit me here. I showed him my archive, and he apologized.
He promised he'd correct his errors in the next edition.
Your last American film was made in 1920. After that, you moved back to France. But you never made another film?
No. I was 40 years old, and my career ended then and there.
I tried to open an antiques shop in the south, but without success.
I ended up selling my furs and jewels.

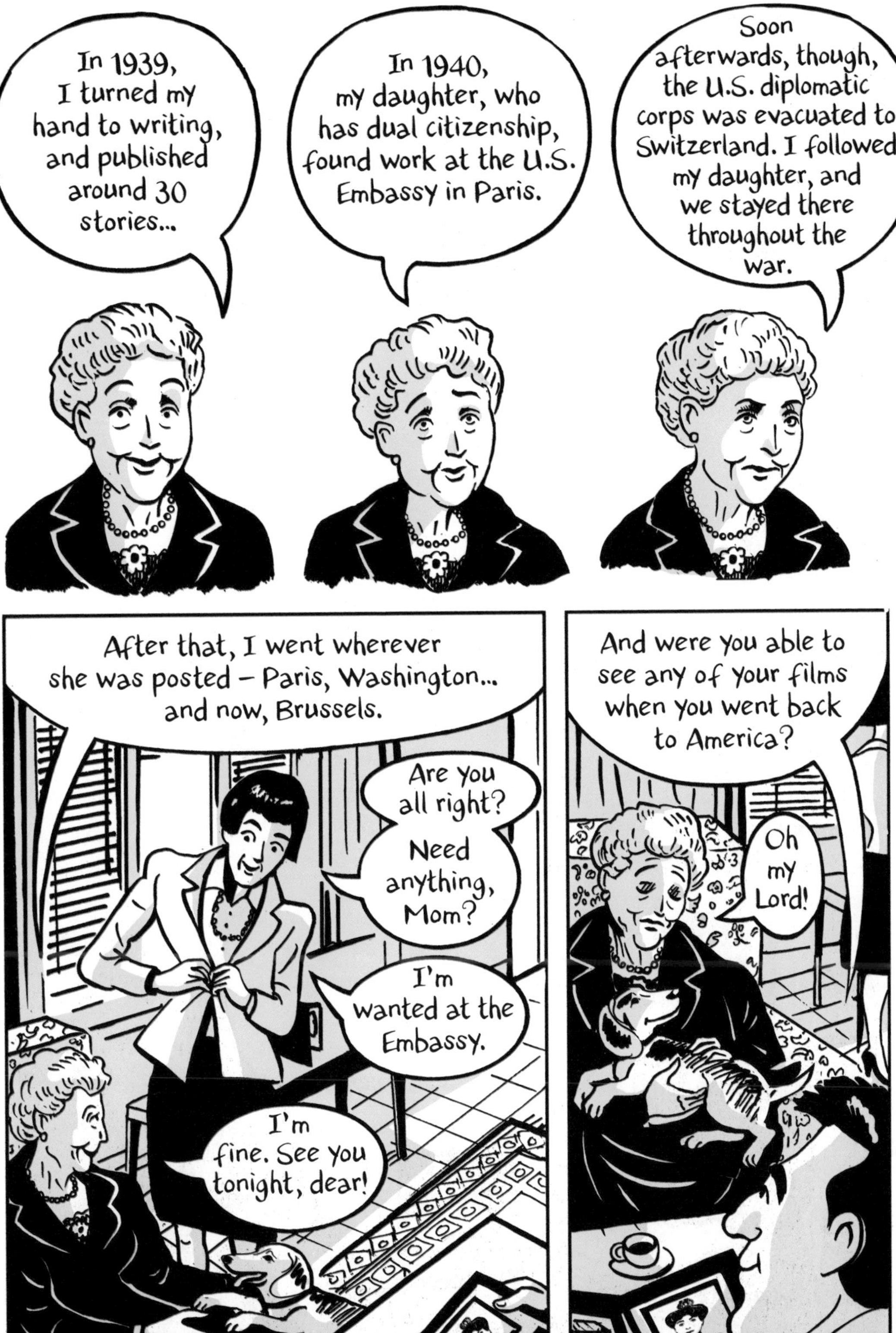
In 1939, I turned my hand to writing, and published around 30 stories...
In 1940, my daughter, who has dual citizenship, found work at the U.S. Embassy in Paris.
Soon afterwards, though, the U.S. diplomatic corps was evacuated to Switzerland. I followed my daughter, and we stayed there throughout the war.
After that, I went wherever she was posted – Paris, Washington... and now, Brussels.
Are you all right?
Need anything, Mom?
I'm wanted at the Embassy.
I'm fine. See you tonight, dear!
And were you able to see any of your films when you went back to America?
Oh my Lord!

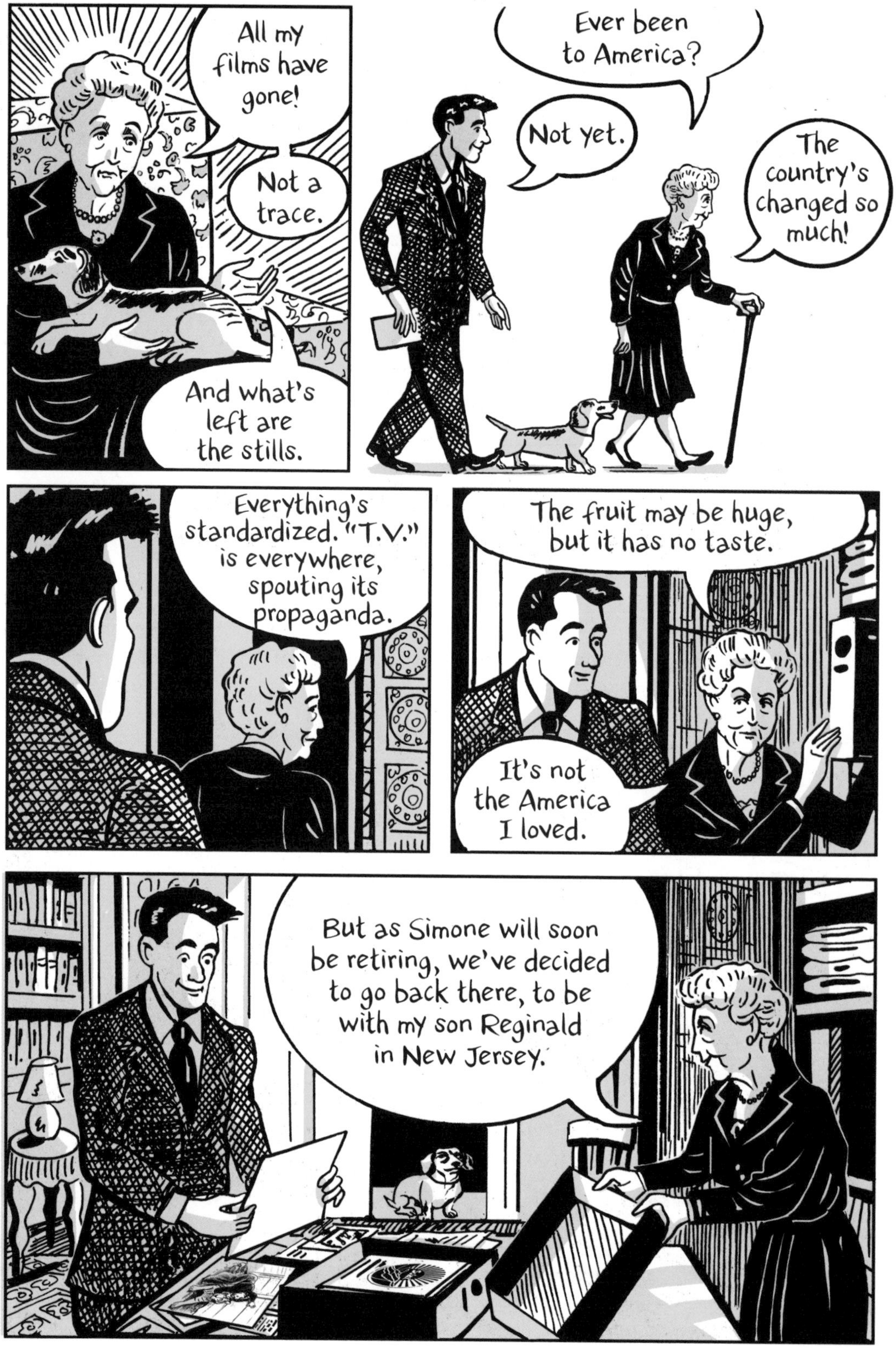
All my films have gone!
Not a trace.
And what's left are the stills.
Ever been to America?
Not yet.
The country's changed so much!
Everything's standardized. "T.V." is everywhere, spouting its propaganda.
The fruit may be huge, but it has no taste.
It's not the America I loved.
But as Simone will soon be retiring, we've decided to go back there, to be with my son Reginald in New Jersey.

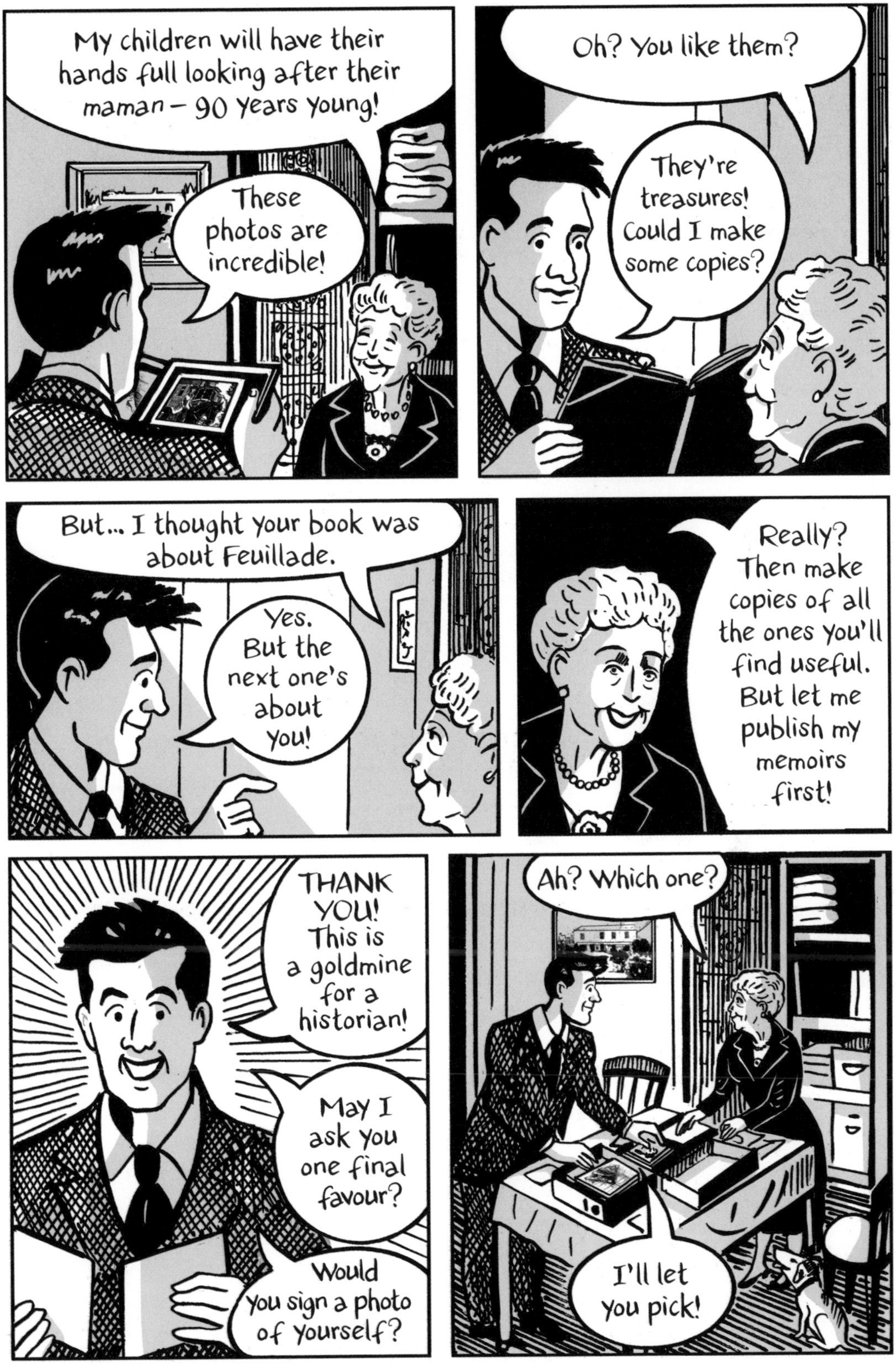
My children will have their hands full looking after their maman – 90 years young!
These photos are incredible!
Oh? You like them?
They're treasures! Could I make some copies?
But... I thought your book was about Feuillade.
Yes. But the next one's about you!
Really? Then make copies of all the ones you'll find useful. But let me publish my memoirs first!
THANK YOU! This is a goldmine for a historian!
May I ask you one final favour?
Would you sign a photo of yourself?
Ah? Which one?
I'll let you pick!

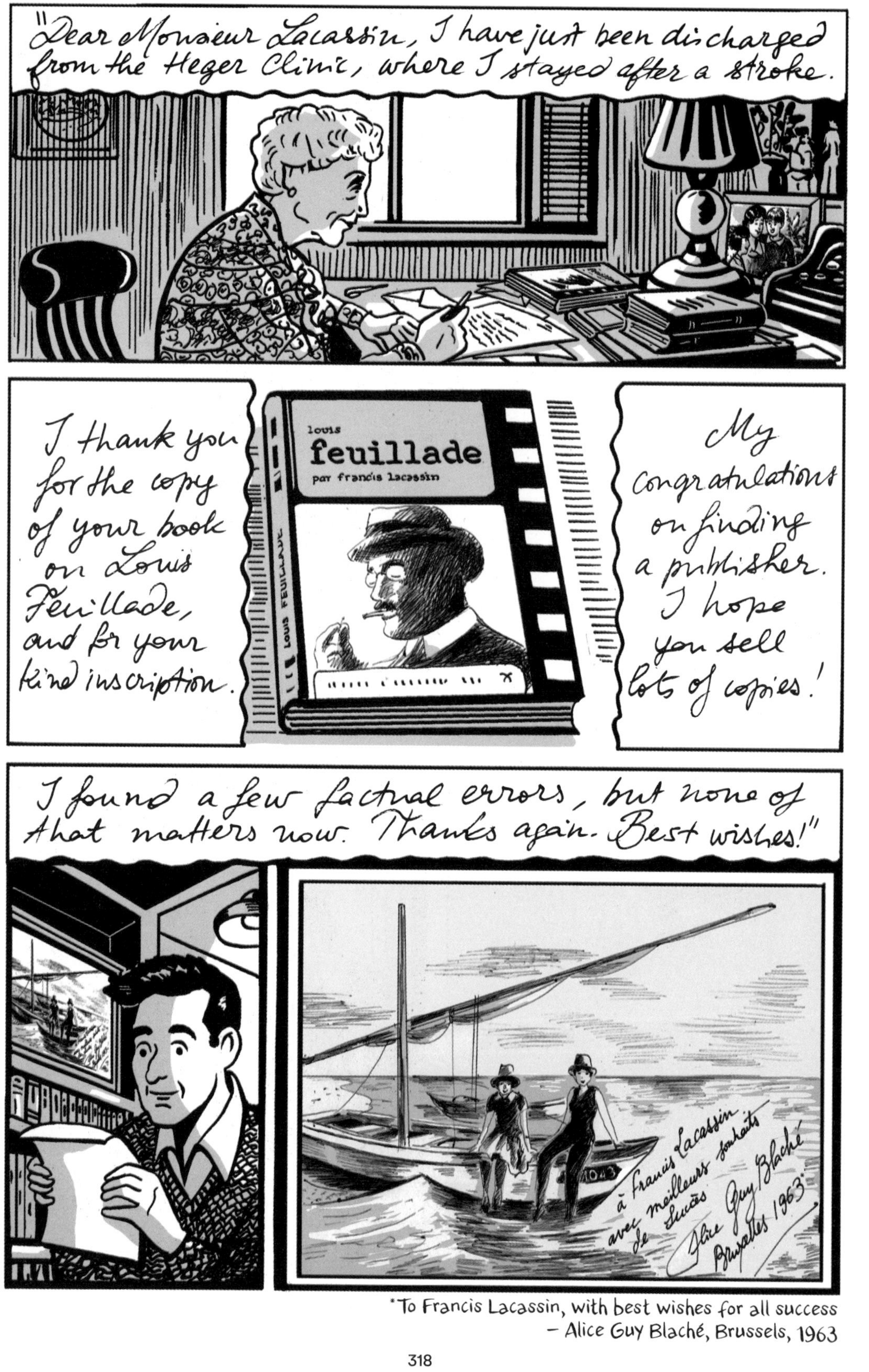
"Dear Monsieur Lacassin, I have just been discharged from the Heger Clinic, where I stayed after a stroke.
I thank you for the copy of your book on Louis Feuillade, and for your kind inscription.
louis
feuillade
par francis lacassin
LOUIS FEUILLADE
My congratulations on finding a publisher. I hope you sell lots of copies!
I found a few factual errors, but none of that matters now. Thanks again. Best wishes!"
à Francis Lacassin avec meilleurs souhaits de succès
Alice Guy Blaché
Bruxelles 1963*

*To Francis Lacassin, with best wishes for all success
– Alice Guy Blaché, Brussels, 1963

24 March 1968 – Wayne – New Jersey – U.S.A.

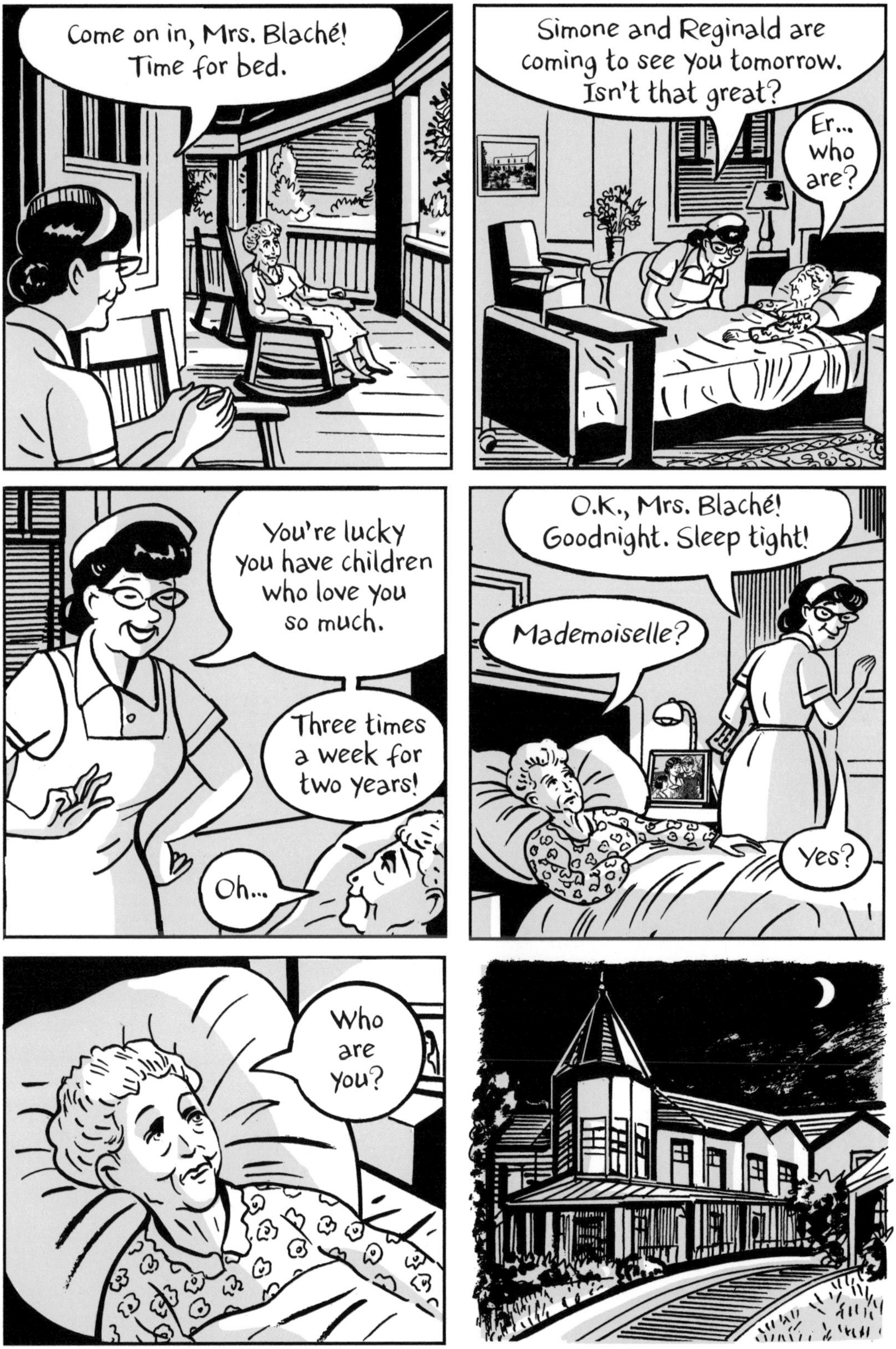
Come on in, Mrs. Blaché! Time for bed.
Simone and Reginald are coming to see you tomorrow. Isn't that great?
Er... who are?
You're lucky you have children who love you so much.
Three times a week for two years!
Oh...
O.K., Mrs. Blaché! Goodnight. Sleep tight!
Mademoiselle?
Yes?
Who are you?

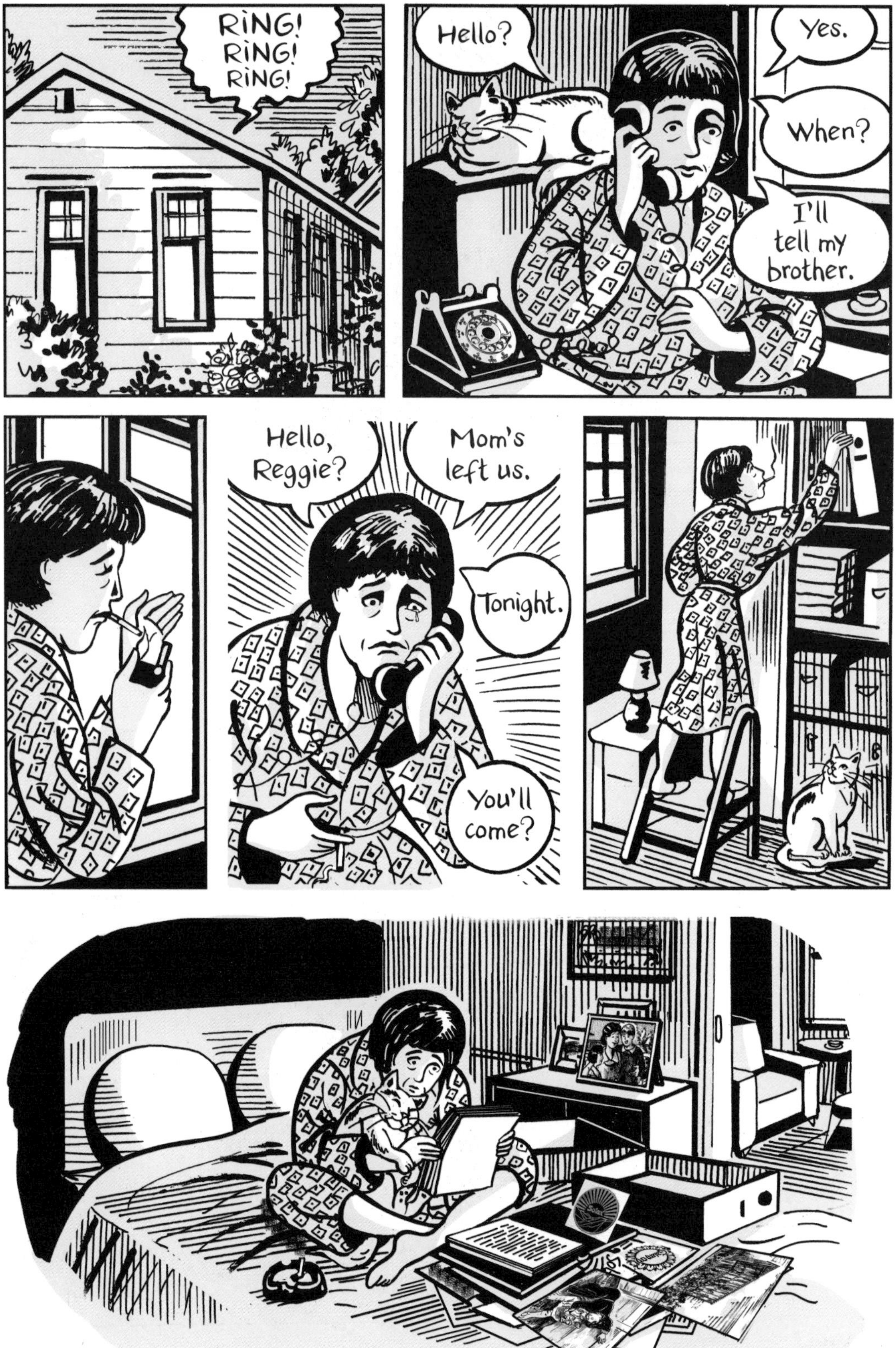
RiNG! RiNG! RiNG!
Hello?
Yes.
When?
I'll tell my brother.
Hello, Reggie?
Mom's left us.
Tonight.
You'll come?

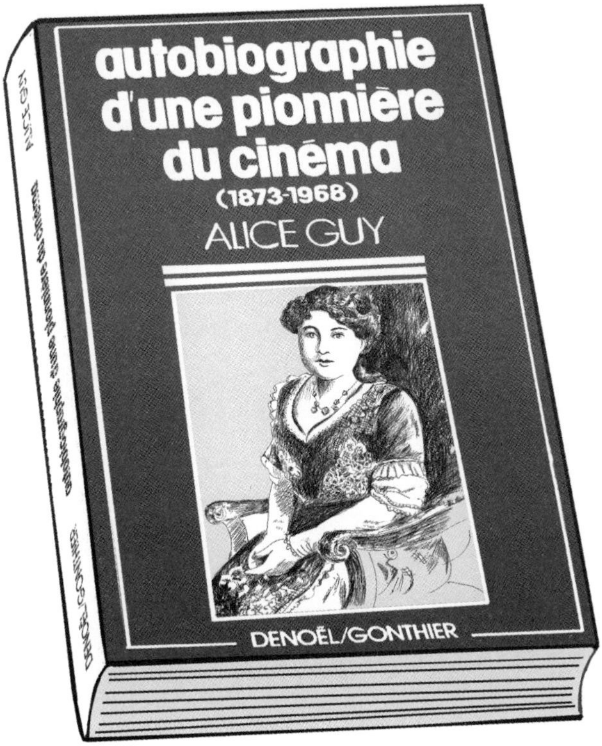
autobiographie
d'une pionnière
du cinéma
(1873-1968)
ALICE GUY
DENOËL/GONTHIER

1976 – Paris – France

TIMELINE

for Alice Guy
and pivotal events in the invention of cinema.

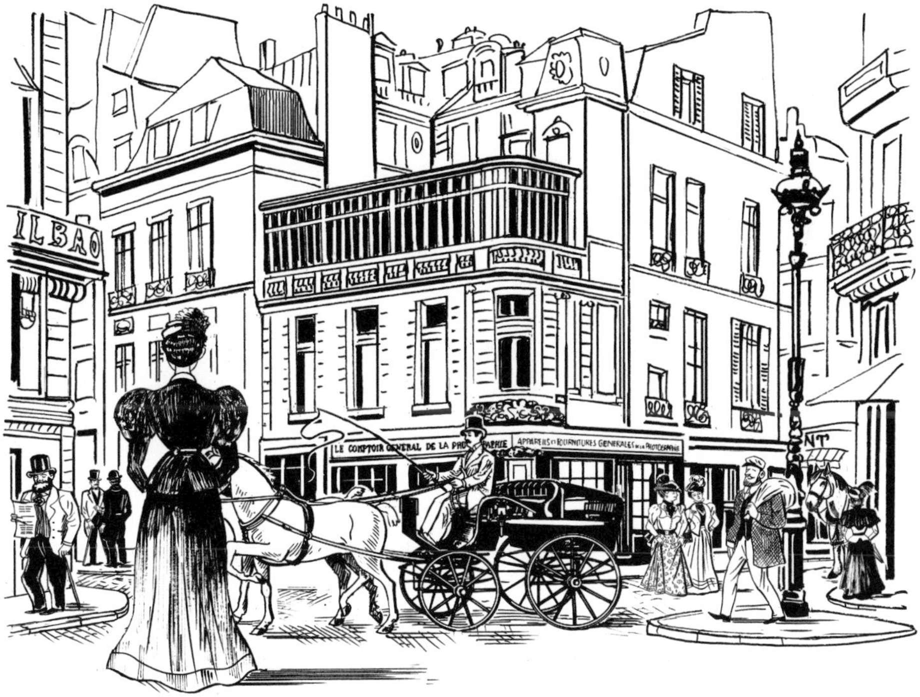
APPAREILS ET FOURNITURES GENERALES DE LA PHOTOGRAPHIE

1827 Nicéphore Niépce takes the first permanent photograph from a window of his house in Saint-Loup-de-Varennes. This amateur inventor is the first to capture and fix an image, but the plate camera he uses to do so dates back to the dawn of time: a simple, sealed black box where light entered through a single hole, projecting the subject the device was aimed at onto a flat surface. The resulting two-dimensional image was reversed and could be drawn or etched. As early as the 4th century B.C.E., the Chinese philosopher Mozi described the principle behind this device. Aristotle did so as well. Its use was especially widespread among 16th-century engravers and painters in the West, when it was given the name "camera obscura". Both Leonardo da Vinci and Johannes Vermeer availed themselves of its use. The desire to fix the resulting image obsessed chemists in the 18th century, but the image always ended up disappearing. In the end it is Niépce, a retired officer in the Revolutionary Army, who perfects the process after 11 years of research and ruinously expensive attempts. At this point, a still life requires an exposure time of a dozen hours.

1832 Although other physicists before him have studied the persistence of retinal vision, the Belgian Joseph Plateau is the first to take a more practical role in his eccentric research. His first noteworthy experiment consists of staring at the noonday sun for 25 seconds – enough to blind himself temporarily. His experiments in optics will lead to permanent loss of vision in 1842, but before then he invents the "phenakistiscope", an optical toy that provides an illusion of movement from the persistence of retinal vision. It is a simple cardboard disc with small rectangular apertures, around which are set a series of around 20 drawn or painted images that break down a single movement. Meanwhile, in Vienna, Simon Ritter von Stampfer invents a similar device, the "stroboscope".
The foundations of cinema have been laid. The first animations have been produced.

1837 Four years after Niépce's death, Louis Daguerre, a former associate of his in Paris, invents a process allowing exposure times to be reduced to a dozen or so minutes. The daguerreotype is born; the French government will acquire the patent two years later. Daguerre will boast of being the inventor of photography, lastingly obscuring the contribution made by his former partner.
5 August: Émile Guy, future father of Alice Guy, is born in Morez, in the Jura.

1847 Clotilde Franceline Marie Aubert, future mother of Alice Guy, is born in Thorens-Glières, in Haute-Savoie.

1850 The use of wet collodion to fix emulsion on a glass plate revolutionizes photography: exposure times are reduced to less than a minute, and development made easier.

1853 Baron von Uchatius combines the magic lantern and the stroboscope to invent the "kinetiscope", the first device to project moving images. The next step will be to replace drawings with photographs.

1865 Émile Guy marries Marie "Mariette" Aubert at the Church of the Madeleine in Paris. Émile is a bookseller and publisher in Chile.

1870 First public showing of animated photos in Columbus, Ohio.
Henry Renno Heyl's "phasmatrope" differs from von Uchatius' device in its use of photographs of successive poses, breaking down movement, but the effect is jerky and inconsistent.

1873 1 July: Alice Ida Antoinette Guy is born in Saint-Mandé, at her parents' home on Rue de la Grange. Alice has three sisters and one brother, all born in Chile. Louis – born 3 August 1866 in Santiago; Julia – born 31 December 1867 in Valparaíso; Fanny or "Henriette" – born 6 November 1869 in Valparaíso; and Marguerite – born 25 May 1871 in Santiago.

1873 –1876. Alice is raised by her grand-mother in Carouge, Switzerland.

1876–1879. Alice's childhood is divided between Santiago and Valparaíso, in Chile.

1878 In Palo Alto, California, English photographer Eadweard Muybridge takes a set of sequential snapshot photographs of motion: a galloping horse. Six years earlier, French physiologist Étienne-Jules Marey had claimed that a galloping horse never has all four hooves in the air when its legs are extended, as artists had been depicting them for centuries. This had become quite a point of contention for scientists and riders from both the

New and Old Worlds. Billionaire and California governor Leland Stanford was of Marey's view, and offered a colossal prize to anyone who could prove or disprove the theory.
Muybridge places a battery of 12 cameras along a racetrack, their shutters automatically triggered when the horse runs by, tripping wires connected to a circuit. In so doing, Muybridge proves Marey's theory.

1879 Alice is reunited with her sisters at the Convent of the Sacred Heart in Veyrier, Switzerland.

1880 16 May: Alice's older brother Louis dies in Paris.

1882 Thanks to Muybridge's work, Marey invents the "chronophotographic gun" to capture animal movements in nature.

1884–1885. Émile Guy files for bankruptcy.
Alice leaves the convent for a boarding school in Ferney-Voltaire.

1885 Entrepreneur George Eastman brings the first celluloid film to market. Flexible and transparent, this invention will enable him to mass-produce the first portable photographic device, the Kodak camera, three years later.

1889 Marey adopts Eastman's film rolls to load the barrels of his chronophotographic gun. He and his collaborator Georges Demenÿ record over 500 scientific films.

1890 The Guy family lives in Paris, at 19, Rue Saint-Sulpice. Alice receives private schooling on Rue Cardinet.

1891 5 January: Émile Guy dies in the family's apartment in Paris, aged 53. Alice lives with her mother and learns stenography. With help from his Scottish protégé William K.L. Dickson, American Thomas Edison invents the first motion picture camera, the "kinetograph". It uses George Eastman's film, but adapts it by perforating the edges so that it can be fed mechanically through both the camera and projector. This system of perforation will remain in use for all cameras and projection devices until the rise of digital technology. To view the images, Dickson develops the "kinetoscope", a single-viewer device. The first (and free) public demonstration of the device features a ten-second short of the inventor doffing his hat. At the International Exposition of Photography in Paris, Demenÿ proceeds with the first public showing of

animated chronophotographic images. Audiences see him in close-up, mouthing the words *"Je vous aime"* ("I love you all").

1892 In March, a patent is filed for a chronophotographic device Demenÿ has developed for Marey: the "phonoscope", an apparatus using glass discs. The Phonoscope Company is founded to commercialize it, but its lack of success drives a wedge between the scientist and his right-hand man.

1893 Alice gets her first professional job in a varnish factory, while living with her mother at 5, Quai Malaquais. In Orange, New Jersey, Dickson builds the first film production studio, nicknamed the "Black Maria". Dickson, the first film director in history, will make the majority of his 148 Edison-produced films there over the next two years.

1894 1 March: Félix-Max Richard hires Léon Gaumont to work at his shop, the Comptoir général de photographie. Gaumont is then admitted to the French Photography Society. Léon Gaumont hires Alice as a stenographer at the Comptoir.
Marey and Demenÿ go their separate ways. The latter develops his own motion picture camera, a new version of the phonoscope, which he renames the "biographe". He intends to bring his invention to market, and seeks backers.
14 April: The Kinetoscope Parlor opens on Broadway in New York. It is the first single-viewer movie theatre to use Edison's invention. A hit with the public, the idea spreads worldwide, making Edison even richer. A few months later, a Kinetoscope Parlor opens on Boulevard Poissonnière in Paris. Antoine Lumière, a photographic plate manufacturer from Lyons, chances upon it.
Kansas man Harvey Henderson Wilcox acquires a plot of 120 acres eight miles outside the city of Los Angeles, California. His wife calls it Hollywood.

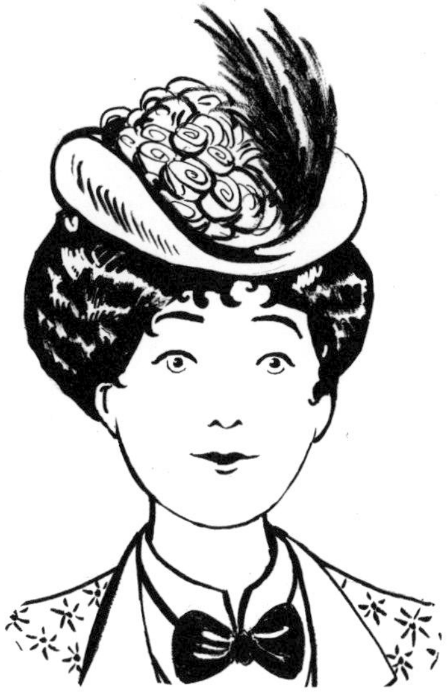

10 August: Léon Gaumont buys up the company, which becomes Léon Gaumont et Cie [Gaumont & Co.].
22 August: Demenÿ files a patent for his biographe.
26 December: Alice's grandmother dies in Carouge.
28 December: The first public projection by the Lumière brothers at the Salon Indien, on Boulevard des Capucines. The world witnesses the birth of cinema.

1895 **Georges Demenÿ offers to let Félix-Max Richard commercialize his phonoscope.**
22 March: In a room of the Society for the Development of Industry on Rue de Rennes in Paris, Alice attends the unveiling and first screening of the "cinematograph", the Lumière brothers' new invention: a reversible camera that projects images on a screen. Edison's single-viewer devices are rendered obsolete.
28 May: A verdict is reached in the lawsuit begun in 1893 between the Richard brothers. Félix-Max is forced to sell the Comptoir.

1896 **May: A patent is filed for commercial rental of a single reversible device, Demenÿ's chronophotograph, marketed by Gaumont, who also publish L'Art dans les projections [The Art of Projection] by Frédéric Dillaye.**
In addition to her work as Léon Gaumont's secretary, Alice takes her first steps as a director. According to the filmography compiled by Victor Bachy in 1993, seven short films can be attributed to Alice Guy between September 1896 and May 1897, including *La Fée aux choux* [The Cabbage Fairy].
28 September: The Pathé brothers found their company. Émile sees to the phonographic side, Charles to the cinematography.
April or October (accounts vary): A projection at the Robert-Houdin Theatre of the first film with special effects – Georges Méliès' *Escamotage d'une dame* [The Vanishing Lady].

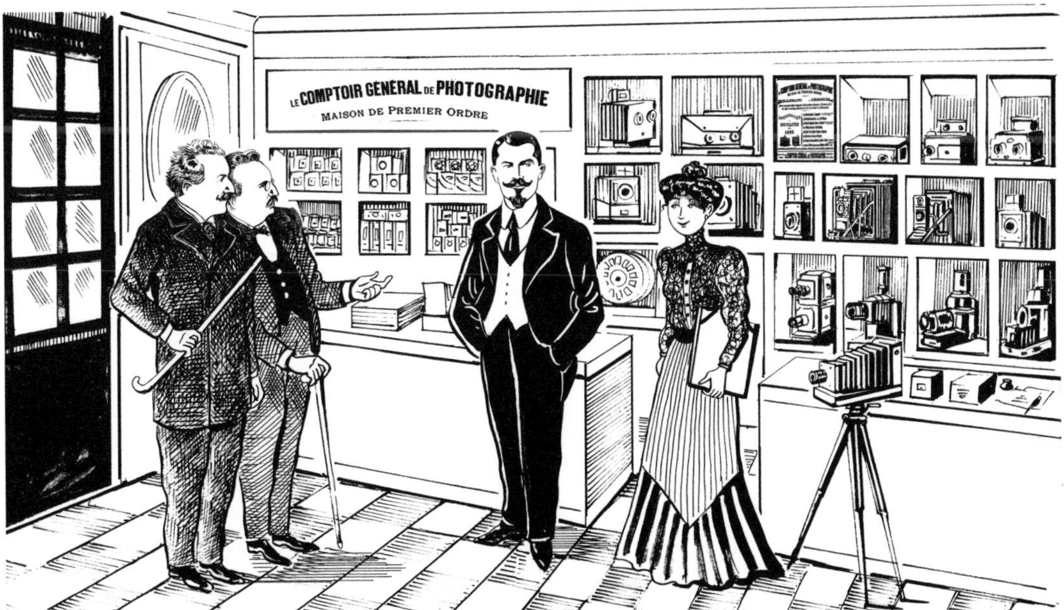
LE COMPTOIR GÉNÉRAL DE PHOTOGRAPHIE
MAISON DE PREMIER ORDRE

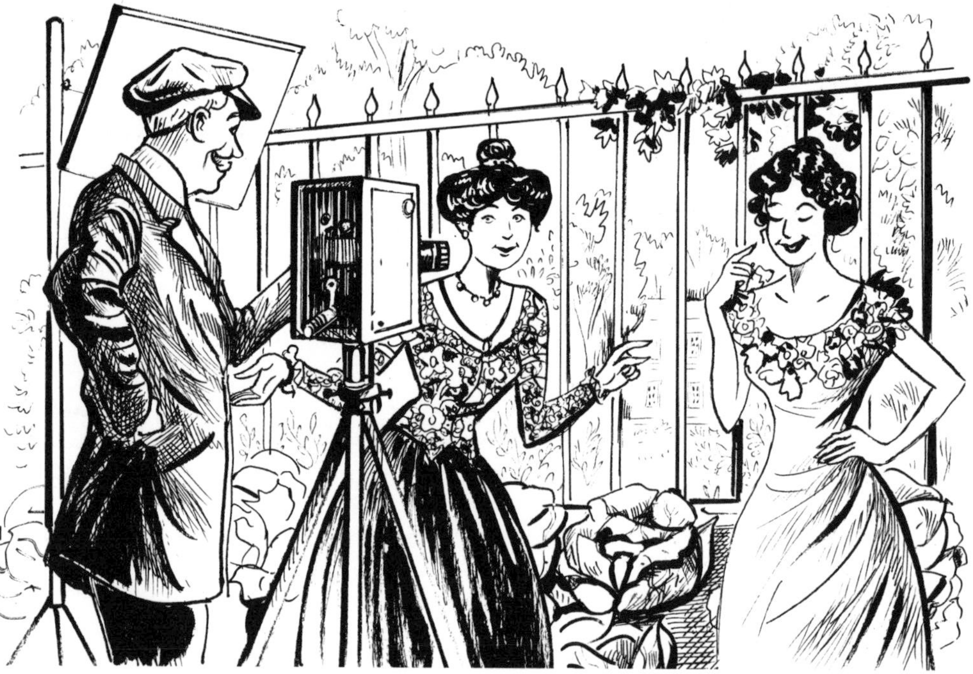

1897 Gaumont & Co. builds its first machine shop in the yard of the property on Ruelle des Sonneries. The Gaumonts rent Alice and her mother a small renovated house at the end of the same property.
According to the first filmography of Alice Guy, compiled by Francis Lacassin in 1976 based on his conversations with her and his analysis of the Gaumont catalogues, in the course of this year the young director makes at least 15 short films (Guy's filmography remains a work in progress. Building on Lacassin's work, several film historians – notably Victor Bachy – have since refined her filmography. But all agree on this figure: 15 films).
4 May: Fire at the Bazar de la Charité.
In the U.S., the Patent Wars begin. Edison leads the charge to monopolize the movie industry. Over the next 11 years, his company files 502 suits. After Edison's offensive, the Lumières' cinematograph is ejected almost by force from the North American continent in summer 1897. Confronted with Edison, only the Biograph Co., backed by the U.S. government, puts up a fight.

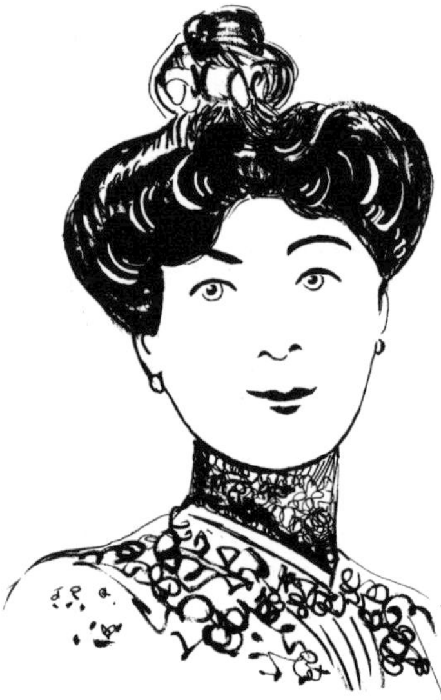

1898 Alice directs 18 short films.

1899 Alice directs another 18 short films.

1900 Gaumont & Co. is an exhibitor at the Universal Exposition in Paris.
Alice is awarded honorary membership in the company. She directs another 53 short films.

1901 Alice directs 11 short films.

1902 "Phono-scenes" go into production. Developed by Gaumont labs, the system is based on synchronizing a phonograph and a motion picture camera. It presages sound cinema, lip synching, and music videos. Over the next five years, Alice makes over 100 of them.

A glass roof is built over the shooting area.
Léon Gaumont entrusts Alice with running the production studio. This year, she directs 26 short films.

Marguerite, the youngest of Alice's sisters, dies in Paris.

1903 Alice hires Ferdinand Zecca as a director. He shoots *Les Méfaits d'une tête de veau* [Crimes of a Calf's Head] – wrongly attributed to Alice Guy for several decades – before joining Pathé as its managing director. Alice directs 29 short films.

1904 Alice directs 12 short films, including *L'Assassinat du courrier de Lyon* [Death of a Courier] in April and *Volée par les bohémiens* [Stolen by Gypsies] in October, both shot in the open air outside the studio.

At the Louisiana Purchase Exposition, or the St. Louis World's Fair, Gaumont productions are awarded a gold medal.

1905 Alice directs 18 short films and phono-scenes. Apart from Zecca's film, she claims responsibility for all the fiction films produced by Gaumont up till now.

She is awarded a gold medal at the Liège International World's Fair.

Shooting begins on *Une Noce au Lac Saint-Fargeau* [A Wedding at St. Fargeau].

Gaumont Studios is built in Buttes-Chaumont to compete with those of Méliès and Pathé.

June: The vast construction project is completed.
September: Alice's first shoot at the new studios: *La Esmeralda* (based on Hugo's *The Hunchback of Notre-Dame*).

Autumn: Alice hires Louis Feuillade as a scriptwriter.

November: Shooting on location in Spain with

camera operator Anatole Thiberville. Alice returns with footage of Barcelona, Zaragoza, Madrid, Córdoba, Seville, Granada, Algeciras, Gibraltar… She makes a fleeting appearance in one of these films.

20 November: Director Étienne Arnaud is hired.

1906 With *La Naissance, la Vie, et la Mort du Christ* [The Birth, Life, and Death of Christ], with its 300 extras and 25 sets, Alice invents the sword-and-sandal epic. The film, which consists of several episodes, is a personal and public triumph.

February/March: Alice shoots 58 opera phono-scenes.

May: Alice shoots five dance phono-scenes.

June: Alice shoots phono-scenes with entertainer Félix Mayol.

July: Gaumont launches its phono-scenes, with accompanying catalogue.

Summer: Alice meets camera operator Herbert Blaché, from Gaumont's London branch. She shoots with him at Saintes-Maries-de-la-Mer in southern France. A romance blossoms.

April to November: At the Milan International World's Fair, *La Vie du Christ* receives a gold medal.

November: Alice and Herbert work together in Germany as Gaumont's ambassadors for the "chronophone", an apparatus developed by the company to synchronize sound and image. Their romance continues.

8 December: Gaumont & Co. becomes the Société des Établissements Gaumont (S.E.G.), with an initial

capital of 2.5 million francs. Alice is a shareholder. Herbert proposes marriage to Alice, who is now 31 years old.

1907 9 January: Alice is filmed directing a phono-scene, *Le Ballet du bal des Capulet* from Gounod's opera *Romeo and Juliet*: the first behind-the-scenes "making-of" sequence in film history.

24 January: At the studio, Alice receives the Ordre des Palmes académiques as a "theatre director". She finds the time to make another nine films this year.
6 March: Alice Guy and Herbert Blaché marry at the town hall in Belleville, Paris. Herbert's brother Charles and Alice's mother Marie witness the wedding. Three days later, they leave for America. Alice suggests that Louis Feuillade replace her at Gaumont.
March: The couple arrive in New York, and then move to Cleveland, where they stay for nine months, representing the Gaumont company and its famous chronophone.
October: In France, Yvonne Serrand, Alice's former assistant, marries Étienne Arnaud.

1908 6 September: To Herbert and Alice, a daughter: Simone.
September: Léon Gaumont's first business trip to New York.
December: The Blaché family moves to Flushing, to be near New York City.
Herbert is named director of Gaumont Studios in Flushing.
The motion picture Patent Wars come to an end. Eastman convinces Edison of the futility of the proceedings. The major American companies sign

an agreement that is also initialled by the French companies Pathé, Gaumont, and Méliès' Star Film.

1909
February: Gaumont returns to New York.
Francis Boggs makes *In the Power of the Sultan* – according to film historian Kevin Brownlow, the first film to be wholly produced in California.

1910
7 September: Alice founds her own production company, Solax Film Co. As both its president and artistic director, she invests $50,000.
21 October: Alice's first American film is released stateside: *A Child's Sacrifice*. Shot at Gaumont Studios in Flushing, it is distributed by General Films (Biograph, Edison, Selig, Vitagraph, Gaumont, Pathé, Méliès…).
Solax is scheduled to produce a one-reel film (approximately 10 to 15 minutes) per week.

1911
March: Solax leaves Gaumont Studios, deeming it too small, and moves into a studio Alice has custom-built on land she owns on Congress Street. On one side of the building are a park and a lake, on the other a western

set with a small hotel, saloon, and general store. Production increases to two one-reelers per week.
July to October: Solax produces 36 one-reelers.
November: Alice expands her studio in Flushing. Production steps up to three one-reelers per week, released every Monday, Wednesday, and Friday. Alice herself makes nine films this year. To keep pace with the increase in production, Alice assembles a permanent stable of actors: the Solax Stock Company.
22 December: *The Violin Maker of Nuremberg* is released – Alice's first major critical and commercial success.
Winter: Alice and Herbert go to Europe to arrange for the distribution of Solax films.
It is a golden age for French filmmakers on the North American continent. Gaumont, Méliès' Star Film, Pathé, and Éclair dominate a market that will very soon become competitive and protectionist.

1912
Early May: Herbert's contract with Gaumont expires. Meanwhile, Solax leaves its distributor, General Films, to team up with Itala, Great Northern, and Gaumont under the aegis of the Exclusive Supply Corporation, of which Herbert becomes president.
May to June: Alice shoots her first three-reeler, *Fra Diavolo*.

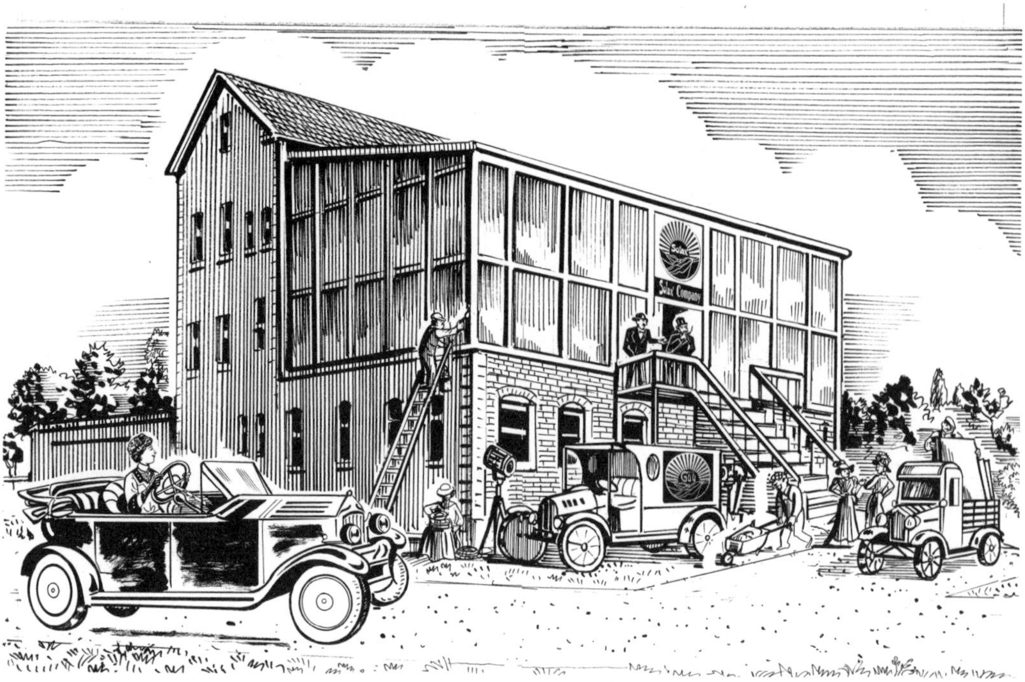
Solax Company

30 June: Alice's son Reginald is born.
Mid-August: Solax moves to its brand-new studio in Fort Lee, New Jersey. Since October 1910, Solax has released about 200 one-reelers. Victor Bachy attributes 119 films to Alice in 1912 alone.

1913 In January, Alice films *Beasts of the Jungle* (with a real tigress), and in March, *Dick Whittington and his Cat*. She writes the scripts for both. In May, Herbert directs *Kelly from the Emerald Isle* from a script co-written with Alice. In August, Alice adapts Poe's *The Pit and the Pendulum*. All four of these three-reelers are hits.
May: The French release of the crime serial *Fantômas*, produced by Gaumont and directed by Louis Feuillade. A worldwide hit.
Late August: Herbert founds his own company, Blaché American Features. In September, he directs B.A.F.'s first production, *The Fight for Millions*.
October: Solax releases its final one-reeler. Alice and Herbert are changing with the market.
December: *Shadows of the Moulin Rouge*, Alice's fourth script and tenth film this year, is released.

1914 May: Solax produces its final film, *The Million Dollar Robbery*, a four-reeler directed by Alice. After flourishing for several years, Alice and Herbert must face a drastic restructuring of the market. Films are going from one to five reels, consolidating investment but also raising the risk of financial loss. From now on, Alice will have to tender her talents and her studio to the highest bidder.
July: Alice shoots *The Lure*, a five-reeler for the Shubert Film Manufacturing Company.
11 July: Madame Alice Blaché publishes her first – and last – article in *The Moving Picture World*, about the place of women in film production.
August: Blaché American Features releases its final film, *The War Extra*, shutting down before the month is out.
September: Herbert founds the U.S. Amusement Corporation. It lasts long enough for him to make two five-reelers.
November: Herbert joins forces with Popular Players and Plays, for whom, over the next three years, he will direct half a dozen films, as will Alice.
7 December: Release of *The Tigress*, with Olga Petrova, directed by Alice for P.P.&P.
France's entry into the First World War sounds the artistic and commercial death knell for French expatriates in Fort Lee, now mobilized under European flags.

1915

19 April: Release of *The Heart of a Painted Woman*, with Olga Petrova. Five reels, directed by Alice for P.P.&P.

9 August: Release of *The Vampire*, with Olga Petrova. Five reels, directed by Alice for P.P.&P.

25 October: Release of *Madonna*, with Olga Petrova. Five reels, directed by Alice for P.P.&P.

November: Alice expands the Solax-Blaché Features studios, now belonging to P.P.&P.

1916

3 January: Release of *What Will People Say?*, with Olga Petrova. Five reels for P.P.&P.

15 May: Release of *The Girl With the Green Eyes*. According to historians, this film may be the work of Alice, Herbert, or both.

August: The Blachés withdraw from Popular Players and Plays and reopen the U.S. Amusement Corporation.

Alice meets the birth control activist Rose Pastor Stokes.

2 November: Release of *The Ocean Waif*. Five reels, directed by Alice for the U.S.A.C. Distributed by the International Film Service founded by William Randolph Hearst.

1917

February: Release of *The Adventurer*, with Bessie Love, based on a work by Upton Sinclair. Five reels, directed by Alice for the U.S.A.C.

11 March: Release of *The Empress*. Five reels, directed by Alice for the U.S.A.C. Distributed by Pathé Exchange.

19 March: Release of *A Man and the Woman*, based on the novel *Nana* by Émile Zola. Five reels, directed by Alice for the U.S.A.C. Distributed by Art Dramas.

2 April: The U.S. enters the war.

May: The Blachés move house, leaving their country villa for a smaller house on the same street as the Solax studios. To pay off their company's debts, they sell 51% of their shares to the Seligmans' bank.

25 June: Release of *House of Cards*, from an original script by Alice and Herbert. Five reels, directed by Alice for the U.S.A.C. Distributed by Art Dramas. Alice also introduces the film at Columbia University in New York. During production, Herbert begins an affair with Catherine Calvert.

13 July: Alice is invited to give a lecture on the art of scriptwriting at Columbia University.

16 July: Release of *When You and I Were Young*. Five reels, directed by Alice for the U.S.A.C./Apollo Pictures. Distributed by Art Dramas.

3 August: Second lecture at Columbia University on scriptwriting.

3 September: Release of *Behind the Mask*, with Catherine Calvert. Five reels, directed by Alice for the U.S.A.C. Distributed by Art Dramas.
Autumn: The U.S.A.C. closes its doors.
The studio in Fort Lee is rented out to other production companies.
Simone (aged nine) and Reginald (five) contract measles. Herbert moves his family to Weaverville in Madison County, North Carolina, where Alice works as a Red Cross volunteer.

1918 10 March: Release of *The Great Adventure*, with Bessie Love. Five reels, for Pathé Players. Distributed by Pathé Exchange.
During Alice's time in North Carolina, Herbert plays the stock market, suffering heavy losses.
While Alice is editing *The Great Adventure*, Herbert leaves her for Catherine Calvert and moves to California. Alice leaves the house in Fort Lee and rents a small apartment at the Bretton Hall Hotel in New York.
11 November: Armistice Day. At the end of the First World War, there are 1,500 movie theatres in France, 3,000 in Italy, 5,300 in the U.K., and an estimated 21,000 in the U.S. Europe's dominance of the global market has gone forever. This year, in the French market alone, 80% of the films screened are American.

1919 Shooting on *Tarnished Reputations*, from a script by Léonce Perret for Perret Pictures.

July: Alice and her children travel to California, where Herbert is working as a director. Though they are separated, she accepts a job as his assistant on *The Brat*, with Alla Nazimova, who becomes her friend.
80% of the movies now being produced in the world are shot in southern California. In just a few years, Hollywood has supplanted Fort Lee.

1920 January: Release of *Stronger Than Death*, with Alla Nazimova, directed by Herbert with Alice assisting. It is the final film of her career. She is 47 years old.
Alice meets Charlie Chaplin, then shooting *The Kid*.
14 March: Release of *Tarnished Reputations*, Alice's final film to hit the screen. Distributed by Pathé Exchange.
The studio in Fort Lee is sold to pay off debts. Having already been damaged in a fire, it will be demolished two years later.
Alice files for divorce.

1922 Divorced from Herbert, Alice returns to France with her two children, but there is no work to be found in the French studios. She settles in Nice with Simone and Reginald. There, a producer interested in buying Victorine Studios commissions a report from Alice. For several weeks, she works tirelessly, consulting producers from Paris to London in order to deliver a clear and professional audit. She has been promised management of the studio – state-of-the-art and custom-built for her, so she imagines – but it falls into rival hands.
Alice's financial situation gets worse. To provide for her children – Simone, now 14, and Reginald, 10 – she sells her books, paintings, jewellery, and furs.
The stock market crash of 1929 will affect Herbert's already sporadic alimony.

1927 Back in the U.S., Alice attempts to track down her American films.
She will spend the rest of her life on this quest, in vain.
6 October: New York premiere of *The Jazz Singer*. Although originally conceived as a silent film, six sequences with songs and dialogue performed by Broadway star Al Jolson are added to it. It is not the first "talkie" but it is the one that, as Kevin Brownlow put it, "precipitated the collapse of the silent film".

1928 Bryan Foy's *Lights of New York* is the first full-scale talkie.

1932 Alice and family move to Paris. With her mother's help, Simone first finds work at the Paris branch of the American company United Artists, then at Fox. Through Léon Gaumont's intervention, Reginald gets a job in a film laboratory.
13 May: Birth of Régine Blaché-Bolton, daughter of Valérie Piquemal and Reginald.

1933 July: Death of Alice's mother Marie Guy. Alice informs Léon Gaumont by letter two months later.
10 September: Reginald leaves France for California, settling near his father.
23 September: The daily newspaper *Le Temps* devotes an article to France's first female director: Germaine Dulac. Alice protests vigorously in writing that same day.
30 September: *Le Temps* issues a correction and apologizes to Madame Blaché.

1934 Gaumont goes bankrupt. The company is bailed out by the government.

1936 To earn a living, Alice writes short stories under the pen name Guy Alix for women's magazines (*La Mode du jour*, *Les Dimanches de la femme*) owned by the Société parisienne d'édition, publisher of the *Reader's Digest*-like annual *Almanach Vermot* and the popular comic *Les Pieds Nickelés*. She also writes novelizations of films for *Le Film complet*, the first French movie magazine.
Alice receives a signed copy from Léon Gaumont of his book, *Les Établissements Gaumont*, which traces the company's history from its founder's perspective. No mention is made of Alice's contribution to the Gaumont saga in a book that begins only after she has left for the U.S. If even Léon Gaumont seems to have forgotten her work, who else in France will remember her?

1939 Seeking to refresh her former boss' memory, Alice sends him eight densely handwritten pages in which she recounts for the first time her cinematographic activities with the Gaumont Company, from Georges Demenÿ's first visit to her departure for the U.S., detailing her various roles and listing her films. From his retirement at the Château des Tourelles in Sainte-Maxime, Léon Gaumont acknowledges receipt of her letter, thanking her and promising to include it in the second edition of the work about the Gaumount Company, to which she was a "devoted contributor from the very start". But her letter goes unpublished in their lifetimes, and the Second World War puts an end to any plans for publication. Will justice never be done?

1940 The war sounds the death knell for the rehabilitation of Alice's reputation that she has so patiently awaited. Her publisher in Nazi-occupied Paris falls victim to Aryanization laws, and closes its doors in June. With no other income than what she earns from writing, Alice lives with her daughter Simone. Bilingual and an American citizen, Simone finds a job at the U.S. Embassy.

1941 Simone is transferred to Vichy, along with her mother.
A few months later, the two women follow the American diplomatic corps to Switzerland.

1946 Death of Léon Gaumont.

1947 Georges Sadoul publishes the second volume of his *Histoire générale du cinéma* [General History of Cinema] devoted to its pioneers, and, in 1949, his *Histoire du cinéma mondial* [History of World Cinema]. All of Alice's films with Gaumont are attributed to a certain Henri Gallet, and the only one attributed to her, *Les Méfaits d'une tête de veau* [Crimes of a Calf's Head], was directed not by her but by one of her temporary assistants, Ferdinand Zecca, who would go on to direct films himself and become managing director at Pathé.

However, in the first volume of their encyclopedic history of film, devoted to French cinema, René Jeanne and Charles Ford give star billing to Alice's pioneering activities for Gaumont.

In Bern, Alice recites sections of what will become her memoirs at meetings of various women's clubs. Towards the end of the year, Alice accompanies Simone when her daughter is posted to Paris.

1948 5 June: The front page of the weekly paper *France-Illustration* (formerly known as *L'Illustration*) features an article with a portrait of Alice: "Les Pionniers du cinéma: Alice Blaché: la première des metteurs en scène" ["Cinema Pioneers: Alice Blaché, the First Director"].

1952 Alice accompanies Simone to her new posting in Washington, D.C., where she continues to search for prints of her vanished films – in vain. She does, however, find their titles listed in the catalogues of the Library of Congress.

1953 Alice begins serious work on her memoirs, which will not find a publisher in her lifetime.
Her second-oldest sister Fanny, known as "Henriette", dies in Issy-les-Moulineaux.

1954 Léon Gaumont's son Louis finds Alice's letter from 15 years earlier in his father's archives. He reaches out to his father's oldest employee and asks her permission to use the letters in a lecture he delivers on 8 December to the members of the Association française des ingénieurs et techniciens du cinéma [French Association of Film Engineers and Technicians]. Entitled "Quelques souvenirs sur Madame Alice Guy-Blaché, la première femme metteur en scène" ["A Few Memories of Madame Alice Guy-Blaché, the First Woman Director"], it is the cornerstone of her reputation's long, slow rehabilitation.
Alice's eldest sister Julia dies in Marseilles.

1955 Simone is posted back to Paris. Louis Gaumont's lecture about Alice is published in the *Bulletin de l'Association française des ingénieurs et techniciens du cinéma*.

1957 15 March: A tribute to Alice at the Cinémathèque Française on Rue Spontini. Louis Gaumont gives a speech. This is the beginning of public recognition of Alice's work; the press runs with the story. *Les Nouvelles littéraires*, *Le Temps*, *France-Soir*, the *New York Herald Tribune*, *Ciné-revue*, *Femmes d'Aujourd'hui*, and *L'Alsace* pay homage to history's first female filmmaker. François Chalais films an interview with her for French TV.

1958 Alice gives a series of lectures at the American Cultural Centre in Paris.
12 December: Thanks to the efforts of author Marcel Pagnol; playwright Roger Ferdinand, former president of the Société des auteurs et compositeurs dramatiques (S.A.C.D.: Society of Theatrical Writers and Composers); and filmmaker Carlo Rim, Alice is made a Chevalier of the Legion of Honour for having been a "director and producer of films". The award, which touches her deeply, is announced in an official bulletin by the French government on 19 December.
Alice accompanies Simone on her posting to Brussels.

1959 Georges Sadoul visits Alice on Avenue de Tervueren in Brussels. Upon seeing Alice's documents, the film historian admits that he was misled by a former actor from the Gaumont stables who'd presented Alice's films as his own. Sadoul goes on to correct these erroneous attributions in his works.

1961 Director Henri Langlois writes to Alice: "I fully intend to emphasize the undeniable fact that you are the first woman ever to have directed films. It is so incontestable an honour that anyone who seeks to deny it will bring shame and ridicule upon themselves."

1963 Researching his biography of Louis Feuillade, journalist Francis Lacassin interviews Alice in Brussels. Immediately afterwards, he sets out to compile her filmography. Belgian academic Victor Bachy conducts a series of interviews with Alice that lead to the 1993 publication of the first monograph devoted to the filmmaker: *Alice Guy-Blaché, la première femme cinéaste du monde* [The World's First Female Filmmaker].

1964 At the age of 91, Alice suffers a stroke. She recovers, but Simone thinks it prudent to retire to help care for her. In the spring, a decision is made to move to America and settle in New Jersey near Reginald, who has started a family there.
Flemish TV does a show on Alice, broadcast in August.

1966 After a series of further strokes, Alice's mental and physical faculties swiftly decline. The situation necessitates her placement in a nursing home.

1968 24 March: Alice Guy passes away in Wayne, New Jersey, at the age of 95. She dies having completely forgotten her past and without ever finding her films. She is buried at Maryrest Cemetery in Mahwah, N.J.

1974 April: During the first Musidora women's film festival in Paris, two films from Alice's American period are screened, at long last found and supplied by the American Film Institute (A.F.I.) in Washington, D.C. Writer Anthony Slide of the A.F.I. board entrusts Alice Guy's memoirs to the Musidora Association, named for the French silent film actress and director.

1976 *Autobiographie d'une pionnière du cinéma* is published by Éditions Denoël/Gonthier. Alice's memoirs are introduced by actress and writer Nicole-Lise Bernheim and director and journalist Claire Clouzot, with a filmography by Francis Lacassin.

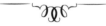

"I believe the Lumière brothers were the first film directors, with *L'Arroseur arrosé* [The Waterer Watered]. All I claim is the title of first female director."

Alice Guy

(Excerpt from a letter to Louis Gaumont, dated 5 January 1954)

BIOGRAPHICAL
NOTES

and portraits of the lead
and supporting characters in
the story of Alice Guy.

In order of appearance...

Émile Guy

Alice Guy's paternal lineage can be traced back to her great-grandparents on her grandfather Marc François Guy's side, and two generations further on the side of her grandmother, Marie-Joséphine *née* Forestier. All originally came from Franche-Comté, an eastern region of France on the Swiss border, but we know that the Guy family has its roots in the Grandvaux plateau of the High Jura, which marks the natural border between Switzerland and France, as a hamlet there bears the family name: Les Guys. Alice's forebears likely crafted watches, raised cattle, and made their own cheese there, but we might also imagine them, like everyone else from Grandvaux, doing a little smuggling on the side – a regional speciality. Up until the French Revolution, it was through these steep and craggy cliffs that banned political and philosophical works printed in Geneva made their way into France. Thanks to their no less lucrative seasonal activities transporting merchandise across France, the Grandvalliers were well-known for their comfortable incomes.

Alice's paternal grandfather Marc was a watchmaker based in Morez (still in the Jura), where he married Marie-Joséphine, whose family had been settled there for several generations. Alice can thus be believed when she asserts that her father was "a man of Franche-Comté from a good family", especially since her grandmother was the aunt of the politician and journalist Étienne Lamy, a member of the Académie Française to whom we owe the 1901 essay "La Femme de demain" ["The Woman of Tomorrow"], which championed education for women.

Émile was born on 5 August 1837 in Morez. His mother was 26 and his father 30. He was the couple's second child and the only boy among five girls. Émile was only 12 when his father died in Paris, at the age of 41. After that, Émile vanishes from the record, only to resurface in 1865, the year of his marriage to Alice's future mother, Marie Aubert, 10 years his junior. Now aged 28, Émile was settled in Chile, where he ran two bookshops named La Librería Universal, one in Santiago and the other in Valparaíso.

Despite his daughter's later claim, he was not the founder of the first French bookshop in Santiago – that dates back to 1849, when Émile was 12. Nor does he seem to have been the first in Valparaíso, that rich and cosmopolitan port then considered one of the pearls of the Pacific. It was the Parisian booksellers Frédéric Rosa and Charles Bouret, specialists in the Spanish-speaking world, who founded the first bookshop there, before selling it to Émile – at least according to an illustrated guidebook published in Chile in 1872. La Librería Universal was located near the port, at 13, Calle de Esmeralda, then Valparaíso's main thoroughfare, known for its luxury boutiques. Nearby were a German bookshop, an English bookshop, and the offices of the *El Mercurio* newspaper. In Santiago, Guy's bookshop was on Calle Estado, smack in the middle of town.

Émile was not only a bookseller, but also a publisher. When the Chilean government opened the country's first public schools in the late 1850s, they needed reference books. Naturally, it cost less to print them domestically than to import them from abroad. Émile seized this opportunity to build his business, which would soon extend beyond Chile to Bolivia and Peru.

From 1865 to 1868, *La Revue des deux mondes*, a monthly magazine of literature, culture, and news, ran several ads indicating a Chilean partnership between Spanish-speaking Parisian bookseller Charles Bouret and a young Émile Guy. Together, they went on to publish many works that bore both their names. In 1872, after Frédéric Rosa's death, Bouret went into partnership with his son. With the younger Bouret, Émile launched *Le Bulletin bibliographique* in 1879, a bilingual French-Spanish monthly intended to keep South American readers abreast of European developments. Such was the cultural context in which Emile met Marie's uncle, Louis Puyo, and through whom he was introduced to her.

Alice doesn't leave much room for family history in her memoirs. In Chile, "I saw very little of my parents. My father was preoccupied by his business affairs." However, growing up in bookish surroundings left young Alice with a taste for reading. She would remember as much when, years later, she pitched Gaumont her first ideas for films: "The daughter of a publisher, I had read a good deal and retained quite a bit."

The early 1880s brought an end to the Chilean dream. In her memoirs, Alice dispenses with this in a single sentence: "In Chile, violent earthquakes, fire, and theft ruined my parents." In a later interview, she would explain that her father was "absolutely destroyed by this failure", a financial collapse whose exact circumstances have never fully come to light. There was indeed an earthquake in Chile in August 1880, and a fire at the port in November 1881. And the war that pitted Chile, Peru, and Bolivia against one another from 1879 to 1884 doubtless played a part in drastically reducing the turnover of La Librería Universal. All we know for sure, however, is that by 1881, both shops were in the hands of a German bookseller named Carlos Niemeyer.

At the same time, the death in 1880 of Louis Alphonse, the Guys' eldest child and only boy, proved the final straw in sending Émile into what seems to have been a deep depression. He passed away in Paris just over a decade later, on 5 January 1891, at the age of 53.

"My father died at 51, more broken by sorrow than by illness." These words – inaccurate about his age – are the last that Alice devotes to her father in her memoirs. To discover how the youngest of the Guy girls felt during her father's slow decline, we could perhaps do worse than to consult her filmography. In 1911, she filmed *Revolutionary Romance*, in which a daughter helps a father who has suffered some setbacks make a fresh start in life. The following year, in *Love of the Flag*, she told the story of an unemployed father whose family sinks into social decline, while in *The High Cost of Living*, a father declares that he would rather die than live a life of poverty. In *The Reformation of Mary*, also from 1912, a six-year-old girl witnesses her father's arrest for a crime he didn't commit. In 1913's *The Quality of Mercy*, a father is taken to the poorhouse, and his young daughter seeks to rescue him. Also in 1913, her film *Ben Bolt* tells the almost identical story of a young girl whose father, a prosperous merchant, meets with financial ruin. The name of the young girl? Alice.

Marie Guy

Françoise Allignet, the great-granddaughter of Henriette, the sister Alice was closest to, can trace her lineage on her mother's side back four generations. The filmmaker's eldest known ancestor, named François Daubert, was born in 1671 and died 73 years later in Meurthe-et-Moselle, eastern France. His son Nicolas was a carpenter, and his grandson Dominique, Alice's great-grandfather on her mother's side, was a master craftsman in the manufacture of Baccarat crystal in Lorraine. His son Alphonse went into the family business and, in 1845, married Catherine Pujo, with whom he had a family of eight children, four of whom died at an early age. The eldest, Clotilde Franceline Marie, born in 1847 at Thorens-Glières in Haute-Savoie, would be Alice's mother. Alphonse never met the youngest of his granddaughters, as he died in Geneva a year before her birth, but his widow Catherine raised Alice in their house in Carouge for the first three years of her life. Later, this beloved grandmother would welcome Alice and her sisters during the vacations from their boarding school, located just a few miles away. But before you can have grandchildren, you need a son-in-law. And it was thanks to Catherine's younger brother, Louis Pujo, that Marie, or "Mariette", met and married one Émile Guy.

According to Alice, the 1848 revolution had driven her mother's uncle and his wife to cross the seas and seek their fortune in South America. At the time, Louis was 26 years old; less than two decades later, he was indeed a rich man. Settled in Santiago, Chile, he owned as many businesses as he did restaurants. He was a town dignitary, a member of the Scientific Society of Chile and the French Legation. In 1864, Louis and his wife, vacationing in France, made the acquaintance of their niece Marie. She was 17, a boarder at the Convent of the Visitation, and full of charm. Her childless South American uncle decided to build her a future and returned to Chile with a photo of her. The following summer, the Pujos were back in France, and with them the man who would become their niece's husband three months later: Émile Guy. He was 10 years older than his future wife. The civil ceremony took place on 18 July 1865 in Clichy, and the religious one the next day at the Church of the Madeleine. Louis Pujo was one of the witnesses for both of these ceremonies. Later, Alice would write: "I do not know if love had a part in the arrangement. At that period, a family decided the future of its daughters… A proper woman must obey her husband, keep her house well, and care for her children. Culture was considered secondary, if not an actual liability." Shortly thereafter, the couple left for Chile, about which Alice says: "The voyage must have been a harsh trial for my poor mama: to leave her country and her beloved parents behind for a distant land whose language she could not speak, her only companions a husband and relations who had been unknown to her a few weeks earlier." In Valparaíso – literally, "paradise valley" – a luxurious hacienda awaited, her uncle's wedding gift. Marie learned Spanish and, as the wife of a prominent town dignitary, took a proper part in the good works of its local charities. Alice adds: "All the Europeans feared the still-untamed Chilean Indians, but the Indians adored my mother for her goodness, and the mere tales of her encounters with them are of interest."

Sadly, Alice was to keep such tales to herself. She also skips rather quickly over her four siblings, each of whom were born in Chile. "My mother was 26 years old when she decided that her fifth child should be truly French, of French birth." The children were: Louis Alphonse Émile, born in 1866; Julia Joséphine, born the following year; Fanny "Henriette" Marie, born in 1869; Marguerite Marie Louise, born in 1871; and finally Alice, two years later. Mariette experienced the tragedy of losing two of her children in her own lifetime: her son and eldest child in 1880, at the age of 14, and Marguerite in 1902, at the age of 30. Marguerite died at 12, Rue des Alouettes, the home that Gaumont rented to Alice and her mother. Marguerite's eldest son, Charles Pin, later joined his aunt in the U.S., where she introduced him to the film industry.

The start of the 1880s seems to have been a chaotic time for the Guys. Although the rest of the family was already in France, Marie was still in Chile, only returning at the news of her son's death. In her novel *Alice Guy, la première femme cinéaste de l'histoire* [The First Female Director in History], Emmanuelle Gaume imagines a love affair between Marie and a Chilean man, an interlude to which Régine Bolton-Blaché – Alice's granddaughter, and the novelist's primary source – did not object. Whatever the truth, in the decade that followed the couple were reconciled, and the Guys made do as best they could in a modest apartment on Rue Saint-Sulpice. Émile's death shattered this precarious balance. "I remained alone with my mother, who had never until then had to concern herself with the realities of life," Alice remarked. In 1892, the newly launched insurance company Mutualité Maternelle offered Mariette the opportunity to coordinate their philanthropic activities. Her task was to assist pregnant textile-industry workers, but this temporary employment came to an end a few months later, after which Mariette's welfare fell to her daughters. Henriette and Marguerite were already married, and Julia was studying to be a teacher. This only left Alice, who trained to be a stenographer and so became the family breadwinner. At first, the two women lived on Rue de Tournon, and then, thanks to Alice's salary from Gaumont, they moved to Quai Malaquais. Around 1896, they moved once again, to be closer to the Gaumont offices in Buttes-Chaumont. There, mother and daughter lived on Rue des Alouettes, in a small house belonging to the Gaumont family. A bathroom was installed, and Alice paid a modest rent. That same year, after divorcing her first husband, Henriette came to live with her mother and sister on Rue des Alouettes. She would stay until her second marriage in 1902. Mariette and Alice remained in the house until Alice married Herbert, when the newly-weds left for the U.S. And what of Mariette then? We may assume that Alice continued to provide for her from across the Atlantic and saw her during her return visits to France.

On 25 September 1933, Alice wrote to inform Léon Gaumont of the death (two months earlier, in July) of her mother, with whom he had been close. Clotilde Franceline Marie, or Mariette, would have been 85. Her great-great-granddaughter has not yet been able to determine exactly when or where she died.

Étienne Paul Barat

Paul Barat is the big mystery of Alice Guy's life. Her first mention of him dates to one of her rare filmed interviews, in 1964. Asked by a Belgian journalist how she had first begun to work in film, Alice replies by saying, "I needed to make a living." Her father was dead, and her mother had no source of income; she herself was 18. "I had a friend," she continues, "who was the nephew of the foundress of Sacré-Coeur. He said to my mother, 'I think the best thing for Alice would be to learn stenography. It's a new thing. She could find work as a secretary in an office.' And indeed, I learned fairly quickly." Then, as if to emphasize this man's formative influence on her life as a grown woman, she says: "He was, I must admit, my first love. But he was 75," she adds with a laugh, "and I was 18. Oh, I'd gladly have married him. I adored that man." Viewers in 1964 would have had no idea who he was, as the allusion to the "foundress of Sacré-Coeur" did not shed any light on his identity. Nor would readers of her memoirs, published posthumously in 1976, be significantly better informed, Alice instead elaborating there on the same story. This man was the "secretary-general of the Syndicate"; the "nephew of the foundress of the convent where we had been educated"; a widower. With the same degree of intimacy – something very rare in her writing – Alice wrote: "'P.B.' must have been 70 years old then. I was 17, but I was perfectly charmed by him."

"Every Thursday evening was a party for me," Alice goes on. "We passed those evenings in P.B.'s home with his two daughters. I sat close to him, my hands in his, while his two daughters served tea or played music and my mother knitted or embroidered." On the basis of these two lines, Alice's American biographer Janelle Dietrick concluded in 2016 that the P.B. in question was none other than Gustave Eiffel, and from this concocted a romance between Alice and the legendary engineer. The year before, in her novel about the director, Emmanuelle Gaume had invented a character called Paul Brehm.

However, two clues lead us down two converging paths. The first concerns the foundress of the Society of the Sacred Heart ("Sacré-Coeur"), a religious congregation devoted to educating young women: Madeleine-Sophie Barat. Born to a barrel-maker in 1779 in Joigny dans l'Yonne, she was 22 when she founded her first boarding school in Amiens. Today, in the 21st century, a community of 3,000 nuns, in over 410 institutions in 45 countries, continue her work. She died in 1865, at the age of 85, and was canonized in 1925. So much for the aunt. She had two brothers, one of whom became a priest, the other staying in Joigny to continue the family business. The second clue concerns P.B.'s social standing. The "Syndicate" of which he was, according to Alice, "secretary-general" was a textile workers' union. Ministry of Commerce archives include two references to a certain "Barat, Étienne Paul", in 1903 and 1913 respectively, with the rank of chevalier. His responsibilities are listed: secretary-general for, among other organizations, the Association générale du commerce et de l'industrie des tissus et matières textiles [Union for the Trade and Industry of Fabrics and Textiles], and a judge at the Joigny commercial court. He lived on Rue de Babylone in Paris. His place of birth is also specified: Joigny dans l'Yonne, which establishes a clear link with the family of Madeleine-Sophie Barat. The most surprising detail in the records, though, is his date of birth: 28 February 1838. If we recall that Alice began her stenography courses in 1892, P.B. would then have been 54 – not an old man in his 70s, as Alice seems to recall, but one in his prime.

We will never know just how serious the relationship between Alice and P.B. was, but one thing is certain: without his progressive prescience, Alice's career would never have intersected with the modern movement that is embodied in cinema.

Léon Gaumont

Léon Ernest Gaumont was born in Paris on 10 May 1864. His father, Auguste, was then 26, from the Orne region, a coachman by trade. His mother Marguerite *née* Dupanloup, hailed from the Haute-Saône and was a chambermaid. At the time of their marriage four years earlier, they gave their address as 68, Rue du Faubourg Saint-Honoré, home of the Count and Countess de Beaumont.

Despite being born below-stairs, Léon benefited from a middle-class education. He was six when he was enrolled at Saint-Pierre boarding school in Dreux, where he took top honours in geography. Six years later, his father enrolled him at Sainte-Barbe preparatory school in Fontenay-aux-Roses. Meanwhile, Auguste had become a horse trader. In 1878, Léon was 14 when he began boarding at the Collège Sainte-Barbe de Paris, in the first year of "a special preparatory course for business and industry". He came top of his class in history, geography, mathematics, physics, and natural sciences, but proved wanting in French; his spelling would always remain shaky. His school reports remarked that he was "somewhat sensitive" and "sulky" by nature. Léon dreamed of going on to attend a prestigious university, but a reversal of his father's fortune flung him into the workforce at the age of 16. Family rumour had it that Auguste lost all his money at the racetrack, but Léon always remained tight-lipped about his father's vicissitudes. However, much later, in 1903, he chose the daisy (in French, *marguerite*) as his company's logo, in reference to his mother's name.

In the early 1880s, this curious young man was often to be seen at the Institut populaire du Progrès [People's Institute for Progress] at the Palais du Trocadéro, where he spent his evenings and weekends taking courses run by the astronomer Léon Jaubert. The prizewinning geography student nursed a dream of joining the next exploratory expedition of Pierre Savorgnan de Brazza, who had established the territory of the French Congo, but Jaubert instead recommended him for a job as secretary to the inventor Jules Carpentier, who ran an optical and precision instrument workshop on Rue Delambre. Having wanted to push the envelope, he found himself a mere pen-pusher.

His term of military service in 1886 renewed his friendship from school with Henry Maillard, the son of architect Charles Maillard, a former deputy mayor of Paris who had died in 1884. While home on leave, Henry introduced Léon to his half-sister Camille, then already 26. Two years later, Léon married this wealthy young woman, four years his senior. The couple moved into the family residence at 61, Rue de la Villette. In 1889, the first of their five children was born. In 1891, Léon left Carpentier to become the director of a lamp factory, but three years later, the very same Carpentier, whom Léon described as his "master", secured his employment as manager of the "Comptoir général de photographie", a shop that sold, among other things, the early cameras known as "photo-jumelles" produced in Carpentier's workshop. Shortly thereafter, this ambitious young man hired the young Alice Guy as his secretary. However, owner Félix-Max Richard was soon forced to sell his business, electing Léon as his successor. Léon had to raise a quarter of the 200,000 francs of capital required, which he achieved with the help of old friends from Sainte-Barbe. In 1895, at the age of 30, this chambermaid's son was now head of a company employing 23 staff. But could a small retail business – albeit one at technology's cutting edge – ever satisfy his ambitions?

It was Gaumont's meeting with Georges Demenÿ that decided the visionary industrialist's destiny. Armed with the scientist's inventions, Léon joined the race to capture and project moving images. Although the Lumière brothers soon emerged as leaders of this new technology, a new market was opening up, taking shape, giving free rein to a generation of pioneers: Georges Méliès, Charles Pathé, Léon Gaumont. The creative stakes of what had not yet been dubbed the "seventh art" seemed trivial enough for the ambitious Gaumont – always more energized by technical challenges – to delegate them to his former assistant. So it was that he developed the "chronophone", which in 1900 enabled sound to be matched to image for the first time, and for which Alice Guy directed almost 200 "phono-scenes". Later, in 1912, Gaumont's engineers perfected the "chronochrome" process, by which, instead of laboriously hand-colouring every frame, "natural colours" were preserved via the "trichromatic "process of a three-colour camera. But the need for exhibitors to constantly be upgrading their costly equipment put the brakes on the development of such technological advances.

While the rivalry between Pathé and Gaumont is still remembered today, it is no doubt because they are the only two historical brands still active in the 21st century. The commercial reality was more prosaic. As early as 1903, the Pathé Company's revenues had largely overtaken those of its French rivals Méliès and Gaumont, enabling it to expand to the U.S. market four years before the Blachés arrived there as Gaumont's representatives. Up until the outbreak of the First World War, Charles Pathé concerned himself little with his French competitors, despite the emergence in 1906 of such new companies as Éclair, Lux, and Éclipse. Regardless of the new corporate status Gaumont sought for his company in 1906 to finance international expansion and the construction of new studios in Buttes-Chaumont (the Cité Elgé, built in part on land owned by his wife), the 65,000 feet of film daily printed there could not compete with the 262,000 feet streaming out of the Pathé labs.

As Léon foresaw, the new century would bring the era of fairground screenings to an end, replaced in future by bespoke movie theatres. In 1911, he turned the Montmartre Hippodrome into the Gaumont-Palace, the "biggest cinema in the world", with a 6,000-seat capacity. It is worth noting that in that same year, Charles Pathé's bulging portfolio of stock included 120 shares in the Gaumont Company.

In 1930, at the age of 66, Léon gave up the reins of his company. Following his wife Camille's death in 1933, the former industrialist lived out his retirement in the South of France at Château de Sainte-Maxime, Les Tourelles, which he had purchased in 1906. His geographical proximity to Charles Pathé, who had retired in 1929 and had been living in nearby Monaco since 1931, saw a friendship blossom between the two ageing pioneers over a weekly lunch. In 1940, the 77-year-old Charles self-published his memoirs, in which he paid tribute to Léon Gaumont ("of my competitors, his name is among those I most enjoy recalling"), conceding him "second place in the French cinematographic industry" up until 1912, and even going so far as to inscribe Gaumont's copy of the book "To my friend and colleague, with regret that 40 years ago we were not the friends we are now".

Léon Gaumont died on 8 August 1946, at the age of 82. Only a single building of the Cité Elgé now remains.

In 2001, the Gaumont and Pathé theatre chains merged, and remain to this day under the complete control of the Pathé Group – a total of more than 1,000 screens across Europe.

The Gaumont Film Company is now the world's oldest cinematic company that is still active.

Caroline Huppert's 1983 TV movie *Elle voulait faire du cinéma* [She Wanted to Make Films], featuring Christine Pascal as Alice Guy, imagined a romantic relationship between Léon and Alice – an interpretation of events that has since all but passed for the truth. There is, however, no documentary evidence that suggests that Alice Guy's success can be credited to anything other than her own talent.

Félix-Max Richard

It all begins with the father, Félix, a man from the Lyons region who opened a barometer factory on Boulevard de la Villette in Paris. Eight years later, now a rich man, he turned to politics and was elected mayor of the 19th arrondissement. To him we owe the first technical training high school, which was to become the model for all such schools in France. It is still operating today, as the Lycée Diderot. Among Félix Richard's assistants were the architect Maillard, whose daughter Camille would later go on to marry a certain Léon Gaumont. In 1876, when the elder Richard died, two of his four sons, Jules and Félix-Maxime (a.k.a. "Max"), took up the torch in the shape of a new company, Richard Frères, dedicated to the manufacture of precision instruments. This expertise led Félix-Max to suggest to Élie Mascart, the director of France's central meteorology office, that a weather station be installed at the top of the Eiffel Tower, then under construction. Engineer Gustave Eiffel was taken with the idea and commissioned Félix-Max to fit out his tower's third storey. In 1890, the very next year, Félix-Max, now expert in extreme challenges, installed his instruments in the laboratory that Joseph Vallot had built at the summit of Mont Blanc. Despite these successes, the two brothers went their separate ways in late 1891. Félix-Max sold his shares for 300,000 francs and promised not to "found or operate, in the future, any business assets or industry whose primary or secondary activity is a related sale or manufacture". Barely three months later, however, Félix-Max invested in the purchase of the Comptoir général de photographie, founded by the Picard brothers a decade earlier. The shop sold all the supplies a photographer might need: stand, plate, and studio cameras; lenses; photographic plates, printing paper and cardstock coated in a suspension of silver bromide in gelatin; shutters and optical glassware. Services on offer included developing, retouching, printing, montage, glazing, enlargements, and reproductions, and even home installation of darkrooms and photographic laboratories, as well as daily photography classes.

The Comptoir's flagship product was the "photo-jumelle", or binocular camera, a high-precision portable photographic device designed and manufactured by Jules Carpentier, Léon Gaumont's first employer and mentor. Félix-Max prided himself on owning the monopoly on the photo-jumelle, much to the irritation of his brother Jules, who believed that Carpentier had copied his work. For, working independently, Jules Richard had perfected the apparatus that would make his fortune from 1893 onwards: the vérascope, a stereo camera for glass plates that popularized stereoscopes and that his shops would continue to sell until the late 1960s. As a result, Jules decided to file a suit against Félix-Max for violating his non-competition clause. On 5 October 1893, the Paris courts banned Félix-Max from continuing his business activities. He appealed, but on 28 May 1895, the verdict was upheld. After that, he had no choice: he had to sell the Comptoir. He chose as his successor a young Léon Gaumont, whom he had hired on 1 March 1894 on Carpentier's recommendation. Félix-Max himself arranged for the financing of the purchase, calling on Gustave Eiffel, Joseph Vallot, and Alfred Besnier (vice president of the merchant shipping company Messageries Maritimes), who brought 50,000, 75,000, and 25,000 francs respectively to add to Gaumont's stake of 50,000. So it was that on 10 August 1895, a limited company was founded under the name "L. Gaumont et Cie".

Afterwards, Félix-Max Richard seems to vanish from the annals of fame, unlike his brother Jules, whose factories adjoined the Cité Elgé studios. Not only did Jules continue to prosper – to him we owe the altimeter used in the first French fighter plane, the Spad, in 1917 – but like their father, he founded a technical high school in his own name, whose doors remain open to this day. A confirmed bachelor and an habitué of the Montmartre cabarets, he would also become known, as a photographer, for his studies of female nudes.

And yet for all his relative obscurity, Max did not entirely abandon the business of innovation. In 1893, he and his younger brother Georges founded the Société des cycles

Georges Richard [Georges Richard Bicycle Company], whose quality products were used both by the armed forces and the post office. The pair went on to found, in 1896, a new venture that included the production of automobiles, and their first two-seater car, dubbed the Poney, rolled out of their factory that same year. The two brothers took part in races up until the year 1900. In the 1897 Paris–Trouville race, Georges finished in 21st place and Max in 32nd. In 1901, they teamed up with Charles-Henri Brasier, inventor of the four-cylinder V-shaped engine. The brothers' company soon went from a small workshop to one of 300 employees. This new responsibility did not prompt Georges to emulate his brother by giving up high-speed racing, however, and in 1903 his participation in the most dangerous of automobile races, the Paris–Madrid, ended when he crashed into a tree. He was badly injured, and Brasier took advantage of his convalescence to jettison the two brothers. Meanwhile, in 1905 the playwright and entrepreneur Henri de Rothschild offered Georges financial assistance to found a new company that would become known for its utility vehicles – taxis, trucks – under the name Unic. Georges died in 1922, after yet another car accident.

Although Jules, the enemy brother, died in 1930, Félix-Max was still alive in 1943, when he wrote a friendly letter to the retired Léon Gaumont. He had just read a piece devoted to the career of the cinema pioneer, and had forgotten nothing of their brief mutual adventure. His words: "Bravo, my dear friend!"

Frédéric Dillaye

Born on 19 January 1848 in Villedieu-les-Poêles, in the region of La Manche, Frédéric Léon Dillaye first arrived in Paris as a civil servant in the Finance Ministry before turning his back on a deskbound career and leaping headlong into the adventurous life of a Parisian journalist. A contributor to many literary and scientific publications, he eventually achieved fame as a novelist. A handful of novels pepper his voluminous bibliography: *Les Millions du Marchouin* [Marchouin's Millions], *Les Émigrants de l'hirondelle rouge* [The Migrants of *The Red Swallow*], *Les Vêpres égyptiennes* [Egyptian Vespers], and *La Filleule de Saint-Louis* [The Girl from Saint-Louis] were all bestsellers. He also wrote plays, a book of childen's games illustrated with 203 etchings, and even a general treatise on vitreous enamel paints for porcelain. But it was for photography that he would go down in posterity.

Violent controversy over the very nature of photography had raged for quite some time. Were photographers artists or technicians? Practitioner, theorist, and historian Frédéric Dillaye was among the crackpots who championed the notion that photography was already an art unto itself. Ever since photography had made its official debut in the history of science in 1839, thanks to Daguerre, it had become ubiquitous in the visual environment of the modern world. Just as swiftly, practitioners believed it had the potential to be something other than a mere documentary record – like a visual poem, perhaps. Seizing upon the lengthy exposure times that governed every photography session, these artists, calling themselves "pictorialists", were able to compose and produce their shots at leisure. From painters they borrowed a sense of composition, the depiction of texture, the play of light. The ensemble of aesthetic criteria from pictorialist theory and practice thus came to inhabit the principles of still photography.

Forty years later, Dillaye was the heir to this first generation of pictorialists – despite the fact that, within a few decades, ceaseless technical progress had decreased exposure times from a few dozen minutes to a fraction of a second. Pictorialists prized careful poses and stately compositions and considered the moving image vulgar. Photography might have been a young art form, but already a "classical" camp was voicing strident opposition to a more "modern" one.

In the late 1880s, Dillaye produced a series of books designed to appeal to the broadest audience of amateurs and enthusiasts. *Le Photographiste* [The Photographer], *Le Développement en photographie* [Developing in Photography], *La Pratique en photographie* [The Practice of Photography], *L'Art en photographie avec le procédé au gélatino-bromure d'argent* [Photographic Art with the Silver Bromide Process], and even *Apprenez la photographie seul et sans maître* [Teach Yourself Photography]. Beginning in 1893, as an annual supplement to his bestseller *La Théorie, la Pratique et l'Art en photographie* [Theory, Practice, and Art in Photography], he edited *Les Nouveautés photographiques* [Advances in Photography], which would survive him, lasting until 1914. In books illustrated with his own images, Dillaye both demonstrated and bequeathed his skill at landscape photography, his great speciality. And when he photographed an unnamed family playing at the beach – in fact his own wife and their seven children – it was to explicate the principles of pyramidal composition.

In the mid-1890s, this expert in the art of photography began working with the Comptoir général de photographie. Hired by Félix-Max Richard, he stayed on with Léon Gaumont, who became his publisher for a single work, *L'Art dans les projections* [The Art of Projection]. He became a silent partner of the Gaumont Company in 1905, then a shareholder the following year. Over 50 years later, Alice would write that Dillaye was "my benevolent professor, especially when I began making films". Although sensitive to the technological advances made by the new chronophotographic devices – in 1894, he wrote an article on Demenÿ's phonoscope – Frédéric Dillaye was, without a doubt, less involved in the artistic revolution happening at the same time. Nevertheless, the man who had devoted his life to photography became a collateral victim of a tragedy tied to the cinematograph. On 4 May 1897, the Bazar de la Charité, a short-lived charity fair, was engulfed in flames due to an operator's handling error during a projection session. In a matter of minutes, over 120 people died in the blaze, most of them women, including the wife of Frédéric Dillaye. Alice Guy and Léon Gaumont witnessed this disaster from beginning to end. Shortly thereafter, *Le Figaro* published a volume with the sombre title *La Catastrophe du Bazar de la Charité avec la liste complète des victimes*, which includes, on page 86 of its "Full List of Victims", a photographic portrait of "Madame Frédéric Dillaye", taken by her husband. Of all this prolific photographer's published works, it is the only image to make explicit reference to his personal life.

One year later, his daughter, who had survived the blaze, died of consumption. Sixty years later, Alice would remark: "It was a long time before Dillaye returned to his usual activities."

He died in 1905, at the age of 57.

Georges Demenÿ

Georges Élie Joseph Demenÿ was born in Douai on 12 June 1850, the second son of Philippe Demenÿ, a professor of music at the municipal Conservatory, and his wife, Adèle de Vignron. Born, respectively, in Walloon Brabant and Holland, Philippe and Adèle had met and married in Paris before settling in the ancient cross-border region of Flanders. At an early age, Georges showed evidence of his intellectual abilities, later claiming he could read and write by the age of three. He was also interested from a young age in music and became an outstanding violinist and cellist. Equally fascinated by science, especially mechanics, he set up an attic workshop at the age of 13, where he worked with wood and metal. After an indifferent education, he received a degree in Science from the University of Lille. His interests differed from those of his elder brother Paul, a future "Parnassian" poet and editor of a poetry review, who in 1870 had made friends with a certain young man passing through Douai called Arthur Rimbaud. It was to Paul, a year later, that the author of *Le Bateau ivre* addressed the famous "Lettre du voyant" ["Letter of the Visionary"], in which he defined a poet as a "thief of fire".

Georges Demenÿ was 24 when he moved to Paris in the summer of 1874. Although he failed to pass the competitive entrance exam for the École centrale des arts et manufactures, his interest was stimulated by a new scientific subject: physiology, the study of the human body. The internationally acknowledged master of the discipline at the time was Étienne-Jules Marey, whose classes Georges took at the Collège de France and the school of medicine at the University of Paris. His frail, sickly childhood and youth had given him a chance to measure the absurdity of the physical education system then in force in schools, and he immediately saw an application for this pioneering research. After settling in Paris, he diligently attended gymnasiums, but soon realized the need for a new "method refined by science". On 1 January 1880, Demenÿ founded the Cercle de gymnastique rationnelle [Circle for Rational Gymnastics], where he taught the "mechanical and physiological analysis of movement". But to go further in the discipline, the self-taught scientific pedagogue needed a mentor. The first meeting between Demenÿ and Marey took place that very year. The former was then 30 years old, the latter 50. Their fruitful collaboration would last a decade.

Without meaning to, Marey had set off an international controversy by claiming in his work *La Machine animale* [The Animal Mechanism], published in 1873 – the year of Alice Guy's birth – that although there comes a moment when all four hooves of a galloping horse are lifted off the ground, this never happens when its legs are extended, and for that split second, one of its hooves is always touching the ground – though invisibly to the naked eye. To confirm or disprove this theory, a wealthy Californian grandee approached English photographer Eadweard Muybridge, a pioneer in photographic motion studies, to record a proper image of his horse at full speed. The landmark experiment proved Marey right, and when the scientist met the photographer in 1881, Marey realized that, as far as his research on motion was concerned, photography was the future.

With the help of grants made available by the Minister of Public Education, Jules Ferry, Marey and Demenÿ set up a facility for physiological research, consisting of a laboratory and a hangar for photography. Together, they would go on to invent chronophotography, which allowed them to isolate, from a single viewpoint and at regular intervals, the various phases of a subject's movement against a black backdrop.

Before their lens paraded horses, elephants, and many varieties of birds – carrier pigeons, seagulls – but also a ball in free fall and the wavelike oscillations of a flexible wooden rod. For his part, Demenÿ was interested most of all in the human body in action and compiled a veritable visual encyclopedia of bodily mechanics.

From photographic motion studies to the reconstruction of movement through a succession of images, the scientist and his assistant paved the way for what would one day become the cinema.

The final stage on the path to the cinematograph would be the replacement of glass photographic plates with the supple celluloid film manufactured by the American George Eastman for his Kodak camera. But until 1891, Marey and Demenÿ were the only people in the world to have reliably captured life on film, as the almost 700 films they made still attest to this day. For Demenÿ, this research led to writing two abundantly illustrated works that would establish him as a cinematic precursor: *Bases de l'enseignement de l'éducation physique dans les écoles publiques* [Bases for the Instruction of Physical Education in Public Schools] in 1888, and above all, *Manuel des exercices gymnastiques et des jeux scolaires* [Gymnastic Exercises and Games for Schools: A Manual] in 1891.

In early 1892, Marey decided to market his chronophotographic apparatuses. It was a total failure. Towards the end of that same year, it was Demenÿ's turn, and he founded the Société générale du phonoscope [General Society for the Phonoscope] with capital from a German chocolatier. Immediately afterwards, he set up a laboratory and studio at the Villa Chaptal in Levallois-Perret. From that moment on, the situation rapidly deteriorated between the master and the disciple, the latter now determined to fly with his own wings in the industry. The stakes were suitably high: who would be known as the father of the phonoscope? A battle of patent applications and threatening letters ensued. Demenÿ ended up losing both his post at the facility and the scientist's friendship. But in the race to monetize moving images, Demenÿ was abruptly overtaken by the American inventor Thomas Edison, who in April 1894 opened the Kinetoscope Parlor in New York, where ten kinetoscope devices allowed the public to view short motion pictures. Although Edison's 30-second shorts were far longer than Demenÿ's, the phonoscope remained – until the arrival of the Lumières – the only chronophotographic apparatus to have a projection system. For all that, by 1895, Demenÿ was on the brink of bankruptcy, having already invested 40,000 francs. After fruitlessly asking the Lumières for financial backing, he met Félix-Max Richard, owner of the Comptoir général de photographie, who seemed to be his last chance. In the end, though, it was Richard's successor, the young Léon Gaumont, who stepped in as Demenÿ's new backer in August of that same year. Two months later, the phonoscope, now renamed the bioscope, was at last on the market, but to no avail. In March 1896 it was his camera's turn to hit the market: the biographe. It fared no better. Meanwhile, the Lumières had pulled ahead of the pack due to the unique nature of their apparatus, an all-in-one camera and projector. Seven months later, Gaumont was already selling a single, reversible device that Demenÿ had developed: the chronophotograph. However, a manufacturer of counterfeits, one Henry Joly, brought a specious suit against them for copying his design, which damaged the impact of their product's launch. Such shenanigans left its inventor distraught. From then on, he withdrew from the scene, leaving Gaumont to take care of business and himself more time to explore the passion that had first set him off on this adventure: physical education. In January 1898, Demenÿ was named an officer of public education. During the Universal Exposition of 1900, he was entrusted with organizing the international conference on physical education. The Minister of War then immediately tasked him with reforming the army's physical training methods. The era as a whole was marked by a craze for exercise, with the number of gym instructors licensed in France reaching vast numbers in the 1900s. In 1908, the inveterate bachelor Georges married Marie Vignerelle, from the Moselle region.

Georges Demenÿ died on 26 October 1917, at the age of 67. The papers paid due tribute to him: "Cinema owes him its existence and its successes"; "The inventor-creator of motion pictures". At a lecture eight years earlier, he had declared: "The cinematograph represents a painful and difficult stage in my life, an unfortunate incursion into business and industry, two slippery slopes down which a man devoted to science ought never to venture."

René Decaux

Every story needs a villain. Alice Guy would refer to hers only by the initial "D". In the first French edition of Alice's memoirs, Claire Clouzot identified this man as "a certain René Decaux".

In 1894, in *Les Nouveautés photographiques* [Innovations in Photography], an annual supplement to his indispensable *La Théorie, la Pratique et l'Art en photographie* [The Theory, Practice, and Art of Photography], Fréderic Dillaye hailed the winner of a competition organized by the Société d'encouragement à l'industrie nationale [Society for the Development of National Industry] that aimed to stimulate the invention of a new model of photographic shutter. A thousand francs were awarded to the young inventor of a pneumatic air-brake shutter whose "high light yield and constancy of speed" – as the Gaumont Company's publicity brochures would later explain – ensured instant success. René Léopold Decaux was just 25 years old when he thus proved himself an engineer to be reckoned with in the world of precision mechanical instruments. A former student at the École des arts et métiers [College of Arts and Trades] in Angers, he had worked under Jules Carpentier, where he met Léon Gaumont, and later under Georges Richard. He then joined the Tavernier-Grenet company, where he became a partner, and in 1895, the Comptoir général de photographie began outsourcing work to him. In the years to come, the Decaux "double-drop" shutter would be standard for all Gaumont Company cameras. But it was the development of the moving image that turned Decaux into a top-tier collaborator in Léon Gaumont's eyes. In early 1896, the Lumières' cinematograph put them far ahead of the biograph that Georges Demenÿ had developed for Gaumont. Léon wanted to catch up, and entrusted the young prodigy Decaux with transforming Demenÿ's device into a reversible camera. Three months later, thanks to his hard work, the chronophotograph, with its perforated 58mm film, emerged. Demenÿ registered the patent in his own name.

Léon Gaumont knew how to recognize talent. The engineer in him, excited by this collaboration, and with so much at stake for the future of his company, saw in Decaux a tech-whiz kindred spirit. On 1 December 1896, he hired Decaux to found and manage the future Elgé factories in Buttes-Chaumont. Decaux was 27. It would be his job to oversee the manufacture of all devices that bore the Gaumont name – chronos, phonos, still and moving picture cameras. On all of Gaumont's experimental ventures, Decaux would be right by his side. First came sound cinema, with the perfection of the chronophone. From the 1910s into the 1920s, Decaux went into partnership with the American company Kodak in trials for colour film. Only one photo of the engineer himself survives, taken from a distance in around 1905, showing him and Léon Gaumont on the construction site of the studios in Buttes-Chaumont.

No one knows exactly when hostilities began between the engineer and Alice, only three years his junior, but although he is never named, Decaux makes his entrance in her memoirs at around the time construction on the studios was completed. Alice was forced to vie with him to secure the post of managing director, "in spite of the ill-temper that led him to commit a thousand pettinesses". She provides an example of one such case from the filming of *The Passion* later that year: "This was for the director of production one more occasion to evidence his desire to collaborate in our success. The winter was very cold, and fearing, he said, that the pipes should burst, he availed himself one night of the scenery flats already built by the set shops and had them sawn up in order to insulate the pipes. This cost us only ten days or so of delay." But it was the man she referred to as "my nemesis" who would, indirectly, change the course of her life. The very next year, when Decaux insisted on shooting a series of phono-scenes himself, Gaumont gave in, and in order to keep Alice away from proceedings, sent her off to Spain with her loyal cameraman Anatole Thiberville. This long voyage would remain one of the most striking memories of Alice's career, but the 50-something Anatole came back completely exhausted, so worn out that he did not want to accompany Alice on her next location shoot in Saintes-Maries-de-la-Mer. He was replaced at the last minute by a younger cameraman, Herbert Blaché. That same year, in December 1906, Alice and her sworn enemy both received shares in Gaumont.

In February 1922, René Decaux, still director of the Gaumont Company's studios, was named a Chevalier of the Legion of Honour, at the age of 53. Little is known of his later life, his name only resurfacing in the record half a century later, and then only because of the belligerence he had displayed towards Alice, which she never forgot or forgave.

Auguste & Louis Lumière

Although Auguste Marie Louis Nicolas Lumière was born on 19 October 1862 in Besançon, and Louis Jean on 5 October 1864 in the same town, the two years between them never prevented them from being as inseparable as twins.

It all began in the darkroom of their father Antoine, who, first in Besançon in the early 1860s, and then in Lyons in the following decade, mined the potential of this new invention of photography, shooting, developing, and manufacturing the prints himself. Auguste, Louis, their younger brother Édouard, and their three sisters divided their upbringing between the studio, with its canvas sets, and the laboratory where wet collodion plates were readied. During summer vacations in Brittany, the two eldest brothers set up a darkroom in a cave known as Goule-aux-Fées [the Fairies' Maw], where they spent their time experimenting with chemical emulsion processes. In the early 1880s, photography underwent a major revolution. The wet collodion process, which entailed heavy, costly equipment and endless exposure times, was replaced by dry plates coated with silver bromide in a gelatin suspension. The savings in time and expensive materials democratized the field. Antoine saw a chance to expand his activities as a portraitist into selling photographic equipment as well, instantly attracting a new clientele of amateurs. Alas, dry plates had to be imported, a few at a time, from Belgium, a fact that Antoine bemoaned aloud in front of Louis. While Auguste was studying for polytechnical school, Louis was often at home alone. Beset by chronic migraines since childhood, he had been taken out of school and spent his days playing the piano or trying his hand at chemistry. Antoine understood next to nothing of this field, but tasked his 17-year-old son with finding a solution to the dilemma. A few months later, Louis invented a method for preparing dry plates that proved even more sensitive than existing ones. Visionary that he was, Antoine decided to build an entire factory to market his son's invention. The usual vagaries of founding a company followed: failures, threats of bankruptcy, countless hours of toil. Auguste abandoned his studies and swooped in to help. By 1885, the Lumière plate, known as the "Étiquette bleue", had been perfected. Its sensitivity enabled snapshots unimaginable a decade earlier. In 1894, the Lumière factories produced over 15 million such plates, sold worldwide. The family's fortune was made. Meanwhile, Auguste and Louis had not neglected their private lives. They had married a pair of sisters and now lived in symmetrical apartments in a single house, where they saw each other for dinner every night. While their father handled the business, the two brothers had fun inventing new things. By the time of their deaths, over 200 patents had been registered in their name.

In the mid-1890s, moving images were no longer a novelty. Edison's kinetoscope had already been operating in Paris since the summer of 1894. When Antoine discovered the apparatus, he immediately bought one and brought it back to Lyons. The idea he put to his sons was quite simple. The kinetoscope could only be used by one person at a time. If a single device could project moving images, then it could attract several paying viewers at once. Three things were widely known: how to photograph movement; how to lend still images the illusion of motion; and the principle behind the magic lantern. But no one had managed to coordinate these inventions in such a way as to enable the projection of moving images. The Lumières would succeed in inventing the definitive solution to this problem, combining a handful of small innovations sporadically made over the previous two centuries or more. Neither of the brothers had a degree, but they conducted long months of research and experimentation in their studios and laboratories. Their mastery of chemistry, optics, and precision instruments nevertheless ran up against a fundamental issue: how to drive the perforated film. It was once more Louis who came up with a solution one sleepless night, picturing a kind of claw-mechanism to hold the film in place, inspired by his mother's sewing machine. "My brother invented the cinematograph overnight!" Auguste would declare.

What happened next is now a matter of cinematic legend: Antoine rents a basement room at the Grand Café on Boulevard des Capucines, Paris, and organizes the first paying public screening in history. On 28 December 1895, the first moving images shot by Louis Lumière are projected. There are few viewers in attendance, but they emerge amazed from the Salon Indien.

A humorous short soon became the toast of the programme. Originally titled *Le Jardinier* [The Gardener], the film has gone down in history in a later version known as *L'Arroseur arrosé* [The Waterer Watered]: the very first fiction film in the history of cinema. The script was not original, however, being an adaptation of a wordless comic strip, "Arrosage public", by Uzès, in an 1885 issue of *Chat Noir*, with further variations on the theme by artists Hermann Vogel in 1887 and Christophe in 1889. Two other short films would become part of film history: *Sortie de l'usine Lumière à Lyon* [Employees Leaving the Lumière Factory] and *L'Arrivée d'un train* [The Arrival of a Train in Ciotat].

In just a few months, projections multiplied in France and abroad. By summer, the cinematograph had already been shown to the Queen of Spain, the Tsar of Russia, and the royal families of Romania and Serbia; it was a triumph in the United States. Antoine refused to sell the device so that he alone could make use of it, but they had to move quickly: the Lumières were convinced that audiences would lose interest as swiftly as they had first become infatuated.

Thanks to the distribution network for the Étiquettes bleue, the Lumières already had over 2,000 dealerships in 85 countries. After having Jules Carpentier build new apparatuses, the next step was to recruit and train "experimenters". To put it more prosaically, these young people from all sorts of backgrounds would act as both the operators and managers of the device. Dispatched to the four corners of the world, they were to film and project onsite, thus constantly providing headquarters with new films: "Offrons le monde au monde!"—"Let us offer the world the world!" After three weeks of training in Lyons under Louis' supervision, 50 two-man crews – a cameraman and his assistant – were sent out to travel the world. In late 1896, 20 or so were criss-crossing the American continent. Other players were quick to react. William Dickson, Edison's former collaborator, with whom he'd perfected the kinetoscope and shot most of his films, joined the American Biograph Company, headed by the brother of the U.S. president, McKinley. A fight to the death began between Biograph – not to be confused with Demenÿ's invention – and Cinematograph. A massive billboard on Broadway proclaimed: "American Biograph – America for Americans." In the summer of 1897, there were 24 Lumière devices on the ground in America, along with their operators, who had declared them at customs to be "tools for personal work". Customs officials became aware that these declarations were bogus, and held Lafont, Cinematograph's director in the States, responsible for this infraction of customs regulations. A warrant was put out for his arrest. Lafont secretly left American soil before he was thrown in jail. The devices were confiscated.

Meanwhile, Edison had launched the Vitascope, but could not manage to make it popular. He switched tactics and put his lawyers on the trail of patents that the Lumières had not registered in the U.S. By late 1898, their American adventure had come to an end. However, in 1900, only five years after the cinematograph was launched, it had already brought in a profit of 3 million francs worldwide.

The Lumière brothers were first and foremost scientists, then industrialists, but certainly not fairground barkers. Leaving the business of spectacle to the Gaumonts, the Pathés, and the Méliès of the world, they now went back to their roots: invention. Against the advice of Auguste, who felt he was wasting his time, Louis Lumière explored colour photography, presenting his first "autochrome" plates to the press in 1906. By 1913, the Montplaisir factory was making 6,000 autochrome plates every day.

Louis ran the Lyons factory until 1922. After his wife died, he left Lyons for Neuilly-sur-Seine, near Paris, where he devoted himself to solo research in his own laboratory. In 1935, the

40th anniversary of the invention of cinema was celebrated, with Louis hailed as the father of cinema. On the occasion, Auguste, whose research in biology had won him membership in the Academy of Medicine, declared that his brother deserved all the credit.

In November 1940, following the Nazi Occupation of France, the brothers made public in the press their unconditional support of the collaborationist Marshal Pétain and his infamous vice-president of the Council of Ministers, Pierre Laval.

On 25 January 1941, Louis was appointed to one of 213 seats in the National Council, an advisory assembly replacing Parliament and comprising, among many notable figures, former deputies, senators, and industrialists. The topics discussed ranged from the drafting of a new constitution to administrative reorganization. In 1943, the Council was suspended. In 1941, Louis Lumière had also joined the sponsorship committee for recruiting new members in Free France for the non-profit association the L.V.F., or Legion of French Volunteers against Bolshevism, which sent several thousand men to fight in German uniforms on the Russian front. When Liberation came, the heroic doings of Auguste's son Henri in the French Resistance outshone his elder brother's disgrace. Louis died on 6 June 1948 in Bandol, at the age of 84, and Auguste on 10 April 1954 in Lyons, aged 92.

In 1995, the Bank of France was preparing to print a 200-franc banknote in honour of the Lumière brothers to commemorate the centenary of the cinematograph when groups of former Resistance fighters protested at their Vichy past. The anniversary banknote was cancelled, replaced at the last minute by a new design featuring Gustave Eiffel – which provided the press with a chance to point out Eiffel's less than luminous role in the "Panama scandals" of the 1890s.

Joseph Vallot

Born on 16 February 1854 in Lodève to a wealthy family from the Hérault region of southern France, Henri Marie Joseph Vallot was a life-long eccentric, devoting his entire fortune to financing his many all-encompassing interests, from astronomy, geography, alpinism, botany, glaciology, engineering, geology, photography, and medicine, to physiology, cartography, meteorology, and speleology (the study of caves). His was an insatiable curiosity, and he never stopped feeding it. After graduating from the Lycée Charlemagne in Paris, Joseph began by studying botany and geology, but his life's great passion, its founding emotional encounter, took place in 1875 in Chamonix, where, invited to a geology conference, he beheld Mont Blanc for the first time. He was 21. The massif had not yet been greatly researched, and no in-depth studies had been done on the life of glaciers or the meteorology of summits. Five years later, Joseph climbed to the top of Mont Blanc for the first time. There, he dreamed of building a laboratory-shelter that would enable him to perform all kinds of scientific experiments. His teachers warned him that such altitudes raised many serious, even lethal, risks to life and limb. Six years later, in 1887, the 33-year-old decided to prove them wrong by meticulously mounting an expedition that would allow him to live, sleep, and work for three days and nights at the top of Mont Blanc. After a triumphant descent, Joseph climbed to the summit five more times that same year.

During the summer of 1890, Joseph financed and led a 110-person expedition that in eight days of ascents brought up to 14,000 feet all the equipment necessary to build his laboratory-shelter. Joseph was in seventh heaven. Eight years later, he had his laboratory expanded from two rooms to eight, one of which he decorated as a Chinese-style salon, full of lacquered furniture, rare rugs, and precious curios. Only then did he feel it appropriate to receive his wife Gabrielle there, herself a renowned speleologist.

That same year, working with his cousin, the engineer Henri Vallot, Joseph began making a map of the Mont Blanc massif at a 1:20,000 scale. It was a lifetime's work, as he had to survey the topography at a 1:1 scale on his own two feet. During his alpine rambles, Joseph took a great many photographs – visual notes for research, to be sure, but also a photographer's expression of the emotion that gripped him when confronted by the awesome sight of these mountains, of which he would never tire. Joseph entrusted the development and printing of his photos to the Comptoir général de photographie, run by his friend Félix-Max Richard. So it was that he often had occasion to converse with Mademoiselle Alice Guy. He was among the group of sponsors who came together in 1894 to provide Léon Gaumont with the capital needed to found his company. Two years later, at the age of 42, he was made a Chevalier of the Legion of Honour for his noteworthy scientific achievements.

At the turn of the century, Joseph introduced his daughter Madeleine to the joys of mountain climbing. She accompanied him to his laboratory, and during their first ascent of Mont Blanc, she was forced to hike her dress up to mid-thigh. No sooner had she made the descent than she decided to go back up, but with better equipment that, this time, she designed herself: trousers. Causing a great scandal among her contemporaries, she went on to climb Mont Blanc in trousers six more times, even setting a few records for the ascent, and emerging as one of the major figures in the history of climbing.

Joseph Vallot died on 11 April 1925 in Nice, at the age of 71.

Gustave Eiffel

Alexandre Gustave Bönickhausen, later "Eiffel", was born on 15 December 1832 in Dijon. His German-sounding name came from his great-grandfather, who hailed from Köln and settled in Paris in 1700. Two generations later, his 16-year-old father enlisted as a hussar in Napoleon's Grande Armée. Joining the army again during the Restoration, he was stationed in Dijon, where he met and married Catherine Moneuse, the daughter of a timber tradesman. Gustave was their first child, followed by two daughters. Meanwhile, Monsieur Eiffel was promoted to captain in the National Guard, while Madame founded a coal-distribution business; mining concessions and two barges enabled them to amass a relative fortune. Gustave was 12 when he visited Paris with his mother for the first time. He found the capital "like a fairy-tale". He went back six years later, in 1850, baccalaureate degree in hand, to attend the Collège Sainte-Barbe. There he studied for the polytechnic institute's entrance exam but failed. However, he did pass the exam for the École centrale des arts et manufactures, a science and engineering university. When he finished his studies there, Madame Eiffel took her son's destiny in hand. Her business had expanded from coal to include metallurgy. In 1856, pulling a few strings with her business connections, she managed to get Gustave into the research bureau for the western railway, the Compagnie des chemins de fer de l'Ouest. Since its inauguration, 21 years earlier, of the first French railway line open to the public, it had become an outpost of industrial modernity. So it was that the young engineer's first mission was to build a metal bridge on the Saint-Germain line. By chance, Gustave found himself hired at the forefront of the movement that would see iron construction take off in the two directions that would make him his fortune and his legendary status: bridges and buildings. The first major structure that forged his reputation in 1858 was a bridge in Bordeaux now known as the Eiffel Passerelle, whose 1,673-foot length forced Gustave to come up with some innovative technical feats. He was 26. On this project, he was aided by his sister Marie, who would go on to be his assistant for the rest of his career. It was she who convinced him to start a family, by acting as a matchmaker with a respectable Dijon family. Afer six unsuccessful attempts, Gustave found a rare pearl: 17-year-old Marie Gaudelet. He was 29 at the time. They were married in 1862. Gustave renamed her Marguerite so as not to confuse her with his sister; she gave birth to a little girl the following year. Two other girls and two boys joined the family over the next ten years. A few hundred bridges, viaducts, and train stations later, by the mid-1880s the brilliant engineer had become a powerful industrialist and businessman, spreading his technological expertise to the four corners of the world, from Egypt to Latin America by way of Spain, Portugal, Hungary, Romania, and Indochina. His mother's capital had helped him found his own factory as early as 1867. In 1876, he officially divested himself of his family name, which had made him a target of unscrupulous attacks after Prussia's victory over France in 1870. In 1877, Marguerite died of internal haemorrhaging at the age of 32.

The year 1884 proved a tipping point for Gustave's career. He finished the Garabit Viaduct, which would remain his masterpiece in that category; he developed the portable or "Saigon" bridge that became his company's bestseller; on Bedloe's (now Liberty) Island, he laid the first stone of the pedestal upon which Bartholdi's Statue of Liberty, featuring an Eiffel-designed inner structure, would one day stand. But above all, in June of that year, he made the first sketch for what would become the Eiffel Tower. Five years later, for the Universal Exposition in 1889, what was then the tallest man-made structure rose in the heart of Paris, a technical feat against which such writers, composers, and painters as Huysmans, Maupassant, Gounod, and Bouguereau railed on aesthetic grounds. Often threatened with demolition, the metal tower would assert itself as a symbol of the Industrial Age.

When Félix-Max Richard called on Eiffel in 1895, the engineer was up to his neck in the worst scandal of the age. He was implicated when the French company building a canal across the Panama isthmus went into liquidation, leaving thousands of small shareholders penniless. Eiffel had reaped over 20 million francs in profit, but this had nothing to do with the embezzlement covered up by politicians. Nevertheless, he was forced to endure a slanderous trial, and was even briefly incarcerated before his name was cleared. Americans later built a canal in 1914, but the engineer's public image would remain tarnished for the rest of his days.

Like Gaumont, Eiffel was a "*barbiste*" – an alumnus of the Collège Sainte-Barbe – and the old school tie no doubt played a part in his being hired to work on the project. However, it was primarily his son-in-law, Adolphe Salles, who acted as his principal liaison in all his dealings with the French Panama Canal Company. Salles played an active role indeed, introducing Gaumont to the Banque Suisse et Française, where he was a manager. While another manager, Pierre Azaria, the former *barbiste* and future founder of the Compagnie générale d'électricité, presided over the board of the Gaumont Company from 1905 to 1927. This did not go down well with another client of the same bank, Charles Pathé, who was outraged when his own shareholders received an offer from the bank to contribute to increasing his competitor's capital.

Alice's memoirs record only pleasant memories of Eiffel, and of "the encouragement with which he always showered me". In 2016, American writer Janelle Dietrick self-published *Alice & Eiffel: A New History of Early Cinema and the Love Story Kept Secret for a Century*. Taking as her starting point two sentences from Alice's memoirs – "'P.B.' must have been 70 years old then. I was 17, but I was perfectly charmed by him" – Dietrick extrapolated an outlandish romance between the young woman and Gustave Eiffel, who would then have been 58. As with the alleged relationship with Léon Gaumont, this otherwise well-researched biography added a new chapter to the legend of Alice's love life.

Gustave Eiffel died on 27 December 1923, at the age of 91. He left behind a colossal fortune in property, as well as a portfolio of holdings that still included shares from the Gaumont Company, listed in his will between those of Nestlé and the Galeries Lafayette department store.

Georges Méliès

Catherine *née* Schveringh was the eldest daughter of a rich bootmaker to Queen Hortense of the Netherlands, but arson destroyed their factory, ruining the family and causing them to flee to France. Catherine was a humble worker in a shoe factory when she met a young cobbler-bootmaker who had just finished his seven years of apprenticeship. It was love at first sight; they married and settled in Paris, where the couple decided to set up shop in a small two-room apartment near the Place de la Bourse. What happened next is another of those late 19th-century Industrial Age fairy-tales. After tireless work, technical innovation, and creative talent, by the late 1850s their fortune was made, and they bought a country house on a vast property in Montreuil, to spend vacations and weekends far from the noise of the capital. Their fourth child, Marie-Georges-Jean Méliès, was born in Paris on 8 December 1861; his eldest sibling was 17 years older than he was.

In 1884, Georges was 19 when his father sent him to London to put distance between him and a certain young woman. There he saw a magic show and became enamoured of illusionism, quickly picking up the basics. Upon his return, he steadfastly refused to take part in the family shoe business. A well-made match with a wealthy heiress, Eugénie Génin, the following year, along with a substantial dowry, made him a young man of independent means. He had a penchant for republican politics, made a name for himself as a talented caricaturist in radical pamphlets, set up a photography studio in his attic, and was often to be found at the Chat Noir cabaret, at the same time assiduously pursuing his apprenticeship as a stage magician.

In 1888, Méliès' father sought to pass the company on to his son, an offer Georges immediately refused. As a parting gift, however, he received the colossal sum of 500,000 francs. On 1 July, just four months after his first daughter was born, Georges made his wildest dream come true: he took over the lease of the Théâtre Robert-Houdin, founded on the Boulevard des Italiens by the great magician himself three decades earlier. Among the small troupe of artistes appearing at this temple of illusion was a young Charlotte Faës, whom Méliès would shape into a star under the name Jehanne d'Alcy – but also into his muse, his mistress, and his second wife.

To Georges' concept of illusionism, the cinematograph appeared like a revelation. As soon as he saw the Lumières' first projection in December 1895, he tried to acquire the reversible camera. Despite his attractive offer, Lumière Senior categorically refused – after all, why lend help to the competition? But Méliès was not discouraged. Crossing the Channel to London, he obtained an apparatus to his liking from his friend Robert W. Paul. A filmmaker himself, Paul had made a name for himself as a skilled counterfeiter of Edison's kinetoscope, the patent for which did not apply to Europe. In the light of the Lumières' success, however, he had just perfected his own projection device. So it was that on 5 April 1896, Méliès was able to offer audiences a series of moving images made possible by Paul and Edison, in addition to his usual illusionist bill of fare. Méliès quickly adapted Paul's theatograph into a camera, and in May 1896, in the garden of the family house in Montreuil, he shot his first film – of a group of men playing cards – lasting less than a minute, and directly copied from the Lumières. He followed it up with a sleight-of-hand trick for which he donned his magician's outfit. That same year, he shot over 90 films, from documentaries such as a train arriving in the station at Vincennes, to staged scenes featuring his daughter Georgette. Meanwhile, he developed his own apparatus: the *kinétographe*, which he sought to sell to fairs and carnivals. One of his customers, Charles Pathé, pointed out that audiences would soon tire of moving images showing the same limited range of subjects. In October 1896, Méliès made his name, combining his skills as an illusionist with his expertise in cinema by making the first-ever film with special effects: *L'Escamotage d'une dame chez Robert-Houdin* [The Vanishing Lady]. It was a huge hit with audiences, and Jehanne d'Alcy became the first-ever movie star.

The next year, Méliès built his first studio on his family property in Montreuil and began colourizing all his films – by hand. What happened next is part of film mythology. Between 1897 and 1914, in a total of 600 films of varying lengths (anything from 1 minute to 40), Méliès was the first to explore the worlds of fairy-tale (*Cinderella*), fantasy (*The Bewitched Inn*), and science fiction (the canonical *A Trip to the Moon*), but also reconstructions of current affairs – in dramatizing the Dreyfus affair in 1899, he invented the film-serial, casting himself as the falsely accused officer's lawyer in successive episodes. With almost godlike powers, Méliès wrote and meticulously planned out his films as *"scénarimages"*, to all intents and purposes inventing the modern storyboard. For each of his films, he designed the sets and costumes, occasionally turned his hand to acting, and devised and perfected the special effects that would become his trademark and secure his legendary status: as cinematic creator, inventor, and entrepreneur. By the dawn of the 20th century, Méliès had established himself as the world leader in his field.

Across the Atlantic, *Cinderella* astonished audiences, but Méliès soon found himself a victim of his own success. In the absence, as yet, of any copyright law, each print he sold in the U.S. was immediately bootlegged in countless copies, including by such well-established counterfeiters as Dickson's Biograph or the Edison Company, who then sold them all over the continent. In 1903, Méliès sent his brother Gaston, who had just bankrupted the family shoe business, to New York to found an American branch of Star Film and stamp out pirate copies. It was a useful move: for the next four years, the massive revenue from this outlet enabled Méliès to invest copiously in his own productions. But he hadn't reckoned with Thomas Edison, who, having neglected to file a patent in Europe for his 35mm film with four perforations per frame (the format still in use today), nonetheless swooped down like a hawk on all infringements of his patent on his native soil. And like everyone else except the Lumières (whose filmstock used only two perforations per frame), Méliès used Edison's stock. In October 1907, American courts ruled in favour of Edison, who now wielded absolute control over any film shot or projected on American soil. George Eastman, however, who had a monopoly on the production of celluloid film, saw things differently, suggesting to Edison that the biggest companies form a trust that would include the French pioneers Pathé and Méliès. This was the beginning of the end for Star Film. In a few short years, cinema had become an industry – and Méliès wished to remain an artist. But his fantastical films were now struggling to find an audience; with such exorbitant production costs, they no longer broke even. Starting in 1911, Charles Pathé, a great admirer, tried to save Star Film, gradually taking over and producing Méliès' final creations, including a remake of *Cinderella*, to widespread indifference. In 1913, at the age of 52, Méliès directed his final film.

In 1923, ruined and disillusioned, he burned his entire cinematographic archive in the garden of the house in Montreuil, from which bailiffs were evicting him. Two years later, he met Jehanne again, now Fanny Manieux after a first marriage and running a toy shop by Montparnasse railway station. They married shortly thereafter.

By the late 1920s, Méliès would nevertheless be honoured and recognized in his lifetime for his pioneering genius. But when he died on 21 January 1938, aged 76, only eight of his films had survived. It was his granddaughter Madeleine, secretary to film archivist Henri Langlois, who travelled the world on behalf of the Cinémathèque Française to reconstitute the pioneer's oeuvre – ironically enough, often by resorting to pirated copies.

In 2011, American filmmaker Martin Scorsese directed *Hugo*, based on a fantasy-tinged adventure novel by Brian Selznick. One of the main protagonists of this movie, produced by Johnny Depp, was a very real historical character: a former filmmaker now reduced to selling toys at Montparnasse railway station. Georges Méliès was played by Ben Kingsley.

Anatole Thiberville

Sixteen years older than her, "Old Man Anatole", as she called him, would be Alice Guy's technical alter ego, the eye in her viewfinder, for her entire French career, from 1896 to 1907.

Born on 31 October 1857 in Berchères-sur-Vesgre in the central Eure-et-Loir region southwest of Paris, Désiré Adolphe Anatole Thiberville was the son of a cooper. He would later tell Mademoiselle Alice that he had raised chickens in Bresse, an eastern province famed for its poultry. This episode probably took place around the early 1880s, for in 1883, he brought a young woman from the Jura in Franche-Comté back to his village and married her: Marie-Thérèse Jaggi. A few months later, she gave birth to their daughter Marie-Joséphine. So how did Anatole wind up at the age of 39 on a terrace patio in Buttes-Chaumont, hand-cranking a phonophotograph to record Alice Guy's first film, *The Cabbage Fairy*? The jump-cut in space and time remains a mystery. The only biographical clue we have is a personal tragedy: that same year, in 1896, Marie-Thérèse died, aged 37. However, the very next year the 40-year-old married again, this time a 32-year-old woman from Brittany named Anne Perrine Le Baut.

Initially hired by Gaumont as a news cameraman, Anatole was probably one of the company's first cinematographers of fiction. Until Alice left for the U.S., Anatole would remain part of her every cinematic adventure, from the early improvised sketches to the 1906 masterpiece of her French career, her *Life of Christ*. Of the 200 films, whether long or short, attributed to Mademoiselle Alice, there can have been few that did not benefit from his experience. It was also with Anatole that Louis Feuillade began his career, before selecting another cameraman in 1907.

Time passes; memories fade. In 1936, Alice received a signed copy of a history of the Gaumont companies from Léon Gaumont himself – which made no mention at all of Alice's body of work, since its story began after her departure for the U.S. So Alice took it upon herself to refresh her former boss' memory. Her first note comprised eight densely handwritten pages in which she listed the titles of films and specified her role in them, as well as those of Demenÿ and her first cameraman, Anatole, whose last name she could not recall, replacing it instead with a series of Xs. Retired and living in the Château des Tourelles in Sainte-Maxime, Léon Gaumont confirmed that he had received the letter and promised to use it in the second edition of the work describing the Établissements Gaumont to which she had been a "devoted contributor from the very start". He enclosed a copy of Alice's notes that he had annotated with detailed corrections, thereby at last crediting Alice's first cinematographer with his surname: Thiberville. Alice would not forget him when she began writing her memoirs a few years later.

Thanks to those memoirs, Old Man Anatole remains associated with fiction film's first steps. He also has a place in the history of the seventh art as cinematographer on the first film by the innovative director Marcel L'Herbier, *Rose-France*, which Gaumont produced for the High Propaganda Commission in 1919. Then 61, he died three years later, on 12 November 1921 in Paris, by now a largely forgotten pioneer of the silver screen.

Yvonne Serrand

Yvonne Mugnier-Serrand was born on 1 January 1886, but her name was added to the margins of early cinema history only posthumously, as the unwitting witness-for-the-prosecution in the controversy surrounding *The Cabbage Fairy*. In her memoirs, Alice Guy maintains that her very first film was shot in 1896. Since then, there have been two rival schools of thought: one that takes Alice at her word, and another – including the majority of specialist historians of cinema – that refuses to. Francis Lacassin was in fact the first to cast doubt on this date, as early as 1963. According to his research, even if almost all the era's films have been lost, the reel in question does not appear until 1900 in the Gaumont catalogues. At best, he claims, it could date back to May 1897. However, after defending this theory for several decades, he disowned it in 1995 in the most recent edition of his biography of Louis Feuillade. Why? Because two versions of the same film had meanwhile been discovered, one of which could indeed date from 1896. For all that, Lacassin repeats the same mistake Alice makes in her memoirs by associating Yvonne with the 1896 shoot, when in fact she only appears in the later, longer version. When Maurice Gianati later pointed out, in his essay "Alice Guy a-t-elle existé?" ["Did Alice Guy Exist?"], that in 1896 Yvonne was 10 years old and so can hardly have taken part in that legendary shoot, it was enough for many people to discredit all of Alice's claims.

On the other hand, the presence of Yvonne along with her sister Germaine in the cast of the final version of *The Cabbage Fairy* – entitled *Sage-femme de première classe* [Midwife, First Class] in the Gaumont Catalogue, a title Alice completely rejected in 1964 – allows us to date her debut with the Gaumont company to around 1902. Hired as a secretary-assistant to Mademoiselle Guy, the 16-year-old would appear in at least two other of Alice's films: *Chez la modiste* [At the Milliner's], a "comic film with special effects" from 1903, and *Mireille*, the 1906 adaptation of Mistral's poem filmed in Saintes-Maries-de-la-Mer, of which no trace remains.

Throughout her life, Alice kept three photographs in her personal archive of herself with her young friend Yvonne. The first is from the filming of the remake of *The Cabbage Fairy*, in which Yvonne is dressed as a fairy and Alice as a farmer. The other two are from the filming of *Mireille*: one where they are wearing traditional Provençal folk dress, and another in which Herbert Blaché had them posing in bathing suits on the beach.

In 1906, in the Gaumont offices in the heights of Belleville, Yvonne met and fell in love with a friend of Louis Feuillade who had come to try his hand at filmmaking: Étienne Arnaud, seven years her senior. They were married in October 1907, and settled at 39, Rue Manin, at the foot of Buttes-Chaumont, in an apartment Étienne had purchased the previous June. The following year saw the birth of their only child, Arlette, whom they nicknamed "La môme Ra" [the Sun Kid]. From then on, although Yvonne accompanied her husband on his weekend rides scouting locations on the Paris outskirts, and kept a close eye on his accounts, she does not seem to have played any further role at Gaumont. Five years later, the small family crossed the Atlantic to settle in Fort Lee, New Jersey. Freshly poached from Gaumont by the Éclair Company, Étienne had come to head the artistic direction of its American studios. But the First World War saw the Arnauds return to France in September 1914, back to Rue Manin, where Yvonne would eventually die, 14 years after Étienne, on 3 June 1969, aged 83. Meanwhile, her daughter would also be drawn to cinema, first as an assistant to the European head of publicity for the American studios MGM, Paramount, and R.K.O., and later as head of publicity for R.K.O. in France.

Thanks to her participation in shooting one of the versions of *The Cabbage Fairy*, Yvonne Serrand has gone down in history in a way that her husband Étienne never did.

Victorin Jasset

Victorin-Hippolyte Jasset was born to a humble family in Fumay, in the Ardennes, on 30 March 1862. In the 1880s, he attended classes with the renowned sculptor and former Paris Commune member Jules Dalou, newly returned from exile. Jasset began his career painting fans, then designing costumes and theatre sets. In 1900, he drew favourable notice as a director of historical re-enactments by organizing the equestrian parade for *Vercingétorix* that inaugurated the Montmartre Hippodrome, the future site of the Gaumont-Palace. The following year, he was head of wardrobe for a variety show, *Avariétés de l'année*, at the Bataclan theatre. His flair for putting on a show also led to work on the Boeuf-Gras parade, a traditional carnival of butchers from Paris' La Villette district, as well as horse shows at the Palais Hippique, which were restaged in the so-called Hall of Machines at the Universal Exposition. In 1905, Gaumont hired him to assist Alice Guy on her very first film at the new glass-roofed Gaumont studios, *La Esmeralda*, based on Victor Hugo's novel *The Hunchback of Notre Dame*. Jasset, 10 years older than Alice, was charged with directing the film's many extras. The following year, his expertise in crowd scenes was also put to good use during the filming of Alice's *Life of Christ*. He is also known to have worked on the shooting of *Descente dans les mines de Fumay* [Descent into the Fumay Mines], which took place in his hometown, although no copies of this film have since been found.

When Victor Bachy interviewed Alice in the early 1960s, she recalled her collaboration with Jasset as follows: "He was truly an extraordinary artist. He had a gift for placing people, colours, for '*mettre en scène*' [composition], which is very important to me. Unfortunately, I asked Gaumont to take him on as an assistant without knowing him personally. I'm not trying to be unpleasant, but it must be said: he was a very peculiar man. He could never hire anyone for a crowd scene without undressing them first. Which shocked me. Many things happened that I can't even talk about. Finally, Gaumont was forced to throw him out. Naturally, he was incredibly angry and blamed me." Shortly after this interview, Alice ended up revealing, on Flemish television, details of the unsavoury episode, in which Jasset and his wife took advantage of a minor, a girl of 14. Her grandmother had complained to Alice, who was horrified and alerted Gaumont to the couple's activities.

After a brief spell at the fledgling company Éclipse, Jasset joined the Éclair Company in 1908 and directed a Beethoven biopic starring the young Harry Baur, who went on to play the composer again for director Abel Gance in 1938. But it was his next film that made him a part of cinema history. By adapting the popular American dime novels featuring master detective Nick Carter for the screen, Jasset was the first to bring the sequel to the big screen, building whole series of films around a single central character. He sailed from one hit to another with *Rifle Bill, King of the Prairie*, *Meskal the Smuggler*, and *Morgan the Pirate*, culminating with the adaptation of the proto-Fantômas figure Zigomar, a master criminal in a red hood. Jasset immediately followed this up with a cross-over picture, *Zigomar v. Nick Carter*, in 1912.

In June 1913, immediately after wrapping the first episode of yet another serial, *Protéa* – which featured the first heroine in a catsuit, a precursor to Feuillade's *Irma Vep* – Jasset was suddenly taken ill, dying three months later at the age of 51.

Ironically enough, Georges Sadoul attributed *La Esmeralda* and *Life of Christ* to Jasset in his monumental history of cinema. But this equally monumental error was to spark Alice's crusade for her body of work to be recognized.

Louis Feuillade

Born on 19 February 1873 in Lunel, in the southern coastal region of Hérault, Louis was the fifth child of Marie Avesque and wine merchant Barthélémy Feuillade. After secondary schooling in Carcassonne, he obtained his baccalaureate degree in classics in Montpellier – taken as proof, in 1891, of a superior intellect – before fulfilling his mandatory military service by spending four years in a company of dragoons. Two months after his discharge, in 1895, he married Léontine Jaujou, who in 1903 became the mother of his only child, Isabelle. At the age of 22, Louis joined the family business, which left him time to pursue his true passions: watching bullfights and reciting his own poems, including "La Bicyclette" ["The Bicycle"], which charmed audiences at the Vélo-Club Lunellois. Following the death of his mother, and soon afterwards his father, in February 1898, it took him just a few weeks to leave the family business to his brothers and set out for Paris. He was 25 and dreamed of a career in literature or journalism. Thanks to his family's Catholic connections, he immediately found a job at Maison de la Bonne Presse – the future Bayard Presse – which published the newspaper *La Croix*, where the volatile Feuillade worked in the accounts department. The cinematograph had not received a very good press at Bonne Presse, ever since the fire at the Bazar de la Charité, which the publisher had sponsored, but Louis did at least manage to befriend the head of the "projections department", Michel Coissac, future author of the very first history of cinema (1925), before his irascible and tempestuous nature led him to tender his resignation in 1902, whereupon he returned to the wine business and launched his own "illustrated political" weekly, *La Tomate*. The venture ended in commercial failure in late 1903, but he soon landed himself an editorial post at *La Revue mondiale*, a highly conservative periodical founded by the vice-president of the Paris Toro-Club, a society of bullfighting enthusiasts, of which Louis was an avid member. He also contributed to the daily paper *Le Soleil* and the magazine *Torero*. Along with fellow Toro-Club member Étienne Arnaud, Louis tried his hand at writing for the stage, with little success, but another bullfighting aficionado, André Heuzé, dangled the prospect of a new potential goldmine in front of him: cinema. Heuzé was already writing scripts for Pathé, and advised his friend to offer his services to "a little company up in Belleville" called Gaumont, whose owner was close friends with Feuillade's old pal Michel Coissac. Thanks to Coissac's schmoozing, Feuillade's pitches landed on Gaumont's desk, from where they made their way to that of the managing director, Alice Guy. And so it was that in the final months of 1905, Alice met Louis Feuillade. The apprentice scriptwriter emerged from the interview with a salary three times what he was getting from *La Revue mondiale*. A filmmaker was born.

Alice and Louis were the same age, Louis her elder by only five months. Though the two had very different characters, they shared a deep bond. "Mademoiselle Guy was a highly likeable individual, and very intelligent, with a strong understanding of what contemporary cinema was," Feuillade would later remark. In return, Alice would come to describe Louis as "an excellent comrade", and his tireless work as principal scriptwriter eventually eventually resulted in 150 films, at a rate of two or three a week, most of which were directed by either Étienne Arnaud or Alice herself.

According to his biographer Francis Lacassin, Mademoiselle Guy's assistant began directing in March 1906, at her boss' insistence. Less than a year later, Alice was preparing to leave France. Who would her successor be? The way Alice told the story on Belgian TV in 1964: "Gaumont told me, 'I'm going to get your successor from Pathé.' And I said, 'Why Pathé? You've got Feuillade right here, he's an excellent director.'"

On 7 January 1907, Feuillade assumed the formal duties of Gaumont Studios' managing director, later becoming its artistic director. Meanwhile his financial position had significantly improved. From the cramped apartment on Rue Laumière, at the foot of Buttes-Chaumont, he moved to a detached house named "Les Roses" in the eastern suburb of Chelles, later moving to an even larger villa in Poissy. Following the death, from T.B., of his first wife Léontine in the south of France in 1909, the director married his second wife, Georgette Lagneau, in 1921.

In the years that followed, Feuillade would explore every conceivable genre, from comedy to period drama to social affairs, adventures to westerns, fantasy to melodrama, burlesque to mythology, chalking up several hundred films, both short and long. But as Gaumont's head of production, he was also in charge of hiring other directors, most of whom would go down in film history. In addition to his friend Étienne Arnaud, other notable discoveries included Émile Cohl (inventor of the animated film), Jean Durand, Léonce Perret, Henri Fescourt, Léon Poirier, Jacques Feyder, and Raymond Bernard. But if Feuillade's name is better remembered today than any of theirs, it was thanks to his shrewd instincts. As early as 1908, Victorin Jasset, working at Éclair, had paved the way for a serial form about crime with his *Nick Carter* and *Zigomar* series. These left audiences wanting more, so Charles Pathé sought to acquire the rights to another successful novel series: Pierre Souvestre and Marcel Allain's books about the master criminal Fantômas. Allain played hard to get with the studios, and Gaumont secured the property by tripling Pathé's offer. Feuillade followed through, and the series' first instalment hit the screens in May 1913. It was an instant smash-hit, even internationally. Film after film followed. Poets of the time – Apollinaire, Cendrars, Cocteau – hailed the cinematic adventures of this genius of crime, but the First World War put a brutal halt to proceedings. René Navarre, the actor who played Fantômas, was conscripted, while Feuillade, the former dragoon, was exempted on the grounds of his weak heart.

Meanwhile, the battle for screen dominance raged on. Pathé triumphed worldwide with his transatlantic series *Les Mystères de New York*, featuring Pearl White, while cinema audiences were treated to Feuillade and Gaumont's rival offering in 1915. So what if men were being mobilized? Feuillade picked out the actress Musidora as his heroine, dressed her in a sleek, black bodysuit, and dubbed her Irma Vep, anagrammatic head of the gang that lent its name to their new series: *Les Vampires*. These ten films would, however, prove to be Feuillade's *other* masterpiece, since in the following year the 12-episode *Judex* (1916) confirmed his dominance of the pulp genre. But although this son of the provinces saw his star outshine those of other successful directors until the end of the war, he subsequently fell out of favour with a new generation of critics and filmmakers who now conceived of cinema as an avant-garde art form.

By the early 1920s, Feuillade was spending most of his time at the Villa Blandine in Nice, where a combination of beautiful natural locations and the Gaumont studios on Chemin de Carras amply supplied all he needed to shoot his films, only travelling to Paris for press screenings of his latest creations. In July 1924, he was on location at Eden Roc, on Cap d'Antibes, shooting scenes for *Stigmate*, a six-episode drama that he co-directed with Maurice Champreux – his cinematographer since 1919 and, since 1922, his son-in-law. A few days after work had finished on the fourth episode, he fell victim to acute appendicitis, which developed into peritonitis. On 26 February 1925, at the age of 52, the man Lacassin called the "master of lions and vampires" passed away.

Étienne Arnaud

Étienne Joseph Germain Arnaud was born on 4 September 1879 in Villeneuve-lès-Béziers in the southern province of Hérault. He was the second child of Louise *née* Castel, 27, and farmer and landowner Jacques Arnaud, 28. After his baccalaureate and compulsory military service, Étienne moved to Paris to study law, unsuccessfully working on his doctorate until 1906, from which one might surmise that his many supposedly extracurricular activities left him little time to study. For no sooner did the 19-year-old reach the capital than he gave free rein to pursuing his passions. An aficionado of the bullring, he was among the founding members of Paris' Toro-Club at a time when bullfighting faced opposition in the press in northern France, and animal charities were actively campaigning to ban it nationwide. Battles over laws and ethics pitted the *aficionados* against the anti-*corridas* for almost a century, coming to an end only in 1951 with the Law of 24 April, which compromised by allowing certain cities to organize *corridas* so long as "an uninterrupted tradition could be invoked". It was in this combative atmosphere of controversy that Étienne befriended his fellow enthusiasts André Heuzé and Louis Feuillade, with whom he shared his other great passion: writing. And although he had put his pen to work for the taurine cause, he dreamed first and foremost of tickling the funnybone. As early as 1900, his contribution to Alphonse Allais' publication *Sourire* [Smile] prefigured the whimsical style that would define his career as a singer, which his biographer, Bernard Bastide, has carefully traced from late 1901 to the spring of 1906. From the Quat'z-Arts cabaret in Montmartre to La Lune Rousse on Rue Pigalle by way of Les Noctambules on the Left Bank, we can follow the path of a young artist surely destined for a theatrical future. Friendship would decide otherwise, however, thanks to Feuillade, with whom Étienne had already shared a few journalistic escapades – from the satirical rag *La Tomate* to *La Revue mondiale*, founded by another member of the Toro-Club. It was Heuzé, already a scriptwriter for Pathé, who advised Louis' friend to seek his fortune with his direct competitor, Gaumont. After Mademoiselle Guy had hired him on the spot, Louis Feuillade recommended his pal Étienne Arnaud to turn his stories into moving images in late 1905. So it was that the two men hit upon a winning formula for splitting the proceeds from this new, unexpected source: one would write, and the other direct. Fourteen months later, when Alice Guy left France for the U.S., moving pictures were central to their artistic and professional concerns. Louis took over Alice's duties, Étienne married her assistant, and together the duo expanded the Gaumont catalogue at the rate of a film or more per week. Specializing at first in farces, comedies, and special-effects films, they turned towards drama and period pieces after the arrival of directors Émile Cohl and Jean Durand, with a predilection for biopics of famous people from history – Columbus; the composers Lully, Mozart, and Chopin; the poet André Chénier; the medieval politician Étienne Marcel; the 16th-century potter and natural scientist Bernard Palissy. Arnaud's own biographer unearthed detailed itineraries tracing his many travels – and if there was one thing Étienne loved, it was travel. On location for his films, he could variously be found at Le Havre, Antibes (on the Riviera), Carcassonne, Fontainebleau, Biarritz, on the island of Belle-Île (off the Breton coast), in the popular holiday village of Vernet-les-Bains in the Pyrenees, at the Breton seaside resort of Concarneau, in Saumur, Azay-le-Rideau, Juan-les-Pins, Cannes, Monte Carlo, Marseille, Tours, Annecy, Gisors… By the time Étienne Arnaud left Gaumont in late 1911, he had made more than 230 films. He had already considered a parting of the ways from the studios in Belleville as early as 1908, when Pathé, via his friend Heuzé, sought to poach his talents. But after a quick calculation, Yvonne and Étienne figured that the percentages would be better if he stuck with Gaumont. In the end, it was the fledgling company Éclair that managed to lure him away from the Cité Elgé by promising him America. The young couple and their four-year-old daughter Arlette landed in Manhattan in 1912. Étienne took over as artistic director of the Éclair studios, founded in Fort Lee, at the same time as pursuing his directing career. He fitted into the small community of mostly French expatriate studio personnel, reuniting with Alice Guy, among others. The letters Bernard Bastide uncovered leave no doubt as to his American ambitions – both artistic and, above all, financial. Étienne was there to put away "marbles in his safe", as he put it, seizing on location shoots all around the U.S., from the Niagara Falls to Florida, by way of Louisiana and Mississippi, to enjoy "at Éclair's expense, vacations worthy of a rich New York banker" – though he never stinted in his work: 23 one- and two-reelers in 1912, 17 in 1913, and another six in 1914, before his American sojourn was brutally cut short by conflict in Europe.

The history of the "seventh art" in America owes to Arnaud the big-screen adaptation of Edgar Allan Poe's "The Raven", the second version of Washington Irving's "The Legend of Sleepy Hollow", and the third to feature the legend of Robin Hood. We also owe him a silent musical, *Oh, You Ragtime!*, but above all *Saved from the Titanic*, which hit screens less than a month after the infamous disaster. Top of the bill was actress Dorothy Gibson, an actual survivor of the shipwreck, whom her lover and producer, Jules Brulatour, had persuaded to relive the tragedy. Far from being cathartic, the shoot sent the star into a deep depression, and she would never again appear in front of the camera. The 11-minute film was an instant worldwide hit, but the fire that devastated the Éclair studios in March 1914 destroyed all copies. None have been found, even in 2021.

The First World War sounded the death knell for Arnaud's career. Mobilized at the age of 36 and sent to the Meurthe-et-Moselle front, he was captured by the Germans on 27 August 1915. He was repatriated in July 1918 and discharged in February 1919. Would he return to making movies? The war had upended everything: the structures, modes, and means of production. And he could no longer count on Feuillade, then at the height of his career, since the two were not on good terms. The man who had once been his friend had taken his departure for America as a personal betrayal. So Arnaud turned to the man who had introduced them all to cinema in the first place: André Heuzé – though it was to theatre that these two reunited friends devoted the years that followed. From 1922 to 1939, Arnaud wrote or co-wrote over 15 plays. Still with Heuzé in the 1930s, he shared a co-writing credit with him on half a dozen films, including such racy titles as *Mam'zelle Spahi* and *La Fille de la Madelon*. He co-wrote one final script with Heuzé in 1938, *L'Enfant de troupe*, then seemed to entirely drop off the radar of artistic creation, at the age of 59. He died 17 years later on 10 March 1955, at home on Rue Manin, a few hundred feet from the studios where he had made his debut the previous century.

Herbert Blaché

Herbert Reginald Gaston Blaché-Bolton was born on 5 October 1882, in London, to a French father, hatter Victor Blaché, a native of Mont-de-Marchan in the Landes region on France's Atlantic coast, and an English mother, actress Mary Elizabeth Bolton, originally from Preston in Lancashire, allegedly of aristocratic descent. They were 24 and 22. In her biographical novel, Emmanuelle Gaume hints at an itinerant life through Europe, fleeing parental ire from both sides of the family, as both plied trades that could be practised anywhere. Following legal proceedings in 1902, Herbert was granted permission to use his mother's name, and thenceforth he would sign all his official papers with both. According to Herbert himself, he finished his studies in England so he could immediately launch a professional career with the British branch of Gaumont, which since 1898 had been run by Alfred Claude Bromhead, then 26. Herbert, only slightly younger, became his assistant. Although he tried his hand at being a cameraman, it was for his fluency in English, French, and German that his contribution to the business was primarily valued, and this caught the eye of Léon Gaumont, who offered him the management of his Berlin branch. Prior to taking up that post, however, he was invited to the Elgé studios in Paris to finish his training. That was where he first met Alice Guy, and where Gaumont asked him, on her behalf and at short notice, to fill in as her cameraman.

In her memoirs, Alice wrote of this first encounter as follows: "He later told me he had never met a woman who left such a cold and distant first impression. No doubt he was right. As a young woman constantly having to assert her authority in her job, I deliberately avoided all familiarity." During the summer of 1906, while shooting *Mireille* in Saintes-Maries-de-la-Mer, a certain familiarity nevertheless seemed to set in between Alice and the man Feuillade nicknamed "the baronet". When the troupe left Saintes-Maries, first for Nîmes before catching the train back to Paris, Alice could not contain her emotion: "We wanted to revisit the Roman amphitheatre in Nîmes. The setting was romantic. That evening made us regret our forthcoming separation. I did not expect to see Herbert Blaché again." No sooner was he back in Paris than the young man set out for Norway to film the coronation of the new king and queen, then took up his post in Berlin. But, as Alice wrote: "We are but playthings in the hands of fate." In Germany, Herbert's clients were experiencing technical difficulties in synchronizing the chronophone. During a 1964 televised interview, Alice recalled that "Gaumont was annoyed he couldn't go himself. He told me to. 'But I don't speak German. I don't know Germany at all!' 'Blaché will be your guide.'" As they roamed from Dresden to Nuremberg by way of Köln and Frankfurt, Herbert proved to be a smooth operator. As Alice put it in 1964: "We didn't get married right then and there, but he did propose. I told him, 'Look, I need some time to think…' I didn't really want to leave France. Indeed, above all, I didn't really want to marry an Englishman. English people aren't very nice…" And she finished off her reminiscence with a little laugh.

The date of their marriage is recorded as 6 March 1907 at the town hall of Paris' 19th arrondissement. Alice was 34 and Herbert 25. The witnesses were Charles Blaché, the groom's brother, and Marie Guy, the bride's mother. Just a few days later, by way of a honeymoon, the couple set sail for New York. "The crossing was miserable," Alice later commented. Seasickness was the primary cause. A certain melancholy also hung over the trip. To follow her husband on the mission with which Gaumont had entrusted him – representing the chronophone on American soil – she had left behind everything she knew in France.

Initially cloistered in Cleveland, far from the heart of the film business, in 1908 the couple moved to Flushing, where Gaumont had just built a modest studio for shooting "phono-scenes" intended for the American market. Herbert was appointed director of the studio. That same year, the couple's first child, Simone, was born. Two years later, Alice founded her own production company, Solax. In 1912 – an eventful year – Herbert left Gaumont to join forces with Alice, and Solax had its own studios built in Fort Lee, New Jersey, where the family now welcomed yet another member,

Reginald. It was also in 1912 that Herbert directed his first film, *Robin Hood*, in collaboration with an old acquaintance, Étienne Arnaud, who had recently arrived in the U.S. Herbert directed his first notable film, *The Fight for Millions*, for Solax in 1913. That same year, he made two more for Solax and, in his first act of infidelity to the family business, a short film for Pathé entitled *A Slave for Satan*.

In 1914, he made three more films for Solax, including *The Million Dollar Robbery*, which Alice later claimed as her own work. Then Herbert founded his own company, the U.S. Amusement Corporation, directing two films for them before joining World Film and the Sun Photoplay Company for two more films distributed by the Warner Company. In 1915, Alice and Herbert went into partnership with Popular Players and Plays, founded by Adolph Zukor, for which Herbert made five films that year, one of them co-written with Alice – *The Song of the Wage Slave* – followed by two more in 1916. In 1917, it was his own company's turn again: the U.S. Amusement Corporation produced all four of his films that year, one of which he co-directed with his wife. *A Man and the Woman* was Alice's adaptation of Émile Zola's novel *Nana*. In the same year, she directed one of the biggest hits of her husband's company, *House of Cards*, starring the actress Catherine Calvert. Herbert shot *Think It Over* with the same actress immediately afterwards. For the Blachés, it was the beginning of the end: "My husband suffered a mid-life crisis," wrote Alice, "and went to California with his leading lady."

In 1918, Herbert directed one last film on the East Coast – *Loaded Dice*, for Pathé – before heading off to California, where he made two films for the Metro Pictures Corporation. The year after that saw him add seven films for the same company to his resumé. For the last of these, *The Brat*, he hired Alice as an assistant when she came to California with the children. She was now 46. It was to be the last time she ever set foot on a film set. Her career was over, but at 37, Herbert's star was rising. 1920 saw him make no less than six features: four produced or distributed by Metro – among them *The Saphead* with Buster Keaton – and a fifth shot in New York. The sixth, *Tarnished Reputations*, is credited as being co-directed by Alice, a fact she neglects to mention in her memoirs. 1921 saw a dip in Herbert's output: two short films for an obscure East Coast production company, and a single feature for the Realart Pictures Corporation, followed by a single short in 1922. But starting in 1923, thanks to Carl Laemmle, who hired him at Universal, Herbert returned to the director's chair with five features that year, followed by two the next, another two in 1925, and just one in 1926. In 1927… nothing.

Co-directed with Henry MacRae for Universal in 1928, *Burning the Wind*, featuring a young Boris Karloff, was Herbert Blaché's final film. Meanwhile, Carl Laemmle had slowly lost control of his company. In 1928, the producer and Herbert's champion was replaced by his own son. Laemmle Junior was 20, and was cleaning house with the arrival of the talkies. Herbert was 46 – the same age Alice had been when her career had come to an end. Between 1912 and 1928, Herbert made a total of 55 films before abruptly disappearing from the annals of cinema. His divorce from Alice was finalized on 24 March 1923 (or 1922); his second marriage was to Nora Hallgran, with whom he ran a lighting business (selling lamps and lampshades) on Melrose Avenue, the couple going on to reinvent themselves as almond growers outside San Francisco before finally settling in Santa Monica, California, as antique dealers. In 1951, they appeared on a list of Hollywood names denounced for ties to the Communist Party.

Herbert Blaché died in Santa Monica on 23 October 1953. Emmanuelle Gaume discovered a letter Alice wrote at the time: "I have never been able to forget that we spent ten happy years together, and he was the father of my children. Although he remarried, I always thought of him as my husband and his partner as nothing but a concubine. May God forgive him, as I myself have done." A decade later, when Belgian historian Victor Bachy asked her about her husband's fate after Solax, Alice summed up their shared adventure in a few lapidary sentences: "Monsieur Blaché was in California where all the studios were going. He worked there, but in reality, he had completely withdrawn from business. And there he died."

Marquis Folco de Baroncelli-Javon

In the 12th century, a Baroncelli, sovereign of Fiesole in Tuscany, fought so valiantly for Otto IV that the Holy Roman Emperor supposedly knelt beside him on the battlefield and, dipping an imperial finger in the dying man's wound, drew three bloody stripes on his shield: "Henceforth, this shall be your family's coat-of-arms." Three centuries later, a Baroncelli took part in the assassination of Giuliano de' Medici in the Duomo of Florence, Santa Maria del Fiore. This Florentine banking family next turns up in the Papal States. In Avignon, the Baroncellis acquired buildings that would become the Hôtel de Javon, a stately town dwelling, and then the Palais du Roure. In the 17th century, Pope Leo X granted the family the marquisate of Javon in the Vaucluse. In the 18th century, the King of France confirmed the title, which would never again leave the family. Skip forward a few generations, and on 1 November 1869, in Aix-en-Provence, Marie Lucien Gabriel Folco was born, the eldest of what would be nine children. His father Raymond was the son of the then-marquis, and his mother a descendant of an old Provençal family, the Chazelles-Lunacs. The future marquis was raised in large part by his maternal grandmother, a woman with the "*fé di biou*" – the Occitan expression for someone of bullish temperament. Every summer, she would take her young grandson with her to Saintes-Maries-de-la-Mer in the Camargue. She died when Folco was 17. He was soon back in Avignon, where his grandfather Gabriel was a patron of the *félibre* poets, who wrote in Occitan. Foremost among them was Frédéric Mistral, who would go on to win the Nobel Prize for literature. Folco met Mistral at the family home in 1889. The following year, having started a job at the local tax office, the 21-year-old discovered that Mistral had appointed him editor-in-chief of a Provençal-language newspaper, *L'Aiòli*. Its offices were set up in the Hôtel de Javon, with Baroncelli Senior as its patron. Starting in the autumn of 1892, Folco fell into the habit of taking regular trips to the Camargue – a journey of almost 40 miles on horseback from Avignon. Two years later, now possessed of a few horses, and embarked on the famous Gypsy Pilgrimage in Saintes-Maries-de-la-Mer since May, he made the acquaintance of Henriette Constantin, the daughter of a vineyard owner in Châteauneuf-du-Pape. They were married the following year. The last stop on their honeymoon was the Camargue. A few months later, the couple settled in Saintes-Maries-de-la-Mer. Folco had decided to devote himself to his own herd, raising both bulls and horses, with the goal of reviving the stock of Camargue purebreds. In 1899, his time at *L'Aiòli* came to an end, though Folco's enthusiasm for Provençal poetry never faltered. The herd meanwhile grew and spread – the Baroncellis took over the Mas de L'Amarée, a farm and ranch of almost 500 acres – and enhanced its reputation. Their bull Provenço would long remain a legend for any Camargue *afeciounado*. Three daughters were born, but during hard weather – winters in the Camargue are especially harsh – Henriette would take refuge with the girls in Avignon or at her father's vineyard, Fines Roches. So it was that in just under a decade, Folco de Baroncelli established himself as a first-rate cattleman, but also as an ambassador for the renaissance of Provençal culture. And such was the scene in 1905 when he first conceived of reaching out to the showman William F. Cody. Better known as Buffalo Bill, Cody was then touring Europe with his monumental "Wild West Show", a spectacle that thought nothing of roping in the skills of local riders, be they Cossacks, Bedouins, or gauchos – and so why not the Camargue's *gardians*? Folco duly travelled to Paris to offer his services. But though the Marquis de Baroncelli never did get to meet Colonel Cody, he was introduced to Joë Hamman, who would shortly go on to invent the movie western in France. Hamman in turn introduced him to his friends Jacob White Eyes and Sam Lone Bear, two Native Americans from Cody's show, with whom he established a lasting friendship, the two of them frequent visitors at Saintes-Maries. A lengthy correspondence followed, and Folco conceived a passion for Native American culture, which made him one of the first so-called *indianers* in France. The stage was thus set on 15 May 1906 when the Marquis de Baroncelli received a letter, on Gaumont & Co.-headed paper, signed by Louis Feuillade, who introduced himself as the editor of *Torero* and mentioned a few of the *félibre* poet friends they had in common before getting down to business: might the marquis be willing to rent out his herd to be "cinematographed"? "We would like many horses, many bulls," Feuillade added, explaining that the footage would be part of a film adaptation of Mistral's *Mirèio* (*Mireille* in French, as in Gounod's opera). The price the cattleman quoted must have suited Gaumont, for a fortnight later, a troupe headed by Alice Guy settled in at Saintes-Maries-de-la-Mer. Alice must have felt at home; in Chile, her parents had been friends with a certain French consul named Baroncelli-Javon, who turned out to be the marquis' uncle. Alice was of the same generation as her hosts – she being 33 and the marquis just five years older. Later, in the U.S., Alice would recall the cattleman's interests and send him postcards of "Cowboys and Indians".

By June, the entire crew was back in Paris. But the footage would never see the light of day. In October 1906, Alice wrote to the marquis explaining that "our lack of success is due to the poor quality of the cameras, which let in light and lacked stability". According to film historian Maurice Gianati, a short film entitled *Drame d'amour* [Tragedy of Love] nevertheless survives. It was not until 1908, under the direction of Henri Cain for Les Films d'Art, that *Mireille* would at last be brought to the screen. During the shoot, the Marquis de Baroncelli first met the woman who would become his muse, the poet and journalist Jeanne de Flandreysy. She later published a book of Folco's poems before buying the Hôtel de Javon – renamed the Palais du Roure by her close friend Mistral – in order to turn it into a Provençal "Villa Medici". In its archives may be found a full-length photo of Jeanne, Folco, and Joë Hamman all posing in authentic Native American chieftain garb.

Although the footage Alice brought back from Saintes-Maries would never be seen, the shoot proved the first of many for Folco and the Camargue. From then on, directors would film on location in the open air, and to the lens, the wide-open spaces of the Camargue were like no other. Over the next four decades, Folco de Baroncelli would be the premier supplier of horses, bulls, and *gardians* – often dressed up as cowboys – to all the film crews who ventured to those lands. The most frequent of these cinematic visitors was doubtless his friend Joë Hamman, who, as both actor and director, notched up over 20 credits in films shot in the Camargue between 1909 and 1950, with Folco himself appearing as an extra in some of these, including *Le Réveil* [The Awakening] in 1925, directed by his younger brother Jacques, whose son Jean would also go on to enjoy a filmmaking career.

Marquis Folco de Baroncelli-Javon died on 15 December 1943 at the age of 74, whereupon the title passed to his brother Jacques. The aristocratic cattleman left an indelible mark on Camargue memory and culture. To this day, his headstone stands facing the sea, along the pilgrimage route in Sainte-Maries-de-la-Mer, on the site of his final farmstead, Le Simbèu, later dynamited by the occupying German forces, and now on the empty ground between two campgrounds.

Ernest Grenier

In a set of manuscript notes titled "Les Premiers Clients" ["The First Clients"], Francis Lacassin wrote that "Alice Guy tells the story of how the Greniers invited her over when they were at the fair in Rouen", going on to record the filmmaker's words: "Theirs was a large family. Six or seven children, I think. They had wonderful trailers, very modern for the time; the mother was the cashier; father and son saw to the tent, which was spacious, and to the projection; the daughters were on stage [during the intermission], dancing and playing instruments, etc. They were tremendously successful and invited me to watch one of my own films, *Le Matelas* [The Mattress]. I was treated like a queen. At the end of the presentation, they gave me a wonderful bouquet of roses. The Greniers were also our first chronophone clients. Afterwards, I heard that one of the daughters became a nun!"

This eye-witness description of a fairground family and its division of labour would come up again in Alice's memoirs, with the exception of the twist at the end. She refers to a film whose complete title is *Le Matelas alcoolique* [The Drunken Mattress], sometimes retitled *Le Matelas épileptique*, which allows us to date the screening to 1906. There was in fact a Théâtre Grenier at the Saint-Romain fair, held every year in late autumn in Rouen, the capital of the Norman *département* of Seine-Maritime. The fair, also known as the Foire du Pardon [Fair of Forgiveness], can be traced back to the Middle Ages and is the second largest in France.

After the cinematograph made a sensation at the Salon Indien in 1895, the Théâtre Grenier added it as an attraction the following autumn. Not content to merely project films, paterfamilias Ernest Grenier made his own "moving images, brought to life by electricity" – local news and human interest stories, to be precise. A poster promoting the Théâtre électrique Grenier at a 1901 fair in Orléans proclaimed that "At every show, Monsieur Grenier will project local scenes wherein audience members may be surprised to find their friends have, unbeknownst to them, become part of the act". It was specified that these scenes were "striking and startling" and that "these wondrous shows would end with over 900 metres of photographic footage of the *Life of Joan of Arc*". There were three one-hour shows daily, six on Sundays.

When Alice went to the Saint-Romain fair in 1906, the Théâtre Grenier no longer had a monopoly on such attractions. The Cirque de Rouen and the Théâtre de l'Alhambra also occasionally projected films. In 1907, the Théâtre Grenier ceased its cinematographic activities at the Saint-Romain fair, and as early as the following year, a downtown businessman got the idea to transform his shop, L'Innovation, into a theatre exclusively dedicated to projecting films. This was the first cinema in Rouen. The pioneering Théâtre Grenier is thus an exemplar in the history of early cinema – in its distribution system, expansion, and financial viability – in the days before such fairground diversions found a permanent home in dedicated theatres.

Jean-Luc Godard dates the history of cinema to the first screening that sold tickets, on 28 December 1895. On that day, when the Lumières rented out the Salon Indien, they achieved a double revolution, at once showing moving pictures to the public and inventing their commercial exploitation. To this extent, their policy was based on a monopoly: the Lumières sold neither their devices nor their films, and thereby retained control over their projections at rented locations. Their junior rivals – Gaumont, Pathé, Méliès – pursued a different strategy, seeking to sell both content and machinery to anyone who was buying, and of these, the first in the queue were fairground owners. At a time when such intellectuals as Ludovic Halévy, a friend of the artist Degas, were openly hostile to these "empty inventions that in any case will vanish after a few months", who could have imagined the cinematograph as a dramatic art instead of a fleeting attraction? And fleeting attractions have always been the domain of the itinerant. "Fit only for the Fête de Neuilly," as one well-dressed lady's damning verdict had put it, upon exiting the Lumières' show at the Salon Indien, to journalist Louis Forest at *L'Illustration* magazine. Had fairground operators not seized upon it, the cinematograph might indeed have remained "an invention without a future", as Louis Lumière remarked.

Méliès knew full well that, even though he had his own theatre for showing his films, the new medium had the potential to reach a great many people. And where did the masses flock to, if not to fairs, tents, and travelling shows? In 1927, the magician told the story of how he convinced a circus-owner from Paris' Foire du Trône, the largest fair in France, to project his *Trip to the Moon* by offering to let him borrow the film for a night for a test screening. "If it's a flop, I'll take it back at midnight, no questions asked. If it's a hit, I'll sell it to you." To which the roustabout replied, "That works for me!" And that very night, according to Méliès, "It was madness. No one had ever seen a film like it before. In short," he concluded, "my roustabout raked in more than he ever had before. He was beaming. So imagine how I felt! I was transfixed by the effect my film had on an actual audience." Nor did Charles Pathé look down his nose at fairground attractions. After all, that was where his phonographs and, later, kinetoscopes had got their first outings; where he'd first become aware of the public's liking for, even infatuation with, moving pictures; and where he'd learned to build an empire on illusions.

The first filmmakers, then, belonged to the world of strongmen, acrobats, clowns, fortune tellers, and lion-tamers. Jacques Deslandes was the first to study the phenomenon in his 1968 *Histoire comparée du Cinéma*, [A Comparative History of Cinema], in which he listed eight fairground operators who, beginning in 1896, reinvented themselves as film exhibitors, including the famous Théâtre Grenier, so dear to Alice. By 1897, there were 19 of them; by 1898, 29; and on the eve of the new century, there were already 47 roaming France with their own projectors and films.

In the self-serving company history that Gaumont published in the 1930s, no reference is made to this first generation of exhibitors, only to the turn that film took towards permanent theatres. "As soon as the success of the cinematograph seemed assured, M. Gaumont deemed it useful for the company to have at its disposal a certain number of projection rooms that would enable his customers to see how films should be shown [...] It seemed to him, and rightly so, that to attract choice audiences, he would need theatres luxuriously and tastefully appointed to desirable standards of cleanliness and comfort." In 1908, Gaumont purchased one of the first permanent cinemas in Paris, to debut the chronophone, and then, in 1911, he bought the 6,000-seat Montmartre Hippodrome, converting it into the Gaumont-Palace. As early as 1906, Pathé was urging entrepreneurs to operate in a theatre bearing the Pathé name on Rue Montmartre in Paris. At the same time, Gaumont and Pathé switched to the American model and began renting their films out instead of selling them.

The invention of the movie theatre was a way for the owners of the means of production to take back control of the entire economic system of film exhibition. The unregulated, unpredictable fairground operators were replaced by managers of permanent cinemas. Gone was the risk that an exhibitor might suddenly decide to stop showing films and bring back the bearded lady because she proved more profitable.

Gaumont and Pathé effectively invented the business model of "vertical integration". Alice wasn't around in France to witness this industrial transformation of a society and business founded on spectacle. She would only encounter it in the U.S., where the Patent Wars over exclusivity raged throughout the 1910s, and where her independence, first as a producer, then as a director, would be taken away. The happy, rough-and-ready days of the fair were already a thing of the past.

Simone Blaché

In her memoirs, Alice Guy mentions her children only in passing: "My two children had just had a bad case of measles." This happened sometime between 1915 and 1917, part of a scene that introduces the family's move to North Carolina for a few brief months. Only in a footnote supplied by the book's editor, Claire Clouzot, are readers informed of the birth of the filmmaker's children a few years earlier.

Simone was born on 6 September 1908 in New York. The children of successful producer-directors, Simone and her younger brother Reginald seemed to grow up with all the comfortable trappings of middle-class prosperity. Wet nurses, nannies, and then boarding school formed the first years of their lives, from the big house in Fort Lee to the tropical bungalows of Hollywood. The Blachés' elder child even appeared in a few of her mother's films. Simone was 14 when her parents divorced, she and her brother following their mother to France, where they settled in Nice.

As she explained to Francis Lacassin in the 1970s, after her father drove the family companies to bankruptcy with disastrous stock market investments, he paid his alimony only intermittently before stopping altogether. Despite help from her sister Julia, Alice was forced to sell her furs, jewels, furniture, and all the last vestiges of her former fortune in order to get by in Nice. When Simone turned 18, she joined the working world and found a job in a bank, but in 1932, mother and daughter left Nice for Paris. Bilingual and an American citizen, Simone was immediately hired by United Artists as a secretary in the publicity department, then held the same position at Fox from 1936 to 1940. When war broke out, Fox removed to Bordeaux, but Simone wished to stay in Paris with her mother. That summer, she was a telephone operator at Time Life, before joining the American Embassy in Paris in September. In February 1941, the Embassy moved to Vichy; Simone was then secretary to the commercial attaché. The Blaché ladies stayed in Pétain's capital for ten months, until the diplomatic corps was transferred to Bern. Simone and Alice remained in Switzerland until 1947, as part of the Embassy's extended family, then moved back to Paris for another five years.

In an era when society still condemned lesbianism, Simone never had any official relationships. Despite her fashionable haircuts and stylishness, she was thus able to cultivate for the public at large the image of an old maid, forever chaperoned by her mother.

In 1952, she returned to America after an absence of 30 years. Simone was stationed in Washington, but two years later, mother and daughter were in Paris again for four more years. In 1958, Simone, still with the American Embassy, was assigned to her final posting, this time in Brussels. But in 1964, Alice had her first stroke. Simone decided to retire and go back to the U.S. to be near her brother and look after her mother. By the time Alice died in 1968, Simone had spent 58 unbroken years with her mother.

When Victor Bachy asked Alice about her daughter in 1953, she replied: "I have a daughter who hates movies because they took over my life back there in Fort Lee. Reporters were always stopping by, people came to ask me for information on this and that. She took quite a dislike to all that." And as the nonagenarian lady brought up her fruitless quest to track down all her American films, she concluded: "But my daughter doesn't see things the same way. She says to me, 'Forget all that, leave it all behind, toss it on the fire.'"

However, when Claire Clouzot contacted her over a decade later while readying Alice's memoirs for French publication, Simone generously supplied some carefully preserved photos and documents. She closes a letter dated 29 April 1975 with these words: "Mama was passionate and generous by nature, blessed with exceptional energy and youthfulness. An open mind, always curious about the latest scientific discoveries and new literary trends. Her deep love of nature and her enthusiasm for life were contagious. She was more a friend than a mother to me, and I owe her the better part of what happiness remains." Some ten years later, under the editorial supervision of historian Anthony Slide, Simone and her sister-in-law Roberta Blaché would adapt their mother's memoirs into English. In the end, Simone tossed none of her mother's things into the fire.

She died in the U.S. in 1995, aged 87.

Reginald Blaché-Bolton

Reginald, the second child of Alice and Herbert, was born on 27 June 1912 in Fort Lee, New Jersey. He was seven when his parents separated and only 10 when he left the U.S. with his mother to live in Europe in the south-eastern region of Alpes-Maritimes. He grew up in Nice, where he became a fencing champion and graduated from the Lycée Masséna. He was 19 when he fell in love with Valérie Piquemal-Cancarou, 11 years his senior. This young woman, from Ariège near the Pyrenees, ran a dry-cleaning business, Vite et Bien, recently opened in the newly built Forum on the Promenade des Anglais. But Valérie became pregnant, and for Alice there was no question but that her young son should honour his responsibilities. The couple married in April 1932, and their daughter, Régine, was born a few months later, then immediately taken in by the Piquemal family. Régine was 13 before she ever met her grandmother, Alice, while holidaying in Bern immediately after the end of the Second World War. This was because her father, Reginald, had left Nice before she was even born, in order to seek work in Paris, which he did alone – according to her grandson, Thierry Peeters – because Valérie did not want to abandon her own mother.

Once in the capital, Reginald set his heart on a career as a sound engineer in film – at a time when silent cinema was being consigned to the dustbin of history – and with help from Léon Gaumont, he found a job at Clément Maurice's laboratory on Rue de la Villette, where he worked under Quittard, one of Alice's former colleagues. A few months later, his mother and sister joined him, and they all three shared an apartment on Rue de l'Atlas in the 19th arrondissement. The family reunion was short-lived. On 10 September 1933, the young man boarded the ocean liner *Majestic*, headed for New York. With his American citizenship, he was able to secure repatriation from the Consular service. He joined his father in California and began working for him, but only briefly, since discord grew between him and his new stepmother.

In 1943, Reginald was back in Europe with the American army, having taken part in Operation Torch the previous November, in which Allied troops wrested back control of the North African coast in Morocco and Algeria from the Vichy regime. Less than a year later, he landed in Sicily under General Patton, then marched on to Naples. From January to May 1944, Allied troops tried to break the entrenched German stranglehold on the Abruzzo mountains, and Reginald was involved in the bloodiest battle of the Italian campaign, Monte Cassino, from which he emerged unscathed.

Alice and Simone would have to wait until 1947 to be reunited with their son and brother in Paris. It is likely that during this time he also saw Régine – now his elder daughter, following the new life he had made for himself in the U.S. with Roberta Meyer, the mother of his second daughter, Adrienne, though the divorce from Régine's mother was not finalized until much later, in 1951. In 1964, Simone and Alice came to live a few miles away from Reginald and his family in Fort Lee, New Jersey, settling there for good.

Reginald died on 3 February 1991, at the age of 78. His French descendants would prove very active in bringing his mother's cinematic works to light. Régine went on to found La Société des Amis d'Alice Guy [The Society for the Friends of Alice Guy], and was a devoted supporter of Emmanuelle Gaume's various research endeavours. Following the death of Régine Blaché-Bolton, her son Thierry Peeters and granddaughter Alice Guy Jr. continue to maintain that work.

James Russell

Almost nothing is now known of James Russell, and this neglect, this life whitewashed from the annals of history, doubtless speaks to the status of African American artists in the early 20th-century American theatre industry. And yet in the early 1910s, according to Alice Guy, James Russell was considered the "King of the Cake-walk" in New York. The dance known as the cake-walk derives from Black slaves in Florida, allegedly inspired by Seminole "Indian" war dances to mock the stateliness of their European oppressors' minuets. Probably originating in the 1800s, it is one of the oldest forms of dance and music to have emerged from African American slave culture. It made the leap from the plantation to the music hall in the early 20th century, though audiences then preferred to watch white performers in blackface. Nevertheless, in 1898 Broadway was home to a cake-walk show that mixed Black and white dancers, marking the very first instance of racial integration on a New York stage. Fourteen years later, when Alice hired James Russell to act in her short film *The Fool and his Money*, there was no doubt that her white actors' refusal to act with her African American discovery shocked her to her core.

Alice came from a country with a slave-owning past, but France and America differed greatly in their collective unconscious. The French kings had limited slavery to their colonies: out of sight, out of mind. Slavery was a colonial business, a dream from beyond the sea, a majority enslaved by a minority. In America, itself a former colony, slavery was an everyday part of society. Hadn't founding father George Washington himself owned slaves? Here the power balance was reversed: a minority enslaved by a majority. And although Northerners and Southerners had torn each other to pieces over the issue of slavery (among others) in a Civil War, and though slavery had been abolished in 1865, the situation for the descendants of slaves in 1912 was hardly a model of integration. Despite the emergence of a new and intellectual middle class, most African Americans remained stuck in a social ghetto surrounded by segregationist barbed wire.

The African American community was thus an invisible minority on the silver screen. Incredibly, even in the earliest film adaptation of *Uncle's Tom Cabin* in 1903, by the cinema pioneer Edwin S. Porter, the title role was played by a white actor in blackface, and the same was true of the next four adaptations, between 1910 and 1913. Not until the sixth adaptation, in 1914, would the role of Uncle Tom go to Sam Lucas, long considered to be the first Black actor hired by a major U.S. film production company. Two years earlier, however, James Russell and his troupe had performed in *The Fool and his Money* for Alice Guy, but the film went unnoticed by historians for almost a century, as no copy had survived. When Victor Bachy summarized the story of the film for his readers in 1993, he did not bring up its rare casting decision, since he largely relied on an article in *The Moving Picture World* from 5 October 1912 that studiously avoided any discussion of the issue. Then, one miraculous day, an engineer in California bought an old trunk at an auction. At the bottom were a few reels of film, including *The Fool and his Money*. After the film was restored, and its director identified, a screening took place in 2018 at Grauman's Egyptian Theatre, the legendary cinema on Hollywood Boulevard built in the very same year that Alice gave up all hope of a new career in California. With poetic justice, it has now been established that Alice Guy was the first to defy prejudice and make a film with an entirely African American cast.

Billy Quirk

William Andrew Quirk was born in the same year as Alice, on 27 March 1873, in Jersey City, New Jersey. Few biographical traces remain of one of the leading members of Madame Blaché's American players.

In 1903, Billy married Patsy Jane Holcomb. The daughter of a Cedar Rapids lawyer, she had been a dancer in revues and vaudeville under the name Jane Frayne, since the age of 14. Her entire professional life would be spent on the stage, and it is assumed that her husband, already 30 by the time they married, had also made a career treading the boards. In fact, though, the name Billy Quirk would leave its mark elsewhere: namely, on film. A comic noted both for his easygoing style and memorable presence, Quirk was already 37 when he turned up for his first job at a film studio, in Fort Lee. This was still the age of hand-cranked one- and two-reelers, and it was Billy's good fortune – as well as that of the history of the seventh art – to find himself face-to-face with the Biograph Company's star director, D.W. (David Wark) Griffith. From 1909 to 1910, on occasion sharing the billing with Mary Pickford or Mack Sennett, Billy acted in 70 shorts directed by the filmmaker (his junior by two years). When Griffith decided to move to California in 1910, Billy preferred to stay put, and, two years later, first appeared in an Alice Guy film, *Canned Harmony*, followed swiftly by *Mignon*, *The Blood Stain*, *Treasures on the Wing*, *Algie the Miner*, *Phantom Paradise*, and (most notably) *Fra Diavolo*, one of Alice's biggest hits. But in that same year, Billy turned down Alice's offer to appear with Black actors in *The Fool and His Money*. A few months later, in the pages of the French paper *Ciné-Journal*, Alice told the story: "They withdrew, slamming the doors, considering it an irremediable disgrace to work alongside people of colour." In conclusion, she wrote: "And that's what racial prejudice is about in free America!"

The very next year – 1913 – Alice and Billy went their separate ways. His path led him to Hollywood, where he reunited with Griffith at the height of his fame in 1916 and acted in the massive production *Intolerance*, which hastened the director's financial ruin.

In the late 1910s, the constant pressure of shooting so many films plunged Billy into deep depression and, in 1920, he attempted suicide. Around this time, he also divorced Jane. After acting in another 10 films, Billy Quirk died in Los Angeles on 20 April 1926, aged only 53.

Catherine Calvert

Born on 20 April 1890 in Baltimore, Maryland, Catherine Cassidy appeared onstage for the first time at the age of 18 in Albany, New York, acting in Rida Johnson Young's play *Brown of Harvard*, whose 1926 Hollywood adaptation saw the debut of John Wayne. Catherine had adopted the stage name Calvert from the start, and on January 1911, this was the name that appeared in lights on Broadway – the Holy Grail for American actresses – when she played the female lead in *The Deep Purple*. Playwright Paul Armstrong, 43, doubtless not immune to the 21-year-old's charms, offered her the lead in *The Escape* in September 1913. Two years later, they were married – just long enough to have a child, Paul Armstrong Jr., before the playwright's sudden death in July 1915. Widowed at 25, Catherine devoted herself to the booming new industry of cinema. She made her debut in a 1916 short, *Partners*, for the Universal Film Manufacturing Company, founded four years earlier by the Austrian Carl Laemmle, but it was Alice Guy's *House of Cards* that made her name the following year. In her memoirs, the director, then 44, tells of how the 27-year-old actress was forced upon her by her backers, "although she limped badly". Alice recounts a tense conversation in a car taking her, Herbert, and Catherine to a party thrown by Ukrainian producer Lewis J. Selznick, father of the future David O.: "En route, Catherine Calvert suddenly said to my husband, 'You know, Mr. Blaché, for a director who would make me a star there would be no limit to my gratitude.' 'You might have to step over some dead bodies,' answered Herbert. 'Oh! That wouldn't bother me!' One of my assistants warned me that she had broken up more than one marriage [...] 'Why don't you propose your trade to Selznick?' I asked our companion. 'How horrible!' she cried, disgusted. Then added, with half-closed eyes, 'But Mr. Blaché is so romantic!'" Alice offers the following words in conclusion: "The wife of a film director in the United States must arm herself with a certain shield of indifference. Many actresses are willing to pay any price."

Herbert would go on to produce and direct Catherine Calvert's next two features, *The Peddler* and *Think It Over*, and Alice had to suffer the indignity of directing yet another film with her rival, *Behind the Mask*. Catherine followed this up with five films produced by the Frank A. Keeney Pictures Corporation – the last they ever made. Two of these were adaptations of plays by her late husband, to which she had retained the rights. In 1919, she played the lead in *Fires of Faith*, joining Famous Players-Lasky, which the Hungarian Adolph Zukor had just merged with Paramount Distribution. Up through 1921, the company, which had offices on both coasts, managed to put out anywhere from two to three feature-length films per week. Catherine's contribution to this boom in production was a single film, *The Career of Katherine Bush*, which she made before joining Vitagraph, founded by the British-American J.S. Blackton, for three films, including *Dead Men Tell No Tales*, and then moving on to Outlook Photoplays for a single film, *You Find It Everywhere*. Calvert, who now only accepted starring roles, filmed *The Green Caravan* in London in 1922 before returning to New York to play the lead in *That Woman*. In 1923, Catherine was back in the U.K. for her last two films, *The Indian Love Lyrics* and *Out to Win*.

With a total of 21 films to her name, Catherine Calvert retired from the screen at the age of 33, two years later marrying Colonel George A. Carrothers, a Canadian billionaire who'd made a fortune in wheat exports. The couple later separated. They had no children.

Catherine Calvert died on 18 January 1971 in Uniondale, on Long Island, New York.

Darwin Karr

Darwin Karr was born on 25 July 1875 in Almond, in upstate New York. In 1910, at the age of 35, he married actress Florence Bindley, seven years his senior. She had been acting since the age of three; at six, under the name Baby Bindley, she had sung and danced for Queen Victoria. She was 12 when she left to conquer the Broadway stage, which she would not leave until her path crossed there with Darwin's.

Darwin made his screen debut in September 1911 in an Edison Company short, *That Winsome Winnie Smile*. He followed up with six more for Edison, until late November. In three short months, at the age of 36, he had become a star. Now parting company with Edison, he acted in a single film for Éclair in November, and in January 1912 joined Solax, where he was directed by Alice for the first time. That film, *A Solax Celebration* – a New Year's sketch – was set and filmed in the Solax offices, with Alice, Herbert, set designer Henri Ménessier, and all the actors in the company playing themselves. Running a studio wasn't just about owning infrastructure and buildings; above all, it required a dedicated stable of actors to feature in the productions. With two or three films being made every week, after all, there was no time to audition a fresh cast for each one, and so it was that Alice came to rely on the dozen or so actors who made up her repertory company. And in 1912, the "star system" was already an important element of film production.

Alice would later refer to Darwin Karr in her memoirs as "my young leading man", and she announced his recruitment to the press in the same terms: "Monsieur Karr comes to us with a very fine reputation. He already has 14 years of experience with the best shows on Broadway, and has made a name for himself in the world of film. With his arrival, I am convinced that Solax is now synonymous with 'profit and pleasure' for film industry professionals. I am not trying to boast. I am simply saying: 'Look!'" For his part, Karr went even further: "I am especially happy to join Solax, as they make the kinds of comedies I love, in which audiences can see the best I have to give." Of his new trade, he said, "I believe that acting in a silent film is far more difficult than acting for the traditional stage, especially when it comes to comedy. One or two words are enough to get a laugh on stage, but when acting for the camera, words are no use. An actor is put to the test in the most demanding way." This sentiment echoed the way Alice conceived of her job as a director. That same year, in 1912, she wrote an article addressing the topic: "In my studio… I say to one of my company, 'This is your part.' He or she takes the script – reads it over – studies it – and works out their interpretation of the role. An American's method of playing the part is an intellectual process, which makes it relatively easy for the director. If at any given point the actor's ideas strike the wrong note, a director can usually correct them by appeal to reason. To the average French actor, though, this is not the way to do it. If their interpretation, as tends to happen with them, arises spontaneously from the heart, it can be more effective, but only if that interpretation happens to be correct. Sometimes, though, it is incorrect, and in such a case, the director is brought to their wits' end in trying to show the player why. 'I feel it in my soul' is the actor's sole riposte to all the intellectual arguments the director can muster. For that reason it is much harder to work with my own people than with Americans."

Darwin Karr had parts in 45 of the 115 one-reel shorts from 1912 whose direction Slide, Lacassin, and Bachy attribute to Alice Guy, as well as in *Fra Diavolo*, her first three-reeler. In March, Solax loaned the actor to Éclair, then being run by Étienne Arnaud, for a single-reeler with Dorothy Gibson, later a survivor of the *Titanic*. Karr also acted in a Solax film that Alice co-directed with Herbert Blaché and Edward Warren – the first assistant she hired that year. 1913 was a year of great transition: audiences now wanted films longer than a single reel, and Solax and its principal director followed this irreversible trend. Out of 94 films made by Alice, most were still one-reelers. Karr acted in 30 of them, but also featured in Alice's first major three-reelers, *Beasts of the Jungle* and *The Pit and the Pendulum*. In September and October, his final two films for Solax were the first shorts credited to Herbert Blaché. From November 1913 onwards, the honeymoon was over between the one-time star of the one-reeler and the Solax company, which completely abandoned the format the following year. Thus it was that in 1914, Darwin Karr could be seen in 16 shorts for Vitagraph, one of the oldest American production companies, founded by the British J. Stuart Blackton and Albert Smith in 1896. In 1915, he appeared in another ten shorts for Vitagraph, and in late September 1915, his first short for Essanay Film, *The Call of the Sea*. Before the year was up, he acted in five other films for this company, which could boast of hiring a rising star from Keystone: Charlie Chaplin. In September 1916, after ten further films for Essanay, Darwin left the company. The title of his final short now seems prophetic: *The Way of Patience*. In 1917, Karr was nowhere to be seen on screen. Now just 42 years old, he was already becoming – like Alice herself – a relic from a bygone era. 1918 marked his return to screens for a supporting role in the feature *The Unbeliever*, with Erich von Stroheim playing, as usual, a German officer.

Two years later, Karr appeared with Mary Pickford in *Suds*, then in one last feature in 1922, *The Sin Flood*. Darwin Karr, now 47, exited the stage of cinema. He died on 31 December 1945 in Los Angeles, at the age of 70, survived by his widow, Florence, who died in 1951.

Rose Pastor Stokes

Rose Harriet Wieslander was born on 18 July 1879 to an Orthodox Jewish family in Augustów, north-eastern Poland, then a province of the Russian Empire. Shortly after her birth, her parents separated, her father Jacob emigrating to the United States. Rose was three when the time came for her mother Anna and her grandparents to emigrate in turn, to London. In an impoverished East End neighbourhood, Anna married Israel Pastor, with whom she had six more children. Rose was 12 when the entire family emigrated to Cleveland, Ohio. The following year, in 1893, Rose began working in a cigar factory. Not long afterwards, her stepfather died, and she was forced to provide for her entire family. Rose was just over 20 when the New York-based *Yidishes Tageblatt* [Jewish Daily News] conducted a survey of its readers on their life and working conditions. Rose sent in a letter, which was immediately published. Thus emboldened, she began submitting regular dispatches on the lives of the working classes. In 1903, the newspaper hired her to write a regular advice column for young women. She moved to New York and, by setting aside some of her $15-a-week salary, managed to bring her family over from Cleveland two years later. Her life changed the day she interviewed multi-millionaire James Graham Phelps Stokes about his social activism. The scion of a wealthy New England family, Graham was a philanthropist with socialist ideals. Rose was 26 and Graham 33 when they married in July 1905, joining the Socialist Party of America soon thereafter. Along with other socialist activists, including writers Jack London and Upton Sinclair, the young couple founded The Intercollegiate Socialist Society, devoted to spreading their progressive ideals to students and colleges. On behalf of this organization, Rose kept company with writer Charlotte Perkins Gilman, a pioneering American feminist, who rallied her to her cause.

Rose and Graham began to drift apart when she began to publicly advocate for birth control, and it was during these years that Alice and Rose met. They worked on a film script together, but it never found a producer. "Selznick laughed in my face," Alice later recalled.

In 1917, when the U.S. entered the First World War, the rift between Rose and Graham widened. Graham enlisted in the army, despite the condemnation by socialists of American involvement. In 1918, after a spat with the *Kansas City Star* that saw Rose accuse the American government of colluding with war profiteers, she was arrested for violating a federal law, the Espionage Act of 1917. Tried in Kansas City, Missouri, she was sentenced to ten years in a state prison, before a successful appeal. Pastor Stokes reacted by moving to the left in her politics, at a time when, in her homeland, the 1917 Russian Revolution was bringing hope to workers throughout the world. In 1919, Rose was among the founding members of the American Communist Party, travelling to Moscow three years later as the American delegate to the Fourth Congress of the Communist International (Comintern).

In 1925, Graham filed for divorce. Four years later, Rose remarried Jerome Isaac Romain, a Jewish Communist intellectual, and like her of Polish-Russian descent. She was 46 and Jerome 29. But her newfound happiness was to prove short-lived. The very next year, she was diagnosed with breast cancer, and she died three years later in Frankfurt, Germany, where she had been receiving treatment. The woman known as "Rose of the Ghetto" for her work with Lower East Side labour activists was 54 years old.

Graham died in New York in 1960.

Léonce Perret

The third child of Marie and Ferdinand Perret, Léonce was born in Niort in the Deux-Sèvres region of east-central France on 14 March 1880. He grew up surrounded by the family carpentry business, and from an early age exhibited a clear penchant for the arts. A delicate child, it was a stay at a Paris hospital that convinced him of his artistic calling. Despite their reluctance, his parents allowed him to study music in the capital, but his first paying jobs were as an extra in the theatre. He was 19 when he followed his company on his first European tour, which took him as far afield as Russia. The following year, he was the male lead at the Théâtre de l'Athénée in Paris, and, three years after that, headlined the Théâtre du Vaudeville, before joining the Théâtre de l'Odéon in 1905. In 1908, he joined the Théâtre Michel and headed off to St. Petersburg, stopping off in Berlin on the return journey a year later to perform in Rostand's *Cyrano de Bergerac*. While there, a colleague informed him that the local Gaumont branch sometimes produced its own films. He went over to introduce himself and was hired on the spot: "I put together and acted in nine films, entirely on an amateur basis," he would declare 15 years later. "I never thought my destiny lay with silent cinema. It was just that I had nothing better to do." Back in Paris, he called in at Boulevard de la Villette. Legend has it that Louis Feuillade had just fired a member of the Comédie-Française mid-shoot, and there and then replaced the unsuitable actor with a rather portly individual who happened to be hanging around at the back of the set: Léonce Perret. He was 29, and would never again abandon his self-styled profession of "cinegraphist". From 1909 onwards, he acted for Feuillade and Arnaud, but also began directing his own films. By 1917, he had acted in 140 films and directed more than 250, including a dozen or so in collaboration with Feuillade. In 1913, he debuted the hit series *Léonce*, which he wrote, directed, and starred in. Describing this highly productive period, the film historian Henri Langlois compared Perret to no less a figure than the first genius of Quattrocento Florence: "In the history of cinema, Léonce Perret is a veritable Masaccio of photography, so far ahead of his time as to astound us."

When Feuillade was mobilized in 1915, Perret, ruled unfit for service due to his poor health, replaced him as head of production at Gaumont. Feuillade later took umbrage on learning that Perret was being paid 4 francs per metre of developed footage – nearly three times more than his own previous rate. Perret, however, had benefited from the negotiating skills of his wife – and now skilled manager – Valentine Petit, a Folies Bergère dancer of Belgian descent who had become one of his top female stars. Gaumont had barely been given a choice in the matter. By 1916, though, Feuillade was back, and with Perret's contract nearing its end, he and his wife seized the opportunity to make the big transatlantic leap.

Léonce Perret was not an unknown quantity to Americans, D.W. Griffith and Mary Pickford having both considered his 1913 short *La Dentellière* [The Lacemaker] a masterpiece. In 1925, he would recall meeting the pioneering American film director in the pages of *Cinématographie française*: "Griffith threw his arms around me and hugged me tight, with these simple words: 'Oh, Perret! I am so happy!' And with that, we both began crying like children."

Between 1917 and 1920, Léonce Perret directed 16 films in the home of the free and the land of the brave, most of which would be financed, via a series of production companies, by Pathé Exchange, an American branch of Pathé dedicated to distribution. So it was that Perret's first trio of films featured the actor Robert Warwick, who was also credited as producer, and likewise the actress Rita Jolivet, who also received producer credit for the patriotic film *Lest We Forget*. In 1918, Léonce and Valentine founded their own company, Perret Production Inc., again distributed and financed by Pathé Exchange, which notched up three films to its name, one of which, the deeply patriotic *Lafayette, We Come*, featured both Valentine Petit and, in a cameo appearance, a certain Frenchman by the name of Marcel Duchamp. *Tarnished Reputations* (1920) was the final feature produced by P.P.I., and was also Alice Guy's last film. An early draft of the script had been titled *A Soul Adrift* and was written by Jean Durand, a former colleague of Perret's at Gaumont. Perret took over the script and production, and offered the gig to Émile Chautard, a former director for Éclair, but he was otherwise engaged and suggested Alice. "The salary was meagre – $2,000 for six weeks of work – but it was better than nothing, and could put me back on my feet. So I accepted." The film, starring Dolores Casinelli, in fact took several long months to shoot, as Perret's script arrived in dribs and drabs, while the studio's technical facilities were at the same time prioritized for his own work. When Alice was at last able to sit down to editing it, she came down with influenza, and it was while she was being nursed by Valentine at the Perrets' house that Herbert Blaché, then passing through New York, apparently took over and completed the job. The film was released in March 1920 as *Tarnished Reputations*. A century on, expert opinion remains divided as to the film's proper directing credit – by turns attributed to Alice, to Herbert, to them both, and sometimes as a three-way joint billing with Léonce Perret himself. It is on this highly confusing note that the directing career of Alice Guy ends.

The Perrets returned to France in the late summer of 1921. Léonce immediately tackled a feature, *L'Écuyère* [The Horsewoman], released the following year, before diving into the adaptation of Pierre Benoit's bestseller, *Koenigsmark*. Three years earlier, Valentine, then in France to negotiate the distribution of her husband's American films, had come across the novel in a bookshop's window display, read the whole thing in one night, and then rushed to secure the rights. The film was one of 1923's major international hits, a comeback thunderous enough to label Perret as "Americanized". As early as 1920, the Fédération de la cinématographie française took him to task, accusing him of promoting "the introduction of American film in another form" and threatening him with "a report to be transmitted to the honourable Ministers of Commerce and Education". Yes, Perret admitted, he had adopted the best of the American style, but only to help the French cinematic sensibility achieve its potential. He didn't mince his words: "From a commercial standpoint, an industry that doesn't make back its costs is doomed to die. The French film industry must organize itself in a logical and methodical fashion so as to put profit above all else, or it will go extinct." These words were manna to the ears of producers, who didn't think twice about funding such mammoth productions of his as *Madame Sans-Gêne* with American star Gloria Swanson, produced in France by Zukor's Paramount in 1924. However, Perret's speech raised hackles in those he defined, within damning quotation marks, as "aesthetes" and "visionaries". But these were the very people upon whom an artist's posterity would depend, irrespective of their popular acclaim. So when Léonce Perret died suddenly on 12 August 1935, at the age of 55, while preparing a sound remake of *Koenigsmark* – he had been the pioneer of the talkie in France since 1929 – the "cinegraphist" almost immediately fell off the radars of film historians. One early critical assassin was Georges Sadoul, who called him "a man without much taste". It was not until the 21st century, with the help of Henri Langlois, that Perret's work, and his crucial place in film history, began to be re-evaluated.

Alice retained enormous gratitude towards Valentine for her nursely devotion during her final cinematic venture, but the two women would never meet again. When Alice's homage to Léonce Perret's wife was published in her memoirs, Valentine had already been dead for 14 years, and Alice for six.

Buster Keaton

Joseph Frank Keaton was born on 4 October 1895 in Piqua, an unincorporated community in southern Kansas, where the family had been millers for three generations before Buster's father Joe went the way of vaudeville along with Buster's mother Myra. For Joe, performing was a calling, and for Myra, the daughter of a carnival manager, it was a living. Family legend has it that Joseph Jr.'s nickname was given to him by none other than Joe's business partner, Harry Houdini. Junior was just months old when when he fell down a flight of stairs and burst into tears. The magician picked him up and said, "My, what a buster!" (meaning a fall). Thus "Buster Keaton" was born: all he had to do now was make an entrance onstage. According to another family legend, this happened less than three years later. Since the family couldn't afford a babysitter every night, baby Buster stayed in the wings, but as soon as he could walk, he kept joining his parents in the limelight. Rather than let his son cause chaos onstage, Senior decided to focus his energies. Joe put Buster in the same Irish workingman's outfit he wore and let him imitate his dance steps. Audiences loved it. From then on, Buster was an integral part of the show, just like, in time, his younger brother and sister. As he later said, "I was their partner, however, as well as their child." It was around this time that the young boy learned how to take a fall: "This was the result of a series of interesting experiments Pop made with me. He began these by carrying me out on the stage and dropping me on the floor. Next he started wiping up the floor with me. When I gave no sign of minding this he began throwing me through the scenery, out into the wings, and dropping me down on the bass drum in the orchestra pit." During these years of his apprenticeship in slapstick, Buster came to a personal realization that would inform his image as a performer: "One of the first things I noticed was that whenever I smiled or let the audience suspect how much I was enjoying myself they didn't seem to laugh as much as usual." The Man Who Never Laughed became his trademark over a 60-year career.

But the Keatons' show, reputed to be the most violent in all vaudeville, came to the attention of child protection agencies. Despite denials from father and son alike concerning the former's mistreatment of the latter, the family troupe was banned from New York theatres for two years. But it was Joe's alcoholism that finally tore the family apart. In February 1917, Buster ditched his dad in Los Angeles and headed straight to New York to find a solo engagement – which he immediately did. During rehearsals, however, he ran into Lou Anger, a fellow vaudevillian then working with Roscoe "Fatty" Arbuckle, former star of Mack Sennett's productions who had recently gone independent. Lou asked Buster over for a tour of the studio. The Keaton family had always been prejudiced against the "flickers", those images wavering on a bedsheet. They'd never "replace vaudeville as the country's favourite form of entertainment". Pop had even turned down an offer from William Randolph Hearst (Welles' model for *Citizen Kane*) to hire the family for a big-screen adaptation of George McManus' comic strip *Bringing up Father*. But Buster admired Fatty's one-reelers, just as Fatty appreciated the Keatons' show and the precision timing of their pratfalls. So it was that when Buster met Fatty, the latter immediately urged him to take a screen test. In just one take – in which Buster gets a sack of flour right to the face – Buster seemed to the manner born: "From the first day on, I hadn't a doubt that I was going to love working in the movies." Never again would Buster show up for rehearsals at the Broadway theatre. He was 22 years old.

Working with Arbuckle meant learning the trade from a man second only to Chaplin in the hearts of audiences. It was a steep learning curve. Between April 1917 and January 1920, Buster appeared beside Roscoe in 14 shorts, developing a recurring character. Meanwhile the crew left New York for Hollywood, and Buster went off to war: in August 1918, he shipped off to France with the 40th Infantry Division, but luckily the war ended before the outfit saw battle on the front.

The year 1920 saw Buster obtain his own independence as an actor. Roscoe's contract had just been bought out by Zukor, who successfully put him into features. Buster accepted an offer from Metro for his own leading role in his first feature. It was an adaptation of the play *The New Henrietta*, in a role originated onstage by Douglas Fairbanks, who had just founded the joint venture company United Artists with his wife Mary Pickford, Charles Chaplin, and D.W. Griffith. Fairbanks could not see himself reprising the role, so he recommended that it be offered to young Buster. Thus, under Herbert Blaché's direction, Buster Keaton played the part of Bertie Van Alstyne in *The Saphead*, released in September 1920 in Metro's theatres. "This picture, the first I starred in, was one of the company's big hits that year," he later recalled.

Buster Keaton was off to a great start, following up with a series of shorts produced by Roscoe's producer, Joseph Schenck. This former accountant of Russian descent had married movie star Norma Talmadge, and introduced the latter's younger sister to his new protégé, who soon became his brother-in-law. Over the course of a dozen-odd films up through September 1921, Buster Keaton refined his image and established himself as a director. It was also in September 1921 that Roscoe was unjustly accused of raping and accidentally killing a girl. Hearst's papers and the morality leagues made up the public's minds long before the trial; eventually exonerated, Roscoe's image became one of Hollywood debauchery and perversity personified. Support from Keaton and Chaplin could not keep his career from utter ruin.

In January 1922, at Schenck's request, Buster Keaton became his own producer with the short *The Paleface*. From then until 1928, under the aegis of Buster Keaton Productions and Buster Keaton Comedies, distributed by MGM or United Artists (of which Schenck became president), Buster Keaton unfurled the full extent of his genius, giving the history of cinema a few silent classics: *The Navigator*, *Sherlock Jr.*, *Seven Chances*. "All our bosses asked of us was that our pictures make fortunes, and our pictures did." But the 1926 spectacular *The General* – the actor-director did not think twice about filming the destruction of an actual locomotive – did not bring in the hoped-for fortune; this reminder of the Civil War failed to make Americans laugh. From then on, his distributor United Artists – and co-producer, in the case of Schenck – which had lost a great deal of money on the film, imposed creative control. The two films that followed were subject to oversight and limited freedom. Still, the final Keaton/Schenck co-production, *Steamboat Bill, Jr.*, was not the hit they were banking on.

In 1928, against advice from his friend Chaplin, Buster Keaton abandoned vague hopes of independence and agreed to sign a contract with Metro-Goldwyn-Mayer. "The worst mistake of my life," Keaton later confessed. Although he was able to wrap his first feature, *The Cameraman*, which added a feather to a cap already full of silent film classics, he lost all subsequent autonomy starting with his next film, with no final control over the script, artistic direction, or casting. For insurance reasons, he was not even allowed to perform his own stunts. He sank into alcoholism and depression, divorcing actress Natalie Talmadge, the mother of his two sons, whom he was not allowed to see for many years. The advent of the talkies seemed to have relegated the stars of silent film to obscurity. At the age of 38, Keaton fled to Paris in 1934 to shoot a film, *Le Roi des Champs-Élysées* (never distributed in the U.S.), then found himself in London the following year for one final European shoot. His return to Hollywood proved less than triumphant. Nothing seemed able to halt the decline of the silent-era star.

In 1940, there was a glimmer of hope: he married a dancer he'd met at MGM, Eleanor Norris, with whose help he was able to moderate his drinking. His life stabilized, and he made do with being a gag writer for MGM In 1950, he appeared in Billy Wilder's *Sunset Boulevard* with Erich von Stroheim and Gloria Swanson – two more stars fallen from the heights of Hollywood fame. Two years later, he and Chaplin formed a duo for the ages in *Limelight*, the latter's final American film before being banned from the U.S. for political reasons.

In the 1950s, with the rise of television as a new mass medium, America (re)discovered Buster Keaton. A good sport, he guest-starred or did cameos on variety shows, talk shows, and various series (including an episode of *The Twilight Zone*), gradually re-establishing his brand: crackerjack timing, precision of movement, the gift of gag. Actor James Mason, who had bought Keaton's former villa, found the negatives of some of his shorts and features; Keaton himself also still had a few. A distributor conceived the idea of restoring the work of the Man Who Never Laughed, so audiences could enjoy him once more.

In 1960, Buster Keaton was awarded an Honorary Academy Award for his body of work.

Keaton was never informed of an advanced lung cancer diagnosis from January 1966, believing until the time of his death that he was battling a serious case of bronchitis, and impatient to be discharged. The night before he died, he was playing cards with friends. He passed away on 1 February, at the age of 70. "I'd like to be buried with a deck of cards in one hand," he is said to have once remarked, "and the rosary in the other, so I can be ready for anything."

Charlie Chaplin

Born on 16 April 1889 in London – although no official record of his birth exists – Charlie Chaplin was the second of three sons, all from different fathers, born to Hannah Hill, who sang and danced under the stage name Lily Harley. His father, Charles Chaplin, was also a music-hall entertainer, and his baritone voice brought him a measure of fame in the 1880s. But alcoholism soon got the better of his career, family, health, and finances, and he died at the age of 38. Soon separated from Chaplin Sr., and then from her next husband, Hannah sank into poverty, malnutrition, and psychosis. She was committed to an asylum, and her children taken away from her. Charlie's childhood is, in every way, like something out of a Dickens novel – right down to its redemption, which in the case of young Chaplin took the form of artistic expression. His first performance onstage, aged five, standing in for his sick mother, has passed into legend. It marked not only the revelation of a calling, but of a means of escape: earning a living by winning the public's love. Despite its precariousness, his mother encouraged him down this path, passing on to him her observational skills, and his father found him a gig with a music-hall troupe that enabled him to practise dancing, singing, and pantomime. He was barely 10. At the turn of the century, he embarked on a career in the theatre, where he first attracted notice in 1903, as a newsboy in the play *Jim, A Romance of Cockayne*.

His performance led to his landing the role of Billy the pageboy in a theatrical version of *Sherlock Holmes* co-written by Arthur Conan Doyle himself. It was a smash hit, and his career took off. His fees allowed him to dress stylishly, right down to a pearl-handled cane, and take care of his mother. He was 16 when he played Billy for the last time. Meanwhile, he also played one of the Lost Boys in J.M. Barrie's *Peter Pan; or, the Boy Who Wouldn't Grow Up*.

Although Chaplin believed himself destined for dramatic roles, his teenage years, spent knocking on doors to get parts in satirical sketches to make ends meet, resulted in his discovery of his own comic potential. One day, while touring in the Channel Islands, he was disconcerted by the fact that the locals did not understand his accent, so he resorted to miming to achieve the desired effect. Charlie Chaplin had found his voice.

Meanwhile his brother Sydney, four years his senior, was also pursuing a career on the boards. Since 1906, he had been acting with a prestigious comedy company headed by Fred Karno. In 1908, Sydney managed to convince the director to hire his younger brother. Two years later, Chaplin was playing lead roles for the Karno Company, critics and audiences alike particularly lauding his inspired routine playing a drunk. The company had a worldwide reputation, and in 1910 set out for a two-year tour of the U.S., where Chaplin once again earned favourable notices, and immediately agreed to cross the Atlantic again when a new tour was scheduled in October 1913. This time, he would not return to the U.K., for he had meanwhile been contacted by the owner of the New York Motion Picture Company, one of whose branches was Keystone Studios, headed by Mack Sennett. Chaplin was offered $150 per week; Karno only paid him $50. So in December 1913, Charlie Chaplin arrived in Glendale, California. He was 24. He went on to shoot 36 shorts for Keystone – long enough to develop and perfect the "Tramp" character he had improvised for the second of these, *Kid Auto Races at Venice*. Chaplin was soon directing his own films and, just as quickly, Sennett increased his weekly salary to $400.

The Englishman had wanted twice as much, but Sennett refused. So when his contract ended in 1914, Charlie's Tramp left Keystone for Essanay Films on a weekly rate of $1,250 – in modern terms, slightly in excess of $30,000. For Essanay, he directed 15 films in 1915, which enabled him to refine his character, introducing pathos and tenderness in *The Tramp*. His reputation as a "control freak" also began to assert itself, including his insistence that he compose his own musical accompaniments for his films. In 1916, he joined the Mutual Film Corporation. His brother Sydney, now his manager, had negotiated a salary of $10,000 a week for him, with an annual bonus of $150,000, plus his exclusive use of a studio to work in. Charlie Chaplin was 26 years old. He made 12 films, of at least two reels apiece, up to the end of 1917. Scholars are generally agreed – with Chaplin himself – in considering the Mutual films the height of his creative genius. *Easy Street, The Immigrant,* and *The Adventurer* would prove to be worldwide hits. Less well known, *Behind the Screen* – in which Chaplin played a hapless stagehand – may be the first film to go behind the scenes of a movie set to tell a fictional story.

In 1918, ever in search of greater artistic independence, he signed a contract directly with a consortium of movie theatre owners, First National Exhibitors' Circuit, which had formed to compete with Zukor's hegemonic Paramount. This time Sydney negotiated a contract for $1 million – the equivalent of $20 million today – for eight films in 18 months. From then on, Chaplin was not only a director, he was his own producer; his own money was on the line. His first act was to build his own studio at the corner of La Brea and Sunset Boulevard, in what was then still the outskirts of Hollywood. That was where Alice Guy came to visit him in 1920. In 1918, the actor had married a 16-year-old actress. They had a child together, who lived for only three days, and a bitter separation and divorce soon followed, miring him in protracted legal proceedings. On the professional front, he had already made five films for his clients, including 1918's *Shoulder Arms,* an artistic triumph that spent two years in cinemas. "That film is certainly drumming up trade," wrote Jean Cocteau in Paris. In 1920, Chaplin was working on his first feature-length film of six reels. Begun the previous year, *The Kid,* which drew on his own childhood for many of its episodes, proved a difficult film to make. Chaplin's perfectionism caused him to shoot up to 53 takes of the same scene. Meanwhile his highly vexatious divorce left him miserable.

It is hard to understand why Alice Guy pitched Charlie Chaplin one of her own scripts. Was she being naïve? Or else either wilfully ignorant or genuinely unaware of his working habits? No wonder, in any case, that the star turned her down. However, the friendly welcome he extended to the pioneering filmmaker – at a time when he was all but inaccessible, shut away in his studio filming night and day – might in itself be seen as a mark of his respect for her.

In 1923, after fulfilling his contractual obligations to First National, he decided to go for complete autonomy. He teamed up with celebrity-couple Mary Pickford and Douglas Fairbanks, as well as director D.W. Griffith, to found United Artists, initially a film distribution company, later an independent production company, established on co-operative principles. From now until his ignominious exile from the U.S. in 1952, he would make his next eight features under his own banner. *The Gold Rush* (1925), *City Lights* (1931), *Modern Times* (1936), and *The Great Dictator* (1940) were instant and immortal classics. Meanwhile, the 35-year-old actor had married another girl of 16, Lita Grey, only to go through a divorce as calamitous as his first, but this time with two children to consider. In 1932, he fell in love with a slightly older actress, 21-year-old Paulette Goddard, with whom he lived happily for about a decade. Faced with the arrival of the talkies, Chaplin took a steadfast stand against sound until 1940; no dialogue was needed, after all, to understand *Modern Times* as a critique of capitalism. *The Great Dictator* was also a vehicle for progressive ideas, but it was in *Monsieur Verdoux,* from an original script by Orson Welles, that his manifestly anti-capitalist message became unignorable for America's witch-hunters in 1947. FBI director J. Edgar Hoover began an official investigation of this Communist sympathizer. The film was a flop. Its follow-up, *Limelight,* tells the story of a music-hall performer's comeback, and guest-starred Buster Keaton. When Chaplin left for London to introduce the film at its world premiere, the U.S. Attorney General revoked the Englishman's re-entry permit. In 1953, Chaplin settled in Switzerland with his final wife, Oona, daughter of playwright Eugene O'Neill. She was 18 when they met. They went on to have eight children together. Chaplin directed two more features: 1957's *A King in New York* (not distributed in the U.S.) and 1967's *A Countess from Hong Kong.* He died 10 years later, on 25 December 1977, at the age of 88. Earlier, in 1972, he had been awarded an honorary Academy Award, and went to Hollywood to accept it in person. The ovation that greeted him was the longest in the history of the Oscars.

And after such a unique life, a no less dramatic posthumous event: in 1978, a Pole and a Bulgarian exhumed the actor's coffin, holding it to a ransom of 100,000 Swiss francs – apparently intended to fund a new garage. In 2014, French actor and director Xavier Beauvois used this story as inspiration for his film *La Rançon de la gloire* [The Price of Fame].

Francis Lacassin

Born on 18 November 1931 in Saint-Jean-de-Valériscle in the Gard region of southern France, Francis Lacassin grew up in Alès, where his parents were shopkeepers. The kids' comics section of the newspapers gave him a lifelong love of reading. He was 24 when he set out to conquer the capital in 1954, having passed a stiff Civil Service entrance exam in Montpellier to study at an Inland Revenue college in Paris. It was only by entrancing himself in daily visits to the Cinémathèque Française, run by Henri Langlois, that Lacassin was able to endure the 24 months of his dull, soporific, bureaucratic training. It became clear to him that he could never be a pen-pusher, that he loved words and images more than numbers. He never looked back. The early 1960s found Francis Lacassin mapping out the territories he would later conquer: genre and adventure novels; the history of early cinema; and graphic novels or "comics" (*bandes dessinées*) – this was his Holy Trinity.

In 1962, when Lacassin founded the Club des Bandes Dessinées – later renamed the Centre d'études des littératures d'expression graphique [Centre for Studies in Graphic Literature] – comics were still published in digest-like periodicals or "*illustrés*", a term that confused form and content. Before the Second World War, the distinguished film historian Georges Sadoul had already claimed that such publications "poured into children's impressionable brains the basest pornography, encouraged an enthusiasm for murder and the exploits of gangsters, fostering a desire for espionage, and the subversive hope of participation in civil war". In 1962, then, for an adolescent to be reading comics was socially unacceptable – and these were prejudicial wrongs that needed righting. At Lacassin's urging, the Club soon turned into an activist cell fighting for comics to be recognized as a major means of expression, an art unto itself. Lacassin found himself in good company: sociologist Évelyne Sullerot; actress Delphine Seyrig; cartoonist Jean-Claude Forest; filmmakers Alain Resnais and Chris Marker; and Pierre Lazareff, proprietor of the newspaper *France-Soir*. Their illustrious ranks were soon joined by writer Raymond Queneau and cartoonists Hergé and René Goscinny. Thanks to them, comics were finally granted an ordinal number: "the ninth art". In 1971, Francis taught the very first class devoted to comics at Université Paris I, and in the following year published *Pour un neuvième art* [Towards a Ninth Art] in the prestigious paperback imprint 10/18 (named for the dimensions of its books).

In 1963, he wrote his first film script, for director Georges Franju: an adaptation of *Judex*, the 12-episode serial that Louis Feuillade had directed in 1916. The following year, with Raymond Bellour, he published his first major work on cinema, *Le Procès Clouzot* [The Clouzot Trial], with with regular biographical studies of other pioneering filmmakers to come over the years, from Louis Feuillade to Jean Durand to Alfred Machin. That same year, 1963, in the pages of *Bizarre* magazine – published by the groundbreaking Jean-Jacques Pauvert – Lacassin supplied a lengthy study of the *Tarzan* stories ("Mythe triomphant, mythe humilié" ["Myth Triumphant, Myth Defeated"]), which he later expanded to book length for 10/18. *Tarzan, ou le Chevalier crispé* [Tarzan: The Awkward Knight] remains the definitive account of this King of the Jungle.

This was his first great accomplishment in the critical field of popular fiction, and Lacassin's memoirs pay homage to a "great vigilante of publishing and a true St.-Bernard for authors buried in neglect". The name of this publisher, who first offered him the opportunity of resuscitating the reputations of any forgotten figure, from any field, that caught his fancy, was Christian Bourgois, the new head of 10/18, who, ever since their first meeting in the early 1970s, demonstrated implicit faith in Lacassin's work. Between then and 1995, Lacassin would edit 221 books under his imprint – Jules Verne, Rudyard Kipling, Conan Doyle, Joseph Kessel, Gaston Leroux, Titaÿna, Léo Malet, Sinclair Lewis, Pierre Mac Orlan, Georges Simenon – and oversee the first translation and publication of Jack London's complete works into French. In just 25 years, Francis Lacassin had compiled his ideal library.

But his great passion, for which cinephiles the world over would come to remember him, was early cinema – a field previously overlooked by historians. In 1960, Francis connected with the Fédération Française des Ciné-clubs, which sent him all over Central France to preach the word of cinema by re-introducing classic and contemporary films to a new generation of suburban audiences. This was his primary livelihood in the years to come, in return for which he contributed a series of unpaid articles for *Cinéma* magazine – the more heartfelt for the independence they afforded his research. From his very first articles in *Cinéma*, Lacassin distinguished himself from his fellow contributors by displaying a true fascination for a subject in which almost no one else was then interested (something of a credo of his): the early pioneers of French filmmaking. Building on the work of Henri Langlois – his only peer – on silent cinema, Lacassin was a trailblazer, expertly marking out this new scholarly territory that he loved so much. An archaeologist of his own childhood memories, Lacassin made it his mission to interview the surviving members of that era, track down prints of their vanished films, and reconstitute the scattered traces of a time at once so close to living memory and yet already so distant from contemporary theoreticians of the seventh art.

In July 1963, on the Avenue de Tervueren in Brussels, Alice Guy, then 90, first received the 32-year-old Francis Lacassin into her home. He had arranged the interview in order to ask Alice some questions for his biography of Louis Feuillade, but Francis returned from Brussels a changed man. Faced with this lively nonagenarian, the young man soon realized that Alice's dealings with Feuillade represented but a tiny part of the immense submerged iceberg of her life – a life devoted to the cinema. Lacassin had found the heroine of his dreams, a new cause to champion – and the two remained in constant contact until the ebullient old lady's return to the U.S. Francis sought to place Alice's memoirs with his own publisher, Pierre Lherminier, who had just founded the Cinéma d'aujourd'hui [Today's Cinema] imprint at Seghers, and had recently sold 200,000 copies of its volume on Jean-Luc Godard. The pitch failed – "an interesting idea" but "unlikely to sell more than 1,000 copies", and so on. Faced with this setback, Lacassin instead conceived an alternative contribution to the cause by compiling the first full filmography of Alice Guy-Blaché – at first with the help of Alice herself, and then with research trips to the States. He rummaged through catalogues; hung around art-house cinemas, collected film-stills; made copies of those Alice sent him – and stored it all in a yellow Kodak box. He was also among the first to notice the absence of *The Cabbage Fairy* from the Gaumont catalogue: since no catalogue can ever be taken as gospel, he reasoned, the 1896 version might have vanished, and the two known versions could *both* be remakes… The jury is still out, but the trial goes on.

In 1971, Lacassin at last managed to publish an article devoted to Alice Guy in the specialist magazine *Cinéma 71*. This was immediately translated for *Sight and Sound*, sending American scholars down this previously unknown path at long last. The following year, his magnum opus, *Pour une contre-histoire du cinéma* [Towards an Alternative History of Cinema], opened with a chapter entitled "Alice Guy, la première femme réalisatrice de films du monde" ["The First Female Film Director in the World"].

Four years later, Alice's long-held dream finally came true, when the feminist Musidora Association prepared her memoirs, *L'Autobiographie d'une pionnière du cinéma*, for publication under an imprint of Denoël's. To it, Lacassin appended the first filmography of Alice's cinematic works, the fruit of twelve years' research.

Alice remained a constant preoccupation of the journalist's for the rest of his life. In 2008 he published "Au secours de la Victorine, un épisode niçois de l'aventure d'Alice Guy" ["Rescuing Victorine Studios: An Episode in the Adventures of Alice Guy"] for a small cinema magazine. The pitch was in the title, its 15-odd pages the culmination of over a decade's worth of research. For the first time, light was shed on Alice's life from 1920 until her death, with the help of oral accounts gathered from her daughter Simone, her granddaughter Régine, and her great-nephew Gabriel Alliguet, as well as Marc Sandberg, grandson of Victorine's founder. This short piece, available online, has become the standard account.

Francis Lacassin died on the night of 11 August 2008, at Paris' Georges Bizet hospital, where he had undergone heart surgery four days earlier. He was 77 years old.

A few months before his passing, while we were working on the second volume of his memoirs, Francis entrusted me with the fruit of all his research on Alice Guy – in a yellow Kodak box – and a mission: to continue fighting for the resurrection of her reputation. He knew, from the very first time we'd met in 1980, that I had found his fascination for the First Lady of Cinema infectious. But I am no scholar, researching the fragments of untold stories; all I know is how to tell them. As it happens, he'd had a chance to appreciate the work that Catel and I had put into our graphic biography of Kiki of Montparnasse. "Come on, José-Louis," he told me. "Alice is a perfect subject for the two of you!"

In 2017, Catel and I decided to open the famous yellow Kodak box at last. It was obviously Francis' destiny to one day turn into a character in a comic book.

FILMOGRAPHY
BIBLIOGRAPHY

Filmography

Available films by Alice Guy

Le Cinéma premier, volume 1. Gaumont.
[The First Films]

Le Pêcheur dans le torrent (0'52" – 1897)
[The Fisherman in the Stream]

Baignade dans un torrent (0'55" – 1897)
[Bathing in a Stream]

Mme Bob-Walter, danse serpentine (1'5" – 1897)
[Serpentine Dance]

Effets de mer (1'40" – 1899)
[Ocean Studies]

Les Cambrioleurs (1'4" – 1898)
[The Robbers]

Chez le magnétiseur (1'0" – 1898)
[At the Hypnotist's]

Scène d'escamotage (0'59" – 1898)
[Disappearing Act]

L'Aveugle fin de siècle (1'0" – 1898)
[The Turn-of-the-Century Blind Man]

Surprise d'une maison au petit jour (1'0" – 1898)
[Surprise Attack on a House at Daybreak]

Au cabaret (0'52" – 1899)
[At the Club]

La Bonne Absinthe (0'56" – 1899)
[Wonderful Absinthe]

Danse pseudo japonaise; Lina Esbrard : danse serpentine; Zambelli (3'29" – 1900)
["Japanese" Dance; Lina Esbrard: Serpentine Dance; and Zambelli]

Au bal de flore (1900)
[At the Floral Ball]

Valse directoire (1900)
[Directorate Waltz]

Les Fredaines de Pierrette (2'0" – 1900)
[Pierrette's Escapades]

Chapellerie et charcuterie mécaniques (0'57" – 1900)
[The Hat-and-Sausage Machine]

Chirurgie fin de siècle (2'11" – 1900)
[Turn-of-the-Century Surgery]

Danse des saisons – L'Hiver, danse de la neige (0'55" – 1900)
[Dance of the Seasons – Winter, Snow Dance]

La Concierge (0'53" – 1900) [The Landlady]

Chez le photographe (1'3" – 1900)
[At the Photographer's]

Avenue de l'Opéra (1'0" – 1900)

La Fée aux choux (1'0" – ?)
[The Cabbage Fairy]

Sage-Femme de première classe (3'30" – 1902)
[First-Class Midwife]

Intervention malencontreuse (0'56" – 1902)
[An Untimely Intrusion]

Les Chiens savants (3'23" – 1902)
[Miss Dundee and Her Performing Dogs]

Faust et Méphistophélès (1'50" – 1903)
[Faust and Mephistopheles]

Comment monsieur prend son bain (1'41" – 1903)
[How Monsieur Takes His Bath]

Cake-Walk (0'32" – 1905)

Les Maçons (2'0" – 1905)
[The Bricklayers]

La Statue (6'0" – 1905)
[The Statue]

La Charité du prestidigitateur (3'0" – 1905)
[The Magician's Alms]

Chien jouant à la balle (2'0" – 1905)
[Dog Playing with Ball]

Le Tango (2'0" – 1905)

La Malagueña y el Torero (2'0" – 1905)
[The Malagueña and the Bullfighter]

L'Anatomie du conscrit (2'27" – 1906)
[Polin sings "Anatomy of a Draftee"]

Mayol chante: "Lilas blanc" (3'0" – 1906)
[Félix Mayol sings "White Lilac"]

La Polka des trottins (2'25" – 1906)
[Félix Mayol sings "The Errand Boys' Polka"]

Questions indiscrètes (4'54" – 1906)
[Félix Mayol sings "Indiscreet Questions"]

Le Vrai Jiu jitsu (2'27" – 1906)
[Dranem sings "The True Jujitsu"]

Five O'Clock Tea (2'56" – 1906)

Le Matelas épileptique (9'30" – 1906)
[The Drunken Mattress]

La Marâtre (7'15" – 1906)
[The Cruel Mother]

Une Noce au Lac Saint-Fargeau (1905)
[A Wedding at St. Fargeau]

La Femme collante (2'30" – 1906)
[A Sticky Woman]

Une course d'obstacles (6'30" – 1906)
[An Obstacle Course]

La Vérité sur l'homme singe (7'30" – 1906)
[The Truth About the Ape-Man]

La Naissance, la Vie, et la Mort du Christ (37'7" – 1906)
[The Birth, Life, and Death of Christ]

Madame a des envies (4'57" – 1906)
[Madame's Cravings]

La Hiérarchie dans l'amour (3'0" – 1906)
[The Hierarchies of Love]

Une Histoire roulante (2'30" – 1906)
[A Story Well-Spun]

Le Noël de monsieur le curé (6'0" – 1906)
[The Parish Priest's Christmas]

Le Fils du garde-chasse (5'30" – 1906)
[The Gamekeeper's Son]

Alice Guy films a phono-scene at the studios in
Buttes-Chaumont (1'40" – 1907)

La Course à la saucisse (4'30" – 1907)
[The Race for the Sausage]

Les Résultats du féminisme (7'0" – 1906)
[The Consequences of Feminism]

Le Piano irrésistible (4'40" – 1907)
[The Irresistible Piano]

Une Héroïne de quatre ans (5'40" – 1907)
[A Four-Year-Old Heroine]

Sur la barricade (4'0" – 1907)
[On the Barricade]

Le Billet de banque (11'3" – 1907)
[The Banknote]

Le Lit à roulettes (3'0" – 1907)
[The Rolling Bed]

La Glu (4'0" – 1907)
[The Glue]

Le Bonnet à poil (5'0" – 1907)
[The Fur Hat]

Le Frotteur (4'0" – 1907)
[The Cleaning Man]

Le Coq dressé (2'0" – 1910)
[The Singing Rooster]

Espagne
[Spain]

Le Ballon dirigeable "Le Patrie" (1'12")
[The Dirigible "Homeland" Takes Flight]

Alice Guy-Blaché, *Les pionnières du cinéma*
[Women Film Pioneers], Volume 1
(Lobster Films).

Falling Leaves (1912)

L'Américanisé (1912)
[Making an American Citizen]

The Girl in the Armchair (1912)

Greater Love Hath no Man (1911)

A Fool and his Money (1912)

For Love of the Flag (1912)

Algie the Miner (1912)

Matrimony's Speed Limit (1913)

Ocean Waif (1916)

Documentaries about Alice Guy

Cinépanorama: entretien avec Alice Guy [Interview].
François Chalais. ORTF. 1957.

Qui est Alice Guy? [Who is Alice Guy]. Nicole
Lise Bernheim and Monique Renault. Télévision
française. 1976.

Le Jardin oublié: la vie et l'oeuvre d'Alice Guy-Blaché
[The Forgotten Garden: The Life and Work of Alice
Guy-Blaché]. Marquise Lepage. 1995.

Alice Guy, l'enfance du cinéma [The Childhood of
Cinema]. Florida Sadki. 1995.

Looking for Alice. Claudia Colla. 2008.

Elle s'appelle Alice Guy [Her Name Is Alice Guy].
Emmanuelle Gaume with Alexandra Lamy. WLC
Production and Gaumont. 2016.

Be Natural: The Untold Story of Alice Guy-Blaché.
Pamela Green with Jodie Foster. 2019.

Alice Guy, l'inconnue du 7ᵉ art [The Unknown
Woman of the Seventh Art]. Valérie Urréa and
Nathalie Masduraud, based on original idea by Catel
and Bocquet. 10.7 productions/Arte. 2021.

TV Movies

Elle voulait faire du cinéma [She Wanted to Make
Movies]. Caroline Huppert. 1983. With Christine
Pascal as Alice Guy and André Dussollier as Léon
Gaumont.

The Prix Alice Guy

A prize founded in 2018 by Véronique Le Bris,
awarded annually to a film directed by a woman.
Winners: Lidia Terki for *Paris la blanche* (Paris
the White, 2018), Catherine Corsini for *Un amour
impossible* (An Impossible Love, 2019), Mounia
Meddour for *Papicha* (2020), and Mamouna
Doucouré for *Mignonnes* (Cuties, 2021).

Bibliography

Bachy, Victor, "Alice Guy, les raisons d'un effacement" [Reasons for an Erasure], in *Les Premiers ans du cinéma français* [The First Years of French Cinema], ed. Pierre Guibbert (Institut Jean Vigo, 1985).

———, *Alice Guy-Blaché, la première femme cinéaste du monde* [The World's First Female Filmmaker] (Institut Jean Vigo, 1993).

Baranger, René, *En Camargue avec Baroncelli* [In the Camargue with Baroncelli] (Nîmes, 1992).

Bastide, Bernard, *Le Marquis & le cinéma : Folco de Baroncelli, ambassadeur du cinéma en Camargue* [The Marquis & The Movies: Folco de Baroncelli, Cinematic Ambassador in the Camargue] (Institut Jean Vigo/Cinémathèque de Toulouse, 1993).

———, *Étienne Arnaud (1875–1955), une biographie*, Mémoire de D.E.A. [Étienne Arnaud (1875–1955): A Biography, Master's dissertation] (Université Paris III/Sorbonne nouvelle, 2001).

———, *Aux sources du cinéma en Camargue : Joë Hamman & Folco de Baroncelli* [Wellsprings of Cinema in the Camargue] (Palais du Roure/Fondation Flandeysy-Espérandieu, 2018).

——— and Jean-Antoine Gili, eds. *Léonce Perret* (Association française de recherche sur l'histoire du cinéma/Cineteca di Bologna, 2003). Bessy, Maurice, and Jean-Louis Chardans, *Dictionnaire du cinéma* (J.-J. Pauvert, 1966).

Bottomore, Stephen, ed., "Correspondance entre Léon Gaumont et Alfred Claude Bromhead, 1906–1908" [Gaumont–Bromhead Letters], *1895: Revue de l'association française de rechercher sur l'histoire du cinema* 37 (2002): <https://www.academia.edu/28858213/Correspondance_entre_L%C3%A9on_Gaumont_et_Alfred_Claude_Bromhead_1906_1908>.

Braquet, Maxime, *Les Industriels Richard* [The Richard Brothers: Industrialists] (Quartiers Libres, 2006).

———, *Léon et Camille Gaumont* [Léon and Camille Gaumont] (Quartiers Libres, 2006).

Brion, Patrick, ed., *D.W. Griffith* (L'Équerre/Centre Georges Pompidou, 1982).

Brownlow, Kevin, *The Parade's Gone By...* (Secker & Warburg, 1968).

———, *Hollywood: The Pioneers* (Harper Collins, 1979).

Carmona, Michel, *Eiffel* (Fayard, 2002).

Carou, Alain, and Laurent Le Forestier, eds., *Louis Feuillade, retour aux sources – correspondance et archives* [Louis Feuillade: A Return to the Sources] (Association française de recherche sur l'histoire du cinéma/Gaumont, 2007).

Chardère, Bernard, *Le Roman des Lumière* [The Story of the Lumières] (Gallimard, 1995).

Chocron, Daniel, *Alice Guy, pionnière du cinéma* [Alice Guy, Film Pioneer] (Le jardin d'essai, 2013).

Corcy, Marie-Sophie, Jacques Malthête, Laurent Mannoni, and Jean-Jacques Meusy, *Les Premières Années de la société L. Gaumont et Cie, correspondance commerciale de Léon Gaumont 1895–1899* [The Gaumont Company's First Years: Léon Gaumont's Commercial Correspondence] (Association française de recherche sur l'histoire du cinéma/Bibliothèque du Film/Gaumont, 1998).

de Araujo, Germana Gonçalves, ed., *Candido de Faria, un illustrateur sergipain des arts appliqués* [Candido de Faria: A Sergipain Illustrator in the Applied Arts] (UFS, 2018).

de Baroncelli, Folco, *L'Élevage en Camargue, le taureau* [Raising Bulls in the Camargue] (L'aucèu libre, 2007).

de Lorde, André, *Pour jouer la comédie de salon* [Amateur Theatre for the Salon] (Hachette, 1908).

Deslandes, Jacques, and Jacques Richard, *Histoire comparée du cinéma, 1896–1906* [A Comparative History of Cinema] (Casterman, 1968).

Dietrick, Janelle, *Alice & Eiffel* (Bookbaby, 2016).

Dillaye, Frédéric, *L'Art en photographie* [The Art of Photography] (La librairie illustrée, 1895).

———, *L'Art dans les projections* [The Art of Projection] (L. Gaumont et Cie, 1896).

Feuillade, Louis, *Chroniques taurines* [Taurine Chronicles], *1899–1907* (Ciné Sud, 1988).

———, *Retour aux sources, correspondance et archives* [Return to the Sources: Correspondence and Archives] (Association française de recherche sur l'histoire du cinéma/Gaumont, 2007).

Florey, Robert, *Filmland* (Éditions de Cinémagazine, 1923).

———, *Hollywood années zéro* [Hollywood Year Zero] (Seghers, 1972).

Gaume, Emmanuelle, *Alice Guy, la première femme cinéaste de l'histoire* [Alice Guy : The First Female Filmmaker in History] (Plon, 2015).

Gaumont, Léon, ed. *Établissements Gaumont* [The Gaumont Companies] (Gaumont, n.d.).

Gaumont, Louis, "Quelques souvenirs sur Mme Alice Guy-Blaché, la première femme 'metteur en scène'" [A Few Remembrances of Madame Alice Guy-Blaché, the First Woman Director], *Bulletin de l'association française des ingénieurs et techniciens du cinéma* (8 December 1954), 23–8.

Gianati, Maurice, "…Les couleurs et les sons se répondent…" [Sounds and Colours Go Together], *1895: Revue de l'association française de rechercher sur l'histoire du cinema* (1993).

——— and Laurent Mannoni, eds. *Alice Guy, Léon Gaumont et les débuts du film sonore* [Alice Guy, Léon Gaumont, and the Beginnings of Sound Film] (John Libbey Publishing, 2012).

Grenon, Charly *Les "temps héroïques" du cinéma dans le Centre-Ouest: des pionniers forains aux derniers "tourneurs"* [The "Heroic Age" of Cinema in the Central Western France: From Fairground Pioneers to the Last "Travelling Projectionists"] (Société d'études folkloriques du Centre-Ouest, 1975).

Grunfeld, Jean-François, *L'Empire du bureau* [The Empire of the Office], *1900–2000* (CNAP/Berger-Levrault, 1984).

Guibbert, Pierre, ed., "Louis Feuillade", *Les Cahiers de la Cinémathèque* 48 (1987).

Guy, Alice, *Autobiographie d'une pionnière du cinéma, 1873-1968* (Denoël/Gonthier, 1976).

———, *The Memoirs of Alice Guy Blaché*, trans. Roberta and Simone Blaché, ed. Anthony Slide (Scarecrow, 1996).

Henshaw, Richard, "Women Directors", *Film Comment* 8/4 (1972).

Huff, Theodore, *Charlie Chaplin* (Cassell & Co., 1952).

Huret, Jules, *La Catastrophe du Bazar de la Charité* [The Bazar de la Charité Disaster] (Juven, 1897).

Jeanne, René, *Cinéma 1900* (Flammarion, 1965).

Kisch, John Duke, *Separate Cinema: The First 100 Years of Black Poster Art* (Reel Art Press, 2014).

Koszarski, Richard, *Fort Lee: The Film Town (1904–2004)* (John Libbey Publishing, 2005).

Kubnick, Henri, *Les frères Lumière* [The Lumière Brothers] (Plon, 1938).

Laborieux, Alain, *Le Taureau et la fête au xixᵉ siècle en Languedoc* [Bulls and Festivals in 19th-century Languedoc] (Gaussen, 2011).

Lacassin, Francis, "Out of Oblivion: Alice Guy Blaché", *Sight and Sound* 4/3 (1971).

———, *Pour une contre-histoire du cinéma* [Towards an Alternative History of Cinema] (10/18 (1972); repr. Institut Lumière/Actes Sud, 1994).

———, *Maître des lions et des vampires, Louis Feuillade* [Master of Lions and Vampires] (Bordas & fils, 1995).

———, *Au secours de la Victorine : un épisode niçois de l'aventure d'Alice Guy* [Rescuing Victorine Studios: An Episode in the Adventures of Alice Guy] (Ciné Nice, 2008).

Leteux, Christine, *Maurice Tourneur, réalisateur sans frontières* [Maurice Tourneur: Director Without Borders] (La Tour verte, 2015).

Lumière, Auguste and Louis, *Les Premières photographies en couleurs* [The First Colour Photographs] (André Barret, 1974).

Malthête-Méliès, Madeleine, *Georges Méliès, l'enchanteur* [Georges Méliès, The Enchanter] (La Tour verte, 2011).

McAvoy, George E., *My Father: A Silent Films Pioneer* (AuthorHouse, 2011).

McMahan, Alison, *Alice Guy Blaché: Lost Visionary of the Cinema* (Continuum, 2002); revised Filmography in "The Feature Films of Alice Guy Blaché" (2009): <https://aliceguyblache.com/sites/default/files/pdfs/Feature_Films_of_Alice_Guy_Blache.pdf>.

Marey, Étienne-Jules, "La Chronophotographie" [Chronophotography], *Revue générale des sciences pures et appliquées* 21 (1891).

Meyers, Tom, ed., *Fort Lee: Birthplace of the Motion Picture Industry* (Fort Lee Film Commission/Arcadia Publishing, 2006).

Mistral, Frédéric, *Mireille, poème provençal* [Mireille, A Provençal Poem] (Librairie Hachette, 1891).

Paillard, Christophe, *Voltaire en son château de Ferney* [Voltaire at Château de Ferney] (Éditions du patrimoine, CMN, 2010).

Pathé, Charles, *Écrits autobiographiques* [Autobiographical Writings] (L'Harmattan, 2006).

Peary, Gerald, "Czarina of the Silent Screen: Solax's Alice Blaché", *The Velvet Light Trap* 6 (1972).

Pessiot, Guy, *Histoire de Rouen, 1900–1939* (PTC, 1982).

Pickett, D. W., "Gypsies: An International Community of Wandering Thieves", unpublished PhD dissertation (Syracuse University, 1970).

Poivert, Michel, *Le Sacrifice du présent, pictorialisme et modernité* [The Sacrifice of the Present: Pictorialism and Modernity] (Études photographiques, 2000).

Pranchère, Victor, "Le Cinéma en couleurs chez la Société des Établissements Gaumont (1909–1921)" [Colour Films at the Gaumont Companies], unpublished PhD thesis (Université Paris I: Panthéon-Sorbonne, 2013).

Rauger, Jean-François, ed., *Universal : 100 ans de cinéma* [Universal: 100 Years of Cinema] (La Martinière/Universal/Cinémathèque Française, 2012).

Richard, Marie-Dominique, *Ministère du commerce : dossiers de proposition pour la légion d'honneur, début xixᵉ siècle à 1939* [Ministry of Commerce: Nominations for the Legion of Honour] (Archives nationales, 2008).

Saccone, Kate, *Alice Guy Blaché at Columbia University: One Hundred Years Later* (Women Film Pioneers Project/Columbia University, 2017).

Sadoul, Georges, *Histoire générale du cinéma 1832–1897* [A General History of Cinema, Vol. 1] (Denoël, 1946).

Salmon, Stéphanie, *Pathé à la conquête du cinéma, 1896–1929* [Pathé and the Conquest of Cinema] (Tallandier, 2014).

Budd Schulberg, *Moving Pictures: Memories of a Hollywood Prince* (Stein & Day, 1982).

Simien, Frédéric, *Saintes-Maries-de-la-Mer*, 2 vols (Alan Sutton, 2018).

Sternberg, Josef von, *Fun in a Chinese Laundry* (Mercury House, 1965).

Toulet, Emmanuelle, "Cinema at the Universal Exposition, Paris, 1900", *Persistence of Vision* 9 (1991), 10–36.

Vermès, Anne, *Entreprendre comme les frères Lumière* [Entrepreneurship the Lumière Way] (Eyrolles, 2013).

Zukor, Adolph, with Dale Kramer, *The Public Is Never Wrong: The Autobiography of Adolph Zukor* (Cassell, 1954).